Exploring Global Issues:
Social, Economic, and Environmental Interconnections

Student Text

Primary Authors

Laura Skelton, M.S.

Sheeba Jacob, M.Ed.

Danica Hendrickson, M.Ed.

Danielle Shaw, J.D.

Facing the Future™

Exploring Global Issues:
Social, Economic, and Environmental Interconnections
Student Text

In general, it is necessary to obtain advance, written permission to copy *Facing the Future* publications. However, given that worksheets, tests, quizzes and other student handouts in *Facing the Future* publications are designed to be copied and distributed in class, it is not necessary for an individual educator to request permission from *Facing the Future* to make copies of these student handouts for use by his or her students in a school or other non-profit educational organization.

Other than the exception outlined above for the non-commercial purposes of teachers and individual classrooms, USERS MAY NOT REPRODUCE, MODIFY, TRANSLATE, SELL OR DISTRIBUTE THE MATERIALS FOR ANY PURPOSE WITHOUT FACING THE FUTURE'S PRIOR WRITTEN AUTHORIZATION. To request written authorization, please contact *Facing the Future* at **office@facingthefuture.org**. Users must provide proper attribution and identifying information for *Facing the Future* as the author and developer of the materials, and may not delete or in any manner alter any copyright, trademark or other proprietary rights notices that have been placed on the materials.

Copyright © *Facing the Future*, 2013

ISBN 978-0-9815577-8-6

Facing the Future is a nonprofit organization that develops and delivers standards-based hands-on lessons, student textbooks, curriculum units, and professional development opportunities for educators that promote critical thinking on global issues, sustainability, and positive solutions. Our curriculum is in use in all 50 U.S. states and over 120 countries by teachers and students in grades K-12, in undergraduate and graduate classes, and across multiple subject areas. For more information, visit **www.facingthefuture.org**.

FACING THE FUTURE
1904 3rd Avenue, Suite 510
Seattle, WA 98101
(206) 264-1503
www.facingthefuture.org

Front Cover Credits
photo 1. © Janis Lacis | Dreamstime.com
photo 2: Riot 68
photo 3: Lauren McClanahan
photo 4: © Branex | Dreamstime.com
photo 5: © Twindesigner | Dreamstime.com

We dedicate this textbook and teacher's guide to our Teacher Advisory Group. Thank you for providing us excellent feedback that helped to push this project forward:

Chris Alejano	Rik Katz
Brook Brayman	Bob Mazelow
Darrellene Canada	Bridgette McGoldrick
Lisa Clarke	Erin Sanchez
James Covi	Ben Wheeler
Wendy Ewbank	David White-Espin

Noah Zeichner

We thank all of the following *Facing the Future* staff, past and present, who have made this textbook what it is today.

Leah Ankeny	Alicia Keefe
Wendy Church	Justine Miley
Kim Corrigan	Bob Oswald
Jack Edgerton	Kim Rakow Bernier
Christie Heyer	Daniel Schafer
Beth Hintz	Dave Wilton

We also want to express our gratitude to our Board of Directors for their incredible support of *Facing the Future's* mission.

Acknowledgements

Primary Authors
Laura Skelton, M.S.
Sheeba Jacob, M.Ed
Danica Hendrickson, M.Ed
Danielle Shaw, J.D.

Contributing Writers
Allison Liddell
Randy Thompson
John de Graaf

Supporting Researchers and Writers
Wren Brennan
Robin Brown
Ann Dold
Jill Falman
Jocelyn MacDonald
Eleanor Runde
Jordan Stalker

Copy Edit
Christie Heyer
Seth Bookey
Cecilia Lund

Design and Production
Print Materials
DECODE, Inc.

Digital Materials
Sparkworks

Production Management
Elizabeth Cromwell/Books in Flight

Field Testing

Thank you to the following educators and their students for field testing this curriculum and providing feedback for its improvement.

Tanya Bartlett
World Geography Teacher
Notre Dame Preparatory High School
Arizona

Jill Berge
History Teacher
Rose Hill Junior High School
Washington

Brook Brayman
Humanities Teacher
Technology Access Foundation
Washington

Gail Chastain
Social Science Teacher
Mercy High School
California

Bev Feldcamp
Global Issues Teacher
Valley Lutheran High School
Michigan

Raelenne Haeberle
Social Studies Teacher
The Epiphany School
North Carolina

Rik Katz
Geography Teacher
Roosevelt High School
Washington

Carole Layton
Social Studies Teacher
Black Hills High School
Washington

Jason Long
Social Studies Teacher
Placer High School
California

Rick Malmstrom
Social Studies Teacher
The Ellis School
Pennsylvania

Bridgette McGoldrick
History Teacher
Annie Wright School
Washington

Kim Nasser
Social Studies Teacher
Wayne High School
North Carolina

Jon Schmidt
Service Learning Manager
Chicago Public Schools
Illinois

Jennifer Syrota
Social Science Teacher
MacLachlan College
Ontario

Kate Trimlett
Environmental Science Teacher
Green Academy
California

Ben Wheeler
Global Studies Teacher
Explorer West Middle School
Washington

Kevin Witte
Social Studies Teacher
Kearney High School
Nebraska

Noah Zeichner
Social Studies Teacher
Chief Sealth High School
Washington

Content Expert Contributions

Thank you to the following experts who reviewed content to ensure that this volume includes the most accurate and up-to-date information available.

Becky Alexander
Assistant Professor, Department of Atmospheric Sciences
University of Washington

Chris Benner
Associate Professor of Human and Community Development
University of California, Davis

Wynn Calder
Director
Sustainable Schools, LLC

Tim Crosby
Director
Slow Money

Erene Dorfmeier
Research Scientist
University of Washington, School of Aquatic and Fishery Sciences

Kerry Coughlin
Regional Director, Americas
Marine Stewardship Council

John de Graaf
Co-Founder
Seattle Happiness Initiative

Roman P. de Jesus, PhD.
Lecturer, School of Marine & Atomspheric Sciences
Stony Brook University

Lynne Dial
Policy Analyst
NW Energy Coalition

Teri Eastburn
Manager, School & Public Programs
Spark UCAR Science Education

ERM (Environmental Resources Management)

Bryan Fiedorczyk
Sustainable West Seattle

Michael Frank, P.E., LEED A.P.
Senior Engineer
McKinstry

Allison Fundis
Ocean Observatories Initiative Education and Public Engagement Liason

Robert Henry Cox
Professor of Political Science and Director of the Walker Institute of International and Area Studies
University of South Carolina

Brett Hill
Assistant Professor of Anthropology
Hendrix College

Mike Hoffman
Economist
Center for Economics at the U.S. Government Accountability Office

AJ Howard
Senior Project Analyst
EMI Consulting

Mathew Isaac
Professor of Marketing
Seattle University

Sheena Jacob
Nursing Director
I-Tech

Laurel Kearns
Associate Professor of Sociology of Religion and Environmental Studies
Drew University

Terry Leitzell
Retired Negotiator & Regulatory Attorney

Nalani Linder
Systems Thinking Consultant
NP Linder Consulting, LLC

Nan Little, PhD
Retired Professor of Anthropology

Peter Locke
Sustainability Consulting Director
McKinstry

Kelly McCusker
Research Assistant, Department of Atmospheric Sciences
University of Washington

Dr. Matthew Moran
Professor of Ecology
Hendrix College

Kerin Ord
Head of International Programs
World Vision Australia

Darshana Patel
Consultant
World Bank
Guyana

Dr. Scott Perkin

Sara Posada
Portfolio Manager
Nike Foundation

Jaisanker Sarma
Global Director of Field Operations
World Vision

Thresia Sebastian MD, MPH
Pediatrician

Julie Shackford-Bradley, PhD
Professor of Peace and Conflict Studies
University of California, Berkeley

Dianna Shandy
Professor of Anthropology
Macalester College

Cindi Smith-Walters, PhD
Professor & Director of MTSU Center for Environmental Education
Middle Tennessee State University

Erin Swanson
Marketing Programs Manager
Water.org

Alan Thein Durning
Executive Director
Sightline Institute

Content Expert Contributions, continued

Dr. Daniel Thornhill
Conservation Scientist
Defenders of Wildlife

Stewart Tolnay
Professor of Sociology
University of Washington

Stephen G. Warren
Professor of Atmospheric Sciences
University of Washington

Jeana C. Wiser
Project Coordinator
Preservation Green Lab, National Trust for Historic Preservation

Roger Valdez
Seattle Researcher and Writer
Director of Housing Programs
Sea Mar Community Health Centers

Anand Yang
Professor of International Studies
University of Washington

Education Experts

Thank you to the following educators who reviewed content and supported us with pedagogy.

Julie Ayers
Service Learning Specialist
Maryland State Department of Education

Christine Benita
Science Specialist
Seattle Public Schools

Lois Brewer
Director, Service Learning Seattle
Seattle Public Schools

Joe Brooks
Executive Director
Community Works Institute

Thomas Chandler, PhD
Adjunct Assistant Professor
Department of Arts & Humanities
Teachers College, Columbia University

Lori Diefenbacher
Coordinator of Education for Global Sustainability
Webster University

Cathy Feyt
Instructional Services Consultant
Michigan

David Grant
Technology Coordinator
King Middle School

Heidi Hayes Jacobs, PhD
President, Curriculum Designers Group and Director
The Curriculum21 Project

Brenda Higa
STEM Curriculum Consultant
Washington MESA

Beth Kelly
Program Supervisor
Learn and Serve America

Kate McPherson
Director
Project Service Leadership

Lauren G. McClanahan, PhD
Professor of Secondary Education
Woodring College of Education
Western Washington University

Jay McTighe
Educational Author and Consultant

Merry M. Merryfield
Professor of Social Studies and Global Education
Ohio State

Andrew Miller
National Faculty
Buck Institute for Education

Paul Miller
Global Initiatives Director
National Association of Independent Schools

Jean Orvis
Founder
Seattle Academy of Arts and Sciences

Rosalie Romano
Professor of Mathematics Education
Western Washington University

Debra Rowe
President
U.S. Partnership for Education for Sustainable Development
Professor of Renewable Energies & Sustainable Living
Oakland Community College

Kurt Sahl
Associate Professor of Technology in the Classroom
Antioch University

Jon Schmidt
Service Learning Manager
Chicago Public Schools

Nancy Skeritt
Assistant Superintendent of Teaching and Learning
Tacoma School District

Bethany Vosburg-Bluem
PhD Candidate
School of Teaching and Learning
Ohio State University

Introduction

Have you ever thought about how a teenager in Vietnam could be linked to the pair of jeans you wear? You are connected to the world in countless ways. Where did tomatoes for the ketchup in your school cafeteria come from? Where were the cars in your school parking lot manufactured? In which country was the computer code for your cellphone written? You might be thinking, "How does all this connect with my life?"

In a world where two people 7,000 miles apart can connect digitally, knowledge of different cultures and customs can prove useful. In a world where we rely more and more on goods and services from other countries, knowledge of international trade and economics is essential. In a world where the air you breathe can be affected by a factory outside your nation's borders, knowledge of wind cycles and international enforcement of environmental standards can be crucial to creating solutions to issues that impact us all.

Everyone benefits from an understanding of global issues. It is the nature of the world in which we live that connections—whether social, economic, or environmental—now occur on a global scale. Global issues, such as poverty, climate change, conflict, and population growth are interrelated and affect the lives of all people around the world. The good news is while these issues can be challenging, they have interconnected solutions that we can develop to create long-lasting, positive change. By thinking of global solutions to global issues, we can begin to create a truly sustainable world.

Exploring Global Issues: Social, Economic, and Environmental Interconnections provides you the opportunity to learn about 24 topics related to global issues and sustainable ways to address these issues. You will learn about the background of the topic, examine how it impacts the world today, draw personal and community connections, and devise solutions to address the issue. Each chapter features young people who are doing work related to the topic. Each chapter also features case studies that present issues in context.

These case studies allow you to see an issue in real life and perhaps from a perspective that you had not considered before. They also provide you with the opportunity to connect your personal experiences and knowledge about an issue with a different part of the world.

As you learn about these topics, you will also participate in activities related to each chapter. These resources are designed to:

- enhance your ability to think critically
- improve your problem-solving abilities
- expand your global perspective
- increase your knowledge of global issues and sustainable solutions

This text will provide you with the foundational knowledge and skills to understand what's happening in the world around you and prepare you to be an engaged citizen. You are capable of creating change locally and globally!

Table of Contents

I. Introductory Materials 7

II. Chapters 10

Introduction to Global Issues and Sustainability

   1. Global Issues 10

   2. Sustainability 24

Essential Human Needs

   3. Food 38

   4. Water 58

   5. Air 76

   6. Energy 96

Our Collective Impact:
Ecological Footprint and Carrying Capacity

   7. Population 116

   8. Consumption 134

   9. Climate Change 152

   10. Biodiversity 172

   11. Oceans 192

Human Health, Security, and Well-being

    12. Quality of Life 212

    13. Governance 230

    14. Health 248

    15. Peace and Conflict 266

    16. Human Rights 284

    17. Gender 302

    18. Human Migration 318

The Global Economy: Economics and Development

    19. Economics 332

    20. Poverty 350

    21. Globalization 368

Creating Sustainable Communities

    22. Community Development 386

    23. Sustainable Design 402

    24. Taking Action 424

III. Glossary 441

IV. Endnotes 447

HANALEI
mi
8779 mi
LOS ANGELES 2613 mi
40 mi
KEKA
RUSSIA
LONDON
10 mi
749 mi
AUSTRALIA 5039 mi

Chapter 1

Global Issues

> **GUIDING QUESTIONS**
> - How do we understand challenges facing the world today?
> - How can youth be involved in creating solutions to global issues?

Introduction to Global Issues

Have you ever stopped to think about how connected people in the world are to each other? In the 21st century, people around the world interact with each other more than ever before. If you have ever used social networking websites like Facebook, you know how easy it is to communicate with individuals from many different locations. Technologies such as the Internet and cell phones help transmit ideas rapidly. These days, you are likely to find youth in very different parts of the world listening to the same music, watching the same movies, and studying similar issues in school.[1]

Today, approximately 50% of the world's population is under 27 years old.[2] What makes youth feel like they are part of a larger global community? Looking at specific trends can help answer this question.

What Connects Us?

Consider the following influences that have brought us closer together around the world:

Cultural Influences

Annually, there are over 190 million people living outside of their home country.[3] These people impact their new communities when they arrive with their own language, culture, and food. *Culture* includes the behaviors and beliefs of a specific group of people. For example, immigrants who have moved from the Dominican Republic to New York City over the last century have brought a number of cultural influences with them like the dance styles of Merengue and Bachata.[4] At the same time, new immigrants adapt to their host country as they learn new customs and traditions and merge their cultural practices with these. A family from Latin America might add plantains, roast pork, black beans, and rice to their Thanksgiving meal, bringing new meaning to the holiday.

The entertainment industry plays a large role in transmitting cultural ideas quickly around the world. The United States is the largest producer of popular culture goods and entertainment.[5] Foreign companies distribute movies, music, television shows, fast food, and clothing from the United States throughout the world. In 2007, the international community spent over $17 billion toward American cinema while Americans spent $9.6 billion.[6]

Entertainment from other countries also has a significant influence on global cultures. Bollywood, the film industry in Mumbai, India, generates the largest amount of feature films in the world. These films are extremely popular in places like Kuwait, Nigeria, Russia, and Scandinavia.[7]

Media Influences

Media is a form of communication. Mass media is a combination of many means of communication, especially newspapers, popular magazines, Internet, radio, and television, which reach and influence large numbers of people. These days, people around the world have wide access to a large number of different types of media. There are approximately 250 television sets per 1,000 people globally.[8] In Mexico it is more common for people to have televisions in their houses than to have showers and refrigerators.[9]

The many people who have access to television are able to watch not only entertainment, but also news coverage of events happening both locally and globally. CNN, an American news network, provides 24-hour reporting to over 200 million households in over 212 countries and territories.[10]

The Associated Press (AP) is an American news agency that is able to distribute stories and images to 1,700 newspapers and 5,000 television and radio broadcasters daily. People around the world are able to access these stories via the Internet.[11]

Technology Influences

Technology is a critical tool in connecting people around the world. The Internet alone has had a huge impact on how news, ideas, and culture

EarthCorps volunteers come together from around the world to restore green spaces.

are spread. Think about how often you use technology throughout the day.

In 1962 the Internet did not yet exist. There were only about 10,000 computers and each one cost hundreds of thousands of dollars.[12] Over the next several decades, computers became less expensive and scientists learned how to connect computers to each other to create the Internet. Currently, over 200 million people use the Internet within the United States[13] and close to 300 million people use the Internet in China.[14] If billions of people around the world have access to the Internet, think about how easily information can spread in a matter of seconds from Thailand to Canada or Mozambique to Chile. Developments in social networking websites all impact the way we communicate with each other.

Cell phones are another technology that has had a major influence. Over one billion people have access to cell phones today, compared to only 33 million people during the 1990s.[15] Cell phones are not only used as a means for social communication, but also for many other practical reasons. Using cell phones, construction workers can send pictures to contractors, residents can pay their heating bills, citizens can vote in electoral campaigns, and paramedics can send pictures of incoming injuries to hospitals. In some countries like Niger, farmers even use cell phones to determine who will give them the best price for their crops.[16]

Around the world, people have taken advantage of these technologies to help solve global issues. For example, the International Campaign to Ban Landmines used the Internet to create a large social movement with over 1,100 groups to educate the world about the dangers of landmines. Landmines are explosive devices used to kill people in times of war or conflict and are highly present in conflict-ridden areas. They were first put in widespread use during World War II. They can remain in a location years after a conflict has finished and severely harm individuals who step on them unknowingly.[17] The director of the International

A young man speaks on a cell phone in India. Cell phones have had a tremendous impact on communication around the world.

Campaign to Ban Landmines mobilized a large group of people to speak out against this weapon of war. The organization was awarded the Nobel Peace Prize for working to decrease the number of landmines in the world.[18] This type of global outreach would have been far more difficult in a time before the Internet.

Globalization Influences

Later in this textbook, you will learn about the process of economic globalization. *Economic globalization* is the increased ease with which countries can do business with each other.

In 1994, the United States, for example, opened up its borders for trade with Mexico and Canada through the North American Free Trade Agreement (NAFTA). This agreement brought the countries and cultures closer together. Those in favor of NAFTA argued that the agreement would raise living standards and create millions of good jobs. Critics believe that there have been a number of unintended consequences. For instance, because these countries opened up their borders, the United States could sell food to Mexicans at much lower prices than local farmers in Mexico might.

As a result, a number of Mexicans migrated to the United States because there was no work available to them within Mexico.[19]

Global Issues and Sustainability

Sustainability represents the idea that we can meet our basic needs and live a good life without compromising future generations' ability to meet their own basic needs. You will be reading how issues in this book relate to this idea of sustainability.

These days, our societies, economies, and environments are more connected than ever. When thinking about sustainability, understanding that our personal choices can have global impacts is key. Similarly, understanding that global issues can have local impacts is important. We have transformed from times when people were separated into kingdoms and feudal systems to a time when people of different backgrounds interact with each other constantly from opposite ends of the globe. Contrast modern societies to the early 1900s when 90% of humanity lived and died within a 50-mile radius. In the United States, 75% of people today move at least 100 miles away from their homes.[20]

People these days may have connections to a global community, a local neighborhood, an ethnic group, a state, a city, a spiritual group, etc. These identities go beyond the traditional

CASE STUDY: Global Response to the 2004 Tsunami[21]

The tsunami on December 26th, 2004 made significant ripples throughout the world. This natural disaster killed over 270,000 people in both Africa and Asia. Some of the most devastated places were within Indonesia and Sri Lanka. Images of the gigantic waves and the resulting damage from those waves was broadcast globally, compelling many people to offer their support for the impacted communities. A Sri Lankan group living in South Africa created a special fund to help millions of Sri Lankans who were made homeless by the tsunami. Indonesian workers who lived in Hong Kong sent money, clothes, food, and other supplies back to Indonesia. Through these efforts, they were able to collect $19,000 in just four days. The tsunami's impact was further felt throughout the world with an increase in global migration caused by the disaster. As a result, Canada declared it would expedite immigration paperwork for any victims who had relatives in Canada. Immigration officers in Toronto even met with local Sri Lankan, Indonesian, Somali, and Indian communities to work with them on how to best help tsunami victims from these countries resettle peacefully in Canada. One thousand applications from tsunami-affected areas were fast-tracked for immigration status.

A fisherman in Sri Lanka works on his boat. One of the most devastated places after the 2004 Tsunami was Sri Lanka.

geographic boundaries that defined people in the past.[22] Consider the example of how the Indian Ocean tsunami of 2004 impacted communities around the world.

Global Issues Today

You've read about the influences that bring us closer together. These global issues impact us far more today than in the past.

So what exactly is a global issue? Let's say you're struggling with a class in school. You decide to speak to your teacher. After discussing ways to improve your grade, you both decide you will come in once a week during lunchtime to receive extra help. You defined a problem and your teacher and you have agreed on a possible solution.

Now, let's say the problem has transformed into something larger. A number of students at your school struggle with this same class and all of you need support or you won't graduate. Your teacher comes to school every few days, but you live in a rural location that is not easy to reach. Your relatives who live in different parts of the country express the same frustrations. In fact, many people have become concerned about the future of your country's youth. The problem has become a national issue. Lately, with no real educational opportunities, many families in your country have started migrating to other neighboring countries in search of opportunity. Some of these neighboring countries don't have the capacity (i.e., social services and natural resources) to meet the needs of new migrants. The issue has now become global.

A **global issue** is complex and can be defined in a number of ways:

- It persists over time.
- It is transnational and transboundary.
- It affects large numbers of people.
- It has underlying causes.
- It is connected to other global issues.

If we look at the topic of education mentioned before, we can see how a lack of education can easily become a global issue. The country

Young children stand in line for water in the country of Sudan.

of Sudan, for example, has struggled with education issues for over a decade. One of the underlying causes of Sudan's education issues was a long civil war that made it difficult for many children to go to school. Only 28% of school-aged children—mostly those who can afford to pay school fees—attend school. Due to this civil war, South Sudan officially divided from Sudan in 2011 and became an independent state. Most schools in Southern Sudan are overcrowded, with few teachers and hardly any school supplies. Teenagers who have had to flee their homes because of the war live in camps for internally displaced persons where they typically cannot attend secondary school. Since there are no other constructive activities for them in these camps, youth often become frustrated and may participate in violence.[23] With few opportunities for education in their home country, some families in South Sudan and Sudan may cross borders to other countries in search of opportunity. The issue now becomes transboundary.

For those who remain in Sudan and South Sudan, a lack of education can reduce economic opportunities and limit people to low-paying jobs. As a result, the struggle with poverty could lead people back into conflict. The good news is that just as global issues connect with each other, so do the solutions to these challenges.

Using Frameworks to Understand Global Issues

A number of frameworks can help us understand global issues on a deeper level:

Global Issues in Balance

Take, for instance, this visual you see below. Notice how Earth is situated at the bottom of this visual with a number of different balls balancing on top. If you slightly move one of the balls, the other balls will move too. Some might even fall to the ground. Think of global issues as being interconnected in a similar way. For instance, if more people are added to the planet, this means all of our needs and our consumption go up. What we consume is drawn from our natural resources and impacts the environment. These two reinforce one another: when resources are scarce, people struggle harder to get what they need and often cause damage. At the same time, as the environment degrades, it is able to produce fewer resources. Access to resources and how they are distributed is a matter of equity and greater inequality often results in poverty among some people. In turn, poverty can be linked to social breakdown and crime. Essentially, if one part of the system is affected, all parts of the system feel the impacts.

The Iceberg Model

The *iceberg model* is another way to understand global issues.[24] We know that an iceberg has only 10% of its total mass above the water, while 90% is under water.[25] But the 90% is what the ocean currents act on and what creates the iceberg's behavior at its tip. Global issues can be looked at in a similar way. We can think of the tip of the iceberg, above the water, as representing events or things we see or hear happening in the world.

If we look below the water line, we start to see patterns, or a recurrence of events. These patterns help us to understand that events are not incidents that happen in isolation.

Toward the bottom of the iceberg are underlying structures or root causes that create these patterns. By looking at root causes,

Global Issues in Balance

we can start to understand and address long-term solutions.

Finally, at the base of the iceberg are assumptions and worldviews that create or sustain the structures above. In solving global issues, the greatest impact comes from changing structures and applying deep currents to move the iceberg and, as a result, change the events at its tip.

Systems Thinking

Systems thinking is a field of study that looks carefully at all important components of a system and how they connect to each other. A system is a group of components that form a complex and unified whole. Systems are everywhere. For example, the circulatory system in your body is made up of components like the heart, blood, and blood vessels that work together to deliver nutrients and oxygen to tissues in the body. Ecological systems and human social systems are living systems; human-made systems such as cars and washing machines are nonliving systems. Most systems thinkers focus their attention on living systems, especially human social systems.

Suppose a landfill in a city becomes full, leaving the citizens without a place to put their garbage. A nonsystems approach to this problem might be to build another landfill or find a landfill in another city that would take the garbage for a fee. A systems thinking approach would look not only at these two options, but also at other aspects of the problem by asking a number of questions: Where does the garbage come from? What's in the garbage? Is there a way to reduce the amount of garbage produced? Answering these questions could give the city a number of alternatives, including starting or expanding a recycling program, raising fees for garbage disposal as an incentive for citizens to create less garbage, or working with manufacturers to produce less packaging for their products.

The global issues in balance visual, iceberg model, and systems thinking framework provide ways of understanding how global issues

ICEBERG MODEL

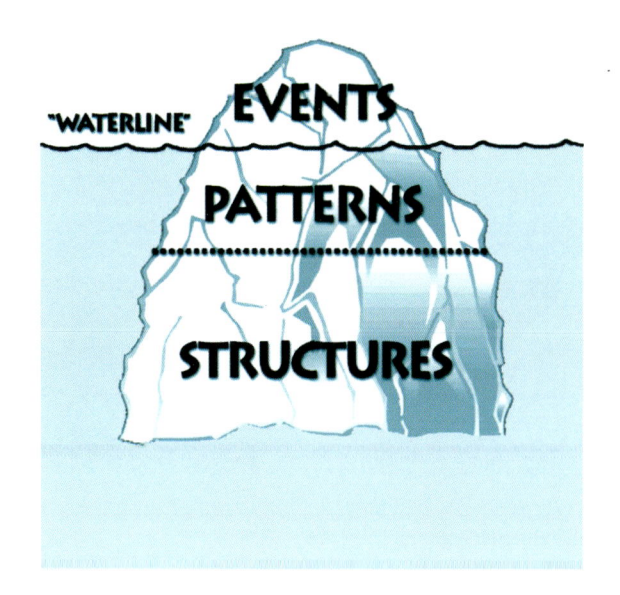

are connected. On the flip side, they can also help us visualize how solutions might be connected. Reducing poverty could help to create a healthy environment, for example. Or providing people a voice in government could help to reduce conflict.

Understanding the World

You've learned different frameworks that can help you to analyze global issues. On a more fundamental level, what are ways we as humans can understand the world around us?

Worldview

Worldview includes a set of assumptions, perspectives, and beliefs held by individuals, cultures, and societies through which we make sense of our lives and the world. Our worldview helps us understand structures, patterns, and events that we experience in life. People's worldviews are often linked to where they live and the environmental, economic, and social issues around them. Worldview is also a way that people can personally relate to global issues.

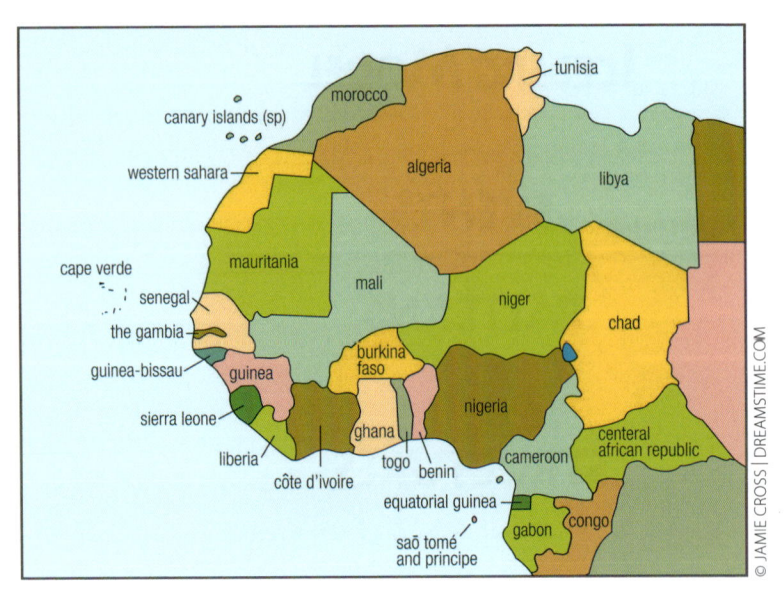

As a Peace Corps volunteer, Roz Wolmmering spent her time in the country of Guinea-Bissau.

An ability to appreciate differences in worldview can help increase understanding among different people throughout the world. Roz Wolmmering learned this fact firsthand when she became a Peace Corps volunteer in the West African country of Guinea-Bissau. The Peace Corps, an organization started in 1960, sends US citizens as volunteers to live and work in developing countries with the aim of increasing world peace.[26] Peace Corps volunteers work in such fields as education, health, business development, agriculture, and youth development.

Roz was assigned to be a teacher in a classroom of 47 students. On the first day of classes, Roz showed up promptly, charged with excitement. Her belief was, "Always wiser to be punctual and prepared than be tardy and unequipped." Imagine her surprise when she found only two students in the classroom playing cards. Eventually, more and more students arrived in the next month, but she had classroom management issues and couldn't seem to get students interested in what they were learning.

Roz finally asked her students what the problem was. They informed her:

- No one comes to school on the first day because students are typically still on farms finishing harvests for their family or trying to register for class.
- Teachers only begin teaching the third week of school.
- Students believed Roz didn't command respect from them because she never told them to wear their school jackets.
- Teachers typically walk in after all students are in the class so students could stand up and honor them. Roz was always in the classroom waiting for her students so they could never honor her.
- While Roz demanded that her students write all the time, Guineans are more used to verbal communication.

Roz's willingness to hear from her students helped to clear up these differences in worldview.[27]

Media Literacy

Think of how much information you receive daily through the Internet, television, radio, and print. The average person potentially sees up to 5,000 advertisements per day. Do you ever question where it comes from or who provides you this information? Have you ever thought about how news a person receives in Egypt could look quite different from news someone might receive in the United States?

Media literacy is the ability to access and evaluate media messages of all kinds in order to understand how these messages create meaning and what impact they have on society. Depending on where the media you read or view is created, it is likely to present a certain point of view or be associated with a certain value.[28] Ten huge conglomerates (companies that own many other companies) run the majority of global news and entertainment media. Well-known ones include Time Warner, Turner Broadcasting, and Twentieth Century Fox. When a few companies control messages that filter through the media, do you think there are some messages that might get left out?

In some places, the government exerts control over the media and may censor certain types of news. For example, when the 2011 Egyptian uprisings happened and President Mubarak was asked to step down, China censored certain websites that used the word "Egypt." The Chinese government was wary of how the social movement in Egypt might spur political reform and demands for democracy within China.[29]

Media messages have economic, political, and social purposes. Media literacy helps to reveal the purposes behind these messages.

When you read newspapers, watch the news, and pay attention to other types of media, you can ask the following questions to help you determine possible bias:

- Who was this message written for?
- Whose perspective is this story told from?
- Whose story is not told in this message?

Asking the right questions about how media portray global issues can help you

CASE STUDY: Global Visionaries

As I continue to develop and reflect on my experiences, it is almost impossible for me to speak about my life without the inclusion of GV—one of the many homes that I was raised in. Here, I learned to be a leader, humility, social responsibility, confidence and above all, to love the work I do with others.

—Marita Phelps, GV participant

Based in Seattle, Washington, the mission of Global Visionaries (GV) is to empower young people to become global leaders in the creation of a just and sustainable future. High school students who participate in GV programs have multiple opportunities to increase their global awareness.

Over the course of one school year, participants in GV's Leadership Program receive cross-cultural training on global awareness, fundraising, and social action. They take part in a cultural immersion trip to Guatemala, where they meet their peers in GV's Guatemala Youth Leadership Program. Together, American and Guatemalan youth undertake work in one of four areas:

Global Visionaries participants volunteer in Guatemala.

- Construction of classrooms for schools
- Reforestation of rural areas by planting trees
- Production of coffee on small, independent farms
- Support of hospital nursing staff with care for premature babies, children, adults, and the elderly

Along with service learning, students experience the local culture by trying different foods, living with Guatemalan families, taking Spanish lessons, and going on trips to the local market.

Participants learn that every action they take has a ripple effect on society and the world as a whole. They become active leaders and global citizens who promote social and environmental justice through education and service at home and abroad.

Anne Mahlum, founder of Back on My Feet, walks with members.

understand the issue through multiple people's point of view instead of hearing only one side of the story.

Global Awareness

To develop **global awareness** is to gain the ability to understand people from other nations and cultures. This awareness also means learning from and working collaboratively with individuals from diverse cultures, religions, and lifestyles.[30] By studying other societies and learning about the connections between various peoples, cultures, and countries, you can understand both your own background and those of others around the world. It has become common for us to interact with people from all over the world. Check out the label on an item of clothing you're wearing. Was it made in this country? If not, what do you know about the country where it's made? How might things going on in that country affect your life?

With this awareness, you can understand why the world functions the way it does, work effectively with different kinds of people, and think critically in order to solve global issues.

Pathways to Progress: Global Issues

Throughout this book you will be reading about a number of interconnected global issues. You'll also be reading about some of the efforts made by individuals, communities, governments and other organizations to find lasting solutions to these issues.

Thinking of solutions to global issues is part of living sustainably; that is, making choices that ensure a healthy natural environment, a flourishing economy, and a thriving society. You might be thinking, how do I have the power to impact the environment, economy, and society? In order to live sustainably, you don't need to solve all the problems related to poverty, climate change, crime, war, and population growth. Taken together, these many problems can be overwhelming and tackling all of them individually is impossible. However, joining others in creating sustainable solutions to one issue can be a powerful way to positively impact your own future and the future of generations to come. Thinking at a local level could be the easiest place to start. Consider the **personal solution** Anne Mahlum created to address poverty in her neighborhood.

Fighting Poverty

Anne Mahlum would get up early in the morning to run through the neighborhoods of Philadelphia. She loved running and had even run a few marathons. On her route in the city, she always passed by a homeless men's shelter and the men would cheer her on. Anne came to realize that while she was always running past these men, they never moved. These were people who lived in her community, but were not able to fulfill their personal goals. Anne wanted to help the men at the shelter accomplish their goals just like she accomplished her goals each time she completed a marathon. She talked to the director of the shelter and started a running club called Back on My Feet. Members of the group run three mornings a week to improve their health. Additionally, the organization helps those who are homeless to improve their lives by providing them with opportunities to go to school and gain computer and job skills.[31]

YOUTH PROFILE
Urban Youth Collaborative

Earlier in this chapter, you read about the iceberg model and how this model helps to understand root causes of global issues. **Structural solutions** involve many people and address root causes of a problem. They are "structural" because they work to change a system—such as health care or education—in order to alleviate a problem. Structural solutions often involve organizations or governments and they can have a lasting impact on people and places around the world. Consider the issue of school bullying: a personal solution to bullying may be to tell one of your peers to stop bullying another student, a structural solution would be to implement policies that prevent bullying on school grounds.

The Urban Youth Collaborative based in New York City focuses on social and economic justice for youth. The organization formed in

The Urban Youth Collaborative marches over the Brooklyn Bridge.

CAREER PROFILE — Journalist

Throughout this book, you will learn about a different career in each chapter. Look for this section at the end of the chapter, where you will read about real people doing jobs related to global issues solutions.

In the space of a few columns of words, journalists map out what's happening where and why it matters. They ask compelling questions, get the facts, and then compose an engaging written piece that grabs the reader's attention and brings even far-off people and places into clear focus. Journalists are good writers and often develop their skills by pursuing a degree, although this is certainly not required. Strong writing, even for your school paper, is the real determining factor in landing this dream job for any deadline-driven, analytical scribe. Some journalists work on the staff of newspapers, magazines, and blogs. Others make a good living by writing about whatever interests them, querying publications and working as freelance writers.

Carley Petesch (right) is a journalist in South Africa for the Associated Press.

Journalism offers you the option of studying something you care about and sharing it with the world.

Carley Petesch is the editor of the Africa Desk for the Associated Press. She collects stories from over 60 correspondents and writes stories from Johannesburg, South Africa about news all over the sub-Saharan region. She says, "I work with colleagues who are at the scenes of plane crashes, coups, or clashes and they tell me what's going on. Sometimes they only send me a text message and I have to write a story to explain what is happening to readers all over the world." For her, going to work is an adventure where she meets all sorts of people and asks all sorts of questions. The reward is giving people access to these stories and explaining why these stories matter. "[Readers] may never travel to remote Congo but they should know that the minerals in their cell phone were in some cases harvested by people under very questionable circumstances." Carley helps keep people in Africa informed about what's going on in other continents and brings information about what's going on in Africa to the rest of the world. As democracy spreads through the Middle East, different parts of the world will read about it, hear about it, and perhaps be inspired. As people read about atrocities in other countries, perhaps they will be encouraged to learn from past mistakes and to reach out to help those in need.

2004 because students wanted a platform to voice their concerns related to overcrowding and safety in schools. One recent Urban Youth Collaborative campaign helped save student MetroCards. For many years, students who attended New York City public schools were allowed to travel to and from school on the bus or subway free of charge. However, in 2009, the Metropolitan Transit Authority (MTA) announced the program would be cut in 2011 because of a $800 million budget deficit. Students taking public transportation would have to pay $1,000 each year to get to school.

The Urban Youth Collaborative spoke out against the cut and campaigned to preserve student access to free MetroCards. They also held a number of press conferences outside MTA offices and met with city officials. To increase the visibility of their campaign, they organized a student-led walk-out of 23 high schools. One thousand students left their schools during the school day, rallied, and marched over the Brooklyn Bridge in support of the cause. The group also met with state legislators over several months, making trips to Albany, New York to discuss the issue. Based on the Urban Youth Collaborative's strategic thinking, state officials made a tentative deal to keep student MetroCards.[32]

Increasing Access to Technology

Leapfrogging is the idea that developing countries do not have to progress in the same way developed nations have done in the past in order to adopt modern technology like the Internet and cell phones. Leapfrogging does not mean that countries invent new technologies, but they are developing ways to "leapfrog" infrastructure needed to support these types of technologies. Certain developing countries have discovered how easy it is to put in cellular phone towers in rural areas compared to landlines. Therefore, cell phone use has exploded throughout these areas.[33]

While limited electricity and illiteracy pose problems for establishing and utilizing conventional computer networks, the technology that outfits mobile phones with Internet access is readily available and is not dependent on computer hardware or landlines. Internet-enabled cell phones have many potential uses beyond simple communication. For example, they can promote education and citizenship, including remote voting.

A cell phone with Internet access will not substitute for the basic and readily available technology that can result in increased food production, fresh water for agricultural and domestic use, or improved health care services. However, it can serve personal and business needs efficiently, even substituting for some of the advantages that more expensive and unlikely Internet access might afford. For example, the business earnings from the average Nigerian cell phone are twice that of the average American's because of the amount and type of business conducted over the phone.[34]

WHAT YOU CAN DO — Global Issues

What issues do you care about? Are there certain things in the world you want to change, or things you want to make sure stay the same? How would you like to impact the world around you?

You can participate in actions now that can significantly affect the future—both your own future and the future of the planet.

Of course, the world is a big place. Not sure where to start? The best place to start is by educating yourself. You can read this textbook to find out more about global issues and solutions happening right now and research events that are impacting your local and global communities. There are millions of people around the world working to create personal and structural solutions to global issues and they would love for you to join them!

What do you care about? How would you like to impact the world around you?

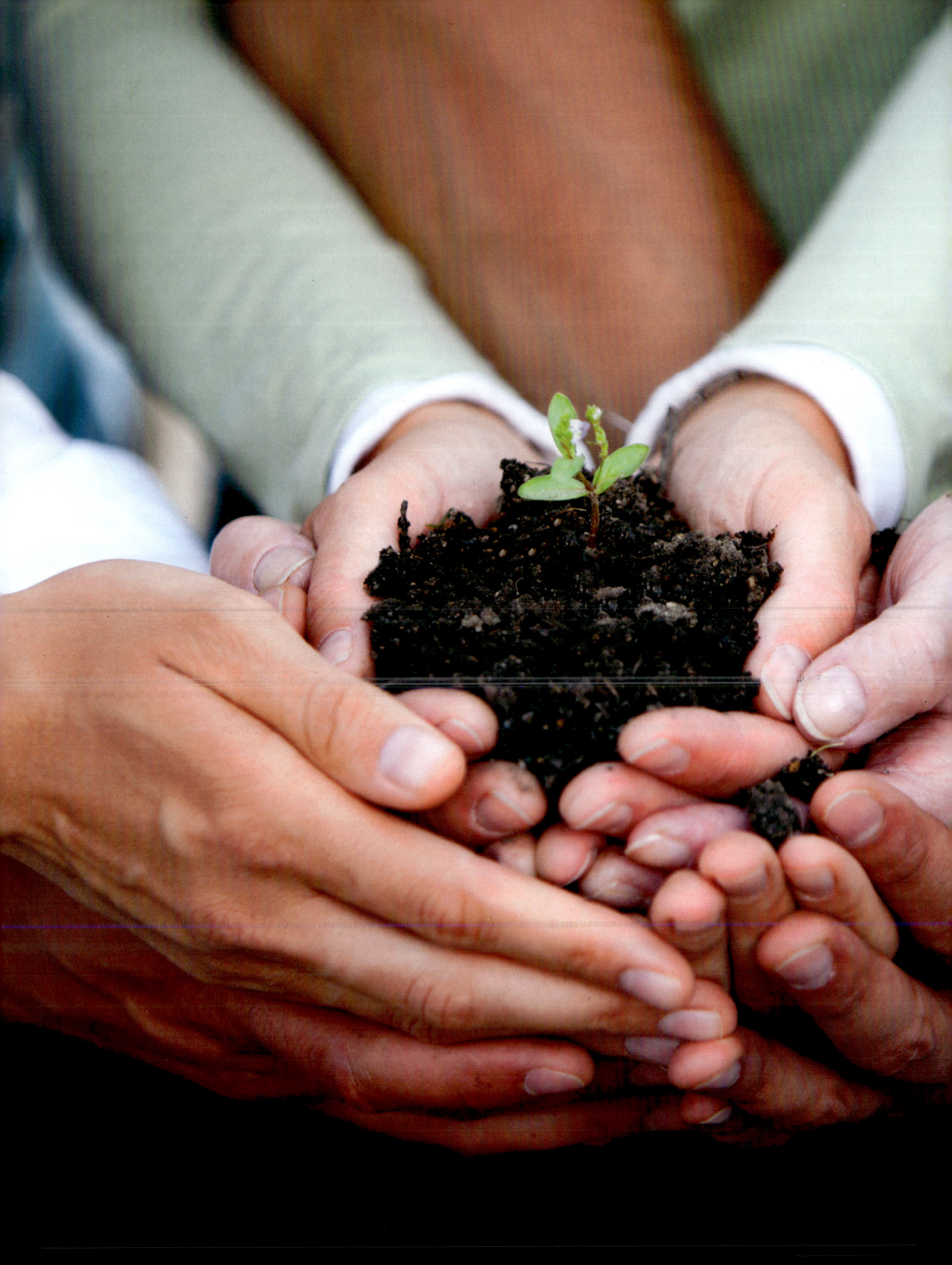

Chapter 2

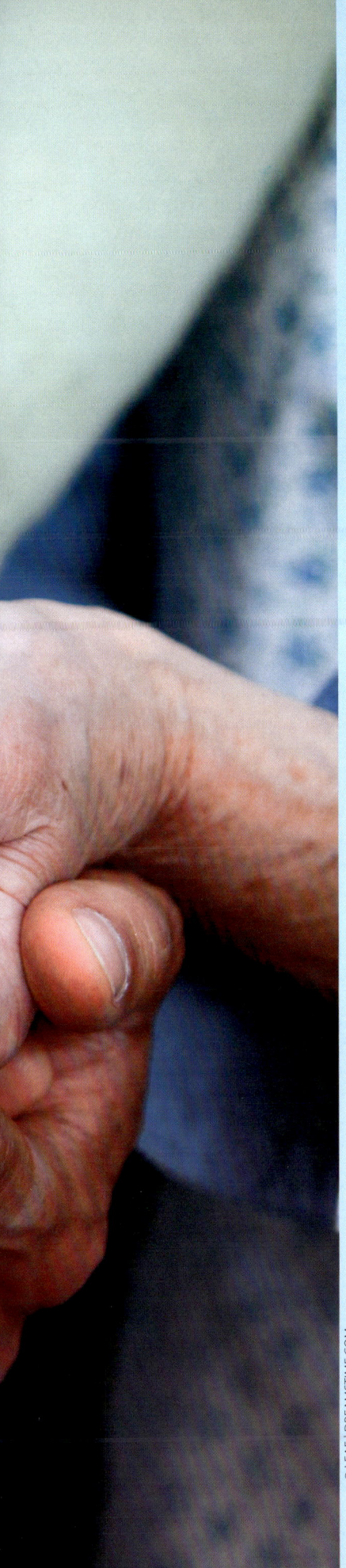

Sustainability

GUIDING QUESTIONS

- How can sustainability promote environmental health, economic development, and human well-being?
- How are people working toward sustainable solutions to local and global issues?

Introduction to Sustainability

Jarid Manos grew up in rural Ohio, where he first fell in love with the prairie ecosystem. The prairie served as a refuge where Jarid could go when life became difficult. Jarid's childhood was not easy. As a teenager, he ran away from home. He spent years moving from one city to another, making money any way he could. As a young man he struggled with depression and drinking and eventually he resorted to selling drugs. During those turbulent times, Jarid yearned to return to the prairies he loved.

Now, Jarid's refuge is a disappearing ecosystem. In the past, prairies were found all over the United States. Today, there are fewer and fewer prairies in North America as people are building homes and farms where prairies used to be.

Jarid eventually grew from a troubled young man into a leader and role model. After spending years building a healthy life, learning about efforts to save America's disappearing prairies, and discovering how to lead a movement for change, Jarid founded the Great Plains Restoration Council (GPRC).

Jarid Manos founded the Great Plains Restoration Council.

The GPRC restores prairie ecosystems in Texas and South Dakota with the help of people from different cultures, backgrounds, and communities. The GPRC works not only to protect natural prairie areas and the wildlife that live there, but also to help young people improve their lives by teaching them leadership skills. The Council strives to build healthy environments and healthy people. Says Jarid, "This is Ecological Health—healing ourselves through healing the Earth."[1]

Jarid's own personal journey and the work of the Great Plains Restoration Council are connected to the idea of sustainability. **Sustainability** is the principle of meeting current needs without limiting the ability of future generations to meet their needs. Perhaps the simplest way to think about it is that sustainability involves the health of people and the planet.

Sustainability comes from the concept of sustainable development. **Sustainable development** is the process of economic, social, and political transformation using practices that raise standards of living for people around the world without depleting Earth's resources. In other words, it involves helping people to meet their needs for a good life without compromising the ability of future generations to meet their needs. If we allow Earth's resources to be depleted, then we limit the ability of people to meet their needs and to have a good quality of life in the years to come.

Two fundamental principles tied to sustainability are:

1. **Intergenerational responsibility:** We have a responsibility to leave ample resources for future generations on Earth.
2. **Interconnectedness:** Natural and human-constructed systems cannot be separated. They interact with and impact each other.

How are intergenerational responsibility and interconnectedness part of the things we do every day? As you participate in an activity, ask yourself if it can be done in a way so that people in the future will have the same opportunities to do this activity as you do today. For example, if you live in an area surrounded by natural beauty you can enjoy your environment in ways that increase your health and happiness. If you also make an effort to maintain your surroundings by keeping the streets clean, recycling, and decreasing air pollution, you will help preserve a healthy environment for future generations. You will also support the health of your community today (for example, a decrease in air pollution can decrease respiratory issues).

When we talk about striving for sustainability, are we talking about something on a global scale or are we talking about something that applies to local communities? Yes and yes! That is, we are talking about both global and local issues. When you think about it, even global problems are local to someone. When these issues become global in scale, it is because of recurring patterns and widespread consequences. Think about the issue of poverty. Approximately 1 billion children around the world live in poverty.[2] This issue is clearly one that needs to be addressed systemically. At a global level, we can look at root causes and solutions (i.e., policies that will decrease poverty by a certain year). At a local level, people can provide more immediate responses to help to alleviate poverty (i.e., food banks, shelters for homeless people).

Frameworks for Envisioning Sustainability

Sustainability is a big idea. Yet, at its core, it is also a simple idea. However, it is not always easy to visualize sustainability. Frameworks have been developed over the years in an attempt to provide a structure for exploring, analyzing, and acting on sustainability issues. As you read the two frameworks presented here, think about which one makes the most sense to you and why. How would you explain sustainability?

Environment as the Base

Some people argue that a healthy environment is the foundation of a sustainable future. Without a thriving natural environment, they argue, there would be no human society because humans rely on resources from nature every day. Take, for instance, the food that you eat. If there was no healthy environment where the food could grow, you would not be able to survive. Thus, the human spheres of society and economy fall within the larger sphere of environment. Similarly, economy is a sub-system of society, so the economic sphere is further nested within the social sphere. The result of this hierarchy is a system of nested circles.

Three Equal Sectors

A different model suggests that all three types of systems—environmental, economic, and social—must be in good working order to support sustainable communities. This puts economy and society on par with environment.

A Venn diagram provides the simplest model for visualizing the role that the three sectors play in sustainability. The area in the middle where the three sectors overlap is where sustainability occurs.

This diagram is useful as a "lens" for looking at the sustainability of any decision, behavior, or object. For example, you can use the diagram to analyze the sustainability of a cup of fair trade coffee. **Fair trade** is the idea that fair prices are paid to those producing goods in developing countries. This coffee

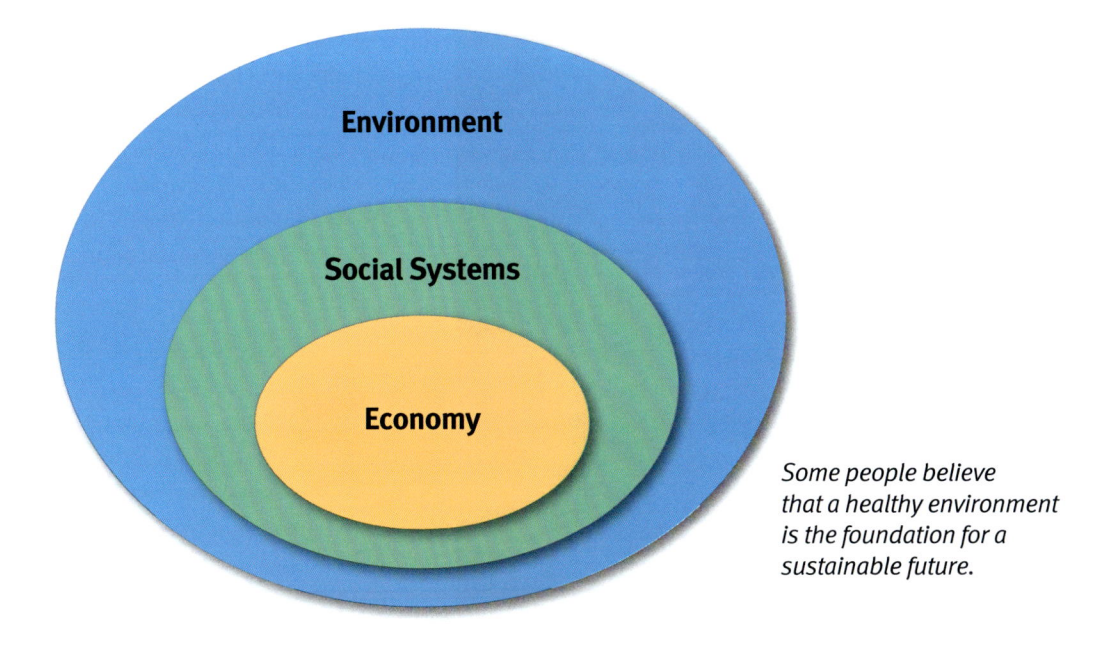

Some people believe that a healthy environment is the foundation for a sustainable future.

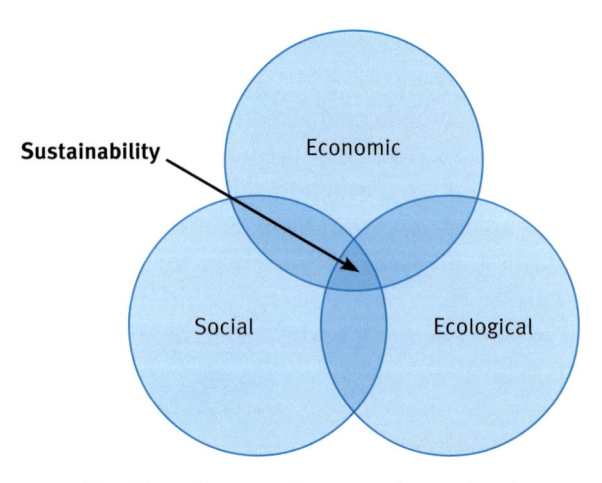

This Venn Diagram illustrates how a thriving society, flourishing economy, and healthy environment support sustainability.

provides a living wage (income necessary to meet one's basic needs) for coffee farmers, so we can say that it promotes economic sustainability for coffee-growing communities. If the coffee is shade-grown, meaning it grows in tropical forests alongside other species and provides habitat for native birds, we can argue that it supports ecological sustainability. Lastly, our cup of coffee can be seen as encouraging social sustainability because the fair trade

The Selva Negra Coffee Farm in Nicaragua offers organic, shade grown, bird-friendly coffee.

model allows farmers in Nicaragua to grow coffee in a traditional manner and to sustain their local culture. If fair trade coffee promotes the well-being of the economy, society, and environment, we can conclude that it is a sustainable choice.

This Venn diagram appears throughout the book as a simple visual tool to show that building sustainable communities requires environmental well-being, social vitality, and economic health. If you take one component of the Venn diagram out, this can lead to instability and possible collapse of the others.

How Sustainability Connects to Us

When you think about the world in 50 years, what do you think it will look like? And what do you hope it will look like? There are many different ways you can help to create your ideal future. Young people around the world today make sustainable choices all the time. These decisions range from the types of things you choose to buy and the career you pursue all the way to how you deal with conflict. Consider the following examples:

- A high school student who has witnessed violence in his local community decides to create music about increasing peace
- a student club works with their school to teach everyone how to save energy within the building
- a homeroom decides to create a public service announcement to teach youth about making sustainable choices when they shop

All of the above examples illustrate different ways we can live more sustainably. The choices we make individually can influence the choices we make as a society. And the choices we make as a society can have a global impact. The case study above illustrates one person's sustainable choices and how his choices support his family and his community.

Raul lives in the town of Chinchero with his family.

YOUTH PROFILE
Raul Quillahuaman Huaman

Raul lives in the town of Chinchero in Peru with his family. He loves life in Chinchero because it is peaceful; people are friendly and help each other. He also loves the mountains that surround the town.

Chinchero is famous for its weaving and boys and girls learn how to weave at a young age. Many people in Chinchero are farmers. In addition to growing potatoes and lima beans, they raise sheep that provide wool for weaving blankets and clothes. The land is very important to people in Chinchero because it provides food and a way to make money. The main language spoken in Chinchero is Quechua and the second language is Spanish.

One challenge in Chinchero is that many people lack the money to complete their education. Students usually stop going to school by the time they are 16, and without a proper education they struggle to earn enough money to support their families and take care of the land.

Raul currently attends university to study tourism so that he can help strengthen his community's economy, sustain the environment, and teach people about his culture. Raul's hope is that Chinchero can attract tourists who will support the town's economy when they eat at local restaurants, take tours of the village, buy blankets or clothes, and rent hotel rooms. The money that local people make through tourism supports their livelihood. Tourism also gives Raul a chance to share his way of life with those who come to learn about his people. He wants to make sure that in 50 years his community and family have good opportunities in life. His career choice helps him pursue this goal.

Background on Sustainability

Human history has taught us lessons related to extinct civilizations and reasons why they were not able to survive. In certain cases, civilizations were not able to make sustainable decisions for the future and this lack of foresight led to their eventual collapse. Jared Diamond, an

American scientist and author, speaks to a number of factors that lead to a civilization's collapse: environmental damage, climate change, conflict, loss of support from friendly trade partners, and responses to environmental problems. Diamond notes that some past societies failed while others succeeded: "The past offers us a rich database from which we can learn in order that we may keep on succeeding."[3]

Even though the term sustainability may be relatively new, the concept behind it is not. Over time, societies have made decisions that allowed them to grow, adapt, and thrive. The Iroquois League, a group of North American tribes that speak the Iroquois language, is credited with the principle of seventh generation sustainability. This principle requires tribal leaders to consider the effects of their actions on their descendants through the next seven generations. How might your actions change if you had to consider whether your choices would benefit your children, grandchildren, and great-grandchildren?

> *Even though the term sustainability may be relatively new, the concept behind it is not.*

In more recent years, the United Nations formed the World Commission on Environment and Development (WECD) in 1983 after realizing that economic and social development—in short, improving people's lives—relied in part on sustaining environmental resources.

Specifically, the UN asked the Commission to focus on:

- Developing environmental strategies for achieving sustainable development
- Translating concern for the environment into greater cooperation among countries and consideration of the connections among people, resources, environment, and development
- Defining shared perceptions of environmental issues and of the efforts needed to successfully protect the environment, an agenda for action during the decades to follow, and long-term goals[4]

In 1987, this commission, led by chairman Gro Harlem Brundtland, released a report titled "Our Common Future."[5] The report provided a vision of hope for transforming *economic development* (increasing the standard of living within a country) into something that also supports environmental health.

Sustainability Today

Some experts working in the field of sustainability suggest that we are now approaching a full—swing revolution—a sustainability revolution, that is.[6] As you read this book, consider whether the evidence supports the idea that we are living in revolutionary times. Is there a critical mass of people working toward sustainability? Do our existing models of sustainability provide a roadmap for ensuring the long-term well-being of people and the planet, or will new models of sustainability be required?

There are more than just a few individuals and organizations striving to create a sustainable future. According to the WiserEarth database, which connects people and organizations working on social justice, environmental stewardship, and indigenous rights, "There are more than one million organizations and many millions of us around the world who are actively working toward ecological sustainability, economic justice, human rights protection, political accountability and peace—issues that are systemically interconnected and intertwined."[7]

The following examples demonstrate the different ways educational organizations, businesses, governments, and religious groups think sustainably.

Education

Both K-12 schools and higher education are making commitments to sustainability. One example is the Goddard School

District in Goddard, Kansas, which uses sustainability as a guiding principle. Each year hundreds of students at Goddard's two high schools take an ecology course that teaches the scientific principles behind waste management, climate change, and alternative energy technologies. Students apply their understanding to implement waste management, recycling, and energy efficiency systems for their school buildings and then teach younger students about sustainability in a district-wide event. The district's emphasis on sustainability influences energy-use policies within classrooms (for example, keeping temperatures at 68°F in winter and 75°F in warmer months and using motion sensors to turn off lights when not being used) and supports the planting of native gardens on school grounds. The Goddard School District is a member of both Eco-Schools USA and the Kansas Green Schools Network, organizations that support educators and students in implementing sustainability measures at their schools.[8]

Over 650 colleges and universities in the United States have signed the American College & University Presidents' Climate Commitment. Leaders at these institutions agree that colleges and universities should model ways to reduce greenhouse gas emissions that contribute to climate change. They are also committed to educating their students about climate change and solutions.[9]

The United Nations declared 2005 to 2014 the Decade of Education for Sustainable Development (DESD). The UN requested countries "to integrate the principles, values and practices of sustainable development into all aspects of education and learning, in order to address the social, economic, cultural and environmental issues we face in the 21st century." For example, DESD efforts in India include a National Curriculum Framework "connecting knowledge to life outside the school," and their Supreme Court directed all schools to include environmental education at all levels. Beyond 2014 this work will be sustained at The Earth Charter Center for Education for Sustainable Development at the University for Peace in Costa Rica.[10]

Goddard students plant a native prairie garden.

Business

Businesses and industries are also starting to incorporate an ethic of sustainability into their operations. Some companies, like the Body Shop, were founded on sustainability principles. Others, like Gap, have adopted strong corporate social responsibility policies, pledging to treat workers, consumers, and the environment with respect.

Major companies—including Dow Chemical, GE, Home Depot, and UPS—are creating "Chief Sustainability Officer" positions. These executives are typically responsible for exploring green product development and reducing the environmental impact of their business.

The green jobs movement in the United States is another example of how sustainability permeates the business world. **Green jobs**, sometimes also called green-collar jobs, are typically career-track jobs that improve the environment and pay a livable wage. Green-collar workers might install solar panels on homes, create landscapes that harvest rainwater, or insulate buildings to prevent heat loss.

Green jobs organizations work in many different communities to encourage government leaders to invest in green jobs and to train the workers who will install and maintain the technologies needed to reduce our negative environmental impacts. One of the most well-known organizations in this movement is Green for All. Green for All's approach is to lift people out of poverty by building a "green economy." A green economy can serve the needs of many by simultaneously providing jobs for thousands of Americans, helping homeowners reduce energy costs, and connecting people with renewable sources of energy.[11]

Government

Governments are also getting involved in sustainability. Some of these efforts are at the local government level, such as in the city of Madison, Wisconsin. Madison has its own City Sustainability Plan. So far, the city has taken many different steps down the path of sustainability, including:

- Signing the Kyoto Protocol, an international agreement to reduce greenhouse gas emissions
- Providing help for homeowners who want to install solar panels
- Requiring recycling companies to comply with the most rigorous standards for handling international e-waste

Photovoltaic cells are attached to the roof of a shelter in a Madison city park.

- Employing green building techniques in the construction of new libraries, a fire station, and a convention center
- Retrofitting a number of existing government buildings for energy efficiency
- Increasing the use of renewable sources of electricity from 3% in 2006 to 22% in 2009
- Purchasing furniture and cleaning products with sustainability in mind[12]

National governments are also part of the story. Federal policies, initiatives, and funding can be used to further realize goals of sustainability. Sweden's Ministry of the Environment works to ensure sustainable development, as does France's Ministry of Ecology, Sustainable Development, Transport and Housing. Going one step further, international efforts between two or more national governments demonstrate how governments can become a powerful force for change. One such international effort resulted in the Montreal Protocol on Substances that Deplete the Ozone Layer.

During the 1980s, scientists discovered that the ozone layer in Earth's atmosphere was thinning in some places. A large hole in the ozone formed above Antarctica. The ozone layer protects us from some of the sun's harmful ultraviolet radiation that can cause skin cancer and eye cataracts. People all over the world were alarmed by the depletion of the ozone layer and its implications for global health. Once scientists traced the damage to halogen gases used in products such as refrigerators and fire extinguishers, it was clear that the ozone would continue to disappear unless people stopped using these gases.

In 1987, the Montreal Protocol established limits on the amounts of ozone-depleting gases any nation could produce or consume, eventually phasing out the destructive gases altogether. Ozone-depleting gases were replaced with other gases that provided the same functions (refrigerants and propellants) without destroying the ozone. The Protocol, now ratified by 196 countries, has been successful at slowing the rate of ozone depletion.

Religions from around the world share similar values around sustainability.

Scientists predict that by the middle of this century, ozone levels will return to pre-halogen gas product levels.[13]

Religion

Many of the world's religions have sustainability-focused principles. For example, the Jewish Torah (or the Christian Old Testament) and the Islamic Qur'an each state that God made all the lands and waters on Earth, as well as all living creatures. The idea that humans have an obligation to care for all the resources on Earth is a form of reverence to God's creation.[14] Though we now refer to this principle as sustainability, you may have also heard it called *stewardship*.

Over the last several decades, many of the world's religious leaders have begun to address global sustainability challenges. Historically, religious leaders have worked on securing social well-being through reducing poverty and suffering. More recently, many of these leaders have come together to work on ensuring environmental well-being.[15] Consider the breadth of just a few of these partnerships:

World Wildlife Fund

In 1986, the World Wildlife Fund (WWF) sponsored an interreligious meeting in Assisi, Italy. Buddhist, Christian, Hindu, Muslim, and Jewish leaders came together to discuss how their faiths could help protect the environment. After that initial meeting, WWF also began working with additional religious groups—Baha'is, Daoists, Jains, and Sikhs—on conservation projects.[16]

The United Nations Environment Programme

The United Nations Environment Programme (UNEP) in North America established an annual Environmental Sabbath and distributes materials to communities of faith in the United States and Canada.[17]

The Parliament of World Religions

In 1993, the Parliament of World Religions held a meeting in Chicago attended by 8,000 people. They issued a resulting statement, *Towards a Global Ethic: An Initial Declaration,* that claims, "Our world is experiencing a *fundamental crisis:* A crisis in global economy, global ecology, and global politics." In response to this crisis, the Parliament put forth a set of common ethical principles that all religious and non-religious persons could agree upon to foster socially beneficial, peaceful, and environmentally friendly ways of living.[18]

Pathways to Progress: Sustainability

What does sustainability look like in action? And what are ways institutions, communities, and people can work to make sustainable choices?

The following examples demonstrate sustainable actions that communities, organizations, and individuals can take.

Community Growth: Moss Point, Mississippi

A sustainable community strives for:[19]

- A better quality of life for everyone in the community, without negatively impacting other communities

Moss Point citizens attend a community meeting.

- Healthy ecosystems
- Effective governance supported by active citizen participation
- Economic security

Moss Point is a city of around 20,000 people that lies along the Gulf Coast of Mississippi. Moss Point was particularly devastated by Hurricane Katrina, which happened in 2005, in part due to previously existing poverty. The hurricane destroyed homes and washed out the entire downtown area. With the help of the Institute for Sustainable Communities, Moss Point turned the devastation into an opportunity to build a stronger community. Rebuilding sustainably means that they are not only rebuilding damaged neighborhoods, but also that citizens and government are working together to solve long-term problems such as environmental degradation, poverty, and loss of jobs and industry.

The Moss Point community is now engaged in developing thriving environmental, social, and economic systems. New city buildings are being constructed with environmentally minded practices. The community now recognizes the need to preserve natural ecosystems such as wetlands, which provide a barrier against powerful storms and can generate tourism. A task force was developed to ensure that a range of affordable housing options is available for all, including low-income residents. In all of Moss Point's rebuilding efforts, citizens are involved in making decisions in partnership with government and nonprofit organizations that are working to restore the community.[20]

Nonprofit Support: Snow Leopard Trust

Snow Leopard Trust is a nonprofit organization that works to protect endangered snow leopards living in the mountains of Central Asia. Although they have roamed the mountains for centuries, snow leopards face threats due to the overlap in landscape and resource use between themselves and humans. Snow

Snow leopards face extinction due to human activities; many are illegally hunted by poachers.

leopards are hunted illegally by poachers and are losing habitat and wild prey as people and their livestock (like goats and sheep) move into new areas. In some cases, livestock herders have killed snow leopards in retaliation for the leopards eating herders' goats and sheep.

The Snow Leopard Trust realized that the people living in snow leopard habitats should be involved in finding a solution to help protect snow leopards. It was also clear that a lasting solution would have to take into account the well-being of both snow leopards and people. Because people in the region make very little money, a long-lasting solution would have to provide livestock herders with income. This approach to conservation of endangered species or wildlands is called community-based conservation; it takes into account the unique challenges, needs, skills, and resources of a particular community.

A unique conservation program developed by Snow Leopard Trust in partnership with communities in Mongolia assists people living in the mountains alongside snow leopards with the sale of wool handicrafts, such as rugs and slippers. To participate in the program, communities in snow leopard areas must agree not

CAREER PROFILE   Ecologist

Do you ever wonder how creatures organize themselves around their landscape? Why one living thing depends on another for its survival? How vital nutrients cycle through an ecosystem? Ecologists make a career out of questions like these; they study how living things interact with each other and with their environments. Ecology is a subset of biology. There are all sorts of careers that apply ecology, from computer-based modeling of ecosystems to conducting field research on wetlands. Opportunities to work in the field are diverse, since ecologists study many different aspects of ecosystems such as biodiversity, habitat, niche, and geography. There are also opportunities to work in the realm of human ecology, contributing to fields such as resource management and urban development.

Sasha Kramer, Ph.D., has a lot of jobs, not the least of which is her work as an ecologist. She is the cofounder of SOIL (Sustainable Organic Integrated Livelihoods), an international aid organization in Haiti, and an adjunct professor of International Studies at the University of Miami. Sasha's training in ecology prepared her for her current work, but it was her passion for human rights that inspired her to begin a civil engineering nongovernmental organization (NGO). "While working as a human rights observer in Haiti in 2004," she says, "I became acutely aware of how much most people in the United States take toilets for granted; it is painfully obvious when you cannot find one and you need one." The absence of sanitation infrastructure and the environmental impact of dumping sewage into aquatic ecosystems create a crisis for human health and ecosystems. SOIL began by building toilets where human wastes, instead of being dumped into waterways, were recycled into organic compost. This compost can then be used to rejuvenate nutrient-depleted soil, which helps crops to grow. SOIL installs toilets designed with ecological sanitation principles in mind in communities throughout Haiti. These seemingly simple toilets effectively handle two of the foremost problems (sanitation and agricultural development) that otherwise compromise human rights and quality of life.

Sasha emerges from a toilet installed by SOIL.

---

to kill snow leopards and their prey. If everyone in a herding community keeps their agreement, herders receive cash bonuses once a year. If just one person in the community breaks her or his agreement, no one receives a bonus. This community-based conservation strategy frees people from poverty while also protecting an endangered species.[21]

Citizens Taking Action

When faced with the big challenges that must be addressed to build a sustainable future, it can be difficult to imagine how a single individual can create real change. You might wonder what personal action you can take. As illustrated by Raul's story earlier in the chapter, it is possible for one person to influence her or his own life and the life of the planet through her or his own choices. Your actions, from small to large, do matter. This might mean taking personal responsibility to recycle or reuse discarded items or to purchase sustainably produced products. You can also make a difference by voting for laws and government representatives that will support sustainability. Or you can take part in your community's efforts to improve quality of life—for example, by volunteering for a community organization—to contribute to lasting change.

If you are passionate about creating a sustainable future, you can help drive change by taking a leadership position. People young and old from all backgrounds can get involved in community decision-making. This might mean becoming a member of a group that works to protect the environment or alleviate poverty, or even becoming a member of a governmental group (like student council). Another approach is to question and change structures that present obstacles to sustainability. Are there policies in your community or state that make it difficult for people to transition out of poverty? Does an absence of laws or restrictions allow people to destroy the natural environment? You might imagine long-term solutions to these issues, such as financial assistance to help people move out of poverty or legislation to prevent forests from being overharvested. And you can take part in making those solutions a reality by joining a social or political movement to effect dramatic and long-term change.

Taking Action: Global Youth Action Network

Global Youth Action Network (GYAN) is a youth-led group that started in 1999. GYAN believes young people have the power to make a difference in the world and that by taking positive action now they can reduce the number of problems in the future. Through programs like Global Youth Service Day, GYAN helps young people in more than 125 countries work on service projects in their communities. For example, teenagers in Bolivia taught their community about the dangers of drinking unclean water. In the United States, youth educated people about the importance of voting. In Thailand, students taught leadership and life skills to children who were orphaned when their parents died of AIDS. Global Youth Action Network is one group of young people who truly believe they can change the world.[22]

WHAT YOU CAN DO | Sustainability

The steps to achieve sustainable solutions are similar to those for any other challenge: first you must gain background knowledge on important issues, build skills needed to create change, and believe that you can change things. This book will provide you with information about a wide variety of sustainability issues that challenge our world, it will help you to develop skills to solve problems, and it will show you how other people just like you are doing things large and small to bring about a more sustainable future.

Remember that you have a place in sustainable development. Keep these simple questions in mind as you read each chapter:

- What issue are we talking about?
- What are obstacles to sustainability related to this issue?
- Why does it matter to me, anyway? How does it connect to my life?
- What are possible solutions that I can be a part of?

When we think about a sustainable future, we consider our actions now and for future generations.

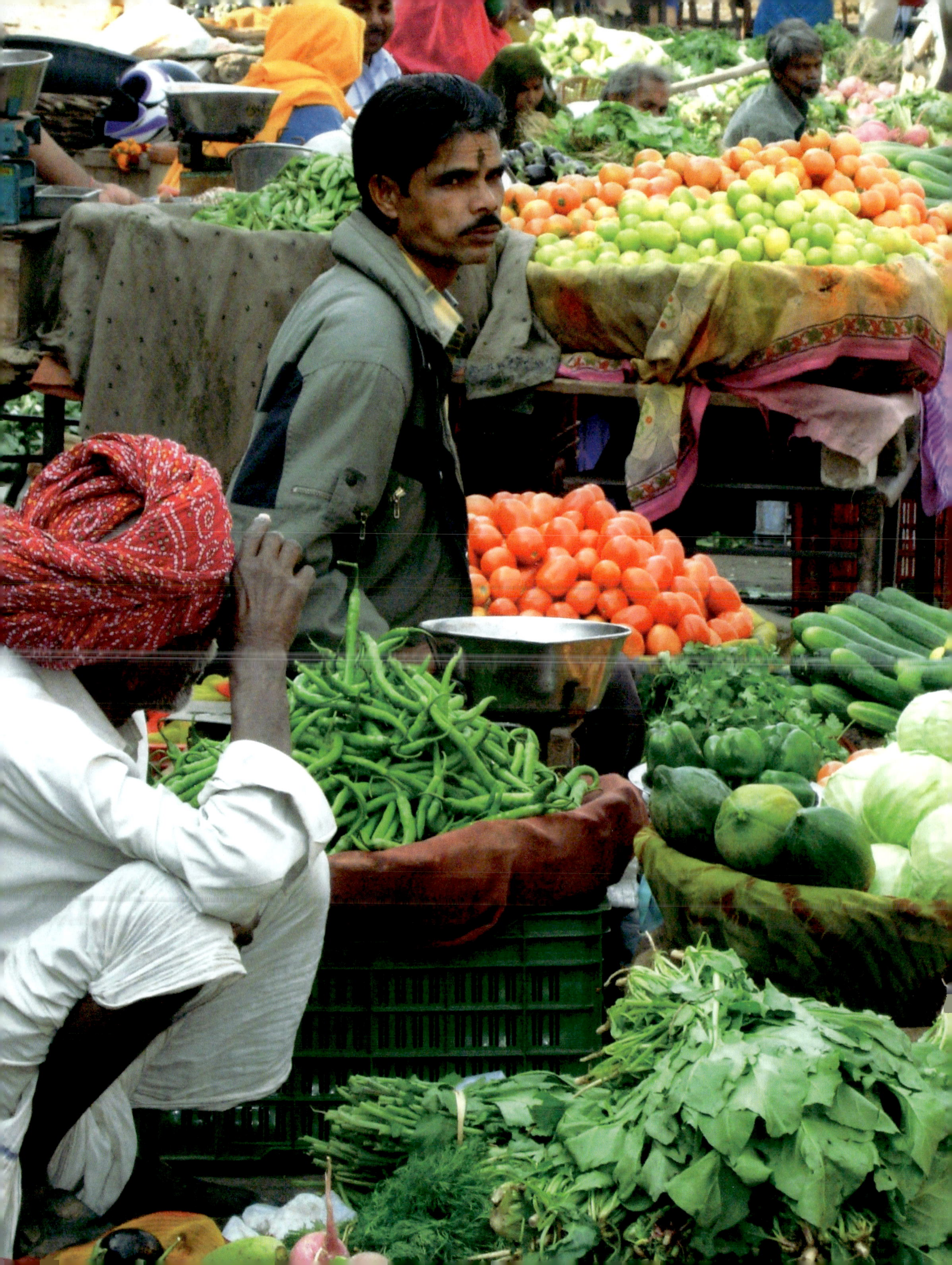

Chapter 3

Food

Food, glorious food!
What is there more handsome?
Gulped, swallowed or chewed—
Still worth a king's ransom!

—Lionel Bart, *Oliver!* the musical

> **GUIDING QUESTIONS**
> - How can we ensure that all people have access to nutritious food?
> - What agricultural practices are compatible with a healthy planet?

Introduction to Food

Have you ever been unable to finish your meal and then heard someone say, "You shouldn't waste food when there are starving people in the world"? It's definitely true that some people in the world do not have enough to eat. But why are they starving? What does it have to do with the way food is grown and distributed? And how do our actions play a part?

Food and Sustainability

Economy

The World Food Summit in 1996 explained **food security** this way: "when all people at all times have access to sufficient, safe, nutritious food to maintain a healthy and active life."[1]

Food security obviously affects individual well-being—we all need to eat. Food security directly relates to sustainability, too. It can affect entire societies, creating unrest and instability and even triggering changes in politics and governance. "Bread riots" have occurred throughout modern times when food prices rise to the extent that many people can no longer afford food staples like bread. Egypt experienced bread riots at several points during the last few decades. Much of Egypt's food is imported, making the country vulnerable to rising market prices. In 2007-2008, high grain prices abroad led to a 37% increase in the price of bread in Egypt.[2] Thousands of Egyptians took to the streets in protest.[3]

In 2010, another wave of bread riots occurred in the region. This time food insecurity ignited a spark that contributed to a series of citizen-led uprisings in Arab countries such as Egypt, Tunisia, and Syria, known as the Arab Spring. Governments in these countries have typically subsidized staple foods like bread to keep costs affordable for citizens. However, as global grain prices soared, government subsidies could not keep pace and consumer prices for food began to climb. Along with other factors, the high cost of bread helped create a shift in public attitudes. Arab Spring protesters began to question the policies of their governments, express their waning confidence with the authoritarian regimes in power, and demonstrate their desire for greater liberty. In this case, what began as bread riots grew into a broader popular movement that ultimately led to the overthrow of national governments.[4]

Bread riots have happened throughout the world when food has become too expensive.

Society

Food security can be undermined by a variety of challenges. Our ability to continue to produce enough food for everyone may be limited by population growth, environmental degradation, and climate change. As more people are added to the world's population, there are more mouths to feed. And as people's lives improve and they become wealthier, food consumption changes. When incomes rise, people tend to eat more meat. Eating meat reduces the potential number of calories available to people around the world because of the resources it takes to produce it. Did you know that it takes at least six pounds of corn to produce one pound of beef?[5]

Environment

Another challenge is environmental degradation. Each year more and more of the world's best farmland becomes unusable. Some agricultural land is overworked; intensive tilling, combined with strong winds or rainfall, removes fertile topsoil and nutrients and reduces the productivity of the land. Farmland is lost to other uses, too. For example, some productive farmland in the United States is turned into suburban neighborhoods because farmers can make more money by selling their land than they can by farming.[6]

Climate change can make it difficult to grow crops in some places.[7] As a result of climate change, natural disasters that destroy crops and farmland can become more severe. It may also result in the spread of agricultural pests and diseases, like fungi and bacteria.

However, agricultural technology is also part of the equation. Past improvements in farming efficiency have allowed us to grow much more food than our ancestors were able to grow.

The challenges facing food production are not the driving force behind food insecurity. Believe it or not, enough food is grown and harvested to feed everyone on the planet. In fact, there is enough food available on Earth for all people to have enough nourishment to lead a healthy, productive life.[8]

Yet even in a world of plenty, poverty and hunger affect many. The Director-General of the United Nations Food and Agriculture Organization, Jacques Diouf, asks: "If our planet produces enough food to feed its entire population, why do 854 million people still go to sleep on an empty stomach?"[9] As you will read later in this chapter, hunger is typically the result of an inability to access available food.

Background on Food

People have not always farmed. For thousands of years, people lived as hunter-gatherers or foragers, following animal migrations and the seasonal growth of plants. During this time, world population remained low and grew slowly—the number of people who died was about the same as the number of people who were born. Around 11,000 to 10,000 people began to grow their own food. Farming maximizes the productivity of plants to supply more energy than what natural ecosystems can provide. Therefore, cultivating their own food allowed populations to grow much more rapidly.[10]

Major ancient civilizations would not have flourished without productive agricultural systems. Part of this process was driven by domestication. For plant species, domestication entailed keeping certain seeds and replanting them. Animal species were domesticated by controlling their reproduction and isolating them from wild populations. Interestingly, agriculture did not just emerge in one place and spread from there; instead, agriculture emerged in different places around the globe independently.[11]

Millions of tons of food waste are generated each year in the United States while millions of people around the world still go hungry.

The development of agricultural practices meant that humans began to alter their environment as never before. They dammed water to irrigate crops, eliminated unwanted species in an area, and deliberately planted particular species of interest to humans.[12] As you will read throughout this chapter, these changes have had varying effects on environments. In some cases, over time the intensive use of environmental resources has led to soil erosion and expansion of deserts. But in other cases, humans have learned to farm in ways that are more cooperative with nature.

The Incas, for example, farmed on steep hillsides using terraces and irrigation techniques. Their methods conserved both water and soil resources while increasing food availability for a growing population.[13] In less mountainous areas, the Incas and other indigenous groups in the Americas, including the Aztecs, grew crops on raised beds. This practice helped mitigate the

CASE STUDY: The Dust Bowl

The famous period in American history known as the Dust Bowl shows the consequences that can result from unsustainable land use. In the 1930s, the Great Plains of the United States and parts of Canada experienced a severe drought and enormous dust storms, the loss of millions of acres of farmland, and massive migration westward from the Great Plains. In the dust storm of May 10, 1934, 12 million tons of dirt landed in Chicago. There were 22 major dust storms in 1934; three years later, the number of dust storms in a year had more than tripled.[15] Constant wind and periodic droughts were not new to the Great Plains region, so why did the Dust Bowl happen in the 1930s and not before?

Encouraged by government incentives and the dream of financial success, people flocked to the Great Plains to set up farms between 1862 and the 1920s. The invention of the tractor enabled people to farm much larger areas of land than before and farmers were encouraged to produce as much as possible, even if there was already plenty of food in the United States. The farming techniques that most farmers used increased erosion. By tilling native grassland to create fields and plant crops, farmers pulled out the support system that held soil in place during dry windy periods. During the drought of the 1930s, topsoil dried out from lack of rain and strong winds blew it off the fields.[16] With their crops and fields ruined and little hope for local employment amidst the Great Depression, 400,000 people migrated west in search of migrant farm labor jobs.[17]

The Dust Bowl changed the way Americans thought about the environment.

The difficult experience of the Dust Bowl changed the way that many people in the United States thought about the relationship between humans and the environment. In 1935, President Franklin Roosevelt signed the Soil Conservation Act, establishing a Soil Conservation Service. The Soil Conservation Service was tasked with conducting soil erosion surveys and helping to prevent further soil erosion.

impact of both drought and heavy rains by increasing water retention when rain was scarce and protecting root systems during periods of heavy rainfall.[14]

Beginning in the 1950s, agriculture—especially in developing countries—went through a transformation called the **Green Revolution**. Hybrid seeds, fertilizers, pesticides, new machinery, and irrigation projects began to be used around the world. These new agricultural practices and technologies dramatically increased crop yields, helping to feed a growing world population. By the 1960s, Green Revolution techniques such as monocultures (fields where only one crop is grown) and heavy dependence on chemical fertilizers, pesticides, and herbicides had become well known in agricultural production worldwide.

While modern farming techniques have allowed for high crop yields and ensured a food surplus, some of those techniques have resulted in exposure to hazardous chemicals, depleted water sources, and soil erosion. Additionally, the loss of genetic variation and crop variety from monoculture practices and hybrid seeds may disrupt natural ecosystems.

Food Today

Despite the lessons learned from the Dust Bowl, many unsustainable farming practices continue today. Whereas some would argue that intensive farming techniques at odds with nature are necessary to produce food, others argue that farming methods can and should be in harmony with natural processes. By examining each stage of food production, we see these two viewpoints emerge again and again.

Starting with a Seed

Tactics to improve the amount and quality of food raised are not just applied to crops already growing in the field. People are also revolutionizing the seeds that will give rise to the crops. For centuries, scientists and farmers have tinkered with seeds, carefully selecting seeds from higher-yielding crops or tastier fruits in an attempt to ensure those traits persist in their next harvest. Other times scientists have created hybrids of existing plants to produce an entirely new plant variety.

Rather than simply selecting seeds from plants that have desirable traits or cross-pollinating two species to produce a hybrid, today's plant breeders are doing revolutionary things. Over the last 30 years, **genetically modified organisms** (GMOs) have transitioned from experiments in the laboratory into agricultural fields worldwide. Genetic modification involves the insertion of genes from one organism into another to produce altered genetic material (DNA). Unlike older methods of genetic manipulation of plants, genetic modification allows genes from very different types of organisms to be inserted into a plant's genome.

Perhaps the most famous GMO is *Bt* corn. *Bt* stands for *Bacillus thuringiensis,* a bacteria that acts as a pesticide. When insects ingest the bacteria, it eventually kills them. Scientists inserted the *Bt* gene into corn to prevent crop loss due to insect feeding. In theory, farmers would not have to apply additional pesticides to *Bt* corn.

GMO seeds like *Bt* corn have their share of critics. Over time, insect species that were once affected by *Bt* have become resistant to it, meaning it no longer kills them. Genetic contamination of non-GMO species is also a concern. Genes from *Bt* corn have been known to contaminate non-*Bt* corn; pollen from the plants is carried by wind from one field to another. Little is known about the long-term impacts of GMOs on human health and some people are worried that health issues may emerge, such as new allergens.[18]

A different set of concerns is related to legal and economic issues presented by

Genes from Bt corn can contaminate non-Bt corn.

GMOs. In 1980, the U.S. Supreme Court ruled in the case of *Diamond* v. *Chakrabarty* that living things could be patented; prior to that time no living organism was patented. The living thing in the Chakrabarty case was a microorganism engineered to eat oil to help clean up oil spills. The court's decision opened the door to patents for other GMOs. Once an organism is patented, no one other than the patent owner is allowed to create or sell that organism. This is intended to help make it profitable for companies to develop new inventions like GMOs, given the time and resources a company must put into the development process.

On the Farm

Turning seeds into edible plants is an age-old process; Mother Nature has done this for thousands of years without help from humans. However, the development of farming techniques has allowed humans

CASE STUDY: Patenting Seeds

A *patent* is a set of rights granted by a government to an inventor. Article I, Section 8 of the U.S. Constitution gives Congress the right "to promote the Progress of Science and useful Arts, by securing for limited Times to Authors and Inventors the exclusive Right to their respective Writings and Discoveries." When an inventor is granted a patent for an invention, he or she is given the right to exclude others from making, using, or selling his/her invention for a certain amount of time.

In the United States, patents can apply to a newly developed or discovered process, machine, composition of matter, design for a manufactured item, or variety of plant. An invention or discovery must be useful, new, and non-obvious in order to be patented.

The ability to patent genetic material has generated a lot of controversy. One of the most famous cases is a patent on basmati rice lines. U.S.-based RiceTec, Inc. filed for a patent on basmati rice varieties in 1997. This outraged farmers, advocates, and government offi-

Canola is used to making cooking oil.

cials in India, where basmati rice has been grown for thousands of years. Critics called the patent an act of biopiracy, essentially a theft of the collective knowledge of the natural world. RiceTec's patent had consequences not only for Indian farmers who grew basmati rice, but also for Indian traders and exporters. Because basmati rice is such a significant component of India's culture, the RiceTec patent was seen as a threat to India's national heritage. In response to protests from India, RiceTec withdrew most of its patents, including the right to refer to their rice varieties as "basmati."[19]

Patent law battles continue to be fought in courtrooms today. Suspicions of violating patent law have led to a slew of lawsuits filed by large agricultural companies who hold patents for seeds. For example, in one case Monsanto successfully sued a farmer in Canada who planted genetically modified canola seeds without paying Monsanto for them.[20]

to produce much more food in a given area of land than what Mother Nature can do on her own. Some farming methods attempt to mimic natural processes in order to encourage maximum plant growth without harming environmental systems. Other farming methods seem to fight natural processes at every step of the way.

Tillage

On a modern farm—one with diesel-powered machinery and laboratory-developed techniques—*tilling* the soil is one of the first steps to growing a crop. Soils are tilled for several reasons: For one thing, tilling compact soils can break them up to make it easier for plant roots to dig deeper into the ground as they grow. For another thing, tillage can incorporate left-over plant matter from previous harvests, which returns nutrients to soils. Also, some farmers use tillage to interfere with weed growth and other unwanted pests.

Unfortunately, over time tillage can destroy healthy soil. Tillage can rob soil of vital nutrients like carbon and nitrogen that help plants to grow.[21] Tillage can also result in *soil erosion;*

Tilling breaks up soil to help control weed growth in between rows of established crops.

when tilled, nutrient-rich topsoil is broken up into smaller particles that can be carried away by wind or water.

Herbicides, Pesticides, and Fertilizers

When thinking about how our food is grown, tilling is not the only thing to consider.

CASE STUDY Natural Systems Agriculture

Natural systems agriculture is just what it sounds like: a method of agriculture that is modeled after natural systems. The Land Institute is a nonprofit research and education organization working to make natural systems agriculture a reality on farms around the world. The Land Institute is located in Kansas, where prairie ecosystems dominate. Land Institute scientists look to processes seen in the native prairie ecosystems around them to inform agricultural methods including crop production, soil conservation, and nutrient cycling.

Long-lived perennial plants (plants that live for multiple years) predominate in the prairie, as they do in most natural ecosystems. Therefore, one aspect of The Land Institute's research focuses on breeding perennial grains. While annual grains such as wheat and corn must be replanted each year, perennial grains provide food for several years in a row. Planting perennial crops saves resources and means fields can be tilled less frequently than with annuals.

Researchers at The Land Institute and their colleagues across the United States and the world have studied perennial breeding in wheat, corn, rice, sorghum, sunflower, and other species. As one example, they are currently working with hybrids of intermediate wheatgrass (a naturally occurring perennial grain) and annual wheat. They work with different hybrids in order to assess useful traits in them like high seed yield and survivability. The ideal perennial wheat species would produce ample grain and continue to produce high yields year after year.

The Green Revolution increased the use of fertilizers and pesticides.

Some farmers and scientists argue that additional chemicals (herbicides) are needed to kill weeds so that crop seeds can get established. Others are finding ways to both reduce tillage and eliminate use of agricultural chemicals.

The Green Revolution resulted in widespread usage of chemical inputs such as fertilizers and pesticides. *Fertilizers* are designed to quickly add nutrients including nitrogen, potassium, and phosphorous to the soil. Just as we need nutrients to grow, so do plants. These nutrients cycle through ecosystems naturally. However, when humans alter natural cycles during farming, nutrients necessary for plant growth have to be applied from outside of the system.

Inorganic fertilizers created in factories have been credited with greatly increasing crop yields around the world. However, there are tradeoffs involved in the world's increasingly heavy usage of and reliance on these fertilizers. They require large amounts of energy to create and they release greenhouse gas emissions that contribute to climate change.

Agricultural chemicals do not only impact the land and environmental resources they come into contact with; they can also impact the health of farm workers and people who live near farms. According to the World Health Organization, poisoning can result when toxic chemicals—including pesticides used to kill weeds and insects—are released into soil, air, and water. Long-term exposure to pesticides can lead to developmental and reproductive disorders, hormone disruption, nervous system impairment, and cancer.[22]

Irrigation

Water is another important resource for agriculture. Agricultural uses account for 75% of worldwide water use, mainly for *irrigation*.[23] While some fields are watered by rainfall, many farmers rely on aquifers to provide irrigation water. *Aquifers* are areas of porous rock below ground where water collects. Some people refer to them as "fossil water" because water in aquifers has been there a very long time. In many places, aquifers are being depleted faster than they can refill. In the United States about 50 billion gallons of water per day are supplied to agriculture from aquifers.[24] Overuse of aquifers can be costly. Water found deeper in the ground requires more energy to pump to the surface and this process may destabilize land. In addition, when aquifers are depleted, groundwater-fed streams begin to dry up.

Livestock

Raising livestock requires tremendous environmental resources, including water and land. One of the world's largest beef producers is Brazil, a country that is home to a large portion of the famous Amazon rainforest. Brazil exports more beef than any other country. To create pasture lands for cattle, ranchers are cutting down trees and burning forest lands.[25] As a result, the rainforest is shrinking in size. Deforestation and overgrazing by cattle also release greenhouse gases into the air, which contributes to climate change.[26]

Grazing animals like cows and sheep can have significant impacts on rangelands. They eat aboveground parts of plants and their hooves compact soils, making it difficult for plant roots to grow. One technique that some ranchers use to minimize the impact that grazing animals have on rangelands is called *intensive rotational grazing*. Instead of allowing animals to graze a large pasture continuously, intensive rotational grazing only leaves animals in any given area for a short time, sometimes just a few days. Then the animals are moved to a new area and the recently grazed area is given time to recover. This helps to prevent overgrazing (when all the plants in an area are grazed so heavily that they cannot grow back) and soil erosion. Plus, it keeps livestock supplied with new plants to eat.

At the Table

Approximately 60% of plant-based calories consumed around the world are supplied by just three crops: wheat, corn, and rice. Although there are people in the world who suffer from hunger, the irony is that enough grain is produced to provide every person in the world with over 3,000 calories per day.[27]

Not all of the cereal crops produced are consumed directly. For example, did you know that only 1% of corn consumed worldwide is actually eaten as whole or processed grain? Over 50% is used to feed livestock (mostly cattle, hogs, and chickens). Most of the rest is consumed as starch or sweeteners like corn syrup.[28]

The portion of our global diet that comes from meat has been increasing over time. While the average person in a developed country eats much more meat than a person in the developing world (80 kg or 176 lbs/person/year in developed countries, versus 30 kg or 66 lbs/person/year in developing countries), meat consumption is rising worldwide.[29] This is due to rising global incomes. Generally, when their incomes rise, people tend to consume more meat and dairy products.[30] While rising incomes are certainly good news for many people, the subsequent demand for meat and dairy may have serious impacts on the environment.

Intensive rotational grazing can prevent overgrazing and supply livestock with new plants to eat.

We Are What We Eat

What we eat impacts more than our environment; it impacts our bodies, too. **Malnutrition** is the result of poor nutrition; it can result from an insufficient, excessive, or unbalanced diet or an inability to absorb foods. While it is often thought of as hunger, malnutrition can also refer to an excess of nutrients that causes bodily harm.[31] According to a research study done by the Worldwatch Institute, nearly two billion adults around the world are overweight.[32] About a quarter of those people are considered obese, meaning they have an excessive amount of body fat.[33] It's not surprising that this trend has been linked to another trend: a rise in preventable medical problems. Obesity has been linked to increased risk for medical conditions including diabetes, heart disease, high blood pressure, and stroke.

Why Hunger Exists Today

By now, you may be thinking that hunger is not really a big problem in the world. After all, more food is grown than what would be needed to sustain the world's population, and many people consume so much food that they are actually overweight. The reality is hunger still exists all over the world. Hunger, or undernutrition, can stunt physical and mental development; young children are especially at risk for long-term damage and death from malnutrition.[34]

While hunger affects people in even the richest countries of the world, hunger tends to affect greater numbers of people in less developed countries. As you may have already guessed, hunger is not the result of insufficient global food production. The problem is really about regional and personal food security.

According to the World Health Organization, food security results when all three of the following conditions are satisfied:

1. Food is available
2. All people have access to it
3. Food can fulfill nutritional needs[35]

Food scarcity in different places is related to a number of factors. While this chapter will not name every possible factor, some of the major causes of food insecurity are discussed here.

Poverty

The leading cause of hunger around the world is poverty. Indeed, poverty and hunger seem to be inseparable. In many cases, hunger within a country is not simply a result of being without food; it often occurs when people are not able to afford the food being produced.

Perhaps you or your elders can remember a time when unemployment in your community spiked. When tough economic times hit, there may be less money for food. People who have the means to meet their basic needs may still cut back on extravagances like eating out in restaurants. Others may turn to support from their community, such as local food banks and soup kitchens. The world's poorest, however, suffer most severely, experiencing hunger, malnutrition, and even starvation.

The link between income and food seems simple. If people do not grow their own food, they must pay for it. So why is it that sometimes people cannot afford to buy food?

Refugee camps such as this one in the Democratic Republic of the Congo can have scarce food resources.

Foreign landowners purchase farmland in poorer countries to grow crops for export, such as tobacco here.

The answer to this question is not as simple. Poverty, and the hunger that results, is caused by many interrelated factors.

Land ownership is one issue linked to hunger. In recent years, the world has seen a so-called *farmland grab* in which wealthier countries (often those in the Middle East and Asia) seek land outside their borders in order to produce food for their citizens. They typically buy land for very low prices in poor countries, where farmers may be completely unaware that a foreign country owns the "community" land they farm. When foreign landowners use some of the best farmland in poor countries to grow food for export, the result is less food available locally and higher prices. The International Food Policy Research Institute reported that 15-20 million hectares (approximately 40-50 million acres) of land in sub-Saharan Africa were purchased by foreign investors between 2006 and 2009.[36]

Another factor that can push people into poverty and hunger is related to changes in the use of agricultural land. Land may be diverted to non-productive uses (such as cash crops like tobacco) or used to grow export crops rather than local staples for domestic consumption. There are various reasons for this, including shifts in production that occurred during colonization and pressure from international lending organizations, such as the International Monetary Fund (IMF) and the World Bank. When the IMF or the World Bank lends money to a nation, the loan may come with specific suggestions designed to encourage economic development within the country, including shifting a country's farming systems from traditional crops to exports that can be sold in a global market.[37]

When farmers do not grow food to be consumed within their own country, their livelihoods are at the mercy of international markets. For example, a farmer in Bangladesh may be tempted by high prices to switch all of his rice fields to tobacco production. As a result, that farmer must rely on his income to eat. If the price for tobacco exports falls, the farmer might not be able to afford to feed his family.[38]

Geographic Constraints

Any time there is a famine, geography is a factor to consider. It is not equally easy to grow food everywhere. Some regions may suffer from food scarcity due to drought and poor soil for growing crops. For example, the Horn of Africa (the region of eastern Africa that includes

This hillside in Haiti is vulnerable to soil erosion due to deforestation.

the countries of Djibouti, Ethiopia, Eritrea, Kenya, Somalia, the Sudan, and Uganda) includes much land area considered arid because it receives very little rainfall. This land is vulnerable to prolonged droughts. Although farmers in the region can do some things to reduce risk of crop failure from drought, such as staggering plantings throughout the growing season, there is little they can do to avoid the devastating impacts of a lengthy period with no rain. It is possible that global climate change will make weather in the region even more unpredictable and farming that much more difficult.[39]

Eastern Africa is not the only place where conditions make agriculture difficult. Another region that has a hot, dry climate is the Middle East. Some agriculture is possible in this climate with the use of irrigation, but much of the region relies on imported food. Whereas regional poverty makes it difficult for those in the Horn of Africa to purchase imported food, strong economies and government subsidies allow many people in the Middle East to purchase food imports. In the Middle East and other places where weather and geography limit people's ability to farm sustainably, food security may be gained through strengthening trade networks rather than increasing agricultural production.[40]

Unsustainable Farming Practices

In some places, food scarcity can be traced to unsustainable farming practices. Soils that were once fertile can be depleted over time if they are not carefully managed. The Caribbean nation of Haiti is an example. Haiti once had nutrient-rich soils, able to support the cultivation of various crops, but those soils are now largely nutrient-depleted. Beginning with the arrival of Spanish and then French explorers, forests in Haiti were cut down to grow crops such as sugar, coffee, and tobacco. Colonial exploitation had a lasting impact on Haiti's forests and soils; it also re-shaped Haitian society through the import of African slaves to work colonial plantations.

Even after Haiti's independence in 1804, good farmland remained concentrated in the hands of a few wealthy landowners and peasant farmers were pushed into hilly areas unsuited for intensive agriculture. Years of intense cultivation of crops such as maize, beans, and cassava on marginal lands combined with deforestation for fuel wood has led to extreme soil erosion. Haiti's inability to grow sufficient food to sustain its population means the country has to rely on imports of staple crops, like rice imported from the United States. Not surprisingly, this means that Haitians are vulnerable to price increases of so-called "Miami rice."[41]

Political Instability and Conflicts

Food scarcity can also result from unstable government and conflict, whether within a single country or between multiple countries. One place where lengthy conflict has impacted food security is the Republic of South Sudan. Prior to achieving statehood in 2011, South Sudan was a part of the northeastern African country of Sudan. Parties in north and south Sudan fought a civil war that lasted from 1983 until peace talks began in 2002 and a formal peace agreement was signed in 2005.[42]

Although the majority of South Sudan's land is suitable for farming, the long civil war devastated agricultural production. Millions of residents were displaced from their homes and those who stayed generally abandoned their fields to avoid being caught in violent raids and attacks.

A UK-based nonprofit organization, FARM-Africa, is working to help people in South Sudan as they return to their fields. According to FARM-Africa, over 80% of South Sudanese make money by rearing livestock and 50% grow crops. Livestock farmers struggle to maintain healthy herds due to limited access to water, pasture, and veterinary services. Farmers who raise crops often lack the tools and knowledge to maximize the land's productivity. FARM-Africa seeks to turn the situation around through programs that establish wells to provide reliable sources of water, provide animal healthcare training, help farmers research the crops best suited to the region, and identify alternate sources of income.[43]

Energy Prices

Poverty, geography, farming practices, and conflict all influence the availability of food. Another factor related to hunger is the cost of food. Food prices might depend on the availability of water, the price of agricultural equipment, or the cost of pesticides. Have you ever thought about how much energy it takes to produce the food that you eat, or how the price of a particular source of energy could even be related to the price of food? A group called the Global Renewable Fuels Alliance argues that the price of one source of energy—petroleum (a.k.a. oil)—directly influences global food prices. When oil is cheap, food is cheap. But the steady climb in oil prices over the last decade has meant a rise in food prices.[44]

South Sudan has land suitable for farming, but civil war devastated its agriculture.

Various agricultural processes involved in growing, transporting, and processing food traditionally depend on petroleum. The biggest need is for diesel fuel or gasoline to operate agricultural machinery and run distribution trucks. In order to make global food prices more predictable, Global Renewable Fuels Alliance advocates for using renewable fuels—primarily biofuels—that are less susceptible to major economic swings.

Interestingly, some research suggests that higher oil prices drive demand for biofuel alternatives (such as ethanol made from corn), which are often made from grain crops. That creates competition with food crops; some cereals are raised to become biofuels rather than food.[45] In a sign of how interconnected our world is, demand for corn-based ethanol in the United States has driven up food prices around the world.[46] Yet other research suggests that demand for biofuels could be coupled with improved food production in Africa. A study that looked at the implications of biofuel investments in Tanzania, Kenya, Mozambique, Zambia, Mali, and Senegal suggests that improved management practices could triple agricultural productivity and free up land to grow crops for biofuels.[47]

Pathways to Progress: Food

There are many examples of positive work being done to increase the availability of food around the world and to grow food in a sustainable manner, from innovative farming methods and government efforts to individual consumption choices. Both personal and structural solutions are important tools to ensure that the world's population has access to food today and in the future.

CASE STUDY: How Much Oil Is in Your Ketchup?

A group of scientists at the Swedish Institute for Food and Biotechnology traced the lifecycle of one food product: ketchup. They attempted to catalog nearly every step in creating ketchup, from growing tomatoes to bottling the final product. They counted 52 steps just for the transportation and processing used to turn tomatoes into that tasty red condiment you know so well. Before the ketchup reached consumers in Sweden, it had logged quite a few miles. The tomatoes were grown and made into tomato paste in Italy. The bags used to store the tomato paste were made in the Netherlands. Once the tomato paste had been created, it was then transported to Sweden.

Scientists counted 52 steps in the lifecycle of ketchup.

The plastic bottles were made of materials from Japan, Italy, Belgium, the United States, and Denmark; the bottle caps were made in Denmark. Other petroleum-based packaging was used, including plastic film.[48]

In the many steps to produce ketchup, various forms of energy are needed: electricity to process the tomatoes into paste, fuel to transport materials, petroleum to make the plastic bottles, and even electricity to run the refrigerator where some people keep their ketchup. The result is that a great amount of energy goes into producing ketchup. It makes you wonder how much energy we get back out of it. As it turns out, the study found that it took four times as much energy to produce, transport, and store ketchup as the energy you could get from eating it.[49]

Sustainable Farming Practices

There are countless methods for sustaining agricultural ecosystems so that they can continue to produce food well into the future. For example, growing species that are well suited for a region's soil and climate can reduce the need for inputs like fertilizers and irrigation. Many researchers and farmers have found ways to preserve precious topsoil through reduced plowing and crop rotation. Incorporating species like legumes and even trees that contribute nitrogen to soils can reduce the need for man-made fertilizers that produce greenhouse gases. Many of these strategies are not revolutionary practices, although they may not be compatible with some of the more resource-intensive methods that emerged during the Green Revolution.

Mark Banik learned about hydroponics and aquaponics at his high school.

YOUTH PROFILE
Mark Banik

When Mark Banik was a freshman at Chicago High School for Agricultural Sciences he was an eager student, but he always avoided one area of his school because of its strong smell. What he didn't know at the time was that it was a crucial part of a sustainable agriculture system. Affectionately called "the fish room," the space has three long soil beds (one planted with lettuce and two with basil) and four huge breeding tanks filled with tilapias (a type of food fish). The tilapias excrete nutrient-rich waste that travels to another tank called a clarifier. Those nutrients are extracted and fed into the soil beds to help the plants grow. The basil stalks take about two months to grow about 10 inches tall before the tops are cut off and harvested.

While hydroponics and aquaponics may look like they mean the same thing, there is one important difference. **Hydroponics** is the technique used to grow plants using nutrient-rich water instead of soil. **Aquaponics** combines that process with fish farming, incorporating the solid waste from the fish into the water's nutrients.

Aquaponics is a method for growing food sustainably by turning waste into a resource. You would normally have to bring nutrients to plants in a hydroponic system, and you would have to remove fish waste from an aquaculture system. Aquaponics allows nutrients to cycle directly from the fish to the plants. The plants then help to filter the water, which can be resupplied to the fish.

Mark eventually got over the smell of the fish room. "Our school is very different and we do this awesome stuff as part of our normal routine," said Mark. The school also harvests and sells honey and wax candles from an on-campus apiary. Each school year, students harvest about 200 pounds of honey. Learning about sustainable agriculture and aquaponics systems like the one at Chicago High School for Agricultural Sciences is not just a learning exercise; it helps prepare students for careers in agriculture.

Consumer Demand

There may be other options to get fresh foods in your neighborhood, such as Community Supported Agriculture programs or even by trying to grow your own food. While you might be craving an avocado in the middle of winter, it might be less tempting when you consider that it was grown halfway around the world. That avocado would have to travel a lot of miles to reach you!

Becoming aware of where your food is grown, how it is grown, and by whom is a critical piece of sustaining food production systems. As a consumer—we all eat!—you have a voice in how you want your food to be produced. You can choose to buy seasonally appropriate food grown by a farmer that lives just 100 miles from you. You can also choose to buy food that was grown according to environmental standards that are important to you. But first you have to be aware of what you're buying, which means asking questions.

One way to learn about how your food is raised is to read the label. But the number of labels on food items can be daunting: organic, natural, wild-caught, locally-grown, hormone-free, grass-fed, cage-free, and on and on. If you know how to decode them, these labels can be helpful in identifying how your food was produced. For example, food that is certified organic is grown largely without the aid of manufactured chemicals, typically used to kill insects and weeds. Beef that is grass-fed does not come from cows that were fattened at feed lots. Pastured chickens are raised outside rather than in large chicken houses. Beyond labels, the best way to learn about where your food comes from is to meet the people who grow it. Shopping at a farmer's market or even visiting a local farm is a great opportunity to ask farmers questions and to let them know what practices are important to you.

Another way to flex your consumer muscle is to help eliminate "food deserts" in your

Farmer's markets can be a source of local and seasonal foods.

community. Do you live in a neighborhood without a grocery store or farmer's market, where you can only get food from a convenience store? If so, you know what a food desert is like. The term food desert describes a neighborhood with high concentrations of people who are far from a source of fresh food, such as a grocery store. If you want your neighborhood store to carry more fresh fruits and vegetables, it probably won't happen until you ask. You can make an even more compelling case by getting others in your neighborhood on board and showing a local food retailer that lots of people will buy fresh foods if they're available.

Government Support

Federal programs can support unsustainable practices or they can be designed to promote sustainable systems of food production. In the United States, a piece of legislation commonly known as the Farm Bill outlines how the federal government will support particular agricultural programs in the country. The bill authorizes direct payments to farmers. In theory, this maintains a farming industry in the United States and keeps food cheap for consumers.

CAREER PROFILE — **Nonprofit Founder**

Do you ever see things you want to change about your community? If you are committed to a cause, you might create change by founding your own nonprofit organization. Although it's called "nonprofit," a nonprofit organization still needs funding to operate. A nonprofit founder or director should enjoy networking with people and have good communication skills to enable him or her to sustain the organization's work by writing grant proposals, soliciting donations, and recruiting volunteers. To run a nonprofit organization, you also need to have excellent management skills to create and prioritize successful projects and to hire the right people to run them. Community service experiences can help you to see how your skills and knowledge can be applied to work in the nonprofit sector. Internships with nonprofits can teach you good management practices for this particular arena of business.

Katy Elliott wanted to connect residents in her community with farm-fresh food and to make sustainable living easy for people through resources, education opportunities, and strong community support. Katy and two other women founded their own nonprofit, the Arkansas Sustainability Network (ASN), in order to hold an expo for community members to learn about sustainability initiatives happening in the state of Arkansas. What started as a one-day expo has bloomed into a multi-faceted social network: it's a food club that connects farmers with consumers, a bike co-op where people can learn bicycle maintenance, and an environmental education program with a student-run garden. ASN's Food Club helps connect Arkansas farmers directly with consumers who want fresh, locally-grown food and allows consumers to meet the people who produce their food. If you want to create change in your community, Katy's advice is, "start small, and go for it!" She suggests small, incremental projects that you can learn from and build on. Maybe one day you, too, will find yourself starting your own nonprofit organization.

Katy Elliot co-founded the Arkansas Sustainability Network.

Corn subsidies have led to an increased supply of cheap corn.

Over the years, U.S. farm bills have supported some unsustainable practices, such as growing an excess of a particular crop. For example, subsidies of corn without limits on production have led to a growing supply of cheap corn and corn-derived products, such as corn syrup. Corn is now included in nearly every kind of processed food you can think of, from chewing gum to beef sticks.[50] But subsidies don't always encourage unsustainable practices; they can be designed for just the opposite outcome.

Federal subsidies for sustainable agricultural practices such as soil and water conservation programs allow more farmers to participate. Some specific examples are provided within the U.S. Farm Bill. The 2008 Farm Bill increased funding over the 2002 legislation for organic programs, providing financial support to farmers transitioning to organic methods. The Farm Bill also encourages school lunch programs to purchase unprocessed, locally-grown foods when possible. Another provision of the bill is that low-income senior community members can qualify to receive fresh, locally-grown foods.[51]

WHAT YOU CAN DO — Food

Food is something you consume every day. Thinking about ways you can play a role in addressing food issues? Consider the following things you can do to get involved:

- Know where your food comes from and what ingredients are included in your food.
- If your grocery store doesn't carry the healthy foods you and your community want, advocate on behalf of your community.
- Participate in local food drives.
- Get involved with global campaigns to fight hunger.

Local fruit is sold at a Bolivian market.

POINT | **COUNTERPOINT**

Should junk food advertising be banned?

The debate on junk food advertising looks at how junk food ads impact parents and children. While some believe ads easily influence children, others believe that parents ultimately have the final decision and can say no to purchasing certain types of food.

Read the following perspectives below taken from the online debate forum, Debatepedia.[52]

POINT

Yes

- **"Children are swayed easily by advertisements to consume junk food.** Most children if they are convinced by an advertisement will want to get the product, in this case, junk food. Eating junk food causes obesity and television advertising during children's programs will just convince innocent children that junk food is good. Stopping these advertisements will help obesity and lower children's intake of unhealthy foods."

- **"Not only does advertising cause obesity, but so too does TV watching.** It is proven that both watching TV and junk food advertising leads to obesity and if a child is watching television in the first place, watching junk food advertisements will not help the world's obesity problem."

COUNTERPOINT

No

- **"Junk food advertising does not force parents to buy the food.** Just because the junk food is being advertised does not mean that parents should buy it for their children or give their children the money to buy it. It is important to recognize that parents have the final say, and also are ultimately responsible for what their children eat. It matters little, therefore, that children might be swayed by advertisements. We should place great onus of responsibility on parents, and if we are concerned that they are buying junk food for their children, we should attempt to address that problem. But this has less to do with junk-food advertising and more to do with informing the health decisions of parents."

- **"If we apply the principle of individual responsibility, advertising is fine.** It is important not to hold businesses and advertisers responsible for the choices of individual consumers. If a consumer wants to purchase a good, the supplier should not be blamed for the consumer finding their good attractive. We must maintain the notion of individual responsibility, or people will start blaming each other for their own bad choices."

Those who believe junk food advertising should be banned think that children are too easily swayed by ads. Do you think this is true?

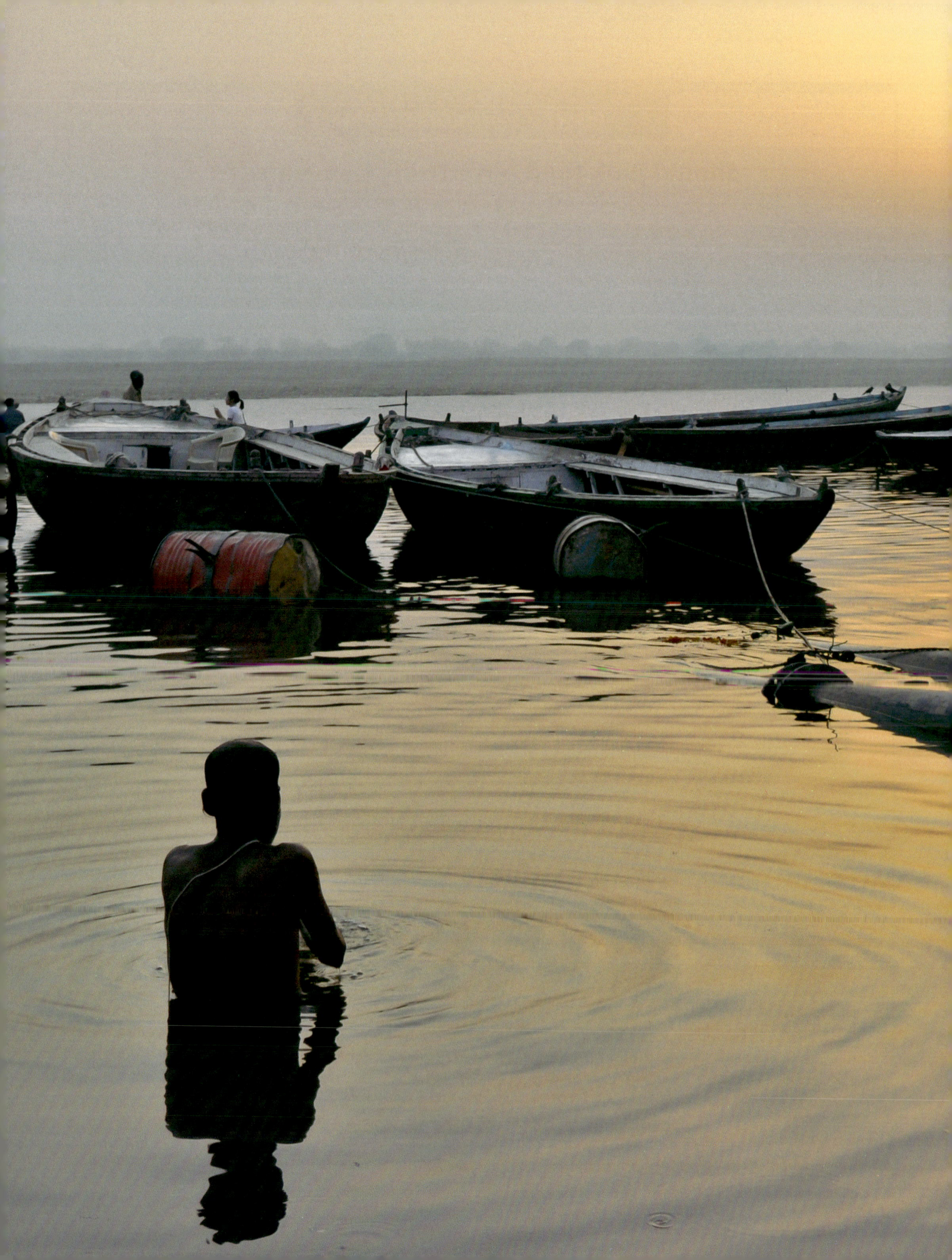

Chapter 4

Water

> **GUIDING QUESTIONS**
> - What makes water plentiful for some people and scarce for others?
> - How can structural and personal decisions around water support sustainability?

Introduction to Water

Water is a sacred symbol in many cultures around the world. For many indigenous peoples, water is the element of creation or the birthplace of the world. Rituals born out of a belief in water's healing powers are present in various cultures and religions: Judaism, Christianity, and Islam all use water for ritual washing and purification, and millions of Hindus make a pilgrimage to sacred rivers such as the Ganges River in India in order to gain salvation through purification by water.[1]

Water and Sustainability

Environment

Water is one of the planet's most precious natural resources—all life depends on it for survival. As water changes form (solid, liquid, or gas) and travels under and over the land, it moves throughout our earth and atmosphere in what is referred to as the *hydrological cycle,* or water cycle. This movement of water can happen quickly or slowly: some water molecules may stay in one place for millions of years (a glacier, for instance), while other water molecules may quickly move from the ocean to our atmosphere by evaporation. Because water constantly cycles through the Earth and its atmosphere, it is considered a *renewable resource.*

Although water is renewable, the total amount of water on the Earth is *finite,* or limited. Furthermore, the majority of water on our planet is salt water (97.5%) and the majority of fresh water is frozen in ice or snow.[2] Less than 1% of all freshwater is available for human and ecosystem use.[3] If global water use is to be sustainable, the whole planet's water needs must be met by this limited amount of water. Yet many regions around the world today are facing **water scarcity**.

The main form of water scarcity that exists in communities and ecosystems around the world is **physical water scarcity**, which exists when the demand for water is greater than local water resources can provide.[4] There are several reasons this might happen. For one thing, the Earth's fresh water is not evenly distributed; rain falls in certain places and not others and the location of mountains determines where it runs once it has fallen. As a result, many arid regions around the world frequently face drought conditions.

Geography is not the only cause of physical water scarcity, however; humans can also play a role. In many places around the world, humans are using groundwater faster than it can be replenished by the hydrological cycle.[5] One dramatic example of this overuse by humans is the shrinking of the Aral Sea. In other places, the alteration of landscapes by humans and human-made pollution is contaminating fresh water. Changes to the natural landscape can destroy an ecosystem's ability to absorb and filter water. For example, trees help ecosystems slow surface water movement and allow water to seep into the ground, where it is naturally filtered before reaching a larger body of water. Deforestation, on the other hand, can cause water to run

The majority of fresh water on Earth is frozen in ice or snow.

CASE STUDY: Aral Sea

In the 1950s, the Soviet Union decided to increase its cotton production. To irrigate the new fields, the government diverted the two main rivers that fed the Aral Sea, an inland basin with no outlet to the ocean. So much water was diverted from the rivers for agricultural use that the rate of evaporation of water from the Aral Sea soon outpaced the amount of water flowing into it and the sea began to shrink.

Over the next 40 years, the Aral Sea lost two-thirds of its water. The salt content of what remains has increased to the point that the sea can no longer support much marine life, ending its fishing industry. The Aral had previously been used for a large amount of shipping, but when the water dried up it became useless for that as well. Its shoreline receded from cities that had been seaports, in some places moving back as much as 150 kilometers. Effectively, the Aral Sea no longer exists.

The Aral Sea does not have the capacity to support marine life. Boats like these represent the end of the fishing industry.

What remains are two separate and much smaller bodies of water and a new desert called the Aralkum that measures hundreds of thousands of square kilometers. The desert generates huge dust storms, visible from outer space, that carry the residue of the pesticides and herbicides that were used on the cotton fields and had washed into the former sea. This residue has affected the health of human populations and reduced crop yields for hundreds of kilometers to the south of the former coastline.[6] These many far-reaching effects in the Aral Sea region were caused by the disruption of one part of the ecosystem.

off the land quickly, eroding soil and carrying pollutants to the nearest body of water.

The contamination of fresh water with human-produced pollutants can occur as a direct result of human activities or as a result of natural disasters that spread human-sourced pollutants far beyond their ordinary reach. For instance, Hurricane Katrina covered 80% of New Orleans in water that contained petroleum products, dead animals, and other contaminants.[7] Whether it comes from sewage, industrial waste, agriculture, or an accident such as an oil spill, human pollution of water can kill wildlife and render waterways unusable for people now and in the future.

In addition to these current challenges, climate change is expected to alter future rainfall patterns and exacerbate water issues. The Intergovernmental Panel on Climate Change, the largest group of climate scientists in the world, predicts that water availability will be even less reliable over the next several decades than it is today. Most dramatically, the intensity of droughts and floods is predicted to increase, straining current water management systems. Scientists expect precipitation patterns to change permanently in some places, turning previously wet regions dry and vice versa. Overall, the negative long-term effects of climate change on water supply are predicted to greatly outweigh any potential benefits.[8]

Society

Water is critical for human survival and recently the United Nations declared water as a human right. Yet 783 million people around the world do not have access to safe drinking water sources such as household connections, public standpipes, or protected wells or streams.[9] Both physical water scarcity and economic water scarcity play a role in this lack of access to water. Recall that physical water scarcity refers to not having enough water to meet a community's needs. **Economic water scarcity**, on the other hand, occurs because of a lack of investment in water resources and typically results in a lack of infrastructure and an unequal distribution of water.[10]

For both the rural and urban poor, a lack of **potable** (drinkable) water means drinking and washing with whatever is available, regardless of contamination or cleanliness. In communities around the world, a lack of potable water contributes to social conflict, food shortages, lack of educational and economic opportunities, disease, and death.

Millions of people around the world do not have access to safe drinking water.

While the vast majority of people living in advanced industrial countries today have access to potable water, around 20% of those in less developed countries cannot obtain even 20 liters of clean water a day,[11] and 2.5 billion do not have any sort of improved sanitation.[12] *Improved sanitation* refers to facilities that safely separate human waste from human contact.[13] Without improved sanitation, water resources that communities use for drinking, cooking, and cleaning can become contaminated with waste and cause serious sickness and even death. According to UN-Water (a body designed to coordinate the water programs of various UN agencies and outside partners), diarrhea is the world's leading cause of sickness and death. Most of these deaths are caused by a lack of sanitation facilities, exacerbated by unsafe drinking water and a lack of water for cleaning.[14]

Water scarcity has other impacts on society. Water shortages can wipe out crops and livestock, causing food shortages. Drought affects food supplies drastically because the amount of water required to raise the plants or animals needed to feed one person is far greater than the amount of water that one person can drink.

Water scarcity can also contribute to political unrest. River basins are almost always shared by more than one nation and disputes over water rights have occurred regularly throughout the past century. For example, Egypt, Sudan, Kenya, and Ethiopia have all contested each others' right to use the waters of the Nile, and conflict over the Jordan River and its tributaries has seriously worsened tensions between Israelis, Lebanese, Jordanians, and Palestinians.

When access to a limited water supply is a matter of life and death, people may resort to armed force to secure their supply. This was the unfortunate result of a relentless drought in East Africa from 2008 to 2011. During the drought most of the region's livestock died, causing the worst famine to hit East Africa in 60 years. Somalia was struck particularly hard due to political instability that prevented the delivery of international relief aid, including food. In the most drought-stricken areas, warlords fought to control wells and springs.[15] With rising global population and the corresponding greater demand on Earth's fixed water supply, it is possible that the wars of the future will be fought over water.

People who do not have access to water at home must spend a significant amount of time collecting it. This household task often falls to women and girls, who, according to one estimate, collectively spend 152 million hours each day gathering water to use in the home.[16] Women and children may face serious educational and economic disadvantages as a result. The time needed to gather water can make it difficult for youth to attend school and for women to hold paying jobs. Such limited opportunities for women have an impact on society that goes beyond gender inequality: helping women find employment outside the home is critical to economic development.[17] Without water, women are not free to participate in and contribute to the economy.

Economy

As the statistics above demonstrate, many communities around the world lack the infrastructure needed to make safe water accessible. In other words, many communities suffer from economic water scarcity.

According to a 2006 United Nations report, 85% of the wealthiest 20% of households in 17 developing countries had piped water connections, but only 25% of the poorest 20% of households had piped connections.[18] There is also often a big difference in the amount that people pay for water around the world—even in the same city. For instance, people that live in informal settlements like slums may pay water prices that are 5-10 times higher than the water prices that wealthier people pay.[19]

Lack of water can also impact the amount of food farmers can produce and sell. In 2012, the United States experienced its worst drought since 1954, which severely decreased crop yields. The combination of this U.S. drought and low crop yields in Asia and Europe is expected to cause food prices to rise.[20]

Agriculture accounts for the greatest share of water use, but almost all other economic activity depends on water in some way. Water powered machines in the first English factories 200 years ago. Even today, making any manufactured product requires at least some water. About 9% of the water withdrawn from rivers and lakes in the United States is put to some industrial use, from making plastics to diluting window-cleaning spray. Paper mills, food-processing plants, and chemical factories all depend directly on freshwater supplies in their production processes.[21]

Droughts such as this one in Saudi Arabia can lead to water scarcity.

Background on Water

Humans and Hydrology

By nature, water flow is unpredictable and powerful. Throughout history, some places have witnessed fairly stable rainfall and river flows; others, like the Yellow River flood plain in China, have seen dramatic cycles that have driven millions of people from their homes time and again. Water constantly challenges our ability to control it—floods can destroy dams and canals, and droughts can make them useless.

Controlling Water

Despite water's challenging nature, it is necessary for human survival. Many early societies have benefitted from water management strategies like irrigation. The world's earliest cities occurred in Sumer, Mesopotamia. It was here that Sumerians developed agricultural methods and irrigation techniques which allowed them to grow crops year round, create a surplus of food, and, therefore, settle in one place.[22]

Digging for Water

To deal with variability in the water supply, humans began digging wells to access **groundwater**. Groundwater is water that has seeped down through the soil and into the porous rock that sits above the impermeable bedrock. To access groundwater, wells must be drilled deep enough to provide a space for this water to pool, just as a hole dug in the sand at the beach will fill with seawater.

Large regions that are permeated with groundwater are called **aquifers**. They can provide water in large enough quantities to be used for irrigation as well as drinking. Aquifers are recharged primarily from precipitation. How quickly they recharge depends on the type of rock that the water must move through and the rate of precipitation. Flash floods, for example, do much less to recharge an aquifer than melting snow does. Some aquifers, however, are made up primarily of fossil water (water from the last Ice Age), which cannot be replenished after it has been used.

The Ogallala Aquifer (also called the High Plains Aquifer) lies beneath 174,000 square miles of the Midwestern United States,

Water flow can be unpredictable and can cause floods.

CASE STUDY: Water and Power in the Cradle of Civilization

Mesopotamia (Greek for "two rivers") was an ancient area located in what is now Iraq, Iran, Syria, and Turkey. In ancient as in modern times, this area was home to two major rivers, the Tigris River and the Euphrates River, which have benefitted humans living in this region for thousands of years.[23]

Modern-day Iraq remains highly dependent on the Tigris and Euphrates for its water supply. These rivers originate in the mountains of Turkey and flow through Syria before reaching Iraqi soil. Any Turkish alteration of the rivers can severely affect the amount of water available to Iraq and Syria, and any Syrian project on the Euphrates affects Iraq. Throughout the 20th century, tensions between these countries increased as their populations grew and demands for electricity generated by damming rivers placed new strains on a limited water flow.

In the past, water projects in the region have led to the brink of war. Both Turkey and Syria completed major dam projects on the Euphrates in 1974. These dams quickly became essential to the electric and water supplies of both countries, but they reduced the Euphrates' downstream flow because water was diverted to fill their newly formed reservoirs. The combined impact on Iraqi water supplies was severe enough that Iraq threatened to bomb the Syrian dam and sent troops to the Syrian border. Mediation by Saudi Arabia and the USSR defused the conflict and Syria committed to release 60% of the river's water to Iraq.

Ten years later, Turkey began construction on the Southeastern Anatolia Development Project (or GAP from its Turkish initials), which includes plans for 22 dams, 19 hydroelectric plants, and the largest water tunnel system in the world. When completed, the GAP will use water from the Tigris and Euphrates to irrigate 4.2 million acres of cropland and generate 27 billion kilowatts of electricity. Its total estimated cost is $32 billion, half of which has already been spent.

Completion of the GAP, projected for 2020, will give Turkey the ability to control the flow of the Euphrates almost completely for the first time in history. Syria perceived the project as a real threat. To pressure the Turkish government, Syria began to fund the Kurdish People's Party (PKK), an ethnic revolutionary movement in the southeast of Turkey, in 2008. Eventually the two countries reached a compromise: Turkey promised to supply its downstream neighbor with approximately half the natural flow of the river and Syria promised to cease funding the PKK.[24]

Water disputes can be complex and difficult to resolve. Even when agreements are reached—such as those between Iraq, Syria, and Turkey—they are temporary and lack methods of enforcement. There are no guarantees about the ability of these three countries to fulfill their promises, either. Ongoing internal conflicts such as the Sunni-Shi'ite divide in Iraq, the uprisings against Bashar al-Assad in Syria, and the question of Kurdish independence from Turkey create a great deal of uncertainty as to whether governments will still be around to honor their agreements in coming years. Thus, the future of water management in the Tigris and Euphrates basins is difficult to predict, but it will have a profound effect on the fate of countries in the region.

The Tigris and Euphrates Rivers supply water to countries in the Middle East.

stretching from South Dakota to Texas and New Mexico. It currently irrigates 13.6 million acres of farmland, about half of which is in Nebraska.[25] Altogether, the Ogallala Aquifer provides about 30% of the water used in the United States for irrigation.[26]

In places where people use an aquifer extensively, they may deplete it faster than it can recharge and thus lower the **water table**, the depth a well must reach in order to find water. The water table of the Ogallala Aquifer has dropped about 100 feet; it would take around 6,000 years for the aquifer to recharge fully via natural processes. As the water table drops, wells must be drilled deeper and at greater cost. Should the aquifer be depleted so far as to make further irrigation impossible, the agricultural production of the United States would drop by about $20 billion.[27]

Water Today

As the world's population grows, so does our water consumption. However, the world's rate of freshwater consumption is growing faster than the rate of population growth due to increasing personal and national water footprints.[28] A *water footprint* is the total volume of freshwater used and polluted directly and indirectly by a person, nation, or industry. Not only are footprints growing in size, but they are becoming increasingly global. For instance, the average American has a water footprint of 2,842 cubic meters per year (the global average per person is 1,385 cubic meters per year). About 20% of this water footprint lies outside the United States (mostly in the Yangtze River basin in China) because many of the water-intensive goods we buy are grown, extracted, or produced in other countries. The burden of any negative impacts on water supply is thus shifted from the importing country to the exporting country.[29]

So what do we use water for? About 70% of global freshwater consumption is for irrigation, 22% for industry, and 8% for domestic use.[30] Let's take a closer look at the direct and indirect ways that humans around the world are using water.

We use a large amount of freshwater for irrigation and production purposes.

Water Use by Sector

Agriculture

As the cases of the Ogallala Aquifer and Aral Sea demonstrate, we use enormous amounts of freshwater to grow crops and raise livestock. In fact, 80% of the water consumed in the United States is for agriculture.[31]

Producing the food we eat requires a large amount of water. For example, growing one kilogram of corn (enough for about 12 corn tortillas) requires an average of 1,220 liters of water.[32] There may not be much water in a corn tortilla itself, but it does require a significant amount of water to produce. The amount of water consumed or polluted to produce a product is often referred to as **virtual water**.[33] Some foods require more virtual water others. An apple, for example, requires an average of about 18 gallons of water. On the other hand, a pound of beef requires about 1,799 gallons, most of which is used to water grain that is used as cattle feed.[34] In general, the water required to grow food increases the farther up the food chain a product sits.

Irrigation refers to the use of water for growing crops. There are many different irrigation techniques and they can vary greatly in how efficiently they use water. Although the water we use in our home may be treated and eventually returned to the environment, only half of the water used to irrigate crops can be reused.[35] Soil can only absorb a certain amount of water at a time and excess water runs off or evaporates without reaching crops. Irrigation techniques such as drip irrigation are more efficient at delivering water directly to crops than flooding a field. Similarly, some crops are more water efficient than others, requiring less water to grow. Growing crops suited to natural rainfall in a region can help decrease the water needed for agriculture.

This form of an irrigation system in Bali uses ecologically sustainable methods.

CASE STUDY: Water Access in the Honduran Highlands

Rainwater is seasonally plentiful throughout Central America, but many regions lack the ability to store and use it throughout the year. Most small coffee farmers in Honduras, for example, lack funds to buy the storage tanks and irrigation systems necessary to grow sustenance crops during the dry season. In order to buy food, they must take out high-interest loans to be repaid out of the next year's coffee harvest.

Several community coffee cooperatives in Honduras have addressed this problem by purchasing very low-cost drip irrigation systems from an American nonprofit design firm, Design Revolution. These systems allow farmers to grow their own food throughout the year, as well as bring their coffee plants into production a year and a half faster than possible with rainfall alone. In these communities, access to water has become much more equitable, democratic, and economical; the cooperatives, in other words, are becoming a sustainable and efficient form of local water governance.[36]

Industry

Industrial water use can be difficult to address because it is intimately tied to energy production. Industry uses water for cooling in power plants and for the production of goods.[37] Water is essential to the production of energy, too. Large amounts of water are required for producing fuel and many power plants operate by heating water to produce steam that turns a generator.[38] These power and processing plants are often several decades old and use far more water than newer facilities, but they are very expensive to replace or modify.

Hydroelectric power, too, involves huge amounts of water loss, despite the fact that water can be used for other purposes once it has passed through hydroelectric turbines. To operate efficiently, the reservoirs of hydroelectric dams must have consistently high water levels. Water evaporates much faster from reservoirs than from rivers, so dams cause huge losses in downstream flow that reduce the amount of water available for other purposes. Since the 1970s, evaporation from reservoirs has exceeded industrial and domestic water consumption around the world.[39]

Just as water is essential for the production of much of our energy, energy is a vital resource for accessing water. Wells, especially large ones, are usually pumped using motors. In water-poor regions with access to the ocean, desalination (the process of removing salt from seawater) requires large amounts of energy.

> *Just as water is essential for the production of much of our energy, energy is a vital resource for accessing water.*

Domestic

Domestic water use refers to the water consumed by people in their homes and commercial businesses. We use water directly for drinking, cooking, and cleaning. We use water to flush our toilets, wash our dishes and clothes, bathe, and brush our teeth. We have many different uses for water, but how much water do we really need?

According to the United Nations, each person needs about 20-50 liters or 5.3-13.2 gallons of water each day to meet their basic water needs (drinking, cooking, and cleaning).[40] On average, people living in developed countries use more water each day than people living in developing countries use. For instance, individuals in the United States and Japan use an average of 350 liters of water each day while individuals in sub-Saharan Africa use an average of 10-20 liters each day.[41]

The challenge for communities that do not have enough water is to increase the quantity and/or the quality of water so that people have enough water not just to drink and cook, but also to keep themselves and their homes clean and sanitary. Sanitation and clean fresh water go hand in hand. Regular hand washing with clean water, for example, could prevent around half of the 1.5 million deaths caused each year by diarrhea.[42] Conversely, when a community lacks basic sanitation this can lead to a contaminated water supply.

Those around the world who use more water than is required to meet their basic needs have a different challenge—water conservation. Although our taps may seem to suggest an infinite amount of water, our supply of fresh water is still finite. In the last five years, almost every region of the United States has faced water shortages.[43] Therefore, it is important to reduce both the amount of water we use and the amount we waste.

On a personal basis, there are many things that we can do to save water. First of all, simply reducing the amount of time that a tap is running is an act of water conservation. You may have noticed that most faucets and toilets provide information about the volume of water they use. For example, most new faucets flow at a rate of 1.5 gallons per minute (or 1.5

CASE STUDY: Mono Lake[44]

Northern California's Mono Lake is an important habitat for more than 80 species of migrating birds and supports a food chain of algae, shrimp, and insects. For most of the 20th century, a system of aqueducts delivered water from Mono Lake, located east of the Sierra Nevada Mountains, across 350 miles of desert to Los Angeles. As Los Angeles' population grew, the demand for water in the city eventually exceeded the amount Mono Lake could supply without damaging the health of the plants and animals that depend on the lake for their survival. By the early 1990s, Mono Lake and its surrounding ecosystem had become stressed.

In 1994, the California State Water Resources Control Board ordered the city of Los Angeles to reduce its use of water from Mono Lake in order to return the lake to a healthy level. The city faced a significant challenge to meeting this goal due to its high population—over 3.6 million people and growing. The only way Los Angeles could comply with the order to reduce overall usage was for each person to use less water.

As they considered various means of water conservation, the California Department of Water and Power hit on a relatively painless way for L.A. residents to reduce their water use: low-flow toilets. Each low-flow toilet installed would save the city 5,000 gallons of water a year. After widespread door-to-door education campaigns by community volunteers, enough Los Angelenos installed low-flow toilets to cut the city's overall water use by 15%, reducing it to a level not seen since 1970. Conservation methods like low-flush toilets can have a significant impact, allowing more people are able to share the same resources.

Mono Lake supplies water to people in the city of Los Angeles.

GPM).[45] When a faucet flows at 1.5 gallons per minute, every second counts! Turning off the faucet while you are brushing your teeth and plugging the drain when you are washing dishes are two simple behaviors that can help conserve water.

At the household level, water consumption can be reduced by fixing leaks and installing water-efficient faucets and appliances. The average home wastes 10,000 gallons of water per year from leaks. This is enough water to fill a swimming pool in your backyard. Yet most common leaks (leaky toilet flaps, dripping faucets, and leaky valves) are easy to fix.[46] Bathrooms are often the largest consumer of water, so installing low-flow toilets or placing an aerator on your shower head can be a great place to start saving water (and the amount of money spent on water bills).[47] When in the market for new appliances such as dishwashers, look for products with the WaterSense label. This label verifies that products are water efficient.[48] As the Mono Lake case study demonstrates, small actions made by many individuals can make a big difference.

Water Management

As we have seen, water is distributed unevenly across the Earth's surface due to a combination of factors. Topography and climate can make water too plentiful in some places and seasons, and extremely scarce in others. Building dams and canals to mitigate physical water scarcity is expensive, so many relatively poor regions lack such infrastructure. And population increases (whether by population growth or migration into cities) can strain existing water infrastructure to the point where it no longer functions and must be rebuilt, replaced, or expanded.

For all these reasons, how people decide to allocate and control the flow of water plays a part in the water shortages that affect so many people. Due to its importance and the difficulty of managing its flow, water almost everywhere is subject to decisions made by groups of people: governments, civic organizations, businesses, and families. The process of making these decisions and putting them into practice is called *water governance*.[49]

Privatization is a form of water governance in which private companies provide water for people rather than publicly-owned utility companies. Privatizing water involves selling government-owned utilities to private companies; people then receive their water (and

---

CAREER PROFILE: Environmental Scientist

Research might remind you of being stuck in the library staring at a computer screen or a stack of books for hours, wishing the necessary facts would rise to the surface and give you the key to writing that book report or science project. But research doesn't have to be tedious; for some people, in fact, it's at the heart of a thrilling career! Research positions exist in virtually all fields and are distinguished by how the research is applied—to the development of products and services like technology or medicine, for instance. Researchers are naturally curious. They seek out answers to pressing questions and find creative solutions in situations where others are content to say, "we haven't found a better way of doing this yet, so we'll stick with the old way even though it has obvious problems." Research is about discovering the unknown and re-discovering the overlooked.

Melissa McCullough is an environmental scientist.

Melissa McCullough works for The U.S. Environmental Protection Agency (EPA) in the office of Research and Development. She holds a Master's of Environmental Management in Applied Ecology and Environmental Toxicology and is on the forefront of developing sustainability policies and education. One such research project looks at stormwater runoff in cities. When it rains, water has to go somewhere. In cities, where so much square footage is paved, excess water has the potential to create flooding and sanitation hazards. The city of Chicago dealt with this problem by retrofitting alleyways with porous paving material, allowing stormwater to drain safely.

The EPA researches sustainable practices in cities all over the country in order to help communities expand without threatening the environment or future generations. Many people, residents and lawmakers alike, do not fully understand the environmental consequences of their choices. Melissa's job is to educate people about sustainable choices and to develop ways to make living sustainably easier. With better information, decision makers and communities can use infrastructure such as porous-paved alleyways to bring human populations into harmony with the ecosystems and atmospheric systems we inhabit.

water bills) from a private company rather than a public utility. Most people in the European Union (except for residents in France) and the United States are provided water by public entities. Many people living in countries in the southern hemisphere, however, receive water through private companies. In the 20th and 21st centuries, institutions, such as the World Bank and International Monetary Fund, that lend money to poorer nations have required countries receiving loans to allow their water to be sold by private companies.[50]

For some, privatization is seen as a "market solution" because it relies on the economic theory that competition will lead to better service at a lower price. Unfortunately, there are many cases in which privatization has made water more expensive—especially for the poor. In the 1990s, for example, the private company Bechtel took over Bolivia's water system, including not only the public water infrastructure but also some informal pumps and wells that people used to retrieve water. The prices for water increased (doubling for some residents) and many were unable to pay these new rates. In 2000, the people of Bolivia took to the streets to protest these unaffordable water prices and ended up forcing Bechtel out of their water supply.[51]

Decisions about water are not always made in a way that includes or benefits everyone involved. Some people have no say in how the water they depend on is managed because they cannot legally participate in the governance process controlling its use. Even if everyone who uses a water source has a say in how it is managed, corruption or lack of resources may prevent some people from taking action.

The coordination of all the government agencies that deal with water rights is another challenge. In many countries, a river used for shipping, fishing, and irrigation would be managed by at least three agencies, each governed by different laws. As water demand grows to outstrip supply, this sort of governance has become unworkable. Many national and local governments have taken steps over the past ten years to coordinate their water governance.[52]

Rain barrels collect rainwater from roofs which can then be used for watering plants or washing cars.

Pathways to Progress: Water

There are many people today working toward sustainable solutions to the water challenges you have read about in this chapter. Some of these solutions involve changes at the personal level, while others involve changes at the structural level.

Personal Solutions

Because a large amount of water is embodied in our food and manufactured goods, our consumption choices are another way for us to shrink our water footprint. For instance, using tap water rather than bottled water saves both water and money. According to the Pacific Institute, it takes 3 liters of water to produce 1 liter of bottled water (not to mention the 3.4 megajoules of energy required to make the plastic bottle and packaging).[53] If you don't like the taste of your tap water or are concerned about water quality, you can install a filter on your tap. Our choices of what to eat can also impact water use. When we eat from lower down the food chain, less water is required to produce our food. Eating smaller portions of meat and dairy (when and where there are alternative sources of the nutrients these foods provide) is a good way to limit the virtual water on our plates. Information on different foods and how much water they contain is readily available through online water calculators.

As the residents of Los Angeles learned in the 1990s, we can reduce our water footprint by installing more water-efficient appliances. Toilets, for instance, are one of the biggest consumers of water in the home. Replacing the older, less water-efficient toilets in the United States could save almost 2 billion gallons of water per day.[54]

Making use of rainfall is another way to reduce strains on water infrastructure. In some places, such as the Pacific Northwest, rain harvesting can provide for all of a household's water needs if what is harvested is used carefully.[55] In others, however, water rights are based on stream flows created by rainwater and harvesting is restricted by law.[56] We can also capture water flows by reusing water, such as by going to a car wash rather than washing a car where water will run into storm drains. Reusing water also limits the pollution of waterways by containing polluted water where it can be treated.

Molly Freed organized World Water Week at her high school.

Community Solutions

Water issues often require collective action. At times, cultural ideas about water use lead to waste. Showering and washing dishes, for example, produces *greywater*, which people commonly consider dirty and unusable for other purposes. On the contrary, greywater is normally fine for flushing toilets or watering lawns, especially if the soap it contains is biodegradable and some care is taken to prevent it from touching food that will not be cooked before it is eaten.[57] Using plants that require frequent watering to decorate our homes is another example of cultural preferences leading us to waste water. An alternative to water-intensive landscaping is xeriscaping, or using only plants that are native to the local climate and can rely primarily on rainfall. Working to develop communities where water conservation is commonplace and aesthetically pleasing is another way that we can collectively address water issues.

YOUTH PROFILE
Molly Freed

Molly Freed cares about water because of its connection to a variety of social and environmental issues—from poverty, starvation, and disease to education and health. She also has a particular familiarity with water after growing up in Seattle, where rain is in no short supply. In 2010, Molly and 12 other high school juniors around the country were chosen for the Bezos Scholars Program. The program selects students and faculty members from public schools across the United States to participate in a dialogue on global leadership at the Aspen Ideas Festival held in the scenic Rocky Mountains. Journalists, scientists, religious figures, Supreme Court justices, and academics present to attendees. When she returned to Seattle after the trip, Molly decided to create World Water Week as her way of actively engaging her community in the issues she learned about at the festival.

Along with a group of volunteers, Molly organized World Water Week at Chief Sealth International High School to increase awareness of water issues and commemorate International World Water Day. Throughout the week, different activities engaged the school community on the topic. Featured events included speeches by members of a local Native American tribe and professionals working in the water industry, and a school-wide challenge called "Carry 5," in which students and staff carried one to five gallons of water around the school's track for 45 minutes to mimic what over a billion

CASE STUDY: Water.org in Ethiopia[58]

Ato Muez Asgede and his son Birhane Muez live in the rural Ethiopian village of Aynalem. Their average annual household income is about 5250 birr ($315 USD). It used to take 30 minutes to walk from their house to the hand-dug well that was their main water source. Ato Muez Asgede rarely collected the water himself; usually his wife and children collected water. The well's water was not always clean and people repeatedly got sick from water-borne diseases.

This all changed when Aynalem worked with the nonprofit organization Water.org to drill a well in the community. Water.org helps communities develop their own solutions to improve the availability and health of local water sources. Aynalem community members formed a water and sanitation (WATSAN) committee and instituted a monthly user fee to maintain and operate the well. Each household contributes 2 birr ($0.06 USD) per month in exchange for access to the well.

Ato Muez Asgede reflected on the importance of having clean water available near his home:

> "My life is changing day after day. The community's life is also changing from day to day. This is because we started to drink potable water, which is much different from before. The new water point is in our vicinity, so community members are now spending their time on other productive activities such as micro-irrigation, trading, and others."

Children stand near a water well in an Ethiopian village.

Following the success of the new well, Ato Muez Asgede attended a training to learn about hygiene and environmental sanitation practices and shared what he learned with his family and neighbors. He recognizes that it will take a community effort to implement these new practices and to keep the water system working properly:

> "To make this water system last, it requires the participation of all of the community members in day-to-day management activities, such as keeping animals away from the water point, supporting the WATSAN committee in the sanitation activities, adjusting the time of the opening and closing of the water point, and holding meetings as necessary."

Birhane Muez shares his father's excitement:

> "There is a huge difference between now and before. Now we start to drink pure water, wash our clothes and body from this source. Before, we used dirty water, which was located far away from our house. My friends and I are very happy about this new program. It has helped us to get clean water nearby and be able to attend school regularly."

people must do each day in order to collect fresh water for their families. Over 75% of those who attended said that they would change the way they used water, from favoring reusable bottles to taking shorter showers.

Thanks to Molly Freed and the Chief Sealth community, World Water Week continues to be a success at the school. Looking back a couple of years later, Molly said,

> "Participating in World Water Week was easily the proudest week of my life. I feel that I was able to touch many people's lives, and open their eyes to issues and solutions that they'd never seen before. To return to my school as I did in December and see a troop of current students busily planning this year's festival gave me hope that World Water Week made a lasting impression."

Structural Solutions

To achieve sustainable global water systems, we must also support the development of water infrastructure in places where it is lacking. In these situations, nonprofit organizations can help communities complete water and sanitation projects by offering resources and expertise.

Cooperative Water Management

Because most major river basins include territory in more than one country, comprehensive and effective water management plans must involve the governments of all those who depend on a river. In essence, water and the services it provides can be delivered more easily if the needs of everyone in the basin are considered together. An ongoing attempt to implement this sort of international cooperation is underway in the Danube River basin, where 18 countries have agreed to manage their waterway collectively.[59] Together these countries have come up with a Danube River Basin Management Plan that provides a legal framework for protecting this river basin as well as ways to measure its health.[60] The countries in this region also hold a "Danube Day" celebration each June to encourage and inspire people across national boundaries to celebrate and care for the river basin.[61]

WHAT YOU CAN DO Water

Wondering how you can get involved in water issues? Here are some ideas:

- Reduce the amount of water you use—Install water-efficient technology in your home and change the way you use your tap!

- Remember virtual water when you shop—By reducing the amount of products you buy (especially products made using water-intensive methods), you can reduce the amount of water used to produce these goods.

- Educate members of your community about how to bring safe, accessible drinking water to those who don't have it.

- Keep your water clean—Organize a river or beach cleanup in your neighborhood. Educate your neighbors about how natural waterways and marine species can be harmed by stormwater runoff.

You can reduce the amount of water you use when you shower or brush your teeth.

POINT | **COUNTERPOINT**

Should water be privatized?

POINT

Yes

- **Freshwater is decreasing considerably around the world.** Lakes, rivers, and aquifers are disappearing rapidly. Privatizing water can help to lower the amount of water use by charging people money when they use the resource.[62]

- **Developing countries desperately need privatized funding of water from international lending institutions in order to economically develop.** These countries are often unable to deal with the nuances of water extraction, treatment, and delivery. Privatized companies can help them manage this part of governance.[63]

COUNTERPOINT

No

- **Water is a human right.** Private water companies tend to increase prices on the water they provide to customers. People living in poverty struggle to afford water. Why privatize water when only wealthy people can afford it?[64]

- **As freshwater continues to disappear throughout the world, the cost of water will continue to increase if privatized.** Countries such as Canada, the United States, and Russia who are able to use large reserves of water and afford to pay for higher costs will be okay, while others such as Syria, India, and Jordan will struggle. Some countries will inevitably go to war because of water shortages and increased costs.[65]

People enjoy the waterfalls in the Dominican Republic. As freshwater disappears around the world, should water be privatized?

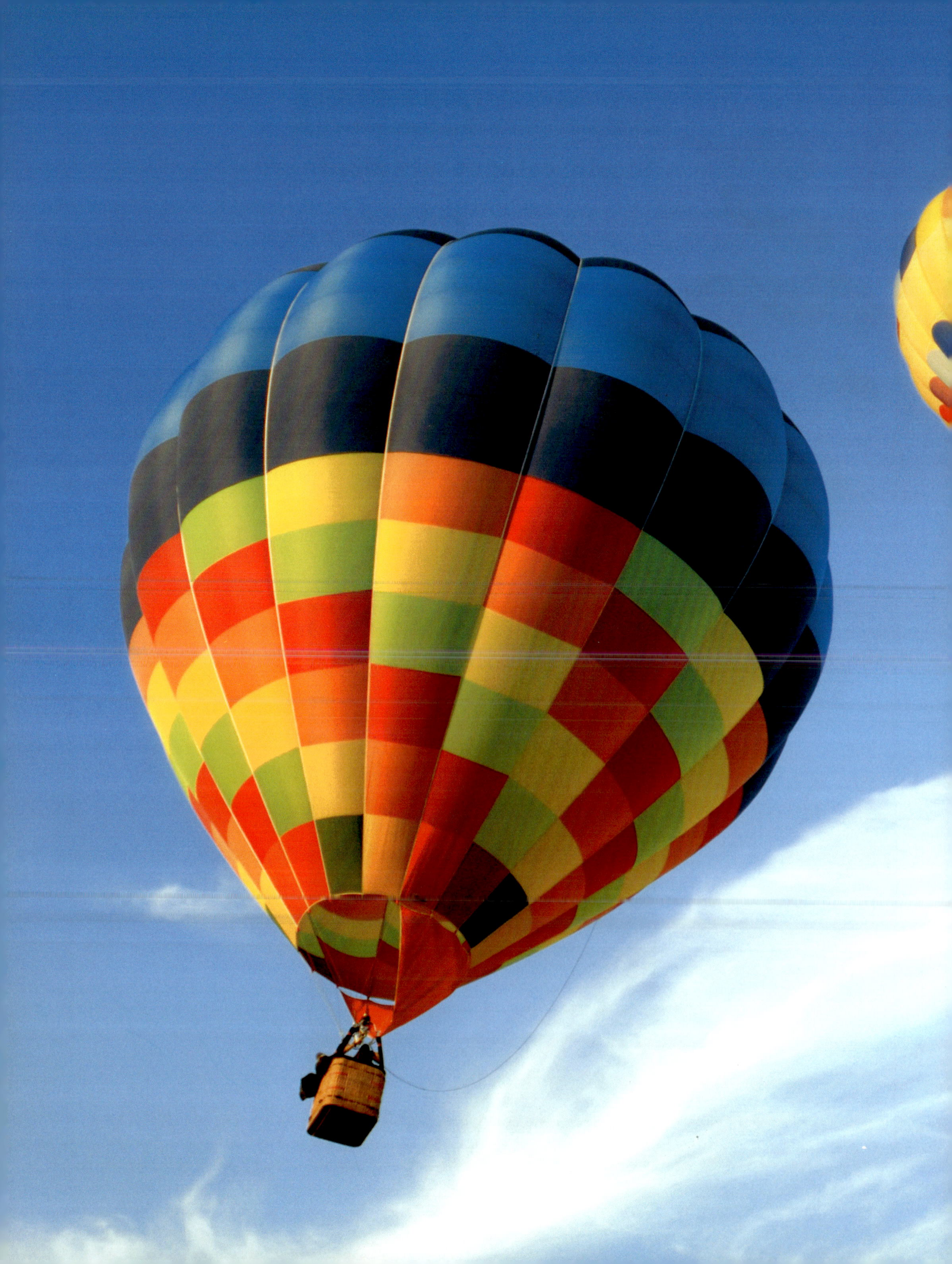

Chapter 5

Air

> **GUIDING QUESTIONS**
> - Why is air considered a common resource?
> - How do people influence the quality of our air?

Introduction to Air

Does it ever feel like something is weighing you down? Well, something is weighing you down. It's air! The weight of air pressing down on each of us is around one ton.[1] Though we have air in our bodies to help balance out this pressure, the air pressure around us pushes in all directions so we are not crushed by the full weight of the air surrounding us.

Air for Life

Air is our most pressing physical need. While we can survive weeks without food and days without water, we cannot go more than a few short minutes without air.

Atmospheric Structure

Broken down, air is a gaseous mixture of mostly nitrogen (78%) and oxygen (21%) along with trace amounts of water vapor, carbon dioxide, argon, and a handful of other elements.[2] The oxygen content is what humans and other animals rely on to breathe and function properly. Carbon dioxide is used by plants for photosynthesis. Air is, simply, an integral part of the planet's environment and essential for many natural processes.

The atmosphere has distinct layers which are impacted by different sources of pollution.

A blanket of air surrounds Earth, referred to as the **atmosphere**. The atmosphere protects us from the harshness of space and the severity of the sun. The composition of air in our atmosphere may change with time and with natural or anthropogenic (man-made) activities. The atmosphere's distinct layers, especially the bottom two, play different roles in fostering life and are impacted by different sources of pollution.

As you may know, air becomes thinner as you move farther from Earth. You might have felt this for yourself if you have ever hiked up a mountainous trail and found it harder to breathe the higher up you go. Think about what the air must be like for someone climbing Mt. Everest. Now imagine sitting up above the clouds near the outer edges of the atmosphere! Why is air "thinner" up there? Gravity pulls much of the air in our atmosphere close to the planet's surface.

The lowest level of the atmosphere is called the troposphere. Take a deep breath in. That air you're inhaling is from the troposphere. This is the layer in which all life on Earth exists. The troposphere is also where weather occurs since the troposphere contains most of the atmosphere's water vapor, allowing for cloud formation.[3]

The next layer is the stratosphere. The stratosphere absorbs large amounts of sunlight, particularly ultraviolet (UV) light. As a result, temperatures are much hotter in the stratosphere than the troposphere.[4]

Some ultraviolet (UV) radiation passes through the stratosphere and troposphere to reach Earth's surface. Small amounts of UV radiation are helpful; for instance, it is a source of vitamin D. However, large amounts of UV radiation can be harmful to plants and animals. For example, sunburns are caused primarily by UV rays and can contribute to skin cancer.

The surface of the planet is protected from high levels of harmful UV radiation by a gas called ozone which is concentrated in a region of the stratosphere known as the **ozone layer**.[5] Ozone is created when UV radiation enters the stratosphere and hits oxygen molecules (O_2), breaking the molecules' two oxygen atoms apart. Some of the free oxygen atoms recombine into a new molecule made of three oxygen atoms, ozone (O_3). The ozone layer makes up only a small fraction of Earth's atmosphere, but it provides a vital shield from UV radiation for the planet's surface.

While ozone in the stratosphere is beneficial, ozone found in the troposphere has a very different effect. Ground-level ozone is considered an air pollutant and is the main ingredient in smog. It is highly reactive and can be dangerous when it comes into direct contact with biological organisms. Ground-level ozone is harmful to breathe in as well as damaging to crops and other vegetation.[6]

Pollution

Both the troposphere and stratosphere are susceptible to **air pollution**, or the concentration of gases, dust, fumes, or odors in amounts that can harm the health of humans, animals, or plants. Different types of pollutants impact different layers of the atmosphere. For example, the troposphere is vulnerable to carbon dioxide emissions, while the stratosphere is vulnerable to human-produced gases containing chlorine and bromine. These gases are used in air conditioners, refrigerators, asthma inhalers, and a variety of other things. They become reactive when circulated in the stratosphere and have caused large holes in the ozone layer.[7]

The sources of air pollutants can be divided into two categories: natural and anthropogenic. A major source of anthropogenic air pollutants is the combustion of fossil fuels (such as coal, oil, and gas) either in vehicles or industrial combustion to produce electricity. **Fossil fuels** are the organic remains of organisms that have been dead and decomposing for millions of years. When you burn these fossils, energy is released. Humans have been burning large amounts of fossil fuels for energy since the Industrial Revolution. However, the combustion of fossil fuels also releases carbon monoxide, carbon dioxide, sulfur, and nitrogen oxides—all forms of air pollution.[8]

Natural pollution, on the other hand, has a history as long as Earth itself. Natural events such as forest fires, volcanic eruptions, and dust storms generated by droughts all contribute to air pollution. In 2004, Alaska had a very warm and dry summer, resulting in the worst wildfires in the state's history.[9] From June through August, the fires produced as much carbon monoxide (CO) as all human activity on the North American continent produces in an entire year. *Carbon monoxide* is a poisonous, colorless, odorless, tasteless gas generated from the incomplete burning of materials containing carbon such as trees or fossil fuels.[10] The map below shows the carbon monoxide levels across the northern hemisphere during the wildfires and then during the same period of time one year later.

The dark red areas in Alaska and Canada displayed in the 2004 map reflect pollution caused by the forest fires. The darker orange areas reflect the wide dispersion of that pollution across the northern hemisphere. In contrast, the 2005 map offers an image of the world with less severe forest fire events. In both maps you can see a large dark red area in East Asia. This concentration of carbon monoxide was not due to forest fires; it is instead linked

The 2004 Alaska wildfires generated carbon monoxide that polluted the air and was carried across the Northern Hemisphere.

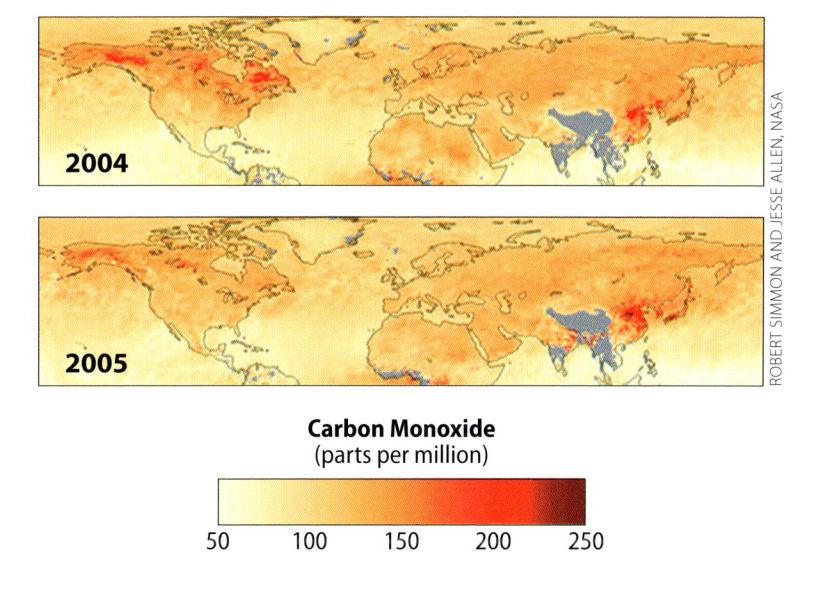

Carbon Monoxide
(parts per million)

50   100   150   200   250

to urban and industrial pollution in China.[11] Such industrial activity occurs regularly and leads to the accumulation of air pollutants in the atmosphere year after year. Natural sources of pollution like forest fires can pose a serious threat, but generally not as great of a threat as human-generated pollutants.[12]

The circulation of air allows the concentration of air pollutants to build up in places where the pollutants may not have originally been produced or released. Recent technological innovation allows us to trace intercontinental air pollution across oceans. For example, coal from each part of the world produces lead pollution with a distinct chemical fingerprint. Scientists can collect air samples anywhere in the world and identify the location the lead particles originated from. A 2011 study collected air samples in Northern California to determine the origin of the lead present in Northern California's air. The study revealed that 29% of this lead had traveled across the Pacific Ocean from Asia, a distance of over 5,000 miles.[13] There were only small amounts of lead detected in the Northern California air samples (not enough to harm human health), but the study illustrates how air pollution moves between continents. Studies of intercontinental pollution, such as the one conducted in Northern California, have shown us that pollutants can stay in the air long enough to follow global wind patterns. In the mid-latitudes of both the northern and southern hemispheres, these winds move from west to east. For instance, in the mid-latitudes of the northern hemisphere, winds bring Asian pollution to North America and North American pollution to Europe. As a result, pollution management is increasingly shaped by the flows of intercontinental air pollution. Neighboring nations are beginning to develop bilateral or multilateral agreements to more effectively address air pollution management.[14]

Air as a Common Resource

How is air classified as a natural resource? Is it a public good or a common resource? Public goods are nonexclusive (that is, no one is prevented from using the resource) and without rivalry in consumption (one person's use of the resource cannot limit another's use).[15] A great example of a public good is a tornado siren. Clean air is a resource available to all but owned by none. However, clean air doesn't seem to fit the requirement to be without rivalry in consumption though.

It may be more accurate to characterize air as a common resource.[16] **Common resources** are rival in consumption but not excludable. While air is a natural resource available to all, one person's actions may diminish the quality of air another person breathes. Keep in mind that people need more than just air to survive; they need air that is free from pollutants. Breathing polluted air has serious health consequences. Living in an area that frequently experiences heavy smog from forest fires or industrial pollution can increase a person's risk of emphysema, asthma, bronchitis, and heart attack.[17]

As with any common resource, if everyone takes care of the air we share, we can all enjoy it. But if a single person pollutes the air, we may all suffer. Clean air is not only one of the most

Air circulation and global wind patterns can spread air pollutants from one part of the world to another.

vital natural resources, it is also one of the most difficult to maintain. While fresh water can be collected behind dams and distributed through canals, air circulates over the entire globe, unrestricted by most physical barriers. Whether it is clean or polluted, all of us share the air to a much greater degree than we share any other resource.

Air and Sustainability

Clean air is necessary for all people and fundamental to social, economic, and environmental stability.

Society

Air pollution can reinforce the divide between rich and poor, disproportionately impacting those with limited financial resources. This statement may seem puzzling at first. After all, we just discussed how air circulates over the entire globe, affecting people regardless of income, race, religion, or social standing.

However, certain areas can experience higher concentrations of air pollutants because of proximity to a major source of air pollution or geological circumstance. When this occurs, people with more money are able to move to areas with better air quality. The mountains that surround Los Angeles, for example, restrict the ability of pollution to leave the city's basin, concentrating air pollutants in a relatively small area. As a result, Southern Los Angeles has worse air quality and higher rates of asthma than the rest of the city. Its residents also have lower per capita income.[18] This correlation between lower incomes and higher rates of asthma also became apparent in a study of hospitalization for severe asthma among different neighborhoods in New York City.[19]

Economy

At the same time, air pollution has an economic effect on everyone, rich or poor. The consequences air pollution can have on human health will also impact the health of our economies. Asthma causes about 15 million missed workdays annually in the United States alone. The estimated cost of productivity lost to these missed workdays is around $3 billion. In addition, students lose about 14 million schooldays to asthma each year, which averages to about eight days for each asthmatic youth.[20]

These economic consequences are considered externalities. An externality is a cost or benefit not reflected in the market price of a good or service. Because businesses and individuals that generate air pollution are not financially responsible for the side effects of that air pollution (such as health complications), these costs are passed on to those who are directly or indirectly impacted by the air pollution.

Additional economic impacts of air pollution include damage to our crops. In 2003, emissions of sulfur dioxide cost Chinese farmers an estimated 30 billion yuan (or about 4.7 billion U.S. dollars) in reduced crop growth.[21] Severe air pollution can obstruct visibility as well. In Beijing during the winter of 2011, limited visibility due to air pollution shut down airports and roadways.[22]

Los Angeles is surrounded by mountains, which restrict the ability of air pollution to leave the city's basin.

Environment

The environmental impacts of air pollution are wide-ranging. Lichens (composite organisms made up of a fungus and an alga) are finely adapted to a certain balance of gases in the atmosphere. In fact, lichens are so sensitive to sulfur dioxide that they can be used more effectively than human-designed instruments to measure the concentration of sulfur dioxide gas in the air.[23] Bushy lichen require very clean air, leafy lichen can tolerate small amounts of sulfur dioxide, and crusty lichen can survive in more polluted air. If no lichen are found in an area they once were, the air is likely to be heavily polluted with sulfur dioxide.[24] This sort of environmental indicator of air pollution provides an inexpensive health advisory to local communities.

The effects of air pollution on plants range from dead leaves to stunted development of flower buds. Forests exposed to chronic air pollution can lose their resistance to insects, leading to widespread tree death throughout a polluted region.[25] As pollutants build up in the soils and waterways over time, fundamental changes will occur within an entire ecosystem—hindering the ecosystem services we rely on such as water filtration, nutrient cycling, and healthy soils. One such change is acidification, caused by acid rain. **Acidification**, or a lowering of pH, prevents new plant growth and interrupts the reproductive cycles of aquatic animals.

Background on Air

Air pollution is not a new phenomenon. In the past, naturally occurring cleansing agents, such as sea salt and hydroxyl radical (OH), helped to keep these pollutants below toxic levels.[26]

Our presence on Earth, due in part to our exponential population growth and our rapid technological progress, has altered the concentration and types of air pollutants found in the atmosphere. Humans are able to generate air pollution on a scale never before seen in nature. We have developed new air pollutants that do not occur naturally. In a sense, it's a testament to the capability of our species. On the other hand, unsustainable industrial activities may be undermining humanity's future.

Lichens are used as an indicator of air quality in the Tongass National Forest of Southeast Alaska, the largest national forest in the United States.

Ancient Air Pollution

One of the earliest forms of human-generated air pollution is linked to our use of fire. Cavemen would often build fires in poorly ventilated caves to keep warm. The drawback was the smoke that filled their lungs and irritated their eyes. As a result, mummified bodies from the Paleolithic era were often discovered to have black lungs.[27]

As humans evolved from a hunter-gatherer lifestyle to an agrarian culture, our population became concentrated—often organizing ourselves into villages and then cities. As a result, air pollution from household fuels, such as wood and charcoal, that were used to keep the home warm became concentrated as well. The more humans urbanized, the more intense our air pollution became.

During the 19th century, England burned coal on a large scale.

Due to the air pollution caused from the combustion of coal, the peppered moth evolved into a darker-colored species that blended with the coal soot.

There is anecdotal evidence of air pollution found in classic Greek and Roman poetry. The Roman poet Horatius (65 B.C.E.–8 C.E.) wrote of buildings in Rome becoming darker and darker from the smoke. The Roman Senate even passed a law some two thousand years ago declaring "Aerem corrumpere non licet" or "Polluting air is not allowed."

Mining for valuable minerals was another early form of human-generated air pollution. Lead was mined in Roman times to be used in face powders, lipstick, and even as a food preservative. Lead, however, is poisonous and those who worked in the mines would experience headaches, nausea, even paralysis as a result.

Noxious Fumes in the Middle Ages

Air pollution from coal was a problem in Europe as early as the Middle Ages. In the 1100s, London artisans began using coal instead of wood to produce heat for blacksmithing, brewing, and other crafts. As noblemen arrived from the countryside to meet for the first sessions of Parliament, they were disgusted by the foul smells and thick smoke produced by burning coal—so much so that the nobles led a public revolt against coal.

King Edward I responded by banning the use of coal in 1306, threatening fines or destruction of furnaces if people were found burning coal.

The ban did not last. By the 1500s, an energy crisis and depleted timber resources forced London's elite to rethink their disdain for coal. Another factor was the widespread appearance of chimneys in poorer households; this source of ventilation enabled the lower classes to burn coal for domestic use.

In the 19th century, England became the first nation to burn coal on a large scale. While there is no available measurement of air pollution generated by coal during this time, writings from the period provide anecdotal evidence of a thick smog that blocked out the sun and a horrid smell that could be detected miles from London. The soot created by coal fires appeared on buildings, furniture, bedding, and clothing. Rain water collected soot as it fell, prompting many people to carry black umbrellas when walking through the streets.[28]

People were not the only ones affected. Due to the amount of air pollution in England during this time, the peppered moth evolved to blend in with buildings and trees covered in coal soot. Through natural selection a darker-colored subspecies grew to vastly outnumber the lighter species of the moth.[29]

Massive deforestation during the Industrial Revolution changed the chemical composition of the atmosphere.

The Modern Era: Impacts of Industry on Air

The Industrial Revolution changed the course of history, but it also led to intense and widespread air pollution. During the 1700s, coal became the primary fuel used in Europe to power factories, move trains, and heat homes. Land was cleared to feed and house a booming population, resulting in massive deforestation. The combination of increased pollution and fewer trees began to change the chemical composition of the atmosphere. The concentration of carbon dioxide in the atmosphere rose exponentially. Rising carbon dioxide levels and resulting climate change continue today as the world continues to generate air pollution from industrial practices.

Increased air pollution has created health complications for people around the world. In October of 1948, a dense fog formed over the small town of Donora, Pennsylvania that lasted five days. Donora was an industrial town, home to a large steel mill and a zinc-reduction plant. A combination of plant and mill pollutants along with some unique weather phenomena (a stagnant weather system and a thermal inversion in the lower atmosphere) created the unusual fog. For those living in Donora, the fog had widespread health effects. At first the elderly and asthmatic had difficulty breathing, but soon the whole town seemed to be experiencing stomach pains, headaches, nausea, and choking. The fog led to 20 deaths in the community. Largely in response to fears of another Donora Smog occurring in other cities and towns, the Air Pollution Control Act was passed in 1955, a precursor to the Clean Air Act of 1970.[30]

Urban areas in other parts of the world also experienced the unfortunate effects of air pollution. In December of 1952, another thick fog settled over the city of London. Large numbers of people with respiratory or cardiovascular problems began arriving at the city's hospitals. It became clear to doctors that the fog was more than water vapor. The coal fires that many people used to heat their homes had laced the fog with sulfur dioxide, nitrogen oxide, and soot. London's Great Smog eventually claimed the lives of about 4,000 people from immediate exposure and approximately 12,000 from exposure-related illness in the weeks and months that followed.[31] This was not the first smog event in London; the smog-producing combination of coal-burning, fog, and calm winds had occurred before in 1873 (costing nearly 700 lives) and 1911 (killing 1,150).[32] However, the Great Smog of 1952 finally provided the catalyst for the British Clean Air Act, passed four years later.[33]

Smog continues to be an issue today. Unlike the black soot generated from coal furnaces, pollutants used today can create less visible, but equally dangerous, forms of air pollution. *Photochemical smog* occurs when air pollutants react with sunlight in stagnant atmospheric conditions and create a brownish haze that may hover above large cities; sometimes the smog can be almost invisible.

Air Today

Air pollution has become a major concern for people all around the world though the types of air pollution people are exposed to on a daily basis varies. The World Health Organization (WHO) estimates that 2 million people die every year from air pollution.[34]

Indoor Air Pollution

What do you think of when you imagine air pollution? The image of brown exhaust coming from a car or smokestack might come to mind. This is an example of outdoor air pollution. However, air pollution also occurs inside homes and buildings.

Indoor air quality can have a far greater impact on human health than outside air quality for two reasons. First, the levels of pollutants inside a building can be far higher than those outside, exposing people to concentrated levels of pollution for hours at a time. Second, many people spend much of their time inside. For instance, in the United States the average person spends about 90% of their life indoors.[35]

Indoor Cooking Fires

Indoor cooking fires in houses with poor ventilation pose a serious risk to the health of billions of people around the world.[36] In India, for example, 72% of all households use stoves fueled by crop husks, straw, dried animal dung, or wood (often referred to collectively as biomass).[37] Such solid fuels produce large amounts of pollutants—especially carbon monoxide and ash, both of which are toxic to humans. Around 2.4 billion people in rural parts of the developing world cook by burning biomass.

Pollutants from these traditional stoves can cause pneumonia, lung cancer, and

---

CASE STUDY: Smokeless Kitchens in Peru[38]

Smoke-filled kitchens are the norm in the small rural village of Usabamba in Peru. Open fires burn in stoves made of adobe bricks in villagers' small homes. Because there is no ventilation to allow smoke to escape, stalactites of soot form on ceilings and walls become black.

The nonprofit organization Crooked Trails is working to address this issue. Crooked Trails trains local volunteers to install new kitchens that allow villagers to live in smoke-free homes for the first time. Each new kitchen costs approximately $230, paid by funds raised by the nonprofit.

Smokeless kitchens include ventilation pipes that allow smoke to escape up and out of a chimney.

The community decides who will receive the next smokeless kitchen based on the greatest need.

The new kitchens include a ventilation pipe to allow smoke to escape up and out through a chimney. The stove itself is enclosed, making it more efficient so that less fuel is wasted. The stove uses small twigs instead of large sticks and heats up rooms by about 20°F—a warm welcome in this cold mountain village. A 15-gallon container of water on the side of the stove provides residents with hot water.

chronic bronchitis, and have been linked to more than two million deaths a year. Since women and children spend the most time near cooking fires in many cultures, they usually suffer the most from this form of indoor air pollution.[39]

Harmful Household Gases

Poor indoor air quality is not unique to homes using traditional stoves and indoor fires for cooking. In fact, the very qualities that make buildings "modern" create their own set of indoor air pollution problems. In the 1970s, efforts to make buildings more energy-efficient led to structures that did not exchange much air with the outside environment. Sealing buildings in this way—as well as using newly invented insulating materials—allowed for lower energy costs for heating and cooling. However, these modern buildings lack ventilation and allow air pollutants to build up over extended periods of time.[40]

Radon is one example of a harmful household gas. Throughout the world, there are small amounts of the radioactive element uranium in soil, rock, and water. As uranium decays, it releases an odorless, colorless gas called radon. Studies of radon's effects on miners have shown that the gas continues to decay long after a person inhales it, releasing radiation that damages lung tissue and can eventually lead to cancer. Indeed, radon inhalation is one of the leading causes of lung cancer in the United States (second only to cigarette smoke), contributing to 21,000 deaths a year.[41] Radon is only a concern indoors; it is dispersed by the free flow of air outdoors. Only inside a mine or a building without adequate ventilation can radon gas reach harmful concentrations.

Another gas that can be harmful when concentrated indoors is carbon monoxide (CO). Carbon monoxide can leak from furnaces or fireplaces, come from automobile or other gas-powered engine fumes, or be released by the incomplete combustion of natural gas in stovetop ranges. At low concentrations, carbon monoxide exposure can lead to fatigue. At higher concentrations, it causes dizziness, blurred vision, headaches, and nausea. These symptoms are often misinterpreted as signs of the flu, but will pass when a person suffering from carbon monoxide exposure leaves the home. At very high concentrations, carbon monoxide can be fatal. Because it is odorless, tasteless, and colorless, people may not realize they are inhaling carbon monoxide, even at fatal levels.[42] One simple way to avoid carbon monoxide poisoning is to install a carbon monoxide detector in your home.

Radon, a colorless and odorless gas, is one example of a harmful household gas.

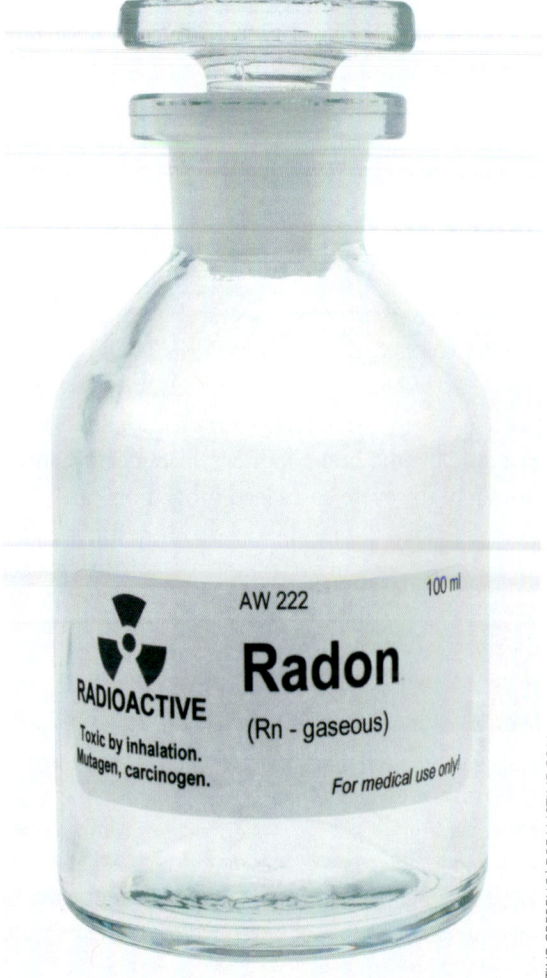

Household Items and Building Materials

Another common source of indoor air pollution are *volatile organic compounds (VOCs)*, carbon-based chemicals that evaporate into gas at room temperature. Many common household chemicals—including aerosol sprays, cosmetics, cleansers, disinfectants, and air fresheners—give off these gases. Such products usually come with a warning label that instructs people to use them only in well-ventilated areas in order for VOCs to disperse without causing harm to human health. This is especially important for cosmetics, which are applied directly to the body.[43]

Much of the VOC pollution inside buildings comes from the building materials themselves. Plywood, construction adhesives, paints, drywall, ceiling panels, and even carpets will *off-gas*, or slowly release VOCs into the air. This off-gassing can occur for years after the materials have been installed. The smell of a new car is another example of off-gassing resulting from the plastics and fabrics inside the car emitting VOCs.

Depending on the materials used during construction, new buildings can emit enough VOCs to make the inside air harmful to your health, in both the short and long term.[44] Within a few hours or days, exposure to high concentrations of VOCs can lead to headaches and nausea and worsen asthma symptoms. Over a longer period of time, VOCs have been associated with kidney and liver damage as well as cancer and complications with the nervous system.[45] Children are more sensitive to VOCs than adults, making the presence of VOCs in schools even more troubling. Much research is being conducted to examine a link between youth exposure to VOCs and developmental disorders.[46]

Outdoor Air Pollution

Outdoor air pollution can also have a significant impact on human health. Outdoor air quality may be particularly poor in places where pollutants are released directly into the air, such as near factories or in cities with heavy traffic. A 2005 *USA Today* report on air quality found that hundreds of schools across the United States are situated in areas with potentially dangerous concentrations of air pollutants.[47]

Toxic Particulate Matter

Metals like manganese and lead do not pollute the air in gaseous form, but as tiny particles less than ten micrometers in size. Metal dust is just one type of particulate contributing to air pollution; others include acids, soil particles, and smoke. Such toxic particulate matter can have profound health impacts, especially because the body often cannot expel the particles once they have been inhaled or ingested.

> *Outdoor air pollution can also have a significant impact on human health.*

Between 2009 and 2011, thousands of residents in certain Chinese villages were found to have toxic levels of lead in their blood—as high as seven times the amount deemed safe by the Chinese government.[48] These people lived near and worked in factories that made lead-acid batteries for electric cars and motorcycles or smelted metal, a process that extracts metal from rock. Both processes generate heavy smoke containing lead particles. When inhaled, this smoke can damage the brain, kidneys, liver, nerves, and stomach. In severe cases lead inhalation can cause seizures, coma, and death. Children are far more vulnerable to lead poisoning because the metal interrupts the development of the nervous system. Lead poisoning in children, even in very small amounts, can lead to permanent learning and behavior disorders.

To prevent exposure to lead, Australia banned leaded gasoline in the 1980s. At the time, leaded gasoline was common worldwide because it increased gasoline's efficiency and power. Many other countries have since followed Australia's example and lead blood levels have dropped significantly in most parts of the world.[49]

Dioxins that are absorbed by smaller organisms move up the food chain due to bioaccumulation.

Dioxins are another type of toxic particulate matter with serious consequences for human health. Formed as an unwanted by-product of various industrial processes ranging from bleaching paper to incinerating solid waste, dioxins are among the most toxic chemicals known to man. Short-term exposure can cause lesions and discoloration of the skin. Long term, the build-up of dioxins in fat cells can lead to reproductive problems and cancer. The U.S. Environmental Protection Agency introduced regulations to limit dioxin emissions in the early 1980s and methods have been invented to trap dioxins in industrial smokestacks before they escape.

Unfortunately, when dioxins make their way into the environment they tend to linger. Dioxins do not break down quickly and can contaminate a wide variety of food sources. Once dioxins find their way into one organism, they work their way up the food chain as the organism is digested by a larger predator. Even if released in low concentrations, dioxins can build up in larger organisms, like humans, over time to toxic levels.[50] This process is referred to as **bioaccumulation**.

Ground-level Ozone

Dioxins and lead are considered primary air pollutants, meaning they are emitted directly into the atmosphere. Secondary pollutants, on the other hand, are created when primary pollutants undergo chemical changes after being released into the air. One of the most common secondary pollutants is ground-level ozone.

As noted earlier, ozone occurs naturally as a gas in the stratosphere, where it filters out some of the UV radiation from the sun. However, ozone can also form in the lower troposphere. This ground-level ozone is created when sunlight interacts with certain air pollutants from cars or manufacturing. When inhaled directly for extended periods of time, ozone irritates the lungs, causing inflammation in the airways. Long-term exposure to ozone has been linked to asthma.[51] Aside from its known health impacts, ground-level ozone is one of the main contributors to smog in metropolitan centers.

Atmospheric Ozone Depletion

As mentioned earlier, ozone concentrated in the stratosphere protects the planet from harmful radiation and is necessary for life as we know it to exist on Earth. When they reach the stratosphere, pollutants such as *chlorofluorocarbons (CFCs),* gases containing chlorine or bromine atoms, can break down existing ozone (O_3) molecules by bonding with one of the oxygen atoms.[52] This reaction can create holes in the ozone layer. These holes

CASE STUDY: Smog in Mexico City[53]

In 1959, the Mexican novelist Carlos Fuentes published his first book, *Where the Air Is Clear*. The title was a reference to the spectacular air quality of Mexico City at the time. The air was considered to be so pristine as to possess therapeutic powers and attracted visitors from around the world with respiratory problems. Half a century later, Mexico City now ranks among the worst cities in the world for air quality. How could air quality change so drastically in just 50 years?

On a rare clear day in Mexico City, visibility can reach 100 kilometers and include awe-inspiring views of three active volcanoes. Most days, however, pollutants such as ground-level ozone and nitrogen dioxide reach two to three times the levels deemed acceptable by the World Health Organization. Air pollution at these levels reduces visibility to just over one kilometer (about half a mile).

Population and resource consumption both play roles in Mexico City's air pollution. Over 21 million people live in Mexico City and the surrounding metropolitan area, four times the population size when Fuentes wrote *Where the Air Is Clear*.[54] As a result of the greater number of people and technological advancement over the years, Mexico City experienced a substantial increase in the combustion of fossil fuels to provide the energy needed to drive cars and produce electricity. Automobile exhaust from the three million private vehicles that take to the streets of Mexico City each day is the greatest contributor to the city's poor air quality.

Car exhaust is largely made up of colorless nitrogen oxides. These gases can be broken apart by sunlight, releasing single oxygen atoms. These oxygen atoms combine with oxygen gas (O_2) present in the air to form ground-level ozone (O_3). This combination of chemicals and light, called photochemical smog, is what gives the city's air its distinctive color.

The geography of Mexico City exacerbates its air pollution problem. The city is more than 7,000 feet above sea level and so naturally has less air pressure than at lower elevations. Reduced air pressure causes fuels such as gasoline, petroleum, and coal to combust only partially; in turn, incomplete combustion of fossil fuels increases pollution. Mexico City also sits within a basin formed by the surrounding mountains, which can trap air pollution.

Automobile exhaust from 3 million private cars contributes to poor air quality in Mexico City.

---

allow high levels of UV radiation to reach the earth's surface. CFCs were once used in almost all refrigeration and air conditioning.

The global production of ozone-depleting gases such as CFCs has led to a seasonal thinning of the ozone layer over each of the poles. The hole over the Antarctic—first discovered in the late 1970s—occurs each year in spring. On rare occasions, this hole extends up and over the southernmost parts of Argentina and Chile, including the city of Punto Arenas. On one occasion in 2008, the city received so much UV radiation that people were sunburnt after about seven minutes' exposure.[55]

In 1987, an international agreement known as the Montreal Protocol on Substances that Deplete the Ozone Layer established limits on the amounts of ozone-depleting gases any nation could produce or consume, eventually phasing out the destructive gases altogether. Ozone-depleting gases were replaced with other gases that provided the same functions (refrigerants and propellants) without destroying ozone. The Protocol, now ratified by 196 countries, has been successful at slowing the rate of ozone depletion. Scientists predict that by the middle of this century, ozone levels will return to normal.[56] If atmospheric ozone continues to rebound, the holes will close for good sometime during the 21st century.[57]

Acid Rain

Volcanic eruptions, forest fires, and burning fossil fuels all release sulfur dioxide and nitric oxide gases into the air. When these gases dissolve in water in the upper atmosphere, sulfur dioxide and nitric oxide become sulfuric and nitric acid and can fall back to earth as acid rain, snow, or fog. While water naturally has a pH (a measure of acidity) close to a neutral 7, the pH of acid rain is usually closer to 5.

Acid rain can damage the leaves or needles of plants by stripping away nutrients. Acid fog has a particularly strong impact on leaves, as it contacts their surfaces for much longer than falling raindrops. While some soils are able to neutralize the extra acid and resist changes to their pH, other soils lack this buffering capacity and gain acidity from rain as it washes through. These acidified soils lose some of the nutrients and minerals necessary for plant life. Over time this can significantly weaken the growth of plants and trees. Lower pH levels also release aluminum into the soil, which is also harmful to plants.

The harmful effects of acid rain continue when it reaches a waterway. Acid rain drops the pH of the water and, if it passes through soil prior to entering a body of water, may carry aluminum. Both low pH and aluminum are toxic to many fish and plants and the impact on aquatic life can be severe. Most fish eggs, for example, cannot hatch in very acidic environments.[58]

Pathways to Progress: Air

There is little that people can do to remove pollution once it is in the air. Air pollutants will work their way out of the atmosphere over time. Oceans, forests, and various other natural ecosystems can speed up this process

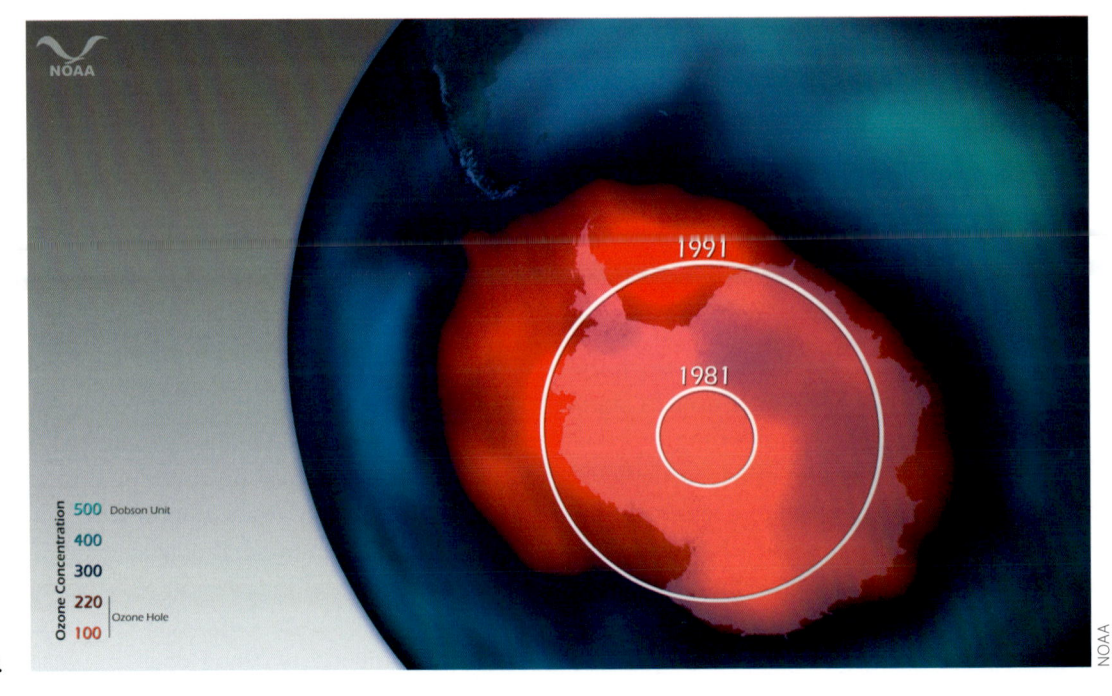

The Montreal Protocol established limits on a country's production and consumption of ozone-depleting gases.

by absorbing pollution. While we cannot eliminate all sources of air pollution—natural sources such as volcanoes and forest fires are beyond our control—we can reduce human contributions to air pollution. We can also help to sustain ecosystems' absorption of air pollution as well as mitigate the effects of pollution on our own health.

Reducing Pollution at the Source

Addressing the sources of air pollution will help reduce the costs associated with air pollution in the long run.

Government Regulations

Government agencies have the ability to regulate air pollution and compel reductions at its source. Cars are one major source of pollution. National standards for emissions, like Corporate Average Fuel Economy (CAFE) standards in the United States, are a common method used by governments to reduce air pollution from cars. In existence since 1975, CAFE standards set a minimum fuel efficiency standard for car manufacturers. Initially, CAFE standards required that each manufacturer's fleet of cars average at least 18 miles per gallon. Over time CAFE standards have risen and may continue to rise to improve fuel efficiency.[59] Greater fuel efficiency means less petroleum is burned by each vehicle and less air pollution is emitted into our atmosphere.

Under government incentive, power plants have also reduced the amount of air pollution they produce. This incentive for reduction often takes one of two forms. The traditional form of government oversight is direct intervention, or command-and-control, mandating certain changes at all power plants to reduce pollution to a fixed level for all polluters. A different form of government oversight, referred to as cap-and-trade, sets a maximum amount of pollution for the industry as a whole. This total amount is then divided up and each plant is given a certain number of pollution allowances that it can emit. For example, if Plant A exceeds its allowances, Plant A will be fined. However, if Plant B emits less than it is allowed, it has the option to sell its extra allowances to Plant A. Plant A would avoid a fine but still pay a price for its additional pollution by purchasing allowances from Plant B. This system caps the total amount of pollution nationwide, but there is a risk of concentrated pollution in one area.

The Puget Sound Clean Air Agency is a government agency that works to protect clean air and our climate.

In 1990, amendments to the U.S. Clean Air Act capped emissions of sulfur dioxide (SO_2) and mandated a lower cap in future years. This legislation set up what came to be known as the Acid Rain Program, since SO_2 is one of the main contributors to acidic precipitation. The program, just one example of cap-and-trade regulation, is widely seen as successful. It reduced the amount of acid deposited into waterways by 40% in just two decades.[60]

National programs are not always sufficient to reduce air pollution for the simple reason that the atmosphere is a common resource and air pollution can easily cross political borders. International programs may be more effective at reducing air pollution and maintaining air

Due to consumer demand, manufacturers have started to produce paints that emit lower amounts of VOC.

quality. One means of ensuring international cooperation is through international treaties that bind the governments of many countries to a commitment to control pollution. An example of such a treaty is the Montreal Protocol, which you read about earlier in this chapter.

Manufacturing Standards

Some manufacturers have reduced their air pollution emissions without government intervention. Their reductions were in response to changing markets and customer demand for healthier products. Manufacturers of paints, for example, have created paints to emit much less VOC pollution largely in response to consumer demand. As a result, the industry established three main certifications for low-VOC paint to help inform consumers about what goes into a can of paint, as well as what gases the paint will emit once out of the can.[61]

Manufacturers' response to consumer demands demonstrate the collective power of individuals to improve the quality of the air that we breathe. Our actions can be most effective when we act both as citizens and consumers, advocating for stricter regulations and making purchases that reflect personal values and concerns.

Sustaining Forests to Clear the Air

We can help improve air quality by preserving those ecosystems that absorb air pollution such as forests. Efforts to protect existing trees from harvest or fire, to plant new trees, or to remove invasive species all help preserve forests. Although forests are vulnerable to the impacts of air pollution (for example, acid rain) these ecosystems are also vital to managing air pollution.

Trees help neutralize air pollution by absorbing carbon dioxide and other harmful gases, producing oxygen, and trapping dust, ash, pollen, and smoke.[62] During the months in which they are in leaf each year, the trees of New York City can take in about 1,800 metric tons of air pollution, roughly equivalent to the annual emissions of about 440 small cars. This absorption has a small effect on the city's overall air quality—dropping levels of ground-level ozone, sulfur dioxide, and nitrogen dioxide by about 0.5%. However, in areas of the city where the trees form a continuous canopy, air quality improves dramatically. In parks, for example, ground-level ozone and sulfur dioxide drop by about 15% and nitrogen dioxide by about 8%.[63]

Mitigating the Effects of Air Pollution: Protecting Your Health

We can also protect ourselves from the effects of outdoor air pollution by paying attention to air quality reports and reacting accordingly, both by staying indoors and by reducing our own contributions to air pollution. If you know that air quality will be worse on a particular day, avoid being outside during peak times of day for air pollutants, especially while exercising and breathing hard. Ground-level ozone, for example, is created only during times when the sunlight is strong, then dissipates when the sun starts going down. On sunny days, morning and evening are the best times to exercise outdoors to avoid breathing in heavy concentrations of ozone. Similarly, staying away from roadways with heavy traffic can help to avoid carbon monoxide emissions.[64]

The U.S. Environmental Protection Agency (EPA) has developed a tool to provide local air quality information to the public, the Air Quality Index. The Air Quality Index provides easy-to-understand updates for the public about the level of air pollution and any related human health risks. Air quality indices have been developed in other parts of the world as well: Canada, China, Hong Kong, Mexico, Singapore, South Korea, Thailand, and the United Kingdom to name a few.

YOUTH PROFILE
Marisol Becerra

As discussed throughout this chapter, air pollution often has a disproportionate effect on the poor. The burden of localized air pollution on poorer neighborhoods rarely provokes policy change, since the affected communities tend to have little influence on decision-making processes. **Environmental justice**, on the other hand, is the fair treatment and involvement of all community members in environmental

CAREER PROFILE: Forester

Rangers working for the U.S. Forest Service manage and care for more than 193 million acres of land, working to sustain the nation's forests and grasslands for a variety of uses. Forestry programs vary in every state, but in general rangers are responsible for maintaining a balance between the protection of natural resources found on public forest land, the control of forest fires, and the sale of timber. In addition, forest rangers monitor air pollution for levels that may pose a threat to human health or health of the forest ecosystems.

Forest rangers usually hold a bachelor's degree in forestry or a related field that includes forestry coursework. Pursuing a master's degree in forest management or park administration may open up opportunities for higher-ranking and higher-paying positions within the Forest Service.

In addition to their work as scientists and conservationists, forest rangers are responsible for

Daniel Richter's work to preserve and manage forests also helps to prevent air pollution.

law enforcement. Many are required to carry guns. Because of this, sober judgment and the ability to stay cool under pressure are highly sought-after qualities for a forest ranger.

Forest ranger Captain Daniel Richter is in charge of the 17 western counties in New York State. Captain Richter and his team of rangers are responsible for "care, custody, and control" of the U.S. forest land within these counties so that competing uses can coexist peacefully. This duty includes managing the sweeping gorge of Letchworth State Park, where visitors enjoy whitewater rafting, and the Allegany Mountains whose forests shade delicate ecosystems and attract hikers and loggers.

Captain Richter's work to preserve and manage forests helps maintain a natural filtration system for air pollution—trees. His team is responsible for inventorying and monitoring each tree in the forest. Captain Richter says, "Our presence by patrol on state forests keeps some sense of stability out there. Even though we sell timber to loggers, we regulate what we want cut and where and how much. If it weren't for forest rangers, there wouldn't be any trees, because people would come in and help themselves." It can be hard work balancing the needs of the public and those of the forest, but being a forest ranger offers adventure and the satisfaction of protecting the environment.

governance. The goal of environmental justice is for all people to have equal access to a healthy environment.[65]

The Little Village neighborhood in Chicago has a large population of Mexican immigrants. Little Village resident Marisol Becerra was a high school freshman when she and her mother went through an environmental training program organized by a local community group, the Little Village Environmental Justice Organization (LVEJO). During this training, Marisol learned about toxic substances in the air. She also learned that 60,000 young people in her neighborhood lived close to coal power plants, which contribute to air pollution.

Angry about the pollution her community was exposed to, Marisol decided to take action. In order to involve more people in the fight for clean air, she created a youth chapter of the Little Village Environmental Justice Organization and put together an online map to educate her community about toxics and pollutants in the neighborhood. The youth chapter of the LVEJO continues to expand and reach more people, improving environmental and social conditions in the neighborhood.

Marisol Becerra

WHAT YOU CAN DO   Air

There are many ways you can help clear the air. The following ideas are just a few solutions.

- Be a savvy consumer: Buy nontoxic household products and low-VOC materials whenever possible to improve indoor air quality and protect your health.

- Contribute to forest regrowth: Lead or join a campaign to plant trees in your community, such as the international Billion Tree Campaign (www.unep.org/billiontreecampaign/).

- Protect forests: Buy sustainably harvested wood products and recycled paper to reduce the demands on our forests and ensure that new trees are grown in place of those that are harvested.

- Travel thoughtfully: To reduce your personal contribution to air pollution and smog, consider ways to travel that are less polluting such as biking, public transportation, or a fuel-efficient car.

- Support air quality legislation: Encourage state and national government representatives to support higher CAFE standards and stricter air quality standards.

One way to address air issues is to contribute to forest regrowth.

POINT | **COUNTERPOINT**

Are cap-and-trade systems more effective than pollution taxes?[66]

A cap-and-trade system sets a cap on pollution for an industry as a whole. The amount of permissible pollution is divided among polluters in the form of a pollution allowance. Those who struggle to keep emissions within their allowance can trade with those who rarely reach their allowance, creating an incentive for low emissions and flexibility for those who cannot yet achieve them. An alternative to a cap-and-trade system are pollution taxes, which automatically fine those who pollute above allowable limits. Which approach do you think would be most effective? Both systems rely on economic incentives but they go about it in very different ways. Consider the following perspectives on the cap-and-trade system and pollution taxes to help you further appreciate this debate about how to address air pollution.

POINT

Yes

- **A cap-and-trade system is certain to reduce emissions.** The act of setting a cap for total emissions is guaranteed to bring down the overall amount of pollution assuming a reasonably effective enforcement mechanism. The cap is a fixed limit and no additional pollution can be emitted. A tax, on the other hand, merely encourages people to emit less by making it more expensive to do so. A tax will only decrease emissions if the cost of cutting emissions is lower than the potential tax. If not, there is no effect on emissions.

- **Cap-and-trade is a fair system.** Pollution-emitting energy industries emerged long ago, before anyone thought about their environmental impacts. Modern energy producers should not be punished for their participation in an industry whose emergence predates concerns about pollution and who provide valuable services to society. Cap-and-trade represents a reasonable approach to reward and punish polluting industries.

- **A cap-and-trade system incentivizes pollution reductions wherever they are most efficient.** The efficiency of a cap-and-trade system comes with the trade part. Let's say you have two power plants, each emitting 100 tons of pollution per hour. The first can reduce its emissions by 20 tons at a cost of $5 per ton, and the second can reduce its emissions by only 10 tons, at a cost of $30 per ton. The most efficient solution is to make the reduction at the first plant, which is cheaper and has a greater impact, and allow the owner of the second plant to pay the owner of the first to offset the costs of the reduction.

COUNTERPOINT

No

- **A cap-and-trade system is vulnerable to companies tricking the system.** The main problem is that baseline emission allowances for companies are often based on their past emissions. For this reason, a company has an incentive to emit as much as possible when these baselines are being established so that the baseline appears high. If a company successfully tricks the system in this way, they will be able to pollute at the same level—or possibly even a higher level—than they had before and no reduction will be achieved.

- **A pollution tax is fairer than cap-and-trade.** A pollution tax considers all pollution emissions harmful to the environment. Everyone is punished proportionally to how much they pollute. A cap-and-trade system only punishes emissions above a certain level, creating an impression that only some kinds of emissions are "bad." A pollution tax, on the other hand, sends a strong message to polluters that all their emissions are harmful and should be phased out.

- **A cap-and-trade system entails substantial administrative costs.** The system demands that a cap be set, monitored, and enforced. This highly complicated process would require substantial administrative oversight. The government would have to determine the emissions baselines for companies, allocate pollution credits, and monitor and enforce the system. Pollution taxes, on the other hand, would be less complex and costly to establish and administer.

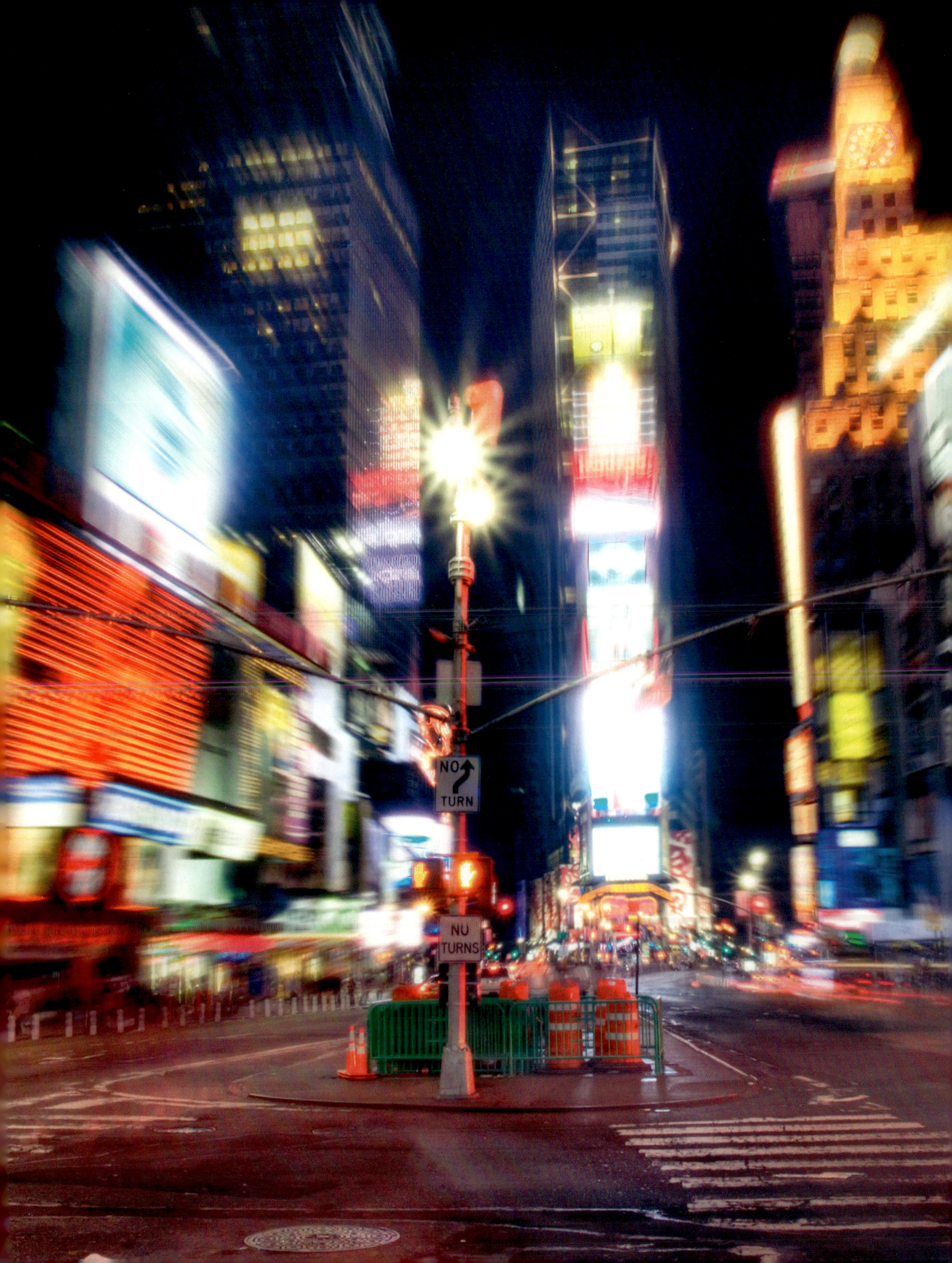
NO TURN
NO TURNS

Chapter 6

Energy

> **GUIDING QUESTIONS**
> - What are the social, economic and environmental consequences of using different sources of energy?
> - How can all humans meet their basic energy needs while ensuring that future generations will be able to do the same?

Introduction to Energy

On a hot summer day in 2003, New York City subways halted and traffic lights went out. A New England Six Flags roller coaster was stopped mid-ride. Over one million residents of Cleveland were faced with dry faucets from out-of-order water pumps,[1] while New York residents were flooded with offers of $1 ice cream bars from store owners who lost refrigeration.[2] During the blackout of 2003, 50 million people in the eastern United States and Canada lost electricity.[3]

What would a day in your life look like without electricity? For many of us, electricity is a modern convenience that we often take for granted. We know that light turns on when we flip a switch, but we may not know if this electricity was generated by burning coal or damming a river. Knowing how we use energy and where our energy comes from can help us make effective energy choices for a sustainable future.

What Is Energy, Anyway?

In our everyday conversations, we often use the term energy to describe many different things: our mood, a sports drink, electricity, and so on. But what is energy, really? Scientists define **energy** as the ability to do work or cause change. This means that some form of energy is required for an object or a system to do things such as move or generate heat and light.

> *Scientists define energy as the ability to do work or cause change.*

Take a car, for instance. What form of energy is necessary in order to drive a car down the road? Most cars use some sort of chemical energy such as gasoline to fuel the engine. When you start the car, the internal combustion engine transforms this chemical energy into motion energy and before you know it you're cruising down the road. Without the energy gasoline provides, the car wouldn't go anywhere.

While there are many different forms of energy such as light, heat, motion, and chemical energy, they can all be classified as either potential or kinetic. *Potential energy*—such as gasoline—is a type of stored energy. When gasoline is burned in an engine, this potential energy is transformed into *kinetic energy*, or the energy of motion. One type of energy can be transformed into another or transferred to a different object. However, energy is never created or destroyed. In fact, there is a constant amount of energy in our universe.

If energy can never be destroyed, then why are so many people concerned with saving or conserving energy? While energy cannot disappear, it can be converted into less useful forms of energy such as heat. Imagine pumping gasoline into a car's gas tank. When burned in the engine, about 14-26% of that gasoline is used to move the car forward; a large amount of the remainder is turned into heat.[4] If you have ever touched the hood of a car after it has been driven, you know that some of this heat warms the body of the car. The rest of it heats up the surrounding air or ground. Unfortunately, this is not a form of energy that is often reused in the tanks of our cars. Therefore, this energy is often referred to as "lost" energy.

In fact, most machines that use energy (including the human body) waste large amounts of energy. For example, many power plants that generate electricity are only 35% efficient.[5] This means that for every three units of fuel used to generate electricity, only one unit of electricity is produced. As with a car, most of the remaining energy is released to the surrounding environment as heat.

Human Energy Needs

Like cars, humans depend on energy to function. First and foremost, we must have energy to stay alive. Energy provided by the foods we eat and the beverages we drink powers the basic operations of our cells and allows our bodies to function on a day-to-day basis. The amount of energy in our bodies also determines our ability to fight off disease and to think clearly.

Secondly, we use energy to perform work and raise our comfort level. For example, energy is used to charge our computers, light and heat our homes, and fuel our transportation. It is also required to manufacture goods such as medicine, clothing, and food. And, how do all of these products get to the store? Energy, of course.

Our Primary Source: The Sun

Where does all of this energy come from? With the exception of geothermal and nuclear energy (which will be discussed later in this chapter), the sun is the main source of energy on Earth. The sun's uneven heating of the air, water, and land produces wind and rain that can be used as energy sources to do work for us.[6] Sunlight is also captured by photosynthesizing organisms such as plants and algae and used to produce chemical energy. Humans and other animals that cannot directly use energy from the sun can get the energy they need by eating plants or other animals that feed off plants. Directly or indirectly, the sun is the original source of food energy for most living organisms on Earth.

In addition to providing food, the sun is one of the primary sources of energy used to power human society. Solar power captures sunlight directly and uses it to create electricity. More significantly, an indirect source of solar energy provides people with a way to harness sunlight that was emitted millions of years ago! Light captured by plants millions of years ago has been stored as chemical energy in fossil fuels. **Fossil fuels** are energy sources created over a long period of time by the decay of organisms such as plants and tiny animals. Years of compression, as layer upon layer of sedimentary rock or large bodies of water formed on top of the decomposed vegetation, resulted in pockets of fossil fuels in the form of coal, oil, and natural gas.

Renewable or Not?

Light and heat are constantly generated by the sun; therefore, solar energy is considered a renewable energy source. A **renewable** energy source is one that is replenished naturally and quickly. Sun, wind, and water power are all examples of renewable energy.

Alternatively, **nonrenewable** energy sources cannot be replaced in a short amount of time. Fossil fuels like coal, oil, and natural gas are considered nonrenewable energy sources because it takes so long for these energy sources to form.

Energy and Sustainability

The amount of energy that the world consumes has been steadily increasing and experts predict that our consumption will continue to increase in the next couple of decades.[7] There are two main energy challenges our world faces. One is that many people around our world still do not have access to reliable forms of energy. Another is that the majority of the world's energy is supplied by oil, coal, and natural gas—all nonrenewable forms of energy that release greenhouse gases when burned.

Economy

In general, as countries become more developed their energy consumption increases. This can improve quality of life for some, but that improvement comes alongside costs such as pollution. For instance, as countries become more developed and incomes rise, more manufacturing occurs and more cars are on the road, leading to even higher use of fossil fuels. If current conditions continue, India is projected to have the highest car density in the world by 2050.[8]

As more and more countries seek to develop their economies, competition will

Wind turbines capture renewable forms of energy.

Women and children are often tasked with collecting biomass.

increase for nonrenewable fossil fuels that are already being depleted. Increasing energy costs—rising gas prices and food prices—can have serious economic and social consequences.

On the other hand, lack of access to energy resources can seriously hinder economic and social development. While many of us take our modern energy resources for granted, about one in five people do not have access to electricity.[9] Countries that lack the resources for energy-intensive forms of industry might not be able to develop economically and compete with energy-rich nations. Furthermore, almost three billion people rely on traditional biomass such as wood, animal dung, or coal to cook their food.[10]

Society

How might this affect a person's opportunities for education, employment, and healthful living? For starters, collecting biomass fuel to cook with such as wood or animal dung is a time-consuming, physically demanding task that is usually borne by women and children.[11]

Time spent collecting fuel is time that is not spent in school or at a paying job. Furthermore, cooking with biomass or coal produces harmful air pollution that can cause serious health problems and even death. In fact, the number of deaths from air pollution inside the home is estimated to be more than 1.45 million people.[12] Using local biomass without replacing it can lead to environmental degradation such as deforestation.

Environment

Energy use is currently the largest contributor to human-produced carbon dioxide emissions. When fuels such as oil and coal are burned in an engine or at a power plant to generate electricity, carbon dioxide and other greenhouse gases are released. A *greenhouse gas* prevents reflected sunlight from leaving the earth's atmosphere and, as a result, enhances Earth's natural greenhouse effect. The greenhouse effect is named for its similarity to the way a greenhouse traps sunlight to make the temperature inside the structure much warmer than outside. As more greenhouse gases accumulate in the atmosphere, the average temperature on Earth goes up. This process alters the earth's climate.

Even before they are burned, the extraction of fossil fuels has significant potential to cause ecological damage. For example, extracting oil requires digging deep into the earth, which can affect landscapes and wildlife habitats. Furthermore, machinery used for extraction, production, and transport of fossil fuels often itself requires large amounts of fuel to operate.

Energy resources such as oil are often transported long distances from the site of extraction.[13] Likely the gasoline at your local gas station traveled across many state lines and possibly even across oceans before reaching you. The distances involved in transporting oil and the methods used to extract it create the potential for accidents, such as oil spills, to occur.[14] One of the biggest oil spills in history was triggered by an explosion on the

Deepwater Horizon oil rig in 2010. This caused an oil leak that released oil and gas into the Gulf of Mexico at a rate of 11,350 tons per day, or around 59,200 barrels of liquid oil per day into coastal waters.[15]

Oil spills can have serious consequences. Wildlife that comes into contact with spilled oil can be harmed or die. Even organisms (including humans) that have not come into direct contact with oil may be harmed if their food sources have been contaminated by oil. Beyond negative impacts on the health of animals and ecosystems, the people whose livelihoods depend on fishing and tourism can face severe economic consequences from an oil spill that may last for years. In fact, the widespread and varying effects of oil spills demonstrate the environmental, economic, and social nature of our energy use.

Other sources of energy such as nuclear and hydroelectric power carry their own environmental risks, as we will discuss later.

Wildlife that comes into contact with oil can be harmed or die.

Background on Energy

For as long as humans have lived, acquiring food has been a top priority. We require a certain amount of *calories* (a unit that measures the amount of energy stored in food) in order to survive. Over time, humans also learned to harness energy resources for purposes beyond basic survival.[16]

One of the first advancements humans made in the field of energy was the utilization of fire. Thousands of years ago, humans learned to use fire to cook their food and provide heat for their bodies. Why would cooking food before eating it be beneficial? Not only can cooking food such as meat kill harmful bacteria, but it also makes the food more digestible.[17] This means that a person's body might be able to absorb more calories from the same source, providing more energy.

Other advancements helped early human societies become more efficient in producing food calories, particularly agriculture. For a long time, however, we relied on direct energy sources, using animals, wind and water for transportation and wood fire for cooking and heating.

Energy Powers a Revolution

By the 1500s, England was using wood energy not only to cook food, but also to fuel its industry. British ships were built from wood and sailed using wind energy. Wood was also burned for fuel to manufacture materials such as steel and iron.[18]

Eventually, the use of wood outpaced regeneration of forests and the English were faced with a wood shortage, known as the timber famine. Between 1500 and 1630, people in England witnessed a sevenfold increase in the price of wood.[19] Although wood was the preferred fuel for heating and manufacturing at the time, the shortage and rising price of wood forced many people to turn to coal for fuel.[20] Coal was used as an energy source for much of human history, often for smelting metals. This replacement of wood with coal not only solved Britain's wood fuel crisis— it revolutionized industry.[21]

As the English began to deplete coal found near the surface of the earth, they started to dig coal mines deeper and deeper. This caused water to seep through the walls of the mines and flood them. To solve this problem, the steam engine was invented to pump water out of the mines. Coincidentally, coal became the main fuel used for steam engines.

People soon developed many other uses for the steam engine; it was used to power machines in factories, move trains, and fuel ships. As a result, people could move around the world faster than ever and machines could perform the work that used to require the labor of hundreds of people or animals. In the early 1700s, producing one kilogram of yarn by hand required 1,100 hours of labor. By the early 1800s, it took only three hours of labor.[22] The widespread use of the steam engine revolutionized industry and established coal as one of its primary sources of energy.

Meanwhile, scientists had been experimenting with electricity. An important advancement came in the early 1800s, when the British physicist Michael Faraday showed that electricity could flow in a metal wire influenced by a changing magnetic field. However, until Nikola Tesla (a Serbian immigrant to the United States and an innovative scientist, engineer, and inventor) demonstrated how to transmit this electricity over long distances in the 1880s, electricity was not a practical supply of energy.[23] **Electricity** is a secondary form of energy resulting from the existence of charged particles, meaning that another form of energy such as coal or wind must be used to produce it.

Petroleum Moves Us

In the mid-1900s, petroleum (or oil) replaced coal as the world's leading fuel source.[24] Humans had been using oil that seeped up to the surface of the earth for thousands of years as adhesives, lubricants, and even medicine. As early as 347 C.E., people in China were using bamboo poles to dig oil wells 800 feet deep.[25] Over time, several historical events created a larger market for petroleum. First came the

Coal has been used throughout human history as an energy source.

CASE STUDY   The Oil Embargo of 1973

In 1973 on Yom Kippur, the holiest day of the year for the Jewish faith, Syria and Egypt attacked Israel in an effort to regain land taken by Israel during the 1967 war. In response, the United States decided to supply Israel with arms and the Soviet Union began supplying Egypt and Syria with arms. Arab members of OPEC were against the U.S. decision to support Israel and announced an embargo, or ban, on trading oil with countries that supported Israel during the war.[26]

The Oil Embargo of 1973 caused global oil prices to spike and limited the supply of oil for a short time. In the United States, this ban—which was characterized by high oil and gas prices and shortages at the pump—prompted the federal government and citizens to adopt ways to conserve energy.[27] Even after the embargo was lifted, the price of gasoline and heating oil remained high and may have contributed to an economic recession in 1974 and 1975.[28]

The Oil Embargo of 1973 limited the supply of oil and gas in the United States.

discovery of kerosene, a fuel made from petroleum. In 1849, a Canadian geologist named Abraham Gesner discovered how to make kerosene for lamp fuel.[29] Kerosene replaced whale oil (oil made from whale blubber), which had been the main energy source for lighting and whose supply was declining. In the early 20th century, the mass production of automobiles as well as the use of military transportation that ran on petroleum-based fuel helped to create a lasting market for oil products.

The Advent of Nuclear Energy

Beyond coal and oil, there have been significant advances in other sources of energy. Scientists knew at the beginning of the 1900s that atoms stored large amounts of energy. They learned that when an atom is split into smaller atoms (a process called *fission*), an incredible amount of heat and radiation is released. In the years leading up to World War II, scientists conducted research into nuclear energy with a focus on creating new weapons.[30]

On August 6, 1945, the United States dropped the first atomic bomb to ever be used in war on Hiroshima, Japan. Three days later the United States dropped a second bomb on Nagasaki, Japan. The official death toll from these bombs was over 200,000. Many of these deaths did not occur immediately; a large number of people died later from exposure to *radiation* (a type of energy given off by nuclear fission that can cause damage to cells, cancer, and death).[31]

Approximately one year later, the U.S. government created the Atomic Energy Commission as an effort to encourage the development of peaceful uses of nuclear energy, primarily as an alternative to fossil fuels to produce electricity. Today several countries around the world use nuclear energy to generate electricity.[32]

Energy Today

The world uses more energy today than ever before, thanks to population growth, increasing transportation of people and products around the world due to globalization, and technology-rich lifestyles that require a constant supply of energy. While oil remains the world's leading fuel, there are many other energy resources used around the globe.

How do we determine which energy sources are most sustainable? One way is to look closely at the economic, environmental, and social consequences of using each source of energy. In the following section, you can learn about the main pros and cons of different non-renewable and renewable energy resources.

Nonrenewables

Oil

As mentioned previously, the energy resource that the world uses more than any other is petroleum, or oil.[33] You probably know that oil is primarily used for transportation: it can be refined (processed) to produce diesel, gasoline, and even jet fuel. But did you also know that oil is an ingredient in many of the products we use such as plastic milk jugs, nylons, cosmetics, medicines, and road materials?[34]

Oil is a fossil fuel that is usually found deep within the earth. It is extracted by drilling through layers of the earth and pumping it to the surface. Oil is not readily found everywhere around the globe, which is why many countries import oil from other countries. The largest oil **reserves** (stores which can be extracted economically using current technology) are found in Saudi Arabia and Venezuela.[35]

As with other nonrenewable resources, there is a limited supply of oil. This can increase competition for this resource and lead to international conflict. Countries that import a large portion of their oil have less control over the price and supply of this resource than they would over a domestic resource.

In addition, at every point of its life cycle—from exploration and extraction to consumer use—oil is linked to pollution. The process of searching for and extracting oil is unpredictable and can impact the health of the surrounding environment. Transporting oil itself requires fuel and creates the potential for oil leaks or spills. Burning oil products in a car, jet, or power plant produces large amounts of pollution that can affect the health of humans, animals, and ecosystems.

However, one main benefit of using oil is that it is energy dense. *Energy density* describes the amount of energy stored in a given volume or space. In fact, oil is more energy dense than natural gas, coal, and biomass. Also, much of the infrastructure needed to refine and distribute oil is already in place. For example, pipelines, roads, gas stations, and most car engines are manufactured to support oil use. Because oil is a form of chemical energy, it can be stored until it is needed (unlike wind or solar energy) and since oil is a liquid, it is easier to transport than coal.

As sources of easily accessible oil are depleted, it will take more and more energy (and money) to extract oil from places that are harder to reach. As it becomes less lucrative to extract fossil fuels like oil, the rate of oil

Oil is a fossil fuel that can be extracted from underground reservoirs.

production may eventually begin to decline. Many people refer to this situation as *peak oil*.[36]

Natural Gas

Natural gas is another fossil fuel found in many places around the world. Although natural gas does emit some pollution when burned, it produces about half the carbon dioxide of coal and is the cleanest fossil fuel to burn.[37] Natural gas is mostly used as a heat source and as an ingredient in products like fertilizers, plastics, glue, and paint.[38] The largest natural gas reserves in the world are found in Russia.[39]

Natural gas has traditionally been extracted from underground reservoirs in porous rock by drilling vertical wells that average about 6,100 feet deep.[40] Once found, natural gas is usually transported from one location to another via underground pipelines. More than 300,000 miles of underground pipeline transport natural gas throughout the United States.[41] The pipelines are relatively cheap to maintain (though expensive to build) and many are already in place.[42]

Recent advances in technology have helped engineers capture natural gas that is trapped in shale formations. Horizontal drilling and hydraulic fracturing, or fracking, are two techniques engineers use to obtain hard-to-reach natural gas. During hydraulic fracturing, water, sand, and chemicals are injected into underground wells to create cracks in the rock. This process forces natural gas up to the surface.[43] Horizontal drilling allows gas to be recovered parallel to rock layers rather than drilling deeper.

Horizontal drilling and hydraulic fracturing make it possible to extract more natural gas from each well. However, fracking uses a large amount of water and produces large amounts of wastewater. If wells are not properly installed, it also has the potential to leak chemicals into nearby water sources and ecosystems. Fracking may lead to land instability and in rare instances may even cause small earthquakes.[44]

Coal

Coal is the third main fossil fuel. Together the United States, Russia, and China have about 60% of the world's coal reserves.[45]

Burning natural gas produces less pollution than other fossil fuels.

Coal is a relatively abundant and inexpensive energy source. It is burned to produce electricity and manufacture products such as steel, which can encourage economic development. In fact, the use of coal is expected to increase in future years, especially in developing countries.[46] For the many countries that can mine it domestically, coal can be more economically and politically secure than oil. Although it is less energy dense than oil or natural gas, it can still provide a good amount of energy.

Coal is extracted from the earth by either surface mining or underground mining. Surface (or strip) mining removes the land above coal deposits.[47] Sometimes explosives are even used to remove land above coal; this is called mountain top removal. The blasted earth often ends

The hot steam generated in nuclear power plants is cooled by cooling towers.

up in valleys or in waterways, which damages ecosystems, wildlife, and water quality. Laws designed to restore the disturbed land after strip mining have had varying degrees of success.[48]

In underground mining, equipment and workers go hundreds of feet below ground to extract coal. People who mine coal are exposed to many dangers: the ground above them can collapse and exposure to years of coal dust can cause health problems such as black lung disease.

Coal is the most polluting of all fossil fuels. The extraction and combustion of coal releases many substances that can affect human health, damage the environment, and contribute to climate change. Burning coal is the leading cause of both sulfur and mercury pollution, which is harmful for humans and ecosystems.[49] Other byproducts of coal can contribute to poor air quality and respiratory problems. Coal mines can release methane (a greenhouse gas) into the atmosphere and, once abandoned, can leak acidic water into the environment.[50]

Nuclear

Nuclear energy is the energy stored within the nucleus of atoms. When atoms are split, the large amount of heat released can be used to generate electricity.

The primary fuel used for nuclear energy is uranium—a nonrenewable resource. Uranium can be found in rocks and extracted from surface or underground mines. Uranium can also be recovered from oceans. Once extracted, uranium is then processed into fuel for nuclear power plants that convert it into electricity. About 13.5% of the world's electricity is generated from nuclear energy and about 30 countries operate nuclear power plants.[51]

One main drawback of nuclear energy is the radiation given off by the process of nuclear fission and the nuclear waste generated by nuclear power plants. This waste will remain radioactive for thousands of years. There is no permanent disposal site for the highly radioactive waste in the United States and most of it is stored at nuclear power plants.[52] Because radioactive materials are hazardous to human health, many people do not want a nuclear reactor or waste near their homes.

The energy released by nuclear fission can heat water up to 520 degrees Fahrenheit![53] Steam from this hot water is used to turn turbines to generate electricity. A large amount of water is then used to cool the steam. This water can come from nearby lakes, rivers, or oceans. Because the hazards of radioactive waste and high heat are so risky (such as negative impacts on nearby aquatic ecosystems), nuclear power plants have many safety systems created to prevent accidents. The failure of these systems can be tragic. For example, in the wake of a 2011 earthquake and tsunami off the coast of Japan, the Fukushima nuclear power plant lost power. A couple small fires started and radioactive waste was released into the air.[54] Due to the risk of radiation, over 100,000 people were evacuated from their homes.[55]

Despite the above concerns, there are many reasons why countries might turn to nuclear power as a source of electricity. Uranium has an incredibly high energy density; one ceramic pellet of uranium is about as big as your fingertip yet has about as much energy as 150 gallons of oil.[56] Although energy (usually from fossil fuels) is required to mine and refine uranium, nuclear fission is a way to produce electricity without creating greenhouse gases and other air pollutants.

Renewables

Water

Water (or hydroelectric) power refers to the kinetic energy of moving water. Fast-flowing water, waterfalls, ocean tides, and waves all contain kinetic energy that can be harnessed to generate electricity. Because water is renewed naturally through the earth's water cycle, water power is considered a renewable energy source.

Most electricity generated from water relies on moving water to turn turbines that capture the water's kinetic energy. This can look different depending on the location and source of water. For example, tidal fences are vertical structures built in the ocean that are embedded with turbines. As the tides move in and out, the flowing water turns the turbines.[57] Hydroelectric power plants, on the other hand, are constructed near freshwater dams. Gates open to release water stored behind the dam so that water flows through turbines to generate electricity.[58]

Producing electricity from moving water does not result in significant carbon dioxide emissions or air pollution because no fuel is burned. However, hydroelectric power may result in some emissions from water reservoirs (bodies of water held by dams). Water is denser than air, so a turbine built for tides can capture more energy than wind. However, this can make the turbine more costly to build because it must be sturdy.[59]

Many countries around the world have built dams in order to generate hydroelectric power. China produces the most hydroelectricity in the world and has created the largest hydroelectric dam in existence.[60] The Three Gorges Dam was built on China's Yangtze River and produces about 85 terawatts (TWh) per year. Eighty-five TWh will meet a tenth of China's current annual electricity need.[61] Hydroelectric power plants provide some of the least expensive electricity to consumers and are about 90% efficient in converting the water's kinetic energy into electricity.[62]

However, building large dams can have high monetary, ecological, and social costs. Often people who live in the area must move to allow the flooding of land to create a reservoir. It is estimated that over 1.4 million people were

Hydroelectric dams convert the kinetic energy of moving water into electricity.

displaced from their homes by the construction of the Three Gorges Dam.[63] In addition, sediments (soil, sand, and leaves) can build up in reservoirs. That sediment reduces water quality for organisms that live in the water and can choke out the sun's light. Changing the path of a stream affects any organisms dependent on that stream. Migrating fish, such as salmon, may have trouble swimming around dams. Damming may also cause erosion along riverbanks. In response to these ecological concerns, there have been some efforts to remove dams and restore rivers and their surrounding ecosystems to their natural state. For instance, the Elwha Dam in Washington State was removed in 2012 to help restore the river and fisheries.[64]

Wood is the most common form of biomass used today.

Biomass

Biomass, or bioenergy, is recently living organic material that can be used as a fuel source. In the process of photosynthesis, plants and organisms like algae capture sunlight and convert it to chemical energy. As you already know, humans have used wood (one type of biomass) for years to provide heat for their homes and cook their food. More recently, people have begun burning biomass to generate electricity and converting it into liquid fuels to run cars and trucks. Wood is still the most common form of biomass used today, but animal dung (waste), grasses, algae, corn, sugarcane, and even garbage or wood waste from construction can be used as fuel.[65]

To accurately evaluate the sustainability of biomass, one would need to take a close look at each type of biomass and the way that it is harvested and grown. However, biomass is considered a renewable energy source because organic matter can be regrown relatively quickly. Biomass provides a way to convert agricultural and forest waste into fuel and can reduce both the amount of waste going to landfills and the amount of oil needed to make gasoline.

Like fossil fuels, burning biomass directly or as transportation fuel produces carbon dioxide emissions. Unlike fossil fuels, the carbon dioxide released by burning biomass was recently absorbed from the atmosphere as part of the natural carbon cycle. If biomass is regrown, it can absorb carbon dioxide from the atmosphere and release oxygen. By contrast, burning fossil fuels releases carbon dioxide that has not been in the atmosphere for millions of years.

However, if biomass is not replanted at the same rate that it is being used, the result will be increased carbon dioxide emissions and deforestation. There are other downsides to biomass energy. Fertilizers and chemical pesticides that might be used to grow biomass are made from fossil fuels. Also, converting land once used to produce food into land that produces biomass for fuel can have negative global impacts on food supply and prices that would likely affect the people in our world that most need food.

YOUTH PROFILE
Whitney M. Young Magnet High School

Sophomore Anna Hernandez wanted to learn more about alternative and green energy technology for a science fair project. She found out about something called biodiesel, a type of fuel made by combining oil with ethanol or methanol. When used in farm machinery or other diesel engines, biodiesel produces fewer greenhouse gases than petroleum-based diesel.

With help from the University of Illinois at Chicago and teacher Brian Sievers, Anna Hernandez and four other students from Chicago's Whitney M. Young Magnet High School created a functional, full-sized biodiesel production system. They converted 1,460 gallons of cooking oil from neighborhood restaurants into biodiesel fuel. They donated biodiesel to farmers and others who use diesel engines.[66]

The students then built and donated a biodiesel system to Mendota High School, a school in rural Illinois, so they could share with the students there what they learned. "They were totally excited to get started making biodiesel," said Sabrina Kwan, a sophomore at Whitney Young. The project even crossed national borders when the students gave a presentation on how to make a biodiesel system to a company in Honduras!

Wind
Wind is produced because the sun heats the surface of the earth unevenly, causing air to circulate. This moving air is a renewable form of energy that can be converted into electricity. When wind turns the blades of a wind turbine, a generator inside the gearbox (at the top of the tower) converts the mechanical action into electricity. Cables inside the tower transmit this energy to a transformer where it is converted to a voltage appropriate for transmission to your home.[67]

The use of wind energy to produce electricity is increasing around the world.[68]

Whitney M. Young students converted used cooking oil into biodiesel.

The main benefit of using wind power is that once a wind farm is set up, it does not produce air or water pollution. There is also no need to buy fuel; wind is free. But wind energy is not consistent and the speed of wind cannot be controlled. This can reduce the reliability of wind turbines or farms to generate electricity.

With new smart grid technologies, however, this problem could be mitigated. An electric grid is made up of all of the equipment (i.e., transmission lines, transformers) necessary to transfer electricity from a power plant to a customer. A smart grid refers to an electric grid that has technology to allow the two-way communication of information about electricity production and consumption to flow from producers to consumers. This information can be used to increase the efficiency of our electricity system.[69]

Wind is not a universally popular source of energy. Wind turbines require large amounts of land and there may be competing interests for the use of this land, such as farming or cattle. Wind farm opponents claim that wind turbines ruin the landscape and cause noise pollution. Wind turbines can kill migrating birds and careful placement is needed to reduce this effect.

For others, wind energy is gaining popularity as turbines become more efficient and cheaper to build. Offshore wind farms are also gaining popularity around the world. While the United States has yet to install wind turbines in oceans, there are 12 countries that have (90% of these are in Europe[70]). Opponents to offshore wind turbines in the United States are concerned about the view of the turbines from the shore. Yet according to the Earth Policy Institute, "Nine of the top 10 carbon dioxide emitting countries in 2010 have more than enough offshore wind energy potential to meet all their current electricity needs."[71]

Geothermal

One renewable form of energy that is not derived from the sun is geothermal energy. Geothermal energy comes from heat produced in the earth's core. This energy can be used to provide heat or generate electricity from steam produced by this heat. At least one quarter of electricity in the Philippines, Iceland, and El Salvador comes from geothermal energy.[72]

Solar cells convert sunlight into electricity.

There is an incredible amount of geothermal energy inside the earth. The amount of heat that flows from the earth into the atmosphere each year is equal to 10 times the amount of energy that the United States uses each year.[73] This type of energy produces very few emissions (1-3% of the carbon dioxide and 3% of the acid rain produced by fossil fuels).[74]

However, some pollution such as hydrogen sulfide (which can contribute to acid rain and smells like rotten eggs) can naturally occur in water heated by geothermal energy. Also, geothermal energy is not located everywhere and the cost of exploratory drilling and the initial setup of power plants can be high. Corrosion can also be a problem with geothermal energy.[75]

Solar

Solar energy comes directly from the earth's star, the sun. This energy can be harnessed passively or actively to heat homes and water or to generate electricity. For years, humans have been building homes and shelters to take advantage of the sun. For example, ancient Roman bathhouses were built facing south toward the sun. In the 1200s, the Anasazi people in North America sheltered themselves in south-facing cliff shelters in order to warm their environments.[76] Many homes today are still built to capture winter sun and deflect summer sun.

Like wind and water, sunlight is free and solar energy is a renewable resource. Photovoltaic cells, or solar cells, allow us to actively capture sunlight and convert it to electricity. Solar cells can be installed on people's homes to provide direct electricity for their needs. Any extra solar energy can be sent back to the city's electrical grid.

Manufacturing photovoltaic cells, however, requires energy and resources such as silica. It also produces waste that must be disposed of properly. Currently, solar cells are fairly inefficient and convert only about 11-27% of the sun's energy into electricity.[77]

Solar energy is also a diffuse form of energy

and concentrating and storing it can be challenging.[78] Like wind, sunlight is not consistent or steady. Time of day, season, latitude, and cloudiness all impact the amount of solar energy available.[79] For example, a desert location can get over six kilowatt-hours per day per square meter, while a cloudy December day in Seattle can receive as little as 0.7 kilowatt-hours per day.[80]

CASE STUDY: Barefoot Solar Engineers[81]

Envision a college where young people, parents, and even grandparents—most of whom cannot read or write—are admitted to train to become solar engineers, water specialists, dentists, doctors, teachers, mechanics, architects, artisans, masons, computer programmers, and accountants.

This is a college that welcomes people who are often seen as "uneducated" and "useless" by society who can indeed learn to build and install solar lighting or manage the primary health care and basic education of thousands of poor children and hundreds of villages across rural India, Africa, Asia, and South America. This place is Barefoot College in the village of Tilonia, in Rajasthan, India.

Barefoot College is a non-governmental organization founded in 1972. Its purpose is to help impoverished rural communities become self-sufficient and sustainable. It seeks to halt the mass migration of unemployed people to overcrowded cities and urban slums, retaining them in their villages with meaningful work. Because the organization believes that successful development must be rooted and managed by the community, their approach is to listen to what communities need and then train through apprenticeship so that people return to their communities prepared to thrive and help others do the same.

Barefoot College trains people from impoverished rural areas to bring sustainable solutions such as solar electrification to their communities.

The Barefoot College asserts—as did the world-renowned Indian leader of nonviolent civil disobedience Mahatma Gandhi—that the skills and wisdom of rural communities should be honored and used to foster lasting change, and that technology should be managed by the locals to prevent the community from becoming exploited or dependent on outside help. The college stresses the importance of demystifying new technologies and decentralizing their use, as well as promoting traditional knowledge and skills that have been employed successfully for millennia. Let's look at one example—bringing solar power to nonelectrified, rural villages.

The process begins with an interested community forming a Village Environmental Energy Committee. This committee communicates with villagers about solar power and will collect a small monthly payment from families participating in the subsidized program. The committee and community select individuals to attend a six-month, in-residence training program at Barefoot College's campus. The college often encourages communities to pick people who struggle to find employment such as single mothers or widows. Upon completion the "Barefoot Solar Engineers" return home, manage the project, and earn a monthly stipend.

At the Barefoot College the message is clear: being educated is about more than reading and writing, it's about caring for yourself, your community, and the world around you.

Pathways to Progress: Energy

With all of these energy resources available, what are the most sustainable ways to supply our world's growing demand for energy? In other words, how do we make sure that all people now have access to reliable forms of energy without compromising the health of the environment, international relations, or the ability of future generations to meet their energy needs?

Energy Conservation

Perhaps the easiest and most practical way we can contribute to sustainable energy solutions is to simply use less energy. Behaviors and actions that save or use less energy—such as turning off the lights when you leave a room—are often referred to as **energy conservation**.

Every choice about energy we make can make a difference in the amount of energy used and the pollution emitted.

Individuals, communities, businesses, and governments all have the ability to address energy conservation. For example, the city of Grand Rapids, Michigan has made an effort to purchase 20% of its energy from renewable sources. The city has also created an inventory of electricity use for all city buildings in order to track usage and reduce energy consumption.[82]

Energy Efficiency

Another way to reduce our energy consumption is by using energy more efficiently. **Energy efficiency** refers to completing a specific task with less energy input than usual.[83] For example, an energy-efficient light bulb—such as an LED or CFL light bulb—requires less energy to produce the same amount of light as other light bulbs.

You may have seen technology and appliances such as light bulbs, computer monitors, or refrigerators that are labeled as energy-efficient. One such label, Energy Star, was created by the U.S. Environmental Protection Agency and Department of Energy as a way for companies

Energy-efficient cars and appliances complete the same tasks as other cars and appliances with less energy.

CAREER PROFILE: NGO Founder

Do you think only governments tackle big social problems? Nongovernmental organizations (NGOs), like governments, often work to address big problems for the benefit of society as a whole or for an underrepresented segment of society.

CEOs and founders of NGOs usually have both a bachelor's degree and business experience. They are savvy in communications, marketing, and management of personnel and finance.

Stacy Noland wants to see major change in the way society powers homes and the work force. After receiving a bachelor's degree in psychology and working as a manager at Microsoft, he founded the Moontown Foundation. The Moontown Foundation is an NGO that creates initiatives with a dual goal:

Stacy Noland founded the nongovernmental organization, Moontown Foundation.

to empower individuals through experiential education and to make immediate impact on climate change and environmental degradation in the communities that need it most. As Stacy states, "It's my personal mission to get the people in poverty to adopt energy conservation, healthy, sustainable living and alternative transportation, first. Those are the hardest people to reach." The Foundation's YES Program (Young Ecopreneurs in Sustainability) and SWITCH Program are focused on creating careers in home energy efficiency and solar energy. They introduce young adults to the mechanics of energy-saving technologies including solar paneling, weatherizing, and low-flow shower heads.

Other projects focus on working with entire communities and considering how to create sustainable solutions to problems. One of these is the Storm Surge project, a documentary film about bringing sustainability to the southeastern states. In the wake of Hurricane Katrina, the 2010 Gulf Oil Spill, and widespread natural disasters, the film looks at how sustainability can be crucial to the health of all states.

---

to let customers know about energy-efficient products and to encourage the reduction of greenhouse gases.[84] According to Energy Star, if each American home replaced one light bulb with an energy-efficient light bulb we could collectively save $600 million in energy costs and prevent 9 million pounds of greenhouse gases from being released into our atmosphere each year.[85] Sometimes an energy-efficient product is more expensive to buy up front. However, it is often more cost-effective in the long term because you will save more money over time on your utility bills.

Policies and Subsidies

At the governmental level, policies can be passed that encourage sustainable energy practices. In response to the oil crisis of the 1970s, Corporate Average Fuel Economy (CAFE) standards were enacted in the United States in 1975. These standards required vehicle manufacturers to create passenger cars and light trucks with improved fuel efficiency (better gas mileage).[86] Today CAFE standards are 33.3 miles per gallon for cars (double that of 1974 vehicles) and 25.4 miles per gallon for light trucks.[87] In 2012, higher efficiency standards were finalized; the goal is for U.S. vehicles to get an average gas mileage of 54.5 miles per gallon by 2025.[88]

Getting better gas mileage means that drivers will need less gas for each mile they drive. Not only can these regulations help drivers save money at the gas pump, but they can also reduce the amount of greenhouse gases emitted by cars. Japan, Canada, Australia, China, and the Republic of Korea have also created standards to improve car fuel economy and other countries are expected to join them.[89]

Governments can also influence the types of energy we use through subsidies. An energy subsidy is an economic benefit provided by a government that reduces the cost of producing a particular energy resource, increases the price received for an energy resource, or reduces the cost of a good or service.[90] In 2010, global fossil fuel subsidies totaled around $409 billion and renewable energy subsidies totaled around $66 billion.[91]

Government institutions can also take part in sustainable energy solutions. The U.S. Department of Defense—the largest consumer of energy in the nation—is promoting renewable and efficient energy use.[92] After several marines were killed while guarding a fleet of fuel trucks, military leaders suggested that reducing the military's reliance on fossil fuels would drastically improve its safety and capability.[93] One energy-saving idea put forth was to insulate military tents. Because temperatures are so high in the desert, a great deal of diesel is used for air conditioning in tents. In Iraq and Afghanistan, these simple measures, along with solar panels at interior bases, cut fossil fuel demand in half and saved the military $95 million in just six months![94] People have begun to refer to officers who promote and encourage the use of sustainable policies and supplies as Green Hawks.

WHAT YOU CAN DO — Energy

Each one of us has the ability to contribute positively to sustainable energy use. The list below suggests a few things that you can do to work toward sustainable energy use. You may even find that, after trying some of these things, there are benefits to these activities beyond a decrease in energy use:

- Commute by foot, bike, public transportation, or carpool.

- If you are shopping for a car, consider its fuel efficiency. By saving on gasoline, you will also save money.

- Educate your community about what they can do to address energy conservation.

- Get involved with global campaigns that work to ensure that all people have access to energy.

- Lobby state and national governments for higher energy-efficiency standards and investments in renewable energy.

Using public transportation is just one way to reduce your personal energy use.

POINT | COUNTERPOINT

Is nuclear power a sustainable energy choice?

POINT

Yes

- **Because wind and solar energy are not constantly available, nuclear power is the only non-fossil fuel that has the capacity to replace the amount of electricity generated by coal-fired power plants.**[95] Coal-fired electric plants in the United States account for approximately 36% of U.S. carbon dioxide emissions. Nuclear power would create far less emissions and is extremely cheap to produce.[96]

- **According to the World Nuclear Association, there have been only three major accidents in the 50 years that people have been generating nuclear power.**[97] These three accidents happened in Three Mile Island, Chernobyl, and Fukushima. This number is small considering there has been nuclear reactor operation in 32 countries. Large-scale testing and analyses have shown that the threat of radioactivity spreading is far less a problem than suspected. Less radioactivity actually escapes from fuel than initially assumed.[98]

COUNTERPOINT

No

- **Nuclear power creates both low- and high-level radioactive waste.** This waste derives from uranium that has to be mined to create fuel for nuclear reactors and can be dangerous for thousands of years. Just in the United States, approximately 103 nuclear operating reactors create over 2,000 metric tons of high-level radioactive waste.[99]

- **Nuclear energy is dangerous and is not worth the investment.** First of all, this kind of energy is costly. A pair of reactors that were originally supposed to cost $660 million at a plant in Georgia in 1971 ended up costing $8.87 billion.[100] The radioactive wastes that these reactors produce can have serious environmental and health implications. Take for instance when a nuclear reactor exploded in the town of Chernobyl, Ukraine in 1986. The reactor released radioactivity that some experts believe was equivalent to 200 Hiroshima and Nagasaki bombs. Millions of people were exposed to this radiation and hundreds of thousands of people were displaced.[101]

Which sources of energy are most sustainable?

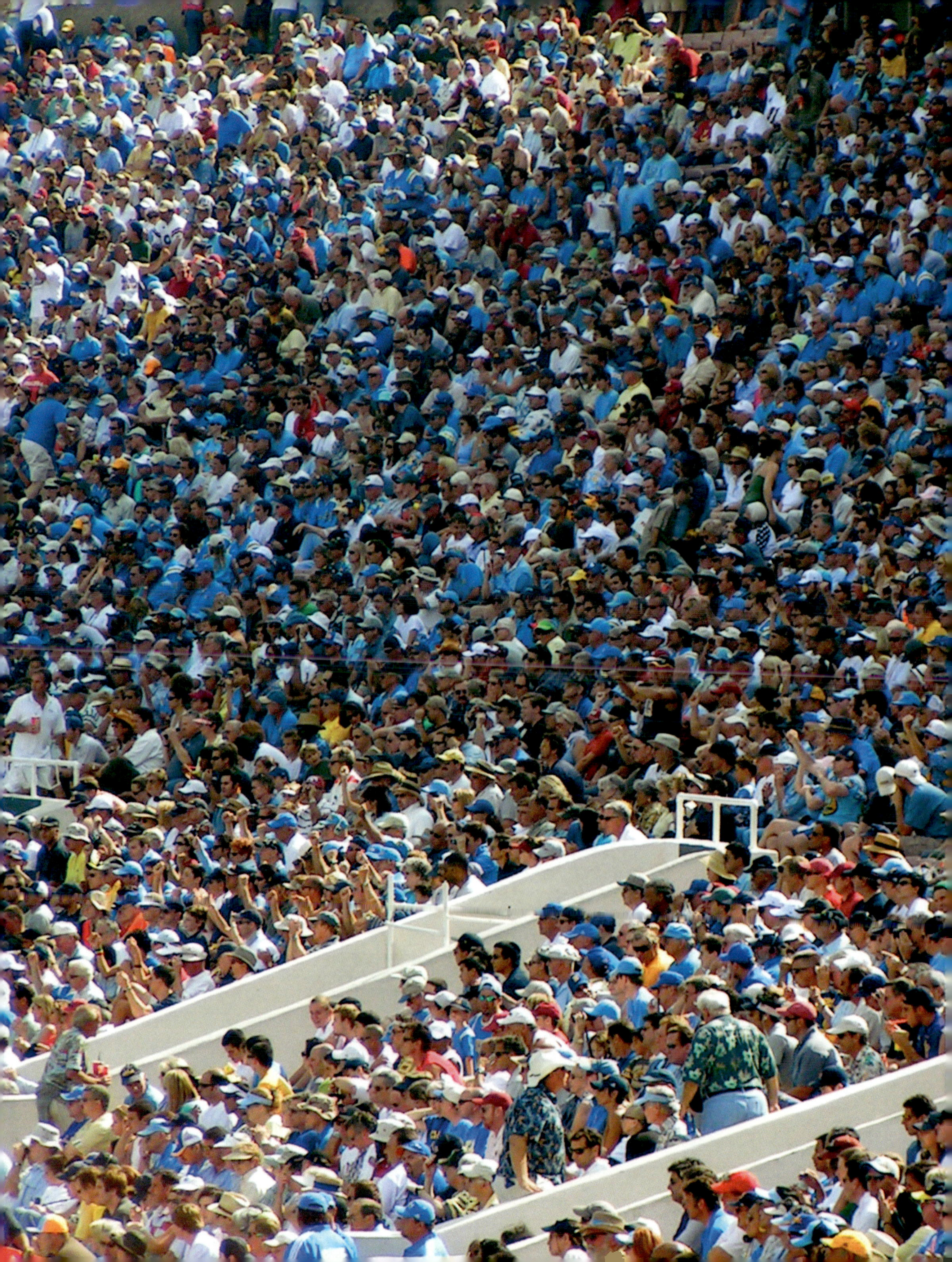

Chapter 7
Population

> **GUIDING QUESTIONS**
> - What causes population to rise or fall?
> - How does global population growth affect our lives and the planet?

Introduction to Population

The total number of people on Earth has doubled since the 1960s and it is still growing at a rapid rate. In 2011, the world's population reached seven billion.[1] By 2025, another billion people will be added to the global population. How do you think a world with 8 billion people will look? Will there be more traffic? Less space? More jobs? As we will learn, a growing population reflects a variety of influences and impacts our lives in countless ways.

You may have heard the term population used in different ways. Ecologists use the term when referring to numbers of individuals belonging to the same species—for example, a population of redwood trees located in Northern California. In this chapter, when we speak about global population trends, we are talking about the human species, *Homo sapiens*.

For most of human history, our species has experienced a positive growth rate. When *demographers*, those who study populations, discuss a **population growth rate**, they are talking about a percent change in population over a period of time. Growth rates can be considered positive (increasing) or negative (decreasing). Humans' positive growth rate is due to the simple fact that there are typically more births than deaths each year. In fact, today for each of the five babies born each second, two people die.[2] That means Earth has a net gain of approximately 180 people every minute.

A positive population growth rate in a country generally reflects two main factors: birth rates and immigration. *Immigration* is the migration of people into a country from other parts of the world and it is another way to grow a country's population. For example, in 2011 the country of Qatar had a positive growth rate of 4.93%.[3] This rate reflected high levels of immigration rather than a baby boom. Qatar has one of the highest per capita GDPs in the world, largely due to its oil and gas reserves.[4] Many people have immigrated to Qatar recently in search of a prosperous future. In fact, four times more people immigrated to Qatar in 2011 than were born in the country.[5]

A negative population growth rate may reflect a high mortality rate. A **mortality rate** is the number of deaths per unit of population (e.g. 100 deaths per 1,000 people) in a given place and time. Negative population growth could also be due to increased *emigration*, or people moving out of a country.

Translating Rates into Numbers

Population growth rates may seem fairly small. For example, when you subtract death rates from birth rates, the annual rate of global population increase is just 1.2%. That doesn't sound like much, but as you can see in the following table it will take us just over 12 years for our population of 7 billion to reach 8 billion if the growth rate remains 1.2%.[6]

People walk in a train station in Mumbai, India; the fifth most populous city in the world.

Population Growth	
Year	Population
1	7,000,000,000
2	7,084,000,000
3	7,169,008,000
4	7,255,036,096
5	7,342,096,529
6	7,430,201,688
7	7,519,364,108
8	7,609,596,477
9	7,700,911,635
10	7,793,322,574
11	7,886,842,445
12	7,981,484,555
13	8,077,262,369

The pattern shown in the table above is an example of exponential growth. *Exponential growth* happens when a constant rate of growth (in this case, 1.2%) is applied to a continuously growing base. In other words, even though the population growth rate does not change, it is applied to a larger population size every year. With an initial population of 7 billion, an exponential growth rate of 1.2% means the addition of 84,000,000 people in Year 1. In Year 2, however, 85,008,000 people are added to the population of 7.08 billion (the original population plus Year 1's 84,000,000 growth). Each year a greater number of people are added than in the year before. As you can see, exponential growth can result in a large population in almost no time.

Whereas it took nearly all of human history for the global population to reach 1 billion, it only took another 123 years to reach 2 billion, 33 additional years to reach 3 billion, 14 years to reach 4 billion, 13 years to reach 5 billion, and 12 years to reach 6 billion.[7]

How long do you think it would take a population of 7 billion to double in size if the population continues to grow 1.2% each year? You might be surprised to learn that it would only take 60 years to reach 14 billion. The phenomenon of *doubling time*—the time it takes a population to double in size—may be explained with this French riddle:

> *Imagine a water lily growing on the surface of a pond. The plant doubles in size every day. You are told that, if left unchecked, the lily would completely cover the pond in thirty days, choking out all other life forms in the pond. Because the lily plant seems so small, you decide you will not cut it back until it covers half the pond. On what day will that be?*[8]

The lily will cover half the pond on the day before it covers the whole pond. Ultimately, the problem, left unchecked, becomes exponentially worse every day or year, making it much more difficult to tackle than if you had done something at the beginning.

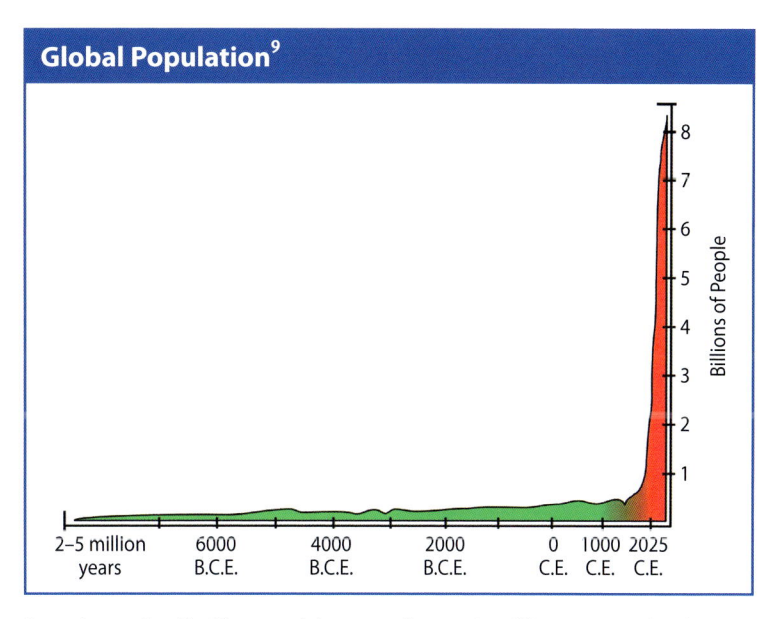

Global Population[9]

It took nearly all of human history—about 50 million years—for the global population to reach 1 billion, but in only another 123 years it reached 2 billion.

A Complex Issue

Population is a hotly debated sustainability issue. Some argue that none of the major issues facing humanity today would be of sufficient magnitude to qualify as global without the pressure of population. Others argue that population growth does not necessarily undermine sustainability if we are able to limit our individual impacts on the planet and carefully manage our natural resources. The entire world population could fit, standing shoulder to shoulder, in an area the size of the city of Los Angeles.[10] It is not necessarily the sheer number of humans that is a concern; rather, it is our behavior, such as resource consumption patterns, that is problematic.

In 1798, a demographer by the name of Thomas Malthus predicted that human population growth would be restrained by food production.[11] Malthus believed a point of crisis would occur when food production could no longer meet our needs, and hunger, disease, and war would result. Others have expressed similar fears. In 1968, a book by biologist Paul Ehrlich entitled *The Population Bomb* once again fueled fears of a rapidly growing global population.

Ehrlich warned of massive famines that would occur due to unrestricted population growth.[12]

Is there evidence to suggest the world will suffer such famines? It's true that there are regions where resources are scarce and famines have occurred. For example, Somalia experienced a devastating famine in 2011 that took tens of thousands of lives.[13] However, we have yet to experience famine on a global scale as both Malthus and Ehrlich predicted.

Professor John Guillebau, who studies reproductive health and family planning at University College London, believes our burgeoning population growth is still the "elephant in the room." Professor Guillebau argues that "unless we reduce the human population humanely through family planning, nature will do it for us, through violence, epidemics, and starvation."[14]

> *"Unless we reduce the human population humanely through family planning, nature will do it for us, through violence, epidemics, and starvation."*

Pandemics for example, can decrease populations. Humanity has experienced pandemics (the widespread outbreak of a disease, usually on a global scale) throughout history—from the bubonic plague of the Middle Ages that took 25 million lives in just 5 years[15] to the Spanish influenza that swept through the world just after World War I, infecting one-fifth of the world's population and killing 50 million people.[16] Ever since the emergence of agrarian societies, humans have lived in close proximity to one another and to a variety of domesticated animals, both factors that can facilitate the emergence of a pandemic.[17] However, through a number of scientific discoveries, including vaccines, the stethoscope, and an understanding of how germs transmit disease, populations have stabilized.

Human ingenuity—technological innovation (Green Revolution), increasing productivity and more efficient use of resources, medical advances, education, and access to family planning—can help offset the negative effects of increasing population.

What do you make of all this? Is population growth "the elephant in the room?" After we explore the topic in greater detail, you will probably start to form your own opinion on the subject. Maybe you'll even start to make your own predictions about future population growth.

Population and Sustainability

Population is more than just a number. With each additional person on Earth there will be a corresponding impact on our society, environment, and economy. For a long time experts have tried to determine Earth's **carrying capacity**—the number of people Earth can support without using resources faster than the planet can replenish them. A population that exceeds Earth's carrying capacity cannot be sustained—food, water, and other vital resources would become overexploited and at some point there would be nothing left to support the population.

The extent of Earth's carrying capacity has been widely debated. It depends on a number of factors: type and quantity of available resources, how those resources are distributed, the amount of resources each person uses.

Society

Human societies can be seriously affected by the pressure population growth places on Earth's resources. For example, some of the most populated places on the planet suffer from water scarcity. Water scarcity arises when water supplies are inadequate to serve the needs of ecosystems and humans. Water scarcity can be caused by water shortages (such as droughts) as well as population pressure. In turn, conflict may arise over who has rights to this scarce but vital resource.

Consider the case of Lake Chad, the largest freshwater resource in the Sahel region of Africa. Lake Chad is bordered by Cameroon, Chad, Niger, and Nigeria. These four countries have an annual population

A growing population leads to rising demand for land and increased water usage.

growth rate of 2.75.[18] Altogether, 30 million people in these countries rely on Lake Chad for drinking water, fishing, farming, or livestock breeding. Lake Chad has also acted as a cultural and economic hub for centuries, facilitating trade between people living north and south of the Sahara.

Over the last three decades, 90% of the lake has disappeared due to natural variation, climate change, and population pressure.[19] Population growth in the four nations surrounding Lake Chad will only continue to put pressure on this vulnerable freshwater resource. Lake Chad may vanish entirely within 20 years. United Nations officials believe the disappearance of Lake Chad would create a humanitarian disaster.[20] If the lake were to disappear, millions of people could face dehydration and starvation.

Environment

The depletion of water resources not only undermines people's ability to meet their basic needs, but it harms our environment as well. Water is a necessity for many species and it helps to naturally filter pollutants, circulate nutrients, and balance ecosystems. Some believe that overpopulation is the root cause of many of our environmental problems.[21] With a growing human population, more water is needed to sustain us, more land is needed to grow our food and house our families, and more pollution is generated by our growing industrialization.

An ecological footprint is a measure of an individual's demand on Earth's resources. With each additional human on Earth comes the addition of another ecological footprint. Some people generate smaller footprints than others. However, given our current rate of population growth, all those additional footprints add up fast and amplify humanity's impact on the planet.

Today, Earth is experiencing a wave of mass extinction. It is estimated that 27,000 species are lost each year.[22] Some of these extinctions might have occurred naturally despite humans and some were caused by humans overexploiting a species for food, but much of this wave of mass extinction has been attributed to habitat loss. The habitats of other species are being destroyed to make room for more people. Other animals are struggling to find a safe place to raise their

A young girl from Ethiopia carries water back to her home.

young, build their homes, and find their traditional sources of nourishment.

Mass species extinction has consequences for humanity. Biodiversity, or the variety of life in a particular ecosystem, is beneficial to human populations in many ways. Half of all the drugs on the U.S. market are derived from plants and animals. Biodiversity among crops facilitates resistance to disease. And the ecosystem services on which people rely in turn rely on a biologically diverse environment.

Economy

A growing population leads to rising demand for additional goods and services and creates the need for significant infrastructure to support modern economies. Yet the supply of many natural resources is finite; as demand grows, we risk exhausting many of the planet's resources. Moreover, increased demand for an exhaustible supply is often associated with rising costs. If resources like water and land become scarce, they will become more expensive. Population growth that exceeds the planet's carrying capacity will create soaring costs and further limit access to basic necessities for the world's poorest people. Throughout the world, poverty continues to be a significant problem. In countries like the Democratic Republic of Congo, approximately 80% of the population lives on less than $2 per day.[23]

Growing populations also require significant investments in infrastructure such as roads and telecommunications, health services, and education. Countries that are poor or that do not have sufficient infrastructure for their populations will face difficulties competing in the global economy.

Background on Population

The first known human lived in Africa. Although scholars continue to debate the exact date, many estimate that *Homo sapiens* first appeared around 250,000 years ago. Over time, humans migrated from Africa to Europe and Asia, later spreading out to Australia and finally into North and South America.[24]

Early Population Growth

Early humans were hunters and foragers who constantly traveled long distances to find food. **Population density**—the amount of people living in a given area—was low. The world population continued to grow during this time, but no large communities of people were present.

Approximately 11,000 to 10,000 years ago, humans began to organize themselves into communities that relied on agriculture. They grew their own food using cultivation techniques and tools.[25] Agrarian communities no longer needed to forage (search for food) as they learned to domesticate plants and animals. Agriculture supplies energy in a more efficient way to growing food crops than can be achieved in the wild: seeds are carefully selected and sown closely together; plants are watered on a regular basis by human efforts; and soils are turned and crops rotated to foster healthy farmland. As a result, agrarian communities benefited from an increased supply of food and populations grew relatively quickly.[26]

About 5,000 years ago, the first city-states appeared. Before the development of city-states, most people lived in small villages and dealt with each other individually, rather than under a formal governance structure with local representatives (e.g., mayors or governors) and public services.

City-states emerged first in Mesopotamia and then in Egypt, India, and China. City-states were marked by hierarchical structures in which some people had power over others. These communities were larger than villages and groups of foragers. As in other communities, agriculture within city-states supported growing populations. In fact, large-scale farming allowed some people to be freed from food production altogether.[27]

About 1,000 years ago, world population reached 250 million.[28] Since that time, population has continued to grow at faster and faster rates. Growth over the last century has been particularly rapid. In 1900, world population was 1.6 billion; by 2000 that figure had risen to over 6 billion.[29] Such a dramatic increase can be largely attributed to reduced mortality rates. The likelihood of surviving past childhood has increased and people are living longer lives. In other words, more people now survive to older ages. This is thanks to advancements in medicine and improved sanitation practices that prevent diseases from spreading.

The Rise of Cities

In the past, the world's population lived primarily in rural areas. Today more than half of the world's people live in urban areas. In 1975, only three cities had populations in excess of 10 million: New York, Tokyo, and Mexico City. By 2009, there were 20 of these so-called *megacities*, half of them in Asia.

Most future population growth is predicted to occur in urban areas. Over the next couple of decades, it is expected that about a third of the increase in urban population will occur in China and India.[30]

Densely populated urban areas can be both negative and positive forces for sustainability. When urban areas grow quickly without adequate

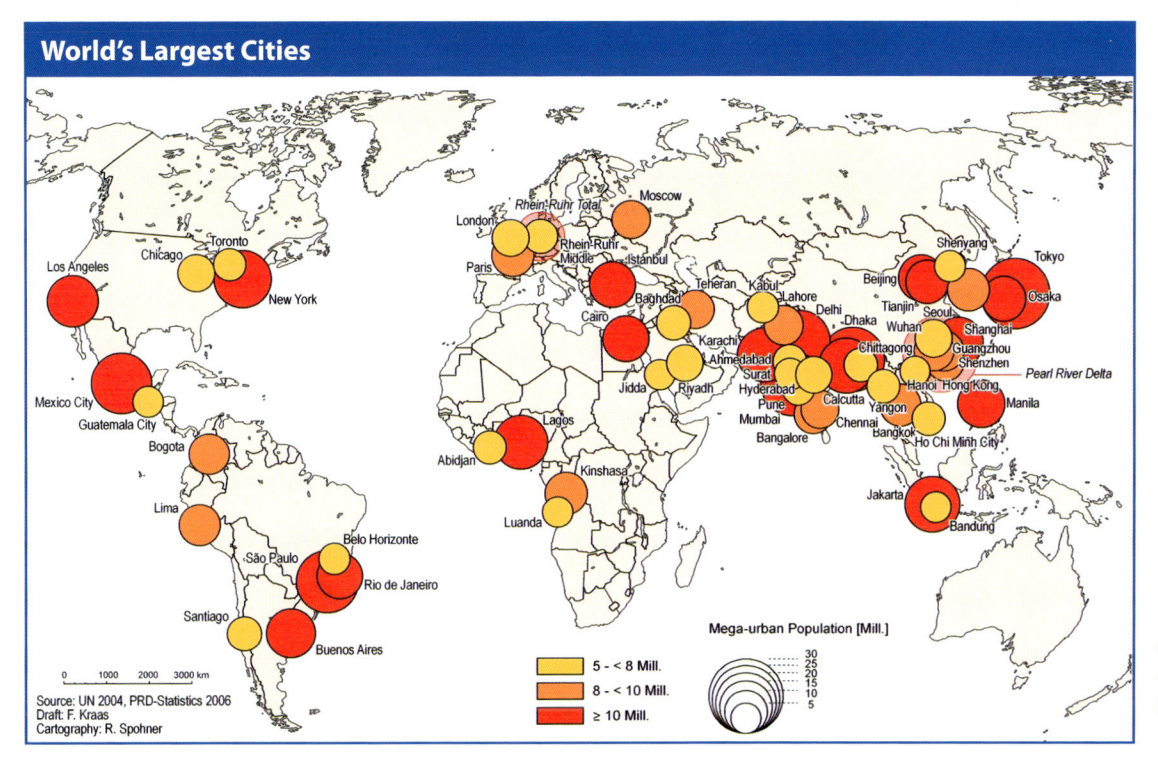

World's Largest Cities

Red dots indicate cities with populations in excess of 10 million.

Commuters ride a crowded train in Japan.

planning and infrastructure, residents are at risk from both natural and man-made hazards. Many of the world's megacities are a result of massive rural to urban migration, which can result in large numbers of people in unsafe, overcrowded, and poorly-built cities.[31] On the other hand, megacities that are designed to accommodate the needs of a growing population can showcase sustainability practices in action. Well-designed urban areas demonstrate efficient use of space and resources, provide wide-ranging economic opportunities for residents, and foster a culturally diverse community.

CASE STUDY: New York, From Wilderness to Metropolis

Can you imagine New York City without its famous skyscrapers and subways? It was not always the megacity that it is today. Times Square was once a wetland and the island of Manhattan was made up of rolling hills and valleys, marshlands, and meadows.[32] Before European colonization, the land was inhabited by the Lenape people, a Native American tribe of hunters, fishermen, and farmers. By the 1600s, Dutch merchants were beginning to settle the area. By 1790, New York City was the largest city in the United States.[33]

In the 19th century, waves of European immigrants began arriving in New York City. Europe was a hard place to live in the 1800s, suffering from events such as a failed revolution in Germany and the Potato Famine in Ireland.[34] People fled to New York City to escape poverty and start a new life. At the time, New York City did not have enough housing for all the people who arrived. Many immigrants had to live in slum-like makeshift housing. Despite these circumstances, waves of immigration continued. By 1950, New York City had become the first megacity with a population over 10 million.[35]

Today, New York City is one of the most famous cities in the world and the idea that it is a place of opportunity persists. It is also the densest city in the United States—over 8 million people live together in an area of just 305 square miles. A number of systems support the needs of New York City's population.

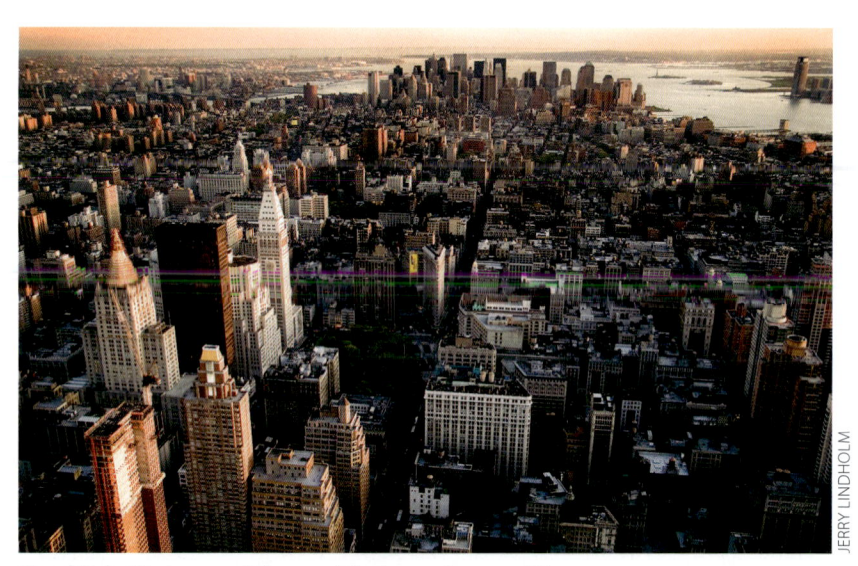

New York City is one of the world's largest megacities.

New York's zoning laws regulate how land in the city is used by restricting the size, use, and location of buildings, as well as ensuring public access to resources such as parks and waterfront areas.[36] Other vital city systems include wastewater treatment, law enforcement, and public transportation. Without these systems in place, the island of Manhattan could not safely support such a large population.

Population Today

Global population growth today is a tale of two trends—a story of both rising numbers and falling rates. While the world's population continues to grow, **fertility rates**, or the average number of children born to each woman, have actually declined in most nations. How can that be? Let's look at an example: in Generation 1 there are three women. If each of those women has three offspring, there will be 9 individuals in Generation 2; the population tripled! If the growth rate then slows, so that each woman in Generation 2 only has two offspring, there will be 18 individuals—double the population from Generation 2. Even though the growth rate slowed down from Generation 2 to Generation 3, the **base population** is still growing, albeit slower than if each individual had three offspring.

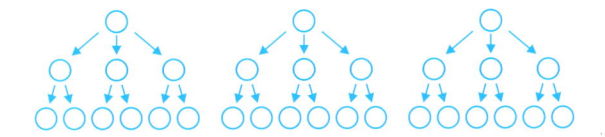

Therefore, despite declining fertility rates, it will still be decades before we see the global population begin to stabilize.

A Developing Issue

Today, there are more people living in developing countries than in developed countries. These populations tend to have high fertility rates and large numbers of young people. Increased access to health care and rising life expectancies in developing countries will further enlarge their populations. Even if growth rates slow, overall growth in these countries will continue as their base populations grow.

As a result, much of the world's projected population growth will occur in developing countries. In fact, this growth will likely be concentrated in just a few nations. The United Nations predicts that just nine countries will account for 50% of the world's population growth from 2010 to 2050: India, Pakistan, Nigeria, Ethiopia, the United States, the Democratic Republic of Congo, the United Republic of Tanzania, China, and Bangladesh.[37]

Fertility Rates

Worldwide, the fertility rate is nearing the **replacement rate** of 2.1. This is the magic number that would result in a stable population. The global average is now 2.4 children per woman[38] and it is expected that the fertility rate will continue to fall, dropping below the replacement rate by 2020.[39]

The rate of population growth in most developing countries has slowed down. For example, Bangladesh's fertility rate has dropped from 6 in 1980 to 2.3 in 2012.[40] There are many other examples of countries where women are having fewer children. Between 1970 and 2008, the fertility rate in India fell from 5.5 to 2.7; in Zimbabwe, the rate fell from 7.4 to 3.4.[41]

Despite the general decline in fertility rates, there remain many developing countries with high fertility rates. These nations are key contributors to global population growth. Countries such as Afghanistan, Burkina Faso, Niger, Somalia, Timor-Leste, and Uganda may not have the largest populations today, but they are growing the fastest because of their high fertility rates.[42]

Nigeria is predicted to have the world's fourth largest population by 2050, right after India, China, and the United States.[43] While Nigeria's fertility rate declined from 6.8 to 5.6 over the past 30 years, it remains high, well above the replacement rate.[44]

Analysts have observed a correlation between high fertility rates and development issues. All seven countries listed above are considered to be at high risk for political instability.[45] All of these nations tend to have high poverty rates as well.[46]

> *Worldwide, the fertility rate is nearing the replacement rate of 2.1. This is the magic number that would result in a stable population.*

CASE STUDY: The United States

Of the nine countries predicted to contribute the most to global population growth, you may have noticed that the United States seems to be an outlier as the only developed country on the list. The United States is one of few developed countries with a growing population. While the U.S. fertility rate is slightly above the average fertility rate for a developed nation (1.9 versus 1.6),[47] much of the population growth in the United States is due to immigration. Ellis Island alone processed 12 million immigrants who came into the United States between 1892 and 1954.[48]

It is estimated that nearly half the people in the United States today are descendants of those immigrants. According to the Pew Research Center, the U.S. population is expected to increase to 438 million by 2050, and immigrants will make up 82% of that population growth.[49]

Ellis Island processed 12 million immigrants who entered the United States between 1892 and 1954.

Afghanistan's Population (age-gender) Pyramid[50]

Based on this 2010 population pyramid, Afghanistan has a large youth population.

Age Matters

When determining how population factors into the sustainability puzzle, it is important to take a look at population age structure. Developing countries tend to have younger populations due to high fertility rates coupled with recent improvements in child survival.[51] These younger populations include a large number of young women in their reproductive prime, which can help to perpetuate high population growth rates.

A youthful age structure has been linked to an increased likelihood of violent conflicts.[52] According to a report published by Population Action International: "During the 1990s, countries with a very young structure were three times more likely to experience civil conflict than countries with a mature age structure." Perhaps not surprisingly, these same countries—categorized as "very young"—have a high likelihood (nearly 90%) of having a government that is autocratic (one ruler with absolute power) or only slightly democratic.

A very young age structure does not necessarily lead to civil conflict or autocracy; likewise, a civil conflict or an autocratic government does not necessarily result in a very young population. Yet, a relationship among these factors seems to exist. Why do you think this is so?

Populations in Transition

The global reduction in population growth has been brought on by a variety of factors, including government policies. In many countries, government policies have been successful in reducing population growth. However, trends do differ across the globe. On the continent of Africa, the population is projected to increase by over 360 million to 1.2 billion by 2025, and to 1.9 billion by 2050.[53] This growth could lead to increased food insecurity, natural resource issues, and conflict if sustainable systems are not put into place to address growth.

CASE STUDY: Iran's Fall and Rise

Iran is another country that has lowered its population growth rate through government initiatives. In Iran prior to the 1980s, women had on average more than six children each. Iran began to feel the pressures of a growing population: cities became crowded and polluted and people struggled to get basic necessities such as food and water. In the late 1980s, the Iranian government started to provide free **family planning services**. A population bulge among young adults in Iran correlates with the period immediately prior to the enactment of their family planning policy in 1989.

Families were encouraged to delay the mother's first pregnancy, to space their children's births farther apart, and to have no more than three children. By 2000, the average number of children per woman had fallen to just two.[55]

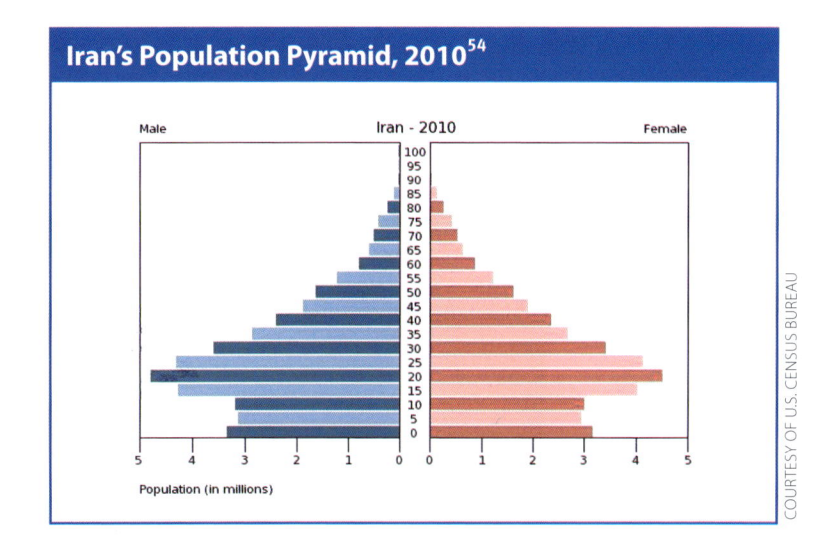

Interestingly, Iran's policy on population recently changed course. In an effort to avoid an aging demographic, President Mahmoud Ahmadinejad is now encouraging families to have more than two children. The government offers a financial incentive: for each child born, money is deposited into an account that the child can access at age 20 to pay for their education, marriage, health, or housing.[56]

Iran's Population Pyramid, 2010[54]

COURTESY OF U.S. CENSUS BUREAU

Some countries create policies that work to decrease population numbers. China enacted a policy to encourage couples to have just one child, which has played a central role in dropping birth rates. While the one-child policy has limited the negative environmental effects of China's growing population (such as stress on natural resources and air and water pollution), it has also had unintended social consequences. The emphasis on one-child families in a society that prizes sons has led to selective abortions of female fetuses. As the "one child generation" grew up, China's sex ratio became lopsided, with a significantly larger male population than female population.[57]

As the Iranian case shows, in some countries government policies to reduce population growth caused population to plummet much faster than expected. As a result, countries around the world with below replacement fertility are starting to encourage population growth once again. Let's explore why shrinking family sizes are causing some nations to rethink their population policies.

The Shrinking Family Dilemma

In a number of countries, including Japan, Canada, and the nations of Europe, fertility rates have fallen below the replacement rate. The average age of first-time mothers in many of these countries today is much older than in past generations.[58] Some women are delaying child bearing in order to pursue educational and career goals. In Japan, where most children are conceived by married couples, fewer and fewer people are getting married.[59]

Unintended Consequences

While population decline reduces pressure on a country's resources, it may also trigger economic difficulties that make it hard to support elderly populations. Some developed countries now have fewer people of working age to maintain their economic productivity and contribute to the government tax base that funds health care and retirement benefits for the elderly.

China enacted a one-child policy to limit the impacts of population growth.

Concern about the unintended consequences of declining fertility rates is not limited to developed countries. As in many countries, people in China worry: "Who will support the elderly?" Whereas the number of young people in China will continue to shrink under the one-child policy, the number of people aged 60 and older will grow dramatically in the next 15 years. An aging population may require national resources to be redirected toward retirement pensions and health care. Smaller families have also brought about changes in social structure. In China, as in many societies, aging parents were historically cared for by their children. Now, as many couples grow old with only one child, or none at all, care of elderly persons is becoming the responsibility of the government.[60]

Declining fertility also means the reduction of a country's working-age population. This is likely to change China's economic status in the global economy; China's economic boom during the last century was fed by a young labor force that will not be entirely replaced.[61]

Finding a Balance

To combat declining populations, some countries have developed policies encouraging citizens to have more children. In Sweden, the government subsidizes daycare and provides parents with paid leave from work of up to 18 months when they have a baby. In the United Kingdom, new mothers can get six months' paid leave. In Germany, families with children receive tax breaks. Mothers in Poland receive a one-time payment for each child they give birth to. In Italy, couples are paid to have a second child.[62] Despite these efforts, fertility rates remain low throughout Europe. On average, European women have 1.6 children.[63]

The Russian government is also trying to counter population loss, in part by encouraging immigration. Russia's efforts to build a larger workforce include welcoming foreign immigrants and encouraging expatriates (people who live outside their native country) to return to Russia.[64]

This woman, Aggie, works with Population Services International and provides family planning counseling to women in Zambia.

Pathways to Progress: Population

On July 11, 2012, World Population Day, United Nations Secretary-General Ban Ki-moon called for an "urgent, concerted action by Member States to bridge the gap between demand and supply for reproductive health care," going on to state that "Investing in universal access to reproductive health is a crucial investment in healthy societies and a more sustainable future."[65]

No matter what the aims of overall population policy, it is clear that people around the world value the choices provided by access to reproductive health care and that such access can transform the lives of young people who might otherwise be trapped in poverty.

Other responses to the issue of sustainable population growth include efforts to minimize our ecological footprint. Often a person's favored response will depend on his or her belief as to the root causes of a population spike or decline.

Supporting Our Women

More than 200 million women in the developing world have an unmet need for family planning and lack access to modern contraceptive methods.[66] Population Services International (PSI) is an organization that helps women and couples achieve their desired family size by educating women about safe family planning options and providing them access to high quality services.[67]

Along with access to family planning services, education is an important component of reproductive health care. Educated women and girls tend to marry later and have fewer children; they also seek medical attention sooner for themselves and their children. According to UNICEF, sending a girl to school makes her more likely to have healthy, well-nourished children and less likely to die during childbirth.[68]

Living Lightly

Humanity's collective footprint is not solely based on our sheer numbers; our resource use has an enormous impact on Earth's carrying capacity. People across the world are tak-

---

CAREER PROFILE — Reproductive Health Manager

Any parent will tell you that raising a child is no easy task. Parenting requires a serious amount of time and energy, not to mention social and financial resources. Planning how many children to have and when to have them can help families provide a safe and nurturing home environment for their kids. Family planning involves everything from sex education to birth control and disease prevention. Family planning is especially important in developing countries where reproductive health resources are scarce. Public health organizations like Population Services International (PSI) partner with local governments to provide family planning services to developing nations. Families with fewer children are better able to provide all of their children with the health care and education they need to succeed. When couples choose a family size based on their available resources, they can help to reduce occurrences of malnutrition and poverty.

PSI encourages safer sex practices and promotes a healthier and more productive life for mothers and their children. In 2010 alone, PSI distributed 28 million mosquito nets to prevent the spread of malaria; stopped 280,000 child deaths from malaria, diarrhea, and pneumonia; minimized disease and unwanted pregnancies by providing contraceptives to 18.6 million couples; and provided 1.8 million people with HIV counseling and testing.

As PSI's Reproductive Health Manager in Mozambique, Wendy Prosser is responsible for creating and maintaining a family planning strategy for the entire country. Wendy works with the national health ministry to secure funding for contraceptives and women's health services. She also works on a local level with pharmacists, nurses, and families to understand the reasons women may or may not be using birth control and how they are spacing their pregnancies.

Despite the cultural and political barriers that have limited family planning services in the past, Wendy believes that the support systems women need to make informed decisions about their reproductive health are coming into place:

Wendy Prosser is a Reproductive Health Manager in Mozambique.

> *Family planning is such a simple, basic and important concept yet so many millions of women don't have access to a birth control method or don't have the information about it. Making sure every woman who wants to plan her family is able to is one of the most important things we can do.*

ing steps to reduce the demand they put on the environment and help ensure adequate resources are available for future generations.

There are many ways we can reduce our demand on the planet's resources. The use of fossil fuels like oil and coal is one of the greatest contributors to our footprint. Moreover, mining for fossil fuels destroys ecosystems and burning them for energy contributes to climate change. Activities like these not only lessen the amount of fossil fuels available, but also have other adverse effects on the biosphere. Reducing fossil fuel use by choosing energy-efficient modes of transportation, limiting air travel, and paying attention to the energy required to heat homes and businesses can contribute to a lessened global footprint. An awareness of resource use in other areas of our lives can also help: using fewer paper products reduces the demand on the world's forests and reconsidering your daily eating habits can shrink your ecological footprint. For example, highly processed foods typically require much more energy to create than raw or whole foods.

The American School of Dubai is one community that is taking the message of living lightly to heart. Dubai is located in the United Arab Emirates, a country with one of the largest ecological footprints in the world. The students at the American School of Dubai undertook the Cool School Challenge to reduce their school's greenhouse gas emissions (which contribute to global climate change). In just one year, students were able to reduce their carbon dioxide emissions by nearly 72,000 pounds. That's like taking six cars off the road for an entire year.[69]

YOUTH PROFILE
Bernadette[70]

Bernadette and her family struggled to make ends meet, let alone afford schooling. Bernadette grew up in the West African nation of Benin, where the adult female literacy rate is 28%, meaning only 28 out of every 100 women can read and write. Benin also has a high population growth rate, the 13th highest in the world. A few years ago, a community organization convinced Bernadette's parents to make

Dubai has one of the largest ecological footprints in the world.

Batonga students

The Batonga Foundation is one organization working to improve the lives of women in Africa through secondary schooling and higher education. The foundation helps to build high schools, provide free school supplies, and teach communities about the importance of educating women. Batonga supports 229 girls in Benin by providing for their school tuition, uniforms, school supplies, and educational activities.

Bernadette says, "I am very happy because now I go to school and have enough to eat. If I go to school, I can learn." With the support of the Batonga Foundation, her community, and her family, Bernadette's future is bright. She is more likely to marry and have children later in life and to decide for herself what her future holds.

the sacrifice and send their daughter to school. Once Bernadette found herself in the classroom, she excelled and soon received a scholarship from the Batonga Foundation.

WHAT YOU CAN DO — Population

There will be moments in all of our lives when we will need to make decisions about family size: choosing if and when to have children, whether or not to adopt, and what steps to take to ensure we do not have children before we are ready. Each one of us will make these choices and all of our choices combined will define future population growth. Because of this, family planning is a critical component of tackling unsustainable population growth and related issues like Earth's carrying capacity. Here are a few things you may want to consider when making these decisions:

- Timing for starting a family—consider your education and your professional aspirations
- Access family planning resources—from birth control to counseling

Changing our consumption habits is another solution to address limited global carrying capacity. Despite having less than 5% of the global population, the United States consumes roughly 30% of the world's resources.[71] The United States also generates an unnecessarily large amount of waste; it is estimated that 40% of food in the United States goes uneaten.[72] Here are a few ideas to get you started:

Reducing the impacts of our consumption is one way to address carrying capacity

- Rethink how you get around town—use your feet, bicycle, or skateboard; consider public transportation or a fuel-efficient car.
- Rethink mealtime—avoid wasting your food and save leftovers for another meal; eat locally-sourced food to reduce the resources it takes to get the food to your table; and try eating one less meal with meat each week (fewer resources are used in the production of non-meat sources of protein).

POINT | **COUNTERPOINT**

Do you agree with China's one-child policy?

How a country chooses to address rising fertility rates among its citizens has often raised debates about government's role in our private lives. In 1979, China implemented a family planning policy encouraging couples to have only one child.

POINT

Yes

- **China has a population of over 1.3 billion people.** If China had not implemented the one-child policy back in 1979, its population today would be far larger—by an estimated 3 to 4 million people—undermining the country's development prospects.[73] An unsustainable population leads to thinly spread government resources and the overexploitation of natural resources. The one-child policy was a drastic measure necessary to secure a bright future for all Chinese citizens and support the country's growing economy. Furthermore, the policy is a temporary measure that will only remain in place until the population stabilizes.

- **Chinese citizens are better off because of the one-child policy.** Chinese women have increased access to health care and family planning services and they enjoy greater choice. Traditionally, Chinese women stayed at home with children as caregivers. Now they do not face the same pressure to bear children and have the opportunity to pursue other careers, increasing both their personal earnings and the national GDP. The policy is beneficial for the economy in other ways as well: limiting unemployment rates, increasing personal savings, and raising overall living standards.[74]

- **While the penalties associated with violating the one-child policy may seem steep, such violations are a well-informed choice made by a couple in their family planning.** Many couples do choose to have a second child, opting to pay the penalty in exchange. The Chinese government has also allowed exceptions under the one-child policy, such as for people living in rural areas or couples who lost their only child during a 2008 earthquake.[75]

COUNTERPOINT

No

- **Alternative family planning programs would better serve China's population predicament.** Sex education campaigns, improved access to contraceptives, and supportive family planning services have been able to reduce fertility rates while preserving personal liberties in Thailand, India, and Indonesia.[76] Alternative family planning programs like these would likely have been just as successful at reducing China's fertility rate as the one-child policy. The one-child policy is an unnecessarily harsh and oppressive method. The right to found a family is a liberty that should never be restricted by a government; according to the United Nations Declaration on Human Rights, it is an inalienable right.

- **The one-child policy has resulted in a gender imbalance.** Traditionally, Chinese culture preferred sons to daughters. Sons were expected to find a career and support their parents in their old age, while daughters, once married, would become part of their husband's family. Under the one-child policy, many couples have used selective abortion, abandoned female infants, or even killed female infants to ensure that their permitted one child is male.[77] As a result, the gender ratio has become skewed. In 2005, government data revealed that for every 100 girls born in China, there are 119 boys born.[78] This gender imbalance can lead to unfortunate social circumstances. It is estimated that by 2020, 40 million Chinese men will be unable to find a wife in their own country. Excess numbers of men have been linked to an increase in sex trafficking, forced prostitution, and illegal marriages.[79]

- **Penalties associated with the one-child policy disproportionately burden the urban poor.** For China's low-income urban community, the fines for having extra children are typically well over the average annual salary. If a couple pregnant with their second child is unable to pay the fine, local family planning officials have forced abortions (even late-term abortions) despite China's central government ban on this practice.[80]

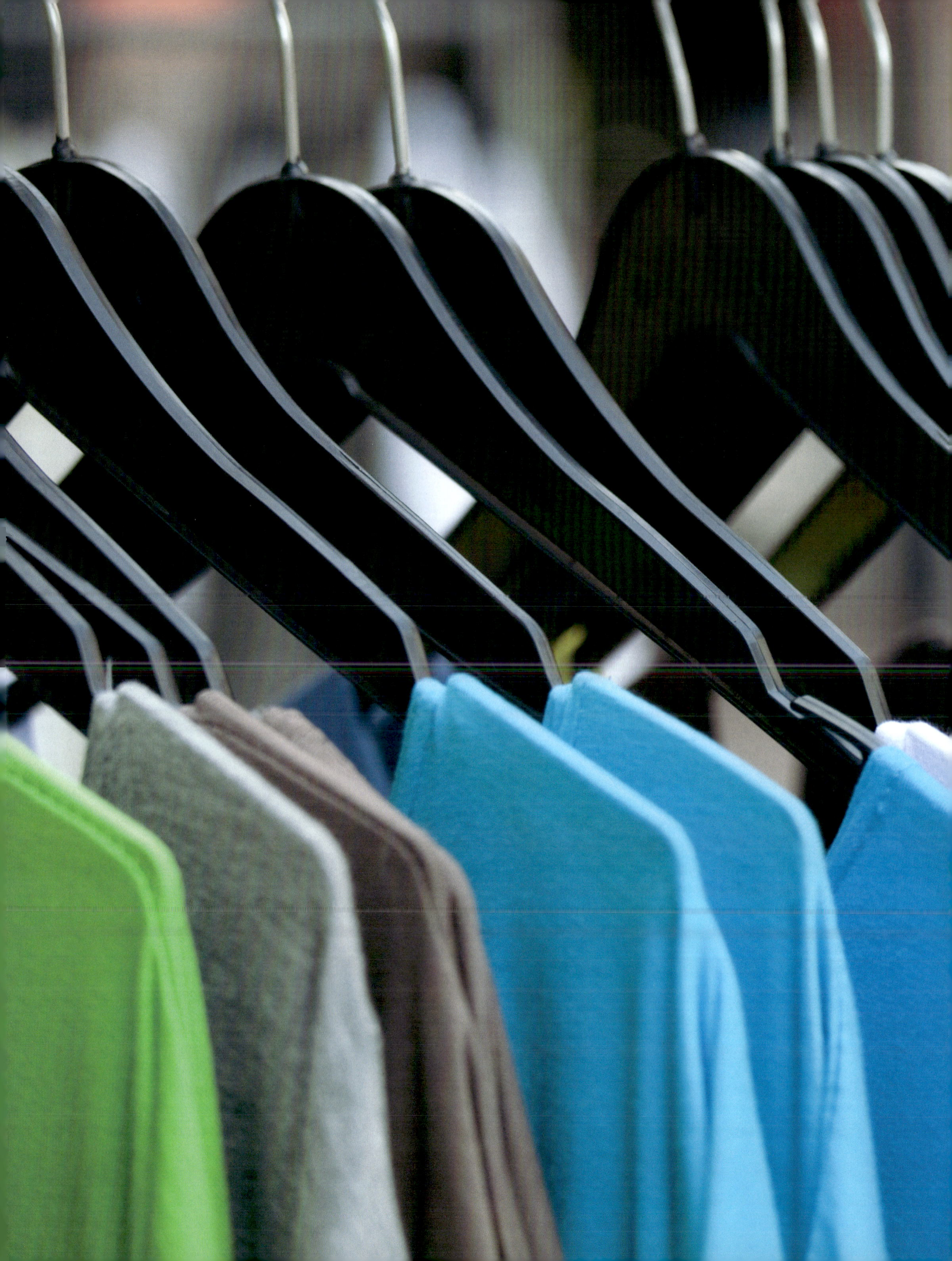

Chapter 8

Consumption

> **GUIDING QUESTIONS**
>
> - How does the use of resources affect people and places around the world?
> - What does sustainable consumption look like?

Introduction to Consumption

Think about the number of advertisements you see every day on television, the Internet, and billboards. Several decades ago, the average person living in a U.S. city saw 2,000 ad messages per day. These days, people see up to 5,000 ads per day.[1] What is the purpose of showing all of these different advertisements? Businesses and companies want people to consume more.

Consumption is a word that can mean different things to different people. In economic terms, consumption refers to the use of goods and services—from eating out at a restaurant to buying a t-shirt. When people purchase goods and services, we call them consumers. Every time we buy groceries, get a haircut, or hire a plumber, we are acting as consumers.

Everyone must consume resources like food and water in order to survive. Our consumption may also be for personal enjoyment, such as with entertainment and leisure. Consumerism is related to consumption, but it describes a particular worldview related to our consumption patterns. **Consumerism** can be defined as "the cultural orientation that leads people to find meaning, contentment, and acceptance through what they consume."[2]

Young people represent a growing proportion of consumers. Consumerism expert Juliet Schor reports that U.S. teens aged 12 to 19 spent an average of $101 per person per week in 2002, amounting to $170 billion in personal spending. In addition to direct purchases, teens also contribute to consumption by influencing adult spending. Before making a purchase for their children, 89% of parents ask for their children's opinions. And two-thirds of car purchases made by parents are influenced by their children's opinions.[3]

Consumption and Sustainability

Economy

Consumption choices are a key sustainability consideration. Consumption is tied to many different global issues, such as pollution and human health. For many nations, consumption is intrinsically linked to economic growth, with rising consumption leading to economic growth.

> *For many nations, consumption is intrinsically linked to economic growth*

If a country's economy is dependent on the ever-increasing consumption of its people, is it sustainable? In 1955, the economist Victor Lebow stated, "Our enormously productive economy…demands that we make consumption our way of life, that we convert the buying and use of goods into rituals, that we seek our spiritual satisfaction, our ego satisfaction, in consumption…We need things consumed, burned up, worn out, replaced, and discarded at an ever increasing rate."

Such economic growth has had consequences: increased demand for goods has increased our need to use natural resources. With a decrease in natural resources, can we continue to consume at the same rate we do now?

Society

What is important to you? Earning a lot of money? Having a family? Enjoying your work? Do your values match your consumption patterns?

Consumption is closely tied to human well-being, for both consumers and for producers. For example, if a company making jeans chooses to pay its workers a very low wage, these workers may struggle to meet their basic needs.

Consumption patterns can have positive and negative impacts. Within a consumer society, we spend less time making things for ourselves and more time working for a wage so that we can purchase products we need and want. When we start to consume beyond our means, we may struggle financially. One of the reasons for the U.S. economic recession in 2008, for example, was that people were purchasing houses they could not afford. When housing prices began to decline and people realized they would lose money, many defaulted on their mortgages and the banks foreclosed on their homes.

Environment

One way to measure the impact of consumption on the environment is by using a tool called ecological footprint. An **ecological footprint** is a measure of how much nature — that is, the amount of land and water resources—a person's lifestyle requires. To support a lifestyle marked by high consumption, many resources will be extracted from the Earth, processed into usable materials, and disposed of as waste. This concept goes hand in hand with population size when we ask the question, "How many people can the Earth support?" Earth's *carrying capacity* is affected not just by the total number of humans on the planet, but also by the degree to which each person's consumption impacts the planet.

What particular natural resources might be required to support a person's lifestyle? The following ecological footprint sectors can help us think about the different ways we use and impact Earth's resources:[4]

- Forests
- Farmland
- Construction and mining
- Wild meat, fish, and seafood
- Water
- Transport, trade, and tourism
- Energy use

Can you think of ways that your lifestyle requires resources in each of these sectors? Compared to other people in the world, do you think you have a relatively small or large ecological footprint?

Let's consider four ecological footprints from four different countries. The average individual living in Malawi or Iraq has a smaller ecological footprint than the world average. In contrast, the average individual living in Libya or the United Arab Emirates (UAE) has a larger ecological footprint than the world average. This means an average person in Libya or the UAE consumes more resources than an average person in Malawi or Iraq.

All together humans are using resources faster than the planet can replenish them. This phenomenon is called **ecological overshoot**. Humanity currently demands 30% more living resources than Earth can regenerate.[5] What could be driving this trend?

The United Arab Emirates (UAE) has the largest per-capita ecological footprint in the world. In response to concerns over its rate of consumption, the UAE is now working to reduce its footprint. The country is working to develop renewable energy sources like solar energy. It is building a new community for 40,000 residents and 1,500 companies; this community is designed to be car free, zero carbon, and zero waste. The UAE also hopes to cultivate a green tourism industry by reducing energy and water usage and waste produced by hotels.[6]

Background on Consumption

Before further exploring how consumption factors into the sustainability picture, let's first look at changes in consumption patterns over time and the emergence of a so-called consumer society.

Humans have always consumed natural resources. Earth's resources, including water and food, are vital to our survival. Early humans foraged to find food and other necessities. As

Dubai is one of seven emirates that make up the United Arab Emirates (UAE).

more sedentary communities began to develop, work grew more specialized. Some people farmed, while others were craftsmen who created tools or provided other services. Farmers and nonfarmers (including priests, builders, soldiers, and artists) traded goods and services with each other.

Population growth between the 8th and 12th centuries contributed to the growth of cities, which fostered expanding trade and consumption. City dwellers shopped and bartered at local markets while regional markets expanded internationally. Merchants traded spices, metals, silk, gemstones, and slaves through trade networks connecting Africa, Europe, and Asia.[7]

By the 16th century, trade networks had become truly global. Navigation tools including the astrolabe (a device that allowed sailors to determine latitude to find their way) and the magnetic compass encouraged the expansion of ocean travel. Europeans established ocean trade routes to aquire goods such as silver from the Americas and spices and silk from Asia.[8]

In modern times, human consumption of resources has continued to grow at ever-increasing rates. Many historians trace this great capacity for consumption to the Industrial Revolution. The Industrial Revolution began in the United Kingdom in the mid-18th century with the development of steam power, more efficient machinery, and factories. The steam engine made the revolution possible by providing a large source of energy. Because steam engines often ran on fossil fuels like coal, the Industrial Revolution also encouraged secondary industries like mining.[9]

Factories fundamentally changed the way goods (products that are bought and sold) were produced. Prior to the emergence of factories, goods were primarily produced close to where they were consumed, in many cases within people's homes. Most people grew their own food, raised livestock, and made their own cloth from wool. The Industrial Revolution introduced new, more efficient ways to produce goods and brought an end to much of this individual production in homes.

Machines in factories made it possible to produce goods faster and in greater quantities than ever before. One new machine was the jenny, created by James Hargreaves to take the place of the spinning wheel. While the spinning wheel produced a single thread, the jenny could spin multiple threads at once. Another advance was the water frame, a machine invented by Richard Arkwright that made the

Steam engines helped to move the Industrial Revolution forward.

Henry Ford designed the Model T in 1908. This car could be mass produced.

creation of stronger threads possible. These machines supported the birth of an industrial textile industry. This model of industrial production soon spread to other types of manufacturing and other places.

By the beginning of the 20th century, the Industrial Revolution had spread throughout Europe and the United States. An important advance by the American automobile maker Henry Ford helped boost industrial productivity and the mass production of consumer goods. At the time, cars were expensive and each one was built to order. In 1908 Ford designed the Model T, a car that could be mass produced rather than custom built. Each Model T was identical, down to the black color. Ford wanted to make the Model T affordable so that most working people could afford to buy one. To lower production costs, Ford developed the moving assembly line. He introduced standard, interchangeable parts that could be created by machines operated by unskilled laborers. Inspired by other industries that used moving belts to bring materials to workers, Ford simplified the process of assembling a Model T into 84 steps and trained workers on an assembly line to each complete just one task. The new process in Ford's factories sped up production and reduced labor costs. Ford then raised the wages of his workers so that, for the first time, they could afford to buy cars of their own.[10]

By the 1920s, ordinary people had become a working consumer class, buying cars, telephones, and radios.[11] World War II (1939-45) shifted industrial production from consumer goods to the manufacture of weapons and other goods for the war.[12] As the war ended, though, Western nations returned to producing the purchasing consumer goods with enthusiasm. Thanks to a booming post-war economy, Americans could afford to purchase more than just basic necessities; they bought televisions, cars, houses, and clothing like never before. A growing advertising industry helped reinforce an American consumer culture with a seemingly endless appetite.[13]

These trends continued in the second half of the 20th century. By 2003 there were more private cars than licensed drivers in the United States.[14] The average size of a house in the United States has more than doubled since 1950, from under 1,000 square feet to 2,500 square feet, despite the fact that each house contains fewer people on average.[15]

The rise of consumerism has not been limited to the United States and Western

Europe. According to the WorldWatch Institute, "worldwide, private consumption expenditures—the amount spent on goods and services at the household level—topped $20 trillion in 2000, a four-fold increase over 1960 (in 1995 dollars)." By 2002, approximately three-quarters of households on the planet contained at least one television. Over one billion mobile lines, enough to supply roughly one out of five people on the planet with a mobile phone, were in use by 2002.[16]

What will consumption look like in the future? How can human consumption support sustainable societies, economies, and environments? Can you think of ways consumption might positively impact people or places? On the other hand, what might be negative consequences of consumption?

These are complex questions, but by the end of this chapter you will have a good deal of information to help you draw your own conclusions about how consumption fits into the sustainability picture.

Consumption is just one step in the materials economy.

Consumption Today

Consumption is really part of a larger system called the materials economy. The **materials economy** includes all the steps involved in producing and consuming goods, including disposal. One way to envision this system is as a series of sequential steps:

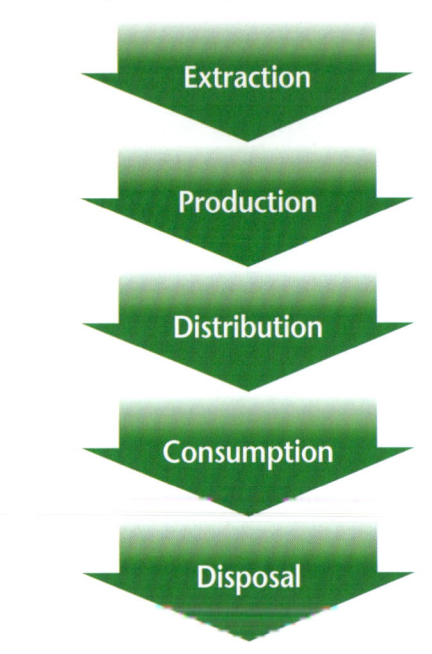

- Extraction
- Production
- Distribution
- Consumption
- Disposal

Seems fairly straightforward, right? Each step represents its own subsystem with a number of impacts on people, economies, and environments. Let's look a little closer at the steps that comprise the materials economy.

Step 1: Extraction

Extraction is the removal of resources from a natural environment. Extraction can refer to harvesting; for example, when trees are harvested to make lumber. Extraction can also refer to mining, such as coal that is mined from deep inside mountains or below the Earth's surface. Water use is also considered a form of extraction; it involves the removal of a natural resource from the environment for human consumption.

Many different materials go into each product you buy. Some things have relatively few ingredients, like a wooden spoon. It's made of…you guessed it, wood! But other resources, including metals used to create machinery to carve the wood and energy sources to fuel the machinery, are required to make this seemingly simple product. Each of these resources—wood, metals, fuel—must be extracted from the Earth. Fuel and metals must be refined and lumber must be cut and treated.

Let's look at a more complex example: a computer. Did you know that more than 2,000 different materials are used to produce a microchip, itself only one small part of a computer?[17] The microchip is made mostly of silicon, an element extracted from the compound silica, commonly found in sand. Metals like copper, gold, and aluminum serve as electrical conductors. The parts of the computer that you see are largely made of plastic (which is made of petroleum-based compounds) and glass (which is made with silica).

The demand for electronics is growing, not only because an increasing number of people are purchasing electronic devices, but also because electronics are replaced frequently (the average lifespan of a cell phone is less than two years).[18] As a result, demand for metals like gold rises, too. Unfortunately, extracting gold can be a dirty business. Open-pit mining is a common means of removing gold from the earth. About three-quarters of the gold produced in the world is extracted using this method. Open-pit mines use huge machines to dig deep into the earth, leaving behind massive pits that can be seen from space.[19]

A large open-pit mine is located on the small island of Sumbawa, Indonesia. Where there once stood a 1,800 foot volcano, there is now a mile-wide pit that reaches 345 feet below sea level and grows deeper every day. The mine is expected to continue to produce gold for about 20 years, at which point it will reach 1,500 feet below sea level.

Open-pit mining is a common means of removing gold from Earth.

There are other concerns about this type of mining. Frequently, open-pit gold mines use a process called cyanide heap-leaching. First, the ore that is extracted from an open-pit mine is dumped into huge piles. Then those heaps are sprayed with a cyanide solution that bonds with tiny bits of gold and silver as it trickles down through the ore. This cyanide is recovered and sprayed again over the heap. Cyanide is extremely toxic—it is a killing agent used in gas chambers. Cyanide in contaminated streams kills fish and wildlife. It can also enter other animals' bodies when they eat contaminated fish.[20]

Another major problem with open-pit mines is the sheer amount of waste they produce. At even the most efficient mines, extracting a single ounce of gold to create a wedding ring requires the removal of 250 tons (that's 500,000 pounds) of rock and ore. The waste rock is spread across surrounding land. On Sumbawa, the disposal of waste rock is destroying what was once pristine rainforest.

Step 2: Production

Production is the process by which raw (and sometimes recycled) materials are turned into manufactured goods. Besides natural resources, many additional kinds of resources are required for this step, including energy and human labor.

In today's interconnected world, many products have a global past. Take the previous example of a computer. Here's one possible map of its production: The computer chip is made of silicon from Washington, copper from Arizona, and gold from South Africa. The microchip is assembled in California and then travels to Malaysia to be built into a package that enables it to be wired to the larger computer. The circuit board includes tin from Brazil and lead from a car battery recycler in Texas. The monitor comes from Japan and is partially composed of plastic created from Saudi Arabian oil. The final assembly is done in California.[21] By the time it reaches a store in North America, a computer has already traveled the globe, using energy at each step of the way.[22]

Power Source

Production is not possible without large amounts of energy. Energy is used throughout the materials economy, and it is a major component of computer manufacturing. One way to get an idea of how much energy is required to produce an item is to examine its carbon footprint. For example, 61% of the greenhouse gas emissions associated with the lifecycle of a common laptop computer result from its production.[24]

Human Resources

Even when high-tech machines are involved in manufacturing products, human labor still plays a major role in production. Fueled by cheap labor, most manufactured products are made in developing countries. Manufacturing plays a key role in many developing country economies and can bring benefits to their people. China is just one example of a country that has built its economy through production of exports.

However, manufacturing in developing countries has downsides. In China, one main concern is working conditions for laborers. Although China has restrictive labor laws, these laws are not always enforced. Some factories maintain two sets of books in order to evade inspectors who visit the factories. One estimate suggests that over half of Chinese suppliers submit false pay records to inspectors, and only a small fraction of Chinese factories obey limitations on daily working hours.[25] In addition to working long hours, the health of factory workers can be impacted by chemicals used to make products. Workers exposed to the toxic chemical n-hexane in a Chinese electronics factory were unable to walk after their exposure.[26] The appearance of cancer clusters in electronics factories in China has become well known. Very young workers have died of leukemia and other cancers.[27]

Factories that do not properly handle dangerous chemicals not only put the health of workers at risk, but they can also affect the health of larger communities. Factory wastes discharged into rivers and the air can lead to illness among people who do not work at the factories. When manufacturing takes place on a large scale and without environmental protections, the cumulative effect of pollution has additional, far-reaching impacts. China's primary energy source for providing electricity to factories is coal, a fossil fuel that contributes to climate change and smog. Hundreds of

Greenhouse gas emissions released during production of computer		
product	kg of CO_2 equivalent released during production	equivalent number of gallons of gasoline burned[23]
15-inch laptop	415 kg	46.80 gallons

Panamax container ships approach the Panama Canal. "Panamax" refers to the largest size of ship that can pass through the locks and enter the canal.

thousands of premature deaths have been traced to China's environmental degradation, in which factories play a significant role.[28]

Other countries, both developing and developed, have experienced harmful health impacts and environmental degradation as a result of manufacturing. Factories building computer components in California in the 1970s left behind 29 hazardous waste sites designated Superfund sites by the Environmental Protection Agency (EPA). These areas were contaminated with toxic chemicals that had leaked out of underground storage tanks at electronics manufacturing plants. The pollution has been linked to birth defects and high rates of miscarriage among women living in the area.[29]

Step 3: Distribution

The *distribution* of a product describes the journey it takes from where it is manufactured to where you can purchase it. This includes moving the manufactured product from a factory to a warehouse or store. It also includes advertising and marketing to sell the product, as well as operating retail stores where people can buy the product.

One key component of distribution is transportation. In our global economy, goods are rarely made close to where they are consumed. Instead, many goods travel across the globe by container ship, truck, and airplane to reach consumers. In most cases, these modes of transportation run on fossil fuels like petroleum (used to create gasoline and diesel) that require millions of years to replenish and contribute to climate change. Burning fossil fuels for transportation releases CO_2, a greenhouse gas that accumulates in the atmosphere. Rising CO_2 levels in Earth's atmosphere correlate with rising average surface temperatures on Earth.[30] These rising temperatures are already affecting ecosystems, resulting in more intense hurricanes, melting glaciers, and spreading disease vectors.[31]

Ninety-nine percent of American overseas trade by weight travels via ship.[32] In addition to releasing greenhouse gases, cargo ships emit other air pollutants like sulfur. It is estimated that ship emissions result in 60,000 cardiopulmonary and lung cancer deaths each year, particularly near coastlines in Europe and Asia.[33]

The size of cargo ships is continually increasing. In 2006, a ship larger than ever before set sail. It was more than three times the size of the Titanic, able to carry 50 million cell phones at one time![34] As the size of ships increase, ports are also increasing in size to accommodate them. This means enlarging canals, including the famous Panama Canal, so that these giant freight carriers can pass through them.[35]

Of course, shipping is just one part of distribution. Once the ship's contents are unloaded onto land, trucks and trains carry goods to

Carbon Footprints for Four Different Distribution Methods[36]

Carbon Dioxide Emissions (g CO_2/metric ton carried/mile)

- Ship: 10
- Rail: 20
- Truck: 54
- Airplane: 570

Step 4: Consumption

The act of buying and using things is known as consumption. This is the most visible step of the materials economy and it drives the whole system—from the extraction of natural resources to the production and distribution of consumer goods.

Of course, consumption is not necessarily a bad thing. We have to consume resources just to live! But let's look at what can happen when we consume more than what we really need, a phenomenon called overconsumption.

People across the globe spend an enormous amount of money on "stuff." Consider these 2003 statistics:

- $18 billion was spent on cosmetics worldwide
- $14 billion was spent on ocean cruises worldwide
- $17 billion was spent on pet food in the United States and Europe[39]

These figures represent an investment of time and energy. Let's look closer at what is happening in the United States, which has the largest economy in the world.[40] A 2008 survey revealed that Americans age 15 and older spend more time purchasing goods and services than they do engaged in housework, caring for household members, educational activities, volunteering, religious activities, or socializing.[41] Altogether Americans spent approximately $1.2 trillion on non-essential consumer goods.[42]

People are buying items like computers and other electronics at faster and faster rates. In 1975, fewer than 50,000 personal computers were sold. In 2009, over 280 million computers were sold worldwide.[43] The average lifespan of one of these computers is three to five years.[44] If you were considering purchasing a computer, what would you want to know? Would you want to know where it was made or who made it? Would you want to know what materials it contains? What about how it performs? Or how long it is expected to last?

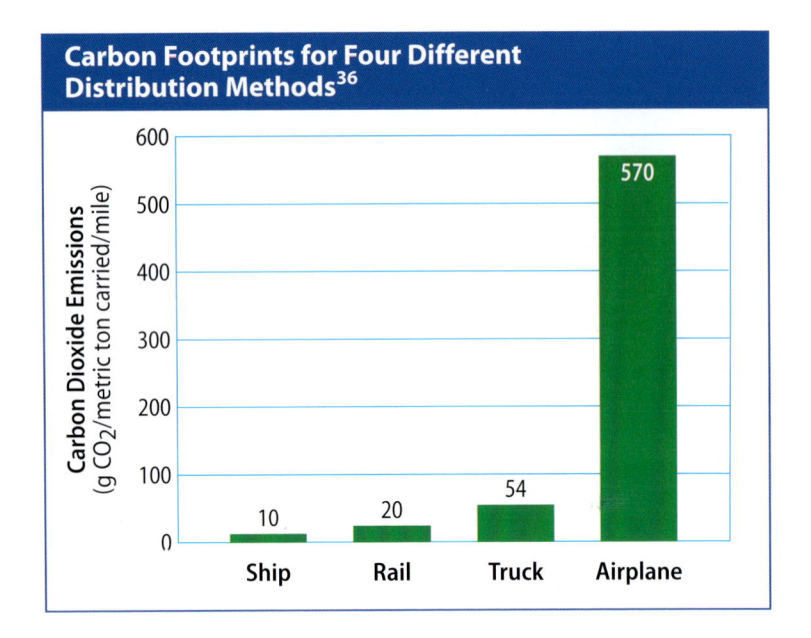

distribution centers and stores. Retails stores where consumers can buy products may also contribute to climate change. If a store's electricity is supplied by a coal-fired power plant (the most common source of electricity),[37] then it contributes to the release of greenhouse gases into the atmosphere.

How consumer goods are distributed has consequences for society. For example, distribution systems can support "big box" stores that consume large amounts of energy, typically include large parking lots, and create competition for smaller local retailers. Distribution methods can encourage particular patterns of community growth, like whether retail stores will be located in cities where many people live or if they will be part of suburban shopping centers. One distribution system might encourage urban density, while another method might encourage suburban sprawl.

The logic of distribution systems impacts workers at retail outlets, too. Some companies only hire part-time workers, keeping wages low and reducing the number of employees eligible for benefits like vacation leave and health care. Even full-time retail workers may not be paid a livable wage. For example, a single parent paid minimum wage earns a salary barely above the poverty level.[38]

The majority of waste ends up in landfills.

There are a lot of reasons that people buy things. A major influence on consumption is advertising and marketing. In 2008, advertisers spent $136.8 billion in the United States alone. (That's $136,800,000,000!)[45] Much of this money is spent marketing to younger and younger consumers. Children in the United States watch an estimated 40,000 commercials each year.[46] Children between ages four and twelve accounted for $30 billion in sales in 2002, and kids aged twelve to nineteen spent $170 billion.[47]

Step 5: Disposal

After a product has been consumed, the last step of the materials economy is *disposal*. Disposal doesn't have to mean throwing something away, though that is how most people have come to think of it.

Think about what happens when something is at the end of its life. Do you try to find a different use for it? Do you give it to someone else who can use it? Do you recycle it or put it in the trash?

Let's go back to our computer example. Computers and other electronics have proven to be very difficult to dispose of sustainably, in part due to the hazardous materials they contain, but also due to the sheer number of different resources and components involved.

Of the 41 million computers and 32 million monitors disposed of in the United States in 2007, about 18% were recycled. The majority of the remaining *e-waste* ended up in landfills.[48] A *landfill* is a place where garbage is buried. Landfills are lined with plastic and dirt is used to cover each day's new garbage. A smaller portion of the e-waste went to incinerators instead of landfills. Incinerators burn trash, resulting in ash that must be buried in a landfill.

Both landfills and incinerators have environmental and social costs. Although landfills have a plastic liner to protect the surrounding soil and groundwater, it is well documented that these eventually break and leak hazardous materials into the environment.[49] Incinerators face a lot of public opposition because burning trash releases chemicals such as lead, mercury, and dioxins. People exposed to lead and mercury can suffer nervous system damage,[50] and dioxins can cause cancer.[51]

The bad news in the case of e-waste is that recycling can also have harmful side effects. Many recycled computers and televisions are shipped to countries in Africa and Asia for "informal" processing—that is, unregulated recycling done by residents in their homes, typically with few safety precautions.[52] Adults or children engaged in informal recycling do not have safety equipment to protect them from hazardous chemicals like lead and mercury, which are often released during recycling.

In the town of Guiyu in China, many residents do this sort of recycling in their homes. The town has the highest levels of cancer-causing dioxins in the world. Children have elevated levels of lead in their blood and pregnant women miscarry six times more than the normal rate.[53] The good news is that there are organizations working to fight this export business by providing more opportunities to recycle electronics domestically where there are stricter safety laws.

Growing Costs of Consumption

As you already know, rising incomes around the world have led to increasing rates of consumption. Let's look a little closer at how escalating consumption is affecting the planet.

Larger Ecological Footprints

Can the rate of human consumption continue to grow as it has in the past? Can the Earth support our consumption and provide us with everything we want? The answers to these questions depend partly on the number of people on Earth. If the planet had fewer people, we would have a smaller collective ecological footprint.

CASE STUDY — **Impacts of a Growing Footprint**[54]

Our consumption can have effects that we may not see or hear about in our daily lives. One example is the cashmere industry. Cashmere goats are typically raised in the arid mountains of China and Mongolia. Their grazing and trampling take a toll on the fragile mountain environment. Prior to the 1980s, only wealthy consumers could afford cashmere sweaters. Starting in the early 1980s, demand for cashmere increased dramatically. Herders began increasing the size of their herds to meet the demand.

Unfortunately, large goat herds have transformed grasslands into desert—the desert is expanding by hundreds of square miles a year. Goats are extremely efficient foragers, destroying any vegetation and causing desertification. Dust storms have become more frequent and far-reaching; dust and air pollution from China can travel across the Pacific Ocean, reaching the west coast of North America. Mongolia has tried to halt desertification by banning grazing in some areas and requiring herders to keep their animals penned up and to feed them by hand.

A woman tends to a cashmere goat herd.

The other part of the equation is the amount of resources that each person consumes. It is estimated that the overall global ecological footprint is already beyond what the planet can support. Experts believe that it takes the Earth a year and a half to regenerate what we use in a year.[55] In other words, we are using resources faster than they can be regenerated. Our collective ecological footprint—a result of the current rate of consumption, the current population, and the current use of technology—cannot be sustained indefinitely.

Externalities

As you read earlier, each step in the materials economy affects people, economies, and environments. Many nations measure their well-being by adding up all of the products and services sold during a year, regardless of whether these services were food for nourishment or treatment for an illness. This aggregate measure of economic well-being, called the Gross Domestic Product (GDP), goes up as people purchase more. If we measure prosperity by indicators like GDP, consumption appears to be the main driver of economic progress.

However, consumption can have negative effects that are not always measured. Many processes involved in making, using, and disposing of consumer products involve costs that are not paid by either the manufacturers or the consumers of those products. Take air pollution, for example. Most people would agree that there are costs associated with air pollution. Smog and particulate matter can cause health problems like asthma. Poor health has a human cost that is hard to quantify, but it also has a monetary cost for individuals, taxpayers, and governments that pay into the health care system.

These hidden costs associated with the materials economy are known in economics as externalities. By definition, externalities are external effects, often unforeseen or unintended, accompanying a process or activity. Externalities can be positive (benefits) or negative (costs). Negative externalities are costs that are not directly paid by manufacturers, such as environmental degradation. Externalities are therefore not included in the purchase price of goods. In other words, these costs are external to the market value of a product. When the purchase price of a good is less than its true cost due to negative externalities, the manufacturers will produce more of it and consumers will buy more of it. In other words, negative externalities help to encourage the overproduction and overconsumption of goods. Positive externalities do just the opposite, they lead to the underproduction of goods that have additional benefits

If we briefly retrace the steps of the materials economy, we will see externalities at each step. First is natural resource extraction. Externalities at this step may include hazards to miners' health or long-term environmental damage. In the next step, production, we find externalities such as unsafe working conditions, worker stress, and air or water pollution from factory discharges. Distribution systems such as retail stores have externalities like withholding health care or other employment benefits from retail employees.

Even in the final step, disposal, a portion of the true cost is often passed along to society at

Air pollution can be an externality.

large. Think about sending trash to a landfill. That landfill is in someone's backyard, possibly leaking toxic materials into neighbors' groundwater. Or consider an incinerator. By burning trash, incinerators reduce its volume, but toxins are also released into the atmosphere. Who, if anyone, do you think pays for these hazards?

So why aren't these externalities included in the purchase price of a product? Well, for one thing, consumers who buy these products pay far less for them than they would if all costs were included. Companies benefit from being able to offer low prices. If a company did want to include these hidden costs in the price of a product, it would be hard to compete with other companies that exclude these costs.

Another problem is that it can be difficult to put a price on externalities. Exactly how much would it cost to remediate air pollution from a textile factory in Mexico? What is the cost of unsustainable deforestation given that forests, if logged sustainably, can be a renewable resource that provides other benefits (air quality, tourism, recreation, and quality of life)? What are the economic repercussions when employees are sick because they do not have health care? Because it can be difficult to calculate exact values for these costs, oftentimes we do not know how great the cost is or who ends up paying it.

Pathways to Progress: Consumption

In response to growing concerns about overconsumption, people around the world are undertaking a variety of actions to improve the well-being of people, places, and economies. The following are just a few examples.

Do More with Less

Kevin and Joan Salwen and their two children lived in a 6,500 square foot home in Atlanta, Georgia. One day while observing a homeless

---

CAREER PROFILE — Sustainable Marketer

Marketers have the power to push and pull consumers' decisions in different directions. Marketers define a brand through packaging, labeling, and advertising a product or service. Marketers may work on a freelance basis, for marketing firms, or within a specific company. They often hold degrees in communications, marketing, or business.

The fastest-growing sector in the field is sustainable marketing, or eco-marketing. Eco-marketers work to highlight a client's commitment to environmental responsibility, sustainability, and the ethical treatment of workers. One woman who is making a name in the field is Jacqueline Ottman.

Jacqueline Ottman is a sustainable marketer.

Jacqueline is the head of her own marketing and consulting agency in Manhattan. Working with some of the biggest names in business, like IBM, Nike, and Stonyfield Farms, Jacqueline delivers a message of corporate responsibility to the consumer. She highlights each brand's commitments to a variety of humanitarian and ecological causes, such as Fair Trade, organic agriculture, or labor rights. Jacqueline emphasizes that people buy green or socially-responsible products because they have added value. They are often of higher quality, more durable, easier to dispose of, or contribute a quantifiable increase in the consumer's quality of life. This is why she believes that all products, even those that are not specifically focused on balancing our present needs with those of future generations, should embrace eco-marketing.

The Salwen family poses with Dr. Naana, the Hunger Project's country director in Ghana.

man from the windows of her family's car, 14-year-old Hannah Salwen thought about how more people in the world could live better lives if some people consumed less. She convinced her family to sell their house and move into a house less than half its size. The Salwens donated half the money from the sale of their house to the Hunger Project, a charity that used the money to help 30 villages in Ghana. The family also gave away half of their belongings.

The result? A smaller house meant that the Salwens saw each other more and spent more time together as a family.[56] They traveled to Ghana to meet the people they had helped and learn about systemic solutions to poverty, such as improvements in education, health care, literacy, and agriculture.

According to the Salwens, consuming less actually improved their lives. Their advice? "Figure out what is 'enough' in your family. So many people get caught up in accumulation of 'stuff,' keeping up with others and adding to their piles. For us it became more satisfying to go the other way, figuring out what we really needed so that we could help others get what they need."[57]

Grow a Local Economy

A movement is building to support and sustain local communities through purchasing locally-made goods. BALLE, the Business Alliance for Local Living Economies, is an organization spearheading this movement. Over 20,000 socially-responsible businesses are already part of BALLE's North American network to create and sustain local living economies.[58]

Local living economies are rooted in the belief that local businesses can uniquely meet the needs of consumers in a community. Because local business owners live within the community where their goods are produced, they have an incentive to produce goods in ways that are mindful of employees (their fellow community members) and environments (their shared neighborhoods and resources). Consumer support of local businesses also allows money earned within a community to stay within that community rather than going to the large multinational corporations who produce many of the world's products.

YOUTH PROFILE
Jessica Assaf

One way to change how consumer products are made is to campaign for structural change. When a teenager from California learned that some makeup products actually had toxics in them that could lead to cancer and other illnesses, she decided to take action to make sure that they were taken off store shelves.

Jessica Assaf worked with the Teens for Safe Cosmetics campaign to create Operation Beauty Drop, which placed large bins in malls for teens to drop off beauty products that contained toxics. Those toxic beauty products were sent back to manufacturers with a petition signed by teenagers demanding the products be made with safer chemicals. Jessica and her friends urged their local senators to pass a bill in California requiring manufacturers to inform the Department of Health Services if their products contained toxics. The bill became law in 2007. As a result, cosmetics manufacturers are now required to label products sold in California if they contain chemicals known to cause birth defects and cancers.[59]

Jessica Assaf

WHAT YOU CAN DO — Consumption

There are many things you can do to **address consumption. These solutions** can range from the personal to the structural:

- Purchase materials that you plan to keep a long time and recycle them when they can no longer be used.

- Research companies to learn if they have social responsibility policies. If a company that creates products you like does not have a commitment to social responsibility, consider contacting them to encourage them do so.

- Support retail stores that are close to where you live, rather than driving long distances to large shopping malls. Are there any stores located close enough to your home that you could walk or take the bus? Shopping close to home can save time and money spent on driving.

- Learn more about companies that sell the products you buy. Think about a catchy ad you have seen recently. Did the ad give you information about how the advertised product affects people or the environment? If not, you can do your own research to learn more about whether or not the product (or the company that makes it) promotes sustainability.

You can learn more about companies that sell products you buy.

POINT | **COUNTERPOINT**

Can voting with your dollars truly support sustainability?

In a time where we have a number of choices as consumers, there is debate whether voting with our dollars will influence the way businesses make decisions. Read the following perspectives to learn more.

POINT

Yes

- **We live in a time where we have many options to choose from when we purchase goods and services.** We can now buy products that are organic, nontoxic, and not made by sweatshops. In the United States, consumer spending accounts for 70% of the GDP.[60] Consumers have a large collective impact, so if we all make choices that are good for people and the planet we can create significant change.

- **There are many issues people face around the world ranging from conflict and poverty to environmental degradation.** It can be overwhelming to learn about these issues and hard to imagine how one person can make a difference. However, by learning about the true costs of a product (such as how much workers are paid and how much pollution a factory emits) and making informed and responsible choices, each individual can be a part of changing the entire system of production and consumption. Consumer choices send a message to businesses; if enough people vote with their dollars, businesses will start making their products more sustainable.

COUNTERPOINT

No

- **Products that are local, organic, or fair trade are more expensive.** In times of economic hardship, these kinds of consumption choices are not truly an option for most people. Voting with one's dollars becomes virtually impossible when goods and services are already unaffordable.

- **While making sustainable choices such as buying things that are fair trade or energy efficient may align with your values, these singular choices don't make a huge difference in the larger landscape of consumption policy.**[61] The greatest potential for change is outside of consumer control—global production, distribution, and disposal accounts for most of the waste, pollution, and negative social effects of consumerism. No matter how eco- or socially-conscious we try to be with our purchasing, we won't change these systems through consumer choice. For example, a few people choosing to buy a fair trade coffee to support farmers in a developing country won't be enough to alleviate poverty in that country. We need to address sustainability through other means, such as voting for policies that will support real change.

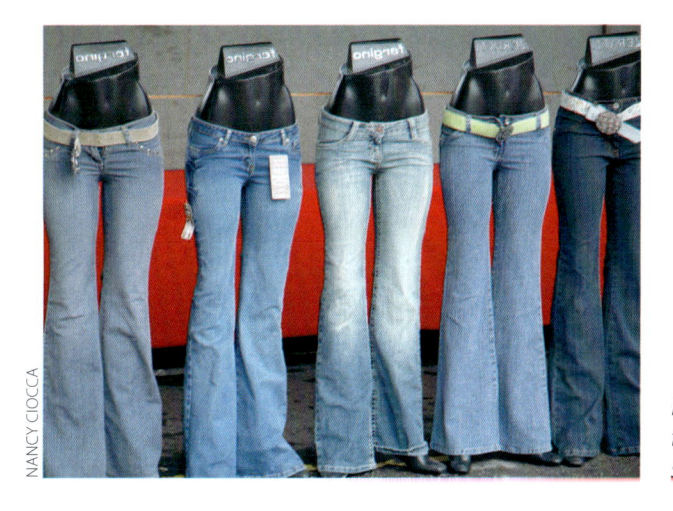

Do consumers have the power to support sustainability?

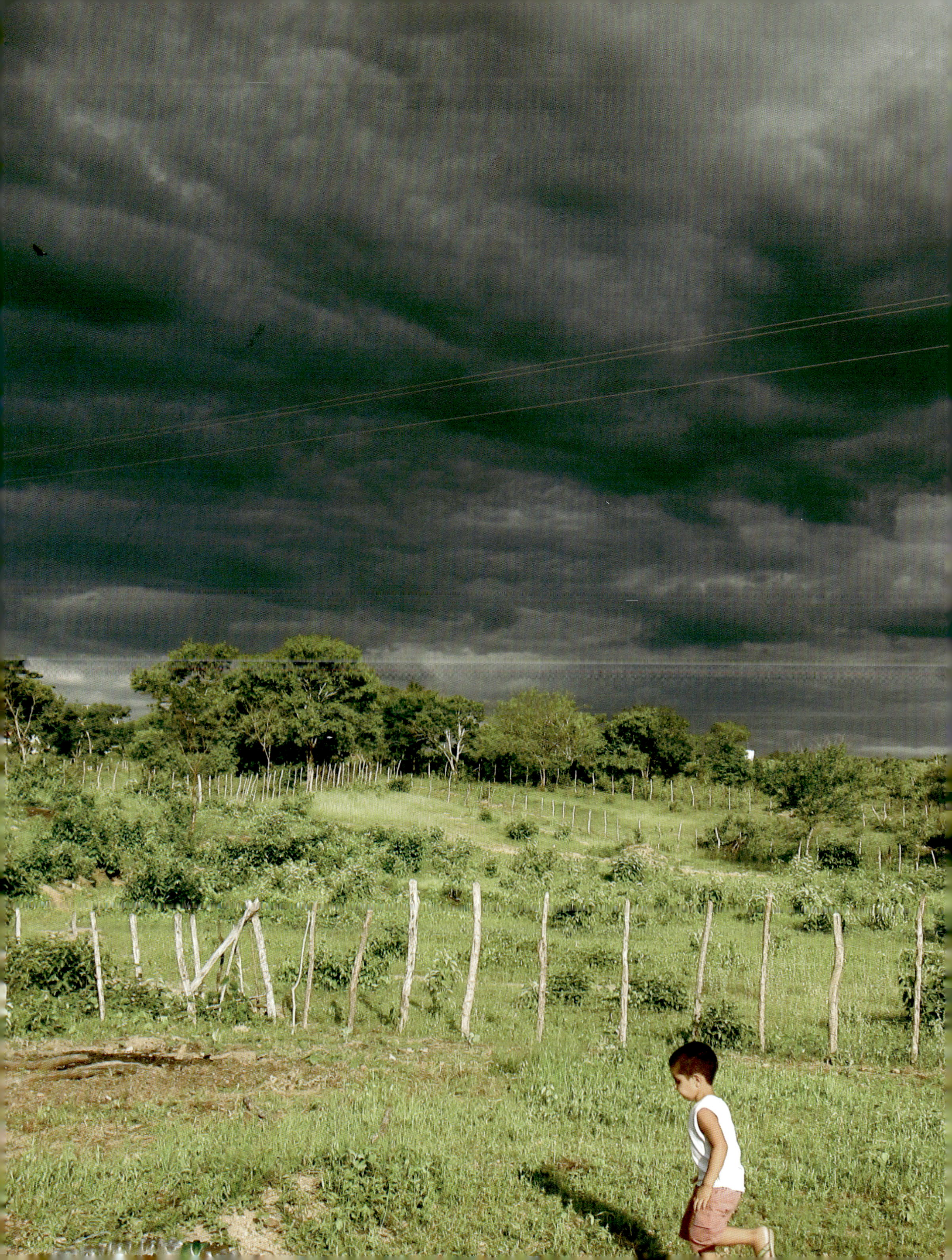

Chapter 9

Climate Change

> **GUIDING QUESTIONS**
> - What natural and anthropogenic processes influence climate change?
> - How can we sustainably address the impacts of changing climate?

Introduction to Climate Change

In Ethiopia, the people of the Gamo Highlands have been farming since agriculture was developed 10,000 years ago. Recently, however, farmers have noticed that rains are becoming unpredictable. Droughts are now occurring on a scale never seen before, causing famine in their community.[1] On the other side of the world, in Peru, people in the southern highlands of the Andes Mountains have long used traditional weather forecast methods to help decide when to plant seeds and to predict the success of a harvest. Farmers watch the nesting patterns of birds and use these observations to project rainfall for the season. For example, if a local species of bird builds their nests up high a rainy season is likely to follow, but if the nests are built low the season will be dry. In recent years, however, rains have begun to arrive early or late, frosts have been unpredictable, and the snow does not stay on the mountaintops as long as it did in the past.[2]

From Ethiopia to Peru, people all over the world are noticing changes in their local climates.

In Canada, Inuit elders of Nunavut have noticed the winds becoming stronger and erratic, the ice growing thinner where they fish for food, and the snowpack retreating earlier and earlier in the spring.[3] Meanwhile in the island nation of Kiribati in the middle of the Pacific Ocean, islanders are watching the sea level rise. Consequently, they are being forced to move their homes farther inland and build sea walls (man-made structures intended to absorb waves before they hit the shoreline) to prevent further erosion of the land. Farmers in Kiribati have seen salt water seeping up from the ground and into their wells, contaminating the fresh rainwater they rely on for drinking and growing food.[4]

Indigenous (or native) communities can often tell us a great deal about the land they live on since they have been living off that particular piece of land for hundreds, if not thousands, of years. For some, the land has become intertwined with their identity and culture. The examples above reveal how ecological knowledge—derived from thoughtful observation—may be passed down over generations in order for a community to live off the land sustainably. However, over the last few decades, these indigenous communities in Ethiopia, Peru, Canada, and Kiribati have noticed unusual changes in their natural environment.

Scientists are beginning to understand what indigenous people have been keenly aware of for decades—Earth's climate is changing.

Understanding Climate

Before we can examine why our climate is changing, we should first understand what we mean when we use the term climate. Many people think of climate and weather interchangeably. While the two are related, climate and weather are not the same thing.

Weather refers to short-term atmospheric conditions. These conditions include temperature, humidity, cloudiness, brightness, visibility, atmospheric pressure, wind, and precipitation (such as snow and rain). For example, a weather report might include a prediction of cloudy skies with a chance of rain.

Climate, on the other hand, refers to long-term prevailing atmospheric conditions. Instead of offering a daily report, climate describes the typical atmospheric conditions of a region averaged over a longer period of time, ranging from years to decades. For example, the climate of a desert might be described as generally hot and arid. To evaluate the planet's overall climate, we should consider trends in average global temperature, general wind patterns, and whether there has been an increase or decrease in the quantity and intensity of extreme weather events.

The Greenhouse Effect

Earth's climate is affected by the composition of our atmosphere, particularly the concentration of chemicals in the atmosphere known as **greenhouse gases**. Naturally occurring greenhouse gases in the atmosphere such as carbon dioxide (CO_2), methane (CH_4), and nitrous oxide (N_2O) comprise less than 1% of the atmosphere. Our atmosphere is primarily composed of two gases: nitrogen (N_2, 78%) and oxygen (O_2, 21%).[5] However, small changes in the amount of greenhouse gases in the atmosphere have a significant impact on the planet's climate.

To understand the impact of greenhouse gases, we must first understand Earth's relationship with the sun. Sunlight is a form of radiant energy. When radiation from the sun reaches Earth, it passes right through the atmosphere. Some of this energy is reflected back into space by clouds, but the majority is absorbed, warming the planet. Earth then re-emits energy back into space as infrared radiation. Here is where greenhouse gases come into play. Greenhouse gases trap some of the outgoing infrared radiation, making surface temperatures on Earth about 61°F (or 34°C) warmer than would be otherwise.[6] Just as a greenhouse allows sunlight to enter but then traps its heat to maintain a warmer temperature inside the structure, greenhouse gases help insulate our planet and make conditions on Earth suitable for life. This phenomenon is called the **greenhouse effect**. Overall temperatures on Earth rise in *correlation* with the increase of the greenhouse effect. The composition of greenhouse gases in the atmosphere can be altered by natural and *anthropogenic* (or human-made: anthropo—from human, genic—generated) activities.

The Carbon Cycle

Carbon dioxide (CO_2) is a powerful greenhouse gas and an integral part of the carbon cycle. CO_2 occurs naturally in Earth's atmosphere, cycling through Earth's systems and traveling from surface of the planet to the atmosphere and back again. For example, CO_2 is released by decaying organisms and absorbed by plants as a part of photosynthesis. Additionally, animals exhale CO_2 as a by-product of cellular respiration (the process of converting food into energy). If CO_2 is not immediately cycled into the atmosphere it may be buried in the ground or at the bottom of the ocean.[7]

Systems, such as wetlands and oceans wherein more CO_2 is absorbed than released, are referred to as **carbon sinks**. For example, a forest may absorb more CO_2 from the atmosphere than it releases since the vegetation in the forest is performing photosynthesis. However, certain events can release the carbon stored in carbon sinks back into the atmosphere. A forest fire will release the CO_2 stored in the forest's vegetation and soil, turning what once was a carbon sink into a **carbon source**.[8]

In addition to natural carbon sources, CO_2 is released into the atmosphere as the result of anthropogenic activities like burning wood and **fossil fuels** (coal, natural gas, and petroleum).[9] Fossil fuels are formed over millions of years by the natural decomposition and compression of

A greenhouse is able to trap heat from the sun, keeping the structure warmer. Likewise, greenhouse gases are able to trap heat from the sun, keeping Earth warmer.

Forest fires release carbon stored in the trees and soil back into the atmosphere.

ancient organisms buried beneath the ground, occurring over millions of years. People typically burn wood and fossil fuels for energy, a process resulting in a carbon source.[10]

Human activities may also transform carbon sinks into carbon sources. Humans cause forest fires, cut down trees for timber, and till soil for farming. All of these processes release CO_2 into the atmosphere.[11] To limit anthropogenic carbon emissions, we can work to prevent widespread deforestation and promote sustainable forestry practices to protect the long-term health of forest ecosystems and their role as carbon sinks. Carbon captured in soils can be protected through soil conservation efforts, such as new agricultural methods that do not rely as heavily on tilling the soil in order to plant crops.[12] To protect land from development, land trusts may be established where a piece of land is purchased with the purpose of preserving it. When land is developed, careful planning of where new buildings, roads, and cities will be built can help protect carbon sinks.

It is important to remember that CO_2 is an essential part of the carbon cycle and is utilized by plants during photosynthesis, which, in turn, produces the oxygen that we breathe.

However, the balance of this natural system has been disrupted by the rapid production of large amounts of CO_2 by human societies.

Beyond Carbon Dioxide

Scientists who study climate change often focus on carbon dioxide to a greater degree than other greenhouse gases. After all, CO_2 accounts for 78% of global greenhouse gas emissions from human activities.[13] Plus CO_2 remains in the atmosphere for a long time—up to 200 years![14] Other greenhouse gases tend to have a much shorter lifetime in the atmosphere, but they too contribute to the greenhouse effect.

Two other greenhouse gases that are commonly produced by human activities are nitrous oxide (N_2O) and methane (CH_4). N_2O is emitted along with CO_2 in the combustion of fossil fuels, mainly from motor vehicles. It is also a by-product of the industrial production of agricultural fertilizers and is released into the air when those fertilizers are applied to soils.[15] CH_4 is the main component of natural gas. The primary source of CH_4 emissions from human activities is livestock production, where CH_4 is released as a by-product of the digestive processes of animals like cows, sheep, and goats and in the storage of animal manure. CH_4 is also released into the atmosphere through the extraction of fossil fuels and as a by-product of the decomposition of organic waste, such as in landfills.[16]

Water vapor is another abundant greenhouse gas—able to absorb and re-emit infrared radiation. Water vapor may seem harmless, but it can further intensify the greenhouse effect. As Earth's temperatures rise as a result of increasing levels of other greenhouse gases, a greater amount of water evaporates from oceans, rivers, and lakes. This additional water vapor in the atmosphere in turn enhances the greenhouse effect and further raises temperatures.[17]

Along with increasing emissions of naturally occurring greenhouse gases, humans have also invented a handful of chemical compounds proven to act as greenhouse gases. Scientists inadvertently developed new greenhouse gases when inventing chemicals to be used in air conditioners, fire extinguishers, and refrigerants. Some of these man-made substances include chlorofluorocarbons (CFCs), hydrofluorocarbons (HFCs), perfluorocarbons (PFCs), and sulfur hexafluoride (SF_6). In the late 1970s, it was discovered that many of these substances are also responsible for the development of holes in the planet's ozone layer.[18]

What Is Climate Change?

Climate change refers to a significant shift in Earth's overall climate over an extended period of time. Today we are experiencing a long-term trend of rising global temperatures, one form of climate change. As we will discuss in more detail later, there is scientific consensus that Earth's average temperature has been rising steadily since the late 19th century.

A variety of natural processes may affect our climate, including the natural change in the Earth's tilt and orbit over time, the intensity of the sun, oceanic currents, plate tectonics, and volcanic eruptions. The climate change we are experiencing today is linked to increases of anthropogenic greenhouse gas emissions.

An increase in Earth's average temperature has varied and complex consequences. Different locations around the planet are affected in different ways by today's changing climate. Some regions may experience drought and extreme heat while others may experience flooding. Coastal regions may be impacted more dramatically than inland regions. Polar regions (North Pole and South Pole) will likely be impacted more severely than regions closer to the equator. This variation is due to alterations in wind patterns and ocean circulation.

Volcanic eruptions release large amounts of water vapor, carbon dioxide, and sulfur dioxide, which can alter the composition of greenhouse gases in Earth's atmosphere.

Climate change can disrupt the circulation between the warmer waters of the tropics and the frigid waters of the North Atlantic region. This disruption can cool the North Atlantic by 14 to 29°F (8 to 16°C).[19] So while average temperatures rise for the planet as a whole, some areas could experience more snow, more rain, and cooler temperatures.

It is not accurate to say that all of the changes we see in our climate today are caused by human activity. Climate change may be the result of both natural processes and human activities. However, our presence on this planet has a distinct effect on climate. As you will learn throughout this chapter, our choices related to lifestyle and consumption have an impact on Earth's atmosphere.

Climate Change and Sustainability

Climate change may alter the planet in profound ways and undermine our efforts to be environmentally, economically, and culturally sustainable. If we set aside land for the preservation of endangered species, what will it matter if that land becomes too arid for those species to thrive? If we work to preserve the language and culture of an isolated tribe, what will it matter if the land that tribe inhabits falls into the sea? If we develop our economy based on shipping routes and prevailing wind patterns, what will it matter if new shipping routes emerge as ice melts and winds change course? Climate change may force us to rethink fundamental aspects of our societies and practices in an effort to achieve global sustainability.

Environment

Climate change is not simply an atmospheric phenomenon. A changing climate has consequences for the hydrosphere (oceans and freshwater), lithosphere (land resources), and biosphere (living organisms). Shifts in climate can affect food production, water availability, biodiversity, and ecosystem resiliency. When the climate changes significantly, it affects the ability of organisms to live in an area they had adapted to and flourished in for thousands of years.

For example, sea turtles are sensitive to climate change. Climate change impacts sea turtle habitat, food sources, and nest selection. Additionally, climate change can have an effect on the ratio of male to female in the sea turtle population. Scientists have found that sea turtle eggs incubated at warmer water temperatures become females and eggs incubated at cooler temperatures become males. At the right temperature, sea turtles will lay a 1:1 ratio of males to females. As water temperatures rise as a result of climate change, the number of female sea turtles will increase while the number of males will decline. As you can imagine, a balanced ratio of male to female eggs is critical to the species' survival. Scientists are worried this trend in sea turtles' male to female ratio is unsustainable and could lead to the extinction of the species.[20]

Economy

Climate change may create a substantial economic burden for people, businesses, and communities around the world in a variety of ways. A few examples of possible economic impacts include: insurance companies that could face increased disaster claims, fishermen that might lose income as their catch disappears, and

Sea turtles are just one species vulnerable to the impacts of climate change.

winemakers at risk of crop loss due to changing temperatures.²¹

One major cost associated with climate change is relocating human communities most at risk from rising sea levels and other environmental changes. The native Alaskan village of Newtok is one community facing severe financial consequences as a result of its forced relocation. The Qaluyaarmiut people, living along the Ninglick River, have watched as the riverbanks bordering their village eroded at a rate of more than 80 feet (approximately 24 meters) a year. Climate change has been a factor in rapidly deteriorating conditions in Newtok. Sea ice, which once protected coastal villages against storm surges, has been shrinking and thinning. Increasing temperatures have caused the ground to warm, leading to thawing permafrost (rock or soil that has been continuously frozen for more than two years). When permafrost thaws, the ground underneath buildings and roads becomes unstable and methane once frozen in the ground is released.²²

In the 1990s, the Newtok Traditional Council began thinking about relocating the village's 350 inhabitants. Working with state and federal representatives, they selected a new site that would be less vulnerable to changing environmental conditions. The estimated price tag for the move is between $80 and 130 million.²³

Although climate change carries significant financial costs as well as biological and social costs, people have also begun to imagine what benefits a warmer world might bring to the global economy. Climate change has the potential to open up trade routes previously blocked by ice. For example, ice melt in the Arctic has allowed ships to navigate a shortened route from Russia to North America.²⁴ Other economic benefits may include increased tourism in regions previously too cold or inaccessible to attract visitors and new agricultural opportunities in parts of the world where the growing season was once too short. In the end, however, the benefits of climate change may be limited, when weighed against the economic consequences.

A changing climate can affect shipping routes.

Society

Just as climate change does not affect all places in the same way, climate change does not affect all people equally. Many environmental hazards, such as water pollution and drought, impact the lives of the poor to a greater degree than the wealthy. Climate change is no exception.

The world's poorest people are likely to be the ones most affected by climate change. Low-income populations often rely solely on local resources, such as water and food, that could be greatly impacted by climate change. The poor, more so than the rich, have few alternatives if these resources disappear. A study conducted by Massachusetts Institute of Technology found that crop yields in India will decline by 4.5-9% over the next 30 years.

This vulnerability is exacerbated by substandard housing, poor health, and limited access to health care—circumstances that often plague poorer communities. Because of these factors, natural disasters have a greater impact on the poor. When a hurricane swept through Honduras in 1998, poor households lost 10-15% of their assets, while the rich lost 3% of their assets.²⁵ Extreme weather events are only expected to increase in frequency with continued climate change.

Background on Climate Change

Understanding how Earth's climate has changed in the past will help us better understand the changes we are witnessing today. At various points throughout Earth's history, global climate patterns have shifted dramatically.

Past Climate Shifts

Earth's climate gradually cycles between glacial periods and interglacial periods. Glacial periods (ice ages) occur when Earth's average temperature is cooler and significant portions of the planet are covered by ice. During these periods, CO_2 levels are lower and there are greater fluctuations in climate patterns. Interglacial periods occur between glacial periods and are characterized by warmer temperatures, higher CO_2 levels, and a more stable climate.

In the past, the cycling between glacial and interglacial periods was the result of natural phenomena. Over time, the shape of Earth's orbit around the sun slowly changes, as does the tilt and direction of Earth's axis. These changes affect the amount of sunlight that reaches Earth, thereby affecting climate. Changes to the sun's intensity also affect climate; reduced intensity of sunlight has resulted in cooling on Earth.

Volcanoes emit ash particles, which can temporarily cause climate cooling by blocking sunlight from reaching Earth. In the early

CASE STUDY: Greenland Norse[26]

Around 1350, the Little Ice Age contributed to the disappearance of an entire group of people, the Greenland Norse. Between 800 and 1300 (during the Medieval Warm Period in Europe), Greenland's climate was fairly mild and it was possible to grow hay and pasture animals. Around 1100, however, average temperatures started to grow colder. The Norse—a group of Vikings from Scandinavia who settled in Greenland—failed to adapt to the colder climate.

Similar to their European ancestors, the Norse raised cows and sheep that were poorly adapted to Greenland's increasingly frigid conditions. The wood they used for fuel was in short supply. Their hunting tools and clothing reflected European influence and were not well adapted for freezing temperatures. In contrast, the Inuit people who shared the island with the Norse

Ruins left after the Norse were unable to adapt to colder, harsher conditions in Greenland during the Little Ice Age.

were able to thrive as the climate grew cooler. Inuits living in Greenland hunted whales and seals in open waters, used sealskins to build boats, built homes designed for warmth, and dressed for extremely cold weather.

With the arrival of the Little Ice Age, temperatures dropped by 7°F (or 4°C) within 80 years. The Norse did not adapt well to the cooler temperatures and were further hindered by lack of trade with Europe, soil erosion, and competition with the Inuit people. As a result, the entire Norse settlement eventually disappeared, whereas Inuit descendants continue to live in Greenland today.

days of Earth's history, carbon dioxide levels were extremely high due to widespread volcanic activity. As Earth aged and volcanic activity decreased, CO_2 levels dropped.

Reconstructing Climate History

Through a variety of methods, scientists have formed a fairly accurate reconstruction of how Earth's climate has changed over the millennia. Most of these methods are called proxy methods, since scientists are unable to go back in time and measure temperature or climate composition directly, rather they assess climate indirectly by examining evidence of the impact of climate on Earth.

Ice cores taken from ancient glaciers provide a window into Earth's climate past. Gas bubbles trapped in the ice can be analyzed to determine the exact air content at the time a bubble was formed. Ice cores from the Russian Vostok Research Station in East Antarctica have allowed scientists to determine CO_2 levels in the atmosphere over 400,000 years ago.

Cores of sediments drilled from the ocean floor also provide clues to Earth's past climate. Scientists are able to gain an idea of past temperatures and atmospheric composition from the remains of tiny organisms found in these ocean sediments, many of which only survive in a narrow temperature range.[27]

Other organisms that help us reconstruct a picture of Earth's previous climate patterns include corals, trees, and other plants. Trees and corals both gain rings or bands as they grow. A tree's rings will appear closer together when experiencing water stress. Similarly, bands in coral shells vary in thickness according to temperature and other environmental conditions.

Pollen buried in lake sediments can be used to reconstruct the natural history of an area. If pollen is discovered from plants that only survive in warm climates, a researcher can make an inference about the past climate of the area.[28]

Today we have the ability to track and analyze climate data with more sophistication than ever before. Over the past 50 years at the Mauna Loa Observatory in Hawaii, scientists have measured daily atmospheric composition and temperature variations. We can use satellite images to measure the seasonal ice cover on Earth's surface and analyze how it changes. We can also measure the rise in sea levels and the concentration of CO_2 in oceans.[29]

Cores retrieved from drilling into ice can be analyzed to determine the composition of atmospheric gases at a given point in time.

Climate Change Today

Earth's climate has experienced fluctuations in the past. However, recent warming trends are occurring at a rate that would not be expected from natural events alone. The Intergovernmental Panel on Climate Change (IPCC)—a group of thousands of scientists around the world who review and analyze climate research—has stated that the evidence suggests that this recent warming is very likely due to human activities.[30]

Evidence of a Warming World

In the last century, Earth's overall surface temperature has risen 1.3°F (0.74°C) and is continuing to warm at the rate of approximately 0.35-0.51°F (0.19-0.28°C) per decade. While a fraction of a degree does not sound like much, even small changes in Earth's climate can greatly impact environmental conditions.

Shifting weather patterns provide additional evidence that the climate is changing. Wind and precipitation patterns have changed in many regions during the past century, resulting in increased rainfall in some places and droughts in others. Ocean currents have changed as well and tropical storms have increased in frequency and intensity.

Retreating glaciers and melting polar ice are visual evidence of a warming climate. The additional volume of liquid water that results from this melting contributes to rising sea levels. Rising temperatures have an impact on sea levels as well. As a body of water heats up, it expands in volume and raises sea levels.[31]

Anthropogenic (human-made) sources of greenhouse gases, such as emissions from power plants, are contributing to climate change.

The Human Element

Scientists have observed a close correlation between fluctuations in CO_2 levels in Earth's atmosphere and fluctuations in average global temperatures over thousands of years. As you can see in the graph above, these variables tend to rise and fall together. There was a sizeable increase in CO_2 levels beginning in the mid-1700s with the start of the Industrial Revolution. As CO_2 concentrations have increased, so has the overall average temperature on Earth's surface.

The combustion (burning) of fossil fuels like coal and petroleum on a large scale releases significant amounts of CO_2 into the air. The IPCC has determined that burning fossil fuels is the main source of increased atmospheric CO_2 concentrations in the last century.[32]

The Industrial Revolution introduced factories powered by coal. Factories that produced items such as textiles and metal pots and pans burned coal to power steam engines and furnaces. Coal was also used to generate electricity and to fuel trains and ships that carried people and goods long distances.

Electricity is a major source of greenhouse gas emissions because coal is still used today to generate electricity. Coal emits more greenhouse gases for the amount of energy generated than any other fossil fuel.[33] We use electricity for all sorts of things: heating and cooling buildings, powering appliances, and creating manufactured products.

In more recent years, industrialized societies have come to rely on petroleum, rather than coal, for transportation. Transportation accounts for 24% of worldwide CO_2 emissions generated from human activities.[34] Gasoline, diesel fuel, and jet fuel—all of which are typically refined from petroleum—account for almost all the energy used for transportation.

Our Carbon Footprint

Carbon footprint is a tool used to assess how our lifestyle generates carbon dioxide emissions. When you participate in an activity or use an

Our daily activities, from our diets to our methods of transportation, can impact the climate. These choices, as a whole, are referred to as our carbon footprint.

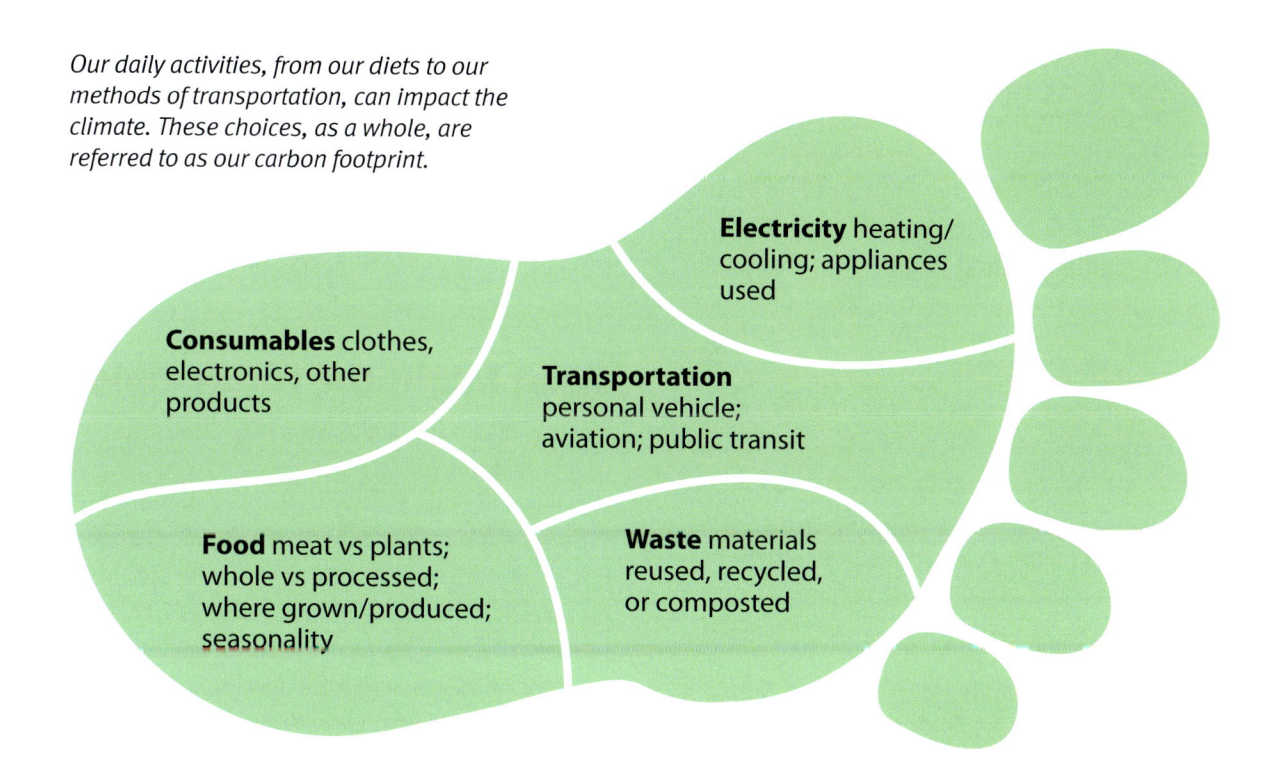

Electricity heating/cooling; appliances used

Consumables clothes, electronics, other products

Transportation personal vehicle; aviation; public transit

Food meat vs plants; whole vs processed; where grown/produced; seasonality

Waste materials reused, recycled, or composted

item that produces greenhouse gases, you leave behind a carbon footprint. This measurement tool can be used to establish a baseline for an individual's actions to help measure progress toward a reduced impact on climate. Two major components of a carbon footprint are related to energy: transportation and electricity.

Carbon footprint can also be calculated for a country or region. A country's total emissions are generally influenced by both the standard of living of its residents and the total number of people living in the country. For example, China has a relatively low per capita carbon footprint—on average, each individual contributes five metric tons of CO_2 each year. But China's large population makes the country's total CO_2 emissions the highest in the world. The United States also has a large total carbon footprint, due not to population density but rather to high per capita emissions—on average, each individual contributes nearly 20 metric tons of CO_2 per year.[35] In general, higher income countries have larger per capita carbon footprints because of their greater usage of fossil fuels.

YOUTH PROFILE

Vedika Khanna and the Cool School Challenge[36]

While a junior at the American School of Dubai, Vedika Khanna read a newspaper article about Dubai's large carbon footprint. That one article transformed her life. It inspired Vedika to change things, starting with her high school. She and other students formed a club called the Global Awareness Inner Awakening (GAIA). The group decided to participate in the Cool School Challenge in order to reduce their school's carbon footprint.

The Cool School Challenge is the brainchild of individuals and organizations in Washington State, halfway across the globe from Dubai. The purpose of the Challenge is to motivate students to lower their emissions of carbon dioxide and other greenhouse gases. Participating schools determine where they can reduce energy use and greenhouse gas emissions. Students, teachers, and administrators then work to set specific goals and implement strategies to reach those goals.

At the American School of Dubai, the first step toward a reduced carbon footprint was to audit the school to see how the building and people's behaviors linked to carbon emissions. GAIA members found that the use of electricity in classrooms and plastic water bottles were two major contributors to the school's carbon footprint. To save electricity, they spoke to teachers and students about turning off printers, computers, and projectors when not in use. GAIA members also made sure that lights were turned off in empty classrooms, especially overnight. To raise awareness among students about how many plastic water bottles they used each week, GAIA members collected and displayed the amount of bottles for one week in a big net on the basketball court. They estimated that students used 90,000 bottles each year! Their solution was to encourage students to use refillable stainless steel water bottles.

Thanks to the work of Vedika and the other GAIA club members, the American School of Dubai reduced its greenhouse gas emissions by almost 72,000 pounds in a single year. They also helped to cut the use of disposable water bottles in half. "I think the most important thing I learned from GAIA and the Cool School Challenge was that I can be a catalyst for change," said Vedika.

What Might the Future Hold?

We can take a look at climate data from the past to help us predict and prepare for what will happen with Earth's climate in the future. However, there are a number of variables and not all of them are well understood or easily predicted. Population growth rate, industrial growth, climate change legislation, technological developments, scientific developments, and Earth's orbit are just a few things that have to be considered. Changes in any of these variables can make the consequences of climate change more or less severe. For example, some climate change predictions assume that people

The American School of Dubai started an organic garden on its campus.

will continue doing what they are currently doing at the same rates. A concerted effort to decrease our impact on the climate could alter these predicted outcomes.

Climate feedback further complicates our ability to predict how the climate system will behave. Feedback refers to an output that feeds back into the system, causing further changes. For example, as surface temperatures rise, the planet's polar ice starts to melt. As the polar ice melts, it lessens the amount of reflective surface (light-colored ice) on the planet and increases the amount of absorptive surface (dark-colored sea). When solar radiation hits reflective surfaces like polar ice, much of the sun's energy reflects back into space. This phenomenon is referred to as the *albedo effect*. As Earth's reflective surfaces vanish, less heat reflects back into the atmosphere and more of the sun's energy is absorbed by the planet, causing the temperature to rise even further.[37] In this example, an effect of climate change (melting polar ice) actually leads to further warming and in turn further melting. This is known as positive feedback, meaning the result further increases the change. In negative feeback, the result decreases change. An example of negative feedback is increased photosynthesis resulting from warmer temperatures that causes plants to absorb more CO_2 from the atmosphere.

While the ice on the left side reflects heat, the darker waters on the right side absorb heat.

Changes in the Natural World

While it is difficult to design a predictive model that will accurately account for all possible contributors to climate change as well as predict how they will interact, research has led to improved climate modeling that allows us to predict future climate change to a certain extent. Here are some forecasts for global climate change predicted by the IPCC:[38]

- Surface Temperature—Average surface temperature is predicted to rise between 1.8 and 4°C by the end of the 21st century. Heat waves will become more frequent occurrences. However, temperature change will not be consistent in all places. Land masses will warm faster than oceans, and higher latitudes (those places farther from the equator) will warm faster than lower latitudes.
- Precipitation—Higher latitudes are likely to experience an increase in precipitation, while most sub-tropical land regions will experience a decrease in precipitation by as much as 20%.
- Storms—Tropical storms will become more frequent and intense with larger peak winds and more precipitation. Storm tracks will also begin to move toward the poles.
- Sea Level—The global sea level will rise between 0.59 and 1.9 feet (0.18 and 0.59 meters) by 2100.
- Ocean Chemistry—Since the Industrial Revolution, the oceans have experienced increased *acidification*. This trend will continue and is directly attributable to human-generated CO_2 emissions.

Changes within Human Communities

While humans have proven to be a resilient species, we are not immune to the impacts of climate change. Climate change may force us to change the way we live, impacting our health, subsistence, and livelihoods, and leave us vulnerable to serious health risks.

- Health Challenges—According to the IPCC, climate change is already contributing to the spread of diseases and early deaths, especially in low-income countries. The World Health Organization has determined that 150,000 deaths a year can be attributed to climate change.[39] As the climate warms, disease vectors (insects and other things that carry disease) like mosquitoes and ticks expand into areas where the population lacks immunity. Without the infrastructure to provide vaccinations and preventive treatment, people in developing countries will be at greater risk of climate-related deaths.[40] Heat-related deaths in countries without widespread access to air conditioning could rise as well.
- Food and Water Availability—Hazardous weather events such as drought or flooding have the potential to decrease the availability of food and fresh water. In addition, as temperatures rise it will become more difficult for farmers to produce crops in already arid regions. They will need to use more water than they did before. This may disproportionately affect countries located in sub-Saharan Africa, where water availability and agricultural output are already a concern. Rapid population growth coupled with increasing urbanization and economic development magnify water stress in this region.
- Migration—In 1990, the IPCC predicted that the greatest impact of climate change would be on human migration. Many people

CASE STUDY: Rising Waters in Tuvalu[41]

Tuvalu is disappearing. The Pacific island nation, located approximately halfway between Australia and Hawaii, is drowning due to sea level rise. Tuvalu consists of nine islands. None of the islands reach higher than ten feet (three meters) above sea level. Because they are so low, even small rises in sea level have a profound effect on the islands.

The visible disappearance of land mass is not the only problem caused by rising sea levels. Even before the islands are completely submerged, the 11,000 inhabitants of Tuvalu will be forced to migrate when salt water from the ocean below seeps through the islands' core and contaminates the people's drinking water and cropland.

Tuvalu is a low-lying Pacific island left vulnerable to the impacts of climate change.

Other impacts of climate change create further challenges for the people of Tuvalu. The coral reefs that surround Tuvalu have provided the islanders with food, medicine, and protection from waves for as long as they can remember. However, corals are sensitive to fluctuations in water temperature and ocean chemistry. As the oceans become more acidic as a result of excess carbon dioxide, corals die. In turn, the fish that thrive in coral reefs are decimated. Fish are a major food resource for islanders.

may be displaced from their homes due to coastal erosion, flooding, and agricultural disruption. It is estimated that by 2050, 200 million people will be forced to move because of climate change.[42]

Pathways to Progress: Climate Change

The impacts of climate change will affect us all, but we don't have to just stand by and watch; we can all contribute to climate solutions. Think about one way that your lifestyle contributes to greenhouse gas emissions. How could you make a change to reduce your carbon footprint?

To *mitigate,* or lessen, the severity of climate change, individuals and governments all over the world are already working on a wide variety of solutions. From changing our daily habits to protecting carbon sinks—efforts large and small can add up.

Because CO_2 remains in the atmosphere for decades, if not longer,[43] solutions to climate change will not instantaneously lower the concentration of CO_2 in the atmosphere. It is especially important to think of climate solutions in the long term as well as solutions that will help us adapt to a changing climate.

Changing Behaviors, Reducing Emissions

Electricity use and transportation choices are two major ways humans contribute to climate change. If you're looking for ways to reduce your carbon footprint, why not start there?

Energy efficiency and conservation is one of the easiest yet most effective ways to decrease your carbon footprint. Efficiency means getting more out of something. For example, energy-efficient light bulbs do the same work as other bulbs while using less electricity. Conservation means using less of something. By unplugging electronics when you are not using them or powering down your computer at night, you can conserve electricity.

In order to reduce emissions associated with your transportation choices, you can carpool, bike, ride public transit, choose a more fuel-efficient car, or even use alternative fuels like biodiesel. When you travel using fossil fuels,

Bike share program in Hangzhou, China helps reduce the combustion of fossil fuel from cars and trucks by offering an alternative mode of transportation.

you could make an effort to offset the impact by planting trees, protecting wetlands, or reducing your carbon footprint elsewhere in exchange.

Governments and Climate Change Policy

Governments can influence behavior through laws, taxes, and benefits. Policymakers have the opportunity to levy taxes on pollution, remove fossil fuel subsidies, add renewable fuel subsidies, and implement international agreements as ways to address climate change. The most famous international effort to address global climate change began with the formation of the United Nations Framework Convention on Climate Change (UNFCCC) in 1992. In 1997, parties to the UNFCCC adopted the Kyoto Protocol, the first formal agreement for industrialized countries to begin reductions in greenhouse gas emissions. The Protocol calls for a reduction in greenhouse gas emissions to at least 5.2% below 1990 levels, to be completed between 2008 and 2012.

The Kyoto Protocol outlines a number of ways nations can cut greenhouse gas emissions. Some of these include:[44]

- Increase energy efficiency to get more energy from less fuel
- Preserve and enhance carbon sinks like oceans and forests

CAREER PROFILE: Low Carbon Business Developer

People working in low carbon business development operate under the belief that using low carbon emitting technologies to develop and grow businesses will not only stimulate the economy in such a way to slow climate change, but will also have a positive impact on human society, now and for future generations. People who work in business development are responsible for cutting-edge concepts to market businesses or develop new products. They love networking, are savvy in business operations, and use science to weigh the environmental costs and benefits of a certain development approach.

Richie Ahuja is the Regional Director in Asia for the Environmental Defense Fund's Climate and Air Program. He works with civil society, businesses, leaders, and governments to creatively address climate change in rapidly developing economies in Asia. Richie began working on environmental issues in high school and he went on to earn an MBA. Now he combines his interest in the environment with his skills in business to help climate-friendly businesses develop in Asia. According to Richie, "Asia is densely populated, with high levels of poverty, and is one of the fastest growing economic regions globally. This means that as the region grows it can either develop in ways that contribute to and increase the climate change problem, or it can follow a smart climate-friendly development path that is different, innovative, and in the process [become] a part of the solution to the climate change problem."

Through his work, Richie has been involved in a wide variety of approaches to mitigating climate change. In the course of one educational project, Richie helped produce a Hindi movie called *Aarohan* (meaning "new beginning" in Hindi). The film is designed to engage and educate rural Indian leaders about the effects of climate change. It has been shown in more than 400 villages in India. When reflecting on his career, Richie states, "This is a great field to get into. It's very fulfilling. There's nothing better than getting up in the morning to work with smart people interested in finding solutions to some of the world's most pressing problems."

Richie Ahuja

- Promote sustainable forestry to harvest trees in such a way that forests continue to thrive
- Promote sustainable agriculture to reduce soil tillage and water use
- Develop renewable energy sources such as solar, wind, and geothermal power
- Reduce subsidies for greenhouse gas-emitting activities to make it less economically advantageous to pollute
- Limit greenhouse gas emissions from cars, airplanes, and other means of transportation

The United States, one of the world's primary greenhouse gas emitters, did not sign the Kyoto Protocol. This has frustrated many people. However, the Kyoto Protocol did have an impact in the United States by inspiring a number of local government officials to take action. In 2005, the mayor of Seattle, Washington launched the U.S. Conference of Mayors Climate Protection Agreement. Over 500 hundred mayors in North America joined him in pledging to meet Kyoto targets for greenhouse gas emissions in their own communities.

The Kyoto Protocol represents an important first step in international climate policy. In December 2011 at the UNFCCC meeting in Durban, South Africa, many of the parties expressed intent to extend the Protocol until 2017 to ensure continued emissions reductions of 25-40% by 2020.[45] Additionally, an agreement was made among the parties to the UNFCCC to launch a negotiation process for a new agreement that would be applicable to both developed and developing countries. Their goal is to implement the agreement, known as the Durban Platform for Enhanced Action, by 2020.[46]

Jonathan Pershing is a member of the United States delegation to UNFCCC meetings.

Green roofs are able to absorb CO_2 and reduce storm-water runoff.

Technology and Industry

While individuals and governments can play a large part in mitigating climate change, businesses and industry can also be a driving force behind climate change solutions.

Some businesses are already working to reduce their greenhouse gas emissions. This is largely due to consumer demand. When people start to ask businesses about their environmental practices, this creates an incentive for businesses to make choices that benefit the environment. Some companies may pursue greenhouse gas reductions to gain public favor with customers who care about climate change. Other companies may reduce energy use to save money. For some, like the outdoor clothing company Patagonia, sustainability is part of their identity.

Technological Innovation

You read about technology that fuels climate change, such as engines powered by fossil fuels. Do you think that technology can also help counteract negative human impacts on the environment? Sustainable energy sources like solar, wind, or water can help reduce dependence on fossil fuels. Many high-tech solutions have been proposed that might help prevent climate change—for example, an artificial volcano that would release sulfur dioxide to temporarily shade Earth from sunlight.[47] However, people are also exploring low-tech solutions that anyone can do, such as planting trees and weatherproofing doors and windows. Did you know that a compact fluorescent light bulb uses 60-80% less energy than a standard incandescent light bulb or halogen light bulb? Think about how much energy you could save by switching to compact fluorescent light bulbs!

WHAT YOU CAN DO — Climate Change

You can probably think of a thousand ways that our daily lives impact climate change. There are just as many ways to reduce or offset our impact. Here are a few ideas. What others can you think of?

- **Conserve forests:** Eat meat raised in a sustainable manner rather than beef grazed on former tropical rainforests.
- **Keep your cool:** Reduce home energy costs through measures such as fans, thicker curtains, improving insulation, and weatherizing your doors and windows. Or simply lower your thermostat a couple of degrees. You'll barely notice the difference.
- **Ditch the car:** When you are not going far, think of low-carbon ways to get there.
- **Recruit others:** Reducing energy costs at home and at school saves money. Educate family, friends, and teachers about this win-win solution.
- **Keep it green:** Remember that plants act as carbon sinks, so get out there and plant some trees! Trees also provide a shady place for humans and animals to hang out.

Planting a tree will help create a carbon sink.

- **Reduce, Reuse, Recycle:** Reduce the resources used to make new things by buying only what you need and reusing and keeping items longer; when it's time to discard something, recycle it.
- **Offset:** If you have to travel far, think of ways that you can offset your carbon emissions, perhaps by helping to protect forest lands or reducing your daily carbon emissions.

POINT | **COUNTERPOINT**

Should developed nations be obligated to reduce their greenhouse gas emissions more than developing nations?

Under the Kyoto Protocol, only industrialized countries and countries in transition toward a market economy (often referred to as developed) are obligated to reduce their greenhouse gas emissions. The Protocol does not include obligations for developing nations. What are the reasons behind this differential treatment? At the time the Protocol was adopted, per capita emissions of developed nations were, on average, 10 times greater than those of developing countries.[48] Many people felt that developed countries should take the lead in tackling climate change out of equitable consideration. This concept is often referred to as "common but differentiated responsibilities"—meaning those who have emitted the most greenhouse gases should feel more obligated to reduce their emissions than others. Developing nations, for the most part, have only recently begun to industrialize and are still working to reach developed status. They have contributed relatively little to climate change thus far. Consider the following perspectives in this debate.

POINT
Yes

- Since the Industrial Revolution began in the mid-1700s, the United States and the European Union have produced the most greenhouse gas emissions by far, with a combined 55% of total historical emissions.[49] Rich countries are responsible for two-thirds of total global emissions since 1850.[50]

- **In 2005, Bolivia emitted 61.8 million metric tons of CO_2.** That seems like a lot, right? Not in comparison with the United States' 6,914.2 million metric tons of CO_2. That is 100 times the amount emitted by Bolivia. Some small developing countries, like Kiribati and Tuvalu, emit below 1 metric ton of CO_2 annually.[51]

- **Developed countries earned their developed status through industrialization.** Historically, industrialization has required the burning of fossil fuels to power large-scale machines and to transport goods. It's convenient for developed countries to say that everyone must now limit their greenhouse gas emissions; they themselves have already industrialized and are able to swiftly transition to clean energy sources due to the wealth and resources they've accumulated through development. This is unfair to developing nations.

COUNTERPOINT
No

- Countries developing today have options that did not exist in the past; they can use green technologies to industrialize and develop their economies without burning large amounts of fossil fuels. To truly tackle climate change, we must rethink our current measures of progress and adjust the pathways to development.

- **It is projected that by 2015 overall emissions from developing nations will surpass overall emissions from developed nations.** This is largely due to China, which is still considered to be a developing nation. When we look at trends in current annual greenhouse gas emissions, China has surpassed the United States as the number one emitter of greenhouse gases. China emits more than the United States and Canada combined, up by 171% since the year 2000. As of 2011, another developing country, India, has taken third place (behind China and the United States) in overall emissions.[52]

- **When we look at the intensity of emissions in a country, developing nations are at the top of the list—specifically, the Central African Republic and the Democratic Republic of the Congo.**[53] These nations may not be emitting as much as the United States in total, but they are ahead of developed nations in terms of how much they emit in comparison to their economic activity. Increased carbon emissions without any connection to economic progress and development should not go unregulated.

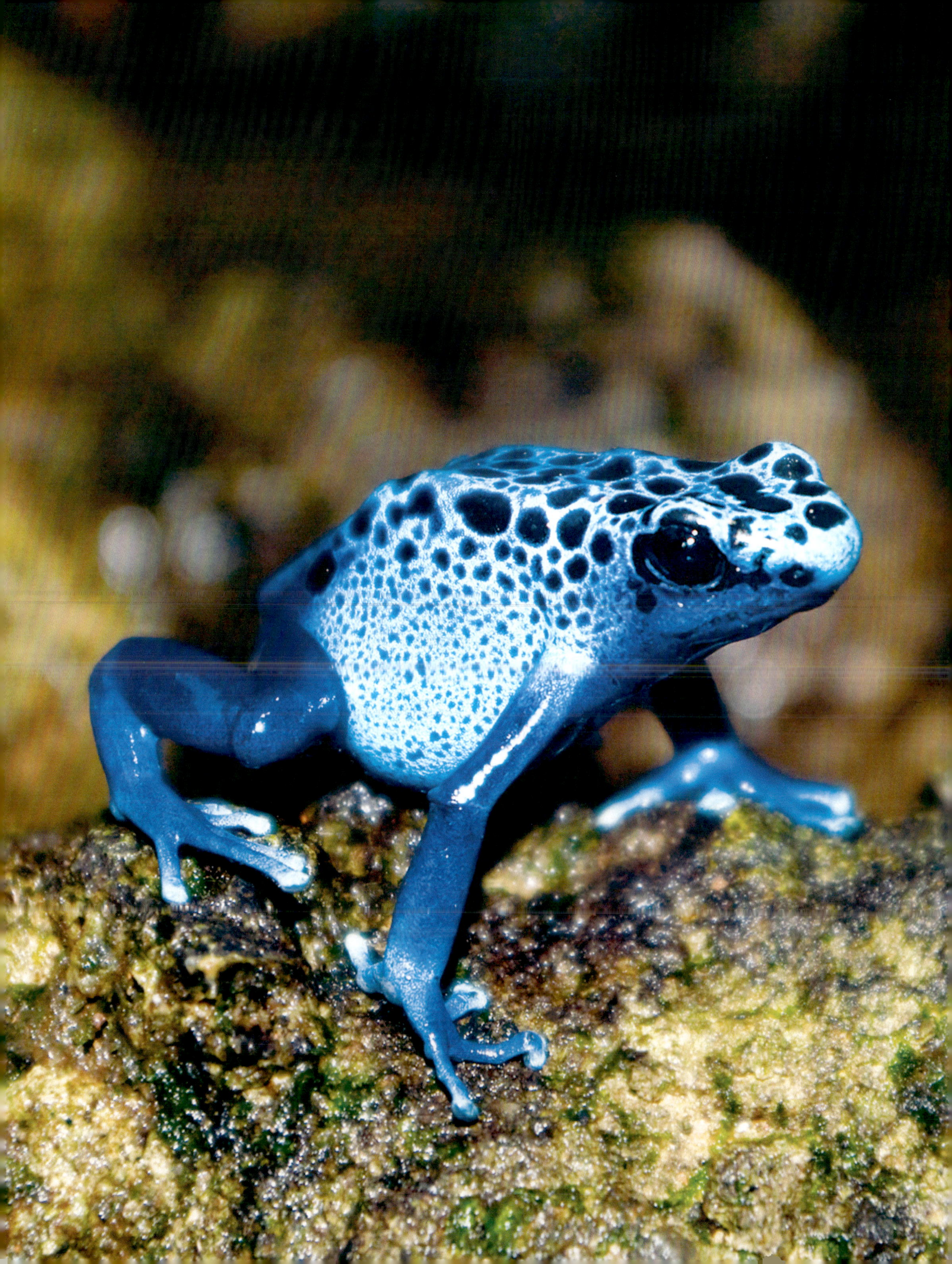

Chapter 10
Biodiversity

> **GUIDING QUESTIONS**
> - What are the benefits of biodiversity?
> - How do humans affect other species in positive and negative ways?

Introduction to Biodiversity

For billions of years, life was simple. Life on Earth consisted of single-celled aquatic organisms. But in the last few hundred million years, life has grown more complex and diverse. This change in biology over time is referred to as **evolution**. Natural selection and genetic mutation have supported evolution in the creation of millions of unique organisms adapted to different environments.[1]

Over 240 million years ago, Earth's continents split and drifted apart.[2] Within continents, geographic barriers like mountain ranges and rivers further separated populations of species. As a result, species on each continent and in geographically isolated areas continued to evolve separately as they adapted to their unique surroundings.

Estimates for the total number of species on Earth range from 2 million to 100 million.[3] A quarter of all known amphibians were only discovered in the last decade and nearly 17,000 new species of plants and animals were discovered in 2006 alone.[4]

Classifying the Diversity

To better study the millions of unique organisms on Earth, the Linnaean system was developed in the 1730s, classifying all organisms into five kingdoms: Monera (prokaryotes, including bacteria), Protista (single-celled eukaryotes, including algae), Fungi, Plant, and Animal.[5] Within these kingdoms there are several subcategories including phyla, classes, orders, families, and genera. Organisms are defined most narrowly by their species, determined by the organisms' ability to reproduce fertile offspring with one another.[6]

The Linnaean system is still in use, though several other systems of classification have since been developed and these are continually being revised to reflect the best scientific knowledge of the time. Today, most scientists have moved toward a three kingdom approach (now referred to as domains) put forward by Carl Woese in 1990. The three domains are Bacteria, Archaea (prokaryotes that are not bacteria), and Eucarya (including plants, animals, and fungi).[7]

Measuring the Variety

Earth's variety of life is known as biological diversity, or **biodiversity**. The more variety of life within a given area, the higher the biodiversity. As you will see in this chapter, biodiversity is important for the planet as well as the continued sustainability of our own species. Scientists study biodiversity at three different levels: species diversity, ecosystem diversity, and genetic diversity. Each of these levels reveals the health of our planet in different ways.

Ecosystems

Ecosystems are composed of a community of organisms and the physical environment they inhabit. They are distinguishable by the types of species, physical characteristics present, and how these elements interact. *Ecosystem diversity* refers to the variety of ecosystem types found within a given region. For example, the San Francisco Bay Delta contains woodland, grassland, wetland, river, ocean, and coastal dune ecosystems—giving it a high level of ecosystem diversity.[8]

Species

Species diversity typically refers to the number and relative abundance of different species found within an area. Species diversity is what most people think of when they talk about biodiversity. High species diversity exists when there are a large number of species in a given area—for example, a pond that contains many different types of fish, frogs, turtles, and algae. Tropical ecosystems are home to 50-90% of plant and

The more variety of life in an area, the higher the biodiversity.

animal species—containing higher species diversity than temperate or boreal ecosystems.[9]

Genetics

Genetic diversity exists where there are a variety of genetic traits within a single species or population. A single species has high genetic diversity when individuals within the species have a wide range of genes. As a result, individuals may look or behave quite differently from one another. A species with high genetic diversity is generally more resilient, or able to withstand change. For example, if a virus attacks a species of apple tree that has significant genetic variation, it is more likely that some of the trees will possess traits that enable them to survive the virus and pass on their genes to offspring. Conversely, if the apple species has little variation, there is a greater risk that most of the trees will be vulnerable to the virus, making the species' chance of survival much slimmer.

Biodiversity and Sustainability

Biodiversity is a key component of building a sustainable future. Every day, humans benefit in various ways from the presence of other species on Earth.

Environment

In general, the less diverse an ecosystem, the more vulnerable it is to changing conditions. If each species in a food web is directly connected to just one other species, the entire ecosystem is left vulnerable to changes that threaten any one species. In contrast, biodiversity makes food webs more robust. For example, in an ecosystem where coyotes eat rabbits, if rabbits disappeared from the food web, coyotes would need a different food source. In a diverse ecosystem, coyotes could survive by switching their diet to prairie dogs or mice. In a less diverse system where alternate prey is lacking, the disappearance of rabbits would cause the coyote population to die out as well.

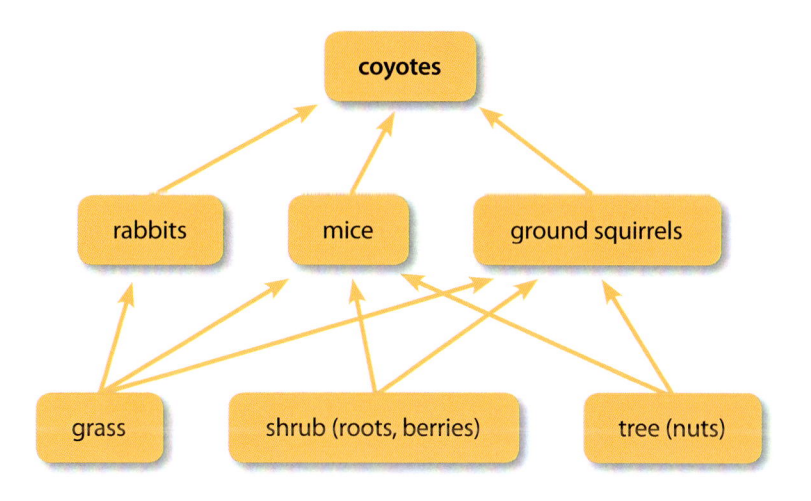

Some species are particularly key to the support of an ecosystem. Known as **keystone species**, these organisms have a disproportionate impact on their ecosystem as compared with other species. Several species of salmon can be considered keystone species in the northern Pacific Ocean. Salmon, including their carcasses and eggs, provide food for a variety of fish, birds, and mammals (bears, for example). They are also the lifeblood of a fishing industry that stretches from Japan to Canada.[10]

Society

Diverse ecosystems are not just beneficial to the species that live in them; they can also contribute to human health and well-being. Ecosystems provide services such as food, fuel, pharmaceuticals (penicillin, for example), air and water purification, pollination, recreational opportunities, and many more things we often take for granted.[11] If the balance of an ecosystem is disturbed, one or more of these **ecosystem services** could be affected.

Additionally, maintaining the biodiversity of a region is often an important part of sustaining native cultures and societies. Indigenous peoples who depend on natural resources are threatened when these resources are overexploited. Deforestation is destroying large sections of rain forest across the globe. Every clear-cut forest endangers and even extinguishes multiple species, some of which may not yet have been discovered.[12] For the indigenous peoples who call these rain forests home and who depend on the rain forest ecosystem to support activities such as hunting, gathering, and the low-impact harvesting of forest products, the consequences can be equally devastating. For generations, the forest has provided the means for these indigenous communities to support themselves; without it, these groups risk not only displacement and poverty, but also the disappearance of their traditional way of life and with it their cultural identity.

Economy

While human communities and economies reap the benefits of ecosystem services, we do not pay for them. These services are generally externalities that are not accounted for when setting prices for goods. If the cost of environmental goods and services were accurately valued, we would pay much higher prices for commodities derived from them and the incentives toward particular economic activities would shift. There have been efforts to place a price tag on ecosystem services. One 1997 estimate found the ecosystem services of the entire planet to be worth somewhere between $16 and $54 trillion per year.[13] For perspective, in 1997, the gross world product was roughly $18 trillion.

Diverse ecosystems also provide direct economic benefits. Areas with high biodiversity tend to experience more tourism. A case study at Skomer Nature Reserve in Wales shows how biodiversity can economically benefit a community in the form of increased tourism revenue. The reserve draws visitors due to its abundance of bird and marine life. These tourists spend money locally during their visit, both on activities related to the marine environment such as

CASE STUDY: People of the Cedar

Western red cedar *(Thuja plicata)* can be considered a "cultural keystone species" for the First Nations peoples of British Columbia, Canada's westernmost province. The tree is a fundamental part of the identity of these groups, who are known as People of the Cedar. They prize red cedar for its value as a building material; it is especially useful for making dugout canoes. The tree also has cultural significance for these First Nations peoples. They regard red cedar as sacred and it has a prominent role in origin stories about where their ancestors came from. Timber companies have harvested much of the cedar in British Columbia, but the People of the Cedar are working to protect cedar forests within their territories.[14]

The Western red cedar is important to the First Nations peoples of British Columbia, Canada.

Visitors are drawn to Skomer Island Nature Preserve for the biodiversity. In turn, this tourism supports the local economy as well.

diving and bird watching, and at local businesses such as hotels, restaurants, and shops.[15]

Similarly, the consequences of biodiversity loss also extend beyond the affected geographical area. Declining fish populations, for example, affect those who make their living from fishing, the communities that support the fishing trade, companies that distribute fish, and families who depend on fish as their primary source of protein.

Background on Biodiversity

As life has evolved into millions of unique species of organisms, some species have disappeared. Scientists believe that approximately one to five species will become extinct each year based on natural selection and predictable fluctuations in a species' environment—this number is considered the natural *background extinction rate*.[16] Scientists also theorize that there have been major extinction events throughout Earth's history that killed off a significant amount of life on Earth.

Mass Extinctions of the Past

Scientists estimate that there have been five major extinction events in Earth's history, each of which eliminated at least half of all species on the planet at the time.[17] These mass extinctions have been attributed to events such as meteor strikes, volcanic eruptions, and natural changes to Earth's climate and sea level.

The Ordovician-Silurian mass extinction occurred 443 million years ago when most living organisms still occupied the oceans. The event was blamed on an ice age and the resulting formation of a huge ice sheet that significantly lowered the sea level and altered the oceans' chemistry. Scientists estimate that 83% of all sea life was killed off.

The Cretaceous-Tertiary mass extinction is the best known. It occurred only 65 million years ago and resulted in the death of the dinosaurs. Scientists theorize that a meteor or comet struck Earth off the coast of Mexico, killing a majority of life (although many species may have already been in decline due to volcanic activity in India and tectonic shifts).[18]

The Current Mass Extinction

Today, many scientists suggest that we are nearing a sixth major extinction event brought on by human activities. Thousands of species around the world are endangered—at risk of extinction within the foreseeable future throughout all or a significant portion of their range. Each of these **endangered species** is part of an ecosystem and has a role in the delicate and complex balance of life that makes ecosystems work.

Ecosystems, when functioning well, rely on the complex interaction of many different species. It's true that ecosystems are always in flux and that dramatic long-term change is part of the natural progression, but rapid loss of species, genetic, and ecosystem diversity puts whole ecosystems at risk and undermines the natural checks and balances that make them sustainable. As more species come under threat, we risk major shifts in the functioning of ecosystems that will affect the entire planet.

E.O. Wilson, a biologist at Harvard University and a world-renowned expert on biodiversity, estimates that the current rate of extinction may be as high as 1,000 times the background rate and could reach 10,000 times the background rate in the next 20 years.[19]

Although it is clear that human activity plays a role in species extinction today, several factors make it difficult to estimate our full impact on the extinction rate. First of all, as we learned earlier in the chapter, no one really knows how many species there are on Earth and many may be lost before they are ever identified by science. For those species that are known, scientists are reluctant to declare a species extinct even when it hasn't been seen for several years because of the possibility that a very small population of the species survives and simply hasn't been spotted. For example, the ivory-billed woodpecker, last sighted in 1944, was long thought to be extinct. A reported sighting in 2004 gave people hope that the species had survived, but the sighting could not be confirmed. It remains unclear whether any members of the species are alive, but if so their numbers are miniscule at best.

Biodiversity Today

Today, there are five major threats to the survival of a species: invasive species; habitat loss and fragmentation; pollution; climate change; and exploitation and overconsumption. Species extinction, in turn, threatens the ecosystem, species, and genetic diversity that is necessary for our planet's long-term sustainability.

Invasive Species

As humans gained the ability to travel around the world, they began crossing oceans to reach new continents. These globetrotters brought things from home with them—animals intentionally taken for companionship, work, and food, and unintentional stowaways like rats, mice, and insects. Similarly, early travelers brought plants to provide food and decor in their new homes, but they also transported seeds stuck to clothing, packing materials, or even animal feed.

When a nonnative plant or animal is introduced into an established ecosystem, one of two things happens. The conditions may be completely unsuited for the newcomer to survive, in which case it will likely die and pose no problem. The other possibility is that the intruder thrives—so much so that it threatens native species. This is typically due to an absence of the intruder's natural predators in the new environment. These nonnative species may breed and spread quickly, outcompeting and threatening native species that occupy a similar ecological niche, or they may prey on native species populations that have not evolved any protections against the invader.

> *Thousands of species around the world are endangered—at risk of extinction within the foreseeable future.*

CASE STUDY: Biocontrol of Tamarisks[20]

The tamarisk tree, also known as saltcedar, is native to Eurasia. Tamarisks were introduced into the United States in the 19th century as method of erosion control along stream banks. There were no natural enemies to the tamarisk in its new environment and it thrived, spreading all over the West. Tamarisks displace native species, change the salinity (saltiness) of the soil, and suck up groundwater. Because of the harm the exotic tree has caused native species and riparian ecosystems in the western United States, it is considered an invasive species.

Getting rid of the tamarisks has proven problematic. You could try to burn the trees—tamarisks burn easily, even when they are green—but they re-seed swiftly after a fire. You could cut them, but that won't keep them from growing back from their roots. Herbicides (that is, chemicals designed to kill certain plants) might be an option, if care is taken not to kill other plants.

In 2001, the U.S. Department of Agriculture (USDA) approved the use of the tamarisk leaf beetle, a natural enemy from the tree's native territory, to help control the tamarisk population in the Colorado river basin. The beetles attack tamarisk trees by eating their leaves repeatedly. This defoliation prevents the plant from performing photosynthesis; the tree eventually dies, typically after three to five years.

A tamarisk (saltcedar) tree near Santa Ana Pueblo, New Mexico is partially defoliated due to the introduction of tamarisk beetles.

Before the USDA approved the beetles' release, they conducted extensive research on the beetles' behavior toward native plants. When the beetles were found to prefer tamarisks to all native plants (to the extent that they would starve to death rather than eat anything else), USDA researchers felt confident enough to release their new weapon. It took a few years for the beetle to adjust to its new environment but eventually it adapted and began defoliating miles of tamarisks all along the Colorado River basin.[21] The approach of using one species to keep the population of another in check is known as *biocontrol*.

Invasive species are more than just an annoyance to homeowners and land stewards. They are costly, both in terms of environmental impacts and economic losses. Invasive species alter natural food webs, decrease biodiversity, and alter ecosystem conditions. Researchers have put some numbers together to estimate the amount of money lost to invasive species each year.

- One single invasive species, the golden apple snail, is responsible for $1.4 trillion of lost revenue worldwide. The snail devours rice crops throughout Asia, where it has no natural predators.[22]
- Invasives result in a loss of $12 billion to Africa's eight major crops. One example is the plant witchweed, which destroys maize and sorghum crops.[23]
- Alien arthropods (insects and their relatives) cause damages totaling $3.7 billion in Europe.[24] One culprit is the citrus longhorn beetle, native to East Asia but now found in

Italy and France, where it kills shrubs and trees, especially citrus fruit trees.[25]
- Invasive species in the United States collectively result in $120 billion in losses. Invasives range from forest pests to fish introduced to freshwater habitats.[26]

Habitat Loss and Fragmentation

Our need for food, housing, and goods leads us to consume land and natural resources. A growing global population and rising levels of consumption require more and more land. People who settle an area typically change the native landscape to plant crops, build houses and factories, and construct roads for access. When we clear the land for our own use, we may destroy other species' habitats.

It's not just the total amount of land developed for human use that's significant. How developed land is spread out plays a part, too. The patterns of our land use can result in habitat fragmentation. Think about how a field would look from an aerial view if you put a road in the

CASE STUDY: Clearing Rain Forests to Raise Cattle[27]

In the Brazilian Amazon, an area the size of France has been cleared for cattle ranching. Ranching is the biggest contributor to deforestation in the region. Over the past 20 years, what used to be a small industry has catapulted into a big threat to rain forest lands. However, awareness about the problem is also growing.

In June 2009, a Greenpeace report titled "Slaughtering the Amazon" named specific corporations that purchased products derived from cattle that were grazed on illegally cleared land. Reaction to the report was immediate. Wal-Mart, Nike, and Timberland all suspended contracts with suppliers who were involved in deforestation and companies began to seek out sustainable supply chains for beef and leather. A federal prosecutor in Brazil filed charges amounting to $1 billion against the cattle industry for environmental damage.

All of this support for the rain forest has heightened awareness of the problem, but rain forest land continues to be cleared for cattle ranching. The difficult question is how to stop the deforestation and still supply the world's insatiable appetite for beef and leather. Standing in the way of a solution are obstacles like corrupt officials who do not enforce Brazilian environmental laws and apathy among beef consumers. A program aimed at providing certification for beef that is grown sustainably on legally cleared land could provide an economic incentive for cattle producers to change their methods if discerning customers were willing to pay a premium for it.

A large amount of land in the Brazilian Amazon has been cleared for cattle ranching.

Chemicals acting as endocrine disruptors in this frog's habitat have caused the specimen to grow without an arm.

middle of it. That road divides the field into two different pieces. All around the world, vast areas of land inhabited by people are fragmented in this way. Habitat fragmentation can disrupt migration patterns and result in loss of genetic variation within a species if fragmentation isolates groups of species and those groups are forced to interbreed with one another.

Pollution

Even in areas where people are not developing land, development has an effect. Human pollution from agricultural, industrial, and residential land use degrades neighboring natural habitats. Chemical runoff from agriculture gets into the water where it affects plants, animals, and ultimately people as well. Trash finds its way into natural areas both on land and at sea with unfortunate consequences for wildlife.

Some pollution is more difficult to see, but it has devastating impacts on biodiversity. Chemicals and compounds from human products can leech into the natural environment. For instance, endocrine disrupting chemicals from pesticides, antibiotics, cosmetics, caffeinated drinks and a variety of other sources, as well as synthetic hormones from oral contraceptives have both been found in nature.[28]

You may wonder how these chemicals could end up in a natural environment. After all, wastewater from our sinks, toilets, and showers passes through wastewater treatment facilities to remove toxins before the water is returned to natural waterways. Unfortunately, treatment of wastewater does not remove pharmaceuticals, including medicines, nor does it remove other chemicals that people ingest, like caffeine. These chemicals are also found in agricultural, industrial, and urban runoff, which can often go entirely untreated.

When they end up in natural environments, these chemicals and compounds can interfere with the endocrine systems of wild animals, affecting reproduction, development, and growth.[29] The effects are most profound for aquatic organisms that live where treated wastewater is released.[30] For instance, chemicals in the environment can disrupt development in amphibians.

Climate Change

Climate change is inevitable; Earth's climate systems are constantly changing. However, evidence is mounting that humans are accelerating and altering natural cycles, including climate shifts. Human activities—in particular, our use of energy from fossil fuels to move our cars and light our

The polar bear has a vast habitat range, therefore, large tracts of their habitat must be conserved to ensure the polar bear's preservation.

homes—accelerate the accumulation of greenhouse gases in Earth's atmosphere. Climate change affects both terrestrial and aquatic environments.

Large species, such as polar bears, lions, and tigers, may be more affected by climate change than smaller species.[31] This is, in part, due to larger animals' need for more energy (from food) than smaller animals, which makes them more vulnerable to a shortage of prey. However, detrimental impacts to larger mammals can help draw attention to the issue of climate change and inspire conservation efforts. Familiar animals like polar bears are often called "charismatic fauna" because they elicit a stronger concern from people than smaller species. Conservation efforts that aim to protect species like the polar bear will have the co-benefit of protecting large areas of polar bear habitat where other species dwell as well.

Another species vulnerable to climate change are corals. Corals play a critical role in the marine ecosystem, even though they only occupy 0.2% of the ocean floor. Corals are animals that build reef structures made from their calcium carbonate exoskeletons. Coral reefs are known for their high biodiversity. They get their coloration from algae that live within coral tissues and provide corals with nutrients that form part of their diet. Attracted by the bright colors, other organisms make their homes in and around reefs, including sponges, fish, sea anemones, and plankton (another food source for corals). Coral ecosystems support over one-third of all marine life.[32]

As oceans grow warmer and more acidic, a common side effect is coral bleaching. Acidic waters damage the algae that color coral reefs and cause the corals to expel the algae, leaving behind a virtually colorless reef. While bleaching does not kill corals immediately (if waters cool and grow less acidic, algae can begin to grow again), over time it may cause the corals to starve to death.[33]

Healthy coral reef ecosystems get their color from algae living within coral tissues.

Acidic waters can damage algae living within coral tissues and cause coral bleaching.

Northern fur seals were once hunted to near extinction for their fur. A law enacted in 1911 protected the seals from overhunting.

Exploitation and Overconsumption

In the absence of regulations, people tend to overfish, overhunt, and overuse natural resources. This is known as the tragedy of the commons.[34] When natural resources are owned in common (meaning that no single person or group has exclusive rights to use them), individuals will usually take more than their fair share. People may not necessarily realize that they are contributing to the overuse of the resource or understand the long-term consequences of their actions. Nevertheless, unregulated hunting and harvesting of natural resources (including plants and animals) can diminish biodiversity. There are numerous examples of species that have been hunted to extinction, including the dodo bird and the Caribbean monk seal. Many more are currently under threat.

The oceans are one of the largest common resources on the planet. No individual or nation has ownership of the high seas. Around the world, there is incredible demand for seafood and huge profits to be made from the fishing industry. As a result, the temptation to overfish the oceans is immense, even though doing so may reduce our ability to harvest fish in the future. Overfishing harms entire marine ecosystems. Seals depend on fish as a source of food. When people kill off fish faster than they can reproduce, seal populations decline. People also hunt seals for their fur, further depleting their population. As the seal population declines, there is less food for the whales and polar bears that prey on seals.

Humans also clear-cut forests for everything from building materials to firewood, wine corks, and baseball bats. Medicinal plants are in high demand, putting pressure on some wild plant populations. Even when regulations to protect resources exist, such as those that place limits on fishing and the trade of medicinal plants, they may not be universally applied or enforced.[35]

Pathways to Progress: Biodiversity

Declining biodiversity threatens more than the existence of the species that face extinction; it also threatens the natural balance that supports all life, including our own species. You've already read about some ways individuals and groups can work to preserve biodiversity, but there are many others.

Biodiversity Hotspots

The British ecologist Norman Myers developed the concept of the **biodiversity hotspot** in 1988 to address and identify the highest priority areas for conserving biodiversity. A region qualifies as a hotspot if it contains at least 1,500 species of vascular plants and has lost at least 70% of its original habitat.[36] There are 34 known hotspots on Earth. They occur both on land and in the ocean. Hotspots cover a small fraction of the Earth's surface, but contain a high number of species. Because of their high diversity, some conservationists focus their efforts and resources on these hotspots.

One biodiversity hotspot is the Tropical Andes, a region that extends down the western edge of South America. The hotspot makes up less than 1% of Earth's total land area yet contains approximately 10% of the whole world's vascular plant species.[37] Vascular plants have an organized tissue system for transporting water, carbohydrates, and minerals back and forth between the roots and leaves. Most of the plants we recognize—trees, bushes, flowers, and grasses—are vascular.

To put the biodiversity of the Tropical Andes in perspective, almost 7% of the world's plants are *endemic* to this region, meaning the Tropical Andes is the only place the plant species are found in nature. Many animal species are also native to this region. There are more than 1,700 species of birds in this hotspot, almost 600 of which are endemic. The Tropical Andes is also home to 570 species of mammals and 600 species of reptiles (almost half of which are endemic).[38]

Thousands of species of amphibians, reptiles, mammals, and plants in the Tropical Andes are considered at risk of extinction, largely from human activities. Several large cities within the hotspot put pressure on the native flora and fauna and more and more land is being used for agriculture or development. Andean farmers clear rain forest land to grow opium poppies—a profitable, though illegal, crop. Armed guards often protect poppy fields, making conservation activities difficult. In addition, mineral and hydrocarbon deposits make the area attractive for mining and industrial development, which can damage forests significantly. On the plus side, 25% of the region's natural habitat remains and there is still time to establish protected nature reserves in some of the still-intact primary forests, mostly in Peru and Bolivia.

While hotspots like the Tropical Andes can be attractive targets for limited conservation budgets, some conservationists argue against focusing conservation efforts exclusively on hotspots because this may cause us to fail to adequately conserve the larger ecosystems and biomes of which they are a part. Neglecting the ecosystem as a whole neglects those species that require larger tracts of habitat, like the polar bear. Efforts focused on hotspots also neglect the protection and maintenance of ecosystems that support all life on the planet. These conservationists suggest that biodiversity should be just one factor among many considered when setting conservation priorities.[39]

The critically endangered yellow-tailed woolly monkey is endemic to Peru.

Governmental Efforts

Efforts by individual governments and international initiatives enacted by multiple governments have played a major role in conservation of biological diversity. The Convention on International Trade in Endangered Species (CITES) is one significant international effort that has severely reduced the hunting, trade, and sale of endangered species.

CITES is an agreement between national governments that protects wildlife from overexploitation and restricts trade of threatened or endangered plants and animals. For example, to protect endangered African and Asian elephant species, CITES makes it illegal to sell or purchase elephant tusks. There are currently 175 countries that are party to the Convention.[40] Participating countries may also have their own laws governing the implementation of CITES provisions at the national level and providing even greater protection for wild species within their borders. In the United States, Congress enacted the Endangered Species Act in 1973.

The whooping crane is an endangered species protected by the Endangered Species Act. It is estimated that less than 400 individuals are alive in the wild.[42]

The Act is administered by the U.S. Fish and Wildlife Service (FWS) and the National Marine Fisheries Service (NMFS). These agencies maintain endangered or threatened species lists for at-risk terrestrial or freshwater

CASE STUDY: Gray Whale Recovery

International laws designed to protect wildlife really can make a difference. Commercial whaling had brought gray whales to near-extinction in the early 20th century. At the time, people used whale products for everything from heating oil to undergarments. In response to plummeting whale populations, 15 nations signed the International Convention on the Regulation of Whaling in December 1946. The agreement established the International Whaling Commission (IWC) to monitor whale populations and regulate whaling operations. The IWC banned commercial killing of gray whales in 1947, though indigenous populations were allowed to continue limited subsistence harvesting.[43] Some nations have taken additional steps to support gray whale populations—Mexico, for example, protects several lagoons in Baja California where the whales return to reproduce. The gray whale population, once so low that the species was on the brink of extinction, now numbers over 20,000.[44] However, many scientists estimate gray whale populations were historically much larger and that the current population remains diminished.[45]

Gray whales were near extinction in the early 20th century, but now have over 20,000 individuals.

species (FWS) and marine species (NMFS). Any species listed as endangered or threatened receives special protections. Federal agencies may not engage in or authorize (such as through federal land use permits) any activity that is likely to threaten the survival of listed species, including destroying critical habitat or interfering in vital breeding or behavioral activities. The Endangered Species Act also makes it illegal for any person to take, kill, sell, or trade any vulnerable species.[41]

Nongovernmental Efforts

Nongovernmental organizations are an important force in conservation efforts. Some nongovernmental organizations work to preserve habitat for species. Other organizations collect research on endangered species in order to advocate for conservation and provide information to decision makers and the public. Yet others work with communities all over the world to develop strategies that simultaneously meet the needs of both human and nonhuman communities.

One of the best-known wildlife conservation organizations is the International Union for Conservation of Nature (IUCN). IUCN is an international network of conservationists made up of representatives from national governments, nongovernmental organizations, and scientists. IUCN publishes the Red List of Threatened Species in order to identify and document species in need of conservation efforts and to track the state of global biodiversity. IUCN works to collect and analyze data, set conservation priorities, and develop better ways to combat decreasing biodiversity.[46]

Another nongovernmental organization that works to protect biodiversity is the Wildlife Conservation Society (WCS). WCS manages about 500 conservation projects worldwide. One project in Zambia aims to stop *poaching*—the illegal take of wildlife in violation of local, national, or international law or agreement. Rather than focus on enforcing poaching laws, WCS addresses the underlying causes of poaching by offering former poachers training in alternative livelihoods such as sustainable farming, beekeeping, and handicrafts through its Community Markets for Conservation co-op (COMACO). In exchange for training, poachers turn over their guns and snares (devices used to capture wild animals). The co-op repurposes wire from the snares to make a line of jewelry called Snarewear that it sells locally and abroad, providing an additional source of income for Zambians who practice conservation.[47]

In addition to their new careers, many former poachers are hired to protect fields from elephants by using muzzle-loaders full of chili powder; this scares and irritates the elephants without significantly harming them. Elephants are sometimes killed to prevent the destruction of villages and crops, but this approach provides a nonlethal way to deter the elephants and keep crops safe.

The Philippine tarsier is identified as near threatened on IUCN's Red List of Threatened Species.

Seed Banks

One way to protect biodiversity is to preserve genetic diversity. *Seed banking* is the practice of harvesting seeds, especially from threatened plants, and storing them somewhere other than their native habitat. This preserves the seeds' genetic information in a safe place in case the species becomes locally extinct.

For example, Britain's Kew Royal Botanical Gardens' Millennium Seed Bank seeks to save plants from extinction by banking their seeds. The bank targets plants and regions most at risk of extinction from climate change or human activities. Currently, it holds over 30,000 species of wild plants; these seeds can later be planted to reintroduce the species in the wild.[48] Another place dedicated to preserving genetic diversity is the Svalbard Global Seed Vault in Norway. In 2004, the government of Norway funded construction of this vault to protect the world's seed collections and ensure future crop diversity. Anyone can store seeds in the vault, and the seeds remain the property of whoever is storing them.[49]

Similar in concept to seed banking, zoos are another resource in the fight to preserve genetic diversity. Some animal species have become extinct in the wild; their only representatives are now in zoos. Many zoos are committed to conservation efforts and have undertaken captive breeding programs to continue the lineage of endangered species. Captive breeding programs also help scientists obtain data that will increase the success of breeding programs in the wild.[50] Along with breeding programs, zoos encourage conservation efforts by educating the public about the importance of each animal species.

CASE STUDY: Endangered Black-Footed Ferrets[51]

There are only three species of ferret on our planet. Of those, the black-footed ferret is the only species native to North America. Black-footed ferrets have been classified as endangered since 1967. The biggest threat to these ferrets is loss of habitat, both for themselves and for their main food source, prairie dogs.

To save the black-footed ferret, scientists removed members of a ferret colony outside of Meeteetse, Wyoming, and started the Black-footed Ferret Species Survival Plan. Six zoos and conservation centers participate in the program, ranging from Arizona to Virginia to Ontario, Canada. Together, these facilities work to breed a genetically diverse ferret population and reintroduce it into the wild. There are currently 19 reintroduction sites scattered throughout the western United States, Canada, and Mexico, where the ferrets bred in captivity are released. While reintroduction sites are carefully selected to ensure maximum survival for the ferrets, the lack of appropriate habitat limits the number of possible reintroduction sites and continues to present a challenge to species recovery efforts.

The biggest threat to the endangered black-footed ferret is loss of habitat for themselves and prairie dogs (their main food source).

Three overpasses were built in Arizona to allow bighorn sheep to access the full range of their habitat which has been fragmented by human development.

Habitat Preservation

Wildlife biologists and conservationists are coming up with increasingly creative solutions that may allow wildlife to survive in areas of heavy human land use. The creation of wildlife corridors, refuges, and preserves is critical to the conservation of biodiversity.

A *wildlife corridor* is a stretch of undeveloped land or water connecting wildlife populations that are otherwise separated by human activities. One example can be found along U.S. Highway 93. This highway is a major access route in the western United States. It is part of the CANAMEX corridor, a transportation network established by the North American Free Trade Agreement (NAFTA) to move goods and people between Canada, the United States, and Mexico. U.S. 93 also travels right through territory of the world's largest herd of desert bighorn sheep.[52] The highway interferes with the connectivity of big horn sheep habitat and poses a challenge for rams trying to get to ewes in different parts of the region, disrupting the species' breeding cycle. The highway also makes it dangerous for sheep to cross in search of drinking water found on the other side of the highway. Vehicle-sheep collisions pose a threat to both sheep and drivers.

The Arizona Department of Transportation, the Federal Highway Administration, and the Arizona Desert Bighorn Sheep Society provided research money to the Arizona Game and Fish Department to come up with a solution. The easiest and most obvious solution was to provide underpasses for the sheep to avoid the road, but unlike deer and elk, desert bighorn sheep will not use underpasses. After outfitting 36 sheep with GPS collars and tracking them for two years, the Arizona Game and Fish Department recommended that three overpasses be built along the ridgelines that the sheep used to access the road. Completed in 2010, these overpasses are the first of their kind to be provided for desert bighorn sheep. Since construction was completed in 2010, sheep have been observed using them to cross the highway.

Conservation-Minded Consumption

As with many aspects of sustainability, the way we choose to spend our money can have a huge impact. The more people become committed to conservation in their approach to consumption, the more producers will listen and respond to demand for sustainable products. As we saw in the case study of the Brazilian Amazon, consumer backlash against the use of cattle products from illegally cleared lands caused companies like Wal-Mart and Nike to reexamine and change their policies for the better.

In some cases, you can consume in ways that directly support conservation efforts. For example, purchasing handicrafts made by herders in Mongolia who work with the Snow Leopard Trust ensures that herders do not kill endangered snow leopards.

YOUTH PROFILE
Phebe Meyers

Even as a young child, Phebe Meyers was concerned about the world. With her sister, Phebe cofounded Change the World Kids when she was just eight years old. The organization is made up of middle- and high-school-age youth undertaking humanitarian and environmental projects to make a positive difference in their local communities and across the globe. Phebe's motto is: "No one can do everything, but everyone can do something."

CAREER PROFILE
Nature Photographer

Artists recreate the world around them through media, whether the medium is paint and paper, words on a page, or sculpted rock. Talent and ingenuity are more important to becoming an artist than training, but to develop raw talent and hone artistic skills many artists benefit from studying under another artist or master craftsman. Artists often have to find unconventional ways to market their work, so having an outgoing personality and a love of networking can be helpful to sustain what is essentially your own small business.

Dudley Edmondson is a freelance nature photographer whose photos are splashed across major natural history publications. Dudley is also an author and filmmaker. He uses these different types of media to explore political and artistic themes in addition to natural landscapes.

Some people may think art

Dudley Edmondson is a freelance nature photographer.

is just for decorating walls, but Dudley Edmondson's photography is intended to build a relationship between people and their environment. By photographing people in nature, especially young people of ethnically diverse backgrounds, Dudley hopes to inspire a commitment to conservation. He says, "The natural world and our public land belong to all people, and if we get everyone participating in conservation we can be sure natural places will be around for future generations."

Dudley's work features diverse scenes: people of color scaling rock faces, grandfathers and granddaughters riding bikes together, and a pack of dogs racing through snowy mountain woods, trailing a sled behind them. These images of people interacting with these familiar and exotic landscapes opens up a world that few experience firsthand. Dudley developed his personal style of nature photography over years of spending time in places of natural beauty. When asked what advice he would give to budding photographers, he says, "It takes a lot of patience and self-motivation, but the rewards are worth it. Develop your own style and bring your passion and emotion into the work. If you can do these things, you will have a very long and successful career."

Growing up in Vermont, Phebe noticed that fewer songbirds visited bird feeders at her house each year. After working with biologists to study this trend, she connected the decline to deforestation occurring within the birds' migration corridor in Central America, where ranchers are clearing patches of rain forest to graze cattle. While visiting Costa Rica, Phebe saw firsthand how songbirds from Vermont were affected by this deforestation. There she held in her hands the state bird from her home state of Vermont,

Phebe Meyers

the Hermit Thrush. These birds migrate from Vermont all the way to Central America.

Phebe and Change the World Kids decided to help protect the rain forest corridor for songbirds and other species by raising money to purchase rain forest land. So far, they've raised $175,000 and preserved 56 acres of rain forest. This land will offer a resting place and a snack for songbirds on their long migration north to Vermont. The organization's goal is to raise $1.8 million to preserve the entire migration corridor.

WHAT YOU CAN DO — Biodiversity

Addressing the threats to biodiversity may seem like a monumental task, but keep in mind that nearly every global issue can be supported by personal and community awareness and a conscious effort to take action.

- Many communities have programs where residents can work with their local parks or conservation groups to help eradicate invasive plants that choke out native species. You don't need to be a botanist to assist—just find a pair of gloves and get to work.

- Become an advocate for biodiversity by keeping an eye on national and international conservation issues and speaking up when you feel it is important. Getting involved can be as simple as writing a letter to your local legislator. Many organizations (the Environmental Defense Fund, for one: www.edf.org) have pre-written letters that you can customize and then send.

- Support the efforts of nongovernmental organizations working to protect global biodiversity. Many of these organizations have programs to direct donations toward specific conservation efforts. For example, you can sponsor a beehive through COMACO (www.itswild.org/) or "adopt" a tiger through WWF (www.worldwildlife.org).

- The Marine Stewardship Council's labeling program and the Monterey Bay Aquarium's Seafood Watch program are both excellent resources to help consumers make seafood purchases with biodiversity in mind.

- Educate yourself about endangered species and the reasons why they are under threat of extinction. You can learn more about species like the black-footed ferret by visiting a zoo or researching online. From there, you can leverage your efforts by sharing what you learn with others, or even holding a fundraiser to collect money to support species conservation.

Just as Phebe Meyers' observations about songbirds—such as this hermit thrush—led her to action, so can your observations about the natural world spark you to action.

POINT | **COUNTERPOINT**

Should wolves be reintroduced into the wild?

In an attempt to restore the wolf populations of the northern Rocky Mountains, wolves are being bred in captivity and then released into the wild. Some commend the program for saving a declining population and supporting biodiversity. Others are against the program because wolves are predators that often prey on livestock.

POINT

Yes[53]

- **Reintroduction of wolves into the wild is necessary to restore their population.** The species is at risk of becoming extinct. While wolves can be found in zoos around the world, this method of preserving biodiversity only goes so far. Wild populations of wolves are a much greater benefit to species diversity since they interact with nature, keeping a balance in the food web.

- **Wolf reintroduction supports healthy ecosystems and even helps restore damaged ecosystems.** Wolves eat elk and deer, keeping their populations at a sustainable level. In addition to direct predation, the presence of wolves creates an "ecology of fear" that keeps deer and elk moving and prevents them from over-grazing any one area. In the absence of wolves, deer and elk can consume too much natural vegetation, limiting that food source for other creatures and further harming biodiversity.

- **The presence of wolves attracts tourists to national parks.** The presence of wolves in Yellowstone National Park increased visitation and ecotourism spending by $35 million in 2005.

COUNTERPOINT

No[54]

- **Wolf reintroduction is a burden on ranchers.** Ranchers already face tough economic times. The loss of each bull that falls prey to a wolf makes it harder for a rancher to get food on the table for his or her family.

- **Livestock supports local economies.** One 1,800-pound bull is valued at $5,000. If a wolf that has been reintroduced to the wild hunts down that $5,000 bull, the financial loss is not only suffered by the rancher, but also the local butcher, the local restaurants, and the local economy.

- **Conservationists and state governments that support reintroduction value the well-being wolf populations over that of human communities.** States often ignore the financial burden placed on local ranchers by wolf reintroduction programs and challenge claims made by ranchers for livestock lost to wolves.

Is the gray wolf a species in need of protection?

Chapter 11

Oceans

The Sea, once it casts its spell,
holds one in its net of wonder forever.

—Jacques-Yves Cousteau

GUIDING QUESTIONS

- How do oceans support life on Earth?
- How do human actions impact marine ecosystems?

Introduction to Oceans

In 1968, Time Magazine published the first photo of Earth taken from space. Accompanying the photo were the words of poet James Dickey: "Behold / The blue planet steeped in its dream / Of reality."[1] From space, Earth's oceans are striking. Over 71% of Earth's surface is covered in water, including five major oceans: the Atlantic, Pacific, Indian, Artic, and Southern Oceans. The amount of water found on Earth is unique among the planets discovered so far and one of the reasons why Earth is abundant with life. What isn't so obvious from space is the immense diversity of life contained within the oceans and dynamic marine ecosystems vital to the sustainability of the planet.

Our Blue Planet

Stop for a moment and consider what life would be like without oceans. No beaches, no boats, no fishing. Did you know our climate would change drastically as well?

Ocean Circulation

Our oceans are composed of water, sea salt, gases (such as oxygen and carbon dioxide), and other substances. Water has a high heat capacity and it takes more energy to raise the temperature of Earth's oceans than it takes to raise the temperature of either air or land. In other words, ocean temperatures are very slow to change. The top layer of the oceans absorbs more than half of energy from the sun that reaches Earth. This high heat capacity helps to moderate onshore weather patterns.

Coastal climates experience less drastic temperature changes than inland climates due to the insulating effect of the oceans. In addition, while most of the sun's energy is concentrated at the equator, ocean currents are able to redistribute that heat, carrying warm water from equatorial areas and cold water from arctic areas. Currents are driven by the winds generated from solar heating and the rotation of the Earth.

There are five main **gyres**, or large-scale circular systems of currents, in the oceans. The Gulf Stream is an oceanic current that is part of the North Atlantic gyre, originating near the tip of Florida and flowing up the U.S. coastline. Without the effect of the Gulf Stream pulling warm water from the tropics to the northeast portion of the Atlantic Ocean, temperatures in Northern Europe would be significantly colder.

Currents become more complex as you dive deeper below the surface of the oceans. Deep-water circulation tends to be slower and can move vertically as well as horizontally.[2]

El Niño and La Niña

Earth's oceans also contribute to our climate through events like El Niño and La Niña that occur periodically and severely alter typical weather patterns. El Niño and La Niña are climatic disturbances caused by changes in ocean surface temperature, oceanic currents, and pressure systems.

El Niño describes an unusually warm current in the eastern Pacific Ocean, occurring every two to ten years. La Niña describes unusually cold temperatures in the eastern to central Pacific Ocean. Both events will cause increased rainfall in some regions and drought in other regions. Both events also cause major ecosystem shifts due to these temperature changes, significantly affecting fish, birds, and mammals. La Niña is often associated with increased hurricane activity in the Atlantic Ocean and snowy winters in the United States.[3] In other regions, drought is a risk; a La Niña event occurring from 2011 to 2012 contributed to droughts in East Africa.[4]

Waves and Tides

The shoreline, where waves crash and the sea ebbs and flows, is often a dramatic place to view the power of the ocean. Waves

A young boy swims as strong currents sweep across the North Shore of Oahu.

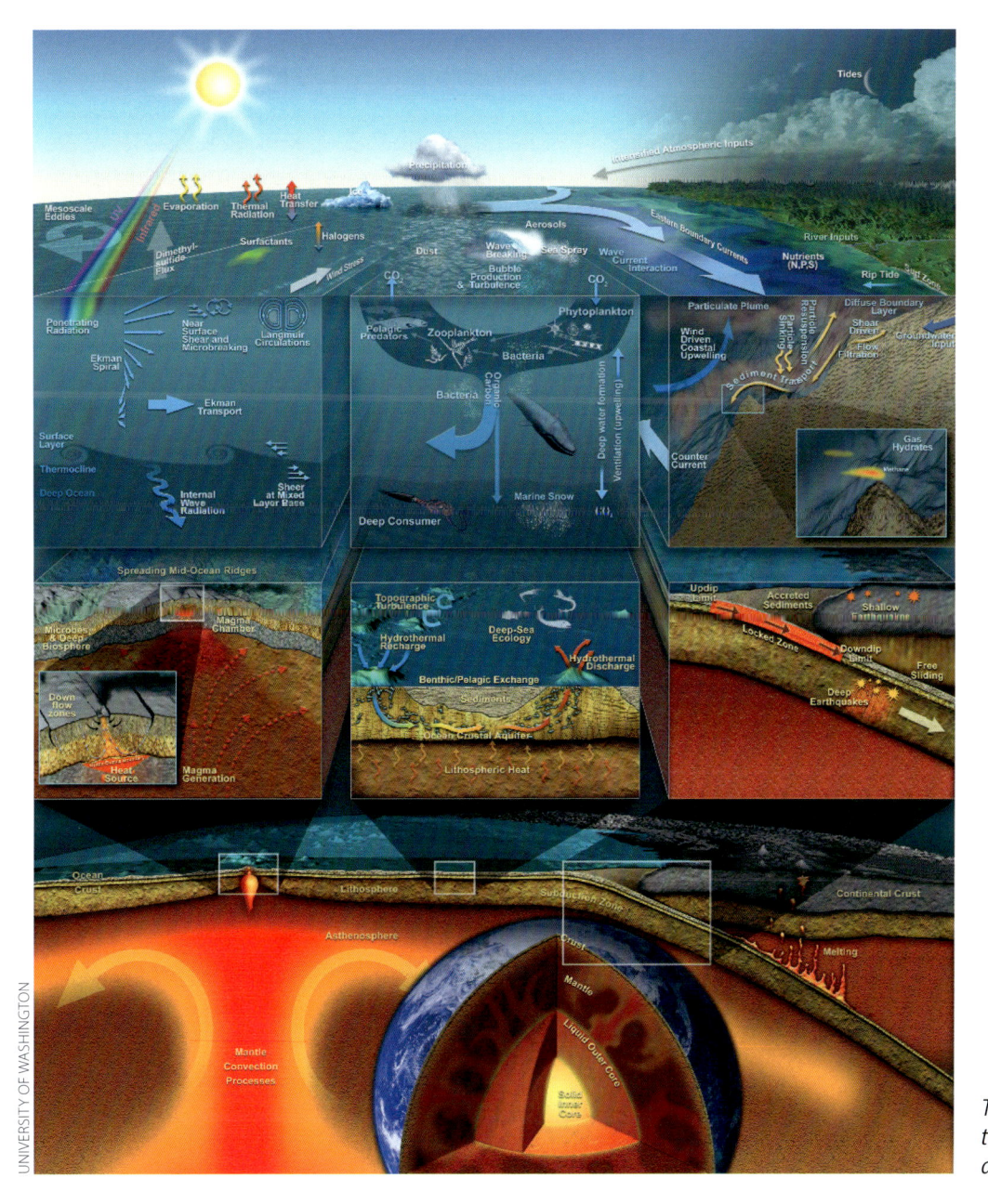

This diagram depicts the diverse processes at play in our oceans.

are a transfer of energy from one part of an ocean to another. They are generated by winds moving over the ocean surface or undersea earthquakes.

Tides, the routine rise and fall of sea level, are orchestrated by the relationship between the moon, the sun, and the rotation of the Earth. The moon's gravity pulls our waters from one direction to another, causing the sea to rise and fall once or twice a day, depending on geographic location.

Marine Ecosystems

Earth's oceans are dynamic and in no way uniform. Different parts of the oceans vary in temperature, salinity, pressure, density, acidity, and dissolved oxygen content (dissolved oxygen is gaseous oxygen diffused in water). Another difference is light. Light does not penetrate deep into the ocean because light waves are quickly absorbed by water. Starting with red and yellow, colors tend to fade as you dive deeper. Most light is absorbed within one meter of the ocean surface and that energy is converted into heat. Most marine plant life is found close to the surface and relies on the sun's energy to sustain life, just like plants on land. Yet the oceans are also home to a variety of organisms that have adapted to the deep, dark waters closer to the ocean floor. As a result of these varying circumstances, the oceans support a variety of ecosystems.

Marine ecosystems support a variety of marine life, commercial fisheries, and recreational opportunities. Some marine ecosystems act as natural buffers between strong seas and coastlines vulnerable to erosion. Other marine ecosystems can help to naturally filter water contaminated with pollutants. Coral reefs, mangrove swamps, and submarine volcanoes are just three types of ecosystems that can be found along our coasts and within our oceans.

Coral Reefs

Coral reefs are formed by millions of tiny organisms called coral that live together in a colony. The Great Barrier Reef off the northern coast of Australia is over 1,200 miles long and can be seen from space. Coral reefs are some of the most diverse and important ecosystems in the world, providing habitat for somewhere between 1 and 9 million species.[5] Coral reefs are highly productive, with more density of life than any other marine ecosystem. Reefs also act as buffers that protect coasts from erosion.

Coral reefs are sensitive to climate change. Rising sea temperatures and pollution can kill off the organisms that give coral reefs their color and provide corals with essential nutrients, leading to a phenomenon known as coral bleaching. Ocean **acidification** is another consequence of climate change that occurs where there is a decrease in the pH level of seawater and an increase in acidity. Because of their extreme sensitivity, scientists can use coral reefs as an indicator of even small changes in ocean temperature or pH level.

Mangrove Swamps

A mangrove is a salt-tolerant tree that grows in tropical and subtropical brackish swamps where oceans meet freshwater resources. Mangrove swamps create an ideal environment for water creatures because of their leaf litter, or all the bits of the tree that fall into the water.

A scuba diver swims near purple soft coral in the Pacific Ocean.

Mangrove swamps offer feeding and breeding grounds for fish, shrimp, crustaceans, and other wildlife. They create an economic boon for fishers as well.

Mangroves are great natural buffers for coastal regions during storm surges and hurricanes because of their unique and extensive root systems. Mangrove habitats not only prevent erosion and limit wave action from moving inland, but mangrove trees saved numerous lives during the 2004 tsunamis in Southeast Asia by preventing people from being swept out to sea, offering them something to cling to.[6] Natural ecosystems are impressively resilient. Studies of the effect of tsunamis have shown that coastal areas protected by mangroves fare far better than communities that have converted mangrove habitat into shrimp farms.[7]

Mangroves are also extremely efficient carbon sinks. They are able to absorb and store vast quantities of carbon dioxide. Mangrove forests, however, are typically located in prime shrimp farming areas. Over half of the world's mangrove swamps have been destroyed due to shrimp farming.[8] The growing market for shrimp (which has replaced tuna as America's most popular seafood) and the profitability of shrimp farms has contributed to the destruction of mangroves.[9]

Submarine Volcanoes

Did you know that more volcanic activity occurs below the ocean surface than on land? Just as on land, the movement of tectonic plates and the upwelling of magma create volcanoes below the sea.

Submarine volcanoes are some of the most extreme environments on Earth. Hydrothermal vents associated with many of these submarine volcanoes emit fluids containing harsh gasses and can reach temperatures up to ~400°C. Despite these extreme conditions and the absence of sunlight needed for photosynthesis, a diversity of life still thrives at hydrothermal vents due to chemosynthesis. Chemosynthesis is a process performed by microbes through which they convert chemicals into food and energy.

Tube worms live near hydrothermal vents.

At submarine volcanoes thousands of feet below the surface of the ocean, you can find tubeworms up to seven feet long and as thick as your arm living near hydrothermal vents.[10] Tubeworms are a marine invertebrate resembling "giant lipsticks." Lacking mouths, eyes, and stomachs, tubeworms survive off bacteria living inside them that can convert gases (such as hydrogen sulfide) emitted from the hydrothermal vents into food for the tubeworm.[11] These bacteria are among the oldest organisms on Earth. Scientists theorize that bacteria that perform chemosynthesis may reveal clues to the origin of life on Earth.[12]

Geologists exploring a mid-ocean ridge off the Galapagos Islands in 1977 were the first to discover marine life thriving in the deep sea.[13] Prior to this discovery, scientists had assumed that all life required sunlight and photosynthesis.

Sustainability and Oceans

Oceans provide 50% of the oxygen we breathe. They sustain economies in coastal communities all over the world. For many people, the sea is intertwined with their cultural identity. For many more, the impact of the ocean may not be easy to explain, but it is deeply felt.

Recreational activities along the coast include boogie boarding.

Environment

The Oceans play a critical role in maintaining Earth's atmosphere. For one thing, oceans provide the oxygen we need to survive. The first free oxygen molecule appeared in the oceans some 3.5 billion years ago.[14] Over 50% of the oxygen we breathe is produced by **phytoplankton**—tiny creatures performing photosynthesis at or just below the ocean surface.[15]

The Oceans also provide the largest carbon sink on the planet. Our oceans absorb vast amounts of carbon dioxide (CO_2), a predominant greenhouse gas linked to climate change. However, with rising CO_2 emissions from human activities, carbon dioxide levels in the oceans are causing acidification. Ocean acidification can have a detrimental affect on a variety of marine species, including coral and shellfish.

Economies

Ocean resources support economies all over the world. Fishing and related activities generate $240 billion in worldwide economic activity.[16] Fish are the most traded global food commodity. Seafood provides the largest source of wild or domestic protein on the planet. However, 15 of the 17 largest fisheries in the world are being severely overfished; tuna, salmon, haddock, halibut, and cod populations have all suffered from overfishing. In addition, fishery *bycatch*, or the creatures and objects caught in fishing nets alongside the intended catch, is the biggest source of biological waste in the oceans. Most bycatch is treated as trash and thrown back overboard, often already dead.[17]

Fishing supports a way of life for coastal communities around the world. For example, the Maori people in New Zealand have strong cultural ties to whaling. And in the northeastern United States, being a fisher is more than just an occupation, it is a calling passed down through many generations.

Society

Additionally, oceans contribute to cultural identities and recreational opportunities. For thousands of years, the sea has offered us a sense of freedom and adventure, inspiring great art and literature.

Herman Melville famously captured the rejuvenating nature of the sea in his 1851 novel *Moby Dick*:

Call me Ishmael. Some years ago—never mind how long precisely—having little or no money in my purse, and nothing particular to interest me on shore, I thought I would sail about a little and see the watery part of the world. It is a way I have of driving off the spleen, and regulating the circulation. Whenever I find myself growing grim about the mouth; whenever it is a damp, drizzly November in my soul; whenever I find myself involuntarily pausing before coffin warehouses, and bringing up the rear of every funeral I meet; and especially whenever my hypos get such an upper hand of me, that it requires a strong moral principle to prevent me from deliberately stepping into the street, and methodically knocking people's hats off—then, I account it high time to get to sea as soon as I can.

Major cities in ancient civilizations were built by the sea, often at the mouths of rivers to facilitate travel and trade. Today, two-thirds of the world population lives within 100 km of the coast.[18] Coastlines offer mild weather, easy transport, access to trade, and a wild food source that, for much of human history, seemed inexhaustible.

Background on Oceans

For centuries the oceans were owned by none and explored by few. Over time, we have greatly expanded our knowledge of the oceans and developed rights and responsibilities associated with oceanic activities.

Oceans as a Commons

The question of who has jurisdiction over the oceans is complicated. *Jurisdiction* is defined as having the power to make legal decisions and judgments. Much of Earth's oceans are considered a classic *commons*, something that is collectively owned or shared among many communities, in this case, the countries of the world.

Although no particular country or government owns the oceans, there are treaties designed to protect and regulate the use of oceans by offering limited authority to specific nations. Under the UN Convention on the Law of the Sea, countries have control over waters less than 200 nautical miles off of their coast—often referred to as the exclusive economic zone or EEZ. This means coastal countries have the ultimate authority over any economic activities, such as fishing or drilling, that happen in the 200-mile band. However, a dilemma arises when two neighboring countries have very different policies governing use of the oceans. Currents and fish migration patterns take no notice of national borders or the EEZ; they flow freely across political boundaries. As a result, the actions of one country can affect what happens in another country's waters.

In the open ocean (also known as the "high seas"), a ship is under the jurisdiction of the nation where it is registered or licensed. Ships from countries with widely differing policies use the same ocean but are governed by different rules. The lack of a common regulatory system undermines attempts by some countries (such as Canada and Sweden) to enforce more stringent and environmentally-responsible ocean regulations.

Mystery and Exploration

Many of the marine species we have uncovered are fascinating, such as bioluminescent organisms. There are many more creatures still waiting to be discovered.

Bioluminescence

Bioluminescence is the emission of light from organisms. Many marine creatures generate bioluminescence, especially deep-sea creatures. You may have witnessed bioluminescence in action if you have ever waded in the ocean at night and seen phosphorescence, a phenomenon resulting from bioluminescent plankton.

Deep water bioluminescent organisms light up the ocean.

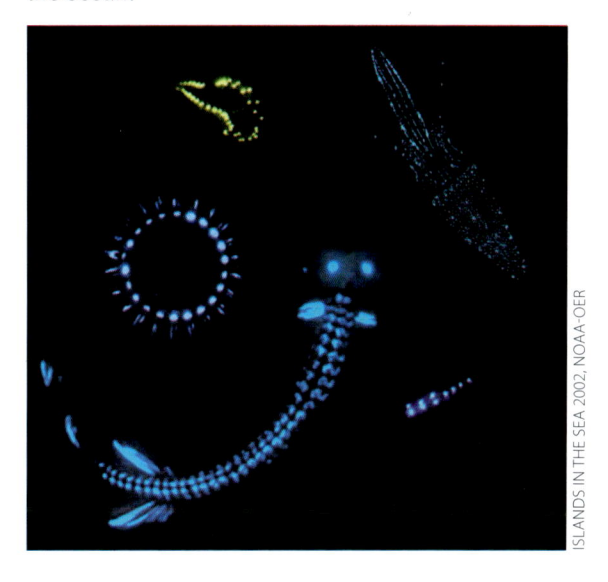

A chemical process with a light-producing compound called luciferin causes bioluminescence. How luciferin makes its way into so many critters and how each one uses its light-generating ability, however, remains a mystery.

Researchers continue to study bioluminescence not only out of scientific interest, but also for its many practical applications. Luciferin has proven valuable in the development of antibacterial agents and cancer-fighting drugs and can help us detect pollutants in our waters.[19] By continuing to explore, understand, and preserve the biodiversity of the oceans, we will likely discover new species of benefit to humanity.

The Scientific Method

In 1872, the first global study of oceanography was undertaken when the Challenger Expedition set sail on a three-and-a-half year voyage to explore Earth's oceans.[20] Many of the scientific techniques pioneered by the Challenger Expedition, such as dragnets, are still used in modern marine exploration.

For centuries, however, oceanic research was limited to intermittent observation and sampling conducted from shore or research vessels. More recent technological innovations have led to a variety of new methods for conducting oceanic research, from scuba divers to submersible vehicles such as underwater remote operated vehicles. One well-known submersible is Alvin, a three-person submarine built by Woods Hole Oceanographic Institute in 1962. Alvin can dive for several hours to depths of 4,500 meters (14,764 feet).

The film director James Cameron (whose films include *Avatar* and *Titanic*) recently made headlines when he undertook a record-breaking dive to the ocean floor in the deepest part of the world's oceans, the Mariana Trench in the western Pacific Ocean, using a newly-developed submarine. Cameron is the first human to reach 6.8 miles below sea level.[21] Innovations like submarines and submersibles have allowed scientists to explore places previously thought to be devoid of life and learn about unique species and processes we had no idea even existed.

During the Galápagos Rift Expedition 2011, scientists and technicians conducted exploratory investigations of deep-sea diversity.

Exploration and innovation continue today. The Ocean Observatories Initiative (OOI), a project funded by the National Science Foundation, is an integrated network of platforms and sensor systems that measure physical, chemical, geological, and biological variables in the ocean and on the seafloor. The project's infrastructure will include high power and bandwidth cables, sensor and instrument packages, mooring, and robotics. Scientific instruments installed in the oceans will provide sustained observations on the ocean floor and throughout the water column above it for the duration of the 25-year program.

The Ocean Observatories Initiative will put real-time ocean observing data in the hands of a vast user community of oceanographers, scientists and researchers, educators, and the public. Anyone with an Internet connection will be able to freely access the project's data.[22]

Oceans Today

Ocean resources are no more immune to the effects of human activities than air and land resources. Around the world, direct contamination and the unintended impact of human activities are threatening the sustainability of our oceans.

Pollution

Amazingly, over 80% of pollution in the ocean comes from land-based activities.[23] Pollution can be sorted into two categories: point source pollution and nonpoint source pollution. Point source pollution describes the release of harmful substances from an identifiable source such as pipe, ditch, ship, or factory smokestack. Nonpoint source pollution includes harmful substances from many different sources that cannot be individually identified. You've probably heard about catastrophic oil spills that dump large amounts of oil into a concentrated area of the ocean, but you might be surprised to learn that the single largest source of oil in the oceans is stormwater runoff, an example of nonpoint source pollution.

Stormwater Runoff

Stormwater runoff is snow or rainfall that flows over impervious surfaces, such as roads, as it makes way toward stormwater drainage systems. Stormwater runoff collects pollutants unable to be absorbed into the ground such as car oil or fertilizersand carry these into bodies of water like streams, rivers, lakes and oceans.

Runoff that contains *nutrients* from animal waste, fertilizers, and industrial agriculture stimulates algae growth. When too many nutrients enter a body of water, unchecked algae growth prevents the water from getting the light or air that it needs to promote other marine life. This phenomenon is called *eutrophication*. While alive, the algae block sunlight from reaching plants near the surface. When the algae die, oxygen is used in their decomposition. A large enough number of decomposing algae can decrease the amount of dissolved oxygen in the water to unhealthy levels and suffocate other marine species.

> *Around the world, direct contamination and the unintended impact of human activities are threatening the sustainability of our oceans.*

Bioaccumulation

There is a misconception that dilution is the solution to pollution because it is thought that when pollutants reach the ocean they are dispersed at less harmful concentrations. However, researchers are finding that these chemicals will build back up in the food chain due to a progression known as *bioaccumulation*. Once a chemical enters a waterway and is ingested by species at the bottom of the food chain, like plankton, the concentration of that chemical increase as it moves up the food chain. For example, if ten plankton ingest a chemical and one shrimp ingests all ten plankton, the shrimp's concentration of the chemical will be ten times that of one plankton. It doesn't stop there. Herring then eat the shrimp, codfish eat the herring, seals eat the codfish, and polar bears eat the seals. By the time we get to polar bears, the concentration of the chemical in a single polar bear is up to 3 billion times greater than the chemical concentration in its environment.

Through bioaccumulation, those at the top of the food chain feel the effects of highly concentrated pollution. One example is orca whales living in Puget Sound, a body of water in the Pacific Northwest region of the United States. Orca whales in Puget Sound have a small population to begin with. They face a decreasing food supply because salmon, the primary component of their diet, is an endangered species. Yet while the salmon population can be rehabilitated, there is another threat that has researchers concerned about the fate of Puget Sound's orca population—the high accumulation of polychlorinated biphenyls (PCBs) in the whales' blubber. PCBs are industrial chemicals with a very long lifespan. PCBs were banned from use in 1979 because they were found to be harmful to humans, but they unfortunately continue to circulate throughout the natural environment. PCBs compromise the whales' immune systems, hinder their development, and cause problems with their reproductive systems. The only thing we can do about PCBs is to clean up the sources of the contaminants.[24]

Solid Waste

In addition to stormwater runoff and chemical pollutants, solid waste is another very real threat to our oceans. Plastic bags, soda bottles, old shoes, balloons, cigarette butts, and medical waste are just a few of the objects that have been found in the sea. Some items were probably dumped intentionally, but others come from land-based trash that has been washed out to sea. Once in the ocean, sea birds and fish mistake the trash for food and pay the price. Birds can get tangled up in soda can holders and strangle themselves. A fish that eats a balloon may die when that balloon cannot be digested.

CASE STUDY: Dead Zones

As mentioned earlier, extensive growth of algae can lead to oxygen-deprived water. Concentrations of oxygen that are below levels necessary to sustain life is called *hypoxia*. When this happens, a **dead zone** is created. The lack of oxygen kills off marine life and those species that survive quickly leave the area.

As the Mississippi River flows into the Gulf of Mexico, it carries with it a massive amount of agricultural waste runoff, leaving a dead zone where the Mississippi meets the Gulf.[25] Like other dead zones, the Gulf of Mexico's dead zone is largest in summer because warmer water is unable to hold as much oxygen as colder water.

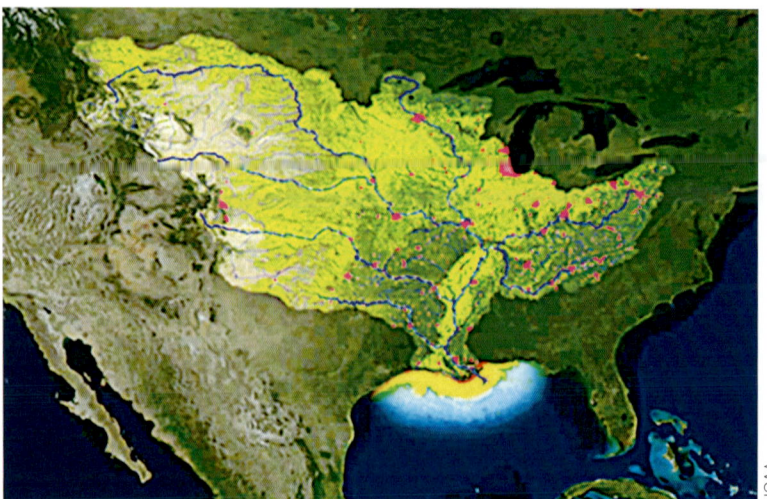

The Gulf of Mexico's dead zone is largest during the summer.

A thousand miles northeast of Hawaii, a mound of trash has been growing in the ocean. This mound, often referred to as the Pacific Ocean garbage patch, is now twice the size of Texas and expected to double in size within a decade. In the mound of trash, you can find everything from light bulbs to kernels of rice to abandoned fishing nets, not to mention lots of plastic. Scientists now believe there are five of these garbage patches in different parts of the oceans where the heavy currents associated with a gyre meet slack winds to form a whirlpool that collects drifting debris.[26]

Offshore Drilling

Most developed nations (as well as many developing nations) are extremely dependent on oil and natural gas for transportation fuels and electricity production. As land-based

---

CASE STUDY: Impacts of the BP Oil Spill[27]

In April 2010, 40 miles off the coast of Louisiana, there was a gas explosion on an offshore drilling rig owned by British Petroleum (BP) called Deepwater Horizon. The explosion killed 11 people and started a fire that lasted for hours until the rig finally sank. The explosion also caused a break in the oil pipeline, releasing an estimated 4.9 million barrels of crude oil into the Gulf of Mexico.

The BP oil spill had devastating environmental impacts on the Gulf Coast. Oil washed up along hundreds of miles of shoreline. Thousands of birds were coated in oil and a majority died as a result of the exposure.[28] Hundreds of dead mammals and turtles were collected.[29] Coral reefs appeared stressed and discolored.[30]

The broken pipeline was capped, but the BP oil spill continues to affect the region. Several communities on the Gulf Coast earn most of their income by extracting fish, shrimp, and shellfish from the sea. The oil spill not only killed off much of the fish and shellfish harvest, but also killed consumer confidence in the shrimp, fish, and oysters that survived the spill. Despite reassurances that Gulf seafood is safe to eat, the perception of a tainted product persists.

The harm done to the economy of these Gulf Coast communities has made a deep impact on the lives of their residents. Psychologists have noticed distinct increases in stress-related behavior among local residents. In places where the livelihood of their entire community has disappeared, people are struggling to survive. In addition to the stress of being without a source of income, Gulf residents now face the additional stresses of defaulting on loans and being unable to afford essential supplies for themselves and their families.

An aerial image of the BP oil spill shows the impact of an open water oil burn.

supplies of these fossil fuels run low, oil and gas companies are increasingly turning to deposits found underwater. The question of who has rights to sub-ocean resources is problematic. The use of ocean resources affects everyone who depends on the ocean commons. In addition, the extraction of oil and natural gas can itself be harmful, as evidenced by the Deepwater Horizon oil spill in the Gulf of Mexico in 2010.

Overfishing

According to a report released by the UN Food and Agriculture Organization (FAO) in January 2011, almost one-third of the world's fish stocks are overexploited, depleted, or recovering.[31] This means that fish are being taken from oceans faster than they can reproduce and replace their populations.

The solution to overfishing is not to halt all commercial fishing. For one thing, the economic consequences of that ban would be wide reaching. Additionally, to replace the amount of ocean-based protein the world consumes with land-based protein, we would have to farm an area equal to 22 times the total area of all of the rainforests on the planet.[32]

Growing awareness of overfishing has already led to the stabilization of some fish populations. With greater emphasis now being placed on sustainable fishing rates and responsible resource use, there is hope that other species will begin to recover.

CASE STUDY: Bluefin Tuna[33]

Atlantic bluefin tuna is a highly migratory species of tuna. Their habitat ranges from the Gulf of Mexico to Newfoundland in the western Atlantic, from the Canary Islands off the northwest coast of Africa to south of Iceland in the eastern Atlantic, and throughout the Mediterranean Sea. Because Bluefin travel so much, they pass through the exclusive economic zones of several different countries. Bluefin tuna are highly sought after for their high fat content, making for excellent sushi and sashimi. Driven by this high demand, the species has been harvested to the brink of extinction.

To prevent the extinction of bluefin tuna, several groups have stepped in to manage the resource, most notably the International Commission for the Conservation of Atlantic Tunas (ICCAT) and national agencies enforcing ICCAT's recommendations, such as the U.S. National Oceanic and Atmospheric Administration (NOAA). Two things complicate management of bluefin tuna populations: the extreme distances that they migrate and the number of countries that fish for Bluefin.

Scientists within ICCAT take stock of the number of Bluefin tuna every couple years. Based on their observations, the member nations of ICCAT adjust their policies for fishing Atlantic bluefin tuna. When ICCAT first began setting quotas in the 1990s, they lacked good data about bluefin populations and as a result compliance with quotas was low. In recent years, however, increased awareness and more scientifically accurate quotas have improved compliance. With continued oversight, the bluefin population is predicted to recover.

A Bluefin tuna is caught off the coast of Italy.

Aquaculture

Aquaculture is the farming of fish, shellfish, and kelp. While seafood is often thought of a wild resource, large-scale domestic production of seafood is emerging all over the world. Today, over one-third of seafood consumed globally is produced by aquaculture.[34] There are many potential benefits to aquaculture. It can be a highly efficient method of producing large amounts of protein for human consumption and may help alleviate pressure on wild fish stocks. Aquaculture can also create jobs, support local economies, and increase recreational opportunities. A link has been discovered between shellfish aquaculture and better water quality.[35]

On the other hand, there are several potential downsides to aquaculture. As we learned earlier, mangrove swamp habitat is being destroyed in areas of Southeast Asia in order to establish shrimp farms. Additionally, within aquaculture operations, when farmed seafood is confined to tight quarters it is vulnerable to the spread of disease and parasites.[36] Farmed fish tend to lack the genetic variation of their wild counterparts. There is a risk that farmed fish could escape and breed with wild fish, reducing the genetic diversity of the wild species.

Aquaculture may also contribute to the spread of invasive species. Invasive species are species that are not native to an area but that thrive due to a lack of natural predators or an ability to outcompete native species for resources. Often, invasive species overwhelm and disrupt the balance of local ecosystems and threaten the survival of native species. Human activities have facilitated the spread of invasive species. In addition to being imported for aquaculture farms, non-native species may stow away on ships or be bought and sold as pets. Methods like these allow a species to enter an ecosystem that would have been difficult for it to reach naturally.

Netpens, such as these off of Catalina Island, are enclosures that house fish and shellfish.

Coastal Development

The urbanization of a coastal area may involve road construction, housing development, port and marina activities, mining, agriculture, and a variety of other human activities. Such coastal development can reduce, fragment, or degrade coastal habitats and reduce the populations of marine plants and animals.

For example, coastal development affects the nesting sites of sea turtles. A female sea turtle will often return to the same nesting site where she was born.[37] However, a sea wall or beachside house may create an obstacle for this maternal instinct. Also, sea turtle hatchlings are drawn back to the ocean by the moonlight.[38] Lights from houses or businesses along the coast can disorient the hatchlings' survival instincts.

These examples will multiply as coastal development continues. Half the U.S. population lives within 50 miles of the coastline and almost half of new development happens near the coast.[39]

Climate Change

Climate change affects the health of our oceans and, in turn, biological diversity and human welfare around the world. Scientists have observed five major areas of change in oceans resulting from climate change: rising ocean temperatures, melting polar ice, rising sea levels, changing currents, and increasing ocean acidification.

Rising ocean temperatures deplete coral populations and alter the nutrient circulation of the world's oceans. These changes each negatively impact fish populations: coral reefs offer protection to fish and nutrient circulation creates rich feeding grounds for fish and other marine life.

Melting polar ice affects the oceans in several ways. As polar ice melts, the ice surface available as habitat for arctic animals such as seals and polar bears is reduced. Arctic animals are hit doubly hard because melting polar ice also reduces their food supply.

Both rising temperatures (which expand water molecules) and melting polar ice contribute to rising sea levels. Rising sea levels reduce coastal habitat, encroach on coastal communities, and in some cases force people to leave their homes.

A changing global climate also affects the currents of the oceans. Rising temperatures alter pressure systems, wind patterns, and, ultimately, ocean currents. The migratory patterns of some animals depend on these currents. In addition, ocean currents greatly impact Earth's weather and climate patterns.

Finally, an increasing concentration of carbon dioxide in Earth's atmosphere has led to the acidification of the oceans. Increasing ocean acidification impacts many organisms, including mollusks, crustaceans, and plankton. Acidity harms shell formation and, as mentioned earlier, leads to a phenomenon called coral bleaching that occurs when organisms that live in and around corals die. If lower levels of the food chain die out, organisms higher up the food chain, including humans, may find their food sources threatened.[40]

Pathways to Progress: Preserving Our Oceans

To put it simply, life on Earth could not be sustained without our oceans. Protecting and conserving our oceans is a way to ensure our own survival.

It is not too late to save our oceans and the creatures that call the seas home. Some changes are unavoidable, but there are measures that are being taken at the national and international level to help protect one of Earth's most important resources. There are also choices you can make and actions that you can take to contribute to responsible ocean stewardship.

Keeping International Agreements

International agreements can be an important component of protecting global commons. The United States has ratified several international treaties aimed at protecting the world's oceans. These treaties cover pollution from land-based sources and activities, vessel pollution, ocean dumping, and the

An octopus is spotted during a deep sea exploration of Indonesia.

preservation of coral reefs and arctic marine environments.[41]

The International Maritime Organization (IMO) is a special branch of the UN with over 169 member countries. Founded in 1948, the IMO's purpose is to improve the safety and security of international shipping and prevent marine pollution from ships. The IMO does not have any law enforcement capacity, however. The organization facilitates the adoption of legislation, but implementation is left up to individual member countries.[42]

Protecting Commercial Fish Stocks

Increased and improved fisheries management programs are having a positive effect on fisheries around the world. Part of their success stems from implementing scientific practices to determine maximum catches for fish stocks to enable fish populations to thrive. Management can take on many aspects, from working directly with fishers to dealing with seafood distributers to educating consumers.

In the United States, fisheries management is delegated to eight regional fisheries councils. Each council is comprised of a variety of stakeholders: a representative from the National Marine Fisheries Service, a representative from each state fishery agency within the region, and a group of private citizens, often from the commercial fishing community. Regional councils also take public testimony and recommendations from scientific and statistical subcommittees into account. Management measures—such as fishing seasons, licenses, and quotas—are discussed in a forum open to the public.[43]

The Marine Stewardship Council (MSC) is a global nonprofit organization that maintains the acknowledged global standard for wild capture seafood, based on three core principles: sustainable fish stocks, effective management, and minimizing environmental impact. The mission of the MSC is to use its ecolabel and fishery certification program to contribute to the health of the world's oceans by recognizing and rewarding sustainable fishing practices, influencing the choices people make when buying seafood, and working with partners to transform the seafood market to a sustainable basis.[44]

The MSC uses its ecolabel pictured here and fishery certification program to contribute to the health of the world's oceans.

Individuals can help protect the diversity of marine life by looking for the Marine Stewardship Council's (MSC) blue ecolabel when shopping for fish. It identifies fish that has been caught in a responsible way and is only awarded to fisheries that meet the MSC's strict environmental standard.

Another place to find information about sustainably harvested seafood is Monterey Bay Aquarium's Seafood Watch program. The aquarium has an online searchable database of many varieties of fish with information such as fishing practices, species endangerment status, whether you should avoid eating the fish, and, if so, what good alternatives are. It provides region-specific pocket guides, and even has an application for mobile devices that you can use while you peruse a restaurant's menu.[45]

Creating Marine Protected Areas

In the United States, a presidential executive order seeks to protect the uniqueness of our oceans by allowing for the creation of Marine Protected Areas (MPAs) by federal, state, local, or tribal governments. The aim of MPAs is not to exclude users from marine areas such as coastal regions, estuaries, inter-tidal zones, and the open ocean, but to manage these areas so that they will remain healthy and biologically diverse for many years to come.[46]

The Florida Keys National Marine Sanctuary is a great example of an area that is managed to the benefit of all users. Created in 1990, the sanctuary encompasses approximately 2,800 nautical square miles of state and federal waters. It features a unique management plan that was developed over six years based on input from all affected user groups. The sanctuary allows public use, but approximately 6% of the sanctuary is protected as ecological reserves, sanctuary preservation areas, or special use areas. These areas are heavily regulated to protect critical habitat, preserve species diversity, and relieve pressure on coral reefs. Even in the less-protected areas of the sanctuary, use is directed toward sustainable practices. Through an extensive education program, the sanctuary seeks to increase public awareness of the importance of caring for and protecting the delicate environment of the Keys.[47]

CAREER PROFILE — Attorney

Turn on a television and it might seem that attorneys spend most of their time sitting in a courtroom, wearing a power suit, and making defendants sweat on the witness stand. In reality, many attorneys never see the inside of a courtroom. An attorney's job is to advise and represent individuals, organizations, or government agencies on legal issues and disputes. An attorney may draft contracts, help settle disputes, negotiate mergers, and lobby the government for favorable policies—all on behalf of their client. The requirements to become an attorney in the United States will vary state by state, but typically you will need to possess a bachelor's degree and a law degree, and also pass the state's written bar exam.

As an attorney and negotiator, Terry Leitzell helped ensure the protection of the marine environment and the proper management of fisheries resources for 38 years. Terry represented the State Department in the 1970s and negotiated on behalf of the United States before the International Maritime Organization (IMO), a UN agency responsible for vessel safety and oil spills. Terry's work contributed to the first oil spill prevention treaty and helped to form the IMO's Marine Environment Protection Committee. This committee brings together representatives from maritime, transportation, and environmental agencies to reach agreements on issues such as ship recycling, controlling emissions, and invasive species.

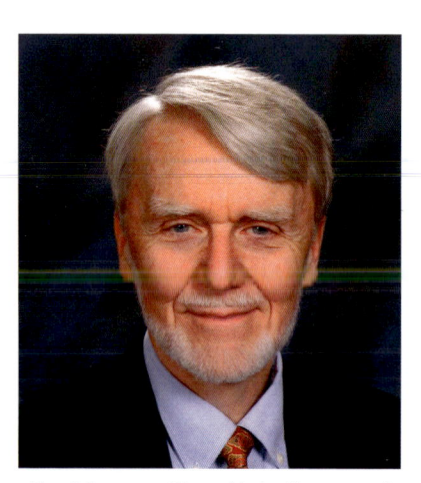

For 38 years, Terry Lietzell ensured protection of the marine environment and proper management of fisheries resources.

From 1978 to 1981, Terry worked at the National Oceanic and Atmospheric Association (NOAA) National Marine Fisheries Service (NMFS). NMFS is responsible for management and regulation of marine fisheries in order to keep environmental protection and industry in a productive balance. Terry Leitzell was the first lawyer to head NMFS; for over 100 years, biologists had headed the agency.

His experience as a negotiator for the government helped to prepare Terry for work in the private sector, where he helped forge relationships between regulators and businesses. Terry represented the fishing industry in Alaska while working for Icicle Seafoods and founded the Marine Conservation Alliance, a unique non-profit working on fishing and environmental issues. Terry did not know that he would specialize in marine resource and environmental law when he was in college, but he found that he was passionate about the subject.

Cleaning Stormwater

Runoff from storm drains is one of the major sources of ocean pollution. Drains empty into nearby bodies of water, which eventually empty into oceans. In many places, stormwater runoff does not go through wastewater treatment plants; instead, pollutants are washed directly into the sea. By monitoring what goes into storm drains, residents can help make sure that what comes out of storm drains is nontoxic.

Education is key. Most people do not think beyond storm drains to where the water will end up. People who would never knowingly dump toxic chemicals into a lake may not give a second thought to making sure those same chemicals don't end up in a storm drain when they wash their cars or fertilize their lawns. To increase awareness, storm drain labeling projects are popping up all over the United States to label storm drains with the name of the waterway that they drain to. This is a simple yet surprisingly effective way to remind people that their actions affect waterways.

Keeping Out the Trash

Since the majority of solid waste, or trash, that ends up in the oceans comes from land-based sources, you can help ocean ecosystems by putting trash in trashcans where it belongs.

People acting together to protect marine habitat can be a powerful force. There are countless examples of local efforts to keep coastal areas litter-free. Take the Alaskan commercial fishing industry, which works together with coastal communities to clean up debris and prevent it from entering the ocean.[48] On the other side of the country, the Blue Ocean Society for Marine Conservation sponsors clean oceans in New Hampshire. They offer adopt-a-beach programs, schedule local cleanup days, do research, and provide educational outreach.[49]

YOUTH PROFILE
Kyle Thiermann

Professional surfer Kyle Thiermann sees the uniting force of oceans as an opportunity to inspire change. Kyle's travels from his hometown of Santa Cruz, California to surf spots in Hawaii, Chile, and Sri Lanka opened his eyes to environmental issues that threaten surfing communities. In response, he created a popular series of short films called "Surfing for Change" that showcases everyday solutions to protect the oceans and the people who depend on them.

In one of his films, Kyle shows the importance of choosing reusable water bottles and bags over the plastic alternatives. He tracks one plastic bag from California to Hawaii, where plastic debris is piling up on the beaches of Oahu. Kyle found that only 5% of plastic products get recycled and even when plastics are recycled, there is no guarantee they will be

Kyle Thiermann is a professional surfer who works to keep our oceans healthy.

properly disposed of. Wind often carries plastic debris out of landfills and other storage facilities and into the oceans, only to wash up on the shores of islands like Hawaii. Sea creatures may mistake plastic debris for food; millions of sea birds die each year because they mistake plastic bags for jellyfish.

In addition to keeping the ocean free of plastic, Kyle promotes shopping for surf gear at locally-owned businesses. Kyle learned that even if clothes are sold locally, most are still made in other parts of the world. So he traveled to Sri Lanka to visit a clothing manufacturer that supplies t-shirts sold in surf shops across the United States, including his local shop in Santa Cruz. Kyle was surprised to find that wages and working conditions at the factory were steadily improving as a result of consumer pressure in the United States. By choosing to shop at local surf shops rather than at larger chains, people were actively changing how clothing factories treated workers. In contrast to multinationals that send profits to their corporate headquarters, local shops use their profits to support the local economy and help boost quality of life for the workers who make their clothing.

In 2011, Kyle won the Brower Youth Award for his "Surfing for Change" series. He continues to create films and speak at high schools and universities on the importance of keeping our oceans healthy, supporting responsible business practices, and keeping small surfing communities afloat.

WHAT YOU CAN DO: Oceans

You have the power to protect the oceans, whether you live on the coast or hundreds of miles from an ocean view. The choices each of us makes, from the foods we choose to the waste we produce, impact the marine environment. Here are a few ways you can support healthy oceans:

- Mind your carbon footprint—reduce energy consumption
- Limit plastic use—avoid plastic bags, unnecessary packaging, and disposable water bottles
- Use a sustainable seafood guide such as the Monterey Seafood Guide when shopping for seafood at a grocery story or ordering at a restaurant
- When you are interacting with the ocean, whether kayaking, canoeing, surfing, or boating, be mindful of the marine life below and don't throw anything overboard
- Make a statement with your wallet—do not purchase products made from coral or shark
- Care for your local beach—leave no trace when you visit the beach and volunteer for beach cleanup
- Investigate if you have any youth programs at your local aquarium or seal sitters programs

Caring for your local beach by picking up trash can be one way to protect oceans.

- Educate yourself and make your voice heard—If you feel your local elected officials aren't doing enough to protect the oceans, write a letter explaining your concern about an ocean issue, why it is important, and what government can do about it

Because the oceans are so immense, they may seem inexhaustible and immune to human activities. As our experience has shown us, this simply isn't true. By understanding our connection to Earth's oceans, we can begin to manage ocean resources in sustainable ways to protect our seas for future generations.

POINT **COUNTERPOINT**

Should indigenous groups continue to hunt endangered whale species?

From the Faroese islanders of the North Atlantic to the Bequia people of St. Vincent and the Grenadines, indigenous groups have hunted whales for centuries. However, many species of whale are now endangered due to human actions. Today international and national regulations limit how many whales can be killed, though these regulations often provide exemptions for native or indigenous groups. Some argue that this is a double standard, while others believe it is a fair approach. Consider the arguments given by both sides below. What do you think?

POINT

Yes

- **Whaling is a critical component of indigenous culture in some parts of the world.** Hunting a handful of whales each year can help indigenous groups connect to the traditional practices of their ancestors. For the Bequia people of the Grenadines (in the Caribbean Sea), whaling is a tradition that pre-dates European settlement and represents skill and bravery.[50] Whalers and whale songs are part of Bequia folk art.

- **Indigenous people often rely on whaling to supply their dietary needs.** The Inupiat and Yup'ik Eskimos of Alaska have hunted bowhead whales for meat for over two thousand years. The hunt is a community activity that helps supply 11 tribes with protein to carry them through Alaska's harsh winters. The International Whaling Commission allows the tribes to take just over 50 bowhead whales a year.[51]

- **The whaling practices of indigenous tribes did not lead to the collapse of Earth's whale populations; commercial whaling was responsible.** Indigenous groups who hunt sustainably in order to preserve their culture and gain nourishment should not be punished.

COUNTERPOINT

No

- **Whaling is inhumane.** Whales are intelligent and social animals able to feel pain and suffer. Traditional forms of whaling are exceptionally cruel, often driving these massive creatures to the beach where they are slaughtered slowly using large knives.[52]

- **In a modern, globalized world, indigenous peoples can adapt their diets.** Tribes have access to a wide variety of food sources now and do not need to rely on whale meat.

- **We must act to protect the population of many whale species.** Whale populations are suffering. For example, despite 45 years of protection, only 1% of the original population of the Antarctic blue whale remains today.[53] Recovery of depleted species has been slower than expected. Even if indigenous groups are not part of the problem, they must be part of the solution if whale populations are to recover.

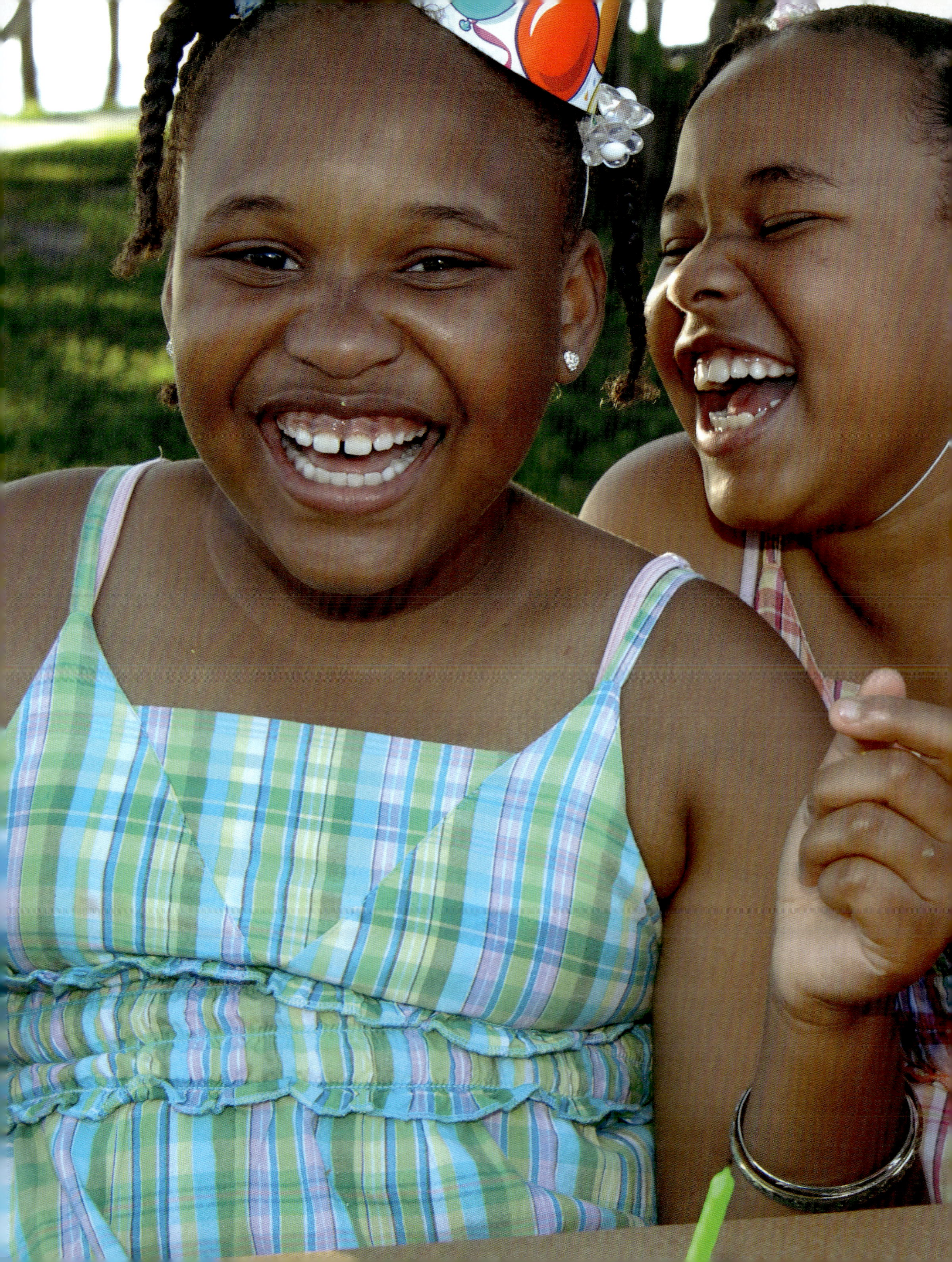

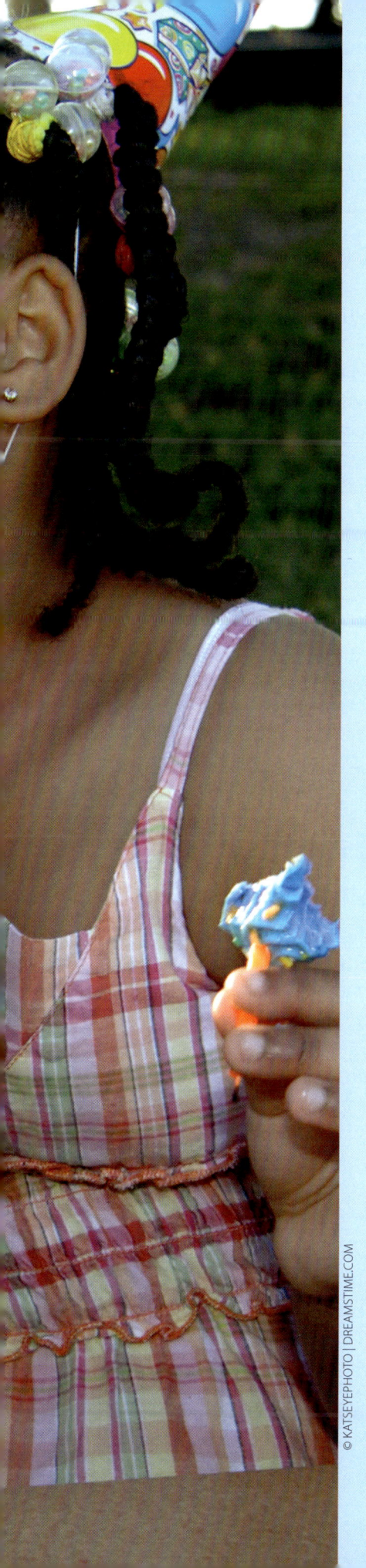

Chapter 12
Quality of Life

> **GUIDING QUESTIONS**
> - How do social, economic, and environmental factors contribute to a higher quality of life?
> - How can addressing global issues like poverty and weak governance improve quality of life?

Introduction to Quality of Life

Imagine the leader of your country decides that the happiness of all citizens is as important as, if not more important than, economic prosperity. Now imagine that this leader is only 16 years old. Would you trust his leadership? In 1972, Bhutan crowned Jigme Singye Wangchuck their king. At the time, he was 16 years old. He believed that focusing only on economic development would limit his country's progress. Instead, he felt that material and spiritual development had to work together to truly achieve a fully developed society. To guide his country on this path, he created the goal of **Gross National Happiness (GNH)**. GNH was a means to measure quality of life in a holistic way beyond economic progress. Decades later, Bhutan still works to increase its GNH by measuring things like psychological well-being, health, time balance, cultural preservation, and community vitality.[1]

Some believe an effort to measure happiness can help improve the quality of life for the citizens of a country. Later in this chapter, you will read about different ways governments measure a country's progress. As you learn about these measurements, consider which might be most effective at improving people's quality of life.

What is Considered a Good Life?

When determining what makes for a higher quality of life, we should first distinguish the term quality of life from a related term, standard of living. While the two terms are interrelated, they describe two distinct concepts.

When most people talk about improving the well-being of a population, they talk about raising their **standard of living**. Standard of living does not have anything to do with how happy you are, how healthy you are, or how much education you have. It is based almost entirely on economic factors, which makes it easy to measure. A nation's standard of living can give us an idea of how much material wealth people have and how comfortable their lives are. It's true that having a good income and some material possessions can make a person's life better. Understanding other factors that contribute to a better life, however, can be useful when making choices at a personal level and at a governmental level.

Quality of life is a more holistic measure of well-being based on a variety of values. Some of these are easy to calculate, such as years of education, while others are more open to interpretation, such as physical and mental health, leisure time, and social activity. This ambiguity makes it difficult for people to agree on a way to measure quality of life across a population. For example, imagine that you live on the outskirts of town and cannot make it into town for a lot of social activities. This suits you because you like reading and would rather stay home than socialize. You consider yourself to have a high quality of life. However, your friend who lives next door craves social activity and is very frustrated to be living in a remote area where there is nothing going on. Her frustration makes her feel like she has a low quality of life.

You can see that a good quality of life depends on people having certain things that they feel are necessary for them to be happy. These things will vary from person to person, but there are some common elements that tend to promote a higher quality of life. Communities that support access to basic resources, democratic governance, civic participation, public safety, and economic opportunity foster high quality of life.[2] In these communities, people feel supported, protected, and respected.

Quality of Life and Sustainability

In many ways, high quality of life is a goal synonymous with sustainability. It is certainly hard to imagine a sustainable community that has not achieved a high quality of life. A community that is not supported by a sustainable economic system, does not protect its environmental resources, and does not promote a culture of equity and equality is less likely to cultivate the happiness of its population. Quality of life is largely a matter of opportunities and access—the more opportunities a person has, the greater that person's happiness and well-being.

Think about spending money. If you always spend more than you really have (using credit, for example), this might cause you to feel stressed and unhappy. The same goes for the earth's resources. Like the money in your bank account, the earth's resources are limited. If we

> *In many ways, high quality of life is a goal synonymous with sustainability. It is certainly hard to imagine a sustainable community that has not achieved a high quality of life.*

Social connections with friends and family can give us a sense of belonging.

use more than we can afford now, we borrow against our future needs, as well as the needs of future generations. As we consider choices we can make to improve quality of life, you might be surprised to know that these choices can complement a sustainable lifestyle. By increasing the sustainability of our local and global communities, we can reduce stress and anxiety about the future and create opportunities for current and future generations to live happier lives. This is true at all levels from the individual all the way up to national policies.

Economics

Not having enough money to cover your basic needs is a barrier to achieving a high quality of life. Therefore, one of the fundamental requirements for a good quality of life is a livable income. Having a livable income means that a person is able to purchase or otherwise obtain basic necessities such as clean water, food, shelter, and clothing. It also means having enough left over to cover an emergency, such as a trip to the hospital. That money provides security, a key factor in quality of life.

A person's job contributes to his or her quality of life when it provides a livable income and security. It's not all about money, though. Meaningful employment, or a job that you enjoy and feel contributes to society, is also an important quality of life consideration.

Society

Our social connections (friends, family, community) are some of the things that make us happy. Social connections give us a sense of security, a sense of belonging, and a sense of identity. People who have a support network of close social connections are less likely to develop stress-related health problems. They also recover more rapidly from trauma or illness.[3]

MTV and the Associated Press commissioned a survey of thousands of young people between the ages of 12 and 24 to see what made them happy. How would you have answered? Think about the three things that make you the happiest.

In the survey results, technology such as cell phones was pretty high on the list, but two other key elements to teen happiness emerged: family, friends, and loved ones, and religion/spirituality. Money and fame showed up on the list, but they did not rank nearly as high as these other elements.[4]

Research shows that while increased income can benefit people—especially those living in poverty—once people reach a middle-class income level increased income does not equate to more happiness.[5]

Environment

Many people feel that a connection to nature and the outdoors is essential to a good quality of life. Researchers at the Human-Environment Research Laboratory at the University of Illinois are just some of the many scientists investigating the ties between our well-being and green spaces, such as parks and wilderness areas. They found several benefits for people with greater access to green spaces, including lower levels of attention deficit hyperactivity disorder (ADHD), improved self-discipline, lower levels of domestic violence, and reduced street crime.[6]

Preserving our environment and providing sustainable access to green spaces will promote well-being for everyone. Additionally, preventing environmental pollution not only keeps the environment healthy, but keeps people healthy as well. Good air quality, for example, can directly contribute to decreased asthma rates. When peak morning traffic in Atlanta decreased by 23% during the Summer Olympic Games in 1996, emergency visits for asthma events in children decreased by 42%.[7]

Background on Quality of Life

The past 200 years have seen a remarkably large worldwide improvement in people's quality of life.[8] Despite many changes over this period of time, the things that most influence people's lives remain centered on day-to-day experiences rather than large crisis events, such as war or economic downturns, or time-dependent events, such as education.

Better living conditions, greater access to medicine, the ability to control the spread of disease, and advancing technology have all led to worldwide increases in **life expectancy**. Life expectancy is the expected number of years a person will live. In the period 1950-1955, the average life expectancy at birth in sub-Saharan Africa was 35.3 years. Just 40 years later, life

Worldwide, life expectancy has increased. A multi-generational family from Kashmir, India poses in this photo.

expectancy in this region had increased to 47 years. A similar increase in life expectancy took place around the world, with the most dramatic changes happening in places where life expectancy was lowest to begin with.

For women, increases in life expectancy have been linked to women getting married at older ages and women having access to different types of contraception. Prior to the widespread introduction of contraceptives for women such as birth control pills and intrauterine devices (IUDs) in the 1960s, women had to rely on birth control methods such as abstinence. Access to contraception lowered birth rates and increased women's health and productivity. Take the example of India. In 1945, a woman in India had a life expectancy (at birth) of only 32.1 years. By 2012, a woman born in India had an average life expectancy of 68.3 years, largely due to access to contraceptives.[9]

Education is another key factor in quality of life. Overall, primary and secondary school enrollment has increased in all parts of the world. The gap between girls and boys enrolled in school is becoming smaller and smaller. However, some countries have shown a decrease in school enrollment in recent years.[10] In some places this is related to violent conflict, as in Afghanistan and Croatia.

Even with all of the progress discussed above, there is still a lot of room for improvement. Quality of life is about equal access to opportunities, but in many countries around the world there are still large gaps between rich and poor and between men and women. Countries with ongoing conflict or fractured governments are unable to make the same progress as more peaceful, stable countries.

Quality of Life Trends

Do people work to live, or live to work? This question is frequently asked when discussing quality of life. When you think about your future career and life aspirations, how do you think you will want work to factor into your life?

In addition to working many hours, people spend a lot of time commuting to and from work.

In today's society, people spend more and more of their time at work. For some, it is because the basic cost of living has increased. For others, it is because their employers want a better bottom line and require their employees to work longer hours. There are also people who just love their jobs. Whatever the reason, decreased leisure time can have a negative impact on quality of life due to the higher stress of working long hours and reduced engagement in other physically, mentally, and emotionally stimulating activities. Overworked people may have less ability or desire to be involved with their families, their neighbors, their friends, and their communities.

In the 1930s, the British economist John Maynard Keynes predicted that improved technology and industrial efficiency would mean that people only had to work for a few hours, if any, per day. To his mind, machines would free up the time people previously spent doing work like weaving textiles by hand. Keynes also thought that if people were left without any purpose in life except to enjoy themselves, it would be bad for the human race and actually decrease our quality of life.[11] Keynes would probably be surprised to find that people in the 21st century are working more than ever before.

CASE STUDY: Longer Work Hours in the United States[12]

In the early 19th century, people in the United States worked approximately 3,000 hours per year. They spent their time doing heavy manual and industrial labor. This averaged out to a 60-hour workweek. Hours began to fall over the years as labor productivity increased (meaning that people could do more work in less time). In 1929, the number of annual work hours had been reduced by 600 hours. This trend continued for several decades. Some of the decrease in work hours can be attributed to workers forming unions to negotiate better working hours. The reduction in the hours worked by the average American leveled off during the 1970s.

Currently, Americans work significantly more than Western Europeans, who receive six-week vacations in addition to other holidays. Americans, on the other hand, tend to have two weeks of vacation each year.

How do longer work hours impact quality of life? Consider the following facts:

- Studies have found that people who work long hours tend to make more resource-intensive choices (e.g., carbon-intensive commutes and eating out for meals).

- Long work hours can increase stress and decrease family and social connections.

Longer work hours can impact a person's quality of life.

Some people have realized these impacts and have made choices to downshift their work. *Downshifting* means that they may choose to work part-time jobs instead of full-time jobs, take positions that have less demanding schedules, and accept lower salaries in exchange for more time outside of work. You may think that decreased salaries could lead to less satisfaction with life, but 85% of people surveyed who made a downshift reported that they were happy to reduce their incomes for increased life satisfaction.[13]

A few corporations have attempted to provide flexibility to their employees so that they do not have to give up their jobs. SAS Institute, for example, is a software company that provides subsidized childcare, unlimited sick time, intramural sports leagues, and a free health care center for its employees.[14]

How is Quality of Life Measured?

Historically, quality of life has been studied by looking at the discrete value of a country's standard of living, largely based on its annual income or *gross domestic product (GDP)*. However, new measurement tools are emerging to take into account how people are doing, not just how much they are earning and spending. Consider the following forms of measuring quality of life:

The Better Life Index

The Organization for Economic Cooperation and Development (OECD) promotes policies that improve the economic and social well-being of people around the world. The OECD has created the Better Life Index, which looks at 11 different components aside from GDP that can improve a nation's quality of life. These include topics like health, life satisfaction, work-life balance, and education.[15]

Several of the countries that have made the most progress in quality of life over the last

50 years have not seen an increase in economic indicators like GDP. Instead, they are marked by increases in the percentage of children in school, lower infant mortality rates, and longer life spans. Turkey, for example, only saw a 26% increase in income levels between 1970 and 2010; in that same time frame, life expectancy increased by 46% and the education rate increased by 64%.[16]

The Human Development Index

The *Human Development Index (HDI)* ranks countries by their human development levels. Rankings indicate whether a country is developed, developing, or under-developed. Human development indicators are used to look at these non-financial aspects of human life. They measure progress in several areas such as education levels.[17] The HDI gives an overall picture of how all these human development indicators come together in each country. Looking at three main categories of health, education, and income enables each country to be assessed according to more than just its economic abilities. The following table gives a snapshot of countries with different HDI rankings.[18]

As you can see from the table, Norway has the world's highest HDI ranking. The other statistics provided support Norway's number one position. In contrast, Zimbabwe's HDI decreased annually by 1.8% between 1980 and 2010 (although there has been a small upturn in some of the country's human development indicators recently). Yet surprisingly, Zimbabwe scores well with respect to education. The country has spent a higher percentage of its

Human Development Index Rankings				
Country	Norway	Bahamas	Fiji	Zimbabwe
HDI Rank (out of 169 countries)	1	43	86	169
	Very High Human Development	High Human Development	Medium Human Development	Low Human Development
Adult (over 15) literacy rate[19]	100%	95.6	93.7	90.7
Average schooling (years)	12.6	11.1	11.0	7.2
CO_2 per capita (tonnes)	8.6	6.5	1.9	0.8
Expenditure on education (GDP)	6.7%	3.6	5.9	4.6
HDI	0.938	0.784	0.669	0.140
Internet users per 100 people	82.5	31.5	12.2	11.4
Life expectancy (years)	81.0	74.4	69.2	47.0
Unemployment rate	2.6%	7.9	4.6	95*
World Happiness Rank[20] (out of 155 countries)	3	Not ranked	Not ranked	115

*This is only an estimate; current economic conditions in Zimbabwe make it impossible to accurately calculate this number.

GDP on education than the Bahamas, has a respectable number of years of schooling completed, and has a much higher than expected literacy rate.

A Focus on Happiness

Perhaps the best measure of quality of life is also one of the hardest to quantify—how happy people are within a given community or state. No matter what your circumstances, if you are happy, you probably have a good quality of life. If you are unhappy, you have a poor quality of life. While happiness is difficult to quantify, several indicators attempt to do just that, including the Gross National Happiness Index, the Happy Planet Index, and the Gallup-Healthways Well-being Index.

These indices take into account a number of different indicators that look at the well-being of an individual and their overall happiness.

CASE STUDY: Which Country is Happiest?

What do you think makes people in a country happy: Fabulous weather? Lots of jobs? Strong sports teams? Low tax rates? Global wealth and power?

Well, summers in the world's happiest country may be sunny, but the temperature rarely gets above 70°F.[21] Winter days experience an average of just one hour of sunlight between November and January, and the high temperature hovers right around freezing. That eliminates weather as the source of happiness. The unemployment rate in the world's happiest country was estimated at 5.9% in 2010, compared to a world average of 8.7%.[22] So availability of jobs might be a factor contributing to happiness. The country does have national sports teams, but individual participation in amateur sports and an active lifestyle are more important. What about taxes? Citizens in this country pay some of the highest taxes in the world, somewhere between 50 and 70% of their incomes! That hurts, until you factor in how this tax money is used: the government covers the entire cost of health care and education and spends the most per capita on children and the elderly of any country in the world.

Denmark has been rated as one of the happiest countries in the world.

So where is this idyllic paradise? Denmark! Denmark came out on top in a number of different surveys including a Gallup Healthways poll and a survey published by the United States National Science Foundation. When asked to rate their happiness on a scale of 1 to 10, most Danes will answer 8 or above.

What makes Danes so happy? Some of the characteristics of Denmark that appear to contribute to the country's happiness include trust, lack of status, and a tightly knit, active society. Danes trust their government to take care of them and they trust each other to do the right thing. Denmark's high tax rates equalize salaries, so there is no particular merit or shame in any type of job. 92% of Danes belong to some form of government-subsidized social club and seem to enjoy getting together with other Danes with very little excuse needed. Denmark's built environment is even structured in a way that emphasizes communal interaction and trust. After 5pm on a weekday, outdoor cafes are filled with people socializing. There are also tables and benches placed along sidewalks so people can stop and chat with others.[23]

Quality of Life Today

While we can't say with certainty that a particular thing or situation will make everyone happy, data has shown that there are some common factors that are more likely to produce a higher quality of life.

Health

Happiness studies have shown that out of health, wealth, and education, good health has the highest influence on perceived happiness.[24] On a personal level, this means having good physical and mental health. On a community level, it relates to health resources, conditions, and policies that impact everyone.

Good physical and mental health have many positive outcomes including fewer health-related expenses and the ability to attend school, go to work, and live a longer life. When a community focuses on public health and disease prevention, good public health can enhance the health status and lengthen the life expectancy of a population.[25]

One example can be found in Rwanda, a country located in central Africa with a population of approximately 11 million people. A massive genocide in the 1990s killed millions of Rwandans and destroyed basic infrastructure for water, sanitation, health, and education. A series of earthquakes in 2008 further damaged the country's infrastructure and ability to provide basic services. However, through the efforts of the Japanese government, UNICEF, and an organization called Caritas Cyangugu, a measure of health and sanitation has been restored to the earthquake-affected southwest corner of Rwanda.[26]

The village of Gihundwe in southwest Rwanda was hit hard by the earthquakes. The village did not have a sewer system and was using broken, unsanitary latrines. As part of a $7.5 million rebuilding effort, the village received 100 new eco-latrines (eco is short for ecological). Steps were taken to source as much

Eco-latrines were installed in the village of Gihundwe. Not only did these eco-latrines help to make the community healthier, waste from the latrines were used to fertilize crops.

material as possible locally, as well as to involve adults in the community in the project to foster a sense of ownership and sustainability. In addition to being much healthier than the old setup, the eco-latrines have another benefit for this agricultural community—the waste from the latrines can be used to fertilize crops. Residents of Gihundwe were also given disease prevention training and learned about the importance of hand washing to keep the community healthy.

Through efforts such as these in Rwanda, communities can learn healthy practices that improve their daily lives.

Income and Economic Opportunities

It's true that money can't buy happiness: income levels doubled in the United States between 1957 and 2002, but the percentage of people who reported being happy stayed the same, or even declined somewhat, in that same period.[27]

CASE STUDY: Poverty Reduction in Savannah[28]

Step Up Savannah, an independent nonprofit organization, came out of the work of Savannah's Anti-Poverty Task Force, convened in 2004 by the mayor of Savannah, Georgia. True to its name, Step Up Savannah has fostered a partnership among local businesses, government, nonprofit organizations, and neighborhood leaders to step up to the challenge of eliminating deep pockets of poverty that have persisted in the city. The organization brings together direct service providers, government agencies and others to address the roots of poverty from different angles.

The Chatham Apprentice Program (CAP) is Step Up's specific workforce development program. CAP provides job and life skills training for motivated residents to allow them to compete for higher-paying jobs. The program is a collaboration among Chatham County government, Step Up, and Savannah Technical College to assist individuals in developing skills to compete in the job market, secure employment, and utilize employment to become more self-sufficient. CAP students receive workforce readiness training, vocational training from Savannah Technical College and job placement assistance. Students have received certificates in Carpentry/Concrete Forming, Masonry, Welding, Historic Preservation, and Warehousing.

Step Up also oversees the Center for Working Families network of direct service providers, which provides GED tutoring and financial literacy coaching. The center also helps eligible families apply for public benefits. Being able to build wealth and financial literacy is another key step to getting out of poverty; without a little help, this is often an unachievable goal. Step Up promotes different solutions to provide that extra push, including financial education and microloans to help small business owners.

Bank On Savannah is a Step Up program that provides banking services to those currently living in poverty. Many people in poverty do not have access to banks and instead rely on non-bank check cashing facilities to provide financial services, often at a high cost. Setting up a basic savings account reduces costs and can help families in case of emergencies.

Step Up also realizes that there are many other factors that influence a person's ability to get and keep a job. Childcare, affordable health care, transportation, and affordable housing are all part of their effort to help families get and stay out of poverty.

Young boys play basketball in Carver Heights, a neighborhood of Savannah, Georgia.

However, money can buy a lot of things that help to promote a person's well-being. In developing countries, a small amount of money can make a big difference in helping to alleviate poverty. The key is to make sure that people have the opportunity to earn more than enough money to cover their basic needs.

Governance

Research on quality of life indicates that people's lives are improved when they are able to participate in the affairs and decision-making processes that affect them and their families.[29] Increased *civic engagement* can benefit many people. The key to increasing civic engagement, however, is not just having a population that is willing to be engaged; the government—city, state, or national—must also encourage involvement.

For example, during the 1980s, the city of Hampton, Virginia faced a number of challenges related to high unemployment and a weak economy. City leaders decided to invest in youth by developing youth leadership skills and engaging young people in governance. At first, the city involved youth in local service projects. They then invited youth to participate on city boards, where they developed more complex skills and had opportunities to make decisions on topics such as school reform and job training.[30]

Decades later, the city has become a model for effective civic engagement in governance. Hampton showed how local government can engage people and involve them in improving their community.[31]

Community Life

We have seen throughout this chapter that social ties and community life are significant factors in a high quality of life. A sense of belonging, security, companionship, and intellectual stimulation all contribute to human well-being. Studies have demonstrated how teenagers who participate in sports teams report feeling healthier and happier in life, not only due to the physical activity, but also because sports teams can increase social connectedness and bonding between members.[32]

Robert Putnam, a professor of Public Policy at Harvard University, confirms this: "the single most common finding from a half century's research on the correlates of life satisfaction…is that happiness is best predicted by the breadth and depth of one's social connections."[33] Civic engagement and social networks have been shown to improve health, lower crime, and lead to greater happiness.[34] These social ties can even lengthen your life span. The results of several studies in Japan, Scandinavia, and the United States show that a person who is isolated is two to five times more likely to die in any given year than a person who is socially active.[35]

Technology can also play a large role in building relationships between people. It is no coincidence that the country with the lowest number of Internet users is also the country with the lowest ranking on the Human Development Index. The Internet is more than just a tool for playing games and keeping in touch with friends. In our information-based society, the Internet is a vast resource of tools that connect people in many different and important ways.

Civic engagement, like these individuals volunteering, has been connected to increased happiness.

Environment

Both our natural and our built environments can contribute to our happiness in the short and long term. Humans spend a lot of time indoors, so we need to pay attention to our built environment as well as the natural environment. An unhealthy building—that is, one with poor air quality or toxins—can make inhabitants sick. On the other hand, healthy built environments, from homes and buildings to streets, parks, and other public spaces, help support human health. Since health is the number one factor in the perception of happiness, we need to do all we can to ensure that we have healthy spaces to work, live, and play.

Aside from the overarching concerns of protecting and preserving the environment, green space is important for our well-being. We use it as a place to exercise, relax, and spend time with other people. In short, unless you have plant allergies there are really no drawbacks to having green space, whether it is natural or manmade.

Pathways to Progress: Quality of Life

UN Millennium Development Goals

In 2000, the United Nations Development Program set eight **Millennium Development Goals (MDGs)** to be achieved by a target

CASE STUDY: Pura Vida in Costa Rica

"Pura Vida" is a phrase commonly associated with the country of Costa Rica. It literally translates to "pure life," but is also associated with the concept of enjoying life expressed by the phrase "this is living!" According to the Happy Life Index, an index that measures sustainability and human well-being, Costa Rica is one of the happiest and greenest countries in the world. Nicoya Peninsula in Costa Rica is one of only a handful of Blue Zones in the world, where people often live to be over 100 years old.[36] Aside from the lush rain forests and beautiful beaches, why exactly does the country have this reputation?

Costa Rica has taken a number of measures to ensure its environmental health. In 1997, it started a carbon tax to pay landowners and indigenous communities money so they would not participate in logging or ranching activities that resulted in deforestation. Oil importers, water-bottling plants, and sewage treatment plants have to pay special taxes if they want to do business in the country.[37] Additionally, 90% of the country's energy supply comes from renewable resources.[38] These decisions are all intended to contribute to environmental sustainability. Do you think Costa Rica's decisions could be applied to other countries throughout the world?

Costa Rica is one of the greenest countries in the world.

New York City has made a commitment to increase civic engagement through service opportunities.

date of 2015. World leaders from 191 UN member countries agreed to work toward the following goals:

- End poverty and hunger
- Ensure all children complete primary school
- Eliminate gender inequality in education
- Improve child and maternal health
- Combat HIV/AIDS
- Promote environmental sustainability
- Develop global partnerships for economic development[39]

These ambitious goals take a multifaceted approach to making the world more peaceful and secure. Ultimately, they aim to improve well-being for all.

The MDGs were not picked at random. They are specific targets to improve the lives of the world's poorest people. The goals reinforce one another to help improve quality of life in other ways. For example, education, a goal in itself, also improves health, increases job opportunities, increases civic engagement, and improves social cohesion.[40]

Increasing Civic Engagement

As mentioned earlier, increasing civic engagement can help to improve quality of life. The city of New York put forth one model for increasing civic engagement through service opportunities. New York City Mayor Michael Bloomberg made commitments to support service in five different categories:

- Help New Yorkers connect to service opportunities more easily
- Create or elevate volunteer opportunities that address the city's most urgent needs
- Support nonprofits and public agencies to use more volunteers, and do so more effectively and strategically
- Promote service as a core part of what it means to be a citizen of New York City
- Measure progress against clear goals[41]

The city's focus on civic engagement has had many positive impacts. Approximately 1.4 million volunteers have participated in New York service initiatives addressing issues related to helping neighbors and communities. As the first deputy mayor Patricia E. Harris has said about this focus on civic engagement, "NYC service is an extraordinary testament to the generosity and compassion of New Yorkers. In every borough, residents have come together to share their unique skills and help keep our communities strong. As our efforts continue to inspire others throughout the nation, I know NYC service will have a long-lasting impact on many citizens throughout our city and country."[42]

Spending Time with Family, Friends, and Neighbors

If we know that spending more time with our family and friends makes us feel better, why do we spend so much time working alone or isolating ourselves? We sometimes get caught up in spending, and we have to work to be able to support that spending. It is easy to understand that after working very hard, people want to treat themselves to a new outfit or a nicer car. However, if we take time to connect with other members of our communities—our friends, family members, and neighbors—we may realize just how much we can support each other in our well-being.

This mutual support can extend across all segments of society. This was the case for Habitat for Humanity in North Carolina when it helped to strengthen social connections between people of different races, religions, and ethnicities. In 1996, the organization encouraged black and white church congregations in Winston-Salem, North Carolina to work together to help build houses. Through building these homes, relationships have developed between both races. They have attended each other's services, swapped choirs, and worked together on education initiatives. Soon after this initial success, a church, temple, and mosque in the area collaborated to sponsor the building of nine more homes. As one homeowner said, "If I were blind, you would have to convince me that these people were not my brothers and sisters."[43]

Assessing Community Happiness[44]

In addition to polling like Gallup-Healthways that assesses happiness at the national level, communities in several countries are starting to do the same at the local level. Using a shortened version of a survey developed for Bhutan, cities, colleges, and businesses in Brazil have been trying to measure their well-being. The process involves many high school and middle school students. One leader in the happiness effort is Susan Andrews, an American who has lived in Brazil since 1992 and runs a model environmentally sustainable eco-village project called Future Vision. She has helped local schools near the city of Sao Paulo train their students to conduct happiness surveys in local neighborhoods and even in impoverished favelas (slums). The students learn about the science of happiness at school and then go door to door in pairs to interview local residents. Students tabulate scores for the communities that are used to guide local dialogues about how quality of life might be improved.

In Victoria, British Columbia, a similar survey is used by city government to assess local well-being as part of the Happiness Index Partnership (HIP). Victoria's mayor, Dean Fortin, says, "It may seem flakey to be

People spend time together in Dolores Park, California.

measuring happiness, but if you can measure it and mark it out you really know what impact your policies are having on your community."

Now, many American cities are starting to use a survey to measure satisfaction in ten areas of life: financial well-being; environment; physical and mental health; confidence in government; time balance; satisfaction with work; community participation; social support; education; and access to arts, culture and recreation.

In the small town of Nevada City, California, high school students have taken the survey door to door as part of a special learning project called the Woolman Semester. As part of the project, they also study the science of happiness and create their own website and videos about the topic.

YOUTH PROFILE
Alfredo Maldonado

Teenagers are sometimes labeled apathetic. It's said that they don't care about what's happening in the world. Despite this claim, there are a number of examples of youth taking charge and making a positive impact in their communities around the world. The Future Project is an organization that believes that when teenagers become inspired, they can do amazing things to improve their own lives and the lives of those around them.

Since its start in 2011, the organization has worked with high school students in New York City, New Haven, and Washington, D.C. to help them identify what most inspires them and how they can channel this energy into 30-day challenges. Students are paired up with coaches who

CAREER PROFILE Wellness Instructor

Do you want to help people stay healthy, but you're not too keen on blood and germs and spending almost all your time in a hospital? One career that provides an opportunity to help people live happier, stronger lives is that of wellness instructor. These educators come in many different forms. Most start with a bachelor's degree and many are nurses or doctors. Others are lecturers that give public talks on specific topics, such as dealing with cancer, talking to kids about sex, or eating a healthy diet. Some work as consultants to companies, delivering instruction and support to employees. Wellness instructors tackle difficult and often taboo topics to help people prevent illness, injury, poor diet, unplanned parenthood, and a host of other ills in their daily lives.

As a wellness instructor, Debi Sibler helps people with their personal health and wellness.

Debi Silber is The Mojo Coach®. Debi is a registered dietician with a master's degree in nutrition, a certified personal trainer, and a certified Whole Health Coach. She teaches people how to strengthen their bodies and minds. A lot of her work is about preventing illness and she cites the prevalence of dangerous but preventable illness (like Type 2 Diabetes) as why her work is so valuable in creating a sustainable future. But for Debi, wellness is about much more than simply not being sick. She says, "There's so much power when we take responsibility for our thoughts, behaviors, actions, habits, and lifestyle because these changes affect us on so many levels. And it's through these changes that we've cleared the path to discover our unique gift, talent, strength and passion." Debi ought to know; it was her own illness that made her decide to become a Whole Health Coach and inspired her to help others achieve spiritual, mental, and physical wellness.

support them in fulfilling these 30-day challenges. The goal is to help youth discover their dreams and purpose so that they can live a meaningful life. Examples of projects have included:

- Creating a dance group and performing two dance routines
- Building a summer skate program for youth
- Introducing people to different types of music

Alfredo Maldonado is one Future Challenge participant. His 30-day challenge was called "Unites Music Inspiration." His idea was to write and produce music that drew on musical traditions of all of the races at the school he attended in New Haven in order to foster dialogue, understanding, and friendship.

Alfredo Maldonado

Alfredo was inspired to start rapping at a young age by his friend Mike and famous artists like Eminem and Tyler the Creator. He learned that it didn't matter how you looked; the music's message and doing what you love were the important things. When asked about how making music relates to improving his quality of life, Alfredo says, "I think it makes life fun. I don't do drugs or drink, or go to parties for that matter at all. So I think music and skating make my life exciting. It makes it worth living. And my life just keeps getting better and better."

Just think—if everyone you knew did something that inspired them, how might their quality of life improve?

WHAT YOU CAN DO — Quality of Life

There are a number of actions that you as an individual can take to improve quality of life for yourself and for others:

- Ask yourself, what contributes to happiness and the "good life?" Consider both material and nonmaterial indicators of well-being.
- Become aware of your consumption patterns. What do you want? What do you need? What do you buy? Consider food, clothing, and recreation.
- Take inventory of how you use your time. Ask yourself, do I spend enough time on things that matter to me and things that help me live a good life?
- Consider ways you could help out a friend or family member in need (e.g., calling a grandparent or helping a friend out with something he or she does not understand in class).
- Participate in projects in your community to improve the quality of life for those who may struggle to meet their basic needs.

This Neighborhood House volunteer reads to children.

- Consider starting a happiness project in your high school. You can find out more at www.happycounts.org.

POINT | COUNTERPOINT

Does money buy happiness?

POINT

Yes

- **Money can definitely buy happiness.** It provides us options and access to opportunities. The key is to spend money on things that lead to more happiness. For example, research shows that people tend to be much happier when they spend money on experiences rather than material possessions. So using your money to purchase a flight in order to go on an African safari may bring more happiness to you than an object you purchase.[45]

- **People with a higher income can afford many things that support well-being, especially related to health.** When you have money for things such as nutritious food and good medical care, it's easier to keep healthy.[46] There is an old adage that says, "Without health, there is no wealth." It may be just as accurate to say, "Without wealth, there is no health."

COUNTERPOINT

No

- **Once a person's income level reaches a certain level, money does not buy happiness.** Purchasing things that have been equated with high status such as a fancy car or big house doesn't actually have a lot to do with being happy. In fact, it's been shown that donating money has a greater link to happiness than spending it.[47]

- **A sense of respect and being valued has more to do with happiness than how much a person makes.** A study from the University of California, Berkeley looked at the happiness of business students pre- and post-graduation and found that happiness was linked more to how much people valued their work than their socioeconomic status.[48]

The country of Bhutan measures Gross National Happiness (GNH). GNH gives equal importance to economic and non-economic aspects of well-being.

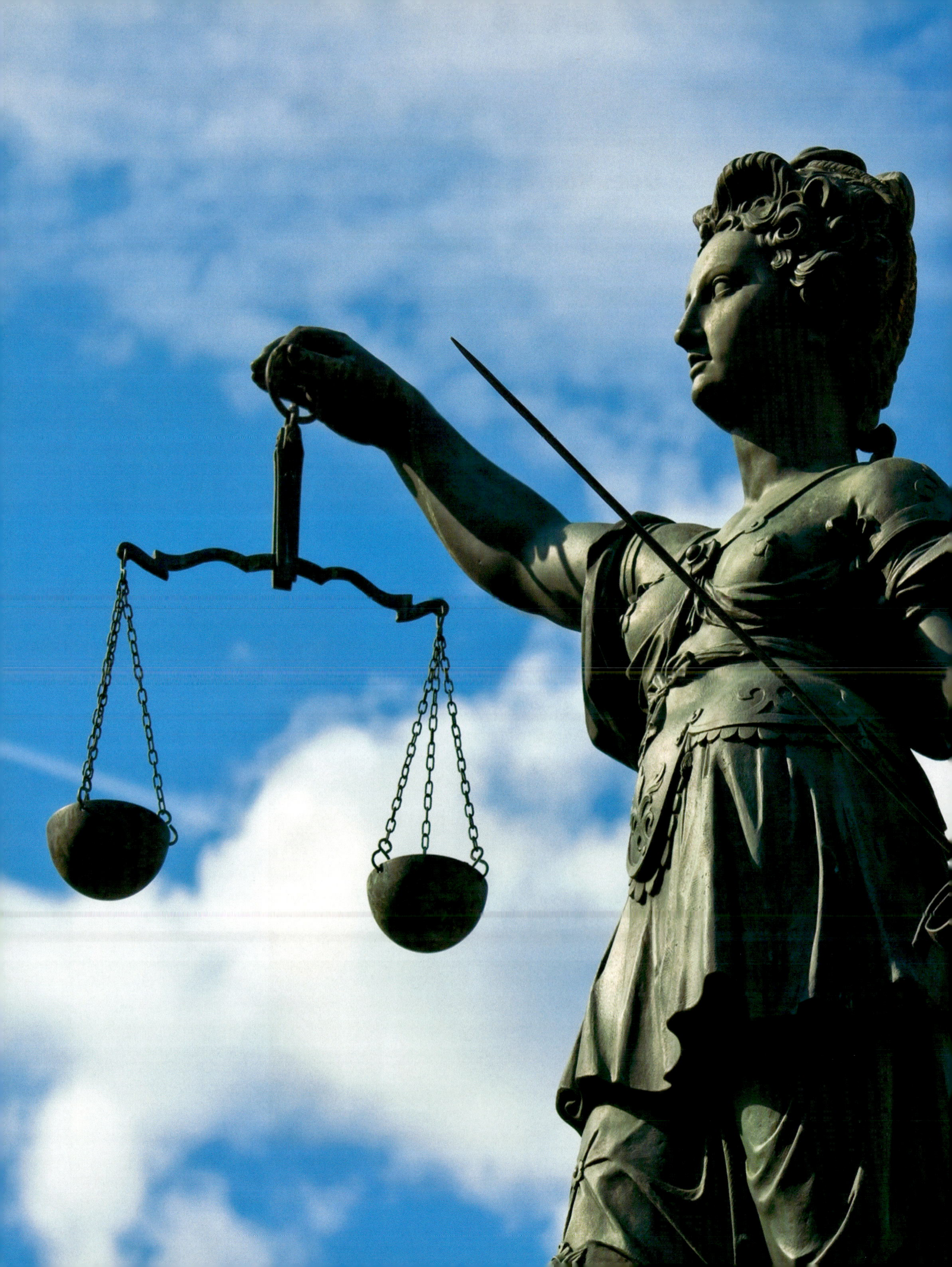

Chapter 13

Governance

> **GUIDING QUESTIONS**
> - How are governance and sustainability connected?
> - What are aspects of good governance?

Introduction to Governance

Have you ever thought about what people your age have the power to do? Have you considered how you can affect the way rules are created in your school or how decisions are made in your local community? Perhaps there is an issue you care deeply about, such as health, music, the environment, or peace. Teenagers around the world have been involved in trying to impact these issues, whether they decide to create murals to beautify their neighborhoods or join committees to change the types of food offered at their school. Many have even worked to create changes in their states, countries, and the world.

Project Citizen is one group working to give youth the tools to participate in local and state government to enact large-scale change. This program teaches young people how to influence public policy related to issues they care about. Among those that have participated in Project Citizen are a group of students from Evergreen High School in Washington State. As these students learned about the U.S. Constitution in their class, they realized that they had not learned about their state government and were unprepared to compare the U.S. Constitution to the constitution of Washington State. The students decided to write a bill that required that teachers instruct high school students about government, economics, and politics so that everyone would know enough to understand and participate in local government. They brought the bill to their state house representative and she agreed to sponsor it. Other officials also endorsed the students' proposal and House Bill 2781 was passed by the state House and Senate on March 27, 2008.[1] By taking initiative and engaging in the democratic process, these students put into motion a change to education policy that affects teenagers' lives throughout Washington State.

Formal decisions about bills and laws are made through a legislative process in the United States.

Examples like this show governance in action. **Governance** refers to the traditions, institutions, and processes that determine how power is exercised, how citizens are given a voice, and how decisions are made on issues of public concern.[2] You might wonder why governance matters. Good governance strives to create systems and structures that promote equity and social welfare for all citizens. Good governance also keeps human development in mind, expanding choices for all people who live within a society.

Governance can be both formal and informal. Formal decisions are guided by a set of rules and laws. The students at Evergreen High School participated in a formal decision when they created a bill that went through the legislative branch of their state government to be passed into law.

Alternately, the students from Evergreen High School could have informally addressed the curriculum issue by discussing it in their classroom. After talking over the students' concerns, the teacher may have decided to teach more about the state constitution or the students may have decided to study these topics on their own. In the end, such informal decisions would have affected students at Evergreen High School, but probably not many more people.

One of the most important aspects of governance is the people involved. The outcome of a decision can be very different depending on who is included (or excluded) from the decision-making process and the degree of influence different parties can bring to bear on the outcome. Take for example, a city governance issue around banning plastic bags in grocery stores. Multiple stakeholders will have different perspectives on the issue. An environmental group might talk about the negative impacts of plastic bag use on the environment. The plastic bag industry may advocate for the use of plastic bags in order to support jobs. If the city proposes charging consumers a small fee to purchase paper bags in place of free plastic bags, social workers might advocate against the fee because of its impact on low-income families. If any one of these stakeholders is left out of the picture, the decision to ban bags does not include all voices.

The Three Parts of Governance

Formal governance consists of three components: government, civil society, and the private sector. These three components help to bring order to society.

Government

Government is the system by which a nation, state, or community is governed. Governments participate in many actions: they keep a country secure through military protection, they provide public services such as health and education to their citizens, and they work to maintain stability in the economy.[3] Government can also represent citizens' voices through elected officials and formal institutions. For example, when you turn 18 years old in the United States, you are granted the right to vote for elected officials such as senators and house representatives. Elected officials from your district will represent your interests as a member of a local community and a citizen of the United States. Government exists at all levels of society, from national legislatures, executives, and other federal governing bodies (like the Department of Labor or the Department of Transportation) to state, county, and municipal governments and agencies.

At a national level, there are many different forms of government. Consider the following in the table below:

Forms of Government	
Afghanistan	Islamic Republic
China	Communist State
Dominican Republic	Democratic Republic
Italy	Republic
Monaco	Constitutional Monarchy
Zimbabwe	Parliamentary Democracy

As a republic, Afghanistan gives its citizens the right to vote for their government representatives.

Some countries have rulers who hold supreme power over everyone in the form of an autocracy. Alexander Lukashenko for example, was elected as the autocratic ruler of Belarus in 1994 and has supreme power over the state and the lives of Belarus' citizens. He was able to alter the constitution to allow himself to serve limitless consecutive terms. His 2010 re-election was the beginning of his fourth term.

Other countries allow adult citizens to have an equal say in the government decisions that impact their lives. Republics, for example, give people the right to choose the representatives they think will best reflect their beliefs.

Civil Society

Influence from outside of government and business is often exercised by civic organizations such as labor unions, churches, and charities. Collectively, these voluntary organizations are referred to as **civil society** and can influence the formal political process in many ways. By making its voice heard, be it through mass demonstrations and protests, education campaigns, or lobbying, civil society has the ability to shape government decision making and drive changes to laws and policies. Civil society can protect the rights of citizens and represent the political face of society.[4] The Civil Rights movement in the United States is one example

One way to help shape government decision-making is through a mass demonstration or protest.

of how civil society significantly changed the way government addressed equality between people.

Civic organizations are as varied as the individual citizens who found them and make up their membership. Their work ranges from education, voter registration, and public health to environmental activism, arts development, and the protection of civil liberties. Well-known civic organizations in the United States include the Sierra Club, an environmental organization; the League of Women Voters, an election organization; and the Red Cross, an international health and emergency relief organization. These groups may be public or private, religious or secular, large or small.

Civic groups often raise important questions for government agencies to consider. They can serve as watchdogs on pressing issues, monitor equity, and provide fresh ideas for sustainable solutions to issues ranging from homelessness to health care to the protection of the environment. A broad range of community, regional, and national civic organizations is a sign of a healthy democracy that provides opportunities for citizens to collaboratively work on and solve local and global issues.

Private Sector

The **private sector**, which includes businesses, industries, and corporations, can have a powerful influence on governance. Businesses also carry on operations that are outside of government but may impact society as a whole, such as the use of natural resources. In many countries, the private sector acts as the primary mechanism of the economy, exchanging goods and services and providing wages and benefits. The private sector has the power to make sustainable choices that support good governance, such as:[5]

- Ensuring that all people have access to credit
- Creating businesses that generate the most jobs and opportunities
- Promoting corporate social responsibility, meaning that businesses adhere to ethical standards and international norms that positively impact the environment, consumers, employees, and communities

The degree to which governments regulate the private sector varies considerably from country to country. Government intervention in the private sector is usually designed to promote equity, access, and health for its citizens.

For example, in addition to subsidies and tax incentives designed to favor certain businesses or discourage others, governments can legislate standards for environmental performance (such as maximum levels of pollution), employee wages and conditions of employment, the role of unions, and restrictions on business monopolies and mergers.

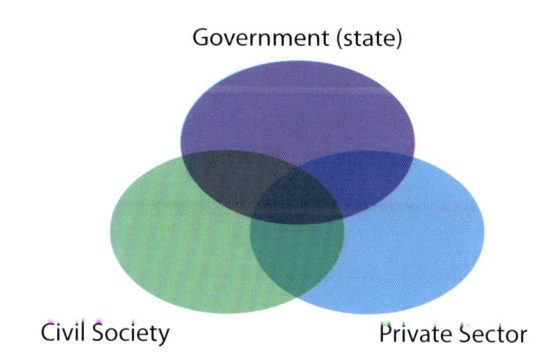

Government (state)

Civil Society   *Private Sector*

Governance and Sustainability

Environmental, social, and economic sustainability are often made possible through good governance. By thinking of the greater good of all people in the long run, governance can create systems that are equitable for people and the planet. For example, in response to government regulation and consumer interest, some automobile manufacturers have begun to address global warming and oil depletion by developing fuel-efficient cars and vehicles that run on alternative fuels. When the private sector, civil society, and government are able to collectively work together, they can achieve sustainable outcomes.

Economy

Good governance is crucial to economic development and poverty reduction within a country. Studies have shown that both autocracies and democracies with well-developed institutions have had much higher rates of economic development than those without established government institutions.[6]

When the economy is effectively controlled by foreign interests or by illegal activities at home, this loss of economic power indicates that traditional governance structures are weak.

Additionally, the concentration of decision-making power in the hands of only a few people is often dictated by the nature of a country's economy. In countries that depend on the extraction of natural resources (like diamonds, gold, oil, or timber) for most of their income, a small number of people may take control of the economy and government for their own benefit. A powerful few are able to exploit resource wealth rather than supporting a sustainable economy that would benefit the country as a whole. Ironically, such resource-rich countries, when burdened with weak governance, tend to remain relatively poor. While a handful of individuals and companies may get rich, the majority of citizens do not benefit.

A country rich in natural resources, such as gold, may still struggle with economic development.

This is known as the **resource curse**, and is most prominent in countries that make most of their money exporting oil or gemstones.

Resource extraction is usually extremely profitable. The large and relatively easy profits that can be made by selling natural resources makes investing in other industries less attractive, creating a situation in which a country's economy is dominated almost completely by resource extraction. If a small elite group can control access to these resources, they can effectively control their country's economy and, if they so choose, use it to enrich themselves. This occurred in Angola in the late 1990s, where members of the ruling class gained enormous oil fortunes over the course of a 27-year civil war while the country collapsed internally.[7]

> *Governance that considers sustainability keeps in mind the civil, cultural, economic, political, and social rights of its citizens.*

The resource curse does not happen to every country that possesses valuable natural resources, however. Norway, for example, has combined oil wealth with highly democratic rule, as well as the establishment of a fund that pays for extensive social services for all Norwegians.[8]

Society

Governance that considers sustainability keeps in mind the civil, cultural, economic, political, and social rights of its citizens. Essentially, this kind of governance promotes human development.[9]

Ineffective governance impacts the quality of life of everyone in a country, from the poorest person, whose basic needs go unmet, to the privileged and wealthy, who risk losing property and wealth due to corruption and unstable economic and political conditions. Ineffective governance can result in diminishing food and water security, depletion of natural resources, lack of personal safety, poor health and education services, human rights abuses, and conflict.

When governance is weak or ineffective, there is often a lack of essential services such as water treatment, sanitation, education, and primary health care for people living in the lower economic levels of society. In countries with ineffective governance, it is often difficult to ensure that people have enough food to eat and fresh drinking water to meet their basic needs. Furthermore, education may be an option for only the wealthy in these places.

Governance involves making decisions about how to allocate resources to address social needs, particularly those needs that cannot be adequately met in the private sector. When decision makers fail to achieve a balance among the many needs of society, it can diminish their ability to respond to new challenges. Crisis situations, in particular, tend to reveal such failures of governance. When Hurricane Katrina hit New Orleans in 2005, for example, the U.S. Federal Emergency Management Agency (FEMA) was unable to effectively coordinate local, state, federal, and private rescue and aid operations.

This breakdown was partially due to a loss of communications from downed cell phone towers, but also was due in part to the federal government's model for crisis management. After the attacks of September 11, 2001, FEMA lost its status as an independent department and was placed within the Department of Homeland Security. The Department of Homeland Security re-oriented FEMA to focus on terrorism and left the agency without the resources it needed to deal with a natural disaster the size of Hurricane Katrina. When the hurricane hit, local and state officials lacked a way to coordinate their efforts and many people were left stranded, waiting for rescue by the Coast Guard.[10]

Environment

Over half the jobs around the world depend on fisheries, forests, or agriculture. Policies and decisions that foster sustainable use of lands and waters can impact individual livelihood and the global economy.[11]

In the long term, ineffective governance can lead to environmental degradation through inefficient natural resource management and the overexploitation of resources. The Amazon rain forest in South America is perhaps one of the most visible examples of this. The unoccupied forest is legally protected, but these laws are rarely enforced. As a result, it is relatively easy and cheap for people to move into forested areas and clear them to create pasture for cattle. Estimates of how much of the rain forest is used to graze cows vary from one-third to over half. Not only does this activity destroy the forest, but grazing cattle is one of the least efficient forms of food production in terms of water and energy.[12] Despite the clear implications for long-term sustainability, people have stepped outside legal channels to exploit the resource for themselves in the only way available to them. Good governance that involves people in the process of forest management and addresses their need for a sustainable way to make a living is an essential part of protecting the Amazon.

In cases where poor governance contributes to environmental degradation, the effects are typically felt most acutely by people who do not have the resources to fight back. It is a well-documented fact that hazardous waste disposal facilities are more likely to be located in low-income neighborhoods. Within these neighborhoods, the percentage of people of color who live near hazardous waste facilities is higher than in areas farther away from the facilities.[13] Decisions about the disposal of waste are often made without consulting with those who will have to live with its long-term effects.

CASE STUDY: Texaco in Ecuador[14]

From 1973 to 1993, Texaco extracted 1.5 billion barrels of oil from heavily forested regions of Ecuador. As is typical for oil drilling, this produced a lot of waste—19 billion gallons. In addition, 16.8 million gallons of crude oil were spilled around drilling sites in the jungle. That's enough petroleum to fill a large tanker.

The waste from Texaco's oil drilling was drained into dirt pits. This disposal method was approved by Texaco's majority partner, the Ecuadorian national oil company Petroecuador. This decision, however, was not made clear to the indigenous tribes that lived in the region, nor did they have a chance to participate in making it. Nevertheless, thousands of indigenous people have been affected by the environmental pollution that resulted from the drilling, in particular, the contamination of water sources.

16.8 million gallons of crude oil were spilled around drilling sites in Ecuadorian forests.

Many suffered serious health consequences, including increased rates of cancer and slow mental development in children. These tribes joined in a lawsuit against Texaco over the environmental damage done to their land. The lawsuit was finally settled in Ecuadorian courts in 2011 after 18 years. The tribes were finally able to join the governance process that they were previously excluded from.

Background on Governance

Governance can take many forms and occur on national, global, and local scales.

National Governance

Almost all states today are built around a nation, or group of people bound together by a shared history, ethnicity, language, and/or religion. A **nation-state**, or country, is a political unit that exercises control and sovereignty over a defined geographic area and provides a socio-cultural identity for its people. There are now nearly 200 nation-states in the world and most people are citizens of one of them. Not all peoples who consider themselves national groups have achieved statehood, but overall states have become the predominant form of governance around the world. Overall, states have become the predominant form of governance around the world.[15]

Most important decisions that impact the majority of people occur at the nation-state level and overrule local decision-making processes. The United States government, for example, is divided into three branches: the executive branch, the judicial branch, and the legislative branch. The decisions of a Supreme Court whose members represent the judicial branch take precedence over those of lower courts from all 50 states.

For much of human history, the largest sovereign states were not nations but empires. Sometimes stretching across multiple continents, empires were usually created through the ascendant power of one national group that subjugated neighboring groups. Not everyone received equal rights under empires. By definition, empires were unequal, with the ascendant national group on top and all others on a sliding scale of privilege beneath them.[16] Nevertheless, empires such as those ruled by the Ottomans, Romans, and Han Chinese did provide a form of international governance by managing the relations between the various peoples over whom they ruled.

Throughout the 19th century, European powers gathered tremendous strength as they attempted to expand globally. The British Empire was one of the largest powers and established many colonies throughout the world.

As in other empires, the colonial rulers did not consider all their subjects equals. This was especially true in colonies, where a native-born person was not considered a citizen and in many cases had no way of becoming one. Administrators appointed by the colonial government had the power to make decisions that affected all aspects of the lives of people living in colonies. Typically, this meant that colonial governance was based on the decisions of foreign elites rather than a broad consensus of those whom it affected.

Colonizers often used part of a native population to help rule the whole. Colonial administrations often took advantage of existing divisions within colonized peoples, offering one group a privileged role in colonial government for their help controlling others. In some places, colonists themselves created divisions, as occurred in Rwanda where Belgian colonial policy divided the indigenous populations into Hutus and Tutsis in order to establish the minority Tutsis as rulers and the majority

The people of Rwanda have worked hard to rebuild a system of good governance and strong community after a turbulent history that left the country divided.

Hutus as subjects. This division eventually set the stage for a bloody civil war in 1994, in which Hutu extremists—who blamed the Tutsis for Rwanda's troubles and the previous oppression of Hutus—incited genocide. By the end of the conflict, 800,000 were dead and many more were refugees.[17]

Over the course of the 20th century, the idea that all peoples have a right to self-government became dominant across most of the globe. People pushed to divide their lands up according to *nationality* (membership within a nation), usually determined by citizenship. Citizenship gave specific rights to those living within a nation; usually, citizens could vote, hold office, give military service, and serve on committees. Many national groups that were ruled by foreign powers drew great hope from the vision of a world made up of self-governing nation-states.[18]

In most of the world, this vision has become a reality. Nearly all formerly colonized nations have declared independence and formed new countries based on national identity. This wave of decolonization is especially visible in Africa. Many of the African countries that exist today were formed between the 1950s and 1970s as the region gained independence from European empires. This process was not always peaceful; revolutionary uprisings were part of establishing independence in a number of African countries. The policies of colonial governments have left legacies that continue to present challenges for governance today. Many other post-colonial states struggle with similar rifts. The instability and violence that they can generate is often a serious barrier to good governance in these countries.

Global Governance

Global governance includes laws, policies, and institutions that work beyond national borders. In an interconnected world where global issues are more and more prevalent, global governance has become more common. We have now agreed

The United Nations is a global governance structure with nearly 200 member states.

to international rules that govern safety at sea and pollution, addressed global health challenges, created norms on weapon control, and developed an International Criminal Court.[19]

The idea of international cooperation has its modern roots in the 19th century, when countries first established international organizations to work together on communication and security issues. The International Telecommunication Union was founded in 1865, and the Universal Postal Union was established in 1874. In 1899, the International Peace Conference was held in The Hague, Netherlands, to develop means for settling crises peacefully, preventing wars, and establishing rules of warfare. After World War I, the 1919 Treaty of Versailles established the League of Nations (now known as the forerunner to the United Nations) to promote international cooperation and achieve peace and security.[20]

In 1945, representatives of 50 countries met in San Francisco at the United Nations Conference on International Organization to draw up the United Nations Charter.[21] The United Nations officially came into existence in October 1945, when the UN Charter was ratified by China, France, the Soviet Union, the United Kingdom, the United States, and a majority of other participating countries. The organization now includes 193 member states and has the following goals:

> *To keep peace throughout the world;*
> *To develop friendly relations among nations;*
> *To help nations work together to improve the lives of poor people, to conquer hunger, disease and illiteracy, and to encourage respect for each other's rights and freedoms;*
> *To be a center for harmonizing the actions of nations to achieve these goals.*[22]

Since its beginnings, the UN has been subject to both harsh criticism and strong support. Critics argue that the UN is an oversized, expensive, and ineffective bureaucracy. To support their claims, they cite examples of the UN's failure to resolve conflicts in Somalia, Rwanda, and Bosnia.[23] Supporters of the UN believe that the UN helps prevent conflicts, mediates disagreements, establishes peacekeeping operations, and assists in the difficult task of post-conflict rebuilding.

For now, the UN exists as the most prominent international body that promotes a global perspective in governance. The work of the UN may never be perfect or complete, but it does have a global vision and its programs undoubtedly improve quality of life for millions of people.

Local Governance

Decision making within a village, town, or neighborhood takes a variety of forms, but such *local governance* often allows for more contact between decision makers and people affected by their decisions simply because of its smaller scale.

In a nation such as the United States, which is made up of various smaller systems, state, city, and county governments could all be considered examples of local governance. Placing power in the hands of local officials can lead to governance that responds more directly to the demands of those it impacts. For example, your school may have a student council that makes decisions related to school dances, events, or budgets.

In India, the local officials in each of the country's 2 million villages are required to hold regularly scheduled gram sabhas (public meetings). These meetings have become one of the largest systems of decision making in human history, involving around 700 million villagers countrywide. The key to the success of gram sabhas is that they exist primarily to ratify (or approve) the decisions of the local government by a majority vote.

A workshop held in Ghana allows these female leaders to gain skills to better participate in good governance.

Gram sabhas commonly discuss the allocation of public funding to development and public works projects, such as repairing a bridge or staffing a new library. The local officials must also present a list of people who they believe are eligible for state welfare at each meeting. Any member of the community may then publicly contest the names that are on the list or petition for others to be added to it.[24]

Another example of local governance is Afghanistan's government-led National Solidarity Program. In 2002, a UN-approved and U.S.-led intervention attempted to drive the Taliban, a group of conservative Islamic revolutionaries, from power in Afghanistan. While the Taliban still controls some regions and villages, the National Solidarity Program's aim is to help the post-Taliban government gain the allegiance of Afghanis. It accomplishes this by offering government grants to communities who form Community Development Councils (CDCs), made up of newly elected representatives. Organizations from Afghanistan and abroad then provide support as the community identifies its most pressing needs, designs solutions, and begins work on projects of their choosing. The budgets and progress of these projects are posted on public boards set up in communities or reported weekly at local mosques in order to increase transparency and hold the members of CDCs accountable. Successful projects have produced wells, schools, electrical stations, and irrigation ditches.

While rebuilding a country with new forms of governance can be challenging, the results of this program have been positive:

- Improved water and roads to rural areas, benefitting 17 million people
- Increased trust in government
- Strengthened democratic culture at the community level[25]

As of 2009, over 20,000 CDCs had been established. Generally, these councils have successfully integrated with traditional governance institutions such as tribal councils and militias. Local elders promoted the program and served to monitor spending and the progress of projects. Previously excluded groups such as women have also been successfully incorporated into decision-making processes in many villages.[26]

Governance Today

What exactly defines good governance? Most people would agree that good governance thrives in the context of democracy. By the beginning of the 21st century, the majority of the world's nations utilized some form of democracy in which citizens exercised their will through voting and representation in government.[27] Local and state governments tend to be more effective when they are founded on democratic principles such as the right to vote, free and fair elections, free speech and press, and economic, civil, and family rights.[28] Democratization is certainly an essential part of building good governance, but it requires ongoing education, the development of government structures and institutions, and time. Once established, democracies need to be tended carefully in order to stay healthy and provide good governance for their people.

The following factors help to contribute to good governance:

> *Most people would agree that good governance thrives in the context of democracy.*

Inclusion

Most generally, good governance rests on the consent of a broad cross-section of the people in a country, rather than only those of one group. In practice, this usually means that governance should include

CASE STUDY: Corrupt Governance in Nicaragua

Bribes and corruption occur in various forms and to varying degrees of visibility in all parts of the world. Corruption can have damaging implications for a nation's economy, especially where global markets are concerned. Some economists have pointed out that if rules are broken too often in a country, companies are less likely to operate there because they will have no legal protection.[29]

In 2003, the leaders of the top two political parties in Nicaragua, the Sandinistas and the Liberals, agreed behind closed doors to lower the percentage of the national vote needed to elect a president from 40% to 35%. The Nicaraguan legislature, where the two parties together formed an overwhelming majority, enacted the change.

Anti-government graffiti represents protest against corruption within Nicaragua's government.

As a result, Daniel Ortega, the leader of the Sandinista party, won the 2006 presidential election with 38% of the vote. Ortega had lost three previous elections. In 2009, Ortega orchestrated the Supreme Court's ruling to end a constitutional ban on consecutive presidential terms, allowing him to run multiple times.

Another Nicaraguan leader, Arnoldo Alemán, stands out as an example of corruption. Alemán was found guilty of embezzling $100 million of government funds during his term as president from 1997-2001. He hid $700,000 of this government money in American banks and attempted to distribute the money to members of his family.[30] Alemán received a 20-year jail sentence for the embezzlement, but Nicaragua's Supreme Court overturned the conviction in 2009.

A lack of transparency has further enabled corruption in Nicaragua. As a result, public confidence in government institutions and leadership has been undermined.

---

everyone, rather than limiting decision-making power to the elite.

If groups that will be affected by decisions have no opportunity to influence the decision-making process, they are less likely to cooperate in the implementation of government policies or programs. The civilian-led uprisings in Tunisia, Egypt, Libya, and elsewhere in the Arab world in the spring of 2011, for example, primarily aimed to challenge leaders who had excluded most people from the governance of their own countries.

Transparency

In order to participate in governance, people need be able to follow the decision-making process and the programs that emerge from it. This requires *transparency*, or the free flow of information to everyone affected by a decision so that they can see what is occurring. This information must be both understandable and easily accessible. Making a law difficult to understand or withholding information can obscure decision making from the public and sometimes hide abuses of power such as mishandled money or sidestepped laws.

Accountability

When people are easily able to understand how decisions are made and participate in the process, they are better able to hold decision-makers accountable, or responsible to the public. Transparency and information about the decision making process is not enough for true accountability, though; there must also be a way for people to challenge decisions and the individuals in power. In the example of local governance mentioned earlier, the gram sabhas in India provide a mechanism for citizens to challenge decisions made by public officials about welfare recipients. Citizens could vote to contest the welfare candidates put forward by officials at the meetings.

Good governance requires *accountability* at all levels. This means that oversight is put in place to ensure that government policies and programs meet their stated objectives and that government responds to the needs of the people it is designed to serve.

Rule of Law

Reliable accountability usually depends on the *rule of law,* or consistent application of legal rules to all people, regardless of who they are. Such impartiality requires a police force and judicial system that are free from corruption and favoritism, as well as independent from all political, social, and economic organizations that might seek to influence them.

When government bodies, civil organizations, and companies are consistently held accountable, through the law or otherwise, they tend to improve their responsiveness to the people they serve. In other words, they generally start to make an effort to serve the interests of all the people who are affected by their decisions.

CASE STUDY: Good Governance in Botswana

According to a continent-wide poll, only about half of the population of Africa has confidence in their government, judicial system, or electoral procedures. Four out of five citizens of Botswana, however, are confident in their country's government. Both the president and parliamentary representatives are elected every five years and the executive (the president) can dissolve the parliament at any time.[31]

Since Botswana's independence in 1966, the country has maintained a regular schedule of elections deemed fair by international observers. Several political parties have consistently shared government power in the Botswana, in marked contrast to other former colonies in Africa that have been ruled for many years by a single party. This clean political track record has accompanied the best economic growth rate in the world over the period 1968-2007, due largely to growth in Botswana's diamond industry. Additionally, economic growth helped the government fund a number of social programs that have improved lives in Botswana, although about one-third of the population still lives on less than a dollar a day.[32]

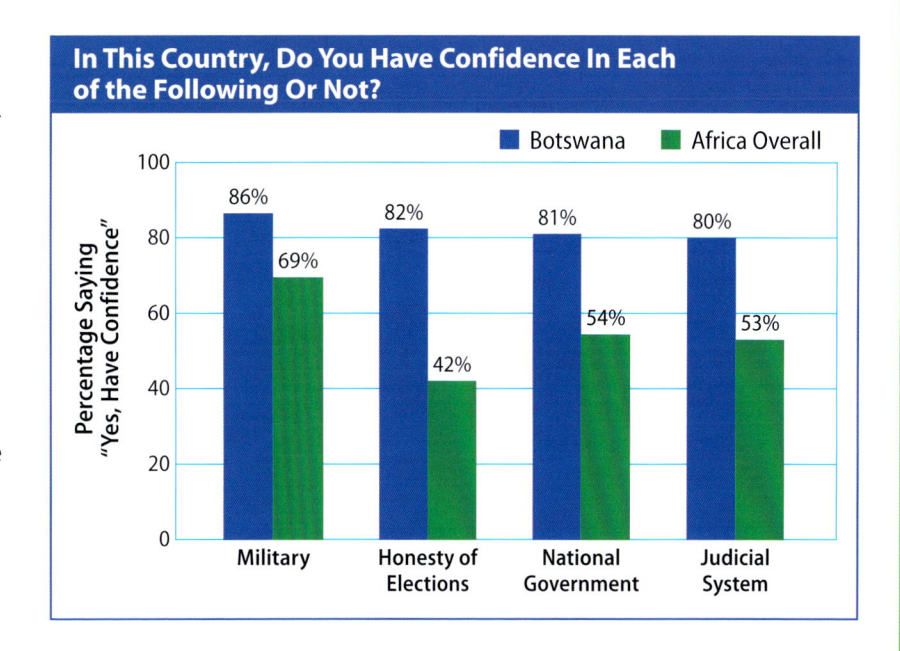

In This Country, Do You Have Confidence In Each of the Following Or Not?

Percentage Saying "Yes, Have Confidence"

	Botswana	Africa Overall
Military	86%	69%
Honesty of Elections	82%	42%
National Government	81%	54%
Judicial System	80%	53%

YOUTH PROFILE
The Little Rock Nine

There are times when governments create laws that justify and institutionalize inequality. Slavery, for example, was legal within the United States until 1865. Even after slavery was abolished, many unfair laws and policies continued. The Civil Rights Movement began as an effort to create equality before the law and equal treatment for all people, regardless of race.

After much debate, in 1954 the U.S. Supreme Court ruled that segregation of black and white people in public places was illegal. The case, *Brown* v. *Board of Education*, deemed segregation unconstitutional. In particular, it required the integration of public institutions like schools and universities. Three years later, the court's ruling was put to the test when nine African-American students enrolled at the previously all-white Central High School in Little Rock, Arkansas.

Orval Faubus, the Governor of Arkansas at the time, defied the ruling.

CAREER PROFILE — World Bank Consultant

The World Bank is an institution collectively owned by 187 countries. Its goal is to end poverty through investment and aid. The Bank provides credit, loans, and grants to populations all over the world to help governments create infrastructure, educational programs, and health care, and to promote the sustainable use of community and environmental resources.

Organizations like the World Bank need communications professionals. These individuals take complex concepts and technical language and bring it to communities in a way they can understand. They talk with communities to help develop projects and policies that meet their needs and they act as the voice of the community when explaining these needs back to the governing organization. If this sounds like an interesting career avenue to you, studying economics, governance, and political science will give you a well-rounded knowledge base, and pursuing a higher-level degree in one of these areas will give you the

DarshanaPatel works in Guyana as a World Bank consultant.

expertise to do this type of work. Needless to say, an ability to effectively communicate ideas to different audiences is a must.

Darshana Patel works in the World Bank Office in Georgetown, Guyana. As a communications professional, she works closely with communities receiving World Bank assistance so that more people are brought into the conversation and more effective solutions can be developed. "I see my role as making development work more bottom-up and democratic. Including many different types of people in a process can certainly make the process more time-consuming and complicated but it ultimately determines whether a development initiative will actually succeed in the long run," she says. For instance, if the World Bank wants to help a community meet its demand for clean drinking water, Darshana makes sure the community understands how to install the systems, how they operate, and how the water is made clean. This information helps ensure that the community will actually make use of the new system. Darshana also facilitates communication in the other direction, from community members to the World Bank. She advises anyone considering work in communications to explore how people express themselves. Whether expressed through an artistic medium, humor, or conversation, every voice is different and important. With sensitivity and an appreciation for peoples' differences, Darshana is able to really listen to people and to respond in the ways they need.

He brought the Arkansas National Guard to Central High School with instructions to prevent any African-American student from entering the school. He claimed the order was given to prevent violence and keep the peace.[36]

On September 4, 1957, the nine African-American students attempted to enter the school to register for classes, but were blocked by the Arkansas National Guard. When students prepared to return to the school and protests looked like they might get out of control, the federal government got involved. President Dwight Eisenhower federalized the Arkansas National Guard, effectively taking it out of Faubus' control, and sent federal troops to Central High School with instructions to enforce integration and protect the nine African-American students. The high school students at the center of this national drama became known as the Little Rock Nine.

Because of the tremendous work of civil society organizations and their influence on the government, the Little Rock Nine were finally able to attend Central High School.

Pathways to Progress: Governance

International Collaboration

Imagine that a popular music group comes to your school to educate you about HIV prevention and how to make positive choices in your life. Members of the group sing traditional songs and bring in speakers who have been impacted by the disease. Now imagine that the group travels throughout your entire country to educate thousands of young people. Vocal Motion 6, an a cappella group in Namibia, has done just that with the support of the ONE campaign and the United States President's Emergency Plan for AIDS Relief (PEPFAR).

The ONE campaign is an organization that works to fight extreme poverty and preventable disease, mostly in Africa. It does so by raising public awareness and pressuring political leaders to support policies that fight poverty. ONE is a partnership of 11 different non-profit organizations, one of which was founded by Bono, the lead singer of the rock band U2.

PEPFAR has supported many educational campaigns to address the AIDS epidemic, including this concert in Vietnam during the country's national action month for HIV.

With over 2.5 million members, ONE works to hold government leaders accountable for their commitments to end world poverty.[33]

Through support from the ONE campaign, PEPFAR funded Vocal Motion 6 on their "Living Positive Tour." The singers reached over 26,000 students throughout Namibia.[34] This is just one example of what can be done through collaboration between international organizations, government agencies, and citizens to help alleviate global issues.

National Collaboration

As with global issues, governance that seeks to address national challenges often requires the collaboration of government, civil society, and the private sector. Hunger, for example, cannot be addressed within a country by just the private sector or a civic organization. Andres Botran, the Secretary for Food Security and Nutrition in Guatemala, realized this when he began to work on the issue. Shocked by the fact that half of Guatemala's children were malnourished, he built relationships with different stakeholders to create a plan to combat hunger and malnutrition. Representatives from the government, civil society, and private sector began working together. Collectively, they convinced the Guatemalan Congress to pass the Food Security and Nutrition Law.[35] This law allowed the government to create policies to ensure that the poorest populations within Guatemala would have access to food.

WHAT YOU CAN DO — Governance

Ultimately, governance impacts all of us. Good governance provides security for people and supports well-being. If we refuse or neglect to participate in the decision-making processes that affect us, we essentially allow other people to decide our future for us.

- Encourage others to vote and vote when you have the ability to do so. Recruitment campaigns like Rock the Vote seek to motivate members of a certain group to register as voters; they also provide nonpartisan information on candidates and initiatives.

- Take part in governance by attending public meetings offered by political officials, candidates, or organizations. Especially at the local level, these meetings provide ways for officials to explain their positions and ideas in detail and listen to feedback.

- Get involved in a campaign for a political candidate, cause, or organization. A campaign is a series of coordinated activities, such as public speaking, designed to achieve a social, political, or commercial goal. Participation in a campaign offers you a chance to learn skills that can be applied to any situation where you want to influence decision makers or the public.

First Lady Eleanor Roosevelt casts her vote in this ballot box in 1936.

- Pursue opportunities to gain hands-on experience in politics. Run for school office. Meet with school administrators to voice your opinions and ideas. Be a student representative to parent and community organizations.

POINT   COUNTERPOINT

Should citizens be allowed to participate in direct democracy?

Direct democracy is when citizens are able to vote directly on policy initiatives instead of having their elected representatives do so for them. This kind of voting allows for greater power by the voters. Should citizens be allowed to participate in direct democracy? The following perspectives are taken from the online forum, Debatepedia.[37]

POINT
Yes

- "Being part of the process is a requirement in a democracy. Citizens identify themselves more closely with the government policies when they are allowed to cast votes. Only when they do so is the government a 'government by the people, of the people and for the people.' This is not a privilege for citizens. It is a responsibility."

- "Direct democracy encourages citizens to educate themselves. It is certainly true that direct democracy requires that citizens participate actively in the political process and that they inform themselves on the issues surrounding them. This creates a strong incentive for citizens to inform themselves on the important issues of the day."

COUNTERPOINT
No

- "Voters are too apathetic to make good laws. The average voter may not be interested in politics and therefore may not participate. In a system with citizen initiatives and direct democracy, high voter apathy may make the subsequent decisions unrepresentative of broader public opinion or possibly just bad policy."

- "Direct democracy fosters emotional decision-making. When presented with a single yes/no question, usually without any information on the issue at hand, people tend to make spur-of-the-moment decisions based on emotions, driven by anger, fear, and hatred."

Voting is a great way to participate in one form of direct democracy.

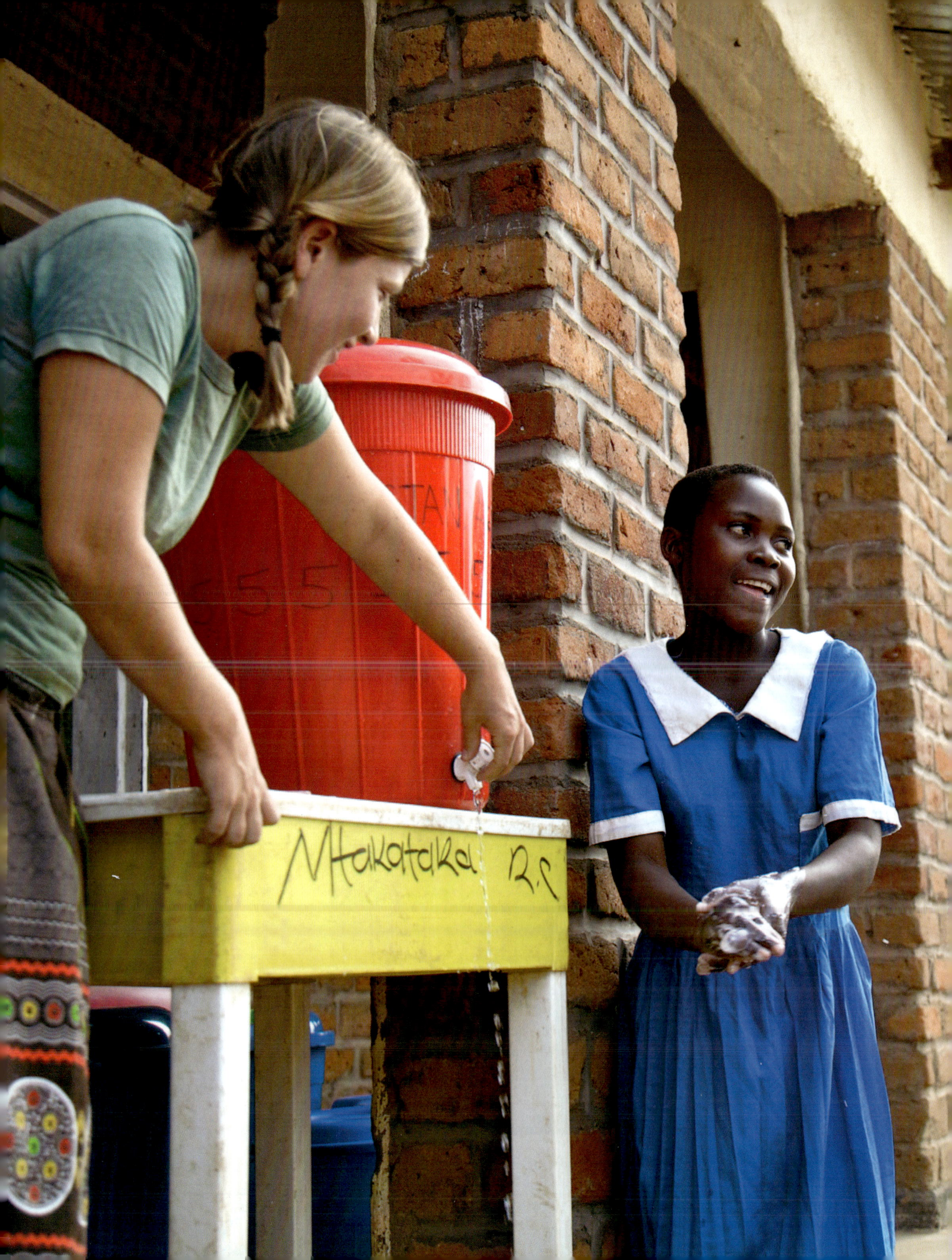
Mtakataka R.S

Chapter 14

Health

> **GUIDING QUESTIONS**
> - How are socioeconomic status and health connected?
> - What personal and structural solutions improve health by addressing root causes of illness and disease?

Introduction to Health

Why is Jason in the hospital?
Because he has a bad infection in his leg.

But why does he have an infection?
Because he has a cut on his leg and it got infected.

But why does he have a cut on his leg?
Because he was playing in the junk yard next to his apartment building and there was some sharp, jagged steel there that he fell on.

But why was he playing in a junk yard?
Because his neighborhood is kind of run down. A lot of kids play there and there is no one to supervise them.

But why does he live in that neighborhood?
Because his parents can't afford a nicer place to live.

But why can't his parents afford a nicer place to live?
Because his Dad is unemployed and his Mom is sick.

But why is his Dad unemployed?
Because he doesn't have much education and he can't find a job.

But why …?"[1]

In Sickness and In Health

As the dialogue you just read highlights, a person's health is influenced by many issues. By looking more closely at all of the factors that affect health, we can also gain ideas for treating and preventing illness.

Many people might not think much about their health until they are sick. Saying someone has a "clean bill of health" is meant to convey that the person has no heart problems, diabetes, infections, parasites, sexually transmitted diseases, broken bones, respiratory problems, and so on. Health is often presented as simply the absence of sickness, but it is much more than that; health is an important foundation of human well-being. The World Health Organization (WHO) was founded on the idea that health is "a state of complete physical, mental, and social well-being and not merely the absence of disease or infirmity."[2] In the long term, such a state of well-being can only exist in connection with social, economic, and environmental sustainability.

Health and Sustainability

Healthy people live in healthy communities. The social, environmental, and economic conditions of the community we live in, as well as how these conditions are distributed among the community, have an enormous effect on our health. Together, these conditions are the **social determinants of health**. In most of the world, living in an impoverished community is strongly related to disease, illness, and preventable death. If people do not have social and economic stability, they are less likely to live long and healthy lives. Similarly, environmental destruction and pollution can cause nearby communities to suffer from birth defects, chronic diseases such as asthma, and even death.[3]

Economy

Health care is critical component of national economies. Health care can be financed by government through taxes and social security. It can also be financed through private insurance or out-of-pocket payments. The amount

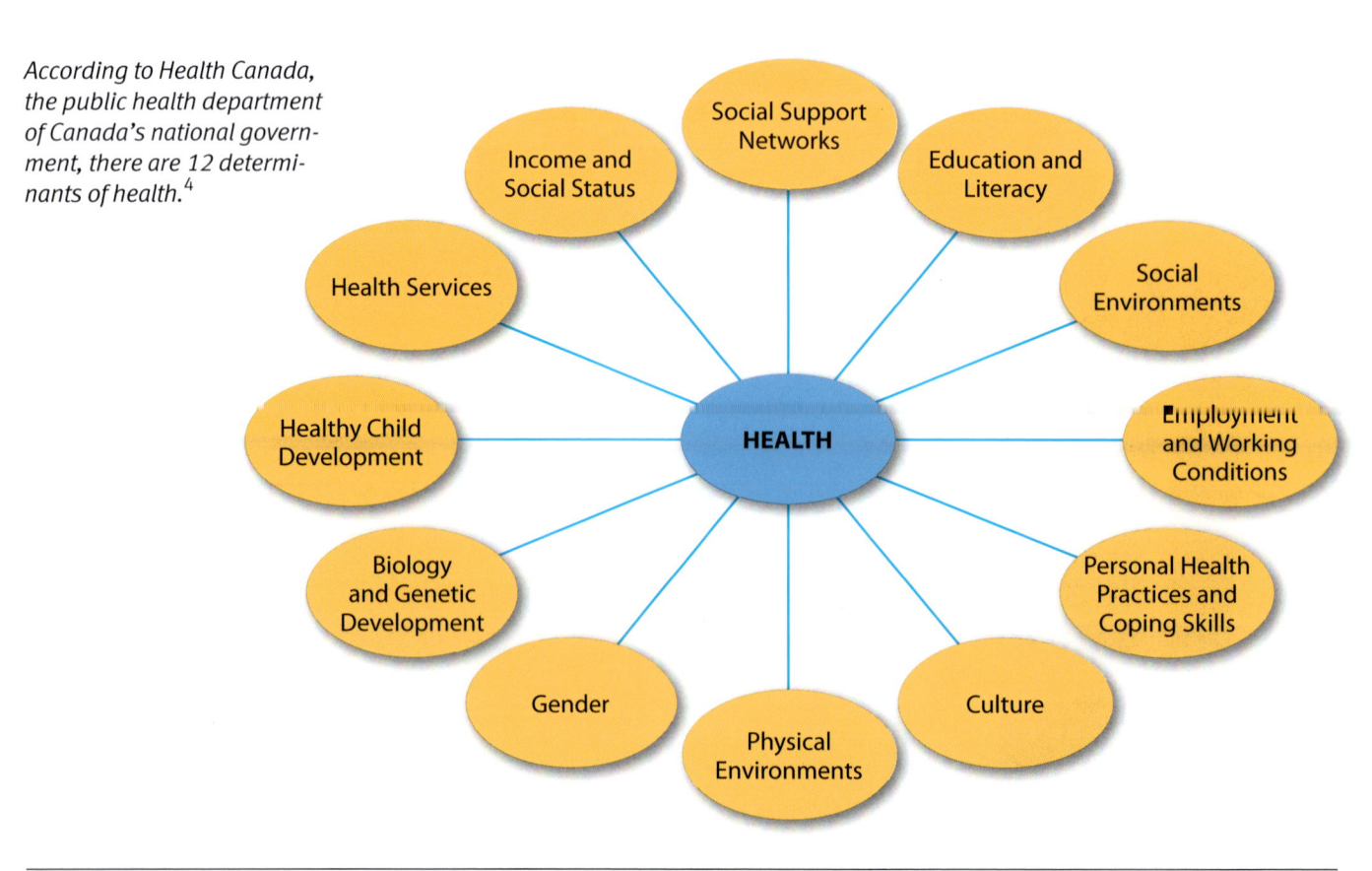

According to Health Canada, the public health department of Canada's national government, there are 12 determinants of health.[4]

The 12 determinants of health surrounding HEALTH:
- Income and Social Status
- Social Support Networks
- Education and Literacy
- Social Environments
- Employment and Working Conditions
- Personal Health Practices and Coping Skills
- Culture
- Physical Environments
- Gender
- Biology and Genetic Development
- Healthy Child Development
- Health Services

of government funds spent on health care differs from country to country as well as the average cost of health care per person. In the United States, an average of $8,233 was spent on health care per person and 48.2% of these costs were financed by the government.[5] In the United Kingdom, $3,433 was spent on health care per person and 83.2% of these costs were financed by the government.[6]

There is a connection between a healthy population and a strong economy. When a population is healthier, employees take fewer sick days and productivity goes up. On the other hand, a population that is vulnerable to the spread of a deadly disease may see productivity and investment in job training go down, limiting the development of new economic sectors. Research has shown that a 10% rise in life expectancy is associated with an annual economic growth of 0.3-0.4%.[7] *Life expectancy* is a statistic that provides a snapshot of the overall health of a population in one number, making it easier to see health disparities between two populations. Life expectancy tells you how long a baby born today is likely to live if current mortality rates remain constant.

Society

As the social determinants of health suggest, the social context in which we live and work influence our health. Social conditions such as access to nutritious food, medical care, and healthy childhood development all impact our health and well-being. Although we make many choices that impact our health, we do not control all aspects of our lives. One of the most obvious factors outside our control is where we are born and grow up. For a number of reasons, it is often difficult for us to leave the communities or places that we are born into. We may desire to be close to our families or be worried about the risk of not finding work in a new town, for instance. Because of this, the health of any one person is often a reflection of the health of the community in which they live. By working at the community level to prevent and treat diseases, health care professionals have an opportunity to implement structural solutions to widespread health challenges rather than just treating the symptoms of each individual.

A volunteer teaches a young girl in Ecuador about the importance of brushing her teeth.

Environment

Our health is closely connected to the environment. Pollution and environmental degradation can have negative impacts on human health. For instance, industrialized and urban areas tend to have poorer air quality which can lead to asthma and other respiratory issues. Also, drinking water supplies contaminated with solid waste can cause serious illness such as cholera.

On the other hand, working to sustain environmental systems can have a positive impact on human health. Healthy ecosystems provide many of the resources humans require to thrive. Trees help filter groundwater as well as absorb CO_2 and other air pollutants.

Our local physical geography may also be a determining factor in our health. For example, tropical regions are prone to the spread of disease through insects such as mosquitoes that thrive in humid, warm regions. Different geographies also present different challenges with respect to access to drinking water and arable land.

Background on Health

The science and art of protecting and improving the health of communities is called **public health**. Public health professionals use a combination of approaches to help groups of people live healthier lives. They may focus on education, such as teaching people about the benefits of washing their hands. They may also design campaigns to promote healthy lifestyles by holding fitness events, for example, or creating advertisements to warn people about the effects of certain street drugs. Where communities lack access to clean water and sanitation, public health measures can help them obtain these necessities. Finally, public health research seeks new ways to prevent disease and injury in communities.

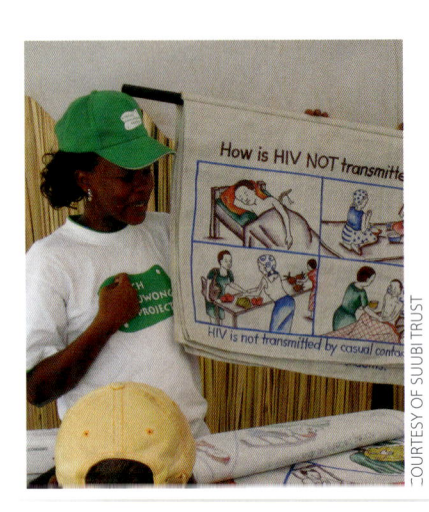

A volunteer supports an HIV public health campaign.

Ancient Public Health Systems

For thousands of years, civilizations around the world have sought to make communities healthier. The ancient Chinese saw the health of the individual and community as intertwined and believed that individual sickness weakened the state as a whole. This perception drove the early development of public health practices in China. As early as 1,000 B.C.E., for example, the Zhou dynasty prohibited excessive eating and drinking and outlawed marriage between family members in order to protect the population's health.[8]

Early Islamic empires also governed over public health. They constructed public hospitals, the first of which opened in 979 C.E. in Baghdad. Several large hospitals were also built in Cairo and Damascus. These ancient hospitals were designed with four wings, each with its own fountain to supply clean water and provide for sanitation. There were separate areas for patients with gastrointestinal problems like dysentery and diarrhea. Physicians made daily rounds and were assisted by orderlies and pharmacists. Hospital services were offered free of charge as a form of charity—an early example of socialized medicine.[9]

CASE STUDY: The Black Death[10]

During the 14th century, plague swept through Europe, killing 25 million people. *Plague* is a bacterial infection most often found in rodents. However, flea bites can transmit the disease from rodents to humans. There are documented cases of plague dating back to 500 B.C.E. However, as Europeans flocked to crowded cities towards the end of the Middle Ages, the disease was able to spread at a much faster rate. The plague killed one-third of the population in Florence, Italy within six months of its arrival.

Plague is often referred to as the Black Death because one of the symptoms of the disease is black blotches on the skin. To protect themselves, medieval doctors wore long robes and beaked masks that typically held flowers or herbs to keep out foul-smelling air, which they believed caused disease.

This illustration of a doctor represents what doctors had to wear when treating patients who had caught the plague.

Birth of Modern Public Health Systems

Public health as it is practiced today did not emerge until the 18th and 19th centuries, in the midst of the Industrial Revolution. During this time many people went to work in newly built factories. Europe witnessed the world's first rapid urbanization as cities sprang up around the new factories without organization or planning.[11]

Epidemics of typhoid, influenza, typhus, and cholera had long caused numerous deaths throughout the world. In the pre-industrial era, outbreaks of these diseases would typically sweep across a region from time to time before dying out. These diseases found a permanent home, however, in Europe's booming cities in the 1830s. By 1839, for every person who died of old age or violence in Great Britain, eight other people died of disease. While general filth was acknowledged to be the source of these diseases, people believed that contagion was carried by miasma (or noxious gases). They had not yet discovered germs.

Emergence of Public Health Laws

In nineteenth-century Europe, most human waste was dumped from chamber pots into the streets, where it drained into community water sources and lead to constantly renewed outbreaks of cholera and other water-borne illnesses. The high concentration of rodents that accompanied the large number of people in cities was another source of illness. Rodents carried fleas and ticks that transmit typhus, a potentially deadly bacterial infection causing fever, rashes, and nausea.[12]

The prevalence of disease provoked the first efforts to develop a modern public health system. In the second half of the 19th century, the British Parliament passed a series of laws called the Public Health Acts. One of these required all new residential construction to include running water and drainage from houses directly into sewers.

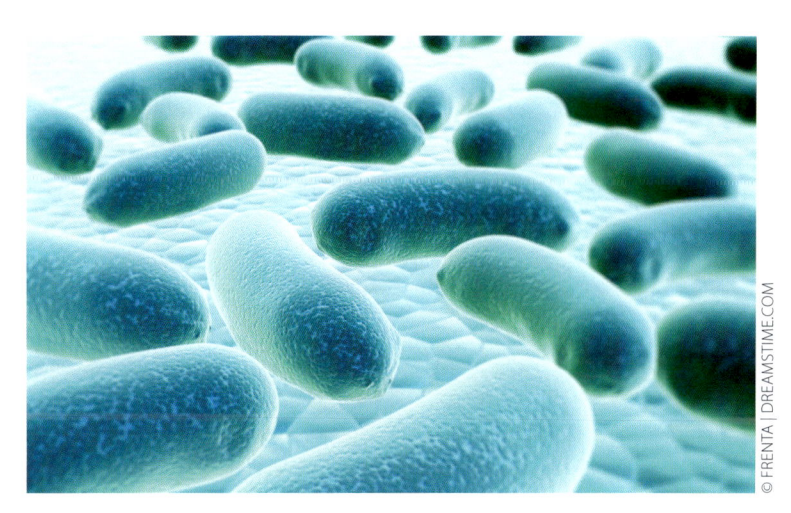

The Germ Theory helped confirm that microbes such as bacteria spread diseases.

Germ Theory of Disease

A vital breakthrough came with the development of the **germ theory of disease**. Microbes such as bacteria had long been associated with the decay of dead tissue, but had been thought to emerge spontaneously from decomposing bodies. It was not until the 1870s that Louis Pasteur showed that these microbes were, in fact, breaking down the decaying tissue. Based on this breakthrough, Pasteur and other researchers made connections between certain microbes and specific diseases. Most importantly, they also theorized that these microbes (or germs) carried disease from one person to another.[13]

The germ theory of disease led to new medical practices and technologies. Antiseptic surgery greatly reduced post-procedure infections and hand-washing by doctors delivering babies ended a form of often-fatal infant fever. Pasteur developed the first vaccines produced in laboratories and a method for killing microbes using heat, now referred to as *pasteurization*. Subjected to a certain amount of heat, potentially harmful **pathogens** (or germs) will die. Pasteurization can kill bacteria like Salmonella and prevent diseases like tuberculosis. By 1900, better sanitation and contributions from bacteriologists had begun to rein in many infectious diseases and extend average lifespans.[14]

Medical advances have helped to increase life expectancy of people around the world.

Over the course of the 20th century, the average lifespan continued to increase in industrialized countries like the United States. Vaccination virtually eradicated smallpox and polio in the United States and brought many other diseases to a point where widespread outbreaks were no longer a day-to-day concern. Campaigns for workplace safety greatly reduced injuries and deaths caused by accidents and environmental hazards, such as exposure to coal dust in mines. Sanitation helped to reduce the spread of infectious disease and antibiotics prevented infections from becoming fatal, improving the survival rate for sicknesses such as pneumonia. Major improvements in emergency medical care increased survival of traumatic injury as well.

Together, these changes led to an unprecedented increase in life expectancy for many populations around the world. Over the past century, the average lifespan of a male in the United States rose from 45 to 75 years old the average lifespan of a woman went from 50 to 80 years old.[15] This rise in life expectancy was accompanied by a dramatic reduction in the number of children the average women gave birth to, or the *fertility rate*. Better health meant that couples could have only two children and expect both children to survive into adulthood.[16]

Health Today

Modern science and technology has made it possible to prevent and treat many of the world's diseases. However, the development of technology and industry has also been accompanied by a new set of health challenges.

Health Issues in Developing Nations

Not all people have shared equally in the health improvements of the past century. There is a health disparity between the world's richest and poorest countries. The life expectancy of an infant born in Burundi in 2007 is 50 years old, while an infant born in Sweden has a life expectancy of 81 years. Part of the reason Swedes tend to live longer lives is that, as in most industrialized countries, most people in Sweden have access to modern medicine and doctors. In contrast, those in Burundi and other developing countries lack reliable access to medical care and as a result are vulnerable to diseases that can be prevented, treated, or cured with access to modern medicine and doctors.[17]

Countries with low life expectancy also commonly have high child mortality rates. A high child mortality rate will significantly decrease a population's life expectancy due to the inclusion of many young children dying at an early age in the average lifespan. Disparities in global health are particularly stark when comparing child mortality in the world's poorest and richest countries. Sub-Saharan Africa, for example, still loses one out of every seven children prior to their fifth birthday, while Europe loses one out of every 250. The good news, however, is that child mortality rates in many developing nations are declining dramatically thanks to improvements in basic health care, sanitation, and education.

Malaria

Malaria is one disease that can be prevented and cured, but remains a serious health issue in many poor countries. Malaria is spread mainly through mosquito bites and bed nets that keep mosquitoes away can reduce the spread of the disease. Even if a person is infected, early diagnosis and immediate treatment can save him or her from death and limit the spread of the disease to other people. Yet malaria still infects hundreds of millions of people each year, mostly in the poorest countries. In 2010, there was an estimated 655,000 malaria deaths worldwide. Most of these occurred in Africa, where it is estimated that each child has malaria fever an average of 1.6 to 5.4 times each year.[18]

Diarrhea

Another disease that highlights the disparity in health between countries is diarrhea. Diarrhea is often caused by the contamination of food or water with fecal matter, a relatively rare occurrence in industrialized countries where water treatment and sewage systems are commonplace.

In developing countries, however, the disease presents a mortal threat to many people. Diarrhea causes rapid and severe dehydration that can lead directly to death or undermine the immune system's ability to fight off other diseases. Diarrhea contributes to more than 4 million deaths each year. It is the second-leading cause of death among children under five, killing around 4,500 each day.[19]

CASE STUDY: Nothing But Nets

The Nothing But Nets campaign began in 2006, after *Sports Illustrated* columnist Rick Reilly challenged each of his readers to donate at least $10 for the purchase of anti-malaria bed nets. Each $10 donation would cover the cost of purchasing a long-lasting insecticide-treated bed net, distributing it, and educating communities on its use. Bed nets have been shown to reduce transmission of malaria by up to 90%.

Mosquitoes carrying malaria bite primarily between 10 P.M. and 4 A.M., making protection during sleep the most important way to prevent infection. Any net that completely covers a sleeping person will provide some protection, but nets treated with a long-term insecticide that is safe for humans are twice as effective as untreated nets. The WHO has approved nets from three companies, including Sumitomo Chemical, which operates net factories in several of the countries where the nets are most needed. One such factory in Tanzania employs 4,000 people and produces 20 million nets per year. All in all, Nothing But Nets has distributed several million nets to African families, many of them in refugee camps.[20]

Mosquito nets treated with long-term insecticides can decrease the transmission of malaria.

Slum Housing

In the developing world, people who move from rural areas into urban centers tend to be poor and only able to afford the cheapest urban housing. This usually means sharing a small room with three or more people in a slum. A *slum* is a structure built out of whatever materials are available and lacking a toilet and clean water.[21] The structures are often clustered tightly together. The concentration of people who lack sanitation means that human waste in these areas is often untreated and uncontained. Furthermore, slums tend to be grouped in marginal environments prone to flooding and landslides, making it likely that the structures will be damaged or destroyed in the event of heavy rainfall or a natural disaster.

As these examples show, a community's social, environmental, and economic conditions play a large role in determining the health of the individuals living in that community. Health disparities within countries and cities point out which places and populations have benefited the most from industrialization and which lack access to modern sanitation and medical care. Public and global health workers continue to seek new ways to bring health services and practices to those communities most vulnerable to illness and death from preventable diseases.

These health disparities highlight how advances in medicine and public health have benefited the industrialized world; they also show how many people do not have much access to modern medicine. However, differences in access to medical care do not tell the whole story. While having doctors available can help identify diseases more accurately and keep people alive after a problem has been spotted, the social and economic conditions that make people ill in the first place are the most significant determinants of the health of a population as a whole.[22] The impact of social and economic conditions on health can be seen most clearly when we examine health disparities within a single country.

> *A community's social, environmental, and economic conditions play a large role in determining the health of the individuals living in that community.*

Health Issues in Developed Nations

Industrialization and development have also been accompanied by an increase in **chronic diseases**, or diseases that last a long time. Some of the world's richest countries suffer from high rates of obesity. Since the 1980s, obesity rates have risen quickly in all but the poorest countries due to an increase in the availability of food and a decrease in physical activity. In 19 out of 34 countries belonging to the Organization for Economic Co-operation and Development (OECD), a group including many of the richest countries on Earth, more than half of the adult population is considered overweight or obese.[23]

Obesity rates are based on a health statistic called *body mass index*, or BMI, a ratio between an individual's height and weight. High obesity rates in a given country indicate that many adults have a body mass index greater than 30, meaning they have reached an unhealthy weight for someone of their height. Body mass index is more than just a measure of how heavy a population is; it also tells us the likelihood that people will have certain health problems.[24] Obese individuals have a life expectancy about 10 years shorter than average, similar to that of smokers.[25] Perhaps not surprisingly, health care expenditures for an obese person are typically much higher than for someone of normal weight. In 2007, health care costs for obese adults averaged about 38% higher than for adults of normal weight.[26]

The danger of obesity lies in close connection with several chronic diseases, especially heart disease and diabetes. Obesity and diabetes (especially when accompanied by stress and high blood pressure) place huge strains on the heart and the circulatory system. Coronary artery disease—in which the build-up of fat in the arteries makes it difficult for the heart to receive blood—is closely related to obesity and can result in death of the heart's muscle tissue. In the worst cases, this results in heart failure and sometimes death.[27]

Together, obesity and diabetes caused around 35 million of the total 58 million deaths worldwide in 2008. These two chronic health problems are the leading causes of death in the United States and are becoming more common in wealthy countries around the world. For example, the prevalence of diabetes rose 5.3% in Japan from 1989-2005 and mortality from obesity-related diabetes in France rose 23% in only seven years.[28]

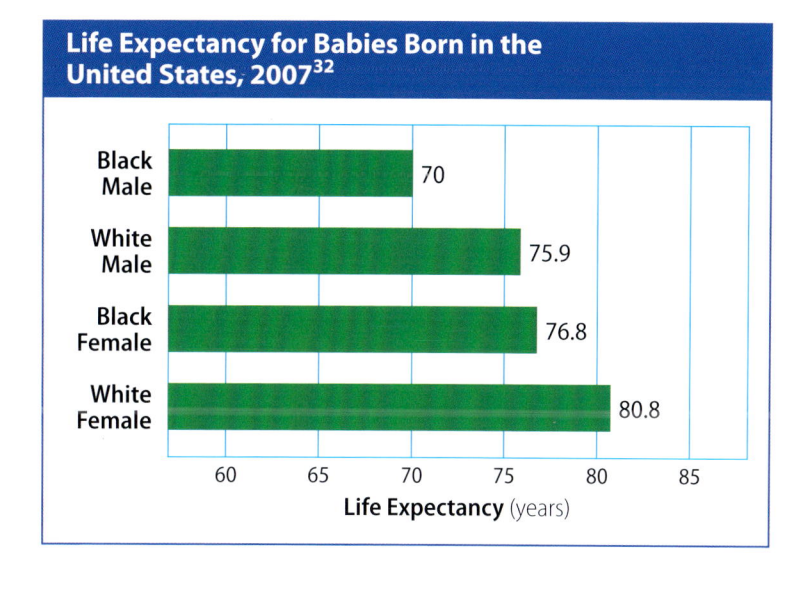

Life Expectancy for Babies Born in the United States, 2007[32]

Group	Life Expectancy (years)
Black Male	70
White Male	75.9
Black Female	76.8
White Female	80.8

Health Disparities within Nations

As was just demonstrated, living in an industrialized country does not guarantee a healthy life, nor does living in a developing country guarantee an early death. Just as populations from different countries can differ in average life expectancy, two populations within the same country can differ as well. The life expectancy of an infant born in the United States in 2007, for example, is about 78 years.[29] However, black males born in Washington, D.C. during that same year have a life expectancy of 57.9 years—just below the life expectancy for men in Bangladesh and Ghana. The life expectancy of a Hispanic woman living in the United States is 5.1 years longer than the average American.[30] Health profiles can be distinct when comparing two different states, as well. Colorado, for example, has the slimmest population in the United States while 34.9% of people in Mississippi are considered obese, the highest average in the country.[31]

In addition to race and ethnicity, socioeconomic status can play a role in health disparities. Take the dramatic differences in health in developing countries for slum inhabitants and for those who are able to live in formal urban housing. The health disparities between slum inhabitants and those who are able to live in formal urban housing in developing nations can be dramatic, too. Studies have found that 150 out of every 1,000 children living in the slums of Nairobi die before reaching the age of five, compared to 90 out of every 1,000 children living in other parts of the city.[33] The social and economic conditions of an individual's local community may play a larger role in determining his or her health than the industrialized status of his or her country of residence. Health disparities within countries and cities point out which places and populations are vulnerable to certain types of disease or lack access to adequate health care. Public and global health workers continue to seek new ways to bring health services and practices to those communities most vulnerable to illness and death from preventable diseases.

Pandemics: Diseases without Borders

Modern transportation has greatly increased the speed with which people travel around the world, but has also made it much easier for a disease to spread from place to place.[34] A **pandemic** is an outbreak of disease that reaches across the globe. The classification of an outbreak as a pandemic refers only to the geographic spread of the disease; it says nothing about the severity of the symptoms or whether it is deadly. Even before the World Health Organization was founded in 1948, nations have sought to coordinate international responses to pandemics. European nations held an international conference in Venice in 1892 to address the spread of cholera. Another conference in 1897 established an international convention to prevent the spread of plague. At that time, pandemics were mainly transmitted across borders by travelers on ships and their spread could be limited by quarantining groups or countries that had been infected.[35]

Quarantines are less feasible today, given the speed with which a disease can jump continents. Diseases can now become global before an outbreak is even detected. Controlling a potential pandemic in a globalized world requires greater collaboration between countries to detect diseases quickly and coordinate national responses. Many countries have already taken steps in this direction. Mexico, for example, closely monitors for new outbreaks during times of the year when the spread of disease is most likely to occur.

However, Mexico's monitoring system has its limits. H1N1, a form of influenza often referred to as swine flu, emerged in Mexico in 2009 during the off-season for flu monitoring. H1N1 spread across much of the world before it was identified and national governments could respond. Another factor contributing to poor international response to H1N1 was the World Health Organization's inability to communicate with its member states due to language barriers—something that could have been avoided with proper planning.

The H1N1 flu killed an estimated 284,500 people.[36] The outbreak highlighted a worldwide vulnerability to severe pandemics and the need for faster response measures.[37] The swine flu pandemic also demonstrated the danger of diseases emerging in livestock and being transmitted to human populations. To mitigate this risk, proper monitoring of illnesses among animals is needed. For instance, after bird flu was detected in Hong Kong in 1997, millions of poultry birds were killed in an attempt to prevent further spread of the disease, which can mutate and spread from birds to humans.

The swine flu pandemic spread quickly around the world.

The Global Challenge of AIDS

HIV/AIDS is a pandemic that has been a major health challenge over the past several decades. In the early 1980s, medical reports shared that a few previously healthy young people in Los Angeles and New York had developed rare forms of cancer and/or pneumonia. As more reports of this condition were released, more patients were diagnosed. In 1982, the term **acquired immunodeficiency syndrome**, or AIDS, was adopted and several cases of AIDS were reported in Europe. Although researchers suspected the disease was spread through sexual contact and the transfer of infected blood, the exact pathogen causing

A Peace Corps volunteer congratulates her student on his creation of an HIV/AIDS mural at the Kerugoya School for the Deaf in Kenya.

the condition was still a mystery. The number of HIV/AIDS infections increased rapidly through the rest of the 1980s. Over the next few years, public health workers developed and promoted strategies to avoid sexual, workplace, and drug-related transmission of this new and unknown pandemic.

As we now know, AIDS is caused by the Human Immunodeficiency Virus, or HIV. Because HIV lives in human immune cells, this virus is spread through blood and bodily fluids (semen, vaginal fluids, and breast milk). The virus is most commonly spread through unprotected sex with someone infected with HIV, using needles that someone with HIV has used, and through mother-to-child transmission during pregnancy, labor, birth, or breastfeeding.[38] HIV can destroy a person's immune system, making the body defenseless against infections and disease.

As control and treatment of the disease has improved, the rate of infection has slowed. By the late 1990s, the number of new cases and deaths had decreased dramatically.[39] Still, there are over 55,000 new cases of HIV/AIDS each year in the United States and more than 18,000 deaths.[40]

HIV/AIDS affects people all around the world and is a global health problem. As of 2010, AIDS had killed 30 million people worldwide.[41] Around 34 million are currently living with the disease.[42] In a pattern similar to that in the United States, the rate of new infections worldwide dropped by 25% between 2001 and 2010. *Antiretroviral drugs*—medications that treat retroviruses such as HIV/AIDS— have played a large part in this reduction. Antiretroviral drugs can reduce the chances of passing the disease on through sex and drop the rate of transmission from an infected mother to her child during pregnancy, labor, or breastfeeding. Despite these advances, there are still about 2.6 million new cases of AIDS each year and the disease is spreading faster than ever in Eastern Europe, the Middle East, and North Africa.[43]

There are a number of positive developments to report in the global fight against AIDS:[44]

- Annual funding to combat AIDS in low- and middle-income countries increased 28-fold between 1996 (when the United Nations program UNAIDS was created) and 2005—from $300 million to $8.3 billion.

- In 2001, 240,000 people in developing countries had access to antiretroviral therapy; this number rose to 6.65 million people in 2010.[45]
- In 58 countries reporting data, 74% of primary schools and 81% of secondary schools now provide HIV/AIDS education.
- Blood for use in transfusions is now routinely screened for HIV in most countries.

Drug Resistance

While many modern drugs have helped drive improvements in global health, the misuse of drugs has led to the development of new and more dangerous forms of the diseases the drugs were meant to treat. The misuse of anti-malarial drugs, for example, has allowed the disease to adapt and gain resistance to anti-malarial drugs. Chloroquine and other drugs that used to halt malaria outbreaks are no longer effective in all cases, making the infection harder to treat and control.

Similar drug resistance has occurred with tuberculosis, or TB, a disease caused by the bacteria *Mycobacterium tuberculosis* that is treated with antibiotics. The tuberculosis bacteria has mutated into new forms that are resistant to traditional drugs (called multidrug-resistant tuberculosis, MDR-TB, or extensively drug-resistant tuberculosis, XDR-TB).[46] The appearance of drug-resistant TB is especially prevalent in poorer countries where people may only be able to afford part of the treatment cycle. When a patient only finishes part of the treatment, some tuberculosis bacteria are exposed to—but not killed by—TB drugs and may develop resistance. Traditional TB drugs will still kill a large portion of wild-type or "normal" TB bacteria, but they cannot kill MDR-TB or XDR-TB. If the full course of TB treatment is not completed, it perpetuates the patient's symptoms and increases his or her chances of dying from the disease.

While new drugs are being developed to create a second line of defense against resistant strains of malaria and TB, they are much more expensive than traditional treatments. Moreover, some of these drugs are only injectable, requiring frequent trips to the hospital or medical clinics for the duration of treatment. And second-line treatment is much longer than the standard six months for wild-type TB bacteria.

Patients receive care in a TB ward at a Partners in Health hospital in Peru.

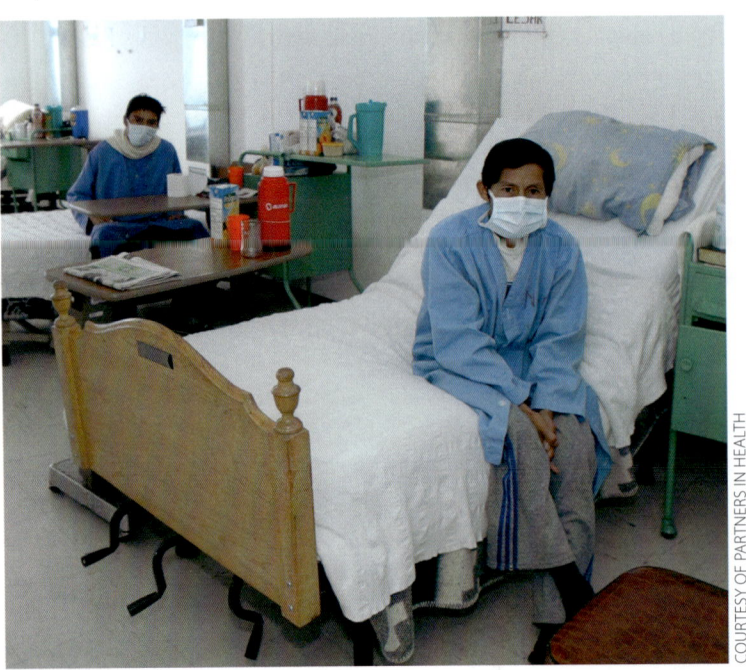

Pathways to Progress: Health

As complex challenges to human health continue to evolve, a variety of solutions will be needed to address health on all levels, from the individual to the structural.

Community Solutions

We can improve the health of our communities by supporting organizations that promote community health. Community health clinics make health care available for those who cannot otherwise afford it, but are often in need of money and volunteers. Community gardens provide a

A community member grows his own food in a City Heights community garden.

way for people to eat better in neighborhoods where nutritious, affordable food is hard to find, such as the City Heights neighborhood of San Diego. Community gardens developed in neighborhoods like these allow residents to feed themselves and even grow produce for sale at farmers markets.[47]

Sometimes community action can make existing health services more effective and improve access to those services for community members. For instance, the chief of one rural district in Malawi decided to take action at the local level in response to a high maternal mortality rate. Almost one out of every hundred deliveries ends in death in Malawi, in part because of the practice of home birth. Traditional beliefs contribute to this practice, such as a belief that a first child must be born at home and that it is the job of the husband to decide when a woman needs medical attention. Under the chief's leadership, the Ntcheu district worked to address the dangers associated with these traditions and, simultaneously, developed a system for registering pregnancies and providing prenatal counseling on nutrition and health.

From 2000 to 2005, not a single mother in the district died while giving birth, in large part due to increases in hospital births. As a consequence, the number of women giving birth at the hospital reached twice the number the maternity ward was designed to handle. The district responded by collecting donations for a clinic to offer basic emergency obstetric services to ease the caseload at the hospital and provide even better maternal and child health care.[48]

Global Solutions

Many people around the world work in the field of global health. **Global health** refers to the collaboration among several different countries in research and practice in order to promote the health of all people.[49] International nongovernmental organizations (NGOs) can support global health issues and health care in communities around the world that are especially vulnerable to social forces working against their health. Often these communities need the help of outside organizations because they do not have the support of their government or the resources to create their own medical facilities. Through advocacy, education, and financial support, international NGOs can level the playing field and give these people a greater chance to be healthy.

Research is another important area of global health work. International NGOs sometimes fund advances in medicine needed to solve health issues in poor communities. PATH, a Seattle-based organization that works on global health issues in developing countries, piloted the deployment of a vaccine for the human papillomavirus (HPV), which is the primary cause of cervical cancer. PATH first contacted government officials in India's Ministries of Health and Education to gain their support for the program and then recruited the World Health Organization and UNICEF to provide international legitimacy. This advocacy for cervical health has created a strong coalition of decision makers who can work with PATH to fund and distribute the vaccine.[50]

While many global health initiatives are big and complex, solutions to some health issues can be fairly simple. Take the Global Soap Project, started by Derreck Kayongo. In his first stay at a

CASE STUDY: Partners in Health[51]

The nonprofit organization Partners in Health (PIH) was founded in 1986 to provide basic medical care for people in rural Haiti. The organization's efforts have since spread to countries all over the world.

One of the biggest health problems in poor countries is tuberculosis (TB). PIH is at the forefront of TB treatment for the poor. In particular, PIH has demonstrated the effectiveness of combining clinical medicine and community action to fight drug-resistant TB, especially in communities with few resources. When an epidemic of MDR-TB (multidrug-resistant tuberculosis) was discovered in the shantytowns of northern Peru in 1996, PIH and a local partner organization, Socios en Salud (SES), created a successful community treatment strategy to cure patients infected with MDR-TB and stop ongoing transmission.

At the time, the World Health Organization and the Peruvian Ministry of Health considered treatment of MDR-TB impractical and unaffordable. The treatment of MDR-TB is complex and involves the administration of drugs several times a day over the course of several months. To overcome this challenge, SES trained and hired people from the community to accompany patients through the long and difficult course of second line drugs. This support made it much more likely that people would complete the treatment and led to one of the highest cure rates for MDR-TB ever reported.

In 1998, PIH took the model established in Peru to Russia, whose epidemic of drug-resistant tuberculosis is among the worst in the world. In Tomsk Oblast, Siberia, for example, 14% of patients newly infected with TB have the multidrug-resistant strain. The TB epidemic is especially complex in the prison system, where drug resistance is even more prevalent. In Russia, PIH has provided TB training for health care workers, worked to improve diagnosis and transmission of TB in hospitals and health clinics, and advocated for institutional change.[52]

On the basis of the success of this program and others modeled after it, the World Health Organization has begun to approve treatment plans for MDR-TB on a country-by-country basis. It also worked with PIH to design a plan to increase the number of MDR-TB patients receiving treatment worldwide from 16,000 in 2006 to a total of 800,000 by 2015.

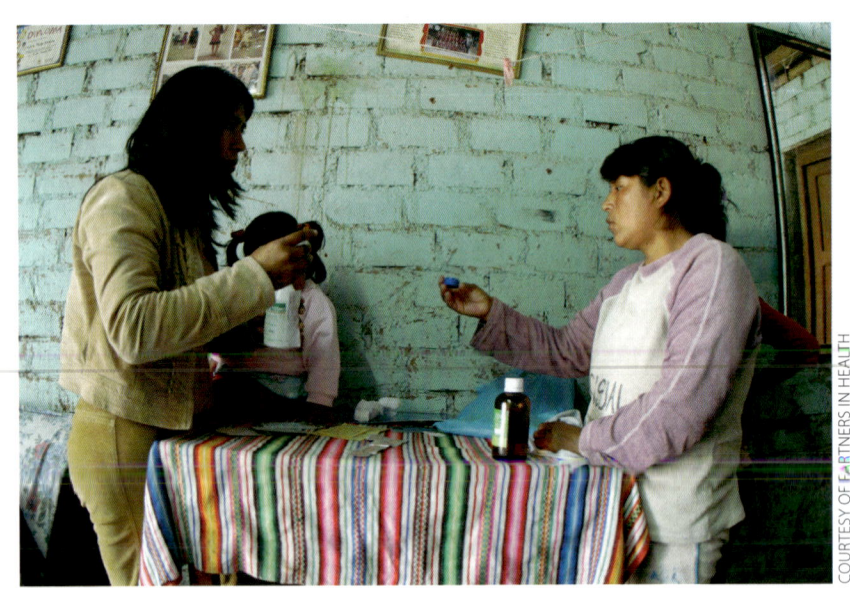

A community health worker with Partners in Health visits a patient to ensure she receives necessary medicines.

hotel in the United States, Derreck, a Ugandan man and son of a soap-maker, was shocked to see that his room was re-stocked with soap each day, even though he had only used the soap a couple of times. In 2009, Derreck began asking hotels if they would donate their used soap for reprocessing and shipment to Uganda, where many people earn just $1 per day, but a bar of soap costs about $0.25. In 2012, the Global Soap project reprocessed and distributed over 482,000 bars of soap around the world and reached people in over 28 countries.[53]

YOUTH PROFILE
Mary Sun

Before she founded NextGEN Policy in 2010, Mary Sun struggled to understand how young people could make concrete changes in the world. Mary watched a close childhood friend battle clinical depression for most of her life; she saw her friend and others her age losing sleep and becoming suicidal. Mary knew she had to do something to help. She learned that current

CAREER PROFILE Infectious Disease Doctor

When you're dreaming up your future career as a kid, being a doctor is right up there with astronaut or ballerina. To become a doctor, you have to enjoy science and math, especially chemistry and biology. You will spend eight years in school after high school and between three and eight years as a resident, or a medical school graduate training in a specialized area of medicine.

As a doctor, you never stop learning, especially if you do both clinical work and research. There are many medical specialties dedicated to treating or preventing specific diseases in adults or children, including surgery, delivering babies, or fixing broken bones. Many doctors choose to specialize in an area that combines intellectual curiosity with a passion for improving the lives of other people.

Shevin Jacob, who holds a medical doctorate and a Master's of Public Health, practices and conducts research in the specialty of infectious diseases at the University of Washington. He was inspired by his father's career as a doctor to enter the field of medicine. Shevin

Shevin Jacob is a doctor who conducts research on infectious diseases.

serves as a consultant for the World Health Organization with a focus on populations in sub-Saharan Africa. He believes regions like sub-Saharan Africa need doctors and advocates because "the burden of disease for severe infections like HIV and malaria disproportionately affects children and adults from poorer countries where there is very little access to health care compared to countries like the United States or Canada." Shevin points out that when individuals are sick, they have a difficult time focusing on providing for their families or their futures. As the number of sick people without access to health care increases, the strength of communities begins to break down. As a result, goals for a flourishing economy, education, and sustainable development take a back seat to survival. If a strong foundation to improve health and access to health services were in place, society would have greater resources to cure and prevent illness for current and future generations.

Shevin is inspired to do his work by the potential to make a positive impact at both the individual and community level:

The ability to see this spectrum of impact is very motivating. It's all about short-term and long-term benefits. In the short term, I can see the smile of a healthy patient after providing her with a life-saving treatment. In the long term, the results of my research can be used to benefit an entire community.

treatments and diagnoses were vastly ineffective. With most teens undertreated and underdiagnosed, depression was just another part of growing up. Mary started doing her own research and launched NextGEN Policy with the hope that new scientific research could have a real-world impact on medical policy and practice.

In just two years, NextGEN has had a lasting effect on science policy advocacy and is now on its way to becoming a fully independent corporation. The organization brings together current scientific research and volunteer advocates to change and improve the health care system. Advocacy efforts include a focus on correct and speedy medical diagnosis, adolescent health policy and youth leadership, and the development of treatments for rare diseases. NextGEN was also involved in lobbying efforts for the Unlocking Lifesaving Treatments for Rare Diseases Act of 2012, recently introduced into Congress.

After graduating high school and looking back on the work that she has done, Mary not only believes in her own ability to make change, but she also expects other young people to do the same. "Founding and continuing to oversee NextGEN Policy has been a remarkably empowering experience," Mary explains. "I now believe very strongly in the ability of youth to make a lasting, positive impact on our world. I have seen this mobilization in action, and I have employed some of the mechanisms which make youth projects so effective."

Mary Sun

WHAT YOU CAN DO — Health

It is important to remember that statistics like life expectancy that represent the health of a group are averages. Averages represent a range of health within a community. But these averages and statistics do not have to define you. You can make choices that promote good health, including:

- Staying fit and eating well—these habits not only improve your own health but relieve pressure on health care systems and contribute to a culture of health in your community
- Washing your hands with soap—each person who doesn't wash their hands puts everyone around them at risk of infection
- Staying home when you are sick—avoiding school, work, and other public places will help to prevent spread of the disease
- Completing the full cycle of prescribed antibiotics—completing the full cycle will help to prevent the creation of drug-resistant forms of disease
- Supporting public health—help educate others on healthy habits and create a public service campaign to build awareness and education around on health concern that disproportionately impacts your community

Derreck Kayongo created a simple solution to addressing sanitation around the world; the Global Soap Project.

POINT | **COUNTERPOINT**

Should governments provide health care to all of their citizens?[54]

Do you believe health care is a basic human right? If so, do you believe this is a right that should be enforced by government-sponsored health care programs rather than private insurance? This debate has raged in countries around the world and is still going on today. National governments have taken a variety of approaches to health care—from Cuba, a country that provides free and universal health care, to Argentina, a country where health care is broken down into a private sector, public sector, and social security sector. Consider the points below taken from the online debate forum Debatepedia. Do any of these arguments sway you one way or the other?

POINT

Yes

- **"The government funds fire-stations, why not universal health care?** The government taxes citizens to fund and provide numerous services universally, including policemen and firemen. These services are comparable to physician services in many ways, particularly in the sense that they help protect the life, safety, or health of citizens. Why shouldn't health care also be provided universally through the same means—taxes?"

- **"Universal health care is a legitimate "burden" on the tax payer.** People pay for public utilities such as road and people pay for education as well. But do people who don't drive recklessly ask for money back when roads are damaged? Do people who send their children to private school ask for all their money back? We place this burden on the state because of equality of opportunity. No man should be denied the right to live his life."

- **"Health care is a basic human right or entitlement.** Health is fundamental to the preservation of all other individual rights. If one is sick in a hospital bed, they cannot be said to have equal opportunity or the ability to exercise free speech and religion. And, of course, one cannot pursue happiness if they are in a hospital bed. This is why health must be considered a basic human right."

COUNTERPOINT

No

- **"Health problems are more about individual choices than fires and crime.** While many people compare health care to police stations and fire stations, they are not the same services. Health care is largely about providing a service to the individual that compensates, often, for poor individual choices. Fire stations and police departments, on the other hand, provide services to a community and focus on protecting individuals against things they have no control over (crime and fires). The differences are very significant in regard to what the state is obligated to provide. The state is obligated to protect citizens from one [sic] another. But, the state is not obligated to protect citizens from themselves. Universal health care is wrongheaded to the extent that it involves protecting individuals from themselves."

- **"People leading healthy lives will be burdened by the unhealthy.** It is not fair for those that lead healthy lives to have to pay for those that lead unhealthy ones. Those that make decisions to smoke cigarettes and eat excessively should pay the consequences."

- **"Universal health care leads to rationing.** Medical resources are rationed in socialized systems so that some people are either denied care or have to wait for it. If a person is "rationed out" of the public health care service (perhaps because the treatment is not considered effective or cost effective enough to warrant intervention) they will be able seek alternative treatment in the private sector. If they cannot afford private care, they may have to go without."

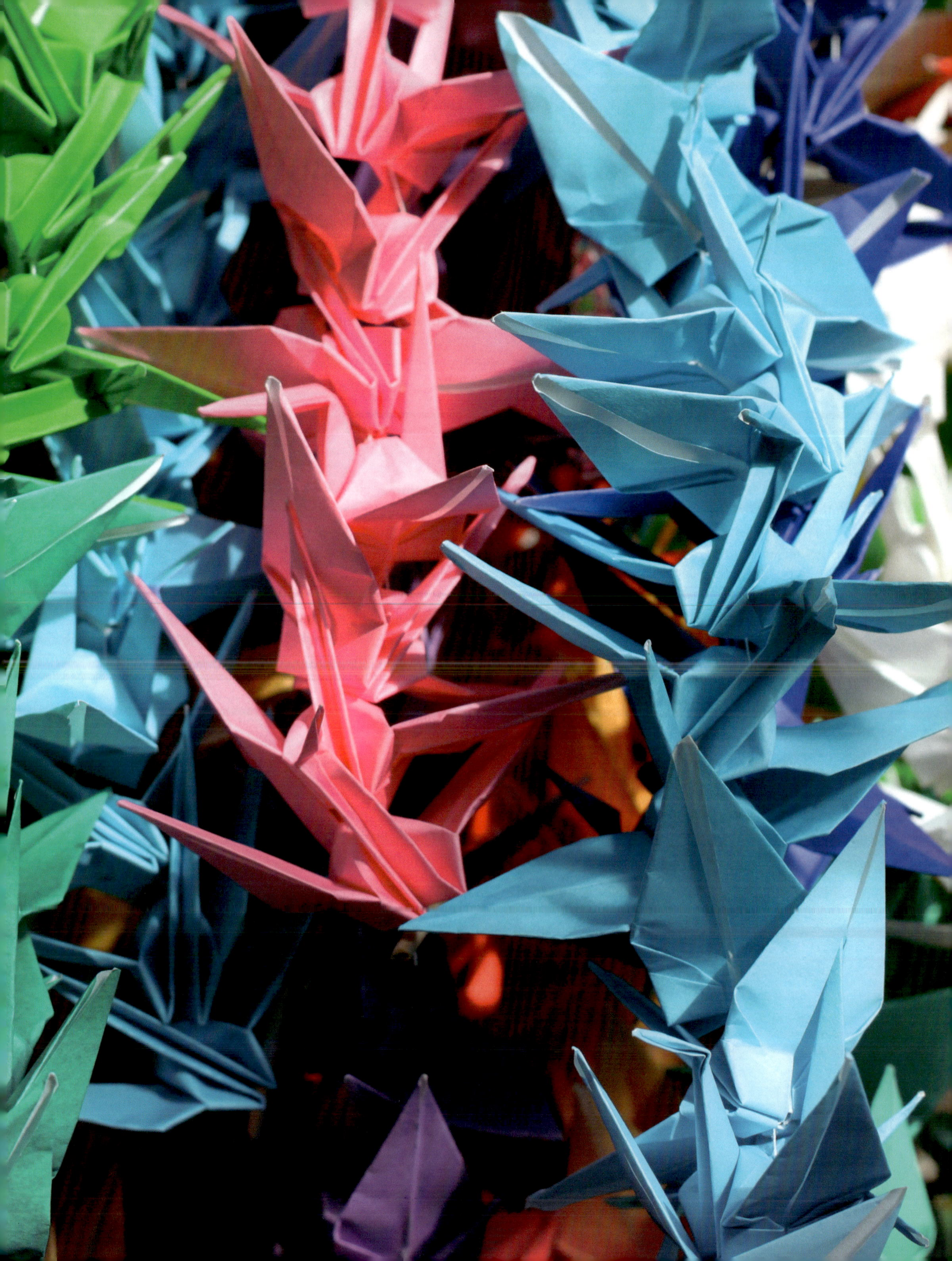

Chapter 15

Peace and Conflict

> **GUIDING QUESTIONS**
> - What causes conflict and why do conflicts persist around the globe?
> - How can we be involved in efforts to decrease conflict and increase peace?

Introduction to Peace and Conflict

Valarie Kaur was 20 years old when the Twin Towers fell on September 11th, 2001. Three days later, her uncle was killed in front of a gas station in Mesa, Arizona. How are the two incidents linked? Valarie comes from a Sikh background, a religion that originated in India. Sikh men often wear turbans and after 9/11 many were mistakenly thought to be Islamic terrorists or terrorist sympathizers in the United States. As a result of this misconception, a number of hate crimes against Sikhs occurred in the wake of 9/11. Valarie decided enough was enough and created a documentary called *Divided We Fall*. The film documents these hate crimes and calls for a deeper understanding of who Americans truly are. She explains how her family has lived in the United States for 100 years, yet they are still viewed as outsiders. The film has won a number of awards and has been screened in over 120 cities with the aim of raising awareness, increasing tolerance among ethnicities, and creating peaceful communities.

Valarie Kaur

What Is Peace?

What leads people to commit acts of terrorism like the September 11th attacks? Why do people develop hatred for others and how does hatred result in conflict? These questions can help us understand what it means to be at peace. Peace can be defined simply as an absence of conflict, but that definition does not address the potential for conflict to flare up again. It is naïve to believe that the people of the world are suddenly going to forget about all of their differences and decide to be friends. A more viable definition of world **peace** is perhaps a world at peace with itself. To be at peace is to respect and embrace differences among people including differences of opinion, religion, ethnicity, etc. Valarie Kaur's work is dedicated to this idea of peace; her film aims to bring people in the United States together in order to learn to respect each other despite their differences.

What Is Conflict?

The most basic definition of **conflict** is a "fight, battle, or struggle, especially a prolonged struggle." On a more personal level, we can define conflict as a state of opposition between persons, ideas, or interests. You could even have an internal conflict—for example, if you're uncertain about which of two choices you should make. Regardless of who the conflicting parties are or what the conflict is about, conflict can be a productive way of overcoming differences in opinion or interest. Other times, however, it can become violent and have a devastating impact.

War and conflict have been around about as long as humans have been around. Conflicts can have wide and long-lasting consequences both for those fighting and for people and places that are not directly involved. Conflict threatens **human security**, people's freedom from danger, poverty, or apprehension. This can happen in violent or nonviolent conflict.

Mild (or nonviolent) conflict, such as two people preferring different sports teams, may get loud, but rarely are they debilitating to a country's people, economy, or environment. Ironically, sporting events have even been known to bring people who are normally at odds with each other together in support of their team or their country. On the other hand, some sporting events, given their popularity, can be the stage for conflict as well.

Peace means not only the absence of conflict, but the ability to embrace differences among people.

CASE STUDY: Prolonged Conflict between Israel and Palestine

Continued tensions exist in the Gaza Strip.

The Wailing Wall is a sacred site for Jews in Israel.

Tensions between Jewish, Christian, and Muslim populations have arisen throughout recorded history. However, the current conflicts between Israel and Palestine began in the 20th century with the development of a new Israeli state.

During World War I, Great Britain was granted the temporary administration of Palestine under the Balfour Declaration of 1917.[1] Before the Great War, Palestine had been absorbed by the Ottoman Empire, but the Turks occupying Palestine during the war were defeated by British troops. Around this time, a movement known as Zionism had begun to take hold, promoting the idea that Jews deserved their own homeland. Britain made a statement in support of a Jewish state in Palestine in the hopes that the statement would encourage influential Zionist leaders in the United States to push for greater U.S. involvement in the Allied war effort. At the close of the Great War, the League of Nations entrusted the British with the construction of a homeland in Palestine for the Jews.

Most of the people living in Palestine at that time were Arabs who did not take kindly to the large number of Jews moving into what they considered to be their land. Great Britain found itself incapable of resolving the differences between the Arabs and the Jews, and after World War II, turned the problem over to the United Nations. The United Nations proposed side-by-side states of Israel and Palestine, with the holy city of Jerusalem divided between the two.

More Jews settled in the area and, in 1948, Israel declared its independence. The new Israeli state occupied three quarters of what was formerly Palestine, including all of Jerusalem—Palestinians were forced to flee. Jordan and Egypt continue to occupy the other quarter of the Palestinian territory. In 1967, Israel initiated the Six-Day War, which ousted Egypt and Jordan from the former Palestinian territory. As a result, Israel gained control over the entire area that once was Palestine. Israel's refusal to give up the territory, despite requests by the Palestinians and the United Nations, sparked waves of violence, including a fatal hostage-taking by the Palestinian terrorist organization Black September of Israeli athletes at the Munich Summer Olympic Games in 1972.

Hope for peace between Israel and Palestine was high in the 1990s, but that peace didn't last past the start of the new millennium. There are continued tensions around issues such as who should control the Gaza Strip, an area allocated to Palestinians with a strong Israeli military presence.[2]

Conflicts can escalate from nonviolent to violent. Violent conflict increases *violence*. The World Health Organization defines violence as "the intentional use of physical force or power, threatened or actual, against oneself, another person, or against a group or community that either results in or has a high likelihood of resulting in injury, death, psychological harm, maldevelopment or deprivation."[3]

Once a conflict escalates to a certain level, it can become more of a habit than an actual dispute with discernable cause. Sometimes a conflict becomes *intractable*, continuing for years or even generations. The conflict between Israel and Palestine is an example of an intractable conflict.

Conflict and Sustainability

Conflict affects all aspects of a country: the stability of its economy, the welfare of its society, and the health of its environment.

Economy

The larger and more prolonged a conflict is, the greater the potential for long-term economic damage. When a country is focused on war, the growth of its economy slows down. If the economy slows to the point that it cannot sustain its citizens, there is a risk that institutions such as banks and businesses will collapse. The result is economic turmoil and chaos, preventing the country from putting the welfare of its people first and foremost.

Society

In times of conflict, refugee and migrant populations increase and so do related health issues and human rights abuses. Refugees who move to refugee camps can develop many types of illnesses. Not only is their exposure level higher in crowded camps, but their resistance to disease is lower most likely due to poorer overall health. A lack of secure access to clean water or proper sanitation worsens these conditions. Epidemics such as malaria and cholera are more likely to spread.[4]

In times of conflict, refugee camps, such as this one in the Democratic Republic of the Congo, can increase.

Violent conflicts can destroy people's homes, their crops, and their livestock. As a result, people get poorer and hungrier the longer a conflict continues. Bomb blasts and bullets can cause damage to *infrastructure* such as roads, buildings, and irrigation systems. One result of infrastructure damage can be water shortages that leave farmers unable to tend to their crops (not to mention themselves or their livestock), assuming they are lucky enough to still have land to farm.[5] Even once the conflict is over, it can leave a mark on the land. Landmines may still be planted, soils may be contaminated, seeds scarce, livestock dead or gone, and infrastructure in need of repair.

Conflict can also have significant effects on soldiers. Many U.S. soldiers coming home from the Iraq War, for example, displayed increases in Post-Traumatic Stress Disorder (PTSD), most likely because they witnessed comrades and civilians killed in war. The Department of Veteran's Affairs hospitals found that more than one in four soldiers came home with psychological or physical problems.[6] In Iraq, PTSD has also been related to the stress of living in a warzone and the constant threat of sudden attack.

Environment
Conflict can be just as hard on the environment as it is on its inhabitants. Chemical warfare, a type of warfare that uses toxic hazardous materials, can cause direct health problems and contaminate water supplies during a conflict. Forests and other wildlife habitat may be destroyed either to provide fuel or offer a tactical advantage to combatants. Land stripped of forests is at risk of soil erosion and flooding. The genocide in Darfur is one example of a conflict that led to widespread destruction of land.[7]

Taken together, the negative impacts of violent conflict make it a barrier to improved human security and environmental sustainability, two key ingredients of a sustainable future.

Background on Peace and Conflict

Interstate Conflicts
Interstate war takes place between two or more different countries, or between a country or countries and a group of people. Interstate wars tend to be caused by either territorial or political disputes. World War II was an interstate war. It began in 1939 when Germany attacked Poland; by early 1942, many countries of the world were involved in the conflict. Interstate wars can also be a result of an outside party's entrance into an intrastate war.

Intrastate Wars
Intrastate wars, also known as civil wars, are internal conflicts within a country. This type of war pits citizens of the same country against each other. You may even find neighbors or members of the same family fighting on opposite sides. The causes of intrastate wars are more varied than those of interstate wars. Violent conflict between citizens of the same nation erupts over such issues as concentration of power by an authoritarian government, or control over a valuable resource. This type of conflict can last decades and cause massive disruption in a country. Arguably, intrastate wars are much more damaging to people than interstate wars, if only because of the fact that both warring parties are occupying the same country. The United States, Ireland, Cambodia, Burma, Sudan, Croatia, Lebanon, and Uganda are just some of the countries that have been ravaged by this type of conflict. Dealing with the aftermath of such wars can take generations of work.

Genocide
Genocide is a term that came into existence in 1944. Created specifically to refer to Nazi crimes against Jewish people, the word genocide was coined by a Polish-Jewish lawyer

CASE STUDY: Genocide in Rwanda[8]

Rwanda is a small landlocked country in central Africa. It supports one of the densest populations on the continent. The population of Rwanda before 1993 consisted of a number of ethnic groups: 85% Hutu, 14% Tutsi, and 1% Twa. Under colonial rule in the early 1900s, Belgium ruled over the country and actively worked to divide these ethnic groups. The Belgian colonial government provided the minority Tutsi group a number of privileges including a western-style education. They reinforced the idea that Tutsis were superior to Hutus because they were taller, lighter, had larger skulls, and supposedly came from Caucasian ancestry. This kind of rationale would also fuel the Nazi plan to exterminate Jews.

After Rwanda gained independence in 1961, tension increased between the two ethnic groups. After years of Tutsi superiority, when the Belgian colonists left they handed power over to a Hutu government elected by Rwanda's Hutu majority. Over the next several decades, a number of smaller massacres of Tutsis took place. By the early 1990s, Hutu extremists increasingly blamed Tutsis for unrest building within Rwanda. While the president at the time worked on peace accords between the two groups and created a multiparty system in the government, Hutu extremists, themselves part of the political elite, became less and less tolerant of Tutsis. At the same time, major Rwandan newspapers and radio shows promoted strong ethnic stereotyping. This type of propaganda, "promoting hatred of the Tutsis," created growing resentment within the country.

In 1994, the plane carrying the Rwandan president—a Hutu—was shot down. Hutus blamed the Tutsis for his death and almost immediately began to kill any Tutsis they could find. The genocide led to the death of 800,000 people, mostly men, leaving Rwanda with an overwhelmingly female population (70%). Many of these women became the primary breadwinners in their households, responsible for supporting themselves, their own children, and the many orphaned children they adopted. Prior to the conflict, these women did not have any training in skills that would support families monetarily. These days, Rwanda has a high rate of female participation in politics and decision-making.

Women for Women International is an organization working to support women in Rwanda. They provide direct financial support, teach women about their legal rights, conduct job skills training, and give emotional support. The organization offers women the opportunity to participate in a one-year program to gain business and leadership skills, receive health education and support, and become active citizens to create lasting change in their communities.

There are many reasons to hope for a brighter future for the people of Rwanda. In 2008, Rwanda made news around the world by electing the first majority female parliament. Women in Rwanda are developing leadership skills to take care of themselves, support their families, and help their country rebuild after the devastation of genocide. Rwanda's success proves that countries have the capacity to restore stability and transform into peaceful societies even after devastating conflicts.

Women for Women International provided opportunities for women in Rwanda after the genocide.

named Raphael Lemkin. He defined it as "a coordinated plan of different actions aiming at the destruction of essential foundations of the life of national groups, with the aim of annihilating the groups themselves."[9] In other words, one group (the Nazis, in this case) seeks to completely wipe out another group (Jews). Genocide in World War II was responsible for the deaths of an estimated 5–6 million Jews.[10] In 1948, the United Nations declared genocide a crime. There are several more recent examples of genocide in Rwanda, the Balkans, and Darfur. What would make one group want to completely destroy another group of people?

Terrorism

Terrorism, as defined by the U.S. Department of Defense, is "the calculated use of unlawful violence or threat of unlawful violence to inculcate fear; intended to coerce or to intimidate governments or societies in the pursuit of goals that are generally political, religious, or ideological."[11] Terrorism thrives on attacking innocent, non-related victims to make a statement or to force another group to act in response. Terrorism is a truly unsettling form of violence because victims don't have any idea of when terrorists could attack. As mentioned earlier, September 11, 2001 was an example of terrorism.

Present-Day International Conflict

The number of international, or interstate, wars and war-related deaths is decreasing. While this is good news, the bad news is that the incidence of intrastate wars is increasing. A unique challenge to ending intrastate conflicts is that Article 2 of the UN Charter prohibits outside nations from intervening in an independent country's internal affairs. The only exception is when sending peacekeeping forces to address issues like genocide or *ethnic cleansing*, a policy designed by one ethnic or religious group to remove by violent means the civilian population of another ethnic or religious group from a given area.

CASE STUDY: Shining Path and Terrorism

During the late 1960s, Abimael Guzmán, a philosophy professor, started the group Shining Path *(Sendero Luminoso)* in Peru. One of the group's intentions was to disrupt and undermine the current government in an effort to form a communist state. During the 1980s, for example, members of the group burned ballot boxes in a small town in order to disrupt democratic elections. But their actions didn't stop there. Members of Shining Path were also involved in a bomb explosion in the city of Lima and a number of other terrorist tactics. They were able to fund many of their operations through narcotrafficking (the smuggling of illegal drugs) and forcing taxes on small businesses and individuals.[12]

This revolutionary group wanted to overthrow the existing government and destroy the government's reputation. While Shining Path initially targeted local authorities like mayors, police, and local political leaders, many others became victim to their violence. By the time Abimael Guzmán was imprisoned on September 12, 1992, over 70,000 people had been killed in the fighting between the Peruvian government and Shining Path.[13]

The Bureau of Counterterrorism within the U.S. Department of State identified Shining Path as a designated foreign terrorist organization. By identifying these groups, the U.S. government is essentially able to isolate these terrorist organizations and prevent any kind of donation or contribution from going to these groups.[14]

Rise of Intrastate Wars and Internal Conflicts

Since the end of World War II, intrastate wars have been more predominant than interstate conflicts. As with the American Civil War, intrastate fighting can be bloody, cruel, and fierce. An estimated 20-30 million people have been killed in these types of wars since 1945, and as many as 50 million more displaced from their homes. By definition, both parties in an intrastate war occupy the same country. This places ordinary citizens in extreme peril. In some civil wars, citizens are used as pawns against the other side; genocide, gang rape, sexual mutilation, torture, and exploitation of child soldiers are among the many cruelties inflicted on innocent citizens during intrastate conflict.[15]

Global Insecurity

The majority of recent armed conflicts have been centered in Africa and Asia. Why is conflict concentrated in these areas? Countries in Africa and Asia have a number of characteristics that can increase the likelihood of internal conflict:[16]

- High populations
- Large population in the 15-24-year-old age bracket
- Low income level
- Low economic growth
- Recent political instability
- Ethnic differences
- Corruption by elites
- Natural resource exploitation
- Country borders arbitrarily drawn by European colonizers
- History of colonization that pitted ethnic groups against one another

Understanding these characteristics of increased likelihood for war can aid in diffusing conflicts. Governments and other groups can create solutions that target these issues to decrease a country's likelihood of violent conflict.

One of the clearest trends in intrastate wars is the way they end. Since the end of World

The Vietnam War began in 1955 and had many casualties.

War II, and especially since the end of the Cold War, intrastate wars have finished with no clear victory by either side; in essence, in a tie. Of the 168 recorded civil wars before 1989, only one (the Mexico-Yucatan Maya war, 1847-1855) is considered not to have ended in a tie. Of the 61 intrastate conflicts that occurred during the Cold War, 20% are considered to have ended in a tie. And since the Cold War, a whopping 38 out of 54 conflicts—that's 70%—have ended with no clear victor. This lack of a decisive victory makes the ensuing peace less stable.[17]

When the parties in an intrastate conflict reach a stalemate, they must agree to stop fighting. Reaching a peace settlement can be challenging for two parties so recently involved in hostilities, and it is often desirable to invite a third party to help broker the peace. Conflicts in Bosnia, Somalia, Haiti, and Cambodia have all been brought to an end through third-party interventions because they couldn't be solved internally.[18] Some bodies that intervene in civil or intrastate conflict include the Council of Europe Commissioner for Human Rights, the United Nations' humanitarian forces, and humanitarian nongovernmental organizations (NGOs). Prominent individuals, such as the leader of a country, can also play a pivotal role in facilitating conflict resolution.

Peace and Conflict Today

You probably already have some ideas about how modern conflicts get started. By exploring this topic in more detail, we can start to get to the roots of many conflicts. Four major factors connected to conflict are: natural resource scarcity, ineffective governance, social division, and limited development.

Natural Resource Scarcity

When resources are scarce, it is only natural for people to want to be in control of them. Dividing up a small pie among many people

A UN peacekeeping soldier greets villagers.

can generate controversy, resentment, and conflict. The party that controls scarce resources will gain money and power, while others may lose out. In the context of the environment, the degradation of resources such as water, forests, or arable land is therefore of concern for its potential to spark human conflict in addition to the harm done to the natural world.

When asked about the conflict in Darfur, Sudan, most people will tell you that it's about ethnic cleansing. This is definitely the case, but a number of other factors—including land degradation, deforestation, and climate change—have contributed to tensions. As northern Sudan's land suffered through drought and underwent desertification, a number of migrants were forced to move south. This large influx of people put pressure on the availability of land and resources. Local tensions around issues such as water scarcity and the mismanagement of

The conflict in Darfur, Sudan created large numbers of internally displaced people.

natural resources already existed in southern Sudan; the arrival of migrants from the north only increased these tensions and made violent conflict more likely.[19]

The origins of the Sudanese conflict demonstrate the role that a stressed environment can play in causing conflict. On the other hand, a focus on environmental sustainability has the potential to prevent conflict or, in the case of Sudan, establish a lasting peace after conflict has occurred. The Executive Director of the United Nations Environment Program (UNEP), Achim Steiner, is optimistic about Sudan's future:

> Just as environmental degradation can contribute to the triggering and perpetuation of conflict, the sustainable management of natural resources can provide the basis for long-term stability, sustainable livelihoods, and development. It is now critical that both national and local leadership prioritize environmental awareness and opportunities for the sustainable management of natural resources in Sudan.[20]

The realization that environmental, political, and social issues are linked is critical to global peace efforts. Sustainable land-use practices and resource consumption will reduce the likelihood of sudden environmental change, creating conditions conducive to peace.

Ineffective Governance

Governance is the exercise of economic, political, and administrative authority to manage a country's affairs at all levels. You have probably noticed the effects of ineffective governance on a local level at some point in your life—perhaps a coach or teacher who couldn't effectively manage a team or classroom. This might result in rebellious behavior, misunderstandings, or unmet goals. At a national level, the consequences of ineffective governance are more serious. At worst, it can lead to insufficient legitimate authority, lack of access to services, high unemployment, and restricted civil rights.

If governance is effective, however, it can prevent conflict. Essentially, effective governance is similar to having a great coach who can really motivate a team—everyone is engaged, goals are clearly stated, and the means to achieve those goals are provided.

In 2003, there were 37 countries in the world emerging from intrastate wars. As they become post-conflict societies, what measures could these countries take to ensure conflict does not recur? There are many things that governments can do to help create a peaceful environment and stable society:[21]

- Reintegrate soldiers back into society
- Control small arms trade
- Reform the constitution
- Allow for free elections and more democracy
- Promote cooperation among ethnic groups
- Satisfy basic social needs of citizens including access to food, water, health, and shelter

Social Division

As we have seen throughout this chapter, social division is a major contributor to conflict around the world. You read about the divisions between the Hutus and Tutsis in Rwanda and how systemic support of this division ultimately resulted in genocide. Throughout history, there have been many examples of tensions related to religion, race, and social class. These tensions create an "us" versus "them" mentality. Different groups of people may not necessarily dislike each other, but peer pressure sometimes prevents them from becoming friends. Research performed in Uganda demonstrates this, showing no difference in productivity when people were asked to work with members of their own ethnic group compared with people outside of it. The study participants were also asked to (theoretically) donate money in two situations: in one, donations were anonymous; in the other, donations were made with the entire group's knowledge. When they gave anonymously, people showed no bias in their donations, but when everyone could see how they gave their money, participants were strongly inclined to give exclusively to their own ethnic group.[22] Effective governance is key in helping prevent peer pressure from escalating ethnic tensions.

Governments have considerable influence over social divisions, for better or worse. A government can increase its own power by pitting different groups against each other. To accomplish this, a government might promote social divisions through propaganda and legislation that create an "us" versus "them" mentality. *Propaganda* is biased information that supports a specific point of view. On the other hand, if leaders are committed to ending ethnic tensions they can also use propaganda and legislation—this time, to promote peace and stability. Effective leadership and the ability to mediate conflicts are examples of tools that a government can use to good effect. However, they will only be successful if leaders from all sides of the conflict are committed to achieving peace and willing to compromise. Diplomatic efforts by governments can help opposed groups set aside their hostility and address issues in a neutral way without descending into violence. Negotiating peace can be a long and complex process, but the end product is worth the struggle.

CASE STUDY: A Newly Democratic South Africa

When the system of Apartheid—or legal racial segregation—ended in South Africa, this did not mean that conflict, racial tensions, and social divisions immediately disappeared. There was still much work to be done in order to create a peaceful society and heal the wounds of South Africa's turbulent history. One important step was the rewriting of the country's constitution to replace existing legal documents that supported Apartheid. A number of people participated in the creation of a new constitution. Among them was Cyril Ramaphosa, the chairperson of the South African Constitutional Assembly. Drafting a new document was an arduous process that frequently brought up unresolved tensions, but Ramaphosa, along with other leaders like President Nelson Mandela, worked hard to ensure that the country was headed toward democracy and away from its socially divisive past.[23]

Children walk down a road together in South Africa.

Limited Opportunities for Development

In some ways, this section could also be titled "The Haves and the Have-nots." When economic opportunities in a country are limited, there are large numbers of people who live in poverty and a small number of wealthy people. The wealthy have much greater access to education and jobs, while the poor continue to be less educated and less able to take advantage of economic opportunities. The educated upper class are most likely to gain positions in the country's government and they may use this power to make political decisions that favor themselves and their peers, further increasing tension between rich and poor. In this way, economic inequality creates social discontent that may lead to conflict.[24]

The riots that took place in Great Britain in 2011 are a good example of this phenomenon. Britain faced a tough economy and the government cut many programs. Lower-income communities struggled with high unemployment among youth and increased racial tensions. When a 29-year-old man was shot by police it was the tipping point that caused many frustrated youth to act out. The riots that erupted throughout London and other cities damaged many buildings and businesses and resulted in injury, loss of life, and hundreds of arrests. In the end, the cost of the riots totaled hundreds of millions of pounds, some of which had to come out of taxpayer money.[25]

Pathways to Progress: Peace and Conflict

As history shows us, conflict is a persistent characteristic of the human race. Nevertheless, there are ways for people to lessen the potential for conflict and live and work together peacefully. No single approach is going to be a quick fix for world peace. Solutions will have to be multifaceted and sustainable over the long run. The following examples illustrate different ways people can work together to build a peaceful world.

The message of this mural in England speaks to creating a more tolerant and peaceful world.

Responding to Abusive Governments

In the aftermath of a conflict, taking steps to hold perpetrators of war crimes and other human rights abuses accountable can be a positive way to reunite a fractured country and promote its stability. In 2002, the Rome Statute established the International Criminal Court (ICC) to do just that. According to the Rome Statute, the ICC can only prosecute cases countries are not prosecuting themselves. Although there had been other international war tribunals, they were always established to deal with a particular issue in a particular time frame. The ICC is the first permanent independent court established to try criminals and crimes of concern to the international community.[26]

The court has opened investigations into crimes committed during conflicts in the Democratic Republic of the Congo, Darfur, the Central African Republic, Kenya, and Libya. For example, in 2006, Thomas Lubanga, the leader of a militia in the Democratic Republic of the Congo, was arrested and brought to trial under the allegation of using child soldiers during warfare.[27] Through prosecutions such as these, the ICC provides a way to hold abusive leaders accountable for their actions.

Protecting Natural Resources and the Environment

Environmental conservation and protection are vital to the continued availability of natural resources to humans and other species. The environment is particularly vulnerable in times of conflict, but people can develop contingency plans to help protect vulnerable areas if conflict should arise. For example, maintaining conservation personnel in the field during and immediately after a conflict can help minimize negative impacts on the environment and natural resources.

Sustainable measures, such as these solar streetlights in Afghanistan, can help to prevent future conflict.

Governments can play a major role in protecting resources and the environment by regulating businesses and other groups. This strategy can have an additional benefit: by ensuring that resource extraction is legal and putting a stop to illegal mining operations, a government can help prevent the escalation of conflicts. In Sierra Leone, for example, illegal diamond mining was used to support the arms trade, which in turn fueled the country's civil war. Imagine how the situation might have been different had the fighters not had access to this valuable natural resource.

Another example is Afghanistan. In the later part of the 20th century, the country suffered through 25 years of conflict. In 2002, Afghanistan's Grand Council met to develop a transitional government structure that will attempt to build a more peaceful future for the country. For the first time, environmental conservation and sustainable development of natural resources were addressed at the ministerial level. The result was the establishment of Afghanistan's National Environmental Protection Agency (NEPA). Given the country's history of civil war and international conflict, not to mention its breakdown of local governments, NEPA faced—and indeed still faces—a monumental task. To help meet the challenge, the European Commission, the Government of Finland, and the Global Environment Facility all contribute to financing conservation efforts in Afghanistan.[28]

Securing Access to Education, Jobs, and Housing

Human security is greatly improved when people have the tools to take care of themselves. As you learned from the example of the 2011 riots in Great Britain, people without the means to support themselves can become frustrated and turn to violence. Efforts to improve access to jobs, housing, and education contribute to stability in a country.

The Basic Education Coalition helps to increase education access to children around the world.

The Basic Education Coalition is one organization working to advance human security by increasing access to education for children around the world. The Coalition works with policymakers in the United States to address the shortfall in education funding that leaves 67 million children worldwide out of school. The Coalition is made up of 15 different organizations including nonprofits such as World Vision, Save the Children, Catholic Relief Services, Creative Associates International, and ChildFund International. Members believe literacy, math, critical thinking, and life skills can help alleviate poverty and that education is essential to civil society, democracy, and political stability.[29]

YOUTH PROFILE
Anderson Sa[30]

When Anderson Sa was only 10 years old, he saw a man shot on the street in his hometown of Rio de Janeiro in Brazil. The neighborhood he lived in is called Vigario Geral; at the time, it was one of the most violent favelas (or slums) in Rio.

By the age of 13, Anderson was already part of a drug cartel. At first, belonging to the cartel's drug army gave Anderson a sense of belonging and helped him to make more money than he could at any other job. But while he was part of the drug army, Anderson lost friends and family to violence. He began to realize the lifestyle he was living was not what he wanted. How could he escape?

While Anderson wondered how to leave the cartel, a DJ by the name of Jose Junior started the Afro Reggae Cultural Group. The group was created to give youth an alternative to involvement in the drug trade. At first, the group published a newspaper for young people to share news about popular music. Soon they opened a community center in Vigario Geral where young people could learn about soccer, music, dance, and capoeira (a type of martial art). The goal was to help youth become positive leaders in the community who could shape their own futures rather than joining drug armies.

Anderson joined the Afro Reggae Cultural Group and was soon an active member of a band. He played different instruments, wrote songs, and taught other young people in the favela about music. During this time, Anderson left the drug army and became a positive role model for many young people through his charisma and leadership. His songs describe the struggles of living in a favela and encourage young people to say no to violence.

A young child stands in front of his favela in Brazil.

CAREER PROFILE: Conflict Mediator

Conflict mediators can help individuals and groups settle disputes and create resolutions. They may specialize in different types of conflict resolution related to families, organizations, nations, or religious groups. While conflicts between people are inevitable, effective resolutions can increase peace and stability. In fact, conflict mediators can play a large role in preventing wars and human rights violations in the future.

Matt Scrimgeour is the program coordinator at the Corrymeela Center, a faith-based nonprofit organization that was created amidst ethno-political conflict in the United Kingdom. Conflict between Ireland and Britain over Ireland's national independence and relationship to Britian is nothing new; it has been going on since the 1600s. However, violence was concentrated and intensified in the 1960s through the 1990s. The Corrymeela Center seeks to "[promote] reconciliation and peace-building through the healing of social, religious, and political divisions in Northern Ireland."

Like a lot of peacebuilding nonprofits, Corrymeela focuses on transforming a culture of conflict by creating a safe opportunity for individuals to confront religious and political divisions in their communities. The Corrymeela Center brings people together in a residence, where people of different backgrounds share meals, conversation, and dorm space. The experience provides an opportunity for participants to reconsider their own assumptions about themselves, each other, and the conflict. Matt is responsible for administration, planning, and problem-solving focused on conflict mediation. Matt admits that "our society will not encounter transformation because of Corrymeela," but he goes on to say that he is witnessing progress: "My experience of growth and change in myself and others nurtures the possibility that significant change is always possible even when at first impression it appears to be a long way from now." Experiential learning in peacebuilding is essential to this career, but Matt also says that pursuing experiences that transform you personally, opening you up to growth and exposing you to people from different backgrounds and worldviews, are just as important.

Matt Scrimgeour works as a conflict mediator in Ireland.

Today, Anderson Sa is the president of the Afro Reggae Cultural Group. In 2006, he helped Afro Reggae expand their programs to reach over 2,000 young people in favelas throughout Rio de Janeiro.[31] Anderson made a huge decision in his life by choosing the path of peace instead of the path of violence. Through this choice, he has taught thousands of others that they also have choices and that they can choose their own future.

Bridging Differences[32]

An organization called Seeds of Peace, founded in 1993, provides the opportunity for youth from conflict-affected countries around the world to come together in a summer camp where they learn about conflict resolution and peaceful coexistence. The camp's programs help teenagers develop leadership skills and overcome social divisions in order to gain respect for other cultures and a deep understanding of others' perspectives. The friendships and channels of communication created at Seeds of Peace camps continue once the young people return home.

A group of 46 Israeli, Palestinian, and Egyptian teenagers met for the first Seeds of Peace International Camp in 1993. These future leaders were selected by their governments. Seeds of Peace empowers youth living in war-impacted countries to break down the social divisions that are often at the root of conflict. In doing so, Seeds of Peace ensures that the future of peace is in the hands of friends rather than enemies.

WHAT YOU CAN DO: Peace and Conflict

Youth can be a major force for establishing peace. Just think about how many young people were involved in the peace movement in the 1960s and the nonviolent protests during the Civil Rights Movement. Young people tend to be very passionate and idealistic. As shown through actions like a high rate of volunteerism, youth and young adults truly believe that they can make a difference. For example, 55% of youth ages 12-18 volunteer in U.S. communities, nearly double the rate of adult volunteerism.[33] This passion and motivation to act can be a strong factor in promoting peace and ending conflict.

There are a number of personal decisions you can make that can help build a more peaceful world. At the local level, learning about conflict management to resolve conflicts you encounter can be useful. Building awareness of and respect for other cultures can help people overcome discrimination and social divisions. Here are a just a few actions you can take:

A mural in New York City spreads a message of peace in different languages.

- Try to resolve disagreements with friends and family peaceably
- Become skilled in mediating conflict
- Support or volunteer with organizations that work to alleviate violence
- Support international peacekeeping efforts with letters to government officials

POINT **COUNTERPOINT**

Should the international community get involved in national affairs related to conflict?[34]

The debate on whether the international community should get involved in a nation's conflicts has been an ongoing debate for quite some time. And if the international community decides to get involved, just how should they do so? There have been atrocities such as the Holocaust and the genocide in Rwanda and uprisings such as those in Iran and Syria that raise the question in this debate.

POINT

Yes

- **When atrocities such as genocide happen within a country, the international community should not just sit and watch.** The international community should get involved and intervene. They can do so through a number of ways. International agencies can stop providing loans and aid to governments that inflict genocide and human rights abuses on their people. War criminals participating in such human rights violations can be sent to the International Criminal Court. After the Holocaust ended in 1945, the international community said, "never again." If the international community can step in and speak out against unjust conflicts in countries, then these types of events can be prevented.

- **Just because conflicts happen within national borders does not mean that the consequences of these conflicts will not spill over into neighboring countries and affect the international community.** If the international community can get involved in conflict prevention, this could be the answer to avoiding such things as increased refugee populations, environmental exploitation of land in bordering countries, drug trafficking, and terrorism.

COUNTERPOINT

No

- **The international community does not have the capacity to get involved in national conflicts.** The World Bank estimates economic costs for conflicts each year of $100 billion. The United States alone provides approximately $2 billion toward the United Nations Department of Peacekeeping Operations' annual budget. Countries around the world should not have to spend their money on issues that do not directly affect them. They can direct their concerns to issues like health care, employment, and education in their own countries.

- **The international community should not get involved in a nation's affairs related to conflicts.** This sets up a dangerous precedent where a nation might lose its rights in dealing with its own internal affairs. Governments should have the ability to manage internal disputes. Countries that get involved with another country's conflicts could worsen the situation. Only when a country asks for help should the international community intervene.

The Auschwitz Concentration Camp pictured here was one of the largest concentration camps that existed during World War II.

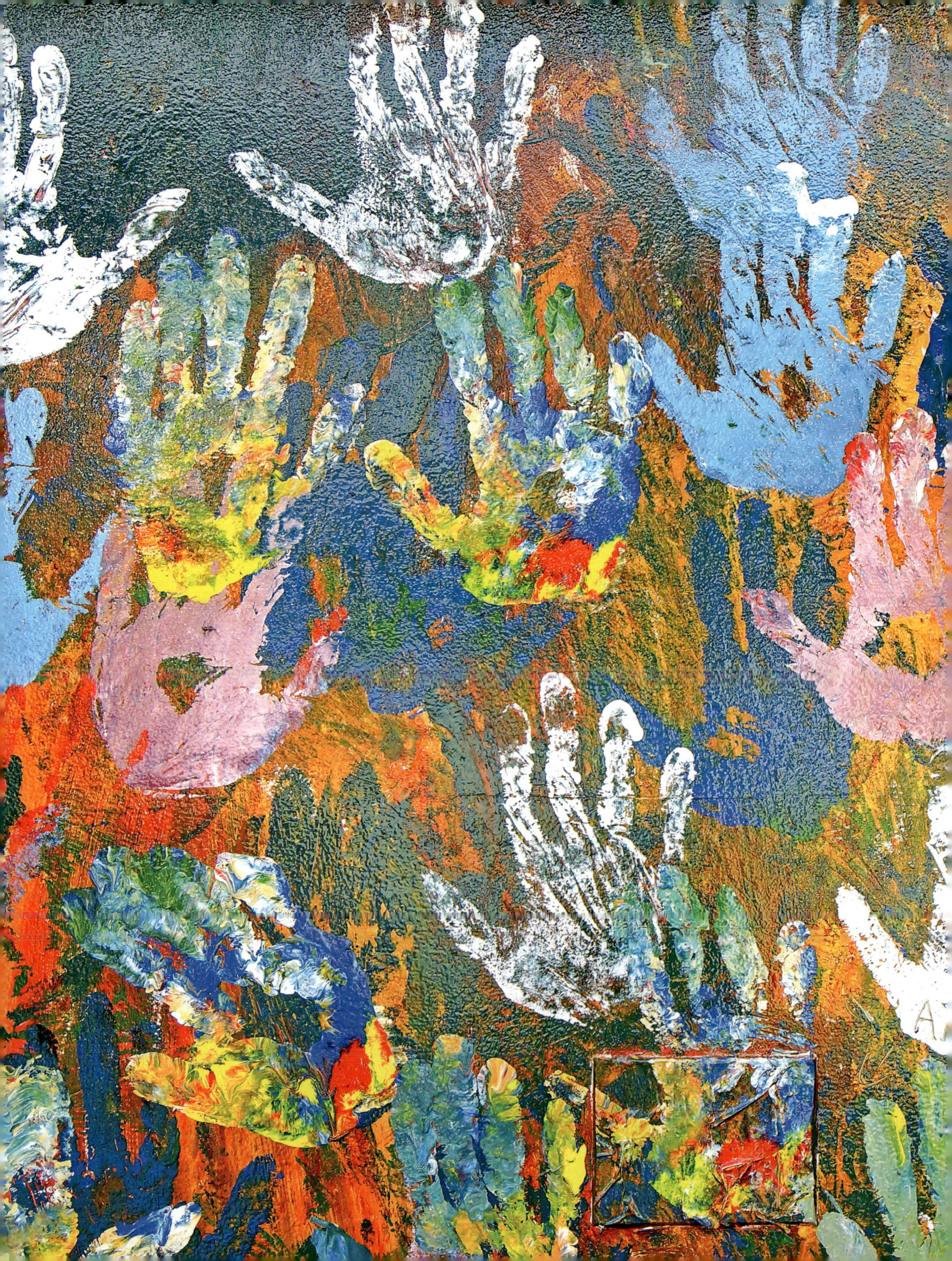

Chapter 16

Human Rights

Peace can only last where human rights are respected, where the people are fed, and where individuals and nations are free.

—His Holiness the 14th Dalai Lama

> **GUIDING QUESTIONS**
> - What are fundamental human rights and how have they been honored or violated throughout history?
> - How do human rights connect to sustainability?

Introduction to Human Rights

When Craig Kielburger was twelve years old, he came across the story of Iqbal Masih while reading the *Toronto Star* newspaper. Iqbal Masih was a Pakistani boy sold into slavery at age four who later spoke out against slavery and in defense of children's rights. At the age of twelve, Iqbal lost his life.

After reading this story, Craig felt the need to do something. He brought his 7th grade classmates together and started the group Free the Children. Today, Free the Children advocates for children's rights and has programs in over 45 countries.[1]

Regardless of where we come from or what we do, we are all born with fundamental human rights. **Human rights** are those basic rights and freedoms to which all humans are entitled, often held to include the right to life and liberty, freedom of thought and expression, and equality before the law.[2] Human rights relate to freedom, justice, and equality. *Freedom* gives you the ability to express yourself religiously, politically, and socially. *Justice* requires individuals be treated fairly and ethically. *Equality* means all people have equal access to rights and opportunities.

Whereas some countries protect and safeguard the basic human rights of their citizens, others have demonstrated glaring human rights abuses. A number of economic, social, and environmental factors can help us understand why these stark global differences exist.

Human Rights and Sustainability

When people are able to live peaceful and secure lives with full access to natural resources, a clean environment, employment, education, and social services, they are more likely to contribute to sustainable communities. However, when people are not able to meet their basic needs or secure their fundamental human rights, they may also lose the ability to participate in social, economic and environmental systems that promote sustainability.

Students in Chicago stand up for human rights

Society

Governments that cannot or will not provide services to their people often pose a risk to citizens and their human rights. These countries are far more likely to experience conflict and instability and are less likely to protect people's rights. When citizens' rights are not observed, they are less likely to participate fully in a society.[3]

The unjust imprisonment, torture, and unfair trial of political prisoners, attacks on journalists and the press, concerns about working conditions, and persecution of religious minorities are all examples of a person's rights being taken away.

What happens to a country when a large portion of its population's rights are violated? Can the country sustain itself and remain stable?

Economy

We live in a global economy. For the most part, countries can trade with each other, borders are open, and businesses can go where they want. This globalized world has the potential to increase jobs and improve the economy. At the same time, certain economic decisions may violate human rights.[4] For example, if a business decides to invest in projects that enforce child labor or human trafficking, that business is responsible for violating people's rights. Working conditions in sweatshops are an issue often raised by human rights organizations. Corporations have come under criticism for forcing people to work in dangerous environments and not paying them a living wage.

Environment

Imagine not having access to clean water or having to breathe in polluted air every day. Access to basic needs like food, water, air, and shelter are necessary to every human being. Pollution is responsible for the death of approximately 2 billion people each year and billions more contract pollution-related diseases. A corporation operating in a developing country that pollutes a local water source and makes it unusable also violates human rights. Other environmental issues such as water shortages, fisheries depletion, and deforestation also threaten people's basic livelihoods and rights. Climate change contributes to environmental degradation and results in increases in human migration, the spread of infectious diseases like malaria, and extreme weather events.[5]

Background on Human Rights

The concept of human rights did not always exist. In the year 539 B.C.E., Cyrus the Great, the founder of the Persian Empire, conquered Babylon. He freed Babylon's slaves, proclaimed the right of all people to choose their own religion, and established racial equality. The principles of Cyrus' rule were written on a baked-clay cylinder that became known as the Cyrus Cylinder. Some regard this cylinder as the first documentation of human rights. Throughout the course of world history, Cyrus the Great's decisions influenced others. In 1215, King John of England signed the Magna Carta, which enshrined in law fundamental human rights for those living under his rule. Hundreds of years later, during the period known as the Enlightenment, support for the idea of human rights grew throughout Europe. Soon after, the Declaration of Independence was signed on July 4, 1776 in the United States, followed by the Declaration of the Rights of Man and Citizen in 1789 in France.[6]

Although these documents spoke of universal rights for all people, before World War II international law gave countries exclusive power over how they dealt with their citizens. A government was free to treat its people however it wished and no other country would interfere. However, during World War II, events such as the Holocaust prompted many leaders to speak out against what they viewed as major human rights violations taking place outside their own national borders. In 1941, U.S. President Franklin Roosevelt spoke to Congress in his State of the Union address about four essential human freedoms: freedom of speech, freedom of worship, freedom from want, and freedom from fear.[7] Many countries around the world accepted these four freedoms and committed to these general ideals.

Despite this international sentiment, by the time World War II ended in 1945, the Nazi regime in Europe had killed over 6 million people, including Jews, gypsies, homosexuals, and people with disabilities. Around the world, people were shocked by this genocide.

In response to these atrocities, 51 countries joined together as a collective international organization called the United Nations to promote peace and security. Although countries still had sovereign authority over citizens, leaders accused of committing crimes against humanity may be tried under international law. The Nuremberg trials of 1945-1946 and the Tokyo Trial of 1946 placed Nazi and Japanese leaders who committed war crimes in front of an international military tribunal.[8] Before this time, these types of crimes were punished predominately under domestic law.[9]

Eleanor Roosevelt, the wife of President Roosevelt, was elected head of the United Nations Human Rights Commission and helped draft a human rights declaration. On October 10, 1948, the General Assembly of the United Nations adopted the **Universal Declaration of Human Rights**, a document outlining a number of rights that all people are born with.[10] When the declaration was initially created, it was not accepted internationally. Some critics believed that the document

> *In 1941, U.S. President Franklin Roosevelt spoke to Congress in his State of the Union address about four essential human freedoms: freedom of speech, freedom of worship, freedom from want, and freedom from fear.*

had too much of a Western focus, with the only input from nonwestern countries coming from China and Lebanon.[11] Others believed that rights to housing, health, and education were better seen as aspirations or public policy goals rather than inalienable rights. Rights were too difficult to guarantee.[12]

At the time when the Universal Declaration of Human Rights was adopted, a number of human rights violations were still happening around the world. Racial segregation was present in the United States. In colonized countries, people often experienced **discrimination**, the unjust treatment of different groups of people. Many wanted an end to colonial rule and used the principle of self-determination to support their claims for independence. **Self-determination** is the right

CASE STUDY: Civil Disobedience in India

British rule in India began in 1757. In the early 20th century, before World War II, Mahatma Gandhi argued that India deserved independence from Britain.[14] There was growing resentment over the way the British treated Indians and their culture. At the same time the British benefited economically from their control over resources in India, including cheap labor. Their restrictions on Indian citizens prohibited Indians themselves from benefiting from industrial and commercial growth.

One such restriction was the British Salt Tax. This law stated that any sale or production of salt not authorized by the British government was a legal offense. While salt was easily available in certain coastal zones of the country, farmers were forced to pay the British government for any salt they harvested.[15] Mahatma Gandhi mobilized people on March 12, 1931 in a nonviolent march against British domination of the salt industry. He used *civil disobedience*, a refusal to obey certain laws of a government, in order to advocate for the human rights of Indian citizens. One hundred people marched 200 miles to the ocean to gather free salt in a protest against the infringement of their rights under British rule.[16] A series of other protests over the next several years would finally usher in India's independence in 1947.

Gandhi used civil disobedience to protest violations of human rights.

288 CHAPTER 16 HUMAN RIGHTS

of all nations to govern themselves without foreign rule or interference. It was seen by many as a fundamental human right they had been denied in the past. Over the next few decades, dozens of countries such as India and Zambia gained independence from their colonizers. Many used articles from the Declaration of Human Rights to support their cause.[13]

Human Rights Today

According to the Universal Declaration of Human Rights, human rights are meant to provide all people with basic protections and securities regardless of where they were born, who they are, what they look like, and what they believe in. By taking a closer look at specific types of rights, we can analyze their significance and how people have worked to secure these rights.

Political Rights

Article 19 of the Declaration of Human Rights states:

> *Everyone has the right to freedom of opinion and expression; this right includes freedom to hold opinions without interference and to seek, receive and impart information and ideas through any media and regardless of frontiers.*

Around the world, certain countries give people complete political freedom, allowing them to express themselves publicly and to assemble peacefully. If you have ever seen a political debate or civic demonstration, then you have seen people expressing themselves publicly. Many of us can't imagine a place where opinions cannot be shared on T-shirts, bumper stickers, and magazines without fear of persecution. Yet that is the reality in some parts of the world. In a country without political freedoms, people may be less likely or less able to participate politically.

Sri Lankan Tamils protest against the genocide occurring in their country.

There are many factors that influence the degree of political freedom a country's citizens enjoy. One factor is the occurrence of major historical events. Events that impact a country's security and stability can affect the government's decision about the political freedoms it provides its citizens. For example, after the attack on the Twin Towers on September 11, 2001, the United States gave priority to the fight against terrorism in exchange for certain civil liberties. The government was given permission to wiretap phones and investigate business records related to any individual suspected of having links to terrorism.[17] This gave the government more access to its citizens' personal lives and impacted people's daily lives.

Another factor that can impact political rights is a country's type of national government. There is a connection between the type of government within a country and the degree of political freedom afforded to citizens. Authoritarian regimes are less likely to allow political participation and rights, while democracies are more likely to encourage civic participation in political matters.[18]

CASE STUDY: The Berlin Wall

After the end of World War II, Germany was divided into occupied zones controlled by the Allied powers. In 1949, tensions between the United States, Great Britain, and France on the one side and the Soviet Union on the other resulted in the formation of two German states: the Federal Republic of Germany, commonly known as West Germany, and the German Democratic Republic, known as East Germany. The division into West and East also took place in the country's capital, Berlin.

The Soviet government strictly controlled life in East Berlin. They restricted access to information media (newspapers and radio) and limited people's ability to express themselves. In contrast, West Berlin, governed by the United States, the United Kingdom, and France, allowed people unrestricted access to media and a number of political freedoms.[19]

On August 13, 1961, in an effort to prevent people from moving from East to West Berlin, the East German government put up a 27-mile-long wall of barbed wire to separate the two sides of the city. The barbed wire was soon replaced by a more permanent wall made of tons of stone and steel. When finished, the wall was 155 kilometers long with armed guards, observation towers, floodlights, and dog patrols.

The Berlin Wall fell on November 9th, 1989.

Before the Berlin Wall was built, over 3.5 million East Germans had left East Berlin between 1945 and 1961. After the wall was erected, the number of people who left decreased to fewer than 6,000.[20] For years, the two sides of Berlin represented very distinct political realities with different political rights. East Berlin was often seen to be oppressive, while West Berlin offered freedom and democracy to its people.

The Berlin Wall was taken down on November 9, 1989, and the East German government resigned. A number of large antigovernment demonstrations precipitated this resignation. Just days earlier, one million people had come together for a pro-democracy demonstration in East Berlin.[21] These demonstrations were an example of people standing up for their human rights.

Gender Rights

Article 2 of the Declaration of Human Rights states:

> *Everyone is entitled to all the rights and freedoms set forth in this Declaration, without distinction of any kind, such as race, color, sex, language, religion, political or other opinion, national or social origin, property, birth or other status.*

Although Article 2 of the Universal Declaration of Human Rights states that human rights apply equally to all persons, women have historically suffered from inequality. Because of gender-based discrimination, women's opportunities to own land, to gain employment, and to earn an education have been very different than those of men. In 1993, the Vienna UN Conference on Human Rights affirmed women's rights as human rights. This confirmation happened 45 years after the Declaration of Human Rights was written.[22] Still today, women face many inequalities. Consider these statistics:

- Women make up 5% of the work force in Saudi Arabia.[23]
- Women own less than 15% of land worldwide.[24]
- Of the 100 million children in the world with no access to primary schooling, 60% are girls.[25]

When a group of people are not considered equal to others in a society, they become more vulnerable to human rights violations. Women have suffered the loss of their rights in a number of different ways: sex trafficking, restrictions to rights in the public sector, slavery, and abuse. Human rights violations against women are often more severe in situations of poverty or conflict. For example, in the Congo, violence against women increased 17-fold between 2004 and 2008 because of conflict and instability within the country.[26]

When women are deemed equal within a society and afforded economic, civic, and political rights, they can help support a country's sustainable development. In fact, developing countries that work toward gender equality are more likely to have lower poverty rates.[27]

Education Rights

Article 26 of the Declaration of Human Rights states:

(1) Everyone has the right to education. Education shall be free, at least in the elementary and fundamental stages. Elementary education shall be compulsory. Technical and professional education shall be made generally available and higher education shall be equally accessible to all on the basis of merit.

(2) Education shall be directed to the full development of the human personality and to the strengthening of respect for human rights and fundamental freedoms. It shall promote understanding, tolerance and friendship among all nations, racial or religious groups, and shall further the activities of the United Nations for the maintenance of peace.

(3) Parents have a prior right to choose the kind of education that shall be given to their children.

Many factors may prevent a child from attending school; conflict, poverty, and distance are just a few. Around the world, 211 million children work instead of attending school to provide financial support to their families. In just one example, 109,000 children in the Ivory Coast work in the cocoa industry. These children work long hours with exposure to dangerous tools,

---

CASE STUDY: Changing Laws in Morocco

Morocco's family law was widely debated for a long period of time. This law, known as Moudouana, prevented women in the country from having many rights within their families. While husbands could easily obtain divorces from their wives without needing their wives' consent, women were forbidden to leave relationships they did not want to be in. Women's groups fought to change the Moudouana. Finally, in 2003, King Mohammed VI gave more rights to women by reforming the country's family law to include these provisions:[28]

In 2003, women in Morocco gained the right to divorce their husbands.

- The minimum age women were allowed to marry was raised from 15 to 18 years old.
- Women gained the right to divorce their husbands.
- Polygamy by married men became illegal.

A young girl participates in her wedding rituals in Bengal, India.

pesticides, and hot temperatures.[29] There can be lasting negative consequences for a country when a large proportion of children work instead of going to school. For example, less than 60% of adults within the Ivory Coast are literate.[30]

While there may be some benefits to child labor, such as an immediate increased household income, the long-term costs can be harmful. When children do not attend school, they are less likely to educate their own children. In addition, children who work instead of attending school are more likely to be low-wage-earning adults.[31]

Childhood Lost

Imagine having to marry at the age of twelve, leaving school to work on a farm at the age of ten, or fighting in a war at the age of eight. Children throughout the world have been forced to do all of these things. Consider the following statistics:

- 300,000 children under the age of 18 are child soldiers. In some cases, they have been kidnapped or forced to join armed conflicts.[32]
- 120 million children between the ages of 5 and 14 work full-time.[33]
- In certain countries within Africa and Southern Asia, over 40% of girls are married before the age of 18.[34]

In 1989, the United Nations General Assembly adopted the Convention on the Rights of the Child. This convention includes 54 articles that were created to protect and uphold the rights of children. A number of governments, non-governmental organizations, and human rights advocates helped to create this document that holds countries accountable for their treatment of children.[35]

Civil Rights

Article 7 of the Declaration of Human Rights states:

> *All are equal before the law and are entitled without any discrimination to equal protection of the law. All are entitled to equal protection against any discrimination in violation of this Declaration and against any incitement to such discrimination.*

Civil rights are rights that protect individuals within a country from unjustifiable actions from the government and give individuals the ability to participate in society without discrimination. The more citizens have a voice within a country, the more they can contribute. On the other hand, when oppression and corruption exist within a country, people are less likely to enjoy political and civil rights.[36]

After slavery in the United States ended in 1865, there remained a number of restrictions that prevented African-American people from participating in civil actions such as voting, and denied them equal access to public spaces and services such as seats on buses and trains or attending school with white children. The Civil Rights Movement, which began in 1948 and continued through the 1970s, involved a number of actions—from court cases to public protests—that laid a foundation for guaranteeing rights for African Americans that did not exist in the past.

Other social movements throughout the world (such as the anti-apartheid movement in South Africa) have also had significant impacts on the civil rights of different groups.

Ending Apartheid

Many countries have a history of denying civil rights to certain groups of people. In South Africa, black South Africans were heavily discriminated against. Whites first came to power in South Africa during the 1650s, when the Dutch government took control of the country. Over the next centuries, Dutch farmers known as Boers seized South African land and forced black Africans to work for them. A number of national laws passed during the early 1900s took away political, civil, and educational rights of black people within South Africa. For example, the Native Lands Act of 1913 allocated only 7.3% of the country's land to black South Africans, although they made up 80% of the population.[37] The Representation of Voters Act of 1936 weakened the rights of Africans in certain regions and allowed them to only vote for white representatives.

During the period known as apartheid, from 1948 to 1993, black citizens could not live or work in "white" areas without special permission. *Apartheid*, meaning separateness, was created by the National Party government to enforce legal segregation. Years later, the anti-apartheid movement in South Africa fought against the discrimination that had taken political and civil rights away from black people.

The African National Congress was one group that sought to liberate South Africa from apartheid. Black South Africans in this political group advocated for peaceful resistance to discriminatory laws. By the 1980s, people around the world were speaking out against apartheid. Finally, the country's discriminatory laws were reversed and blacks achieved the rights they had lost over the last hundred years. Nelson Mandela, a black South African who was imprisoned for 27 years because of his resistance against apartheid, was elected president of South Africa in 1994.[38]

Apartheid was finally dismantled in the early 1990s.

Religious Rights

Article 18 of the Declaration of Human Rights states:

> Everyone has the right to freedom of thought, conscience and religion; this right includes freedom to change his religion or belief, and freedom, either alone or in community with others and in public or private, to manifest his religion or belief in teaching, practice, worship and observance.

Around the world, people practice a great number of different religions ranging from Buddhism, Christianity, and Islam to Judaism, Jainism, and Hinduism. For centuries, people of different religious backgrounds have lived alongside each other. France, for example, has a population that includes Roman Catholics, Muslims, Protestants, Buddhists, Jews, and unaffiliated individuals.[39] People can live peacefully in countries that have a multitude of different religions, but there are also times when religious minorities face persecution and discrimination.

Most religions ask their followers to accept certain core beliefs. When people of different religions interact, the differences in their fundamental beliefs about the world and faith can cause intolerance, discrimination, and tension.[40] Conflict between Hindus and Muslims in India is one of many examples related to religious tensions throughout history.

Teaching Tolerance[41]

The Modesto School District in California has taken a unique approach to religious tolerance and understanding. Modesto's population is around 200,000. Within the city, there are a number of people who identify as Christian and Jewish as well as growing religious communities of Sikhs, Hindus, and Muslims. In 2000, the district began to use public schools to teach about respect for religious freedoms. All 9th grade students are required to take an independent course on world religions. The course first looks at the United States and its history of religious liberty. A study conducted by the district that surveyed 400 students over nine months found that the course had a positive impact on students' respect for other religions.

Religious tolerance is one way to support human rights.

Rights to Health and Well-Being

Article 26 of the Declaration of Human Rights states:

> (1) Everyone has the right to a standard of living adequate for the health and well-being of himself and of his family, including food, clothing, housing and medical care and necessary social services, and the right to security in the event of unemployment, sickness, disability, widowhood, old age or other lack of livelihood in circumstances beyond his control.
>
> (2) Motherhood and childhood are entitled to special care and assistance. All children, whether born in or out of wedlock, shall enjoy the same social protection.

As mentioned earlier, before an individual's civil, political, and religious needs are met, basic needs like access to food, water, shelter, and sanitation are necessary for survival. According to the World Health Organization, "the enjoyment of the highest attainable standard of health is one of the fundamental rights of every human being."[42] When people have access to health care, nutritious food, disease prevention, clothing, and social services, their basic needs and individual rights related to health are met.

Many people struggle to meet these needs. Around the world, there are over one billion people who do not have access to health care systems and who live on less than $1 per day.[43] Without these health services, people may be more prone to poor health and poverty. Those living in poverty often do not have access to safe drinking water, food, education, and adequate housing. As a result of these factors, life expectancy may decrease. For example, in countries like Mozambique, Malawi, and Rwanda, the average life expectancy is below 40 years old.[44] Without intervention, this cycle can continue from generation to generation.

The Star of Hope project provides children in Haiti with nutritious food.

Partners in Health

Paul Farmer is a doctor and anthropologist who cofounded an organization called Partners in Health (PIH) in 1987. Based on the idea that health care is a human right, PIH works in eight different countries including Russia, Peru, and Malawi to treat health problems effectively in poor communities. The organization focuses on five principles:[45]

- Universal access to primary health care
- Free health care and education for the poor
- Community partnerships
- Addressing basic social and economic needs
- Serving the poor through the public sector

PIH has facilitated the training and education of medical practitioners in some of the poorest and most remote communities in several countries. Through local partnerships and the establishment of regional and national education centers in Haiti, Peru, Russia, and Rwanda, PIH has helped clinicians and health administrators attain practical training. As a result, health outcomes in these poor communities have improved. For example, Rwandan health care workers have learned how to use ultrasound technology to diagnose illnesses that would otherwise have gone untreated.

A laborer mines for gold in Madagascar.

Labor Rights

Article 24 of the Declaration of Human Rights states:

> (1) *Everyone has the right to work, to free choice of employment, to just and favourable conditions of work and to protection against unemployment.*
>
> (2) *Everyone, without any discrimination, has the right to equal pay for equal work.*
>
> (3) *Everyone who works has the right to just and favourable remuneration ensuring for himself and his family an existence worthy of human dignity, and supplemented, if necessary, by other means of social protection.*
>
> (4) *Everyone has the right to form and to join trade unions for the protection of his interests.*

Labor rights include respect for human life in the workplace. Throughout the world, people are forced to work for low wages and in unsafe conditions. Some countries use migrant workers to fill labor shortages, especially with jobs that are low paying, dangerous, and poorly regulated. Human rights abuses are more likely to happen in these types of situations because migrants may not have legal status or speak the language of the host country.[46]

Some workers around the world do not have the freedom to choose their employment or even to be paid for their work. Did you know that there are many more slaves in the world today than there were during four centuries of the trans-Atlantic slave trade? The large numbers are due in part to global population growth.[47] Many are debt slaves who are under debt bondage to lenders, while others are trafficked for prostitution. Approximately 12 million people are considered modern-day slaves.[48] Forty-three percent of those who are trafficked are used for commercial sex exploitation. Thirty-two percent are used for forced economic exploitation.[49]

Forced Labor

In Myanmar during the 1990s, U.S. oil companies made an agreement with the government to build a pipeline that would deliver gas to Thailand. The creation of this pipeline would help bring millions of dollars to Myanmar. Between 1993 and 1996, oil companies and the government cleared lands and built roads to support this effort. Pipeline construction took place between 1996 and 1998. Throughout this period, human rights groups reported abuses related to pipeline construction. Myanmar's military government used forced labor, making villagers relocate and work under harsh conditions. If they chose not to work, they faced either imprisonment or execution.[50] The villagers finally spoke out against a U.S.-based oil company, bringing it to federal court in the United States. They ended up receiving an out-of-court settlement that rewarded them financially and protected their rights within the region where they lived. Programs were also created to improve the health and living conditions for the villagers.[51]

Pathways to Progress: Human Rights

Around the world, governments, organizations, and individuals have spoken out against human rights violations in an attempt to secure human rights for all. At times, this intervention has caused tensions in the international community, as some believe that a country's human rights issues are its own business and foreign nations and organizations should not intervene. Others believe that an international commitment to human rights has given voice to many who previously were not able to advocate for themselves.

Advocacy

The organization Amnesty International was founded in 1961 to safeguard human rights for people around the world. Amnesty International has offices in over 80 countries and a membership of 2.8 million people. The organization believes that human rights should be respected and protected for all people. They research human rights abuses and campaign internationally to protect people whose rights have been violated, including female victims of violence, refugees and migrants, political dissidents, and people in poverty.[52]

Throughout the world, youth participate in Amnesty International and write letters to different governments asking them to stop human rights violations.

Transitional Justice

Transitional justice is a response to large-scale human rights violations that happen within a country. This justice includes measures by different countries that address massive human

Amnesty International is an organization that promotes human rights around the world.

Two Japanese American children wait for the evacuation bus that will take them to an internment camp.

rights abuses. A national government may decide that when people's rights are violated it will seek justice for the victims through criminal prosecutions, truth commissions, or reparations programs.[53]

For example, during World War II, thousands of Japanese Americans were forced to relocate and live in internment camps out of fear they were a threat to national security. After the attack on Pearl Harbor on December 7, 1941, the FBI began rounding up leaders of the Japanese-American community and questioning them. Soon after, President Roosevelt signed an act that forced 110,000 Japanese Americans to relocate to 10 internment camps across the United States. The camps were fenced in and guarded. Many of them were located in deserts. Japanese Americans who interned in the camps often received meager portions at meals and some died because of inadequate medical care.[54] Several years later, on June 30, 1947, hundreds were released from these camps.

In 1979, a U.S. House Representative introduced the World War II Japanese-American Human Rights Violations Act to Congress. The act proposed that each victim of an internment camp should be paid $15,000 in reparation for their internment. In 1981, the Commission on Wartime Relocation and Internment of Civilians gave hundreds of Japanese Americans the opportunity to recount their wartime experiences. In 1988, President Ronald Reagan signed a law that paid $20,000 to each surviving internee.[55]

Governance

Governance and human rights reinforce each other. Human rights can provide governments with a framework to work by when developing policies and allocating budgets to certain sectors such as education and health. Good governance supports human rights through transparency and by encouraging public participation from citizens in a positive way.[56] This type of governance can also help to strengthen democracy, give all groups a voice, and improve services to support basic needs like health and education.

Take the example of the Brazilian government's response to the HIV/AIDS health crisis. During the 1990s, 600,000 people were living with HIV in Brazil. The government established a Parliamentary Group in 2000 to respond to this issue. Their goal was to make sure legislation was adopted to support the human rights of those with HIV/AIDS. The group also worked to strengthen the state and municipal governments' ability to respond to the HIV/AIDS crisis. Because of the Parliamentary Group's work, communication between different levels of government improved and the distribution of medicines to people increased.[57]

YOUTH PROFILE
Free the Children

One way to advocate for human rights is to support organizations that are working toward improving the rights of children around the world.

As mentioned earlier in the chapter, Free the Children is an organization that has involved more than one million youth in programs across 45 countries. The organization received a human rights award known as the World's Children's Prize for the Rights of the Child. Based on the work of Craig Kielburger, Free the Children now provides a number of opportunities for young people

CAREER PROFILE — Social Studies Teacher

Did you ever imagine that being a teacher could impact human rights? Liz Devine had a severe stuttering problem when she was young, making her the victim of jokes by other students. Her fourth grade teacher helped her to gain confidence in herself and she eventually overcame her speech problem. Liz realized she wanted to pass on that gift to others by becoming a teacher. She went to college in New York and proceeded to get her Master in Teaching.

Fast-forward 32 years: Liz has spent her adult life teaching high school social studies classes including Human Rights, Government, United States History, American Studies, and American History. According to Liz, "The way to work for positive change in our communities, our nation, and the world is to nurture and encourage advocacy in our young people. In order to create advocates, we need to educate and inspire students. I see the job of education as pivotal in the quest for a better world." By providing tools to analyze history and events, social studies teachers such as Liz can help students understand what influences governments, organizations, and individuals to make specific decisions and how these decisions impact people's rights.

Liz says that the most rewarding class she teaches is Human Rights. Her students end the semester with an action project where they create and implement an action plan on topics ranging from child labor and hunger to human trafficking and voting rights. Many people inspire Liz to teach human rights: colleagues in her department, students who volunteer, and community activists like Ishmael Beah and Emmanuel Jal. She also appreciates the efforts of former presidents like Jimmy Carter and Bill Clinton and celebrities like Bono and George Clooney. Liz believes that education provides hope and opportunity for young people.

Liz Devine teaches about human rights in her social studies class.

to get involved in campaigns supporting projects like building schools, providing clean water to families, and helping women start businesses. These projects support human rights for people around the world. For example, actions like building schools help prevent child labor by giving children the opportunity to receive an education. Since its inception, Free the Children has done the following:[58]

- Helped educate 55,000 children every day
- Shipped $16 million worth of medical supplies to countries around the world
- Provided clean water, health care, and sanitation to one million people

Craig Keilburger, founder of Free the Children, reads with students.

WHAT YOU CAN DO — Human Rights

Think about some of the examples in this chapter of people standing up for human rights in their local and global communities. In East Berlin, people expressed their opinions and rallied for change. Today, young people such as those involved with Free the Children help others around the world by building schools and sending health kits to people in need. What's important to you? What should be changed where you live? Are there injustices that could be prevented? Here are a few ways you can get involved:

- Learn about human rights issues happening both locally and globally by reading the newspaper, watching documentaries, reading books, or talking to experts.
- Volunteer with a human rights organization to learn more about a specific human rights campaign.
- Research local community members involved in human rights work. Work with your teacher to bring community members to your classroom to speak to your classmates.

Students attend a climate change rally; an issue some believe will have devastating impacts on human rights around the world.

POINT | **COUNTERPOINT**

Should a government sacrifice civil liberties for security purposes?[59]

The Patriot Act was signed into law on October 26, 2001 after the attacks on the Twin Towers. The act was meant to allow law enforcement agencies to do things such as wiretap phones and search business records. Is it acceptable to sacrifice civil liberties and rights for security purposes? The following are some perspectives offered by people in the online forum Debatepedia on this topic.

POINT
Yes

- **"There is a large threat to our security.** The current level of international tensions is likely to increase, leading to more and more dissatisfaction with American policies, which in turn may result in more terrorist attacks. The nature of contemporary terrorism has become far more frightening with fundamentalists ready to commit suicide, and fears that terror groups are seeking access to biological, chemical and nuclear materials. Old-fashioned terrorism has transformed into high intelligence networks of hard-to-track terrorist cells. It is not possible to curb terrorism without curbing some of the rights of citizens."

- **"Negative cases of security abuse are few.** In any wide-scale attempt to fight terrorism, there are bound to be a few cases of abuse of security measures. Therefore it is not a good idea to shut down all security measures under a pretext that they violate rights. The majority of the measures are intended to safeguard those civil liberties instead of abusing them."

COUNTERPOINT
No

- **"If the United States, the example-setting country of cherished civil liberties, allows the loss of its liberties to terrorism, it will show that terrorists have succeeded in forcing us to change our way of life.** Lots of apparently minor measures can quickly add up to a significant loss of liberty. Other countries will take their cue from the United States and use security as an excuse for a crackdown on political opposition movements and minority groups (examples of this can be found in Russia, China, Hong Kong, India, Liberia and the Central Asian republics). Rights mean nothing if they are ignored and eroded as soon as hard cases come along."

- **"Governments are likely to use terror as a convenient excuse for tightening laws and restricting freedoms in order to crack down in areas such as immigration, drug smuggling, fraud, etc., with insufficient public debate.** Such an erosion of liberties has a long-term impact and, in practice, is unlikely ever to be reversed as it is not the nature of state bureaucracies ever to give up power. Democratic mandates are insufficient reason to erode liberties; a key purpose of civil liberties is to protect minorities from the tyranny of the majority."

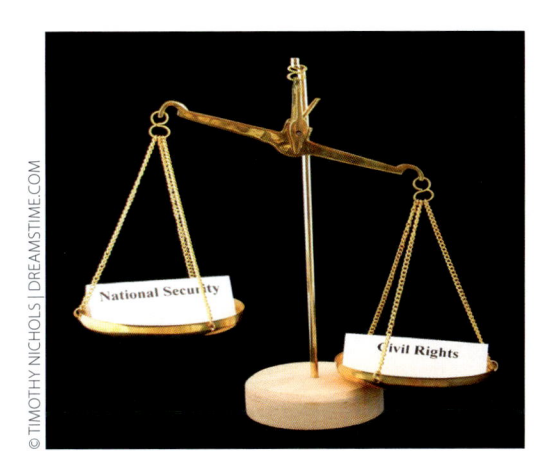

Does national security outweigh civil liberties when your country is under threat of terrorism?

boy ♂

girl ♀

Chapter 17
Gender

> **GUIDING QUESTIONS**
> - How does gender equity relate to sustainability?
> - What are modern trends related to gender equity?
> - What are ways to personally and structurally address gender inequities?

Introduction to Gender

As she walked across the football field to receive her crown, one Michigan high school teen looked slightly different than your typical homecoming queen. Instead of a dress, she was wearing a football jersey, having just walked off the field at the homecoming game with the rest of her team.[1] If this image seems unfamiliar to you, it is probably because women traditionally have not played football. Have you ever wondered why that is? Where do we get these ideas about who should be playing certain types of sports, working certain jobs, or participating in specific activities?

What is Gender?

Gender includes the range of characteristics, such as attitude, behavior, roles, and attributes that a society associates with men and women. Throughout history, societies have designated specific social roles to males and females. You'll read more about this creation of gender roles later in the chapter. But for now, consider the following questions: Have you ever paid close attention to commercials on television or advertisements in magazines? How are males and females portrayed? Are certain **stereotypes** (widely held and oversimplified beliefs about people and things) reinforced through these advertisements? In a study done on advertisements, researchers found that girls were more likely to be portrayed as shy and giggly while boys were powerful and assertive.[2] Can you think of other gender stereotypes?

While media and culture play a role in creating gender dynamics, other systems (i.e., policies and laws) also contribute to the way we think about gender. Policies or laws can enforce inequity between genders. On the contrary, **gender equity** happens when men and women are treated fairly in accordance with their differing needs. Policies that reinforce inequity may include not allowing women to own property or not giving women the right to vote. Inequity and discrimination based on gender can have consequences for social well-being, economic development, and even environmental preservation.

Gender stereotypes can perpetuate gender inequity.

Gender-Based Inequities

Most people assume gender-based issues primarily refer to women. However, men can face a number of these issues, too. Consider the disparities between genders shown in the following statistics:

Men
- Boys in the United States are twice as likely to be threatened or injured with a weapon at school as girls.[3]
- According to the World Health Organization, suicide rates around the world are typically three times higher for men than for women.[4]
- In colleges and universities in the United States, men represent 43% of the student population while women account for 57% of students.[5]

Women
- Approximately 66% of illiterate adults are female.[6]
- Only 19% of the world's parliamentarians are women.[7]
- Women perform 66% of the world's work, yet earn 10% of the income.[8]
- Only 1% of the world's landowners are women.[9]

While men do face a number of gender-based issues, the consequences of these issues may be felt more strongly by women. This is because most women have historically lived in a **patriarchal society**, that is, a society in which the male is the dominant authority figure. While a number of societies have shifted to more egalitarian systems, patriarchal systems are still present throughout the world. Within these societies, legal, political, and economic power is more often given to men than women.[10]

Therefore, while men and women face inequality, as evidenced by the statistics above, women face more inequity than men. They have a more difficult time overcoming factors that prevent them from sharing equal power with men, even when they enjoy equal opportunity.

Women and men have different strengths that they bring to their families, their communities, and their work. Involving women in sustainability efforts worldwide requires the support of men, who often have central roles in family, community, and societal decision-making.[11] While women have certainly featured prominently in sustainable development efforts thus far, many around the world do not have access to the same education and employment rights.

Gender and Sustainability

Sustainable development simply is not possible without equal rights, equal opportunities, and equal access to resources for both men and women. In order to build a sustainable future, both men and women must be part of solutions for improved economic, social, and environmental well-being.

Economy

Economic growth increases when women's work is formally recognized. Much of women's work is informal—in the home, in the fields, or in cottage industries. Without an officially recognized "job," it is nearly impossible to secure credit to do something like buy a cow or start a small business. When women are able to get loans for activities like these, their families benefit from increased opportunity and they contribute to the larger economy. Studies in both developed and developing countries have shown the benefits of providing women monetary income. In highly industrialized countries, a woman's increased participation in paid employment has been shown to strengthen financial status for her and her family in addition to improving her mental and physical health.[12] In impoverished countries, women farmers who earn income usually spend their money on children's education, nutrition, and health.[13]

In many countries within Africa, credit associations and export crop marketing cooperatives have only allowed male household heads to become members, excluding married and unmarried women.[14] Organizations such as the World Bank have worked to help expand the role of women in developing economies. One way they have tried to help is through legal arrangements to give women more equality when it comes to accessing credit. In Ethiopia, a World Bank pilot project tested a simple change to land title forms: space for a second name and picture was added to the form, allowing two people to jointly be listed as landowners. The result was a great increase in the number of women who officially had land ownership.[15]

Liberia elected its first female president, Ellen Johnson Sirleaf, in 2005.

Society

Increasing gender equality can improve physical and mental well-being. Evidence suggests that empowering girls and women through education and poverty alleviation leads to healthier families. As stated before, many studies have found that women are more likely than men to spend their money on improving living conditions for their family rather than spending earnings on themselves.[16] In the United States, for example, sociologist Catherine Kenney has noted that children experienced less food insecurity in low- to moderate-income two-parent households when the mother controlled the income instead of the father.[17] In this way, supporting women benefits an entire community.

The benefits of gender equality can extend well beyond the walls of a family's home, perhaps even impacting a nation's politics. A 100-country study found that decreasing the gap between male and female primary school completion rates increases democracy.[18] In other words, countries where girls and boys have more similar rates of completing primary school are also more democratic.

Environment

In developing countries, women spend a disproportionate amount of time in the natural environment doing agricultural work or collecting water and firewood. Collecting firewood without replanting trees can lead to the degradation of forests, which in turn can lead to increased resource scarcity. Women can be part of the solution when thinking about how to preserve these forests. The Green Belt Movement is one example of how women joined forces to protect the environment and empower themselves.

In 1977, Wangari Maathai started the Green Belt Movement in Nairobi, Kenya. Her goal was both to protect the environment and to empower Kenyan women. To do this, the movement organized rural women in order to help them stop deforestation, become trained in skills like forestry and beekeeping, and promote ecotourism. Since the time Wangari Maathai started the program, over 30,000 women have been trained and over 40 million trees have been planted. She received the Nobel Peace Prize in 2004 to commend her lifetime of work and its immense benefit for women and the environment.[19]

Background on Gender

For quite a large portion of human history, in most places men have enjoyed rights that their female counterparts have not. As societies slowly shifted from hunter-gather groups to agricultural settlements, the *stratification* or distinction between men and women became even more pronounced. In the past, women shared similar status to men because they participated in equal amounts of labor. However, when advanced technology was introduced to improve food systems in certain areas (i.e., the plough), women's labor outside the home was needed less and less.[20]

Of course, traditional male roles also demand some pretty hefty responsibilities. In societies where men are seen as the "stronger sex," men are expected to provide food, shelter, and protection for their families. Women's responsibilities are different, but equally important. Women prepare the food, maintain the shelter, and raise the children. In many places, including both developed and developing nations, elements of these roles persist today. Nevertheless, women around the world slowly gained rights they were largely denied in the past.

Voting Rights

During the 19th century, women's roles in the United States were defined by certain values referred to as the "cult of true womanhood." Women were reminded of how they should act in sermons at churches and in women's magazines. They were meant to run their households, take care of their husbands and children, uphold religious beliefs, and maintain an even temperament through it all. However, women were not supposed to participate in hard labor or political life. Men were the ones who earned money for their work; women's labor fell outside the cash economy. Nevertheless, 19th century women began pushing boundaries. More and more women participated in the economy, got involved in reform movements related to slavery and women's rights, wrote for newspapers, and lobbied political bodies.[21] As a result, women's roles slowly transformed and they earned a political voice.

Women in the United States finally gained the right to vote through the 19th Amendment to the U.S. Constitution, adopted in 1920. Women in Great Britain, provided they were over 30, gained the right to vote in 1918. Most European countries granted women the right to vote by 1931, though some notable exceptions include France (1944), Belgium and Italy (1946), Switzerland (1971), and Liechtenstein (1984). Women were voting in most Asian countries by 1960. Many African nations also gave women the right to vote by 1960, although in those countries men and women typically received the right to vote at the same time as formerly colonized African nations gained their independence.[22] In more recent history, Saudi Arabia granted women the right to vote in September of 2011. The country's ruler, King Abdullah, also allowed women to run for local office and serve on his advisory board.[23]

Property Rights

Similar to voting rights, women did not have property rights for a long period of U.S. history. In 1769, the 13 colonies adopted the same system of property rights used in England. Married women were not allowed to own property in their own name and they could not keep any income they earned; instead, this money went to their husbands. By 1900, every state passed legislation that allowed women to keep their earnings and to own property.[24]

The right to own property is still an important issue for women around the world. Women currently own only 1-2% of all titled land worldwide. Land ownership can bring social status and is often a prerequisite for securing loans and credit. Those who do not own land are often more vulnerable, especially during times of famine and unrest.[25]

Reproductive Rights

For many young women today, it would probably be difficult to contemplate not having control over the number of children they give birth to. However, many women throughout the world face this issue and continue to struggle for *reproductive rights*, especially in developing countries. Reproductive rights are legal rights and freedoms regarding reproduction and reproductive health. These rights include such things as voluntary choice in marriage and determining the number of children a woman has.[26] According to the World Health Organization, one third of women in the developing world face illnesses related to pregnancy, childbirth, HIV, and other related reproductive health issues. Many of these illnesses could be prevented with better reproductive health systems and rights for women.[27]

Changing Economic Roles

The Industrial Revolution began in 1750 and increased the need for women in the work force. There weren't enough men to fill all of the factory positions, so factory owners had to hire women and children. Factory owners still did not see women as primary employees, however, and did not give women workers the same rights as men.

The next major shift in economic roles started with the two great wars in the beginning of the 20th century. Wartime in an industrial economy forces many changes on society. World War II is a perfect example of how conflict forced industry to allow women workers to do jobs more typically reserved for men. With so many of the world's men away fighting, there was no one to work in the factories except the women left at home. Women were not allowed to fight in the war, so many saw factory work as a way of fulfilling their patriotic duty. Many women who entered

This image of Rosie the Riveter represents the women who worked during World War II in jobs traditionally held by men.

Total Fall Enrollment in Degree-granting Institutions within the United States by Gender[28]

engineers. Your mother expects you to be a doctor, lawyer, or engineer."[29] Indeed, more and more women within the United States have pursued degrees in higher education. Women hold 60% of bachelor's degrees, 60% of master's degrees, about half of all medical and law degrees, and just over 40% of all M.B.A. (Master of Business Administration) degrees. Men are much more likely now than women to only hold a high-school diploma.[30] In 2010, just over half of management and professional positions in the United States were held by women. However, in Fortune 500 companies, only 14.4% of the executive officer positions were held by women,[31] showing that in terms of high finance, there is still a bias toward men.

Around the world, the gap between genders is shrinking in education, health, and politics. Consider the following gender-related facts from the 21st century:[32]

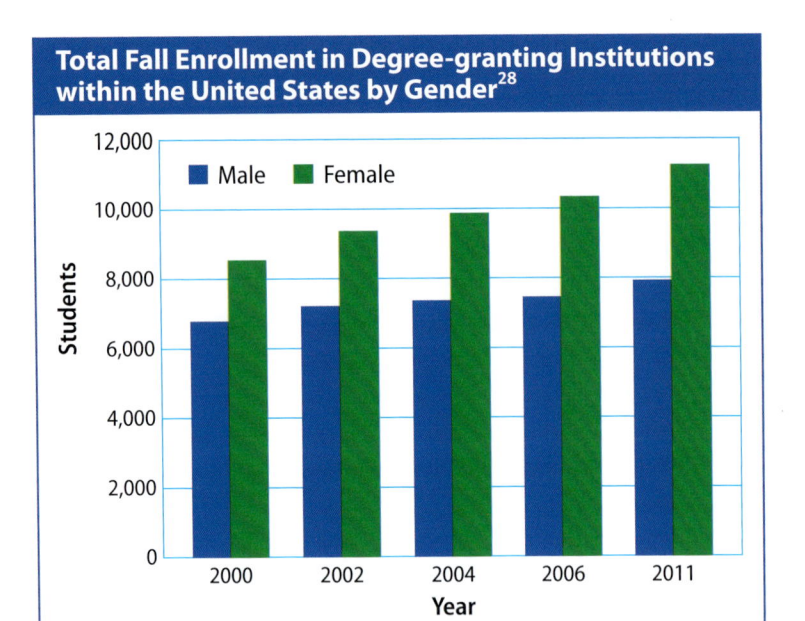

the work force during World War II discovered that they enjoyed working and continued once the war was over, setting the stage for the women's movements of the second half of the 20th century.

Women born in the early and mid 20th century had differing expectations for their daughters. One woman, born in 1918, put it very succinctly when giving career advice to her granddaughter: "In my day, I expected my daughters to marry doctors or lawyers or

- In the country of Iceland, only 6% of women do not work. Comparatively, 5% of men do not work in formal jobs.
- In Cyprus, Mongolia, Cuba, and Bulgaria 60% of university students are women.
- In Turkey, women no longer need permission from their husbands to work outside the home and they enjoy equal property rights.

CASE STUDY: Rwanda's Parliament[33]

In 1994, an estimated 800,000 people were killed in the country of Rwanda as a result of genocide. Given Rwanda's history of conflict, you might not expect Rwanda today to have the world's highest proportion of women in parliament. In fact, that very same bloody history is what has allowed the country's women to form the majority of the nation's leadership. One of the reasons that women were able to gain such political power is the number of men who were killed during the Rwandan genocide; 70% of the population remaining after Rwanda's genocide was female. Women were forced to step into leadership roles, and the role of women in Rwandan society expanded by default. Women are still in the majority in Rwanda, though by a much smaller margin than in the 1990s.

During the post-genocide transition period, Rwanda redrafted its constitution. The revision process allowed for input and participation by and from women, which was not previously allowed. Adopted in 2003, Rwanda's constitution guarantees at least 30% of the parliamentary positions to women.

Gender Today

As you can see from the discussion above, progress truly has been made toward providing women and men equal opportunities. Girls and women attend school at higher rates than in the past. Women enjoy more legal rights, are healthier, and participate in the world's work force more than ever before.[34]

Yet there is still much progress to be made. As you will read, some women in the world do not even enjoy basic human rights. And in extreme cases, such as conflict or poverty, women and children are the most vulnerable populations.

Trafficking

Slavery is a centuries-old practice. The Roman Empire exploited the labor of thousands, if not millions, of prisoners of war. Ancient Egyptian culture was heavily dependent on slave labor. The forced import of Africans to the United States enabled the plantation lifestyle that defined the American South.

Slavery is enforced labor with no compensation. You may have thought that slavery ended with the abolition movement and the U.S. Civil War. Slave labor, while illegal, is still widely used. In fact, there are 27 million slaves in the world today, more than at any time in history.[35] While many of the world's slaves live in places where laws go unenforced, slaves continue to be illegally bought and sold into some of the world's most wealthy developed countries.

People who deal in buying and selling human beings, especially with the purpose of promoting slavery, are human traffickers. Trafficking in general means dealing or trading in something illegal. Trafficking of human beings is a gross abuse of human rights. People are forced into many different types of slavery—domestic service, forced labor, or sexual favors. A 2005 report from the U.S. State Department estimates that between 600,000 and 800,000 people are trafficked across international borders annually.[36] Almost 75% of 21st-century slaves are female, and 50% are children.[37]

There are several reasons that **human trafficking** exists today. Extreme poverty can lead people into desperate action, including selling wives and children for profit. This has been the case in recent years in Cambodia and human trafficking there has had serious consequences for women. Women and children are enticed from rural areas by promises of domestic jobs in the city, only to be coerced into sexual slavery once they arrive. Traffickers are not only organized crime syndicates, but can also be parents, friends, relatives, or neighbors. In addition to sexual slavery, women and children are trafficked for other purposes; forced labor in factories, domestic servitude, begging, and street vending are all areas where trafficking has gotten a foothold.[38] While this type of activity is illegal, it often goes unnoticed or unreported. Reports have documented how human traffickers are connected to international criminal organizations and are difficult to prosecute.[39] While trafficking can have serious impacts on communities, there are a number of people taking action in different ways to address this issue.

YOUTH PROFILE
Maddy Berry and Will Putnam

In his book *Half the Sky*, journalist Nicholas Kristof chronicled the trafficking of women and children in Pailin, Cambodia, a community that also suffers from related challenges like poverty and disease.

Inspired by Kristof's book, a group of students and teachers from Washington state is working to provide a brighter future for children in Pailin. Students at the Overlake School in Redmond, Washington worked together

Maddy Berry poses with young students in Pailin, Cambodia.

Violence Against Women

Trafficking is only one form of violence against women and children. Physical and emotional abuse also occur more often against women and children than against men. The World Health Organization studied women's health and domestic violence in 10 countries including Bangladesh, Brazil, Ethiopia, Japan, and Samoa.[41] Many women in the study reported that their first sexual encounter was against their will. In addition, the study shared how approximately 5,000 women are murdered each year by family members in the name of honor. Women and children are still forced into marriage, particularly in rural areas within Asia, the Middle East, and sub-Saharan Africa.

Experiencing violence can harm a woman's well-being in many ways, including physical injuries and poor mental health. The factors that put women and children at increased risk can be divided into these categories:

- An individual's low level of education, socioeconomic disadvantage, or substance abuse can put her at risk of being a victim of violence. If a woman's partner has a low education level, abuses drugs or alcohol, or has a poor attitude toward women, these factors may contribute.
- Women who were abused or witnessed domestic violence as children are also at higher risk.
- In a family, marital discord, a history of male dominance, and economic stress are tangible factors that put women and children at higher risk for violence.
- A community that lacks cohesion and gender equality puts women and children at risk.
- Lastly, societies that are repressive or restrictive toward women seem to permit gender-based violence, especially domestic violence.[42]

to raise money to build a primary school in Pailin. The students put on a series of fundraising events, ranging from bake sales to talent shows. With the help of the nonprofit organization American Assistance for Cambodia and matching funds from the World Bank, the Overlake School in Pailin opened in 2003.

Overlake students Maddy Berry and Will Putnam traveled to Pailin in 2010 to visit their "sister school."[40] They brought school supplies with them and taught for a week at the school. Together with their classmates, they also helped to put together a library and computer center.

Maddy and Will saw firsthand the difficult choices faced by families in Pailin. According to Will, "A lot of the kids, and the families too, come up against the challenge of 'how are they going to take care of their families?'" Although Pailin faces many challenges—the lingering effects of genocide, poverty, malaria, AIDS, and human trafficking—there is hope for children there. Maddy says, "I feel like the way to combat most of those, if not all of them, is through education." Thanks to the opportunities that education provides—and new friends from across the world—the youth of Pailin have new possibilities to look forward to.

Victims of Conflict

In places where violent conflicts terrorize daily life, women are disproportionately affected by war. The majority of combatants are men. Women and children are left at home, where they become more vulnerable to sexual violence, including rape and forced prostitution. The threat of this type of violence affects children's ability to go to school safely; women gathering firewood or water are targets as well.

After a conflict ends and a society begins to rebuild, both men's and women's roles need to be taken into consideration. With men gone during conflict, women are often forced to be the primary family caretakers and breadwinners. Women have more responsibility and must make decisions and grow into new roles. After the conflict ends and men return to their normal lives, women may face hostile attitudes as both genders attempt to readjust. Men who return to their communities to find women expressing greater authority and independence may feel threatened. This can generate hostility toward women and put them at risk of violence.

Maternal Health

When women do well, their children are healthier. But not all women around the world have access to **maternal health care**. Maternal health care is the health care women receive during pregnancy, childbirth, and after. They can receive services that support their

CASE STUDY: HEAL Africa

Violence and war have a long history in the Democratic Republic of the Congo (DRC), from the brutal colonization of the country in the 1800s by King Leopold II of Belgium to current regional conflicts. The most recent conflict in DRC is between government and rebel forces and involves other countries in the region, including Rwanda, Uganda, Angola, Namibia, and Zimbabwe.

The conflict has taken a large toll on citizens of DRC. An estimated 5 million people have died during the recent war, either as a direct result of fighting or through malnutrition and disease that resulted from the conflict.[43] An estimated 2 million people have been displaced from their homes due to the fighting.[44] As a result of the war, thousands of children have been forced into service as child soldiers.[45] Women have also suffered greatly from the violence; thousands have been subjected to rape and torture.[46]

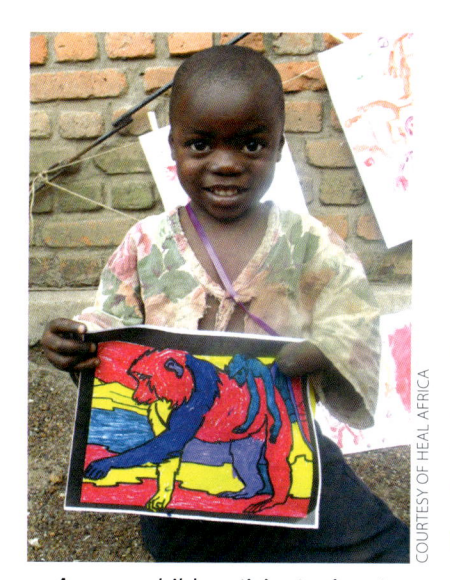

A young child participates in art camp through HEAL Africa.

HEAL Africa is one organization that works to address the effects of the war. HEAL stands for Health—Education—Action—Leadership. The organization works to help survivors of violent conflict, including women who have been brutally raped, heal physically and emotionally. In addition, HEAL Africa provides a multitude of services such as micro-insurance loans that help women pay for health care, agricultural education, and training for local doctors and nurses. By helping women get back on their feet, these programs enable them to contribute to the well-being of their families and society.

The organization has also worked to promote gender equity within the DRC by doing the following:[47]

- Training religious and community leaders to be advocates of gender equity

- Creating opportunities for men to engage in dialogue about how to change perceptions of masculinity

- Training teachers in primary and secondary schools to speak about gender issues

education in safe birthing options, nutrition, and how to identify danger signs while pregnant.[48] Women in developing countries are disproportionately affected by the negative impacts of substandard health care. For example, a woman in a developing country is 36 times more likely to die from pregnancy-related complications than a woman in a developed country.[49]

While poverty plays a role in women's access to health care for themselves and their children, culture is also a factor. One example is *child marriage*, which occurs when one or both of the people married is under 18. The majority of those married before their 18th birthday are girls, often called "child brides." Global rates of child marriage have declined over the last 30 years, but it still happens at an alarmingly high rate, especially in extremely poor rural areas. As of 2007, 77% of girls in Niger, 72% in Chad, and 69% in Bangladesh were married before their 18th birthday.[50]

Marrying at such an early age can have lifelong consequences for these child brides and their children. Death due to pregnancy-related complications is five times more likely in girls younger than 15 than it is in older women. Additionally, babies of child brides have a 75% higher mortality rate. Babies that do survive have a good chance of being born prematurely with a low birth weight and a higher risk of contracting HIV/AIDS. Other consequences of marrying so young can include illiteracy, poverty, domestic abuse, and abandonment by the woman's spouse.[51]

The good news is that education can be a highly effective preventive measure. Girls who have a secondary education are up to six times less likely to become child brides. This is largely due to the fact that education provides

CASE STUDY: Empowered Mothers in Bangladesh[52]

The Interagency Gender Working Group of USAID did a study on six rural villages in Bangladesh between 2001 and 2003. All six villages in the study area were typical rural villages where people are poor and men control most family decisions. The study looked at whether mothers and mothers-in-law who were empowered were more likely to encourage positive behavior in the next generation of women. Empowerment in this context means the ability for people to make strategic life choices where they previously weren't allowed. Empowered women have a key role in the economic and decision-making processes of their families and communities, are assertive, and are recognized for their abilities and accomplishments by their families and communities.

A mother from Bangladesh laughs with her child.

Researchers interviewed 186 women and 13 men. They chose women—mothers, mothers-in-law, daughters, and daughters-in-law—whom the researchers considered to be empowered. Mothers-in-law were included in the study because Bangladeshi women typically marry young and live with their husband's family, where her mother-in-law becomes a girl's primary role model.

The study found that empowered women recognize their ability to change the quality of their family's lives through their actions and that they desire to do so. Some common findings included a wish to delay marriage and the birth of a first child and support for the use of modern contraceptives.

so many other opportunities for a girl; each of these opportunities can be seen as an alternative to early marriage.[53]

Gender Gap

All over the world, women performing the same jobs as men are paid significantly less for their work. This is not because women are less capable or less skilled, but is largely a matter of inequity.[54] Even though society has changed and many women are now an equal contributor to family income (or in some cases the only contributor), social perceptions have not changed at the same pace. A gap in earnings between men and women can be observed even in very wealthy countries; in poor communities, gender disparities tend to be more pronounced.

The widening gap between the number of men and the number of women in poverty is referred to as the **feminization of poverty**. Women form a much higher percentage of the 1.5 billion people worldwide who live below the poverty threshold than men.[55] While many countries are starting to realize that there is a gender aspect to poverty and are crafting new policies accordingly, great disparities still exist. In rural Asia, for example, households that are led by women are typically poorer than those run by men. Children in families headed by women, especially female children, are more likely to drop out of school to help their mothers. Consequently, the lower education level of these children will make it even more difficult for them to escape poverty. Another factor restricting women's access to education and later opportunities is largely cultural. In many cases, if a family has more than one child but only enough resources to send one child to school, that child is typically the oldest male.[56]

In certain places around the world, when girls are able to stay in school they often do not receive the same quality of education as their male counterparts. They might be pushed toward female-centered careers such as social work and teaching and steered away from science and math. Quality education that does not discriminate between genders benefits both boys and girls.

Paying close attention to trends in different countries can help to ensure that girls and boys are doing equally well in school. For example, boys are 30% more likely to drop out of school in the United States than girls.[57] Prison and the cycle of poverty have proven to have serious consequences on certain populations of men within the United States. Low education levels correlate to increased incarceration rates.[58] Creating preventative measures to ensure all children can be successful in the classroom and less inclined to drop out can be a powerful solution.

> *All over the world, women performing the same jobs as men are paid significantly less for their work.*

Pathways to Progress: Gender

Slowly but surely changes are being made to create equitable opportunities for both men and women. Breaking the cycle of poverty, investing in education, and involving women in decision-making and leadership roles are all positive changes being made today.

Breaking the Cycle of Poverty

Many women work long, hard hours with little to no compensation and no formal recognition of their labor. The Self Employed Women's Association (SEWA) of India seeks to change that, at least in India. SEWA is a trade union for poor, self-employed women workers.[59] These unrecognized and often lonely laborers come together as one body and use their strength in numbers to get benefits that they would not be able to obtain on their own. SEWA helps members organize services such as savings and credit, insurance, health care, and legal aid. This cooperation gives members valuable life skills and knowledge that make them more self-sufficient and more likely to be able to move past poverty.

Investing in Girls' Education

In many parts of the developing world, by the time a girl is 12 years old she has most probably left school in order to take care of the household, cook, and clean.[60] In sub-Saharan Africa, fewer than one in five girls attend secondary school and almost half are married by age 18.[61] Educating girls can be instrumental to improving gender equality and it has additional beneficial impacts, such as supporting economic growth.[62]

In response to the reality faced by adolescent girls in developing nations around the world, the organization Girl Up raises funds to help girls gain access to education and health opportunities. In Liberia, Girl Up helped to launch a program that helped support costs for uniforms and school supplies and provide space for counseling services. In Guatemala, Girl Up helped create a peer education program in which girls learned to teach health education to their friends.[63]

Promoting Women's Health

Healthy women are strong women. Many women around the world are denied access to even basic health care—including vaccinations and pregnancy-related check-ups—that most women in developed countries take for granted. One of the biggest areas of inequality is in reproductive and sexual health. Lack of access to birth control results in more than 70 million unintended pregnancies each year in the developing world. Women may lack knowledge about birth control, they may be too poor to afford it, they may not be allowed to use it because it is not socially acceptable or for religious reasons, or they simply may not have anywhere to get it.[64] Whatever the reason, the resulting unintended pregnancies can contribute to a cycle of poverty if a mother is unable to adequately feed, clothe, and shelter her children.

SEWA provides its members life skills that help them to move out of poverty.

Transforming Perceptions of Women

As mentioned earlier in the chapter, what you see in the media can influence the way you might think about gender. According to the World Health Organization, public awareness campaigns and other media interventions can be effective in changing gender attitudes and norms.[65] One organization working to do just that is Reel Grrls. The group's mission is to empower young women from diverse communities to realize the power, talent, and influence they have through media production.

Reel Grrls teaches teenage girls skills like animation and script writing.

CAREER PROFILE: Gender Advisor

Organizations everywhere struggle to find solutions to the complex issues related to human rights, gender equality, and public health. These issues are multifaceted and require deep understanding and diverse approaches. Some organizations choose to focus on domestic violence, others on access to education, and still others on equal legal rights.

Floriza Gennari is one of these women. She is the Program Management and Partnership Specialist at the Gender, Diversity and Human Rights Office at the Pan American Health Organization (PAHO). PAHO is an "international public health agency with almost 110 years of experience working to improve health and living standards in the countries of the Americas." Floriza works in countries that PAHO has prioritized due to their socioeconomic circumstances, such as Bolivia, Guyana, Haiti, Honduras and Nicaragua. Her job is to help to make sure that PAHO's projects, meant to improve health services in the countries, benefit men and women equally. She decided to pursue a career focused on gender equality because she believes that equal and equitable opportunities for boys and girls will help all human beings achieve their full potential.

Floriza Gennari works to ensure health services are equally given to men and women.

She believes that gender issues cannot be addressed in a vacuum and that a person's ethnic background, sexual orientation, educational or socioeconomic status all relate to how women and men are treated. For example, she notes that indigenous women are at a higher risk of maternal mortality than other women. Likewise, gay men in Latin America are more likely than straight men to contract HIV because of discrimination against them which limits their access to information and important health services. She says that the best way to change lives in the long term, to make a sustainable difference, is to change government policies. This is especially true in the pursuit of gender equality, but it isn't easy to alter the laws or beliefs of a country's leaders, so PAHO works with several sectors, such as Ministries of Health, Ministries of Women's Affairs, and Ministries of Finance in various countries to come up with funds and strategies for their health care objectives.

Undeterred by the challenges of her job, Floriza says that she believes in a world where "women do not have to live in fear of violence, are equally represented in governments, and participate equally in the economic and social sphere."

Reel Grrls teaches teenage girls skills related to animation, cinematography, scriptwriting, and other elements of film. In addition, the girls are able to meet women filmmakers and form lasting relationships that help them to develop a critical lens of what they see in the media and how they can change perceptions of gender. In the words of one participant, "Ever since participating in Reel Grrls, I see the world through new eyes."[66]

Supporting Gender Equity

People can address gender equity in a number of ways. The Convention on the Elimination of All Forms of Discrimination against Women (CEDAW), for example, is often referred to as the international bill of rights for women. The Convention was created in 1979 and over time it has been signed and ratified by 186 countries. CEDAW offers a way to challenge discriminatory laws against women and girls. Its influence has prompted countries to take initiative to address women's rights. For example, in 2007 Mexico strengthened its laws on violence against women.[67]

Support for gender equity can come from individuals, too. Questioning inequities and stereotypes is an essential first step toward gender equality and requires the participation of both women and men. Programs throughout the world have helped support boys and men in conversations about gender so that they can, in turn, contribute to building gender equity in their communities. In certain cases, high-ranking officials such as religious leaders have stepped in to speak to men about making decisions to create healthy families. In recent years:[68]

- Monks in Cambodia taught men about HIV prevention.
- Clerics in Saudi Arabia instructed fathers not to force their daughters to get married.
- State officials in Brazil spoke to men about ending domestic violence.

Changing gender-based perceptions and ways of doing things to reinforce equity can be a powerful way of making change within a society.

WHAT YOU CAN DO — Gender

Are you wondering what you can do to address gender issues at a personal level? Consider the following ways to get involved:

- Learn more about campaigns around the world working to provide equal rights to women
- Work with your friends, classmates, and school community to challenge gender-based stereotypes that could be harmful to males and females
- Volunteer with an organization that provides educational opportunities for girls around the world
- Get involved with drop-out prevention programs for both males and females

Young students wait to attend school in Malaysia.

POINT | **COUNTERPOINT**

Should school be single-sex instead of co-ed?[69]

In the United States, education was single-sex until the 19th century. Research came out in the following years that spoke to the benefits and the consequences of co-ed classrooms. Interest in single-sex schools started gathering momentum during the 1990s.[70] Today, the debate continues. Should schools be single-sex or co-ed?

POINT

Yes

- **Single-sex schooling can be an effective approach when teachers use techniques that support lessons developmentally appropriate for boys that are separate from those that are appropriate for girls.**

- **There are a number of pressures that males and females may face when they are in the same classroom.** However, when girls are able to attend all-girls schools, they are more likely to study subjects such as math and computer science. In fact, a number of studies have shown that girls of all academic abilities perform better in single-sex schools than co-ed schools.[71]

COUNTERPOINT

No

- **Boys and girls should not be separated when they are in school.** They can learn a lot from each other if they are put together in the same classroom. Once separated, they may have difficulty dealing with mixed gender settings later in their life. As an adult, it is a rare situation where men and women are separated from each other. Why set children up for failure in single-sex schools?[72]

- **Success in the classroom is not related to separation of the sexes.** As the National Coalition for Women and Girls in Education has noted, success in the classroom is related to great teachers, small class sizes, core academics, and parental involvement.[73] Why separate genders, when there are a number of other factors that contribute to student success?

A number of studies have shown that girls academically perform better in single-sex classrooms.

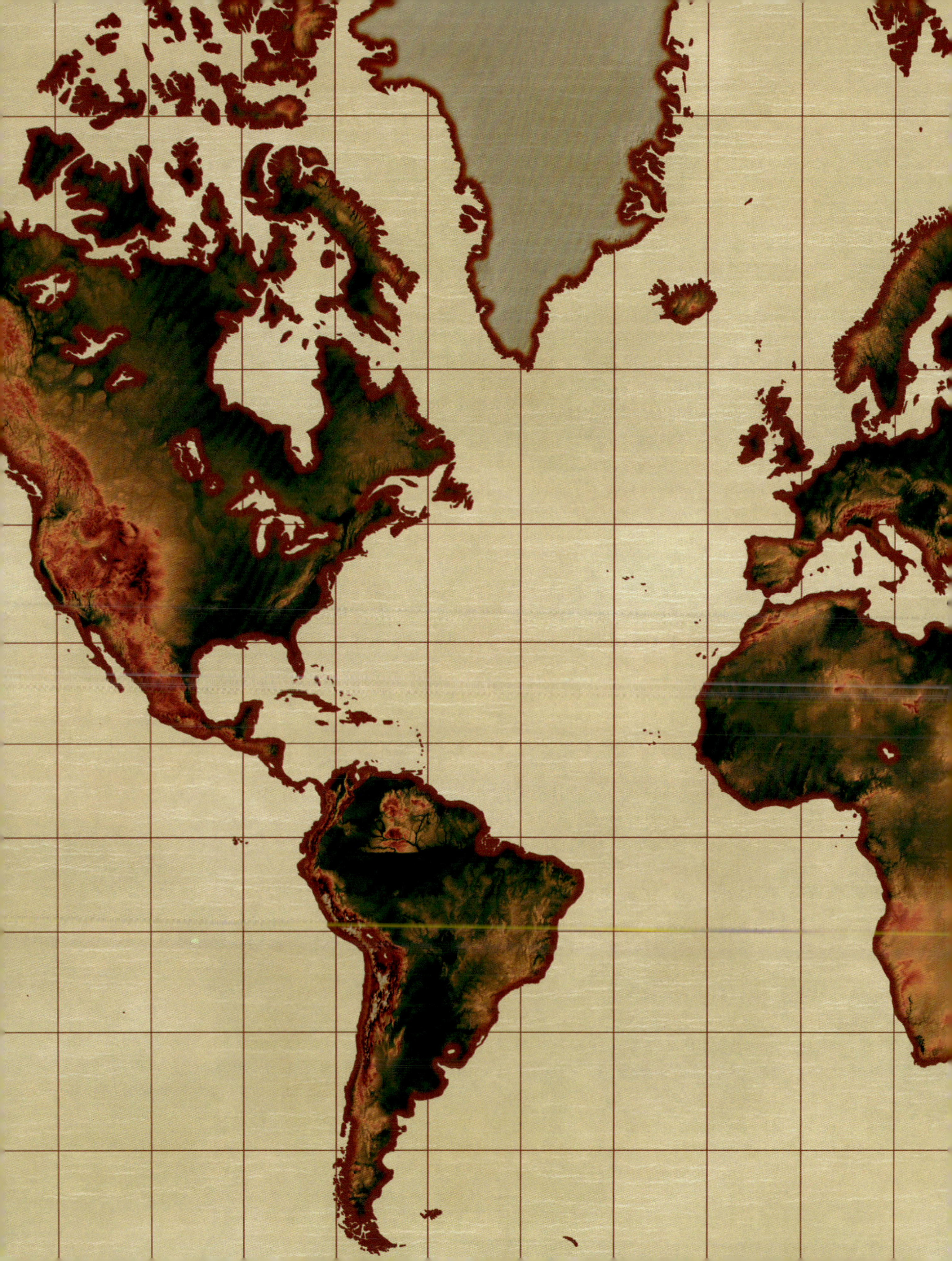

Chapter 18

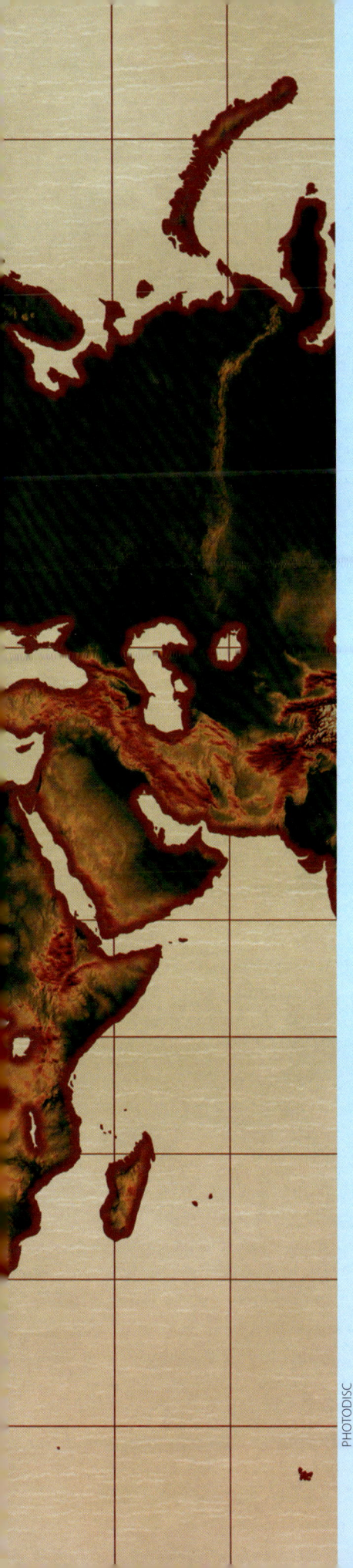

Human Migration

> **GUIDING QUESTIONS**
> - What are global impacts of forced and voluntary migration?
> - What does human migration look like in a sustainable world?

Introduction to Human Migration

Walking among San Francisco's different neighborhoods, you might hear a number of languages ranging from Hindi, Spanish, and Vietnamese to Mandarin, Arabic, and English. In the neighborhood of Poble Sec in Barcelona, Spain, you can find people from Pakistan, Morocco, Ecuador, the Philippines, and the Dominican Republic living right next to each other. In fact, if you were to travel throughout the world to most major metropolitan cities, you would find diverse populations living in nearly all of them.

Rural areas can have diverse populations, too. If you were to visit small towns in the United States, you may be surprised to find immigrants from Somalia, Cambodia, or Guatemala. For example, a large number of Muslim refugees from Somalia have resettled in the town of Shelbyville, Tennessee.

A parade in San Francisco celebrates different cultures.

What created these diverse communities? **Human migration** is the permanent or semi-permanent relocation of a person or group of people from one location to another. The United Nations defines a migrant as someone who lives outside of his or her country for over one year.[1] There are countless stories of migration dating as far back as over 80,000 years ago. Because of economic, environmental, cultural, and religious reasons, over 200 million people currently live outside of their country of origin.[2] The population of Brazil, for instance, includes people who have migrated both voluntarily and involuntarily over the past 500 years from Africa, Europe, Asia, and the Middle East.[3]

Human Migration and Sustainability

Why would people decide to leave their homes and migrate to other places around the world? We can use the framework of push and pull theory to help explain the motives of migrants.[4] On the one hand are pull factors that can draw people toward another country: lower crime rates, better educational opportunities, political security, and a more attractive quality of life. On the other hand, push factors force people to move due to circumstances such as poverty, war, unemployment, and drought. These migrants often have little or no choice in the matter.

All of these factors—push and pull, negative and positive—connect to sustainability. Likewise, the many effects of human migration are connected to the sustainability of both the communities that take in immigrants and the countries immigrants leave behind.

Human Migration and Economics

When groups of people move from one country to another, they may decide to do so for economic reasons. People who face high unemployment in their home country may decide to migrate in search of opportunities to improve their standard of living.

As migrants move from one country to another and are fully integrated into their new host country, they can work and contribute economically both to their country of residence and to their country of origin. Migrants who move from developing to developed countries who are able to find employment have the potential to earn an income that is 20 to 30 times higher than what they would have earned in their home country.[5] Through their jobs, these migrants contribute to the economy of their host country; they also generate economic activity by purchasing products and services locally and by paying taxes.

Migrants are also connected to the economies of their countries of origin. Many migrants send *remittances* back to their home country where economic opportunities may be more limited. A remittance is money sent by migrants to their families. This source of income can help stabilize a struggling country's economy and improve people's standard of living. For example, some remittances sent back to people in Ghana have helped reduce poverty, while remittances sent back to Pakistan have been used to increase educational opportunities for girls.[6]

Not everyone agrees that migration is economically beneficial for all. Critics argue that new immigrants take away jobs that should be filled by citizens of the host country. They claim that immigrants are, in fact, more of a burden on a country's economy than a support.

Human Migration and Society

When a new culture settles into a community, there is no question that it will influence the community. The reverse is true too; immigrants become heavily influenced by the culture they have joined.

New York City, with a population of 8 million people, is known as a global city. It has a diverse cultural life, boasts the world's largest foreign-born population, and is home to a large number of international organizations such as the United Nations.[7] Immigrants have established many different neighborhoods throughout the city, from Chinatown to Little Italy. New York City would indeed be very different if not for the cultural influences of its many immigrant populations.

When immigrants are fully accepted and integrated into a new society, they bring with them knowledge about different skills, traditions, foods, and ways of living. A number of famous immigrants, including Albert Einstein and former U.S. Secretary of State Madeline Albright, have made large impacts on society within America.

Different countries adopt different policies toward immigrants and refugees. Certain countries expect migrants to fully assimilate and learn the language and customs of their host country, while others allow migrants to integrate only as much as they choose. Policies can encourage immigration or make it difficult for people to obtain citizenship.[8] When immigrants do not share the same language, religion, or customs as citizens of their host country, they may even experience *xenophobia*. Xenophobia is a fear or hatred of foreigners. Negative attitudes toward immigrants can influence a country's policies and result in the limitation of freedoms for foreigners, harassment, and even riots.[9] During World War II, for example, Japanese Americans experienced xenophobia. The U.S. government detained approximately 120,000 people of Japanese ancestry after the bombing of Pearl Harbor by Japan.[10]

Some governments emphasize multiculturalism and support these types of policies. **Multiculturalism** is the idea that people who come from many different cultural and ethnic backgrounds can coexist peacefully and equitably in one country. Multicultural policies, such as policies in Canada, do such things as providing citizens the opportunity for dual citizenship, funding bilingual education, and supporting multiculturalism in school curricula.[11] Other governments create policies that emphasize assimilation rather than multiculturalism. In 2004, France passed a ban that made it illegal for students to wear religious symbols in public schools. Religious symbols such as the headscarf worn by Muslim women, the turban worn by Sikh men, the yarmulke worn by Jewish men, and large Christian crucifixes were banned. Supporters of the ban argued that the world's religious conflicts should not be brought into the classroom and students who wore religious symbols might incite tensions.[12]

> *Immigrants become heavily influenced by the culture they have joined.*

In 2011, another bill passed that made it illegal for a person in a public space to wear anything that hid the face, including burqas (loose body covering with head covering) and niqabs (face veils). President Nicolas Sarkozy enforced this ban because he believed that the veil imprisons women and that it contradicts the values of a secular country.[13]

Human Migration and the Environment

When natural resources such as water and food are scarce, groups of people may be forced to relocate from one place to another simply to survive. When natural disasters or changes in climate destroy a community's environment, people are often left with little choice but to migrate.

CASE STUDY: The Earthquake in Haiti

When an earthquake registering 8.0 on the Richter scale struck Haiti in January 2010, thousands of Haitians tried to flee for safety. Neighboring countries braced themselves for an influx of people whose homes and lives were destroyed by this natural disaster. One would-be migrant was Jean-Louis Elifaute, a 49-year-old Haitian man who attempted to escape to Miami in a boat just days after the earthquake. On the way, the mast of the boat broke and the boat ended up capsizing. Jean-Louis returned to Haiti, but he has every intention of trying to migrate out of the country again in search of greater opportunity.[14]

The earthquake in Haiti led to increased migration out of Haiti.

As Jean-Louis's story shows, although the earthquake was an important factor in Haitian migration in 2010, it's not the whole story. The reality is Haitians have been migrating for years. They have moved to countries as diverse as the Dominican Republic, the United States, and France. A number of economic, environmental, and societal issues plaguing the country have led large numbers of Haitians to emigrate ever since the time of the country's independence.

Prior to gaining independence in 1801, Haiti was a slave colony under French rule. Throughout its history as an independent nation, it witnessed economic instability, dictatorship, and a number of natural disasters.[15] Tens of thousands of Haitians were desperate to escape oppression at home.[16] Under the rule of Francois Duvalier from 1957 to 1971, a large number of educated professionals fled the country. Today, approximately eight out of ten Haitians with college degrees live outside of Haiti.[17]

Poverty also drove large numbers of people to leave the country. Haiti is one of the poorest nations in the Western Hemisphere, with 80% of the population living in poverty.[18] The country's unemployment rate is 60-70% and the minimum wage is $1.50.[19]

While the 2010 earthquake spurred a huge increase in migration out of Haiti, the fundamental question to ask is why so many people were desperate to flee the country rather than remain in Haiti to pick up the pieces. What was missing within the country that would have given people the opportunity to build sustainable communities at home? How do these immigration patterns impact other countries?

In countries that receive large numbers of immigrants, there may be a negative impact on the health of the environment. It can be a challenge for a country's land and resources to support new immigrant populations while continuing to meet the needs of those who already live within a country.

A host country's environment is often especially at risk in refugee situations. **Refugees** are people who flee their home country for safety. There are approximately 15 million refugees across the globe. When they first leave their countries, 75% of these refugees cross the border to a neighboring country.[20] However, countries receiving refugees may not be equipped to support their needs, especially if these countries are struggling to meet their own citizens' needs.

Background on Migration

Since the beginning of human history, people have been on the move. Starting approximately 80,000 years ago, humans began to migrate from Africa to other parts of the world. Initial migration mostly occurred in Europe and Asia. Then, around 15,000 years ago, humans crossed from Asia to the Americas via the Bering Strait.[21]

Human migration over the past several hundred years was the result of a combination of forced and voluntary factors.

The following are examples of forced migrations:[22]

- Slaves from Western Africa were brought to the United States, Central America, South America, and the Caribbean during the 16th to 19th centuries. This transatlantic slave trade of approximately 11 million people from the west coast of Africa was the largest form of forced migration that has happened in world history.
- After countries abolished slavery, *indentured servants* from colonized countries dispersed throughout the world. Indentured servants were people who did work for a fixed period of time and were given certain provisions such as shelter, transportation, and food. They worked to extract gold, sugar, cotton, coffee, and tobacco. They also helped to build railroads. Most indentured servants came from India and China and they were often exploited by their employers.

The following are examples of voluntary migrations:[23]

- When European countries such as Spain, the United Kingdom, and Germany colonized countries in Africa and Asia, a number of people migrated from Europe to live in these new colonies. British policy actually encouraged its citizens to move to British colonies in an effort to support domination over colonized areas.
- The United States became an industrial power in the mid-1850s. North American economic growth attracted large numbers of Europeans who came in search of work. Over 50 million people emigrated from Europe to the United States during this time.
- Beginning in the 1940s after the end of World War II, there was an economic boom in the industrial world. A large amount of labor was necessary to support growing economies throughout Europe. People from Southern European countries such as Italy, Greece, and Turkey migrated to Northwestern Europe to work in factories, where they were needed for routine jobs to support the mass production of goods.
- After the 1980s, many immigrants from Asia, North Africa, and Eastern Europe moved to Southern Europe. A wide variety of jobs available in fields like construction, tourism, and domestic care attracted unskilled foreign labor from these countries.

Human Migration Today

As the previous cases show, migration has occurred throughout the ages as a result of both forced and voluntary factors. This continues today.

Voluntary Migration

People who move voluntarily to other places often do so to pursue economic or educational opportunities. In 2006, 2.7 million people left their home country to seek education abroad. Many choose to go to developed countries to pursue academic degrees and training.[26]

Along with education, economic opportunity is often a powerful pull that attracts voluntary migrants. This type of migration can benefit both people who choose to pursue work outside their home country and the host countries where they go to work. Some host countries may develop policies that encourage the immigration of skilled workers and provide a pathway to legal employment and eventual citizenship. For example, the United States offers H-1B visas for highly skilled migrants such as doctors and engineers. On average, the United States offers 65,000 of these visas per year.[27] Another example of a country encouraging immigration to support economic expansion is the United Arab Emirates. Many people came to the U.A.E. over the past four decades to work in jobs linked to the oil industry and construction. In fact, the U.A.E's labor force consists of over 80% of foreigners.[28]

Typically, voluntary migration flows occur from developing to developed countries. In developing countries, factors like poverty, resource scarcity, conflict, and gender inequality can limit educational or economic opportunities. As a result, many people seek out opportunities abroad and look to migration as a way to better their lives.

Brain Drain

As mentioned, developed countries including the United States and Canada have a strong interest in attracting skilled workers such as doctors or computer scientists to help support their economies. These skilled workers leave their home countries to pursue economic opportunities. Many highly skilled migrant workers in the developed world come from countries such as China, India, Mexico, and the

CASE STUDY: Diverse Peoples in Trinidad and Tobago

Historical migration patterns can help us to understand why countries have certain demographics today. Trinidad and Tobago is an island situated between the Caribbean Sea and the Atlantic Ocean. The country is known for its cultural diversity, a result of both forced and voluntary migration. Slaves from Africa were brought to the island under British rule during the 18th and 19th centuries. After Trinidad and Tobago abolished slavery, over 143,000 indentured servants from India came to do similar work on sugar cane plantations. The island also attracted voluntary immigrants such as fabric traders from the Middle East and vineyard workers from Portugal.[24]

Due to the immigration of different people to Trinidad and Tobago, the country's population today is 40% Indian, 37.5% African, and 20.5% multiracial. Languages spoken include English, Hindi, French, Spanish, and Chinese.[25]

This young child from Trinidad and Tobago represents the diverse landscape of people who live in the country.

Philippines.[29] What do you think happens in these countries when skilled workers leave?

If a large enough number of skilled workers emigrate from a country, it can experience a shortage of skilled workers often referred to as *brain drain*.[30] The loss of doctors, engineers, and computer scientists can equate to a loss of local knowledge from these fields. Imagine the consequences when a country has severe health epidemics such as HIV, malaria, or tuberculosis and does not have enough doctors and health care providers to treat patients.

Forced Migration

Refugees and IDPs

If you were forced to leave your home, what would you take with you? How would you adapt to a new place? People may be forced to leave their homes due to conflict, persecution, natural disaster, or loss of personal liberty through coercion, enslavement or human trafficking.

Those forced to leave their homes often become refugees or internally displaced persons. As mentioned earlier, refugees are people who flee their country for safety. **Internally displaced persons (IDPs)** are those people who cannot flee to another country and are forced to find safety within their own national borders. There are approximately 26 million IDPs living throughout the world in places with ongoing violent conflict. In some countries experiencing conflict, IDP numbers are relatively low. For example, Somalia has 1.5 million IDPs and Pakistan has 980,000.[31] Compare this to the large number of IDPs in Sudan (2.4 million people)[32] and Colombia (3.9 million people), countries with some of the largest IDP populations.[33]

Refugees can apply for asylum in other countries. An **asylum-seeker** is a person who applies for protection and the right of residence in a foreign country. Asylum can be offered to citizens of countries that are experiencing violent conflict, religious persecution, or political instability and who may not be safe in their home country. Many asylum applications are sent to four countries: France, the United States, Australia, and Canada.[34] Acceptance is based on criteria from the 1951 United Nations Convention Relating to the Status of Refugees. Not all asylum seekers are granted refugee status. The time it takes to process applications can be long. They then face the challenge of living in their host country without legal status. This can restrict their ability to work and access social services, and in some cases it may lead to deportation.

Sudanese refugees walk through a refugee camp.

The first refugees under the 1951 UN Convention were Jews escaping from Nazi Germany during World War II. After the war, refugees from around the world continued to leave home because of weak governance, instability, and lingering conflict.[35] In recent years, large refugee populations have emerged from Afghanistan, Iraq, the Democratic Republic of the Congo, and Sudan.

When host countries do not have the capacity to house refugees or provide them space, refugees typically live in temporary camps. Refugee camps are intended to be an intermediate step for people who flee their own countries. At times, refugees have spent much longer in these camps than expected. For example, a number of refugees from Somalia have lived in refugee camps in Kenya since 1991. And some Palestinian refugees have lived in camps within Lebanon for over 50 years.[36] Those living in camps often do not have much access to employment skills and education due to a lack of money and resources to support these needs.[37] If a teenager moves to a camp and must stay there for several years, what kind of future prospects might he or she have?

> *Tensions between a host country's citizens and refugees are more likely to happen when resource scarcity already exists.*

The largest refugee populations are found in the Middle East and North Africa. The African nation of Chad houses over 200,000 refugees.[38] A large number have fled to Chad to get away from the escalating conflict and genocide within the Darfur region of Sudan. Most refugees settled in the east side of Chad, known for its arid climate and lack of vegetation. People in Chad were already struggling to meet their basic needs; over 80% of Chad's population lives below the poverty line. When refugees from Darfur began entering the country, competition over food, land, and water increased.

Tensions between a host country's citizens and refugees are more likely to happen when resource scarcity already exists. The United Nations refugee agency (UNHCR) has worked to decrease some of these tensions in Chad through the following efforts:[39]

- Teaching women in refugee camps how to use fuel-efficient stoves in order to prevent them from collecting firewood and depleting forests
- Providing 300,000 seedlings to refugee camps to grow more trees for firewood
- Installing water pumps near refugee camps

YOUTH PROFILE
Thanh Nguyen, Firsthand Account of a Refugee

For my parents, escaping Vietnam was the only choice they had. Shortly after the communists took over in 1975, my dad had to work in a reeducation or labor camp like many South Vietnamese men. In the reeducation camp, the communists tried to assimilate my dad into the new political system through hard labor and propaganda classes. My dad didn't do anything criminal except for being on the losing side of the war. He felt like a prisoner in his own country. Everywhere he went, he had to check in with the local officials. There was no freedom of movement. It wasn't the country he or my mom knew or wanted their children to grow up in. They had to flee Vietnam.

My parents faced a lot of failures trying to escape. There was always something that went wrong, like some officials found out or they didn't have enough money. These failures wore them down, but they didn't give up. Fortunately, they heard about another escape attempt by boat. The boatman wanted three bars of gold as payment to get us to Malaysia, a first asylum country. They decided to pay the boatman and take the risk.

I was three at the time, so everything was a blur. During the night, my dad came into the room and woke my sister, brother, and me. It was time to go. We took nothing except water, boiled eggs, and some fruit. We separated into three small groups so we wouldn't be noticed. Two uncles took my brother. Another uncle took my sister and a cousin. My dad took me and two other cousins. Our plan was to take different routes and meet up at the boat.

When we met up at the boat, everyone was there except my mom. The boat took off, but we had no choice; we couldn't go back for my mom. (To this day, I'm still unsure why she wasn't there. I really don't want to know. I just know that for my mother, not being with her children was one of the most painful experiences she had to live with for 11 years.)

Getting on the boat was the first step. Surviving the journey was the next step. The boat overflowed with a mishmash of adults and children. My dad didn't trust the boatman. He knew the stories of capsizing boats or pirating. He knew there was no certainty of success and something could go terribly wrong. It did. The sun's heat started taking its toll; people, especially the elderly, were starting to become dehydrated. The water supply was tainted which made it undrinkable. People were dying and had to be cast off into the South China Sea. We drank whatever was left from our water bottles as the boat continued to drift.

Eventually, we were spotted by a naval ship, which gave us supplies and hauled us to a refugee camp in Malaysia. After a few months in the refugee camp, we were sent to the U.S. military base in the Philippines to be processed as refugees. Luckily, another uncle had escaped prior to us and sponsored us to be resettled in Philadelphia. Under the Refugee Act of 1980, we needed proof of status to enter the United States. Being from Vietnam was proof enough after the Vietnam War.

When we arrived in the United States, we stayed with my uncle and his family in Philadelphia. Being Catholics, one of the most important supports was the local church, St. Francis de Sales, and Catholic Charities. De Sales also had a dedicated Vietnamese priest and a Vietnamese friar running English as a Second Language classes to prepare us for school. We were even given clothes from the church thrift shop. They helped us to resettle and become Americans.

It's been 31 years since my family fled Vietnam. We're a complete family now. My mom eventually came over when I was 14. I'm currently an elementary teacher, educating fifth graders at a public school in southeast D.C.

Undocumented or Illegal Immigrants

Undocumented or illegal immigrants are people who do not have legal status in their

Thanh Nguyen (front left) lived at a military base in the Philippines with his family.

country of residence. They may have chosen to leave their country of origin voluntarily or they may have been forced. These migrants usually do not have documentation like visas or passports when crossing borders. Some may have crossed the border legally but overstayed their designated time in their host country; others may not ever have been given permission to enter the country.[40] People may resort to illegal migration when policies do not allow them to legally migrate or the process to become legal takes too long.

Some of these migrants take risks when trying to enter another country: paying smugglers to bring them across borders by car or boat, or traveling dangerous routes that involve remote desert crossings or journeys by sea. Each year, hundreds of thousands of Mexicans attempt to cross the border from Mexico to the United States. Other countries face similar challenges. Around the world, tensions related to illegal migration are escalating.[41] See the Point-Counterpoint section to learn more about this global issue.

Pathways to Progress: Human Migration

Trends show that migration is on the rise due to factors related to globalization, technology, environment, and economy.[42] Some migrants are desperate to meet basic needs such as food, water, and shelter. Others want to improve their quality of life in the areas of education, human rights, and health. Yet others are forced to move because of global issues such as war and human trafficking. A number of people, organizations, and governments have created solutions to meet the challenges faced by both immigrants and the communities that receive them. The following are just a few examples.

Organizations Supporting Refugees

Civil war within Sierra Leone during the 1990s forced hundreds of thousands of people to flee,

---

CASE STUDY: The Fight against Human Trafficking

Human trafficking is the act of taking people through force, fraud, or deception in order to exploit them.[43] There are around 2.5 million people in the world who are forced into labor and not paid for their work. The majority of people trafficked are from Asia and most are women.[44] Trafficking may involve the physical abduction of a person. Human traffickers also frequently take advantage of people in desperate situations who are looking for opportunities abroad to escape poverty. Traffickers deceive these people with promises of economic opportunity to get them to agree to be smuggled away from their homes. Rather than the promised prosperity, many instead find themselves forced into jobs as domestic workers, prostitutes, or farmers, often with no pay at all.

The sex slave trade is the third most profitable criminal industry in the world, bringing in $12 billion per year. Somaly Mam learned this firsthand when she was sold into slavery at the age of 12. She was born in Cambodia to a family from a tribal minority that lived in extreme poverty. A man who posed as her grandfather made the decision to sell her. For years, Somaly was forced to work in a brothel, but she finally escaped.

Today, she helps to run the Somaly Mam Foundation. The mission of the Foundation is to end modern-day slavery around the world. It does so by helping to eradicate human trafficking, liberate its victims, and empower survivors. As a result of Somaly's inspiring work, she has received various honors, including being named one of *Time Magazine's* 100 most influential people in 2009 and one of *Newsweek Magazine's* 150 women who shake the world.[45]

Somaly Mam sits with girls served by her foundation.

CAREER PROFILE: Program Officer

People are drawn out of their home countries for a variety of reasons, as you have learned in this chapter, but they do not always understand the laws and restrictions facing them when they arrive in a new country. Some immigrants end up in jail and face a difficult and complicated situation. The Women's Refugee Commission (WRC) is one organization working to help secure legal rights for immigrants and refugees. Most people who work in organizations such as the WRC hold degrees in international relations, human rights, and/or international law. Many of them also speak multiple languages. Strong written and verbal communication is key in this line of work. Emily Butera followed this path.

Emily didn't grow up dreaming she'd be the Program Officer for the WRC's Detention and Asylum Program, researching, advocating, and influencing policy on behalf of immigrants. She says she was drawn into it when she began interning at a nearby prison with a large population of immigrant detainees. Today, her job involves going to detention centers all over the country and talking to detainees to find out what kinds of conditions they were living in before moving to the United States and what their lives are like in detention. Without help from groups like the WRC, detainees may not be able to communicate their most basic needs.

Emily Butera creates policy initiatives that improve detention facilities for immigrants.

Immigrants put themselves at the mercy of a large and complicated system in order to integrate and become naturalized citizens; Emily helps them to navigate that system. In addition to helping individual detainees, Emily crafts policy initiatives to improve detention conditions and to influence immigration law. Although her job is difficult she says she must do it. She finds it rewarding to be able to help people who have been made virtually invisible, to listen to them and care about them. To anyone thinking about entering this kind of work, she recommends starting with reaching out to people at church or school. Volunteering or interning is the best way to get your foot in the door and to make sure you are ready to commit. She also recommends traveling abroad to learn about other people's values and culture firsthand.

---

seeking safety. Reuben Koromo and Francis Lamgba were among the Sierra Leonean refugees living in a refugee camp in Guinea. Both men had a love for music and wanted to continue playing, so they decided to put together a band to entertain others within the camp. They used acoustic guitars and wrote their own songs. After some time, a Canadian refugee organization provided them electric guitars and other instruments. Soon, the band expanded to six people, including a talented teenaged rapper. They began traveling between camps to share their music with other refugees. The group became the international pop stars known as the Refugee All Stars. Their music with positive messages of hope continues to inspire people all over the world.[46]

The Refugee All Stars practice together.

International Governance

The United Nations High Commissioner for Refugees (UNHCR) is a refugee agency created by the UN on December 14, 1950 to help refugees and internally displaced persons throughout the world. UNHCR works toward solutions at a number of different levels. It advocates for refugees and IDPs by working with different countries to help create laws, policies, and standards that help protect migrants.

- It uses an emergency response system to respond to as many as 500,000 people who may be fleeing their home countries due to conflict or natural disaster.
- It helps prevent environmental degradation such as deforestation caused by the use of wood for fire and water scarcity resulting from an influx of refugees moving into a new country.[47]

UNHCR's multilayered approach to migration issues allows it to make an impact on many different levels, from on-the-ground assistance to meet refugees' basic needs to changes in international law, with the aim of improving the quality of life for refugees and IDPs.

Creating Sustainable Growth in a Country

As mentioned earlier, brain drain can lead to a country not having enough trained professionals such as doctors and engineers to support sustainable growth.

The U.K. London School of Hygiene and Tropical Medicine has created a distance learning program that allows those in developing countries to take courses online so that they do not have to leave their home country to pursue educational opportunities. This type of program is one way to help medical professionals remain within their own countries instead of having to migrate elsewhere.[48]

WHAT YOU CAN DO: Human Migration

There are a number of things you can do to address human migration issues and contribute to healthy and sustainable communities.

- Still need to learn more? Educate yourself on what's happening with immigration in your local community and within your country. Analyze the debates.

- If you are concerned about refugees and IDPs around the word, start a fundraiser at your school to donate money to support refugees in specific countries.

- Increase tolerance within your school and community by raising awareness and understanding of different people's backgrounds and cultures. What new groups have arrived in your community? What cultures, traditions, and experiences do they bring with them that help define or enrich your community? How can you share your community's culture with others?

You can educate yourself on what's happening with immigration in your local community and within your country.

POINT | COUNTERPOINT

Was the DREAM Act fair?

The DREAM Act (Development Relief and Education for Alien Minors) was legislation first introduced in the United States by Republicans and Democrats in 2001. Its goal was to address one of the issues faced by a particular group of illegal immigrants: young people. The act would give students who grew up in the United States but are not legal immigrants an opportunity to participate in the military or complete their higher education degree. There are specific provisions in the DREAM Act that would allow for a young person to stay in the country, including:[49]

- The person must be 15 years old or younger when he or she entered the United States.
- The person must have lived in the United States for at least five years before the bill was enacted.
- The person must have graduated from high school or obtained a GED and also must have been accepted into a college or university.
- The person must be between 12 and 35 years old at the time of application.

There are many who supported and many who were against this legislation. By 2012, President Barack Obama made significant changes to U.S. deportation policy that reflected much of the DREAM Act criteria. The following perspectives show some of the debate around the DREAM Act and immigration.

POINT
Yes

- **Imagine you are brought to the United States when you are three years old.** You do all of your schooling from kindergarten through 12th grade in the United States, adapt well to the culture, and excel in the classroom; in short, you are a model student. Then when it comes time for you to attend college, you are told that you are undocumented and will not receive financial aid. The DREAM Act would change your status and allow you to attend college.

- **With the DREAM Act in place, a young person given legal status would be able to contribute immensely to the U.S. economy.** Based on the American Integration and Development Center, if the DREAM Act were passed the bill would add up to $3.6 trillion in income across the next few decades. The federal deficit would be reduced by $1.4 billion.[50] There would also be an increase in an educated and skilled workforce that is both multicultural and multilingual.

COUNTERPOINT
No

- **What if a person who sped through a red light were rewarded with a cash incentive?** It seems absurd, but in many ways, this is what would happen if the DREAM Act were passed. Undocumented students would be rewarded for doing something illegal, living in the United States without legal status. Taxpayers pay money to help finance schooling of young people in their communities. The DREAM Act would force taxpayers to likewise support the education of illegal students. In California for example, the Supreme Court has passed a ruling that would allow illegal immigrants who are accepted to in-state universities to pay in-state tuition rather than out-of-state tuition.[51] All of the students who attempt to go to school through the proper channels would have to compete with students who did not follow immigration guidelines.

- **Support of the DREAM Act essentially negates the significance of immigration laws within the United States.** The passing of this act would indicate that parents should bring their children across the border so they can reap the benefits of living in the United States.[52] Meanwhile, legal immigrants who come to the United States on student visas do not benefit from these tuition perks.[53] Additionally, when students become citizens they can soon sponsor their parents for citizenship.[54]

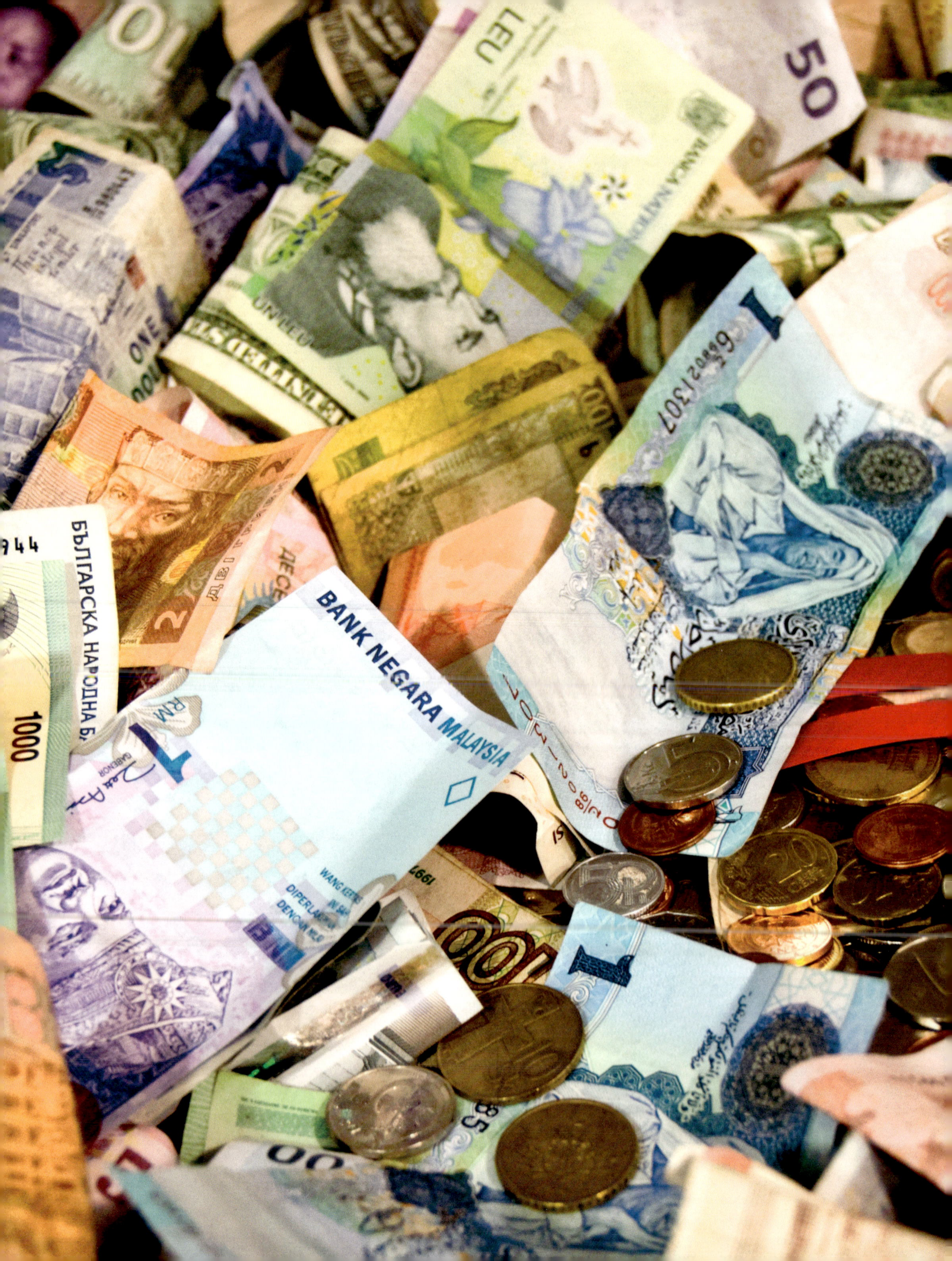
BANK NEGARA MALAYSIA
LEU
БЪЛГАРСКА НАРОДНА
1000
50

Chapter 19

Economics

GUIDING QUESTIONS

- How do we define and measure economic progress?
- How can economic progress be sustainable?

Introduction to Economics

Think about the things you have purchased over the last month. As you decide what to buy, what influences your decisions? Have you considered how your decisions as a consumer influence the world around you or even how spending choices affect your own life?

There are approximately 25.2 million teenagers between the ages of 13 and 18 living in the United States. Considering they make up over 20% of the U.S. population,[1] this group significantly influences the economy. During the 1960s, spending by teenagers in the United States totaled $5 billion per year. Fast-forward to today and teens spend approximately $192 billion per year! Teenagers with an income typically spend their money on the following items: clothing, food, music, shoes, electronics, and games.[2]

Teenagers contribute significantly to the U.S. economy.

Have you ever thought about where goods like these come from? Those who work to produce goods are also part of the economy. Across the globe, approximately 250 million children between the ages of 5 and 14 are working as child laborers.[3] Poorer families may feel they need to send their children to work instead of school in order to provide income for the family. It is very possible that at least one of the products a teenager purchases in the United States was made somewhere else by children.

Economic choices are one of many ideas that will be discussed in this chapter. The word economy comes from the Greek word "oikonomia," meaning management of household. **Economy** includes not only the exchange of money and goods but also everything and everyone involved in making these goods. Economics is the study of how a society manages its scarce resources. Economists analyze the production, distribution, and consumption of goods and services—in other words, the things we buy and sell.

Within each household, there are scarce resources. On a small scale of the economy, household management involves making decisions about how to allocate these resources (and usually this involves decisions about what to buy). Take food, for example. We only have so much land we can use to grow food. Most resources have similar limitations to their availability.

On a larger scale of the economy, management of resources also includes decisions about production, and so involves everything and everyone necessary to create goods and services.

Our current global economic model is based on buying and selling consumer goods and services. We didn't always have stores where we could purchase things. This current market system can be traced back to the beginning of the Industrial Revolution and the mass production of consumer goods. For the first time, people could buy consumer goods rather than making things for themselves or purchasing handcrafted goods from artisans. The roots of this economic model will be discussed later in this chapter.

A **market** is a system or structure whereby buyers and sellers exchange goods, services, or information. Both individuals and countries interact with markets. **Microeconomics** looks at the relationship of consumers with the market (i.e., how people decide to purchase certain goods and services). **Macroeconomics**, on the other hand, looks at an entire economy—often the economy of one nation—and the issues that affect that economy (i.e., inflation, economic growth, and unemployment). Global macroeconomics looks at the same issues affecting national economies, but on a global scale.

Principles of Economics

The choices we make every day shape the economy. To understand why people make certain decisions, it is important to consider some of the guiding principles of economics.

Trade-offs

We face trade-offs. People have to constantly make decisions that involve giving one thing up for another because our budget is typically limited or constrained. If you've ever saved money to buy something, you've experienced tradeoffs. Say you want to save money to buy a video game. In order to save, you might decide not to purchase something else—such as a new pair of shoes—that you don't want as much as the game.

Incentives

We respond to incentives. An incentive is something that motivates or encourages a person to do something. There can be positive and negative incentives. For example, if a city wants its people to ride the bus more, charging a toll for people who drive would be a negative incentive. Offering an employer-sponsored bus card discount would be a positive incentive. Business can also receive financial incentives in the form of **subsidies**. These subsidies are typically some type of assistance given by governments that encourage businesses to make certain kinds of decisions, such as decreasing their carbon footprints or selling certain products.

Costs

All choices involve costs. Each time you make a choice there is a cost. For example, take a city that produces more waste than the city's current landfill can hold. The city needs to decide whether to expand the capacity of its current landfill (costing $400,000 and the expanded landfill will be able to handle 10 more years of waste, based on current rates of waste generation) or build a new landfill (costing $2.1 million and able to handle 35 more years of waste, based on current rates of waste generation). The city could also elect to make efforts in waste reduction, perhaps involving a public awareness campaign and financial incentive for citizens who reduce their waste, such as a deduction on their garbage bill. All of these choices involve different costs. Additionally, there will be environmental costs from additional waste that are not factored in directly.

Economics and Sustainability

Some experts claim that the goal of an economy should be to sustainably improve human well-being and quality of life.[4] We can make economic decisions at the individual and societal level that both improve our lives and contribute to the well-being of the planet.

These days, our economic choices are often connected to a number of global issues that

Many cell phones are manufactured in China and then distributed around the world.

may seem remote from our daily lives. Take the act of purchasing a cell phone. If you trace where your cell phone came from you'll learn that one of the essential materials used to create cell phones is coltan—a resource extracted from mines in the Congo. The phones are then manufactured in factories in places such as China. Based on market need, the phones are distributed to stores around the world where consumers purchase them. When your cell phone stops working, you dispose of it and the cycle begins again. Understanding how the global economy works can help us make specific sustainable choices that support the environment and society.

Environment

When two individuals or groups of people conduct a transaction that has an effect on an uninvolved third party, an **externality** is created. Externalities can be either positive or negative. A negative externality harms the third party in some way; a positive externality benefits the third party. To help evaluate whether an externality is positive or negative, economists look at the private and social costs of a transaction. Private costs are those costs paid by a business or firm that produces the services and goods. Social costs are those costs paid by people in a society.

When the social cost of producing a product is higher than the private cost, you have a negative externality. Consider the following example: a manufacturing factory emits pollution. The factory has to pay private costs, but the factory does not have to pay for the social costs of the pollution. There are both direct (the presence of pollutants) and indirect social costs (the impact of pollution on human and environmental health) that would be considered negative externalities.

When an economic transaction results in a social cost that is lower than the private cost, you have a positive externality. For example,

CASE STUDY: Mining Public Lands

Common resources can also be used to illustrate the impacts of externalities. Common resources are those resources that all members of a community may use such as oceans and land. Public lands in the United States are also common resources; they are owned collectively by society rather than by any individual or private group.

Remember that all choices involve costs. The use of a common resource by one person or company can inadvertently decrease another's ability to use or enjoy it. As an example, mining public lands for minerals and metals often results in negative externalities. Mined metals are used in all sorts of goods. The metal in some of the goods you own—blue jeans with metal rivets, a bicycle, or a cell phone—could have been mined on public lands.

Believe it or not, the General Mining Law of 1872 still governs the mining of gold, uranium, and other metals on U.S. public lands. The law was enacted to promote development of the West. The law allows citizens of the United States and those who declare their intention to become citizens to freely explore public lands for mineral deposits. According to the Pew Campaign for Responsible Mining, the following provisions are included in the General Mining Law:

Mining has priority status on public lands.

- Mining companies are allowed to mine approximately $1 billion worth of gold and other metals from public land each year without paying anything for the privilege.

- Mining has priority status on most public lands, which makes it almost impossible to prohibit or restrict mining even in famous locations such as Grand Canyon National Park.

Mining allowed under the General Mining Law creates various negative externalities. The most immediate are the environmental costs: mountains are destroyed to extract mineral resources and bodies of water are polluted by waste rock and erosion. Mining is one of the nation's most polluting industries and yet is controlled by very few regulations. Because of this lack of regulation, abandoned mines often leave behind toxic waste. Over $2 billion in taxpayer spending has been used over the past 10 years to clean up mine waste.

When individuals or companies are granted free access to common resources and are not held responsible for the environmental or social damage done by their activities, there is no incentive to use the resource sustainably. This is known as the tragedy of the tragedy of the commons. Keeping negative externalities like these in mind can be a powerful way to support sustainable economic decisions.[5]

a local manufacturer decides to redesign its manufacturing process by using energy-efficiency measures and reducing waste. The manufacturer pays to make these changes (a private cost), and because of these changes, the surrounding community benefits. After implementing the changes, the company uses less fuel to transport its goods. This reduces air pollution in the area which decreases human health issues and also limits the company's consumption of petroleum, a nonrenewable resource.

Changes can also made to reduce and re-use the materials involved in the manufacturing process. The result is that less recyclable material goes to the local landfill, conserving the community's natural resources.

Society

You make personal economic choices every day that influence your well-being and that of those around you—from the types of food, clothing, and music you buy to investments you make in your health and education. Purchasing certain things instead of others has *opportunity costs,* meaning that choosing one opportunity limits your ability to pursue a different one.

In other words, every dollar that you spend on one thing leaves you with one less dollar to spend on other things. For example, what if you decide to put all your money toward a college education? What are the benefits and consequences of this investment? Or what if a pair of jeans you want to purchase is only affordable because it was made by children in a developing country? What are the costs and the benefits of purchasing these jeans?

At the national level, the government creates a budget and decides how to spend its money (including investments in health, education, and the military). How a government decides to spend public money impacts the well-being of its citizens. If a country invests money in its education system rather than its military, how do you think this spending will impact its citizens? The following graph[6] illustrates how specific countries have allocated money to different sectors.

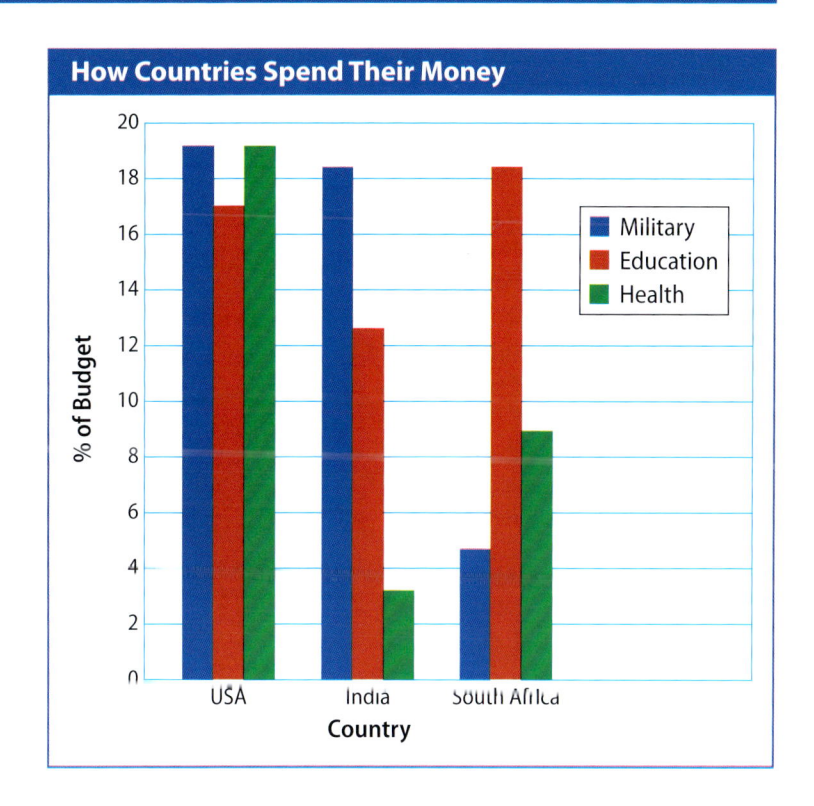

Opportunity costs are an inevitable part of any economic decision. Being aware of these costs and paying close attention to aligning our priorities with our overall distribution of resources can allow individuals and societies to make good decisions that avoid unintended opportunity costs.

Take a look at India's spending. In 2010, India chose to invest heavily in education and the military. These investments may have greatly benefited the country, but the opportunity cost was felt in the comparatively small percentage of the budget left over for health care spending. Without government investment, health care costs in India have pushed 39 million people into poverty each year. As a result of limited public health spending, those struggling to afford health care also face shortages of doctors and medicines.[7] People who do not have access to proper health care may miss work due to illness or otherwise be unable to contribute to the economy. The long-term consequences of allocating less money to health care in India could affect the prosperity of the country itself.

CASE STUDY: Porto Alegre's Budget Process[8]

How would you and your neighbors like to spend $200 million? Beginning in 1989, 50,000 of the 1.5 million poor and middle-class residents of Porto Alegre, Brazil undertook a bold experiment in improving governance involving local government, civic organizations, and the private sector. Normally, citizens pay taxes and the government decides how to spend the money. In this case, the citizens of Porto Alegre chose how the city would budget public money.

At the heart of the effort was a budgeting process involving local citizens. Budgeting (how money is generated and spent) can be a complicated process, so the city began by providing citizens with some basic training on how budgets are constructed. They then held dozens of meetings across the city that aimed to include those who experienced discrimination in Brazilian life—the poor and middle class, those with little education, and blacks. Each meeting attracted more than 1,000 residents to address topics such as transportation, health, education, sports, and economic development. The city then shared information from the meetings with the public.

The government in Porto Alegre, Brazil allowed for citizens to support decision-making around the city's budget.

Since this experiment in self-government and local control of the budgeting process began in 1989, Porto Alegre has seen numerous and impressive benefits. During the project's first 12 years:

- Homes with running and treated freshwater increased from 75% to 99%
- Housing assistance rose from serving 1,700 families to 29,000 families
- The number of public schools increased from 29 to 86, and literacy rates reached 98%
- Government corruption virtually disappeared

Due to its approach to budgeting, Porto Alegre has become one of Brazil's most livable cities. Residents who participated in the process gained skills that helped them improve their own quality of life. This model of economic governance has since spread to 100 other cities in South America.

Background on Economics

The Industrial Revolution

The Industrial Revolution shifted small-scale economies to economies defined by mass production. The Industrial Revolution began in the United Kingdom in the mid-1700s, but soon spread and had a major influence in the rest of the world. According to Robert E. Lucas, Jr., a Nobel Prize-winning economist: "For the first time in history, the living standards of the masses of ordinary people have begun to undergo sustained growth…. Nothing remotely like this economic behavior has happened before."[9] Economies based on manual labor and working animals changed to economies based on machine manufacturing. Throughout this time, the number of goods produced grew exponentially due to the increased manufacturing capacity of machines and improved transportation technologies that allowed goods, services, and ideas to travel more quickly from one place to another.

By the late 19th century, mass production of goods started to globalize the world economy.[10] As goods and services traveled across borders in greater volume, goods could be bought far from where they were made. Economic growth depended heavily on this idea of mass productivity and global trade.

However, when the U.S. stock market crashed in 1929, Americans slowly began to stop purchasing goods. Many withdrew all their money from banks. Suddenly, banks could not provide loans to people. Nearly 5,000 banks failed.[11] An economy dependent on continual economic growth could not survive if people did not buy anything.

During the Great Depression that followed the stock market crash, the U.S. federal government tried to find ways to restart the economy. They needed a tool to look at the big picture of the country's economic activity. In 1934, an American economist and Nobel Prize laureate named Simon Kuznets created gross domestic product (GDP) as a tool to measure economic growth. **Gross domestic product (GDP)** measures the total value of goods and services produced by and within a country. Although GDP was not originally intended to measure a country's well-being, the federal government adopted it as an indicator of economic progress. There were many positive benefits to using GDP. Most significantly, it allowed policy-makers and economists to analyze the impacts of policies on the economy.[12] By the end of World War II, countries around the world had adopted GDP.

There are limitations to using GDP as a measure of economic health. In 1962, Kuznets himself warned against overreliance on GDP among economists and policy-makers. He believed a country's well-being could not necessarily be measured by national income.[13] Despite his warning, GDP continues to be widely used as an indicator of national progress. These days, whether or not GDP is a useful tool to measure economic growth is a debatable topic.

Different Types of Economies

Countries throughout the world follow different economic models. Some follow a market-based economy model while others follow a command economy. Almost all economies fall at some point on this continuum with a mix of market and command forces.

The Great Depression followed the U.S. stock market crash in 1929.

Market Economies

In 1776, Adam Smith, a famous economist, wrote *An Inquiry into the Nature and Causes of the Wealth of Nations*. This book spoke about how too much government intervention in a free-market economy might stifle economic growth.

Market economies are decentralized economies, meaning that they have no government oversight. The economy relies on the freedom of consumers to choose what kinds of goods and services they want and the freedom of producers to create businesses however they see fit and charge prices based on changes in the market. For example, if a business decides to create a pair of jeans and charge a certain price, another business can compete by charging less or offering different styles of jeans. The abundance of different types of goods and services in market economies relates to how so many different businesses are allowed to compete with each other.[14]

Mixed Economies

The U.S. economy, like that of many economies in developed and developing countries, is a *mixed economy*. This means that there is a balance between public and private involvement. Private businesses can produce goods and services that the public can buy. Government agencies provide other types of services such as national defense (the military) and law enforcement (police). Other countries with mixed economies include Japan, India, Canada, Australia, and Italy.

Since the birth of the United States, there has been an emphasis on private control of commerce within the country. The Founding Fathers were wary of allowing the government to have too much power. They were very specific when crafting the country's constitution to limit the amount of influence that the government has over individuals.

These days, the United States economy operates on the premise that the economy is more efficient when it is largely controlled by private corporations and businesses. However, there have been periods in U.S. history when the government had far more control over the economy and how money was spent. For example, during Franklin Roosevelt's presidency, the federal government had a huge amount of power

President Franklin Roosevelt believed the Great Depression happened because of the actions of bankers and businesses. The federal government therefore had more control over the economy for several years.

over banks and businesses. Roosevelt believed the United States experienced the Great Depression as a result of actions by bankers and businesses and he wanted to avoid another depression by taking a hands-on approach to the banking industry. As years passed, regulation of the private sector lessened as businesses pushed for more freedom to make decisions.

In mixed economies such as that of the United States, the private sector provides the majority of the goods and services. The stores you go to for groceries, clothes, electronics, and so on are owned by corporations or private companies, not the government. The government's role is to watch over the market. It creates laws and policies to address externalities like pollution and to prevent one company from monopolizing the market, which can have negative consequences for consumers. Governments also step in when there are disruptions to the market such as natural disasters. Without government intervention, such events could devastate an economy.

People can influence a market economy through consumer choices and by electing officials who support particular economic policies. One of the benefits of a consumer economy is its readiness to adapt to prevailing conditions. As more people commit to sustainable choices, the market may favor companies that implement sustainable practices. Companies that do not make changes could fail in the market if consumers refuse to buy their products.

Command Economies[15]

Command economies are different than mixed and market economies because the government heavily regulates production of goods and services. Countries like North Korea and Cuba follow this kind of model. Private businesses and state-owned enterprises do not make decisions on their own. Rather, governments guide them in what they should do. Therefore, instead of many businesses competing with each other to create a pair of jeans, the government decides who will create jeans and how much to charge for them.

The United States is a mixed economy in which the private sector provides the majority of goods and services.

Economics Today

There are certain forces that have a strong influence on economies throughout the world today: the way we measure economic growth, the process of globalization, and the influence of international economic institutions.

Economic Indicators

As mentioned in the previous section, GDP was created in order to be a tool for economic analysis that measures economic activity and the standard of living within a country. This measurement has guided governments in making policy decisions about how to distribute money. In fact, the White House monitors the GDP of the United States in order to prepare the annual federal budget.

Economic indicators are intended to be objective measures, but they can play a role in supporting or inhibiting sustainable development. For many years GDP has been used by economists to measure the health of nations in areas that extend far beyond their economic output. Some people use GDP to measure how well "developed" a nation is. The underlying

When considering sustainable development in a globalized economy, businesses and governments provide people equitable livelihoods.

premise is that if a nation's economy is doing well, so are its people.

As concern about global issues increases, people all over the world are starting to question the use of GDP as an indicator of true well-being. Does having more money make our lives better? What's missing from the picture? After all, GDP only measures the market economy. It does not include issues that are external to markets like air and water quality, health, education, and unpaid labor, even though these are all important factors in the productivity of an economy.[16]

In 1974, Richard Easterlin, an economist at the University of Southern California, noticed something unusual about the relationship between a nation's GDP and the happiness of its people. The Easterlin Paradox asserts that as a country gets richer its inhabitants do not necessarily get happier. It's like the old adage says: money doesn't buy happiness. Easterlin's research on 37 different countries, both developed and developing, confirms the paradox.[17] He acknowledges that in the short term, happiness and income increase together; until basic human needs are met, there is a strong relationship between income and well-being. Once a certain level of income is met, however, the relationship fades.

Globalization

Globalization presents new challenges for people and the planet, but also new potential for solving global economic issues. Globalization has spurred rapid economic growth in countries like China and India, helping to reduce poverty. For nations such as these that were very poor as little as 20 years ago, this represents significant progress. On the other hand, some of the economic growth resulting from globalization has led to concerns about increasing economic inequalities and environmental degradation in newly developed and rapidly developing countries. In these situations, there have been opportunity costs related to economic growth.[18]

When working toward sustainable development, we must consider how an increasingly globalized economy can balance the desire for profit with the need to provide people in both developed and developing countries with equitable livelihoods. Supporters of economic globalization argue that the tremendous power of free trade can bring both higher incomes and economic development to poorer nations. **Free trade** is the policy of unrestricted international trade; that is, governments do not impose tariffs or quotas on imports, or subsidies on exports. Borders between countries become more open and it is easier for people to trade goods and services. According to free trade proponents, any attempt to restrict the profits, investments, or operations of regional or multinational business will hinder badly needed economic growth in poorer nations.

On the other hand, some experts point to globalization and free trade policies as a driving force for global income inequality. They argue that through globalization, poor countries become increasingly dependent on richer countries for their economic survival. This lopsided arrangement can drive poorer countries to make decisions that may ultimately slow down their economic development. For example, in order to produce goods to export to developed countries, poor nations may allow child labor or deplete natural resources.

Large multinational corporations formed in the 20th and 21st centuries have gained increasing economic power, especially over the agricultural economies of Africa, Asia, and Latin America. These companies operate under a *free market system* in which products and services are produced based on people's demand for them. Within this system, large corporations focus on ways to generate as large a profit as possible to ensure that their *shareholders* (people who own shares of stock in the company) get a return on their investment. Sometimes this focus on profit can create situations of poverty and environmental destruction in the poorer countries where multinationals operate.[19]

When corporations and governments lower costs by reducing environmental protection and employee wages, there are often negative consequences. This phenomenon has been called race to the bottom because the company or nation with the lowest costs of production gains more business in the short term but the environment and society suffer in the long term.

International Economic Institutions

The *International Monetary Fund (IMF)*, founded in 1944, is an international organization of 184 member countries. It was established to promote international monetary cooperation and economic stability, to foster economic growth and high levels of employment, and to provide temporary financial assistance to countries in need. The IMF works toward these goals by monitoring countries' economic activities and lending money to nations to enable conditions for sustained economic growth.

The *World Bank* is another international financial organization that makes loans to developing countries. It is a specialized agency of the United Nations that provides loans, policy advice, technical assistance, and information to low- and middle-income countries in order to support them in reducing poverty and improving living standards. As of 2012, the World Bank had lent its support to more than 1,800 projects in the developing world. Past funding has been used to raise AIDS awareness, support education of girls,

International organizations, such as the World Bank pictured here, provide loans to developing countries.

and improve health care delivery.

The IMF and World Bank were both created after World War II to support the economies of countries impacted by the war. The World Bank's first loans were to Western European countries. Once European economies stabilized, the Bank began helping developing nations. Since 1940, it has loaned more than $330 billion to developing countries. This lending is intended to raise productivity so people can live better lives.[20]

Critics of the IMF and World Bank claim that these institutions actually reinforce poverty, debt, and inequality in poorer countries. These critics assert that the borrowing countries have to make sacrifices to pay back their loan debts, such as adopting certain trade policies or allowing extraction of natural resources. They end up spending money on certain expenses that take away from others like education and health. Some even suggest that in order to help poorer countries reach economic stability these debts should be canceled. This would allow governments in developing countries to spend money on human needs instead of debt repayment.[21]

Critics of the IMF believe that the organization reinforces debt and poverty in poorer countries.

Pathways to Progress: Economics

Alternative Indicators of the Economy

GDP is a starting point when considering economic growth. Three alternative progress indicators are explored below.

Genuine Progress Indicator

The Genuine Progress Indicator (GPI) is an alternative system that looks at a holistic picture of what is happening inside an economic system. Essentially, GPI adjusts the picture provided by GDP to ensure that the end number reflects the relative positive and negative contributions of everything that goes into GDP, including factors that actually reduce our quality of life.

Some economic activities that produce monetary profits also involve costs such as natural resource depletion, pollution, family breakdown, and crime. Economic growth can also include money that contributes to negative social outcomes. For example, GDP incorporates the following into its measure of economic growth: medical costs, legal fees, divorce, and car wrecks.[22]

To calculate economic progress, the Genuine Progress Indicator assesses positive value to things not included in GDP. These include the value of higher education and volunteer work and services provided to society such as highways and streets. It also subtracts some negative impacts not included in GDP such as the costs of air pollution, commuting, and damage from carbon dioxide emissions.

Human Development Index

The Human Development Index (HDI) was created by the United Nations Development Program. It assesses a nation's well-being according to three criteria: standard of living, educational attainment, and life span. Each factor is weighted equally.

The Genuine Progress Indicator considers negative impacts of the GDP such as air pollution.

The HDI does not have any direct environmental components; it is strictly a tool to measure a country's well-being based on the capabilities of its people. It is intended to help analyze and question policy decisions in support of the ultimate aim of improving people's standard of living, educational attainment, and longevity. According to the United Nations Development Program, New Zealand and the Bahamas have approximately the same per capita income. However, New Zealanders have a higher life expectancy and are expected to go to school longer, resulting in a much higher HDI value for New Zealand.[23]

Index of Social Health

The Index of Social Health is the product of the Institute for Innovation in Social Policy at Vassar College. This organization looks at social indicators at the state, national, and international level.[24] It has published the Index of Social Health annually since 1987. The Index looks at 16 related and overlapping social indicators, grouped by the following age categories: children, youth, adults, and the elderly. It measures indicators such as infant mortality, child poverty, high school dropout rates, weekly wages, and affordable housing.

In the United States, the Index score decreased from 64.9 points (out of 100 points) in 1970 to 51.7 points in 2009. During this time period six indicators improved: infant mortality, teenage drug abuse, high school dropout rates, poverty of those over 65 years old, homicides, and alcohol-related traffic fatalities. However, 10 indicators worsened, including child poverty, weekly wages, unemployment, and food insecurity.[25]

Subsidies for Sustainability

Subsidies, or financial incentives, can influence the way people make economic decisions. Subsidies may be intended to encourage the development of a particular industry or support people in making economic choices that benefit society. For example, subsidies may support the development of solar energy by helping homeowners purchase solar panels

CASE STUDY: The Body Shop[26]

The Body Shop is one example of a company that has paid attention to what is happening in the world and changed its business practices accordingly. Body Shop founder Anita Roddick believes that a company does not have to compromise its principles to make a profit. She saw an opportunity to use her company as an example to others to promote responsible business practices.

Some people may associate The Body Shop with soaps and lotions, but that is just one part of the company's work. The Body Shop opposes animal testing, supports fair trade, and believes in protecting the planet. The company has several campaigns that defend human rights, including programs to stop child sex trafficking, prevent the spread of HIV, and address domestic violence.

In 2007, The Body Shop became the first retailer in the cosmetics and toiletries industry to use sustainably grown palm oil. Palm oil is a key ingredient in many widely used cosmetics and toiletries. Unsustainable production of this oil commonly involves cutting down rainforests to clear land for palm oil plantations. Such practices have taken a drastic toll on primary rainforests, particularly in Southeast Asia. The Body Shop worked for several years to introduce sustainable palm oil, and encouraged other manufacturers and retailers to stop using the unsustainably grown palm oil.

Palm oil plantations such as this one in Indonesia can harm rainforests. The Body Shop uses sustainably-grown palm oil.

---

that they could not otherwise afford. While some subsidies can promote unsustainable economic choices, such as increased reliance on nonrenewable fossil fuels, others can promote sustainable behaviors.

In Chile, for example, the price of crude oil increased significantly in 2003. During 2003 to 2006, bus fare increased because of these fuel prices. As a result, bus authorities provided bus transfers to poorer households to support them while public transport and fuel costs were high. In 2005, the Chile Solidario program began providing subsidies for families earning less than $350 per month. Forty percent of Chilean households were eligible. By providing these subsidies to poorer families, the country could prevent the consequences of rising transport costs (e.g., not being able to travel to work because of a lack of transportation options).[27]

Investing in Sustainability

Globalization has had a major impact on how people, governments, and companies make economic decisions. Now more than ever, there is a push for businesses to develop a more sustainable means of determining their profitability, one that includes consideration of externalities. Is a company that makes huge profits at the expense of the environment or its employees truly profitable? Does it contribute to prosperity? Triple bottom line accounting is one way to determine these kinds of profits.

Triple Bottom Line Accounting

A financial bottom line looks at how much a company has spent (outflow) over a certain period in relation to how much the company has made (income) over the same time frame. Very simply, if income is greater than outflow, the company has made a profit. If outflow is greater than income, the company has suffered a loss.

Triple bottom line accounting is a method that uses the three pillars of sustainability—economic, societal, and environmental health—to determine how well a business is doing. The three-pillar model of sustainability is built on the idea that sustainability not only allows us to maintain a flourishing environment, but can also help maintain a thriving economy and society. The three pillars are also sometimes referred to as people, planet, and profit. The goal of triple bottom line accounting is not only to improve a company's profits, but also to do so in a way that improves people's lives and the environment.

YOUTH PROFILE
Alejandro Velez and Nikhil Arora

Youth in the United States between the ages of 18 and 24 years old spend 30% of their monthly income on debt repayment.[28] At a personal level and for society as a whole, the accumulation of debt at a young age is not a sustainable path toward economic growth. Many young people lack knowledge about savings, loans, and debt that could help them avoid debt accumulation.

Biz Kid$ is a public TV series that teaches youth about financial literacy and economic concepts. The show features a number of teenagers and young adults who create their own businesses and make sustainable economic choices.

Alejandro Velez and Nikhil Arora, the founders of Back to the Roots, were featured

CAREER PROFILE   Economist

Economists are trained to predict trends in economies. They are scientists and mathematicians; they analyze data and statistics in order to evaluate where the market is and where it's likely to go. They may work in the private sector, advising businesses on how to act in a particular economic climate. They also work in universities where they research, teach, and publish their findings. Others work for governments as analysts and policy advisors to help predict trends and avoid possible economic depressions. Those who pursue degrees in economics can specialize in jobs related to finance, international trade, agriculture, law, and global development.

Meenakshi Rishi is an economist who teaches about international economic development.

Meenakshi Rishi is an associate professor of economics at Seattle University. She loved learning about economics in high school and college and decided to pursue a PhD in the subject. Her research looks at emerging markets in developing countries such as India and problems related to economic development. To Meenakshi, economics is primarily about common sense and making optimal decisions under conditions of scarcity. She wants her students to understand how international economics and politics are connected and how power and wealth are interrelated. In her classes, she attempts to show her students how economics applies to the real world.

Ultimately, Meenakshi believes that economists are "in the business of making the world a better place" and that meaningful economic research can strongly influence policy and social justice.

Alejandro and Nikhil received a $5,000 grant to start Back to the Roots, a business that supplies restaurants and grocery stores with gourmet mushrooms.

on Biz Kid$ because of a creative business idea they decided to pursue. When they were in their last semester at UC Berkeley, they learned that gourmet mushrooms could be grown from coffee grounds. They had the idea to turn the waste from coffee shops into economic gain by using coffee grounds that would otherwise be disposed of to produce mushrooms. Through experimentation, they learned how to grow oyster mushrooms in coffee grounds.

Soon after, they received a $5,000 grant from UC Berkeley to support their business venture. Alejandro and Nikhil became full-time mushroom farmers and founded the business Back to the Roots. They began supplying restaurants and grocery stores with gourmet mushrooms, then expanded and created grow-at-home mushroom kits that can now be found in Whole Foods stores across the country. Their mission is to create unique, enjoyable, and sustainable products for their customers. As Alejandro puts it, "We're really trying to prove you can operate a successful, profitable business and still take care of your community, environment, and stakeholders."[29]

WHAT YOU CAN DO   Economics

In the beginning of this chapter, you learned about how teenagers and young adults impact economic growth. When thinking about the economic decisions you make on a daily basis, consider how you can support economic sustainability for yourself and those around you.

- Evaluate your spending patterns for one month: Can you afford what you buy? If you borrow money, do you pay it back quickly?
- Support businesses that are environmentally sustainable and that build equity through good wages, employment, conditions, and benefits.
- Pay attention to economic trends by following the news.
- Watch the economic decisions your government makes.

You can evaluate your spending patterns when you shop by checking to see if you can afford what you buy.

POINT **COUNTERPOINT**

Is GDP a good measure of a country's well-being?

While some believe that GDP is a good way to measure a country's well-being, others believe it doesn't capture all of the necessary indicators that can truly improve people's standard of living.

POINT

Yes

- **Using the GDP as a starting point to measure a country's standard of living helps to provide an understanding of just how productive that country truly is.** As GDP increases, the economy grows; as the economy grows, the country is then able to provide more for its citizens.

- **The Great Depression demonstrated that we needed a tool to measure economic progress within a country.** GDP provides us a way to analyze economic stability and instability and to make important decisions that will improve economic growth. With economic growth, a country's economy can support more jobs, which can increase people's ability to obtain food, housing, and medical care.

COUNTERPOINT

No

- **GDP does not separate costs from benefits. While a country's GDP may be high, the factors contributing to this number could be of negative consequence to its citizens.** For example, rising health care costs may be difficult for families to afford; however, these rising costs actually boost GDP.[30]

- **While GDP measures the economic output of a country, it does not measure the amount of natural resources available to a country or the health, wealth, or well-being of its people.** Even if a country does well financially, economic wealth does not necessarily equate to improved quality of life. For example, the United States has one of the highest GDPs in the world, but it also offers some of the least amount of vacation time for its people.

Some people believe that using the GDP to measure a country's standard of living can help to understand the country's productivity.

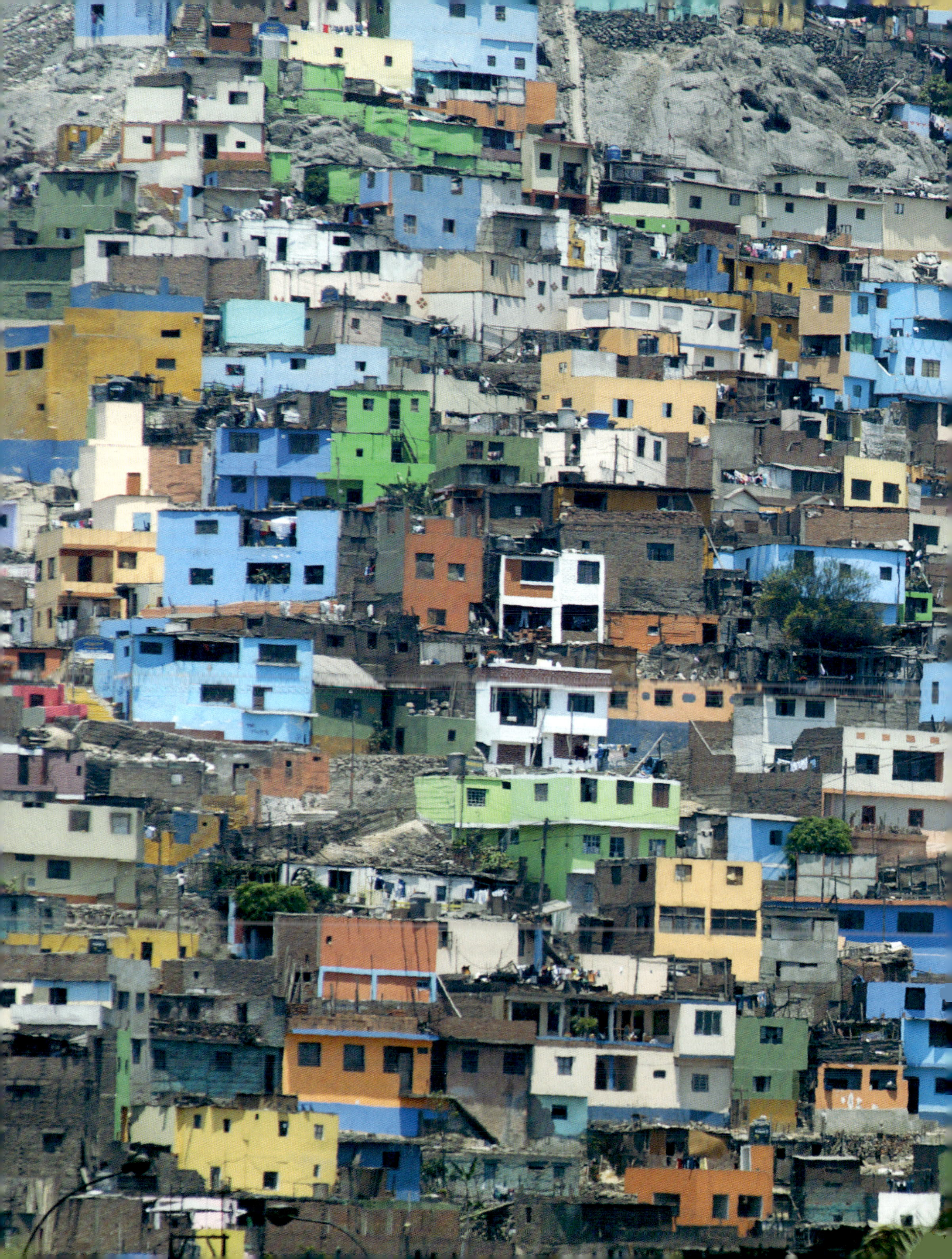

Chapter 20

Poverty

> **GUIDING QUESTIONS**
> - What factors contribute to poverty and the unequal distribution of resources?
> - What steps can individuals, organizations, and governments take to alleviate poverty?

Introduction to Poverty

Jill Paull was working as a hotel housekeeper when she realized two things: the cleaning products she used were making her sick and she wasn't earning enough to take care of her children. She decided to join a program called Washington CASH. This organization was founded to help people find a way out of poverty through loans and job training. After she joined, Jill began making and selling her own ecofriendly cleaning products that used natural ingredients like baking soda, lavender, and tea tree oil. It wasn't easy, but with support from the program Jill was able to grow her business. She remembers starting out with $5 in her business bank account. Now she is able to make a deposit every day. Washington CASH gave Jill the tools she needed to lift herself out of poverty.[1]

What is Poverty?

So, what exactly is poverty? According to the World Bank, **poverty** is a decrease in well-being when basic needs are not met. This condition arises when people have inadequate income, education, health, and shelter. Typically, economists measure poverty by looking at income. Those living on less than $1.25 per day in developing countries live in *extreme poverty*. You may be surprised to learn that around the world approximately 1.4 billion people live under these conditions.[2]

Take a look at the graph below.[3] You'll notice there are certain regions where a greater percentage of people live in poverty than others. You may wonder why these disparities exist and what is driving high poverty rates in certain areas of the world.

Part of the reason for the high rate of poverty in these regions is structural poverty. *Structural poverty* happens when the poor are unable to accumulate resources needed to rise out of their condition due to wider social and economic realities. For the most part, people living in structural poverty are born and raised in conditions of limited opportunity. As adults, they continue to live in poverty in what is known as the cycle of poverty. In other words, a child born in poverty is more likely to become an adult living in poverty and give birth to children who will live in poverty. Extreme poverty continues to be a serious challenge in the world today. Progress has been made in certain developing regions such as South Asia, but extreme poverty has increased in other areas like sub-Saharan Africa.

This chapter will introduce you to the realities of people living in poverty around the world, root causes of this global issue, reasons why people in certain areas are impacted more than others, and different kinds of solutions.

Who Lives in Poverty?

When thinking about poverty, it's helpful to understand there are different levels of poverty ranging from relative to extreme. *Relative poverty* occurs when a family's income level is below a certain proportion of the average national income.[4] For example, in 2012 the poverty line in the United States was defined at the income level of $23,050 for a family of four.[5] Keep in mind that the median income for a U.S family of four during this time was approximately $50,000.[6] While that may be a good deal of money in some places, it can represent financial strife for a family living

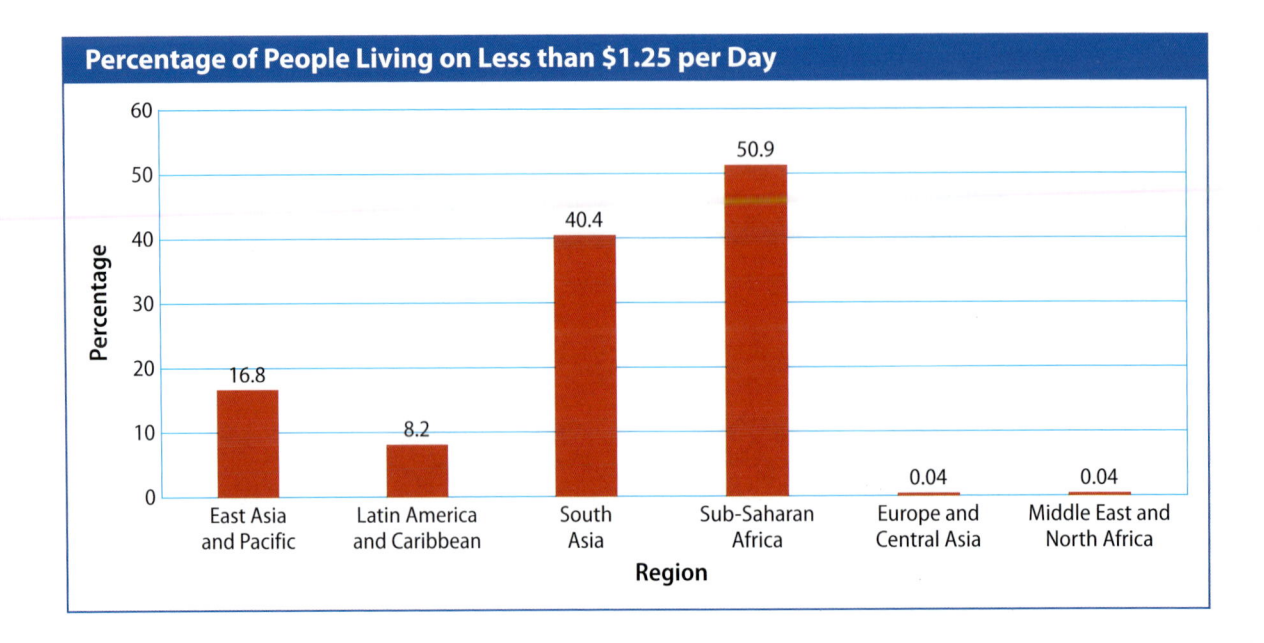

Percentage of People Living on Less than $1.25 per Day

Region	Percentage
East Asia and Pacific	16.8
Latin America and Caribbean	8.2
South Asia	40.4
Sub-Saharan Africa	50.9
Europe and Central Asia	0.04
Middle East and North Africa	0.04

in a U.S. city. This range of what constitutes poverty should be kept in mind when considering poverty from region to region.[7]

There are 37 million people living in relative poverty within the United States, but would you recognize one of these people if you saw her? Of these 37 million people, 43% own homes, 75% own a car, and 47% have their own personal computer. Despite owning material possessions, these people may struggle to buy groceries or gas to commute to work, or be unable to pay for heating and electricity.

The condition of *extreme poverty* is different from relative poverty and is an issue of utmost concern to the United Nations. The UN has developed targets for eliminating extreme poverty by 2015. When a family lives in this type of poverty, their inability to meet basic needs makes their survival uncertain. The extremely poor do not have reliable health care, shelter, or education and do not have access to safe drinking water or sanitation. In these cases, families must spend all their money on basic needs such as food, water, and shelter; no money is left over to pay for things like school fees, immunizations, or new clothes.

Only when incomes rise can families purchase other things that improve the quality of their lives. Even very small increases in income for extremely poor families in the developing world can improve lives. For example, a little extra income can allow a family to purchase bed netting or window screens to keep out disease-bearing mosquitoes. Mosquito nets cost $5 each and can reduce the incidence of malaria and other illnesses. Small investments can also help a family in poverty purchase clean-burning propane stoves to replace dangerous and polluting wood fires.[8]

How Poverty Is Measured

There are different ways countries and international organizations measure poverty. As previously discussed, one way to measure poverty is through income. Economic organizations and governments often use this measurement

Bangladeshi children play on a mud floor.

to decide how to provide aid and funding to poorer countries. Supporting those living in poverty through such aid relates to the idea of **economic development**, which is a concerted effort by policymakers and community members to promote economic health and a stable standard of living. There continues to be debate about whether aid from wealthier nations and institutions like the World Bank or the International Monetary Fund helps those living in poverty or if this aid actually increases debt in poorer countries.

In an effort to look beyond income when assessing poverty, the United Nations Development Program and Oxford University's Poverty and Human Development Initiative created another metric. The Multidimensional Poverty Index (MPI) measures poverty based on factors such as: if a family home has a dirt or dung floor, if family members have to walk more than 30 minutes to get clean drinking water, if a family lives without electricity, and if school-aged children are not enrolled in school.[9] These indicators are related to **human development**, the idea that people develop to their fullest potential and lead productive lives by fulfilling their needs and interests.[10] This type of development is about much more than the rise or fall of incomes. It is about creating a world in which all people have the opportunity to lead happy, healthy, creative lives.

Think about the kinds of things in your life that you consider essential. These may include such things as finishing school, finding a job, and having the freedom to make your own decisions in life. Those same things are considered essential for human development. The basic goals of human development are for people to live long and healthy lives, have access to education and a decent standard of living, and be able to make personal life decisions and participate in the life of the community. Without these aspects of human development, many opportunities in life are simply not available.

> *Children in poverty are less likely to have access to good health care. This inequity is even more pronounced between boys and girls.*

The way that poverty is measured can impact how international aid is distributed. For example, based on the traditional index of poverty (personal income), 40% of people in Ethiopia live in poverty. However, according to the Multidimensional Poverty Index, the number of Ethiopians living in poverty is 90%.[11] The amount of international aid given to Ethiopia may be different depending on which of these measurements of poverty is used.

Poverty and Sustainability

Society

Poverty affects health and education. Children in poverty are less likely to have access to good health care. This inequity is even more pronounced between boys and girls. When children do not have access to health care, they become more susceptible to diseases. They are also more likely to be malnourished, which can stunt their physical, intellectual, and emotional development. All of these factors can decrease the likelihood of receiving a quality education.[12] Studies have shown that employment increases with higher levels of education and that an individual's income can increase with more education.[13]

Life expectancy is another factor related to poverty. Life expectancy between different socioeconomic groups within the United States increased between the years of 1980 and 2000. Life expectancy improved for more affluent groups over the course of these two decades, but poorer groups did not share these gains.[14] The gap in life expectancy grew from less than 3 years between 1980 and 1982 to 4.5 years between 1998 and 2000.[15]

Additional studies have looked at the poorest counties in the United States. They found that life expectancy either stayed the same or declined by 1.3 years between 2000 and 2007. In five specific counties within Mississippi, women had lower life expectancies than people living in Honduras, El Salvador, and Peru.[16] This decrease in life expectancy is correlated to chronic diseases related to obesity, smoking, and high blood pressure.[17]

Seventy percent of the world's poor are women.[18] They have less access to education, health care, and employment and are often paid less than men. They are more likely to participate in insecure and unsafe work because of these social inequalities. However, there is a link between women's employment and economic growth. For example, if women were paid the same salaries as men, America's GDP would increase at least 9%.[19]

Environment

Poverty can have many environmental consequences. Poorer countries may need to extract and export scarce natural resources from their land in order to pay off debts they owe to international lending organizations like the World Bank. Mass extraction of natural resources can lead to environmental damage and reduce biodiversity and agriculturally productive land, increasing poverty in the long term.

Gold is an example of a scarce natural resource that is found in many developing countries. High demand for this resource frequently leads to large-scale mining operations. Gold mining has been happening in the region of Tarkwa in Ghana since the 19th century.[20] On October 16, 2001, a tailings dam burst at the Tarkwa Gold Mine, dumping a large quantity of mine waste into a nearby river. Many of the fish species in this river were found dead because of these toxins. Thousands of people were left without access to drinking water and were unable to produce or sell anything on the farms surrounding the river.[21] In this case, natural resource extraction had a negative effect on the livelihoods of the people in the community, rather than contributing to the community's economic growth.

The impacts of poverty on individuals within a society can be just as debilitating. Poverty can force people to cut down trees for wood and overuse farmlands for greater yields. While these types of actions can have short-term benefits, the long-term results may lead to increased poverty.[22]

Economy

Many countries that struggle with economic growth have high numbers of people living in poverty. Within these developing countries, people may start off living in rural areas. However, they may find themselves having to migrate to cities if they cannot find meaningful work. Changes to the rural economy, such as the transformation of small farms owned by individual farmers into larger farms owned by corporations, may also lead people to migrate to cities.

What many of these urban migrants don't expect is that poverty is often very high in the crowded cities where they seek work. Instead of finding employment to support their families, many of these migrants find themselves living in sub-standard housing, sometimes in dangerous situations.

CASE STUDY: Fabretto, Working to Alleviate Poverty

A major challenge in Nicaragua is poverty. Nicaragua is considered the second poorest nation in the Western Hemisphere, behind only Haiti. Many citizens of Nicaragua, especially those in rural areas, do not have access to adequate food, clean water, health care, education, and economic opportunities.

An organization working to change this is the Fabretto Children's Foundation. In 1948, Father Rafael Fabretto traveled to Nicaragua from Italy and was concerned about the number of poor children he encountered. He founded a group of children's homes in different parts of the country. His idea was to provide basic services (food, clothing, education) to children who were in high-risk situations. Today, Fabretto's foundation works to break the cycle of poverty by providing education, improved nutrition, health care, and other services to impoverished children and their communities in Nicaragua. The organization has seven centers throughout the country and also runs educational enrichment and teacher training programs in more than 50 public elementary schools.

These students in Nicaragua have benefitted from the work of Fabretto.

Known by many names, slums, favelas, and shantytowns are urban neighborhoods that house large numbers of poor people. These are often places where the cycle of poverty persists. Neighborhoods like these areas typically lack infrastructure such as sewer systems and electricity and many of their residents are unable to secure some of their most basic needs. Currently, more than half of the world's population live in cities.

Many people living in poverty within India's slums are forced to live without these basic needs. The Census of India defines a slum as a "compact area of at least 300 in population or about 60-70 households of poorly built, congested tenements in an unhygienic environment with inadequate infrastructure and lacking proper sanitary and drinking water facilities." Homes in a majority of these slums have only one room for many people, dirt floors, and poor ventilation. More than two-thirds of people living in slums do not have access to safe drinking water.[23]

By 2030, almost five billion people will live in cities. Cities designed to meet the needs of people from all socioeconomic backgrounds will be extremely important to economic and human development in coming years.[24] With such large populations living within urban areas, governments will want to address issues like reducing health risks, improving sanitation, improving living conditions in slums, and decreasing pollution. By preparing for these challenges now, people in cities all over the world will be better prepared to live sustainably and help people break the cycle of poverty.

Background on Poverty

Poverty affects a lot of people around the world today.

CASE STUDY: Agros International

Alleviating poverty in rural areas can also help to decrease the amount of people migrating to cities and falling into urban poverty. In countries like El Salvador, Guatemala, and Nicaragua, underemployment and unemployment are common in many rural areas, leading to urban migration. Agros International is an organization that understands this reality and works to provide those living in rural poverty with opportunities to free themselves from poverty. The organization helps families and communities purchase land through low-interest loans and provides assistance and training to help them to grow crops and launch agriculturally-based businesses.

Agros International's approach to sustainable development helps families by teaching them about:

- soil conservation and composting
- how to improve production of grain crops
- how to create effective local community government[25]

Sustainable economic and human development can break the cycle of poverty. Higher incomes provide the benefit of stabilizing population growth through lower fertility rates. Households with higher income and education levels tend to have fewer children, which means that they will be more likely to be able to afford education and health care for their children. These children will in turn be less likely to live in poverty as adults.[26]

Agros International supports sustainable development for families living in rural poverty.

- Approximately 28% of children in the developing world are undernourished or stunted from growth.
- Around the turn of the 21st century, one billion people were unable to read a book or sign their names.
- 1.1 billion people in developing nations don't have access to sanitized water.[27]

Why are so many people in the 21st century living in poverty? Was it always this way?

Looking Back at Poverty

Thousands of years ago, large divides between the wealthy and poor did not exist. Most people were poor, and no one was what you would consider rich.[28] Poverty during these times was mostly linked to hunger. Since there were not large supplies of food available, any disaster such as flood, drought, or warfare had an immediate impact. In ancient Athens between 403 and 323 B.C.E., for example, one in every six years was marked by food scarcity.[29]

During medieval times in Europe, the economy was dependent on agriculture. By the early 14th century, population growth started to deplete the amount of available agricultural land. This population increase, combined with a decline in the economy, social unrest, and severe winter weather, contributed to the Great Famine between 1315 and 1317 C.E.[30]

Food insecurity has been a major cause of poverty throughout history. Other factors contributed to poverty in certain societies as time progressed. For example, when empires began to expand throughout the world and the Age of Discovery (15th–17th centuries) introduced European countries to new lands in Latin America, Asia, and Africa, those in power looked for opportunities to expand their rule and increase profits. Between the early 15th and 19th centuries, European empires established new territories and began to use slaves.[31]

These empires participated in **colonization**, the act of establishing a population in new territory that maintains allegiance to the parent country. Those colonizing new land had advantages over the indigenous populations they encountered. Europeans had developed steel ships and weaponry that gave them military strength.[32] When Europeans came to these new territories, they also brought diseases with them that were new to indigenous populations and against which they had no defense. Smallpox and measles killed between 10 and 20 million indigenous people in the Americas.[33]

During this time, some countries also started importing slaves from other parts of the world. These slaves would participate in labor such as picking cotton from plantations, mining gold, and constructing railroads. Most slaves in Europe and its colonies came from Central and West Africa and were made to work under harsh conditions with no rights.

A second wave of colonization happened during the 19th and 20th centuries. European powers seeking continued economic expansion colonized and ruled more nations, mostly in Africa. Those in power had unequal economic, cultural, and territorial relationships with those they ruled over. During the height of colonialism in the late 1800s, Western powers like France, Portugal, England, and Spain ruled over 85% of the world's territory. This expansion was fueled by

King Leopold II was known for his brutal rule over the Belgium colony in the Congo during the 1800s.

the Industrial Revolution, which created a need for cheap labor, new markets, and raw materials. Industrialized countries sought to exploit these resources from colonized territories.[34]

As you can see, the reasons for poverty range from food scarcity to conflict and power struggles. Learning about the historical roots of poverty can help you to understand the state of global poverty today.

Poverty Today

Poverty in modern times is caused by a number of interrelated factors. Analyzing these root causes of poverty can help you understand why poverty exists and how it can be overcome.

The Legacy of Colonization

The impacts of colonization were devastating in places around the world. For instance, take the continent of Africa. Before developed countries dominated this region, 80% of the continent was ruled by local control. Then European nations began fighting for different parts of Africa. At the Berlin Conference held on November 15, 1884, they divided the continent into regions under the control of 14 different European countries. The division of the continent did not take into account the cultural and linguistic boundaries created by those already living in Africa. Instead, the colonizers drew new political boundaries.[35] Africans were brutally exploited and exposed to violence during these years of colonial rule.

By the time colonial powers withdrew from countries in Africa, Asia, and the Caribbean, the former colonies faced major instability. In many countries, creating effective governance under the new system left behind by colonial rulers was a challenge. For example, the country of Malawi also struggled to develop a strong economy in the face of widespread poverty. Other countries had to depend on foreign investments and loans in order to survive. When they could not afford to make payments on these loans, indebted countries were forced to pay added interest, putting them further into debt.

Many of the modern-day boundaries within Africa were created during European colonization.

Social Inequity and Discrimination

Social inequity can lead to increased poverty. This inequity can manifest itself as a lack of access to education, labor, and health care systems. Without access to these important services, individuals struggle to achieve a decent quality of life. In fact, those living in poverty are more likely to have a lower life expectancy.

Signs of inequality are visible in most countries. These inequalities can occur due to ethnicity, religion, gender, or even disability. When a member of a society does not have equal economic opportunities, this can lead to a power imbalance within a society. These impacts can be even greater when two or more identifiers combine (i.e., a woman who is a religious minority).

Looking at South Africa's history, you can see patterns of unequal wealth distribution. In fact, the country is considered to be one of the world's most unequal societies.[36] Ties with colonial exploitation and Apartheid led to discrimination against black Africans. Apartheid was a system of legal segregation in South Africa. During the time of Apartheid, black Africans did not have access to land rights, business ownership, or high-quality education. For years many were forced to migrate to parts of the country with poor-quality soil and little water.

Today widespread poverty and inequality still exist in South Africa. While the poorest 20% earn 2.3% of the country's income, the richest 20% earn 70%.[37] Even though South Africa is considered a middle-income country, 48% of its citizens live in poverty. This inequality has created challenges for the country. In contrast, countries that have a strong middle class—a sign of greater equality—have been shown to benefit from an increased national income, better infrastructure, and greater political stability.[38]

Weak Governance

Kofi Annan, former Secretary-General of the United Nations, said, "Good governance is perhaps the single most important factor in eradicating poverty and promoting development." Governance refers to employing power over a country's affairs at a number of levels.

CASE STUDY: Economic Progress in Botswana

When the country of Botswana in southern Africa gained independence from Britain in 1966, it was one of the poorest countries in the world. Life expectancy was 37 years, and there were only 12 kilometers (or less than 8 miles) of paved roads. Forty years later, in 2007, life expectancy had increased to 60 years and there were 7,000 kilometers of paved roads. The country is considered to have one of the world's fastest-growing economies since 1965.[39] These days, Botswana has been compared to upper middle class countries like Chile or Argentina. How did this landlocked country in Africa rise above poverty?

Botswana is mineral rich in diamonds, but this is not the main reason it has done so well. Good governance has directly contributed to stability, reduced poverty, and economic progress. Botswana's government has been known for its transparency (meaning it is accountable to the nation's citizens) and its vision to serve people and promote development. As a result, people have put trust in their government and the country has achieved a number of victories. For one, Botswana does not need much economic assistance from other countries; in fact, assistance is less than 3% of the national budget.[40]

Botswana was once one of the poorest countries in the world, but has made progress under practices of good governance.

Often, in times of war, men are called away from their families to become soldiers.

Good governance ensures that people from all socioeconomic backgrounds are given what they need to thrive within a society. A country that is politically stable and whose government allows its citizens a voice will have less poverty.[41] Additionally, when governments include those living in poverty in decision-making, the people themselves can be involved in eliminating poverty.[42] For example, when sufficient transportation options are available throughout a city, people can easily travel to find employment. However, if it's challenging to access roads to get to work, people may be unable to find jobs. In this situation, a government that encourages the participation of poor communities when making decisions about roads and transportation infrastructure can give those communities a way to eliminate a barrier keeping them in poverty.

Violent Conflicts

Conflict within countries can have detrimental effects, including an increase in the number of people living in poverty. Conflicts happen because of a number of factors such as weak governance and resource scarcity. When violent conflicts persist, a society's fabric, the ties that connect citizens with each other and with their government, starts to break down. As a result, during conflicts natural resources are often overexploited, land is destroyed, and human rights are not protected.

During wars, men are often called to become soldiers and are taken away from their families. Because men are typically the ones who contribute the most economically in their households and communities, the collective economic drain caused by their absence can impact sustainable development within a country. In fact, during times of conflict economies grow 1-2% slower than during times of peace. Conflict can also divert a country's financial resources away from development. Money is often used to support war activities rather than to support poverty reduction or to invest in a nation's infrastructure and its citizens' well-being.[43]

Male soldiers are not the only ones impacted by violent conflict; children and women's lives are also disrupted. For example, in the early 2000s during the civil war in Southern Sudan, approximately 200,000 women and children were enslaved.[44] In addition to other hardships, those abducted had no access to education or employment. Imagine the lasting impacts on a country's economy when children are unable to attend school for months, even years.

Governments can make decisions to help reduce conflict and the resulting poverty it brings. For example, after the Ugandan Civil War (1981-1986) the government decided it was important to lower the risk of conflict and reduce poverty. Through a number of measures, they were able to do so. They had learned that when soldiers reenter civilian society without receiving proper supporting resources, they are more likely to involve themselves in new conflicts. Therefore, the government provided financial and material assistance to soldiers who had finished their call of duty. Uganda's government also increased educational opportunities, created strong democratic policies such as the right to free press, and allowed local governments to make their own decisions. These efforts had positive impacts throughout the country for several years.[45]

Resource Scarcity

When you wake up in the morning and go to brush your teeth, you can probably turn on a faucet and get an endless flow of water. What would happen if this water was not so easily available and you had to walk miles to gather it? How would your life transform?

CASE STUDY: Decreasing Hunger in Brazil

The country of Brazil provides an example of how a national program can both fight hunger and decrease poverty. In 2003, Brazilian President Luiz Inácio Lula de Silva launched the Fome Zero (Zero Hunger) Program. The program's goal was simple: to give each Brazilian citizen the opportunity to have at least three meals a day. The Zero Hunger Program was made up of dozens of actions to eradicate hunger. The program aimed to create a national policy that would provide food security to millions of Brazilians who did not have enough money to purchase food. It included two goals: first, to increase immediate access to nourishment for those living below the poverty line; and second, to help people move out of poverty and take care of themselves in the future.[46] Through the program, water cisterns were put in semiarid areas to increase access to water. People were also educated about how to eat in healthy ways and taught about sustainable family farming practices.

By the end of de Silva's second term in 2010, 93% of children in Brazil and 82% of adults had access to three meals per day. Because of his dedication to fighting hunger in Brazil, de Silva won the World Food Prize in 2011. This award is given each year to individuals who advance human development by increasing the availability of food in the world.[47]

Farmers grow green beans at a Landless Worker's Movement settlement in Brazil.

In more impoverished countries, a flowing faucet is a dream, not an everyday reality. In some places, hardly any water comes from taps and children spend countless hours collecting water instead of attending school.[48] Lack of access to piped water is a major issue that can contribute to poverty in many developing countries. In some of the world's poorest countries, only 25% of the poorest households have access to piped water, compared to 85% of the wealthiest households. In the slums of Manila, the capital city of the Philippines, people pay 5-10 times more for water per unit than in wealthier areas.[49] That would be like paying $5-10 for a 20-ounce bottle of water in the United States.

Water scarcity is one type of **resource scarcity** that can contribute to poverty. Harsh climates, poor-quality soil, and inconsistent rainfall can also limit quality of life. Under these conditions it is difficult to grow enough food.[50] In turn, food and water scarcity have significant impacts on human and economic development. When people have to spend time meeting basic needs like food and water, they can't spend as much time engaged in educational or employment activities that could lift them out of poverty. Unless these issues are addressed, the cycle of poverty continues.

Debt in Developing Countries

Developing countries are countries that have a low level of economic development, low life expectancy, and high rate of poverty. There are a number of reasons developing countries might incur debt:

- Inheritance of debt from colonial governments
- Financial mismanagement
- Government corruption
- Loans from international lending organizations or developed countries

In an attempt to help these countries become more developed, wealthy governments and organizations like the *World Bank* and *International Monetary Fund (IMF)* have been providing loans to developing countries for several decades. Often, this aid comes with the

A young girl gathers water at a well.

requirement that developing countries follow certain trade policies such as growing crops for international export. The World Bank and IMF have promoted these policies through *structural adjustment programs (SAPs)*. Proponents believe this kind of aid can support countries in need. Critics believe these policies further push poor countries into debt.[51] As debt increases each year, poverty within indebted countries can increase as well.

Pathways to Progress: Poverty

Because poverty impacts many people in very different places, it's helpful to realize there are a variety of ways individuals, communities, governments, and international organizations can work to alleviate poverty. Different communities will no doubt require different solutions. Below are just a few examples of solutions, large and small, used to tackle poverty.

YouthBuild participants build a home in Washington D.C.

United States and has built over 21,000 units of affordable housing for people in 45 states. The program focuses on giving low-income youth the tools necessary to help rebuild their communities, pull people out of poverty, and improve their lives.[52]

Individuals and Communities

In 1978, Dorothy Stoneman was an educator in New York City. She asked youth in the city's East Harlem neighborhood how they would go about improving their community. They replied, "We'd rebuild the houses. We'd take empty buildings back from the drug dealers and eliminate crime." Out of this conversation a Youth Action Program was formed and young people began renovating housing in East Harlem. A few years later, the program grew into a citywide coalition that spread this model to other neighborhoods, providing education and job training skills for 20,000 youth in New York City.

The success of the program in East Harlem and a growing national demand for ways to involve youth in breaking the cycle of poverty led Dorothy Stoneman and Leroy Looper to cofound YouthBuild USA in 1990. YouthBuild now runs 273 programs throughout the

Social Entrepreneurship

Microcredit is the act of providing small amounts of money at low interest to people in poverty. This practice can be especially useful in places where many people live in poverty. Muhammad Yunus was born in 1940 in Bangladesh. He was the third of 14 children. While his dad pushed him to get an education, his mother taught him about helping the poor. Muhammad grew up to become an economics professor. After a trip with his students to a poor village, he realized that providing small loans (such as $100) had the potential to help lift people out of poverty.[53]

Inspired by this idea, Muhammad Yunus helped establish the Grameen Bank in 1983 to provide loans to poor Bangladeshis. Since its inception, the bank has loaned money to more than seven million people.[54] As with any form of credit, borrowers pay back the money they are loaned with interest. Due to the limited financial means of those living in poverty, these loans are usually quite small. However, they can allow poor people to make investments that would otherwise be out of reach, such as starting or expanding a small business. For example, the money might be used to buy materials for a store that sells basic household supplies or to buy a pot and ingredients to sell snack foods on the street.

National Governments

Governments can improve economic growth in a number of ways. The government of China has undertaken efforts over the last several decades to reduce poverty throughout the country. One specific program that made a significant impact was the 8-7 National Poverty Reduction Program. The program aimed to lift 80 million poor people above the government poverty line during a span of seven years (1994-2000). This large-scale reduction in poverty was made possible through a number of initiatives:

- Assisting poor households with land improvement
- Increasing cash crop and livestock production
- Providing townships with roads
- Improving access to drinking water in poor villages
- Providing universal primary education and basic preventative health care[55]

According to the World Bank's measure of poverty, the number of poor people in China

---

CASE STUDY: Investing in Unity

In 2003, Jessica Jackley and Matt Flannery were newly engaged and living in Palo Alto, California. He wrote computer software and she worked at the Stanford Business School. One day, Jessica invited Matt to listen to a speech given by Muhammad Yunus. Influenced by Yunus and the idea of microfinance, the two cofounded the organization known as Kiva.

Kiva means unity and agreement in the language of Swahili. The mission of the organization is to connect people globally through lending in order to alleviate poverty. People anywhere in the world can lend amounts as small as $25 in order to help others start a business. Kiva works with over 59 countries and has given over $222 million in microcredit loans that have helped people finance small business ventures ranging from running a beauty salon and selling clothing to selling food at markets.[56]

Through Kiva, people have given those living in poverty opportunities to purchase mosquito nets, locks for their doors, sugar for their tea, and education for their children. Meeting these basic needs can help to alleviate poverty in the long term.[57]

A loan of $825 through Kiva helped this young woman purchase a piping machine, fabrics, and accessories for her sewing services in the Philippines.

CAREER PROFILE: Education Coordinator

Becoming a teacher doesn't have to mean you will spend all your time back in school. One teaching career outside the classroom is the job of education coordinator. These teaching specialists design programs, develop budgets, and teach programs in the service of a particular organization. Education coordinators have great communication skills, as they are responsible for teaching, supervising teachers, and securing funding and resources for the programs they develop. They usually have a bachelor's degree in a field related to the organization's work and often a Master's in Teaching to support their work administering programs.

Todd Montgomery serves as the Manager of Adult Education at Heifer International, a nonprofit that donates livestock (e.g., sheep, ducks, chickens, and cows) to people struggling in poverty around the world. Livestock can serve as a source of nutrition and income for families. At Heifer Ranch, the organization's working farm in Arkansas, Heifer offers programs that educate people about the causes of hunger and poverty.

Todd used to believe "like a lot of people do, that certain people were poor because they were lazy or unintelligent." He developed a new perspective through exposure to people of different backgrounds around the world and through volunteer work with Heifer International as a college student. Todd learned that intelligence and a good work ethic is "evenly spread throughout the world," but resources are not so evenly spread. Now he teaches people that global hunger and poverty are connected to choices we all make every day. "Educating the public here in the U.S. and abroad about the causes of hunger and poverty and the necessary steps to overcome them is the only sustainable way to end these problems once and for all," he says. One of Heifer's cornerstones is the idea of "passing on the gift." This means sharing your talents, resources, and ideas with others.

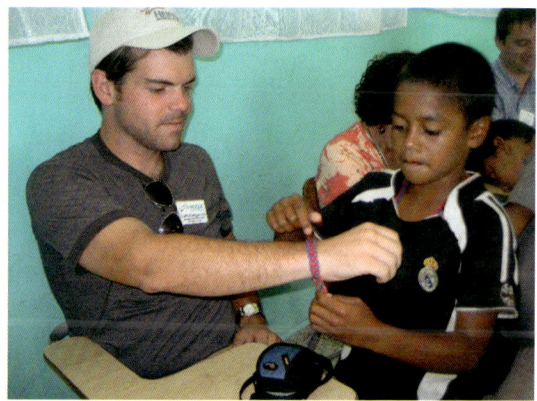

Todd Montgomery spends time in Honduras through his work with Heifer International.

---

has decreased from 490 million to 88 million over the course of 20 years.[58] Poverty reduction programs have played a part in this dramatic decrease in poverty.

The Millennium Development Goals

International collaboration between governments and organizations can significantly impact global poverty. The Millennium Development Goals (MDGs) were created in order to target specific international development goals including eradicating extreme poverty, reducing child poverty, and fighting epidemics like AIDS. These goals were adopted by 192 United Nations members and over 23 international organizations who pledged to work collaboratively to reduce global poverty and suffering.

One major goal is to cut in half the number of people living in poverty by 2015. In order to focus efforts to meet the MDGs, the United Nations created an MDG Acceleration Framework in 2010 to help countries create their own action plans for poverty reduction.

Since the MDGs were created, there have been a number of success stories. For example, Nicaragua reduced its hunger rate by more than half, from 52% to 21%. Kenya enrolled two million more students in school by eliminating school fees.[59] Worldwide, the number of people in poverty has slowly decreased. In 1990, there were 1.8 billion people living below the poverty line; in 2005, this number was 1.4 billion.[60]

Foreign Aid

Foreign aid for poor countries is a controversial topic, as you read earlier. There are ways that foreign aid can help countries rise out of poverty. In the last 50 years, aid has had success in different regions, especially when it is part of a global effort with tangible goals. Specific interventions have proven to be successful: microfinance, electricity generation, cell phone and Internet access, and health improvements.

Effective interventions use low-cost technology, they are easy to deliver, they have clear goals (like polio eradication) rather than vague ones (like economic growth), and they are multilateral. Multilateral aid means that aid is given from a number of governments, international agencies, and private individuals and organizations.[61]

The Private Sector

Businesses and corporations can also play a large role in helping to alleviate poverty. For example, the Coca-Cola Company has done research to produce a drink that can provide micronutrients to help prevent malnutrition among those living in poverty. Hewlett-Packard has partnered with international nongovernmental organizations and the Grameen Bank in Bangladesh to provide HP products and services to the poor. Pharmaceutical companies and biomedical institutes have researched new drugs that could prevent diseases common to poor countries, such as malaria. These types of private initiatives happen when businesses take people into consideration when making decisions about company objectives.[62]

WHAT YOU CAN DO: Poverty

As stated earlier, there are a number of solutions to global poverty ranging from individual to multilateral action. Wondering how to get involved? Here are some ideas:

- Support businesses that demonstrate support for communities where they work. This kind of support by businesses may take the form of providing employees with livable wages, healthy and safe working conditions, and benefits such as insurance or health services.

- Volunteer with homeless shelters, food banks, and other social service organizations that help reduce poverty in communities.

- Learn about organizations working to fight global poverty and campaign with them to raise awareness, lobby for poverty relief efforts, or fundraise to support specific development projects.

Youth volunteers at a Red Cross Service Center serve meals to flood victims.

POINT | **COUNTERPOINT**

Should the debt owed by developing countries be canceled?

The debate on whether developing countries should have to continue paying debts they have incurred over time has been a controversial one. The following thoughts are taken from Debatepedia, an online forum of the International Debate Education Association.

POINT

Yes[63]

- "Debt forces countries to produce 'cash crops' that don't help famine. In order to raise the cash for debt repayments, poor countries have to produce goods which they can sell around the world. Often this means growing so-called 'cash crops' such as coffee, instead of food to support their population. People in fertile countries can find themselves starving, as they cannot afford to buy the food which then has to be bought from other countries, while their own fields produce coffee for the developed world."

- "Poor countries need a fresh start with debt cancellation. While the economies are dominated by the need to repay debt, it is impossible for them to truly invest in infrastructure and education, sowing the seeds for development in the future. By cancelling debt, we would give them a fresh start, and the opportunity to build successful economies which would supply the needs of generations to come."

COUNTERPOINT

No[64]

- "Debt usually cannot be attributed as the cause of deaths in poor countries. There are many reasons for the current problems in the world's poorest nations; often they also have heavy debt burdens, but the debt is not necessarily the cause of the problems. Many countries spend huge amounts of money on weapons in order to fight local wars, instead of investing in their people. Many are led by dictators, or other corrupt governments, whose incompetence or greed are killing their own population. The money to pay for healthcare and social programs at the same time as repaying debt may well exist, but it is instead being wasted in other areas."

- "Famine is the result of many things, not just debt. Again, there are many potential causes for starvation—famines are caused by war or by freak weather conditions, not by debt. While growing cash crops can seem to be counter-intuitive, the money they bring in helps to boost the country's economy. The idea that a nation could and should be self-sufficient is outdated; if (for example) a country is well-suited to growing coffee, it should grow coffee, and buy food crops (for example corn, or wheat) from other countries suited to growing them."

Two young refugees in the country of Kosovo carry bread for their family.

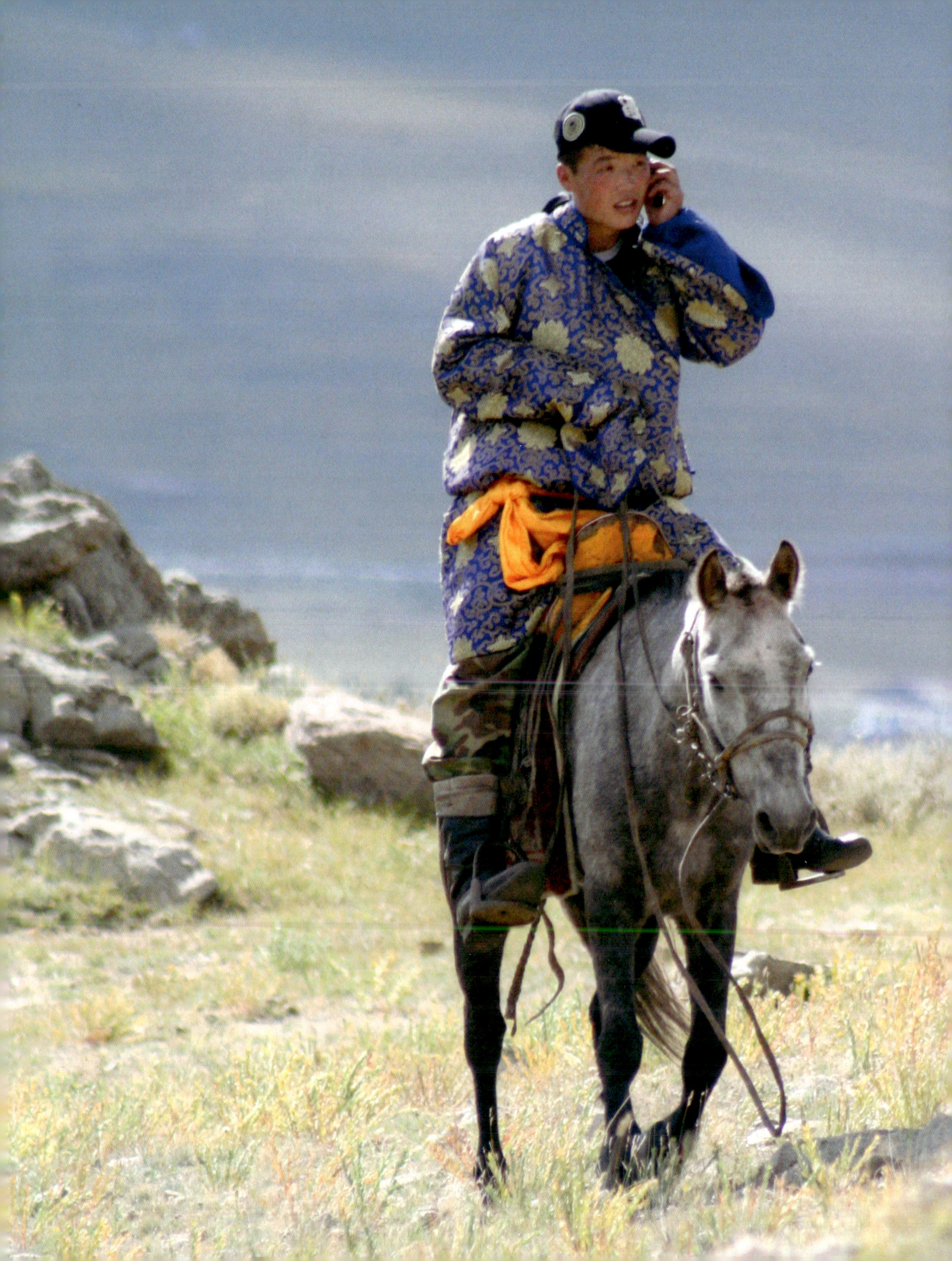

Chapter 21
Globalization

> **GUIDING QUESTIONS**
> - What are benefits and drawbacks of economic globalization?
> - How can we live sustainably in an increasingly globalized world?

Introduction to Globalization

Hip-hop was born in New York City during the 1970s. Elements of hip-hop culture include rapping, DJing, break-dancing, and graffiti art. Although hip-hop originated in the United States, you can find it all over the world, in places like South Africa, Germany, Brazil, and Japan. Some hip-hop artists in different countries have used music as a political tool to voice their opinions on global issues such as poverty and inequity. How does music and art from one part of the world reach other places? Understanding globalization will help you to understand this trend.

Young Soldiers are a hip-hop group from South Africa.

While globalization is a fairly new word, this phenomenon has been happening for thousands of years. You'll learn in this chapter how globalization is connected to economics and how globalization can impact culture, language, and ideas.

When you start looking, you'll find that signs of cultural globalization are everywhere. Sushi and karaoke, originating in Japan, can be found in most parts of the world. American blue jeans are popular in Germany. And while most countries have a national cuisine, it is not unusual to find an increasing variety of international food available in major cities around the globe. Signs of economic globalization are everywhere too.

There are some questions that we can ask to investigate how globalization relates to sustainable development:

- Is increasing globalization inevitable? Is it sustainable?
- If it isn't sustainable, how can it be made sustainable?

What Is Globalization?

According to the United Nations, **globalization** is "the reduction and removal of barriers between national borders in order to facilitate the flow of goods, capital, services and labour."[1] In other words, globalization is the increasing ease with which countries can do business with each other. Globalization is what makes it possible for an exchange student from the United States to go to Italy and use a debit card at an Italian ATM to retrieve money from a U.S. bank account.

You can also see the effects of globalization in the clothing industry. Clothes you are wearing right now might illustrate the process of globalization. Most clothing items have a tag that says where they were made. For example, your T-shirt might bear a label that says "Made in Singapore." But this may only be part of the story. Most garments have a complex past and the label of your shirt may not capture the entire history of where it has been before it reached you.

To help consumers understand the history of their clothes, the outdoor clothing company Patagonia created Footprint Chronicles. These chronicles paint a portrait of how globalized a single shirt can be. While it may be spun, knitted, and dyed in one country, the shirt could be cut and sewn in another country, and then finally distributed in yet another one.

The clothes you are wearing now may also have a much more complex globalized history than you know.

Used garments provide fabric patches for the repairs department at the Patagonia Distribution Center in Reno, Nevada.

Globalization and Sustainability

Globalization has benefits and costs. As we will see throughout this chapter, the impacts of globalization have not been distributed equally around the world. Today's globalized world is made up of a web of international connections related to the environment, trade, culture, media, human rights, technology, and many other global issues.

Economy

In terms of economics, it is hard to say whether globalization has an overall positive or negative impact. It can be very efficient to have a global economy. In the previously discussed example of the Patagonia clothing company, goods are produced using raw materials and labor from many countries. Workers at Patagonia's sewing factory in Mexico are paid less than their U.S. counterparts would be, but still make about three times more than the minimum wage where they live.[2] Lower wages in Mexico keep the price of the shirt lower for U.S. consumers and the company provides good jobs for Mexican workers.

There can be negative consequences to globalized production, too. When U.S. companies look outside their national borders for cheaper labor, U.S. manufacturing plants are often shut down and people lose jobs.

Environment

The seafood industry provides another example of how globalization and sustainability intersect. In the 1990s, the United States wanted to protect sea turtles by banning the import of shrimp that were caught without turtle excluder devices (these devices, attached to shrimp nets, allow turtles that are accidentally caught to escape). Turtles caught in shrimp nets had become a big problem and the turtle population was at risk. However, the U.S. ban was overturned in 1998 by the World Trade Organization, a body that governs trade among nations. Shrimp fishers in the Southeast Asian countries most affected

A U.S. ban of imported shrimp caught without sea turtle excluder devices was overturned in 1998 by the WTO.

by the ban could not afford the devices and the countries claimed the ban would adversely affect their economic growth.[3] This brings up several critical questions:[4]

- How can you balance environmental protection and economic development?
- Whose responsibility is it to decide how to balance the environmental and economic impacts of international trade policies?
- What are the roles and responsibilities of richer, more developed nations in respect to poorer, less developed countries in international trade agreements?

Society

There is substantial evidence to suggest that embracing a global economy could increase a country's trade, income, and quality of life. According to Gary Clyde Hufbauer of the Peterson Institute for International Economics (an organization that researches global economic policies), countries that have increased their per capita Gross Domestic Product (or the average income) in the 20th century all have one thing in common: they actively participate in the global economy.[5]

CASE STUDY: Globalization of the Banana

Think of how common bananas are in our lives—there's banana pudding, banana bread, even banana-flavored candy. Before the 1900s, bananas were not a popular product within the United States. But by 1910, three billion bananas were being imported to the United States each year. In the 1950s, students in classrooms throughout the country watched "Journey to Bananaland," a film used by fruit companies to promote the sale of bananas.[11]

Increasing demand for bananas in the United States and other places around the world gave countries in the Caribbean and Central America an incentive to grow more bananas. Major fruit companies were able to increase banana production by clearing rainforests in Latin America, creating transportation networks that allowed bananas to travel easily across borders, and using technology that helped to control the ripening of the fruit. Fruit companies created entire towns around banana plantations. Many countries producing bananas were reliant on this one export to support economic growth, so they cooperated with fruit companies and agreed to lower wages for their workers.

In some places, this dependency on the export of bananas led to the destruction of small farms in favor of banana plantations. As a result, farmers grew fewer local crops and many had only one place to turn for employment—the banana plantation. The Los Alamos plantation in Ecuador, for example, supplies 25% of bananas imported to the United States. This 3,000-acre plantation has 1,300 employees. Workers have frequently mobilized against low wages and human rights abuses. The Los Alamos plantation is one example of what can happen in a race to the bottom.[14]

Increased banana sales have placed a demand on countries that grow bananas.

Another result of a global market is more competition between countries to attract business. This can result in a *race to the bottom*, a phrase coined by U.S. Supreme Court Justice Louis Brandeis in the first part of the 20th century.[6] The term refers to the practice of relaxing health, safety, environmental, or other standards and regulations in order to make a region or a country more appealing to foreign businesses and investors.

One example of the race to the bottom is the practice of shipping electronic waste (e-waste) to countries where there are no laws in place to protect those who recycle the toxic materials. Residents of wealthy developed countries are disposing of technology such as computers and cell phones at increasingly faster rates. People in Britain dispose of 100,000 tons of e-waste per year, including televisions, computers, and cell phones. Most of that waste is shipped to other countries where it is recycled or left in a landfill. Some of this e-waste from England has ended up in West Africa in countries like Nigeria and Ghana.[7]

Many people try to be responsible and take their used electronics to a specialized recycling facility. Yet sometimes these facilities are willing to break international export laws and sell items, especially computer monitors, overseas for scavengers to pick apart (a process known as informal recycling). The workers doing the recycling are exposed to extremely hazardous materials, many times with absolutely no protection. They are willing to do the work because it pays better than other, safer jobs.[8] Workers involved in informal recycling in locations as diverse as Ghana and Pakistan may not even know that these materials are dangerous to handle without protective equipment.[9] Improperly disposing of e-waste can be harmful to the health of the environment in these countries, too; toxic pollution and environmental damage are hazards faced by e-waste importers.[10]

Background on Globalization

International business and global relations are as old as trade itself. It's only the term globalization that's new. Throughout time, technology has enabled people to trade and interact over great distances. Seaworthy boats, air travel, computers, cell phones and the Internet are only a few of the technologies that have resulted in the expansion of the global marketplace. Think how much easier things would have been for Christopher Columbus if he had been able to pull up Google Maps on his cell phone in the middle of the Atlantic Ocean! Can you imagine what technologies will be developed in the next five hundred years to bring people around the world even closer together?

Cross-cultural and Transboundary Trading

In ancient times, spices were as valuable as gold and silver. Used for everything from flavoring food to treating illness to paying rent, spices such as pepper, ginger, cloves, nutmeg, and cinnamon were rare and desirable. The search for spices went hand in hand with increasing global trade. Four thousand years ago, the spice trade led to the development of many trade routes and the establishment of distribution centers.

These new trade routes brought Western cultures and Eastern cultures into contact with each other. Traders brought pepper and cloves from India, cinnamon and nutmeg from the Spice Islands, and amber and ginger from China to the markets of Egypt, Persia, and Rome. There were fortunes to be made from the spice trade.

The Vikings offer another example of the beginnings of globalization. The Vikings became prominent international traders toward the end of the 8th century B.C.E. They were very skilled sailors and used this skill to travel to other countries and trade for things that they could not get or produce at home. Scandinavian countries at that time were heavily forested and, as today, very mountainous. Viking traders took items that they could easily produce, such as hides, fur, and ivory, to Europe, Russia, and even Asia to trade for goods such as wine, textiles, pottery, and glassware.[13]

In the 19th and 20th centuries, the introduction of powered ships, trains, and vehicles all helped to revolutionize economic exchange and increase the speed and efficiency of trade.[14]

Thousands of years ago, the spice trade increased the number of trade routes and distribution centers around the world.

As the use and sophistication of technology has increased, so has the pace and extent of globalization. The innovations of the last 50 years have made new kinds of global interconnections possible. For instance, people can email and video conference with friends and colleagues across the world.

Globalization and the New Global Economy

The Ripple Effect

As countries become more and more economically interconnected through trade, they also become more connected to events that occur in other countries. As shown in the graph below, the United States has the world's largest economy with a gross domestic product (GDP) of $15.7 trillion.[15] This position allows the U.S. economy to have a substantial influence on the global markets. When the U.S. housing market crashed in 2008, it caused a ripple effect throughout the world.

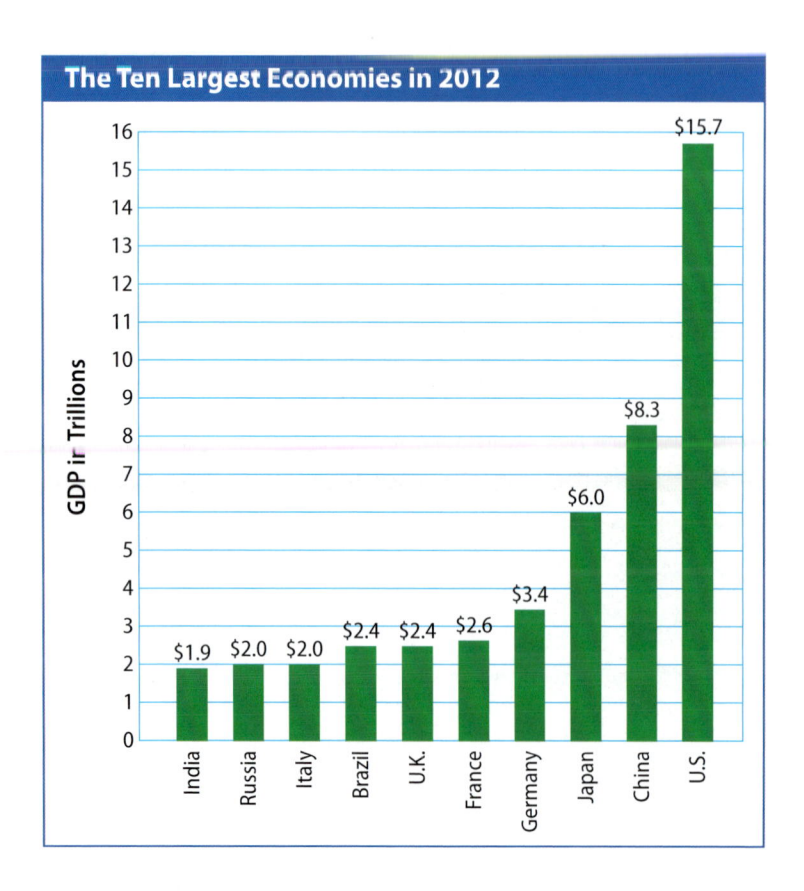

The housing crash created a virtual lockdown on credit, which meant that Americans had less money to spend on imported goods. These events in the United States caused a slowdown of the global economy and triggered similar housing and credit crises in other countries.[16]

Tariffs and Imports

Not all nations are keen to trade with others. Sometimes nations impose tariffs to protect national industries, local employment, and regional control of natural resources. Sometimes nations impose tariffs on imported goods to encourage citizens within their borders to buy domestic products. A **tariff** is the fee (like a tax) a government imposes on imports or exports. In other words, companies or individuals have to pay for the privilege of doing business in other countries.

One catalyst of today's growing economic globalization was the *General Agreement on Tariffs and Trade (GATT)*, designed to reduce tariffs among countries. Signed by 23 countries in 1947, this agreement was the result of efforts by the United States and the Allied forces to promote international trade after World War II. GATT nations lowered trade barriers and tariffs, making it easier for them to buy and sell goods across their borders. Eventually, more than 100 countries signed the agreement. GATT was replaced by the *World Trade Organization (WTO)* in 1995.[17]

The example of global banana trade was discussed earlier in the chapter. In 1993, the *European Union (EU)* decided to impose a tariff on banana producers in Latin America. At the same time, former European colonies in Africa and the Caribbean were exempted from the tariff due to their ties to countries now in the EU. Latin American countries like Ecuador complained about these tariffs to the World Trade Organization and a series of trade disputes known as the Banana Wars began.

The Ten Largest Economies in 2012

Country	GDP in Trillions
India	$1.9
Russia	$2.0
Italy	$2.0
Brazil	$2.4
U.K.	$2.4
France	$2.6
Germany	$3.4
Japan	$6.0
China	$8.3
U.S.	$15.7

The United States got involved to protect the interests of U.S.-run companies that were some of the largest banana producers in Latin America. In 2009, the EU finally decided to sign an agreement with banana producers in Latin America that would cut tariffs on bananas. With tariffs lowered, the market offered Latin American countries the opportunity to compete fairly with other countries in Africa and the Caribbean.[18]

Governance and Policies

The World Trade Organization (WTO) governs trade rules among countries. The WTO provides guidance to help countries settle their trade disagreements. According to the WTO, it provides the following benefits:[19]

1. It helps promote peace by building international confidence and cooperation through fair systems of trade.

CASE STUDY: The European Union

In the years immediately after World War II, Europe was very fragmented. It was a time for rebuilding. In 1950, French Foreign Minister Robert Schuman proposed the establishment of the European Coal and Steel Community (ECSC). This "community" would place the production of coal and steel in Europe under one common authority in order to maximize profits, unlike the previous system in which each nation acted independently. The idea was that all nations could increase their profits by coordinating production rather than competing with each other.[20]

A common market was established in 1957. The six nations that comprised this market—known as the European Economic Community—were Belgium, France, Germany, Italy, Luxembourg, and the Netherlands. The European Union officially formed in 1993, transforming Europe into a free trade area. A common European currency, the Euro, was introduced in 2002. Today, the European Union consists of 27 member countries. By combining their economies, these countries created a larger, more powerful regional economy with greater global importance than any one EU country would have on its own.[21]

The establishment of the single market is one of the greatest achievements of the European Union. In essence, it has removed barriers to trade and free competition among member countries. In order to achieve this single market, the EU had to develop common taxation methods and implement technological standards such as telephone system requirements.

The EU faces new challenges today. Not all EU members have equally strong national economies.

The European Union is an economic and political union of 27 countries.

2. It handles disputes constructively through a set of rules that all countries are required to conform to.
3. It reduces inequalities between countries and makes life easier by giving equal rights to all.
4. It supports freer trade, which leads to a lower cost of living.
5. It allows increased imports that give consumers a greater choice of products and services.
6. It supports lowered trade barriers, which increases trade and incomes.
7. It stimulates economic growth and job creation through increased trade.
8. It increases the efficiency of the global economy by promoting an international division of labor and optimal distribution of resources, as well as offering standardized and simplified trade rules.
9. It protects governments from the lobbying of specialized interest groups by focusing on all sectors of the economy.
10. It encourages good government by holding countries accountable for their commitments, emphasizing transparency, and limiting opportunities for corruption.

A billboard in Uganda speaks to the dangers of corruption.

The WTO is a membership-based organization. As of today, there are over 150 member countries.

WTO trade policies have had positive and negative impacts on countries. Some WTO policies benefit people by protecting inventions and original creations. For example, when the Bangladeshi rock band Miles realized that a popular song they had written had been placed on a Hindi movie soundtrack in India without their permission, they decided to bring the issue to court. Reproducing this song without payment was a violation of intellectual property rights recognized by the WTO. Since both India and Bangladesh became members of the WTO in 1995, both were supposed to comply with the WTO's rules governing intellectual property. After hearing Miles' case, the judge ruled that the song must be removed from the soundtrack.[22]

On the other hand, some people have suffered as a result of liberalized trade policies. Certain WTO trade policies helped eliminate tariffs on imports, which benefits foreign markets but hurts local competition. As low-cost foreign goods enter a country, local businesses may not be able to compete with these cheaper imports. Haitian farmers experienced this phenomenon during the 1990s. Before the 1990s, local farmers were the main producers of rice in Haiti. However, with new trade policies, the amount of rice imported into Haiti increased and the local rice industry suffered as a result.[23]

Many critics have spoken out about the negative impacts of WTO policies, especially for poor countries. When the World Trade Organization met in Seattle, Washington on November 30, 1999, over 40,000 people demonstrated against the organization and the outcomes of its policies which protesters claimed exploited poorer countries, outsourced American jobs, wreaked environmental degradation, and put a downward pressure on living wages around the world. A number of different organizations, both national and international, protested against WTO policies that they considered unfair and not protective of labor and environmental standards.

Globalization Today

As you can see, globalization presents both benefits and challenges for economies, societies, and environments.

Connecting Individuals

Information access is at an all-time high. Technology that was unheard of 50 years ago is now available to the masses. Today's teenagers, for example, rely heavily on cell phones for everything from Internet access to text messaging with friends. Consider the following 2010 statistics on global digital communications and how much the world has changed since then:[24]

- There were 1.88 billion email users worldwide (25% of the world's population), an increase of 480 million (more than a 50% increase) from the previous year.
- There were 2.9 billion email accounts worldwide, 25% of which were business accounts.
- As of December 2010, there were 255 million English websites, 21.4 million of which were added in 2010.
- 2 billion videos were watched on YouTube each day.
- There were more than 5 billion estimated cell phone users around the world.

Cell phones are a major contributor to mobility around the globe. In addition to being able to talk from almost anywhere, users can send and view pictures and videos, access the Internet, and purchase products using their phones. Cell phones have been close to miraculous in many developing African countries with minimal infrastructure and for many people have quickly become their most valued possession. Many developing countries do not have a national telephone system, so cell phones allow them to stay connected where no connection was previously possible. Cell phone technology has also been mobilized globally to help disaster victims by allowing users to make charitable donations via text message and helping coordinate aid efforts. When there was flooding in the Phillipines in 2012, citizens and government agencies were able to access social media outlets using their cell phones to spread information around for relief efforts.[25]

While abroad, a soldier is able to video chat with his family back home using the latest technology.

Economic Efficiency

The theory of **comparative advantage** proposes that two countries, regardless of their development status, can benefit from a division of labor through trade.[26]

For example, Country X is equally able to produce toothbrushes and cooking pots. Country Z can produce toothbrushes four times more effectively than it can produce cooking pots. To make the most of its comparative advantage, Country Z should only focus on producing toothbrushes, and stop making cooking pots. Country Z can begin to trade with Country X for cooking pots. Country X can shift some of its production of toothbrushes to cooking pots to benefit from increased trade with Country Z.

The comparative advantage theory applies only when there are few or no trade barriers in place. The reduction of trade barriers through globalization can allow countries to specialize in particular industries and maximize the efficiency of their economies. However, the specialization of economies can also be part of creating instabilities and imbalances in labor and national self-sufficiency.

Rising Standards of Living

Supporters of globalization contend that it raises the standard of living in developing countries. When people in developed countries invest in developing countries (which may be able to make those toothbrushes much more cheaply), the hope is that this money will go toward improvements in infrastructure such as roads, buildings, and telecommunications. The result is a higher standard of living for all people in the developing country.[27]

In addition to supporting the expansion of infrastructure, foreign investment in developing countries often creates manufacturing jobs.

A young Afghani girl smiles while at school. Some believe globalization may help improve the standard of living in developing countries.

While these jobs may not always seem appealing to workers in developed countries, factory jobs may be highly coveted in places where the alternative could be scavenging recyclable materials from the garbage dump. Sweatshops conjure up a bad image—and rightfully so, since they exploit people for low wages, often with inadequate precautions for workers' health and safety. However, Nicholas Kristof, an American journalist and frequent commentator on human rights, argued in an opinion piece for *The New York Times* that "the central challenge in the poorest countries is not that sweatshops exploit too many people, but that they don't exploit enough."[28] He claims that in some cases sweatshop manufacturing jobs offer cleaner, safer working conditions than the available alternatives. Closing down sweatshops would eliminate these jobs and force people to take jobs with worse conditions or face the prospect of no job at all. How might globalized economies be more equitably designed to benefit a larger number of the world's people?

Spread of Ideas

Perhaps one of the biggest advantages of globalization is the spread of ideas. Not only does globalization give people a chance to benefit financially through trade, but it also allows people in all parts of the world to learn about ideas from other places. Concepts that are commonplace in one country can spread around the world, aided by access to stories and images of people in distant places. Values related to human rights, democracy, and health have spread and begun to influence new policies made on these topics. The entertainment industry contributes to this spread of ideas through movies, music, and publications that are easily accessed via the Internet in many different countries.

With more and more global accountability, it is harder for crimes against people to go unnoticed. WITNESS, for example, is an organization that partners with human rights organizations to teach people how to document and share human rights abuses.[29] Examples of such videos have included the documenting of:

- Juvenile justice issues in the United States
- Internally displaced people in Burma
- Educational rights for Romani children in Bulgaria

The Impacts of Multinational Corporations

As globalization has expanded trade and helped spur economic growth, the world has seen an enormous growth in the power and size of multinational corporations. A **multinational corporation** is a corporation that manages and delivers services in more than one country. Powerful multinational corporations can sometimes undermine local authority and cripple domestic decision-making ability. A company that is not based in a country where its products are manufactured may not necessarily have a vested interest in promoting fair and sustainable business practices in that country. In extreme cases, the desire to avoid these practices may be the reason the company sought to do business outside its own borders in the first place. Globalization has allowed some multinational

---

CASE STUDY: Maquiladoras

The *North American Free Trade Agreement (NAFTA)* started in 1994. NAFTA's goal was to reduce the rules and regulations governing trade between the countries of Mexico, Canada, and the United States to allow freer trade in North America. NAFTA was designed to create manufacturing jobs in Mexico due to the lower cost of Mexican labor.[30] Under NAFTA, thousands of new manufacturing plants known as *maquiladoras* popped up on the border between the United States and Mexico. Maquiladoras provided multinational corporations with opportunities to lower production costs (i.e., labor and transportation) on manufactured goods. At times, NAFTA's rules allowed foreign companies to own and manage factories with special customs treatment. As a result, the import of machinery, equipment, parts and materials, and administrative equipment to these factories was not taxed.[31]

The number of jobs created by maquiladoras was a positive outcome of the phenomenon for Mexican workers. However, there were also negative outcomes for ordinary Mexicans. Many maquiladora workers endured extremely poor working conditions in dirty facilities where they were exposed to toxic chemicals.[32] Due to Mexico's lack of storage for waste and unenforced environmental regulations, the maquiladoras have made the border area one of the most polluted areas in Mexico.[33] In recent years, many maquiladoras have shut down as companies discovered cheaper labor in Asia and Africa and moved their operations, thus defeating one of the purposes of NAFTA: to provide more jobs in North American countries.

A maquiladora is a factory in Mexico run by a foreign company and exporting its products to that company's country.

corporations to dominate local markets and take control away from local producers. Local loss of production can lead to economic instability for people within a country.

The growth of multinational corporations has impacted developed countries, too. Critics of globalization in developed countries cite outsourcing as one of its major drawbacks. *Outsourcing* is the practice of moving certain jobs overseas to be done by foreign workers for lower wages. Customer service and call center jobs are some of the jobs most commonly moved overseas. While many Americans feel that outsourcing takes away jobs that should stay in the United States, most people also want to buy products and services as cheaply as possible. What is the relationship between these two realities?

Illicit Trade[34]

International trade and exchange is on the increase, but not everyone follows the rules. Illict (illegal) trade has grown with globalization as new technologies provide opportunities to skirt trade laws. Moises Naim, a Venezuelan writer and Senior Associate in the International Economics Program at the Carnegie Endowment for International Peace, describes five wars of globalization: arms, drugs, human beings, intellectual property, and money. Increased illegal activities related to all five have been made possible by open borders between countries. Networks of people can participate in these activities throughout the world without government knowledge. Illicit trade has taken on many different forms, such as:

- A factory in the Philippines producing licensed goods and then running a second shift creating methamphetamine drugs and bootleg videos
- Flourishing online markets for prostitution that make it easy to traffic women and children across borders

Environmental Degradation

Economic globalization leads to an increased need for natural resources such as oil, timber, and metals. If the global economy depends on these resources, but the resources are finite, problems can start to arise when they begin to disappear. Between the years 1950 and 2004, the world's population doubled. Water use tripled and consumption of oil, coal, and gas increased fivefold. Because these resources are finite, resource scarcity has fueled conflicts.[35] In our current economy, fossil fuels, clean water, and food security are essential needs. How might conflict over these natural resources be eliminated?

Cultural Homogenization

Critics of globalization worry that it could cause the extinction of languages and cultures. In a global marketplace, it makes sense to

Opium production in Afghanistan continues to prosper and contribute to illicit drug trade.

have a small number of languages so that people can communicate with each other. As a result, schools may teach children only the main languages used when conducting international trade.[36] What kinds of positive or negative consequences would result if languages are lost?

Traditional cultures face similar challenges when people in developing countries are exposed to other ways of life that may appear to be more appealing than their own. For example, introducing fast food or processed food can encroach on traditional diets. This happened in the Pacific Islands when fatty meat was imported from countries such as New Zealand and the United States. Pacific Islanders welcomed the tasty, low-cost meat, unaware that their bodies were evolutionally ill-suited to eating it. When Islanders stopped eating a traditional diet, they became highly susceptible to metabolic syndrome, heart disease, and other related problems. With the introduction of fast food, obesity-related "Western" diseases such as diabetes and hypertension started running rampant. In 1999, Fiji banned the import of low-grade fatty meat and in 2007 the Independent State of Samoa banned imports of turkey tail meat and chicken backs, which have particularly high fat content.[37]

Pathways to Progress: Globalization

It is clear that globalization is already well underway and so is the debate about what globalization means for people and the planet. Recall the questions posed in the beginning of the chapter: Is increasing globalization inevitable? Is it sustainable? If it isn't sustainable, how can it be made sustainable? Consider the following examples, which highlight efforts being taken to sustain local economies, societies, and environments in our increasingly connected world. As you read, think about how these examples

Peter Benfaremo, the Lemon Ice King of Corona, was inducted into the People's Hall of Fame in New York City.

can work alongside, rather than in opposition to, globalization.

Preserving Cultural Identities

Local establishments that have been present within a community for an extended period of time are part of the cultural identity of a given area. Communities can recognize the cultural value of these establishments by helping to preserve them. The Lemon Ice King of Corona, New York, is an Italian ice shop that has been in business for over 60 years. The owner of the shop was inducted into the People's Hall of Fame in New York City, an organization that works to preserve the rich cultural heritage of New York City.

Peter Benfaremo built The Lemon Ice King of Corona after he returned from World War II. The shop has been around for so long, it has become an important part of history in

Corona. Offering 42 different flavors, Benfaremo's shop is famous for its standard lemon ice and a number of other interesting flavors like spicy licorice, sweet cantaloupe, and peanut-speckled peanut butter.[38]

YOUTH PROFILE
Philmon Haile

Ignorance can lead to discrimination and hatred. If we start sharing ideas and promoting understanding with people who are primed to learn, we can help to end ignorance and increase cross-cultural understanding.

Philmon Haile has taken the idea of global citizenship to heart. He was born in Sudan and immigrated to Seattle, Washington with his family after the Eritrean War of Independence. He is fluent in the Eritrean language of Tigrinya, as well as Mandarin Chinese and English. In high school, Philmon studied and interned in Washington, D.C. before spending his senior year at a school in northeastern China. His global education continued in college. He attended Swarthmore College in Pennsylvania and returned to study in China two more times, all before his 21st birthday!

Philmon has made an increasingly globalized world work to his advantage. While attending high school in Seattle, he discovered the OneWorld Now! (OWN) program that provides opportunities for underserved youth to study abroad, gain leadership skills, and study foreign languages. He studied Mandarin Chinese through OWN and developed leadership skills as an intern for the U.S. House of Representatives Page Program. He received an OWN scholarship to study at a high school outside Anshan, China, where he attended classes with local students for 10 hours a day, six days a week. Participating in OWN showed him that foreign travel was no longer restricted to the upper class; in the age of globalization, cultural enrichment programs are now available to people of all backgrounds.

At Swarthmore, Philmon won a grant to lead a Hansen's disease (leprosy) recovery camp in southern China. He spent a year at a university in Harbin, China, where he studied Chinese literature. He was also part of the Western China Education Team and taught English and Math to children in an area affected by the 2008 Sichuan earthquake. In that village, most locals had never encountered a foreign student like him. They were fascinated by Philmon's presence in their community.

Philmon believes that technology has made the world a more interconnected and accessible place for his generation. As a result, he looks for any opportunity to interact with people with backgrounds or worldviews that are different from his own. As Philmon explains, all his travel and cultural immersion has been worth it because "[b]arriers of time, distance, and culture keep us apart. Current political and economic conversation is ever-changing and operates in multiple languages and sociocultural norms. Students need to be able to communicate across cultures in order to engage in this global conversation."

Philmon Haile has taken global citizenship to heart with his work in China.

Addressing Global Economic Instability

Globalization presents governments with a big challenge: they must balance their desire to enter the global marketplace with policies and regulations that make sure they still provide a good quality of life for their citizens. As we consider this challenge, we can see that current forms of globalization are not natural or inevitable. Instead, they are shaped by the policy decisions of individiual governments, multinational corporations, and a number of other stakeholders. These decisions determine how the global marketplace functions. When people's actions and preferences show that they care about equity, social justice, and environmental protection, they can encourage governments and businesses to make policy decisions that support sustainable globalization.

Fair trade was created in response to globalization to support sustainability. The idea behind fair trade is that producers in developing countries are provided "fair" wages for their work. Considering the fact that a cup of coffee sold in France might

---

CAREER PROFILE — Fair Trade Business Owner

Global trade affects almost every product that you buy. More and more, people recognize the need to balance the costs and benefits of global trade for both producers and consumers. One way to do this for trade from developing countries to developed countries is through fair trade. Fair trade certified products claim to pay fair prices to the producers and ensure that workers are in safe environments and are adequately compensated for their labor. Some business owners go a step further, getting to know their producers personally (just as you can do at a farmers market) and engaging in direct trade.

Running this sort of business requires an outgoing and personable demeanor in order to connect and work with lots of individual producers. It requires good algebra skills, especially because working with producers directly requires a lot of travel; you might not always have a computer with you when you are visiting a farm or dealing with an exchange rate that changes on a daily basis. A successful fair trade business owner will be excited to reorganize the business' supply, product, and labor force to respond to a highly dynamic market.

Sebastian Simsch runs Seattle Coffee Works, where he roasts coffee beans and creates the sort of rich espresso that has made Seattle famous for its coffee. He created Seattle Coffee Works because he loves cafe culture—meeting new people and having compelling conversation over a steaming mug. Sebastian learned about the coffee business through advice from other roasters, going to workshops at coffee conferences, reading a number of books on the subject, and spending countless hours trying to make different types of coffee.

He's also interested in making coffee creation sustainable. On the local level this means providing a positive work environment for his employees. On the supply chain side of the business, Sebastian tries to work directly with farmers to negotiate a price that's fair for both sides. By working with the farmers he can be sure that workers are earning a livable wage and that they avoid pesticides and inorganic fertilizers. Sebastian is even trying to find ways to brew coffee with less electricity and fewer materials. He says, "we're now down to boiling water, a good grinder, and a sock. This is a Costa Rican method."

Sebastian Simsch (right), owner of Seattle Coffee Works, negotiates directly with farmers to reach a fair price.

cost a few dollars, how much would you expect the farmer who grew the beans to earn from that cup of coffee—50 cents? You might be surprised to learn that an Ethiopian coffee bean farmer might only make a couple of pennies per day. The rest of the cost of the cup of coffee goes to other people involved in the global coffee trade. In addition to supporting higher wages for farmers and other producers, fair trade attempts to raise social and environmental standards in places where goods are produced, creating better working conditions and improving the quality of life for people around the world.

Let's look at the example of the banana trade one last time. In 1997, 14 small-scale banana farmers in Ecuador decided that instead of going through a middleman (who buys bananas and resells them to foreign companies), they would ship one container (38,400 pounds) of bananas directly to a supermarket in Europe. The cost was no greater to the supermarket, but the farmers would be able to make more money. The sale was a success; suddenly, the banana farmers found themselves interacting directly with the international market. They continued to sell bananas through this fair trade process and decided to use the proceeds for education, health care, and environmental projects in their community. This cooperative was run jointly by farmers who shared the profits and benefits. These days, the farmer-run cooperative El Guabo includes 450 small-scale banana farmers and is an example of what can be achieved through fair trade.[39]

WHAT YOU CAN DO — Globalization

There are a number of ways you can begin addressing impacts of globalization:

- Think critically about how you spend your money. It is a good idea to research companies and look at policies before you make a major purchase. What would you want to know about a company that you support with your hard-earned dollars? How they treat their employees? How they support the local communities they work in? Whether the jobs provided by the company actually improve people's lives? How you spend your money really can make an impact.

- Document your family's history. Most of us have connections to ancestors in other parts of the world; learning more about our own history can help connect us to those places. What are the roots of your identity? What are the traditions of your community and your neighborhood? What stories can you learn from your elders? Preserving this knowledge can help protect history, culture, and communities.

Students from Seattle visit students in Rwanda on a cultural exchange.

- Be open to cultural exchanges. Globalization has opened up borders and made possible many forms of international exchange that did not exist or were not as easily accessible in the past. Consider learning new languages and learning more about other cultures.

POINT | **COUNTERPOINT**

Do globalization and free trade help to decrease poverty?

There have been arguments on both sides of the globalization debate. Some people believe that globalization supports poverty alleviation while others believe globalization increases poverty.

POINT

Yes

- **Approximately 820 million people live on less than $1.25 a day.** However, since 2000, poverty has been reduced at a sustained rate. This progress could relate heavily to rapid economic growth. Those countries that have chosen to participate in the global economy and actively chosen effective strategic policies have been able to trade successfully and create jobs.[40]

- **When countries are able to open themselves up to trade, they have a much easier time participating in the global economy.** This participation can help in alleviating poverty. For example, when the country of Zimbabwe began to open up its trade policies, its economy improved between 1991 and 1997.[41]

COUNTERPOINT

No

- **Free trade allows for industries to move across borders to any part of the world.** If industries offer money to countries in need, this money can be a major incentive. As a result, countries may lower environmental standards in order to retain these businesses.[42] Lowered environmental standards can lead to increased pollution and negative health consequences to workers. Increased pollution does not help to alleviate poverty. If anything, increased pollution can lead to more environmental degradation, which could then lead to fewer natural resources for people.

- **Globalization can lead to higher unemployment and possible declines in wages.** When countries outsource jobs to other countries, their economy can suffer. Similarly, when countries are able to import goods into another country at far cheaper prices, a country can struggle as the need to make these goods domestically isn't needed.[43]

Open borders between countries have allowed for fast food chains like McDonalds to spread around the world.

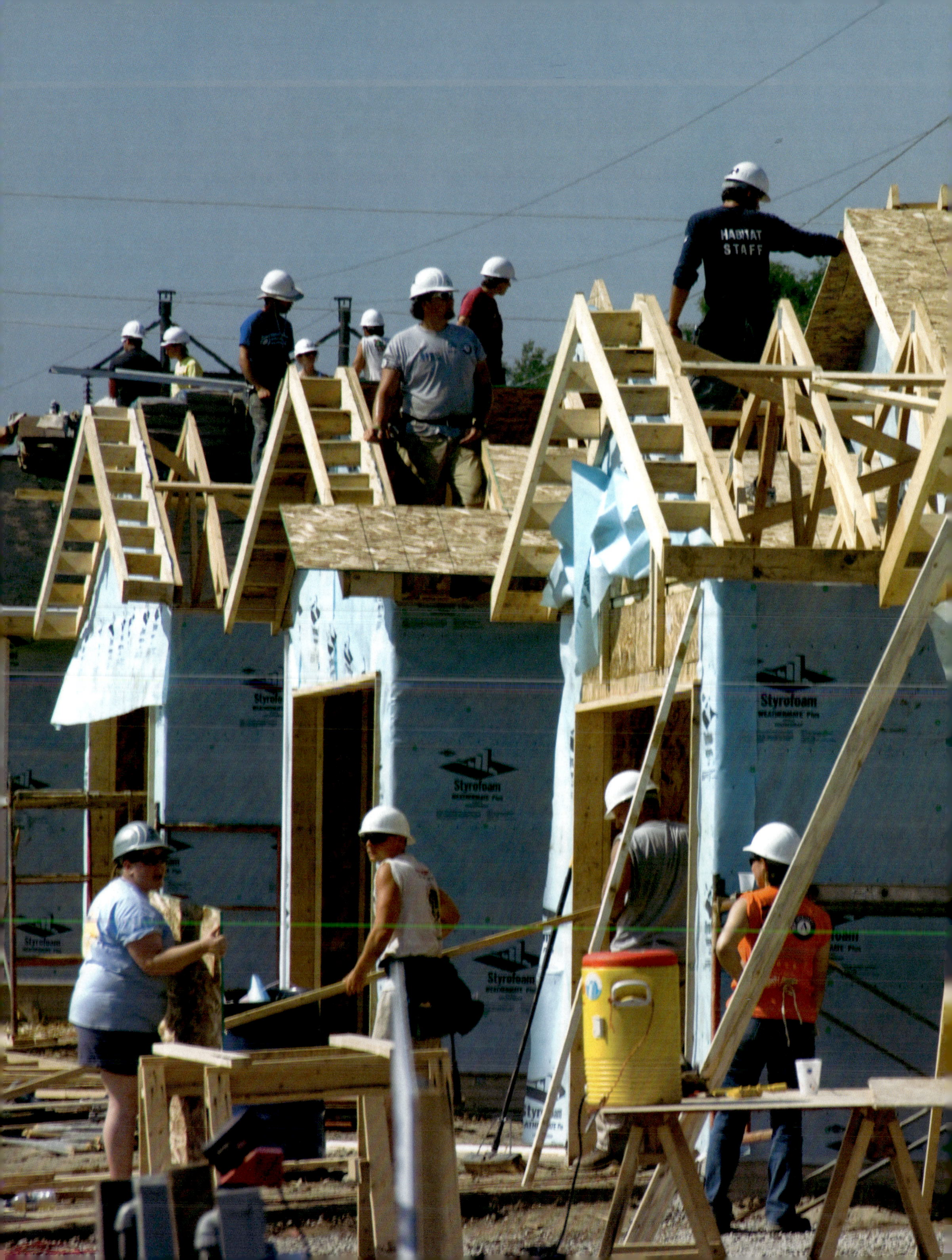
HABITAT
STAFF
Styrofoam
Styrofoam
Styrofoam

Chapter 22
Community Development

> **GUIDING QUESTIONS**
> - Why are communities stronger together?
> - What approaches can help build and strengthen communal assets?

Introduction to Community Development

PeacePlayers International runs youth basketball programs in South Africa, Northern Ireland, Israel and the West Bank, and Cyprus. The teams consist of young people who would normally not communicate with each other. For example, Israelis and Palestinians have long been at odds since the state of Israel was created in 1948 on land previously occupied by Palestinians. PeacePlayers International brings families from both groups together to watch their young people play on the same side and form personal bonds across political lines. The players themselves participate in peace education and life skills activities and form lasting friendships.

PeacePlayers International promotes positive interactions between young people from communities often in conflict.

During the 2010-2011 season, the group entered two "all-star" teams into the prestigious Israeli National Basketball League. They were the first fully integrated teams in the league's history.[1] As one participant states, "The best part was learning things from new players and different areas coming together. I learned you don't have to judge a person based on his religion."[2] Can overcoming differences build stronger communities in the long run?

Many of the problems facing people around the world seem far away. When you think of major challenges like poverty, war, and climate change, you may think, "What can I do? I'm only one person." It is true that solving these problems alone would be difficult. That is why it is imperative that people work together to find solutions.

Beyond the doors of your household, you interact with people in many different contexts. Some, such as other students who attend your school, you see and speak with daily. Others you interact with less frequently. You may play sports, practice music, or participate in a hobby with people that you meet weekly or monthly. In each case some commonality brings you together; the result is a **community**.

Religious communities are brought together by a shared faith.

What Defines Community?

Communities exist within societies. There are many different types of communities. Just a few examples include:

- local community—people who live together in a neighborhood, town, or city
- global community—people from around the world who work together on a common cause
- religious community—people with a shared faith who worship together
- ethnic community—people with a shared ethnicity
- online community—people connected by the Internet
- school community—people who attend the same school

Stronger Together

Communities can be a powerful force for change when their members work together. However, many communities are not united. Some may not even think of themselves as a community. Consider the students at your school: teachers, principals, and even senators make decisions every day that affect you all, but do you see yourselves as a community with the power to have a say in those decisions?

When students work together, they have incredible power. Take for example a group of high school students in Cambridge, Massachusetts. Students at Cambridge Rindge & Latin School identified and took action on a few problems affecting their school community, including dirty bathrooms. With the support of the Boston Youth Organizing Project, the students learned skills that allowed them to set up meetings with school officials. They met with the school district's chief operating officer and the school principal to express their concerns. As a result, school administrators and students made a commitment to keep the bathrooms cleaner.[3]

When the students at Cambridge Rindge & Latin School came together as a community to gain control over the decision-making processes that impacted them, they engaged in **community development**. At its core, community development is about building ties between community members to create a network that can successfully adapt to challenges or opportunities. Communities with strong ties among their members tend to be more resilient in the face of adversity.[4] A strong community can also provide people with a tangible sense of belonging and security, as well as a sense of duty to support one another.

Social Capital: The Fabric of Community

Connections between members of a community form one of the most important resources for accomplishing anything: **social capital**. In economics, capital is defined as goods and services that have value. In a similar way, social capital places a value on people and interpersonal relationships. Social capital includes the networks, norms, and mutual trust that allow people to coordinate and cooperate for the benefit of a community. Social capital, in other words, is made up of the relationships between people that help them to get things done.

Without relationships and trust, businesses could not operate and political processes would not work. Even getting a job would be very difficult, as 80% of all positions in the United States are filled through personal networks rather than anonymous job listings.[5] Creating resilient communities can be important for any undertaking.

Social capital is an important community attribute because in most places more social capital can mean healthier and better-educated children, longer life spans, and better government and economic performance. Communities with low social capital, on the other hand, could have lower civic engagement and less trust between people in the community.[6]

According to Anirudh Krishna, a scholar of social capital, social capital strengthens democracy and promotes development. Those who seek to further democracy and development are therefore interested in learning how to increase social capital. Krishna set out to study the factors that result in social capital growth within communities, collecting data from 61 villages in the state of Rajasthan, India. Krishna found that the following elements were related to social capital:[7]

Women and girls in Rajasthan collect water together from a village well.

- Dealing with crop diseases jointly—Would a crop disease that affects everyone's fields be dealt with together?
- Managing common village land—Are common village areas managed by all members of the community?
- Resolving disputes—Are disputes among community members resolved with the help of the larger community?
- Reciprocity—Do people in the community help to guide each other's children when they do wrong?
- Solidarity—Do community members protect natural resources in order to unite the community?
- Trust—Would people in the community rather work together than individually?

Can you guess how the answers to the questions above might relate to social capital? Krishna found that affirmative answers to these questions were linked to higher social capital within the Rajasthani villages studied. What other elements might increase social capital?

Community Development and Sustainability

Most communities are local. It's true that there are a growing number of international communities, including online networks that connect people all over the world. However, the majority of communities today are still made up of people who live, work, learn, and worship near each other. We interact with the people living near us every day. We influence the environmental, social, and economic conditions in which they live.

All three aspects of sustainability—economic, social, and environmental—depend on people's ability to work together as community. A sustainable local community has a healthy economy, environment, and society, and is also able to bring people together to respond effectively to problems.

> *All three aspects of sustainability—economic, social, and environmental—depend on people's ability to work together as community.*

Economy

Many of the factors necessary for economic sustainability are connected to thriving communities. For example, sustainable economies have diverse forms of economic activity (rather than overreliance on one industry) and they feature businesses that reinvest in the local economy. Such economic diversity and reinvestment can help to create meaningful employment opportunities for people in the community. This is especially important in times of economic hardship when any single industry can collapse suddenly, leading to mass unemployment.[8] The city of Detroit, for example, has long been heavily dependent on auto manufacturing. As that industry shrank between 2000 and 2010 and people moved elsewhere in search of work, the city lost 25% of its population.[9] Job training and education programs can help prevent such mass unemployment by allowing a community's workforce to adapt as the labor needs of the local economy change over time.

Society

Social sustainability at the local level requires, at minimum, the satisfaction of basic human needs such as medical treatment, safe housing, and protection against persecution and physical harm. Access to education is also necessary to foster civic participation and a strong workforce. Finally, cultural and religious customs and traditions must be respected, protected, and even enhanced. This is important because the repression of such practices can lead to divisions within a community and make it more difficult to deal with economic, political, and environmental pressures.

Environment

Environmental conditions also bind local communities together. Common resources such as clean air and water are generally available either to all community members or to none of them; therefore, all community members have a stake in the protection and equitable distribution of these resources. Minimizing pollution requires the participation of the whole community because even a small number of polluters can impact air quality for everyone in the area.

Background on Community Development

The origins of community development are difficult to determine. You can imagine that as long as people have been living together in groups, they have been working together to solve problems and improve their living conditions. There are many examples of communities

CASE STUDY: The Dudley Street Neighborhood Initiative

During the 1960s and 1970s, the Dudley neighborhood in Boston witnessed two decades of neglect and destructive fires, which led to the flight of residents and businesses. By the 1980s, 20% of the neighborhood lay vacant. In the face of redevelopment plans that would dramatically change the neighborhood, the remaining residents came together to discuss ways to *revitalize* their community through locally-owned economic projects.

The result of their discussions was the creation of the Dudley Street Neighborhood Initiative (DSNI). The group was formed from the neighborhood's four major ethnic groups (Black, Latino, White, and Cape Verdean) and included representatives from businesses, churches, and nonprofit organizations. In 1987, the DSNI convinced the Boston City Council to grant it eminent domain over vacant lots, giving ownership of those properties to the community as a whole. The group began to build affordable housing, community centers, schools, a community greenhouse and orchard, and several parks and playgrounds.

The Dudley Street Neighborhood Initiative works to revitalize their community—developing housing using green design techniques such as solar heating.

The DSNI's long-term goal is the creation of a community where food, services, jobs, art, and entertainment are available in a walkable urban village. By 2011, over half of the 1,300 vacant properties given over to the DSNI had been revitalized. New businesses had set up shop, including two small-scale manufacturers that employ neighborhood residents and two mid-sized grocery stores that get most of their produce from the neighborhood's agricultural plots. The most recent housing built by the DSNI is at the leading edge of green building, highly insulated and solar-heated. In the future, the group is considering building its own biological sewage treatment facilities to establish control over its own waste management and save residents money. By incorporating many stakeholders in the revitalization process, the DSNI has been able to create a healthier and more resilient community.[10]

---

that have farmed, foraged, hunted, defended, traded, and otherwise worked cooperatively for the benefit of the entire group. For example, certain Native American tribes hunted together communally as far back as 6,500 B.C.E.[11]

The city-state of Athens in ancient Greece provides an early example of people within a community working together and making decisions cooperatively. In Greece, people who lived in a *polis* (a city, town, or village and its surrounding area) gathered together in public buildings for purposes of entertainment and commerce. Community members of a polis shared a common identity and common goals. Around 500 B.C.E. in the city-state of Athens, members of a polis were granted decision-making powers; prior to that time Athens was governed by monarchs and aristocrats. In this new democracy, male citizens were allowed to publicly debate and vote on issues that affected their community.

Modern-day community development has emerged in various forms. The Settlement Movement in London in the 1800s was an attempt to raise living standards for people within a neighborhood. Many people living in London at that time were unemployed; those who were employed were often paid so little that they remained in poverty. Established by religious leaders, settlement houses were community centers designed to improve the well-being of people in poor neighborhoods. They helped community members by providing job training, education, childcare, and other services.[12]

The Settlement Movement was an early form of **community organizing**, a way for people to work together to overcome problems that affect community members. In the late 1930s, community organizing was further developed in the United States. The Back of the Yards Neighborhood Council (BYNC) is one example. It was formed in 1939 in the Chicago neighborhood known then as the Back of the Yards (named for its proximity to the Union Stock Yards, the epicenter of the meatpacking industry at that time). The BYNC brought together different ethnic groups in the neighborhood to cope with widespread poverty during the Great Depression. One product of this effort was a school lunch program that provided free and reduced-price lunches to children living in poverty. This school lunch model soon spread to schools throughout the nation.[13]

By the 1950s, another form of community development emerged. Neighborhood associations and civic clubs formed to make improvements to physical infrastructure, such as building new parks and making street repairs. Membership rates in these sorts of civic clubs were at their height during the 1960s.[14] While these groups generally worked to promote the welfare of all neighborhood residents, not all civic associations were beneficial for everyone. For example, some sought to prevent racial integration.[15]

Declining Social Capital?

In 1995, Robert Putnam, a political scientist at Harvard University, famously reported that members of American society are becoming more and more disconnected from each other. In his book, *Bowling Alone*, Putnam reported that while more people than ever are bowling, they are no longer bowling as teams in bowling leagues.

Solitary bowling is just one example of how our social fabric may be changing. Between the 1960s and 1990s, the number of U.S. citizens who voted in national elections dropped by almost 25%. Over the same period, the proportion of the population who attended public meetings on town or school issues or who attended political speeches or rallies dropped by half, from 23% to 12%. Membership in fraternal organizations, such as the Elks and the Masons, dropped by at least as much, while volunteer numbers for the Boy Scouts and Red Cross dropped by 23% and 61%, respectively.[16]

Such civic activities and organizations are one way people form bonds with others in their communities. Putnam links the decrease in these civic activities to increasingly individualized leisure time caused by advances in technology (especially television and the Internet). When fewer people join parent-teacher associations, form clubs that meet regularly, or volunteer for extended periods of time with a single organization, there are fewer personal connections made within a community. As a result, the local network of community members becomes weaker and is less able to take advantage of collective opportunities or respond to collective challenges. This process can be described as a loss of social capital.

Volunteering within your local community can help increase social capital.

It should be pointed out that the current state of affairs is not all bad news for community development and social capital. While membership in many traditional community associations may have declined, participation in other types of groups has grown. Groups of people interested in a particular set of issues— such as the Sierra Club, an organization that works to protect environmental resources; the American Association of Retired Persons (AARP), a group that works to secure rights for older people; and the National Organization of Women (NOW), a group that works for women's equality—have seen sizable increases in membership during the same time that membership in community-based clubs has declined.[17] Another interesting trend is the dramatic increase in youth volunteerism. A 2009 study indicated that 73% of youth ages 12-17 have volunteered. That's a sizable increase from the 60% who volunteered just 15 years earlier.[18]

A low level of social capital may be connected to crime, health, and the loss of economic opportunity. All of these things can harm the immediate health and well-being of community members and present a challenge to sustainable development. Communities caught in the cycle of declining social capital may not be able to adapt effectively to new economic, social, and environmental pressures.

Inequity and Social Divisions

One manifestation of low social capital is increased isolation both between and within ethnic groups. In the short run, people who live in communities with higher racial diversity tend to have less trust in their neighbors, whether those neighbors share their ethnic background or not. These diverse communities of individuals are often a result of immigration. People move in and out of neighborhoods without forming relationships that allow them to trust each other.[19] As the U.S. population continues to become more racially diverse over the next 50 years,[20] learning how to use diversity to our advantage will become increasingly important.

Abandoned homes can be an indication of communities with declining social capital.

Limited Economic Opportunities

Low social capital and frequent crime drive businesses and residents out of communities. As businesses leave, people in the community lose access to goods and services. This removes an important source of connection between neighbors. Local stores, in particular, serve as places that residents of a neighborhood or community can identify with and claim as their own. When local stores close, people are forced to go outside their community to do their shopping.

The local economy is also harmed by the loss of businesses in a community. Fewer local jobs lead to an increased number of people living under or near the poverty line. This has significant long-term consequences. Children, in particular, are impacted by poverty in ways that often shape the rest of their lives. For example, one in 10 students in low-income areas of the United States drop out of school, compared to one in 100 in high-income areas. Children living in poverty are more likely to develop nutrition issues like obesity and undernourishment throughout their childhood. They are also more likely to develop emotional problems, such as depression, and behavior problems, such as attention deficit disorder.[21]

Health and Safety Concerns

A faltering local economy and decline in social capital create conditions that may contribute to greater crime rates in a community. In particular, there is more incentive and opportunity for people to turn to illegal activities to make money, such as robbery or selling drugs. The presence of these activities can expose all community members to an increased risk of violence and further undermine people's trust in their community.

Community Development Today

No matter a community's location or economic status, community development can successfully join people together by building a sense of common purpose. This enables people to accomplish goals that they could not achieve alone, including finding ways to live sustainably. In other words, community development seeks to foster education, employment, trust, and solidarity.

> *Problem solving is at the core of community development.*

Community development can originate solely from within a community, or it can be fostered by the intervention of outside organizations. For example, school districts in the United States that need support and additional resources to better serve their students can contact an organization called Communities In Schools. Communities In Schools is a national network of professionals who work within the public school system, determining student needs and establishing relationships with local businesses, social service agencies, health care providers, and parent and volunteer organizations to provide resources that students need in order to be successful in school. They essentially build a community of support for students. To visualize the process of community development, we can look to the Communities In Schools model.[22]

The Process: Stages of Community Development

Identifying the Problem

Problem solving is at the core of community development.[23] Naturally, the first step of community development is usually to identify the problem. The problem may be well known or it may be something that many community members are not aware of. When community development is aimed at sustainability, it also involves assessing how current trends, such as resource consumption, will affect future generations. Let's consider the example of one school district that worked with Communities In Schools to identify and solve a problem. The Seattle Public Schools, with the help of a site coordinator from Communities In Schools, recognized that one challenge to student success was that a number of students lacked basic school supplies.[24]

Making a Plan

The second step in the process of community development involves determining how to address the problem and building the community's ability to deal with problems. This step usually consists of getting as many community members as possible working together and thinking about solutions, generating ideas about what to do and a plan for how it can be accomplished. For Communities In Schools, this step consists of forming a team of community members who can serve the student needs identified by the site coordinator in step one.[25] To address Seattle students' lack of school supplies, a team of people came together to

Respect for other cultures can strengthen bonds within a diverse community.

coordinate the collection of school supply donations from individuals and organizations. They named the program Stuff the Bus.[26]

Taking Action

The planning stage leads into the third step of community development: taking action to address the problem. This can mean starting a nonprofit organization to gather resources and oversee programs, advocating a solution in front of government decision makers, or taking some other approach. Communities In Schools took action on the problem of school supplies by publicizing and running a Stuff the Bus campaign before school starts each fall.[27] They collect supplies from all over the city and distribute them directly to schools where they can be given to students with the greatest need.

Evaluating Results

A final stage of community development involves evaluating the results of an effort. A community will not know whether its efforts were successful at solving a problem unless they evaluate their progress. The Stuff the Bus program provides school supplies to 8,500 students in 32 Seattle schools each year. In a district of 45,000 students where 40% live in poverty, this alleviates a significant burden on families, who spend an average of $60-100 getting a child ready for the first day of school.[28]

The Result: Characteristics of Sustainable Communities

Respect and Diversity

Cultivating and demonstrating respect for diverse cultures can help a community build social capital and work together effectively. Consider the conditions that would make a person feel more inclined to participate in community decisions and help solve problems. Which do you think would be more conducive to building community: a culture where all people are respected, or a culture where some people are not respected? It probably seems like an obvious choice; when individuals within a community feel respected and valued, they are more likely to participate in community endeavors.

One way to create mutual respect between all cultures in a community is to provide opportunities for each cultural group to be involved in making decisions. For example, the Dudley Street Neighborhood Initiative includes representatives from each of the four major ethnic groups in the Dudley neighborhood.[29] These formal arrangements, however, depend on informal ties of friendship and respect between cultures,[30] which develop when people from different cultures work, play, and talk face-to-face. Even if there are rules at your school telling you to respect people of all cultures, your experience has probably shown you that whether students of different backgrounds get along ultimately depends on whether they respect and value each other's culture. Conversely, ignorance or disrespect of someone's heritage is likely to provoke conflict and mistrust.

Civic Participation

Another way to develop community is by involving more people in civic participation, especially those who have not traditionally had a role in making the decisions that affect their lives. **Civic participation** is the ability of citizens to participate in both individual and collective decisions around issues that affect them publicly. This type of participation can range from volunteering with an organization that works to feed the homeless to becoming involved with political decisions that affect teenagers. When decisions about money and power are made by representatives from across the community, the decision-making process takes the interests of the community as a whole into account. In other words, broad participation fosters community-level thinking.

However, not all ways of including people in governance are equal. Some decision makers might consult with people only after decisions have been made or they may consult with the public in a superficial way that denies the public any real power to make change. These weak forms of participation stand in contrast to those in which the whole community has the ability to affect the outcome of decision-making processes.[31]

Equal Opportunities

Securing access to resources such as education, safe housing, and public transit is a key component of building sustainable communities. You may have heard the adage, "It takes a village to raise a child." Certainly raising children is easier when a parent has help from the surrounding family and community. A good example can be found in a hundred-block section of Harlem called the Harlem Children's Zone that has built a network to support kids and their families from birth to college. The premise behind the program is that kids do well when their families do well, and families do well when their community does well.

In the Harlem Children's Zone, parents of newborns can attend "baby college" to learn about how to care for their younger children. Many school-age children attend the Promise Academy Charter School and others receive support for their public school education from the Harlem Children's Zone. After-school programming for high school students focus on career skills and media literacy, helping 100% of the students who participate go on to college. All of these programs operate in the midst of a network of support services for families. Community members can receive drug and alcohol rehabilitation support services, family and truancy counseling to provide stable homes, and education about managing obesity and asthma.[32] In 2010, the federal government took the vision of the Children's Zone—to

Registering people to vote is one form of civic participation.

provide all children in Central Harlem access to great schools and strong systems of family and community support—and applied it to 21 other communities across the country.[33]

YOUTH PROFILE
Alex Epstein

As mentioned in the beginning of the chapter, communities can take various forms; a community might be a school, a sports team, a neighborhood, or a network of friends and family in many cities and towns. For Alex Epstein, the idea of community has grown over time to encompass his high school in New York City, the ninth ward of New Orleans, and finally North Philadelphia, where he is now part of a team working on community development projects. These projects include community centers, urban farms, fresh food markets, and other sustainability efforts.

When Alex traveled from New York to New Orleans after Hurricane Katrina, he was 14 years old. He expected to check off some community service hours and return home. But after his first visit, Alex was compelled to help create change both in the ninth ward in New Orleans and at home in New York. In 2007, he cofounded the New York 2 New Orleans Coalition (NY2NO)—a youth-run network seeking to address inequalities and educate students on ways to create change through community organizing efforts. In the two years since Alex graduated from high school, NY2NO has sent over 1,500 students to New Orleans on 43 separate trips.

While attending college in Philadelphia, Alex cofounded the Philadelphia Urban Creators (PUC). PUC is a youth-led nonprofit organization that works with residents of all ages in North Philadelphia to develop some of the nearly 10,000 vacant lots in the area. Their current project is an educational urban farm that provides a safe space for young people to learn about social and environmental issues

PUC lead organizers stand with Alex (third from right) in front of their urban farm.

and practice sustainable agriculture. The farm also provides fresh, healthy food for the whole community. Together, residents and volunteers transformed a two-acre plot of land into a community garden. In the summer of 2011, the PUC held their first community farmer's market where they sold crops grown in the garden. In more recent times, PUC now sells produce to restaurants downtown. They also help schools to start school gardens.

Social Connections

Sustainable communities are characterized by strong social connections. These connections also build resilience within a community to face adverse times. As people recognize the importance of community and connection, they are finding new ways to build social networks. Some examples are:[34]

- A mentoring and reading program in Philadelphia that brings together retirees and elementary school children to the benefit of both—the children get help reading and the retirees have a richer, more purposeful life
- A group of sixth-grade activists in a small Wisconsin town who persuaded local authorities to improve safety at a railroad crossing, learning a valuable lesson in civic activism through the process
- A regional food council in Los Angeles that

brought together farmers, food distributors, chefs, journalists, public health leaders, architects, and city planners to craft policy recommendations for the mayor of L.A. on how to create a sustainable "foodshed" in Southern California[35]

- A community effort in the impoverished Rio Grande Valley, one of the poorest regions in the United States, that brought such basic services as electricity, roads, and health care to the region's mostly Spanish-speaking residents

All of these efforts create relationships of **reciprocity**, in which people feel inclined to do things for one another.[36] These sentiments are not just nice feelings; they are bonds that tie people together into networks that are responsible, healthy, safe, adaptable, and resilient—in other words, into sustainable communities.

Pathways to Progress: Community Development

There are many ways to help strengthen communities. Advocating for legislative change is one method. Advocacy may be done by residents themselves or by organizations working to change a particular issue. Another way that people transform communities is through community organizing and citizen-led efforts to solve problems. A third way is to provide services that improve the well-being of community members. These different approaches are further explained below.

Community development can be led or supported by government policies.

Laws and Legislation

Community development can be led or supported by government policies. When legislators see a community or a group of communities in need of support, they can shape government policy to help, usually by providing funding for community development projects. Citizens can play a role in this process through voting and advocating for a particular policy to their elected representatives.

Rural communities in North America face a variety of challenges. Relative to their urban counterparts, people living in towns of fewer than 25,000 tend to be poorer and have less access to health care. They are educated at schools that have less funding than those in urban areas. The rural population has been declining for over 100 years and continues to do so today. In particular, many young people from rural areas move to larger cities after graduating high school.[37] This urban migration in pursuit of economic opportunities does not only occur in North America; it is a global phenomenon.

The resulting population decline in rural areas leaves communities in need of vital services, from hospitals to grocery stores. Both the United States and Canada have passed legislation intended to help sustain their rural communities. State policies are also being developed to assist community development in rural areas. For example, the state of New York has initiated a program to fund the construction and restoration of buildings that will help rural towns keep their historic downtowns intact. Many buildings in these small historic districts have fallen into disrepair, but are central to the historic feel of these towns. New York's Rural Area Revitalization Program focuses on providing healthy and sustainable housing, attractive economic facilities, and public spaces where the community can gather.[38]

Citizen-led Initiatives[39]

While government support can be a powerful catalyst for change, you don't have to wait for the government to begin strengthening your community. Groups of citizens can create powerful networks on their own, even when times are hard. One form that these networks can take is that of a *cooperative*, a collection of businesses that workers own and manage collectively.

Twenty-five percent of the people living in Cleveland's Greater University Circle neighborhood are unemployed and the average household income is less than $20,000 per year. In contrast, the university and several hospitals located within the neighborhood control considerable wealth; in 2006, they collectively spent over $3 billion, mostly outside the community. Residents began to sketch out a system of worker-owned businesses that would serve to keep some of that money in the community while also becoming the greenest in their respective industries. These businesses came to be known as the Evergreen Cooperatives.

One of the cooperatives is a laundry service designed around water and energy efficiency. The laundry service found a niche servicing local nursing homes and has been constantly growing since it was founded in 2009. Profits made by the cooperative are shared among its worker-owners. Of course, if the cooperative loses money, workers also run the risk of sharing in its losses.

Investing Individually in Your Community

There are many ways that you can take part in community development. One of the simplest is to meet, talk to, and help other members of your community. What if you could teach someone in your community how to cook a meal and, in exchange, they would help you mow your lawn? This is essentially the premise that lies behind

---

CAREER PROFILE: Community Organizer

A community organizer facilitates the process of community organizing, helping people who live in a common area to gain power to influence decisions that affect them and their neighbors. To do this, a community organizer helps to develop leaders within the community to enable them to campaign for improvements.

Diana Lopez works as a community organizer with the Southwest Workers' Union, which provides education and support for underrepresented and underserved people in San Antonio, Texas. Growing up in San Antonio, she saw firsthand the problems facing her community. Diana wanted to help eliminate health conditions like high blood pressure and diabetes. She led a project to help citizens of San Antonio's East Side learn about nutrition and agriculture.

As part of the project, the Southwest Worker's Union helped build a community garden. "We wanted something that allowed young people to focus on the positive aspects of life," Diana said. "The garden is a safe space for young people to hang out and get to know each other." The community garden, called Roots of Change, allows members of the community to grow and harvest organic so that they do not have to rely on the often less nutritious foods available at large grocery stores.

"I find myself having responsibility for many people and many functions that a 'normal' 23-year-old may not take on. I went from being very shy to being very outspoken. I am now the complete opposite of the person who I was four years ago," she said, because she looked in her community and saw what needed to change. Diana encourages other young people to get involved in community organizing: "I want young people to envision what their community could look like."

Diana Lopez works as a community organizer in San Antonio, Texas.

Time banks, such as this one in Michigan, give people an opportunity to share services with others in their community.

the idea of a *time bank,* an organization through which members can offer their time in many capacities, then bank the hours and call on the help of another member later. The currency in these exchanges is time, rather than money.

There are over 300 time banks in 23 countries around the world. One of the largest time banks—the Community Connections TimeBank, run by the Visiting Nurse Service of New York—has over 2,000 members. Members list what services they can offer on the time bank's website. Just a few services offered are financial planning, clothing alterations, cooking, and visiting those who are house-bound. Each hour spent in service is worth the same amount in the bank, regardless of what service is rendered.

Time banks have a direct impact on community building. Many of the pairings arranged through the bank bring together people from very different religious, ethnic, economic, and even linguistic backgrounds—people who might not otherwise interact. A 2009 survey of members of the Community Connections Time Bank in New York found that 90% of those over 60 years old made new friends through the bank and 71% saw those friends at least once a week.[40]

WHAT YOU CAN DO — Community Development

You have read about various ways that people can work together to improve the quality of life in their communities. Here are a few ways that you can be part of community development efforts where you live:

- Share your time and talents with others in your community—you could even start your own time bank.
- Attend school board and city council meetings to learn about issues that are important to the community.
- Get involved in a community improvement project.
- Write to a city council member about a change you want to see in your community.
- Organize an event that brings community members together, such as a neighborhood barbecue or an "open mic" night.

There are countless ways for you to get involved in community development.

- Plan events in your neighborhood where neighbors can meet each other and build relationships.
- Organize an event that brings community members together, such as a neighborhood barbecue or an open mic night

POINT | **COUNTERPOINT**

Does social media foster the growth of social capital?

As mentioned earlier, technologies such as the Internet and cell phones have changed the way we communicate with each other. They have also stretched the way we think about communities. *Social media,* such as blogs, social networking websites, and podcasts, have created new forms of communities online. Some believe social media increases social capital, while others believe social media decreases social capital.

POINT

Yes

- **Social media has not destroyed community; it has transformed community into something that can be "long distance" and thus more adaptable.**[41] Cars and telephones have long allowed people to keep in touch with family and friends who do not live near them. The rise of social media takes this trend one step further and makes social networks more adaptable as people move. In a time when more and more people have to move to find work, this adaptability is vital for maintaining social capital.

- **Social media has already played a vital role in organizing political resistance.** Almost nothing requires greater social capital than a political uprising. Social media was important to the 2011 uprisings in Egypt and Tunisia. Protestors were able to post plans on social media sites.

COUNTERPOINT

No

- **Social media may bring more people into contact, but it could also reduce the depth of those relationships.** Studies have shown that as people begin to use the Internet heavily, they become more depressed and stressed and have fewer friends.[42] Social media is a way to contact new people. However, relationships formed online are mostly used simply for entertainment. People do not often receive any real support (other than kind words) from those they meet online. In short, online relationships are more about the transfer of information than a means to build true friendships.

- **Any real social capital involved with social media comes from relationships that are built offline.** Most of the connections that people make on social media sites follow face-to-face meetings: for example, "friending" people online who are already your friends or acquaintances.

Some believe that social media improves social capital while others believe it can greatly diminish social capital.

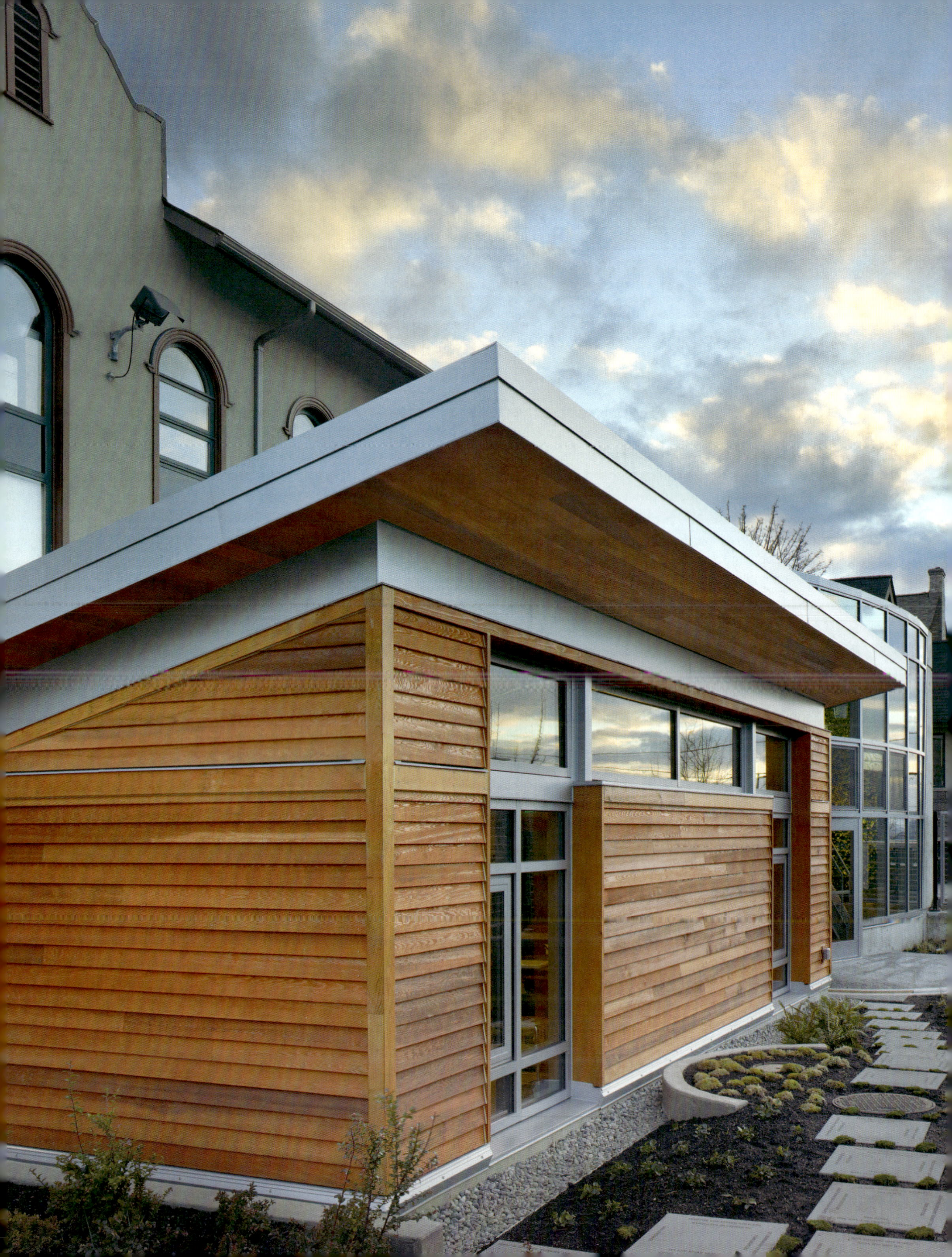

Chapter 23

Sustainable Design

GUIDING QUESTIONS
- How can the built environment be designed sustainably?
- How can sustainable design revitalize a community?
- What can individuals do to create more sustainable environments?

Introduction to Sustainable Design

Buildings modeled after termite mounds, homes powered by the sun, science labs with composting toilets, and municipal waste programs that reduce trash and help low income residents: science fiction, or sustainable design?

What Is Sustainable Design?

Sustainable design brings the perspective of sustainability into the *built environment*—spaces that have been built or changed by humans. Specifically, **sustainable design** refers to creating products and buildings in a way that maximizes benefits to the environment, economy, and society. This kind of design can focus on a single building (i.e., materials used to create the building) all the way to city-wide planning (i.e., how can the design of the city meet the needs of people and the environment?).

Design and Sustainability

Environment

According to U.S. Green Building Council, buildings in the United States account for about 30% of raw material use, 36% of the nation's total energy use, and 12% of potable water use.[1]

To understand why buildings have such an impact on the environment, think about all the steps involved in designing just one building: a site to build on is chosen, designs are drawn up, building materials and products are bought, construction takes place, and waste is generated. Once built, residents of the building use energy and water to operate it, and eventually materials need to be replaced and the building demolished at the end of its life cycle. Each one of these steps has an impact—either immediate or gradual—on natural resources, ecosystems, and wildlife.

Homes, buildings, and communities can be designed to reduce the amount of natural resources they use and emissions they release.

However, homes, buildings, and communities can be designed to reduce the amount of natural resources used and emissions released. One approach to design that encourages people to account for the environmental impact of the built environment is green building. **Green building** is a term that describes the practice of making structures that are environmentally responsible and resource efficient for the entire life cycle of the building, from choosing a site for the structure to deconstruction of the structure.[2] Traditionally, buildings have been constructed with economics, function, resilience, and comfort in mind.[3] In other words, the focus of design has been on creating a building that is affordable, serves the purpose for which it was intended, lasts a long time, and is comfortable for its residents. Green building considers these factors in addition to the building's environmental footprint.

Another approach utilized in sustainable design is biomimicry. **Biomimicry** is a field of science in which nature is used as model to help create sustainable, human-designed products and solutions. Left to itself, nature is both adaptable and sustainable. Consider the example of termites living in extreme weather in Zimbabwe, where outside temperatures range from 35 to 104 degrees Fahrenheit. In order to keep the fungus they feed on alive, these termites build up very large mounds with a complex ventilation system so that the temperature within the mound stays near 87 degrees. The termites maintain a consistent temperature by blocking old vents and digging new ones to create effective air flow.[4]

The architecture firm ARUP worked with architect Mick Pearce to create a shopping center using these termite mounds as a model. The Eastgate Centre Shopping and Office Complex in Harare, Zimbabwe is designed so that air is drawn in and either cooled or heated by the building's concrete material. This air then moves throughout the building before leaving through chimneys at its top. The Eastgate Centre Office Complex has no mechanically controlled heating or air conditioning systems and uses less than 10% of the energy used by buildings of a similar size.[5]

Economy

As the example above suggests, designing buildings with the environment in mind can also have financial benefits. For instance, most sustainably designed buildings are oriented to passively take advantage of free sunlight and natural air movement. This passive design reduces the need for mechanical climate control, or systems such as air conditioners that require an energy input and machinery to operate. Reducing the amount of energy and water that a building uses can save money on utility bills and other operating costs.

Often green buildings will also use materials and appliances that are built to last, which can prevent the need to purchase frequent replacements. The U.S. Environmental Protection

Agency also suggests a further economic benefit: green buildings can improve the productivity of the people who work and live in the building.[6]

Society

Sustainably designed buildings and communities can play a positive role in human health and interaction among community members and provide residents with opportunities to make sustainable lifestyle choices.

We spend a lot of time inside buildings. On average, people in industrialized countries spend 90% of their time indoors.[7] Therefore, the materials used to construct a building and the design of a building can affect human health. Homes and offices can contain biological contaminants such as mold and bacteria as well as chemical contaminants such as by-products from heating systems and formaldehyde from some pressed-wood products. Couple these contaminants with inadequate air flow and there could be negative impacts on the health and productivity of the people in that building.[8]

On the other hand, a building's design can positively impact human health. Buildings that are more energy efficient and better ventilated can be more comfortable and reduce the risk of health problems from extreme weather conditions, indoor air pollution, or the transmission of airborne disease.[9] Buildings can also have materials that do not emit toxins.

Sustainable design strategies can promote better focus and better health, especially for those students with asthma. According to the U.S. Department of Education, over 20% of public schools report unsatisfactory indoor air quality.[10] Studies have shown that there is a 41% health improvement rate when the indoor air quality of a building improves.[11]

Perhaps one of the most pleasant aspects of sustainable design on the human level is the sense of community it can foster. Sustainable design can facilitate human interaction by building streets that encourage walking or parks for community members to enjoy. Conversely, design that does not include

Green building takes into account the entire life cycle of a building.

accessible public spaces or adequate public transportation can isolate people from their larger community and even their neighbors. Poorly designed communities can result in people spending hours of their day in traffic rather than spending time at home with their families or enjoying one of their favorite hobbies. It can also prevent those unable to drive, such as the elderly and individuals with disabilities, from being able to access community resources like libraries and parks.

All of these examples suggest the significance of sustainable design. However, it may be people's daily choices that ultimately determine whether the benefits of a sustainably designed building are maximized. For instance, neighborhoods and cities can be designed to provide residents with the option to take public transportation or walk to work or school, reducing strain on transportation infrastructure. **Infrastructure** refers to the basic facilities and services for the functioning of a community or society, such as transportation and communication systems, water and power systems, and public institutions. Yet, if residents continue to drive alone in their cars, then these options do not provide any of the benefits for which they were intended.

People stand near a skerm hut in a Bushmen village in Namibia.

Background on Sustainable Design

The built environment is nothing new; humans have been building shelters for thousands of years. Variation in the design of man-made environments is wide, ranging from temporary single-room huts to multi-story glass and steel buildings. Whether in a pre-urban setting or the heart of a modern megacity, the design of these dwellings is influenced by the physical environment in which people live as well as the social, economic, religious, and political views held by the community.[12]

For instance, lifestyle impacts a housing design. People living a nomadic lifestyle must be able to construct dwellings quickly and easily with materials found close by. The African Bushmen of the Kalahari Desert live a hunter-gatherer lifestyle and, since food is scarce for the majority of the year, they are constantly moving in search of new food. They construct shelters in just one to two hours and leave them after a few days. These skerm, or circular grass shelters, are made by driving a few branches into the ground and arching them to create a frame that is covered by grass.[13]

The climate and natural resources of an area also impact the design of dwellings. The cliff dwellings in what is now southwestern Colorado serve as one example of how humans learned to take advantage of sunlight for warmth in winter. In the 1200s, the Anasazi people built homes into the cliffs. These homes were south-facing and had cliff overhangs above them.[14] This placement meant that homes received heat from the sun during the winter and were shaded during the summer.[15]

People living in areas that are hot during the day and cool at night have learned to utilize building materials that keep their dwellings at a comfortable temperature. Have you ever walked inside a concrete building after a hot day and noticed how cool it was inside? Materials such as concrete and adobe have high *thermal mass*—

the ability to absorb, store, and release heat.[16] In the past, pueblo structures in the plateaus of Arizona and New Mexico were covered inside and out with compact clay mud. The outer walls absorbed solar energy during the hot days and this heat traveled through the walls to the inside of the homes during the cool nights. By morning, the walls would have cooled significantly to give inhabitants a cool refuge from the heat during the day. Today the same effect is created by using adobe brick or stone and adobe mortar.[17]

The Glass Box

In the 1900s some dramatic changes had an impact on the sustainability of the built environment. New manufactured technologies such as structural steel, reflective glass, and low-wattage fluorescent lighting started to change the way buildings were designed and how cities looked. Large heating and air conditioning systems powered by fossil fuels allowed humans to moderate their environment more than ever before and "glass box" style buildings became increasingly popular.[18] With electricity, air conditioning, and other new technologies, homes, office buildings, and shopping centers could be built with little thought to a region's climate or natural resources.

There are many benefits of this type of design, but there are also some significant consequences. For example, buildings that use mechanical and electrical systems such as pumps, fans, and air conditioning for climate control (rather than passive systems such as windows and materials that naturally absorb heat and distribute air) require significant amounts of energy.[19] This can increase a building's operating costs and, depending on the type of energy source used, can release greenhouse gases into the atmosphere. Furthermore, building materials that became common during this period, such as asbestos and lead-based paint, have now been found harmful to human health.

Structural steel and reflective glass changed the look of buildings.

Green Building Movement

Examples of sustainably designed buildings can be found throughout human history. However, the modern green building movement began gaining momentum with the environmental movement of the 1960s and the oil embargo of the 1970s. One consequence of the 1970s energy crisis associated with the oil embargo was a greater awareness of the amount of energy used in the built environment.

The American Institute of Architects responded to increasing energy awareness in a number of ways. They formed an energy task force and a Committee on Energy. Eventually, with funding from the U.S. Environmental Protection Agency (EPA), they published the Environmental Resource Guide (ERG) in 1992. This pivotal document provides information on building products based on their life cycle. Many people credit the ERG with encouraging manufacturers to make products more environmentally friendly.[20]

Several other events helped to power the green building movement. One important element was a clear definition for the term sustainable development, offered by Gro Harlem Brundtland (the Norwegian prime minister at the time) in 1987. *Sustainable development* is development that meets the needs of the present without compromising the ability of future generations to meet their own needs. Another was U.S. President Bill Clinton's announcement of the "Greening of the White House Initiative" on Earth Day in 1993. This same year, the United States Green Building Council (USGBC) was formed.

In 1998, the USGBC started the Leadership in Energy and Environmental Design (LEED) program.[21] LEED created a framework with useful and measurable ways to design, construct, operate, and maintain buildings sustainably.[22] The LEED certification program uses a rating system to verify whether a home, building, or community was designed and built with high standards for environmental and human health.[23] Depending on the number of points it receives, a building can earn certified, silver, gold, or platinum status.[24] The certification program evaluates and awards points for the following features of a building site:[25]

- Sustainability of a site—Does the location of a building have minimal impact on the surrounding environment, such as waterways and ecosystems? Is the building site already developed land or undeveloped land? (It is preferable to preserve undeveloped land.)
- Water efficiency—Is water used efficiently both inside and outside the building?
- Energy and atmosphere—Is energy used in a way that prevents waste and encourages efficiency? Are renewable energy sources used?
- Materials and resources—Is the amount of waste that is generated by a building reduced and recycled? Are the materials used for a building sustainably grown, produced, and transported?
- Indoor environmental quality—Does the building have clean air, access to natural light, and good acoustics?

Students walk past a LEED certified building on the Central Michigan University campus.

- Locations and linkages—Is a building built away from environmentally sensitive areas? Is a home built close to existing infrastructure, community resources, and open space so that people can walk or enjoy the outdoors?
- Awareness and education—Have developers made an effort to educate the building's occupants about how to take full advantage of the green features of the building?
- Innovation in design—Does the project involve a LEED Accredited Professional? Does the project use new methods and ideas that go above and beyond LEED standards?
- Regional priority—Does the project respond appropriately to the unique environmental needs of the region?[26]

Sustainable design practices are catching on across the world and the LEED International Program provides guidance for green building efforts in various countries. Green Building Councils have formed in nations as diverse as Colombia, Jordan, and South Korea, to name a few.[27]

There are other programs that evaluate the sustainability of design and construction. For example, the Building Research Establishment Environmental Assessment Method (BREEAM) is widely used in Europe and the United Kingdom to implement sustainable building practices and to measure effectiveness.[28] Taking green building a step further, the Living Building Challenge identifies and encourages use of design methods found to be the most sustainable. It is comprised of the following seven performance areas, each with its own requirements: site, water, energy, health, materials, equity, and beauty.[29]

Each of these programs provides strategies for sustainable design. But what does sustainable design look like when it is carried out? The following section gives an overview of sustainable design at various scales, from the design of materials to individual homes to large cities.

Sustainable Design Today

Designing Sustainable Materials

When you buy a product, do you ever consider what will happen to it when it no longer works or fits? Companies that choose to design sustainable products sure do. In fact, the *Cradle to Cradle®* approach considers how a product at the end of its useful life can be recycled into something new or even changed into something more valuable than the previous product.[30] Rather than focus only on the linear life of a product from its creation (cradle) to the end of its useful life (grave), the Environmental Protection Encouragement Agency (EPEA) encourages manufacturers to base their designs on the way natural systems continuously cycle nutrients throughout an ecosystem.

> *Sustainable design practices are catching on across the world.*

Think about a leaf that falls off a tree. In an ecosystem, this would not be left as useless waste; the leaf is eaten by microbes and the nutrients in the leaf are returned to the soil to be used again by the tree or another organism.[31] Designers who adopt this model strive to design products that will biodegrade and return nutrients back to the earth or use materials that can be recycled over and over. This helps prevent useful materials from heading to a landfill and reduces the likelihood of natural resource exhaustion.

The Cradle to Cradle® Products Innovation Institute offers certification at four different levels. Each level indicates the degree to which Cradle to Cradle® principles are incorporated into a product's design. Building materials, cleaning supplies, and even toilet paper have been certified. In fact, the Dutch company van Houtum is the first to manufacture both Cradle to Cradle® certified toilet paper and paper towels. The company has achieved a silver level certification, meaning that they have extensive knowledge about where all of their supplies come from, how much recycled content they use, how much water they use, and what social consequences result from their paper manufacture. The toilet paper is made from 100% recycled material, 85% of which is post-consumer. Using the Cradle to Cradle® philosophy and methodology has improved van Houtum's image and their customers' satisfaction. It hasn't hurt their bottom line, either.[32]

Manufacturers of products are not the only ones in the sustainable materials market. Consumers can also use Cradle to Cradle® thinking when buying or disposing of materials. According to USGBC, an average of 3.9 pounds of waste is created for every one square foot of commercial building constructed. At the end of a building's life, an average of 155 pounds of waste is generated for every one square foot of a commercial building demolished.[33] In the United States, this means about 135 million tons of waste is sent to landfills each year.[34] Those managing construction and demolition can work to reduce waste and divert it from going to the landfills. In fact, there are many organizations working to reduce this type of waste. One nonprofit, The RE Store, will pick up waste from homes for free and either recycle it or sell it for reuse at one of its stores.[35] Not only does this protect the environment, but the unique and vintage salvage materials and furniture can add character to a building.

Sustainably designed building materials are part of the foundation of a sustainable home. Recall that the LEED certification program awards credits for using materials and resources sustainably when designing or renovating homes and buildings. In fact, LEED certification requires buildings to have an area where occupants can recycle materials and it is suggested that measures are taken to reduce the amount of waste that goes to the landfill during construction by recycling or saving materials that could be used again. Points are also awarded to projects that build with materials that are locally harvested and manufactured, recycled, and made from renewable materials or certified wood.[36] All of these options can help protect natural resources.

Solar panels take advantage of a renewable source of energy—the sun.

Residences

You don't have to construct a home from the ground up or perform a complete remodel to make changes that positively contribute to your comfort, your wallet, and your environment. Simply how we maintain and operate our homes—whether apartments, mobile homes, or single-family homes—can also make a difference on the health of our environment, society, and economy.

Think about our energy use, for instance. Energy is used to light and heat our homes. It powers our refrigerators, runs our electronics, and heats our water. In the first part of the millennium, the U.S. residential sector consumed about 23% of the energy used in the country.[37]

Unfortunately, a lot of this energy is wasted due to drafty windows or inefficient appliances. Over 30% of heated or cooled air can escape a home through things such as leaky windows, doors, vents, and fireplaces. Up to 30-50% of this air may be lost through leaky air ducts alone. Fixing these leaks can keep hot or cool air inside your home and save you money on your utility bills.[38] There are many other ways that people can save energy in their homes. For example, replacing incandescent light bulbs with fluorescent bulbs can reduce the amount of electricity you use. Replacing one regular bulb with a fluorescent bulb in every U.S. home could save the country $600 million in energy costs.[39] Not only do these actions save you money, they can also contribute to reducing the environmental impact of electricity generation, such as the amount of greenhouse gases released from non-renewable energy sources.

People shopping for new electronics or appliances can use their consumer power to reduce their energy consumption. For example, selecting energy-efficient appliances when replacing older ones is one way to conserve natural resources and save money on energy bills. In some regions, people may even have the option to purchase electricity generated by renewable resources.

Electric meters measure the amount of electricity used in a building.

Another natural resource used in homes is water. According to the Save Water Today campaign, 36 states may face significant water shortages by 2013 and yet the amount of water wasted from leaks in U.S. homes could be over one trillion gallons per year (the same as the amount of water used by Los Angeles, Chicago, and Miami together)![40] Reducing the amount of water we use and waste is one way to protect the water needs of all people and conserve the amount of water in lakes, streams, and rivers.

There are many things we can do to save water. To begin with, we can take shorter showers and turn off the faucet while brushing our teeth. We can also check and fix leaky faucets and toilets and install low-flow shower and faucet nozzles and toilets.

Even the plants we choose to place in our yard can help us conserve resources. Trees and plants that are native to your region rely on local rainfall and generally do not need to be watered frequently. Planting native trees that provide shade can also cool your residence in the summer. You can collect and store rainwater at home to use for plants in dry periods. Choices like these can help save both water and money.

In addition to consuming energy at home, we also generate wastes. Think about all the things you dispose of: soda cans, water bottles, glass jars, food scraps, leftovers, and so on. Rather than sending all our trash to the landfill, we can first try to reduce what we consume and then recycle, reuse, and compost what we can. Recycling the aluminum, glass, plastic, and paper produced by a household prevents the extraction of more natural resources, creates jobs, and saves energy. In fact, producing cans from recycled aluminum takes 95% less energy than producing cans from virgin ore.[41] So just tossing an aluminum can into a recycling bin rather than a trash can is an act of energy conservation.

Another useful resource that many of us toss out is food and yard waste. If we think about the role of these wastes in the ecosystem, however, then we might remember that this organic matter is rich with nutrients that could be composted and reused by nature. *Compost* is decomposed organic waste that is dark in color, odorless, and nutrient rich. It can be added to soil in order to grow new plants or add to existing landscapes.[42] Unlike composting, when organic waste heads to the landfill, it rots and produces methane (a greenhouse gas). In the United States, food waste is a significant source of methane; 33 million tons of food was thrown away in the early 2000s.[43] If instead we composted this yard and food waste, we could capture the benefits of this nutrient-rich waste and prevent unnecessary greenhouse gases from being released into the atmosphere. Of course, reducing the amount of food waste we produce in the first place is a way to consume even more sustainably.

School and Office Buildings

Ideas for household energy conservation and sustainability can also be implemented on a larger scale. Think about how waste is handled in your school: Is trash separated from recyclables? Does food waste get composted? What happens to your electronics when they break? Many schools are turning toward more sustainable consumption of waste, energy, and water—and saving money doing it. In fact, many such school-wide efforts are initiated by students. For example, after a group of students conducted a waste audit at Bainbridge High School in Washington State, they found out that the school's waste was made of 18% paper lunch trays and 30% food scraps and other organic matter. These students created a goal to reduce school trash by 50% by establishing recycling, reuse, and composting systems. In two years, the students reduced their school's trash costs from $14,000 per year to $10,600 per year.[44]

When constructing a building from the ground up, architects and engineers have the chance to situate the building with respect to its natural surroundings so that it utilizes natural sunlight and air flow. **Passive solar design** involves design techniques and building materials that naturally collect, store, and distribute heat rather than using energy to run mechanical and electrical systems.[45] For example, in the northern hemisphere, buildings like homes and greenhouses may be built with large, south-facing windows to capture heat and light from the low sun in the winter. To keep these buildings cool in the summer, overhangs (roofs, balconies, or screens that stick out beyond the walls of a building) can be placed above windows to shade buildings from the high summer sun. Architects can provide these same passive solar benefits to buildings in the southern hemisphere by using large north-facing windows.[46]

Passive solar design techniques were used to create this housing plan.

Neighborhoods

Beyond greening buildings, how might a *neighborhood* (a smaller region within a city or town) be designed to promote environmental, economic, and social sustainability?

One factor that contributes to the sustainability of a neighborhood is walkability. According to Walk Score, a neighborhood that is walkable can benefit human and environmental health, individual finances, and communities. For example, people who live in a walkable city tend to weigh 6-10 pounds less than those living elsewhere. Also, when people are able to walk or bike rather than drive, pollution goes down. So does the cost of living; cars are the second highest expense for U.S. households. Studies also suggest that the more time a person spends commuting in a car, the less time they spend participating in community activities.[47]

So what makes a neighborhood walkable? A walkable neighborhood is designed so that schools, workplaces, and businesses are close enough for people to access by foot and affordable housing is available in the same area. A walkable neighborhood will also have some sort of city center,

CASE STUDY: Bertschi's Living Science Wing

At Bertschi School, an independent elementary school in Seattle, Washington, sustainability is not just a concept integrated into the curricula, it is also the model that guided the design of its science building. The building was the product of a partnership between Bertschi School and the Restorative Design Collective, a group of design professionals inspired by the Living Building Challenge to create the most sustainable buildings possible. In 2009, Bertschi needed a new science building and the Restorative Design Collective offered to create a building design on the leading edge of sustainability for free, saving the school over $500,000 in design costs.[48] The resulting science wing, which opened in 2011, is Washington State's first Living Building and the world's first building to meet the Living Building Challenge 2.0 standards.[49]

The Living Science Wing's indoor green wall filters grey water through the process of evapotranspiration.

The Living Building Science Wing is not only a model for the global sustainable design community, but it is also a teaching tool for Bertschi School's students. In science class, students can witness rainwater harvesting firsthand by watching rain flow from the roof through a transparent channel in the classroom. This water is then filtered for reuse or used to water an outdoor garden. A moss mat on the roof absorbs storm water and grey water is cleaned through the process of evapotranspiration by an indoor green wall! No black water is produced because the building has composting toilets.[50] These features make the science wing net-zero for water consumption. It is also net-zero for energy consumption—solar panels generate electricity for the building and its infrastructure helps to conserve energy.[51]

The Living Building Science Wing is not a place in which science is simply taught, but a place "where science lives."[52]

Walkable neighborhoods often have community spaces for residents to enjoy.

parks and public spaces for people to enjoy, and enough people to support thriving businesses and widespread public transportation.[53]

Safety is another factor important to sustainable neighborhoods. According to Jane Jacobs (a community activist and writer who encouraged a community-based planning approach[54]), a street that is well used is more likely to be a safe street than a street that is empty. When many people are present at all hours of the day, they watch and monitor what's going on, even if only out of curiosity.[55] In order to encourage many different people to use the streets throughout the day, then, a street should have a variety of shops with windows or porches that face the sidewalks and streets.[56] Mixed-use development, that is the inclusion of residential, commercial, industrial, and other land uses in the same area, is another way to attract a variety of people to a neighborhood and encourage well-used streets.

Another factor that contributes to a neighborhood's sustainability is energy consumption. Neighborhoods can be designed to be more energy-efficient and to rely more on renewable sources of energy. One way to do this is to build District Energy Systems.

District Energy Systems have a central plant that creates steam, hot water, or cold water. This is then sent via underground pipes to individual buildings where people can use it to control their indoor climate.[57] This is beneficial because separate buildings no longer need to fuel a boiler or air conditioning on site. The system can save building managers and residents money on the operation and maintenance of these machines and make the site safer (free of fuel). If the central plants used to generate hot and cold water are built to use renewable energy, District Energy Systems can also help reduce pollution.[58]

District Energy Systems can even be built to use cogeneration—combined heat and power to produce heating and cooling as well as electricity for buildings. While most power plants lose about 60% of the heat produced by burning fuel in order to generate electricity, combined heat and power plants are designed to capture this wasted heat and use it to provide heating and cooling to buildings.[59] Cogeneration is yet another way that neighborhoods can increase their energy efficiency.

Cities

Urban areas, or cities, are places that include several neighborhoods and have a higher **population density** (number of people per unit area) than suburban and rural areas. Today, more than half of the world's population lives in urban areas and it is expected that, as the world population increases, urban areas will absorb this population growth.[60] What implications does this have for sustainability and how can cities be designed to encourage sustainable lifestyles?

A growing number of people in a city presents both opportunities and challenges with respect to sustainability. While cities can be places where jobs, services, and opportunities are centralized, they may also be places where air pollution, physical inactivity, traffic injuries, and violence are concentrated.[61] Additionally, those living in cities often have unequal access to resources.

Among those who lack access to basic services are the approximately 828 million people living in slum households around the world. Slum households are defined as homes that lack one or more of the following conditions: safe water, safe sanitation, sufficient living area (no more than three people per room), durable housing (safe location and quality construction), and protection from eviction.[62] One of the world's larger slums is Dharavi, located in the city of Mumbai, India. Around one million people live in an area of one square mile.

Another challenge of urbanization is that as buildings and paved roads have replaced natural vegetation, cities can become "heat islands" (regions that have hotter temperatures than neighboring rural areas).[63] These higher temperatures can contribute to increased energy consumption (and, therefore, more pollution) as people attempt to cool themselves with air conditioning or electric fans in the summer. People may suffer discomfort or serious heat-related illnesses due to higher temperatures. The environment is at risk, too. Storm water can be warmed as it passes over hot rooftops and roads. When it flows into aquatic ecosystems like rivers, lakes, and wetlands, this warm water can be harmful.[64]

Despite these major concerns, there exists a great opportunity to design or redesign cities to be more sustainable. **Urban planning**, or city planning, is a branch of architecture focused on the design and organization of urban space and activities. Urban planners develop short- and long-term plans for city development and look at the best use of a city's resources and land. They also develop policies such as zoning ordinances that limit what can be built where. Urban planners work with a wide variety of people at all levels of government and private industry.

There are many strategies that urban planners can take to increase the sustainability of cities. To counteract the heat island effect, for example, urban planners might increase the amount of trees and vegetation in a city. They might also install roofs that reflect rather than absorb heat or create green rooftops with gardens or other vegetation to reduce the temperature of a city. Chicago's City Hall installed a green roof with native grasses, hardy ornamental grasses, and a couple of types of trees to test out its ability to cool the building and to serve as a green roof demonstration for the area.[65] Another technique planners can use to reduce the heat island effect is to choose materials for pavement that reflect solar energy and/or allow water to permeate it.[66]

Designing city streets to provide residents with options for transportation can also reduce the energy consumption of a city. According to the National Complete Streets Coalition, the transportation sector has the fastest-growing rate of carbon dioxide emissions in the United

Increasing the amount of vegetation in a city can reduce the heat island effect.

States.[67] Designing streets that have safe sidewalks, bicycle lanes (or wide shoulders), and accessible public transportation stops can encourage people to use more ecofriendly transportation options and allow people of all ages and abilities to be more mobile in cities. There are many public health benefits as well. Streets that are designed for all types of transportation can improve safety, encourage healthful walking and biking, lower transportation costs, and also encourage community.[68]

New Yorkers: Public Transit Trendsetters

One could say that New York City is a place of extremes. Compared to other U.S. cities, New York City has the highest population density, the highest rate of residents that use public transportation (50%), and the lowest average energy consumption and greenhouse gas emissions.[69] New York's Transit Authority is also the first in the United States to attempt to measure its impact on local greenhouse gas emissions.[70]

The city continues to emphasize sustainability. The New York City Department of Transportation, with input from the community, recently redesigned streets and sidewalks surrounding Union Square to have safer pedestrian crossings and add bike lanes and streetscape improvements. For a city square that can see as many as 200,000 people on a summer day, these improvements aim to increase the accessibility of this area while reducing traffic accidents.[71]

Along with conserving energy, sustainable design can help cities conserve other natural resources. Take water, for example. All of the water that goes down our sinks and is flushed from our toilets is called wastewater. This wastewater then goes to a wastewater treatment center. Reducing the amount of wastewater that needs to be treated can save freshwater and energy. One way to do this is to reuse grey water. *Grey water* is the wastewater from baths and showers, bathroom sinks, and washing machines. Instead of sending grey water to a wastewater treatment facility, this water can be used directly for non-drinking purposes such as irrigating landscapes or flushing toilets. There are several other ways to reduce wastewater production including composting toilets and waterless urinals.

In addition to reducing wastewater, a city can reduce and recycle solid waste that usually goes to a landfill or incinerator. The City of Seattle has a municipal recycling program similar to those found in many cities in the United States. However, one unique component of

Grey water is used to water this El Paso prison garden.

CASE STUDY: Students Conduct ECOoffice Audits

ECOoffice is a community service learning activity for students who work directly with local businesses to conduct a basic carbon footprint analysis. From this analysis, youths prepare a report that includes results and recommendations of affordable, achievable actions the company can take to reduce energy consumption, save office resources and lower operating costs.

ECOoffice is one component of the Jane Goodall Institute-Shanghai Roots & Shoots' Eco Audit Educational Program. The company brings together local businesses, college students and high school students in a collaborative effort to promote environmentally responsible practices in the business environment.

In April 2009, a trained student group from Shanghai High School International Division conducted an ECOoffice audit of the Unilever Corporation offices in Shangai. Using a standardized ECOoffice Checklist as their evaluation guide for measuring the office's sustainable practices, the students conducted the audit which consists of three parts:
- walkthrough observations
- administrative interviews
- employee surveys

These students conducted an ECOoffice audit of the Unilever Corporation offices in Shangai.

With Unilever-Shanghai and Shanghai Roots & Shoots support, the students submitted an audit report which contained positive and negative points about company operations and employee behaviors. The report included practical suggestions for improving the company's environmental impact.

After implementing the students' suggestions throughout following year; in 2010, the employees reduced their resource consumption and the company's operating costs. Unilever management realized the sustainable improvements brought by ECOoffice project also would benefit the company financially; therefore, they wished to bring green concepts to more employees.

A business professional from Seattle learned about the positive impacts ECOoffice had on the Shanghai business community and asked Shanghai Roots & Shoots if the program could be brought to the Seattle area. Since that time, 141 students have conducted 38 ECOoffice audits at various workplaces throughout Washington State impacting 2,698 employees. These workplaces included architectural and engineering firms, fire stations, restaurants and retail shops, a local YMCA and a few Washington State Governmental offices. The auditors consisted of students of various ages and numbers: from small independent groups of one or two students, to curriculum programs at a college, three high schools and even a very small eighth grade class.

The ECOaudit Program was also brought to New Delhi, India; and is run as a program of the Indian Youth Climate Network (IYCN). Since then, 55 college students from New Delhi audited 13 companies impacting 1320 employees. Re-audits will be conducted beginning the fall of 2011.

Seattle's program is that the city made it illegal for residents and commercial businesses to throw out recyclable materials. If more than 10% recyclable materials are in a trash can, that can will be tagged and receive a warning. The third time this happens, the trash can owner can be fined.[76]

The city also provides food and yard waste collection—the waste picked up is turned into compost. Currently, about one third of Seattle's waste is food waste. When it's put in the trash, this food waste travels 300 miles on a train to a landfill in Oregon where it takes up space and produces methane gas. Rather than send this food waste to the landfill, Seattle residents can place it in the yard waste bin and it will be turned into compost.[77]

Beyond the City

How does sustainable design relate to communities that have developed outside cities? Both suburban and rural communities are characterized by lower population densities and are located outside a dense urban core.

Suburbs

Located on the outskirts of a city, suburban communities provide some benefits that people might not find in a city. Residents of the suburbs often enjoy larger homes and properties, a greener outdoor environment, and more options for driving and parking.[78]

Suburban developments are typically separated into housing subdivisions, shopping centers, office parks, and public buildings, rather than groups of mixed-use buildings as you would find in a city. These different components are connected via roads.[79] Such separation of buildings by type has its roots in 19th century Europe. During this time, industrialization had created very unhealthy conditions in European cities and city planners advocated for the separation of factories from homes. Within decades of implementing this plan, cities such as London, Paris, and Barcelona were much healthier places to live. In fact, life expectancies of residents in these cities actually rose.[80]

Yet this separation of sectors and building types is now presenting some challenges to the sustainability of suburbs. One main challenge is that most suburban areas are not designed to promote travel by foot or public transportation. When homes are separated a significant distance from stores, schools, offices, or cultural buildings, this encourages or even necessitates driving in order to shop for groceries, get to school, or go to the bank. Suburban streets are often designed to be wider and blocks longer than in cities, making them less pedestrian-friendly. Not only does this emphasis on the automobile contribute to air pollution, but it also puts people that cannot drive or afford cars at a disadvantage as well as reducing the health benefits of walking.[81]

The combination of a lower population density and a separation of building types (housing developments, industrial plants, etc.) requires a large amount of infrastructure such as pipes and roads. As this infrastructure ages and requires maintenance, local residents will usually witness tax increases.[82] The layout of suburban communities can also decrease people's interaction with each other and their participation in the public realm.

Rural Areas

According to the U.S. Census Bureau, rural areas are made up of open country and have fewer than 2,500 residents.[83] In the past, small towns and cities often developed in order to produce goods and extract resources from the surrounding land. These communities were often located near a train station or port where the goods could be shipped to other locations. Many also had a compact, main street where residents could participate in civic, cultural, and social activities.[84]

Today, some rural communities are under pressure to develop in order to accommodate people moving into the area while other communities are facing population decline due to lack of employment and other opportunities. Also, there are generally fewer people, financial, and technical resources in rural areas, which can

In the suburbs, housing is usually segregated from offices and public services.

impact the maintenance of aging infrastructure such as roads. How can these areas maintain their characteristic small-town feel while prospering economically?

In the early 2000s, the U.S. Department of Transportation, U.S. Department of Housing and Urban Development, and the U.S. Environmental Protection Agency created the Partnership for Sustainable Communities in order to help urban, suburban, and rural communities to grow economically, provide residents with more housing and transportation options, and keep air and water clean. The partnership's goal to build sustainable rural communities has at its foundation an understanding of the unique relationship between a town's residents and its surrounding geography.[85] The partnership is guided by a framework called the Livability Principles. These principles are:

- Provide more transportation choices
- Promote equitable, affordable housing
- Enhance economic competitiveness
- Support existing communities
- Coordinate and leverage federal policies and investment
- Value communities and neighborhoods

Lake Village, Arkansas, a small town with less than 3,000 residents, put some of these principles into practice to revitalize their community. Over the years, Lake Village had seen economic decline and many shops and services had moved from central Main Street locations to the edges of the town. In fact, the offices of the mayor, police, and court clerk were located in different places and using space inefficiently. In an effort to revitalize the community and bring people and money back to Main Street, Mayor JoAnne Bush and the City Council members decided to use a historical John L. Tushek (National Register) building to house these public services. In 2010, the town received funding from USDA-Rural Development and the Department of Energy for this project. The funds helped to restore this building using LEED standards and creative design practices such as insulating the walls with old jeans.[86]

The historic John L. Tushek building was renovated using LEED standards.

YOUTH PROFILE
Evans Wadongo

When Evans Wadongo was younger, the only way he could study was by the light of a kerosene lamp. His family had only one lamp and it was too weak for the whole family to use at once, restricting the amount of time Evans could study at night. Because of this, Evans didn't perform as well as he thought he could on exams. The dim light and smoke from the kerosene lamp also damaged his eyesight. Evans was not alone; in his village, many

Evans stands with a recipient of the MwangaBora lantern.

families did not have access to electricity. Many students who lacked proper lighting eventually ended up dropping out of school. Without a complete education, students like these often remain in poverty.[87]

Evans, however, did pursue his education and went on to study at a Kenyan university. One day, he had an idea for something that would transform his village: a solar-powered LED lantern (LED stands for light-emitting

CAREER PROFILE — Architect and Engineer

Many different professionals are involved in the creation of the built environment. Architects, for instance, are professionals who plan and design the structures that we see around us. Not only do architects consider the appearance of a building or structure, but they also consider the safety, cost, and people who will be using the structure.[88] Architects collaborate and communicate with many different people: the clients who have hired them to design a structure, construction teams who will build the structure, and different types of engineers. For instance, structural engineers are knowledgeable about materials involved in the construction of a building and help to design buildings that are structurally appropriate for the environment in which they are built.[89]

Elizabeth English is unusual in that she is both an architect and an engineer. From the time that she graduated from high school, Elizabeth thought that she might want to be an architect and chose a university where she could study architecture. When Elizabeth realized that it was more difficult for her than for her male peers to get exposure to the technical side of design by getting a summer job in construction, she decided to learn about building technology by studying engineering. Through her studies and work experience, she has essentially crafted an interdisciplinary background that is helping her to make a real difference in the world whether it is teaching at the University of Waterloo's School of Architecture in Cambridge, Ontario, or working to help prevent flood damage to homes in southern Louisiana.

Dr. Elizabeth English is both an architect and an engineer.

Elizabeth was conducting hurricane wind research at Louisiana State University when Hurricane Katrina hit. After Hurricanes Katrina and Rita, residents of South Louisiana were required to adapt their homes to meet new elevation requirements. One way to do this is by raising the house on permanent stilts. Unfortunately, this makes the home more vulnerable to wind damage, makes homes difficult to access for the elderly and disabled, and significantly impacts the appearance of the neighborhoods and the residents' way of life—the "front porch" culture of the area. Also, this is costly to implement, especially for low-income families. Because of her background in architecture, Dr. English is sensitive to the social impacts of architectural solutions, and, because of her engineering background, she is aware of the structural challenges presented by recurrent flooding and wind.

This interdisciplinary approach led Dr. English to found the Buoyant Foundation Project. This research project advocates for another approach to flood damage prevention: retrofitting houses with foundations that float! Essentially, buoyant foundations are added to existing houses that are connected to poles, so that the houses can slide up and down. Homes remain on the ground when there is no flooding and can rise with the waters when it does flood. These foundations, also known as amphibious foundations, are a low-cost and effective way to keep the people of Louisiana safe while preserving their culture and architecture. This sustainable solution is the outcome of Dr. English's unique background and interests. As she says, "the best thing about having put together an interdisciplinary background is that I can move back and forth between engineering and architecture as well as bring a different perspective to each field."

diode, a reliable, energy-efficient light source). An artisan helped him construct the lamp and family and friends helped him out financially. Evans named these lamps "MwangaBora," Swahili for "better light."

Evans gained support for the project from the organization Sustainable Development for All—Kenya; eventually, the organization invited Evans to be a partner and chairman of the board. The lanterns are constructed by volunteers. Local women's groups and governments help determine which families are most in need of the lamps. Evans' goal is to create MwangaBora for people living in rural areas throughout Kenya. These lights have many benefits:

- Construction of the lamps leads to local jobs
- Use of the lamps reduces the amount of money a family has to spend on kerosene
- Use of the lamps gives more children a fair opportunity for education
- Replacement of kerosene lamps with LED-powered lamps reduces respiratory illnesses, eye problems, and hazards for fires[90]

Pathways to Progress: Sustainable Design

According to the American Institute of Architects, in the early 2000s buildings and construction were responsible for almost half of the greenhouse gas emissions and energy used each year in the United States.[91] This included the energy required to create building materials, transport them to construction sites, and operate completed buildings. The numbers are even higher for global building and construction.[92] As you know, greenhouse gas emissions and environmental degradation such as deforestation can contribute to climate change.

While these statistics can be sobering, they also suggest that those who design and construct buildings as well as those of us who live in them can make a big difference, if we take action. At each scale of the design process—from choosing a building site in a new construction project to weatherizing buildings for energy conservation—it is possible to reduce the amount of energy and resources used in the built environment. In fact, communities and governments all around the world are turning toward design to promote environmental, economic, and social sustainability. Consider the following examples.

Curitiba, Brazil

Take the city of Curitiba in Brazil. It has established a system for waste that responds to local environmental, economic, and social issues. The Garbage Purchase Program, created with lower-income areas in mind, allows low-income residents to get a bag of food, public transit tokens, or school notebooks in exchange for turning in bags of trash.[93]

Additionally, the design of the city's transportation systems is creative and inexpensive. Throughout the city, there are five different "citizenship streets"—pedestrian-only malls that contain branch offices of many government departments in addition to libraries, community meeting rooms, markets, and sports facilities.[94] The city also has a trinary road system in which wide, one-way roads quickly lead people into and out of the city. These roads surround a middle road that has lanes for express buses only and two lanes for local use.[95]

> *In the early 2000s buildings and construction were responsible for almost half of the greenhouse gas emissions and energy used each year in the United States.*

Denver, Colorado

In Colorado, the Denver Housing Authority is working together with individual residents and community stakeholders of the Mariposa Homes housing development in order to create a redevelopment plan. The intent is to revitalize this community, which is home to a higher than average crime rate and concentrated poverty. Through one-on-one interviews with residents and a committee made up of locals and community stakeholders, the Denver Housing Authority is working with the Lincoln Park/La Alma community to create an environmentally sustainable, culturally diverse, and economically viable region.[96] They plan to use green design practices to construct mixed-use buildings with housing as well as business. Because the project will be performed in phases, people who already live in the neighborhood will not be forced to move to other areas.[97]

Portland, Oregon

Progress is also being made in Oregon State. In 2009, the City of Portland and Multnomah County passed a Climate Change Action Plan to reduce their emissions by 2050.[98] This Oregon county has already been working for years to reduce carbon dioxide emissions through public transit projects and green building policies. Although the population of the area has grown, its emissions have dropped—a promising success story for the rest of the nation.[99]

One area of focus in Portland's plan is reducing emissions from transportation. Portland now boasts the highest percentage of bicycle commuters of any city in the United States. Yet, as noted in the city's Climate Change Action Plan, it is not enough to simply plan for and create infrastructure that allows for safe bicycle travel and accessible public transportation.[100] Individuals must ultimately choose to take advantage of eco-friendly options that are offered by sustainable design—as well as all of the health, environmental, and financial benefits that come along with it.

WHAT YOU CAN DO — Sustainable Design

Wondering what you can do to promote sustainability and sustainable design?

- Attend and participate in public meetings where city planners give opportunities for community input.
- Work to reduce greenhouse gas emissions and energy use by taking public transit, walking, cycling, or carpooling with friends.
- Use your consumer power. The next time you go to buy a product, consider choosing an item that is made of and packaged with materials that can be reused or recycled when you are finished with it, rather than a product that will end up in a landfill.
- Start a Green Team. Join forces with other students and staff at your school to help your school deal with waste, water, and energy more sustainably.

Students in a school in Japan address waste issues.

POINT | COUNTERPOINT

Are historic buildings worth preserving?

POINT

Yes

- **The demolition of historic buildings is costly.** But the reuse of these buildings provides environmental savings. Creating new buildings has climate change impacts and it can take between 10 and 80 years for new buildings to overcome these impacts. On the other hand, reusing materials and retrofitting buildings can significantly reduce these effects on the environment.[101]

- **New is not always better.** Historic buildings have a lot to offer. Take for instance historic neighborhood schools. These schools located in neighborhoods provide the opportunity for students to walk or bike to them. They can foster community and civic pride. When new schools are created, they may have to be created on the outskirts of a town. Often, the new architecture does not reflect a sense of pride and its life span is less than 30 years.[102]

COUNTERPOINT

No

- **Preserving historic buildings can cost taxpayers billions of dollars and threaten public safety.** Are they worth the cost? Some believe that these buildings are meant to sustain cultural values. Historic buildings can create a sense of place and provide historical associations.[103] But the cost is not worth the preservation.

- **Historic buildings are very susceptible to damage from earthquakes.** While these buildings can be retrofitted to meet new construction requirements, the very things that make them historic are lost during this transformation.[104] Historic buildings are typically not designed to absorb the impacts of sudden movements from earthquakes.

The historic John L. Tushek building has been renovated in an effort to revitalize downtown Lake Village, Arkansas.

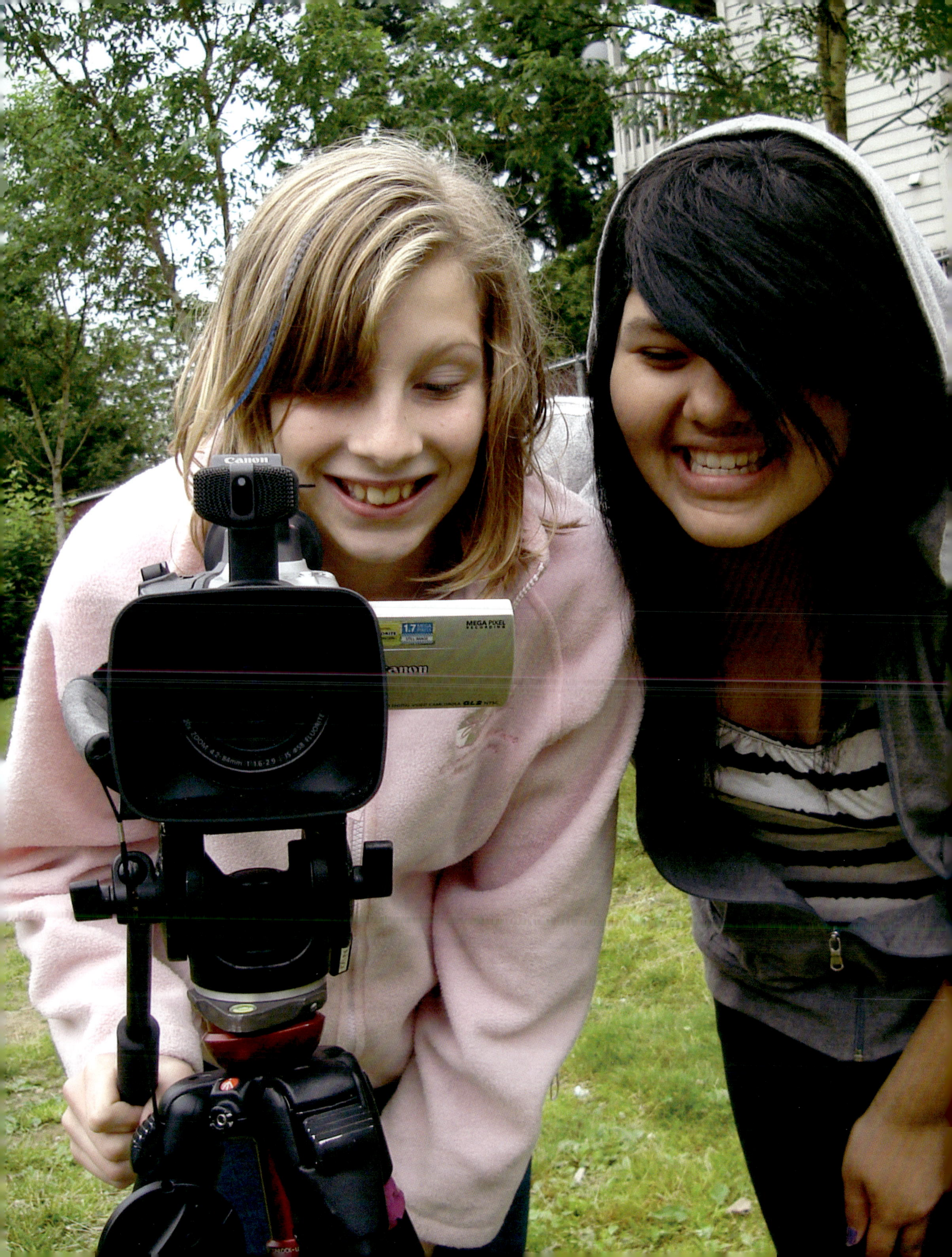
Canon
MEGA PIXEL

Chapter 24

Taking Action

> **GUIDING QUESTIONS**
> - What motivates individuals and groups to work for change?
> - What steps can you personally take to start addressing an issue you care about?

Introduction to Taking Action

Consider the following: a little girl born in London, England receives a stuffed chimpanzee when she is two years old. Throughout her childhood, she's a decent student, but more than anything, she loves being outdoors and learning about animals. One time, she spends five hours studying about how a hen lays an egg. By the time she is 10 years old, she dreams of traveling to Africa to live with animals. She grows up during a war and her dad goes off to fight. After the war, her parents get divorced. When she finishes high school at the age of 18, she does not have the money to attend university. Instead, she works as a secretary, assistant editor at a film studio, and as a waitress, all with the intention of saving money to travel to Africa. Finally she has enough money to travel. At age 26, she heads to Gombe National Park in Tanzania to begin her studies of chimpanzees. Decades later, she continues to study chimpanzees and works to conserve chimpanzee habitat. Her work becomes globally recognized and inspires many others.

This is the true story of Jane Goodall, a famous primatologist known for her groundbreaking case study on the interactions of wild chimpanzees in Tanzania in the 1960s. She was a young girl who had a dream, persisted through many challenges, and ultimately took action to follow her dream.[1]

What about you? What is your story and what motivates you to take action? Perhaps a friend or family member encouraged you to get involved in playing a sport or you watched a movie that challenged you to think about a certain topic in a new way.

On a general level, what motivates people to take action? There has been considerable research on human motivation. In 1943, the psychologist Abraham Maslow wrote a paper on human motivation in which he described a hierarchy of needs. At the bottom of **Maslow's hierarchy of needs** are physiological needs like food, water, and sleep. Next are physiological needs related to safety, such as health and employment. At the top of the hierarchy are needs such as creativity and morality. We are motivated to act in order to meet, or satisfy, these needs.[2]

Imagine a community struggling with violence and low rates of employment. People are afraid to leave their houses at night and children don't have safe places they can gather after school. Because of high rates of unemployment, many families struggle with basic needs. The challenges faced by students who struggle with poor health and inadequate sleep or nutrition make it difficult for them to achieve in school. And while they strive to achieve, their unmet physiological and safety needs prevent these students from fully focusing on needs higher up Maslow's hierarchy. How might these youth take action in positive ways to support their personal lives and their surrounding community? Who are other stakeholders and groups that might help support their needs?

Abraham Maslow's theory of motivation is based on a hierarchy of human needs.

Self-Actualization
morality, creativity, problem solving

Esteem
self-esteem, achievement, respect

Love/Belonging
friendship, family, sexual intimacy

Safety
security of body, employment, resources, morality, family, health

Physiological
breathing, food, water, sex, sleep, excretion

The Power of Action

You watch the news and hear about ethnic cleansing in a country. You pull up a blog and read about high air pollution levels in Los Angeles. You read an article in a magazine about how economic recession has affected a small town in Michigan.

We hear stories about problems in the world all the time. But these aren't the only stories out there. In the same news broadcast, you might hear about students speaking out for a more nutritious school lunch or a community making a concerted effort to decrease air pollution from a local factory. You might listen to a radio program about nurses improving patient care in developing countries by using cell phones to remind their patients to take tuberculosis or HIV medicine. You might read about a clinic striving to increase access to preventive health care for low-income members of your own community.

As the examples throughout this book show, taking action can happen at both personal and structural levels. Just as previous generations faced challenges that were both local and global in scope, so will your generation. Some challenges will be inherited from previous generations; others will be new. And just as people have come together to address global and local issues in the past, your generation has the power to take action, too.

Taking Action and Sustainability

Envision the world you believe we will live in 50 years from now. Now, envision the world you want us to be living in 50 years from now. Are these two visions different from each other? If so, why? What kinds of actions can you take to create the world you want to live in 50 years?

Sustainable actions are actions that help meet the needs of people today as well as future generations. At their best, sustainable actions make connections between three facets of sustainability—society, economy, and environment—to create long-lasting change. Before taking action, there are many questions you can ask to help you understand an issue. Consider the following questions related to sustainable water use:

As you begin to answer these questions, you will learn about the many factors that may be part of a sustainable solution to the issue.

Economics
Is the cost of water affordable for all people?

Society
Why do certain people have access to clean water and certain people do not? What are root causes of these differences?

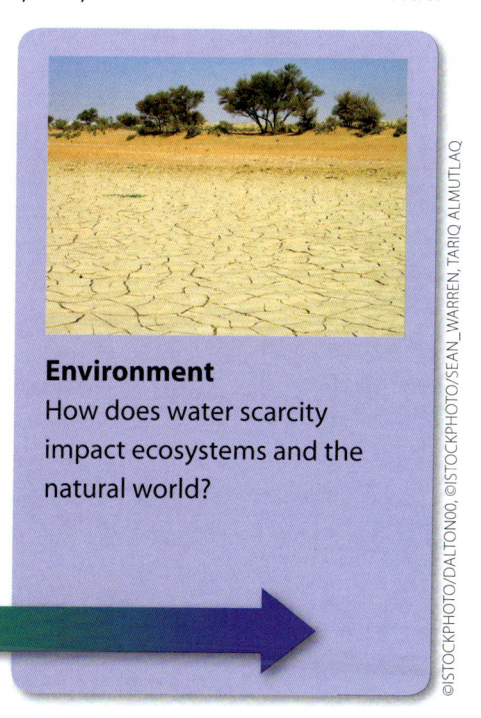

Environment
How does water scarcity impact ecosystems and the natural world?

Sustainable Solutions to Water Scarcity

Economy
- create responsible investments in water technology so more people can have access to water
- internalize costs associated with wasted water

Society
- install low-flow showerheads, faucets, and toilets
- use water conservatively when brushing your teeth, taking a shower, doing dishes, or cooking
- create policies that provide clean water equitably

Environment
- create a system to adequately take care of wastewater
- avoid depleting a natural water source to a level that cannot meet the needs of the local ecosystem

---

Many of the world's greatest challenges today are related to sustainability. Population growth, resource scarcity, and environmental degradation are happening more quickly and on a larger scale than ever before. Living sustainably is a way to meet our needs now in a way that considers future generations. You have read about many different ways people have taken action toward sustainability: high school students who have engaged their school in thinking about water scarcity, entrepreneurs who have created ways to sell organic food and recycle coffee grounds, and government leaders who have addressed hunger within their country. Taking sustainable action does not have to be a life-altering experience. You can participate in actions that are small or large depending on your resources and abilities. These sustainable actions not only help people today, but also create a better world for tomorrow.

Background on Taking Action

As you've seen throughout this book, people in previous generations have actively worked toward sustainable solutions to all sorts of issues. Through these historic endeavors, humanity has demonstrated its ability to make changes for the better. Each generation experiences different challenges and finds different ways to address these challenges, but we can learn from past discoveries and experiences to help us take informed action for the future.

Many of the most effective changes made by previous generations happened at a systemic level. But why do people take action in the first place? What motivates groups of people such as those in governments or scientific communities to work for change? Often change may begin with an increasing awareness that current institutions—political, social, or scientific—are no longer effective. Perhaps a government continues to deny a large segment of the population equal rights under the law. Or maybe the scientific theories of the day no longer effectively explain the natural world. When people come to recognize ineffective systems like these, it can lead to a crisis and then a revolution.[3] For instance, in the 16th century astronomers began to realize that the leading theory of the day (that Earth was the center of the universe) did not accurately explain their observations of the natural world. Following Ptolemy's model of the solar system, astrologers expected to see the moon appearing larger and smaller as it moved closer and farther from the Earth. Yet this is not what scientists observed.[4] This crisis eventually led to the Copernican Revolution and the proposal of a new theory (that the sun was the center of the universe) to guide future scientific inquiry.[5]

When people live under institutions that no longer meet their needs, they may come together to create change through a social movement. **Social movements** are a type of group action that focuses on change at a systemic level. Throughout history, people have participated in various movements that have heavily influenced the world we live in today: the civil rights movement, the women's suffrage movement, the labor movement, and the environmental movement. Change does not happen suddenly. Social movements often begin with one generation who identifies a challenge and is inspired to take action. The work of these early pioneers provides a base for following generations to build on. Each generation's progress can be a springboard for present and future movements.

The civil rights movement started during the 1950s, but there were many earlier events that set the stage for the movement. For example, the National Association for the Advancement of Colored People (NAACP) was formed in 1909 in order to "ensure political, educational, social, and economic equality of rights of all persons and to eliminate racial hatred and racial discrimination."[6] In the beginning, the group worked to end Jim Crow laws that legalized segregation. Later, throughout the civil rights movement, the NAACP helped to desegregate schools. The formation of this organization and the power it was able to accrue over the years gave strength to the civil rights movement.

Movements can gain momentum through all kinds of actions. As mentioned before, small actions can be just as powerful as large actions in supporting change and creating long-lasting results.

The Spectrum of Action during the Civil Rights Movement: From Small to Large

Personal Action
A white student stands up for a black student in a school that has just become integrated.

Community Action
Student volunteers travel to the South in order to support new laws meant to desegregate bus and railway stations.

National Action
The 24th Amendment abolishes the poll tax, which was originally created to make it difficult for poor black people to vote.

Advances in Science

Advances in science and new scientific theories can deepen the way we understand the world around us and change the way we respond to and approach problems. One famous example is the acceptance of the *germ theory of disease* in the 19th century. Before the germ theory of disease was developed, people generally believed that disease was caused by miasma, a toxic vapor that arose from standing water and feces. Although scientists had observed bacteria in wounds and tissues affected by disease, they believed that bacteria appeared spontaneously and did not recognize them as the cause of disease or infection. Although some scientists suggested otherwise (such as Leeuwenhoek in the 17th century), the miasma theory of disease was generally accepted by scientists, doctors, and the public and affected how people behaved. As a result, doctors were often powerless to cure disease or infection, and childhood deaths and death during pregnancy were common.[7]

In the late 19th century, French scientist Louis Pasteur and German scientist Robert Koch suggested that microbes, or germs, did not simply appear spontaneously in diseased tissue, but were actually the cause of disease. Those that accepted the evidence for germ theory changed the way they approached health problems. Upon reading about Pasteur's

CASE STUDY: The Modern Environmental Movement

The modern environmental movement can trace its roots back to the mid-20th century, when deteriorating water quality, polluted air, and the heavy use of chemicals such as DDT led people to question the pursuit of industrial progress without consideration for the natural environment. Public support for the movement was galvanized by events such as the 1948 smog in Donora, Pennsylvania. The smog was laced with sulfur dioxide from the town's steel and wire plant, leading to the death of 20 people and the hospitalization of hundreds more. This event prompted the first U.S. air pollution conference in 1950.[8]

Scientific research helped to inform and strengthen the modern environmental movement. In 1949, the zoologist Paul Ehrlich noted the disappearance of butterflies in New Jersey and attributed this disappearance to use of the chemical DDT. In 1951, a group of ecologists established the nonprofit organization the Nature Conservancy to protect ecologically important lands and waters around the world. In 1953, Jacques Cousteau's documentary *The Silent World* generated a growing public interest in oceans and sea life that launched exploration and marine conservation efforts.

One of the biggest moments for the modern environmental movement was the publication of *Silent Spring* by Rachel Carson in 1962. The book brought widespread attention to the dangers of synthetic chemicals like DDT and established Rachel Carson as a pioneer of the environmental movement. Following the book's publication, President John F. Kennedy asked his Science Advisory Committee to review its claims. As a result, the use of DDT was banned in 1972. Momentum behind the movement continued to mount in 1970, as 20 million Americans participated in the first Earth Day celebration on April 22nd and President Richard Nixon created the Environmental Protection Agency (EPA) as a federal agency responsible for U.S. environmental policy.[9]

The environmental movement has faced its share of challenges. The 1980s brought about cuts to the EPA under the Reagan Administration as public perception of environmentalism shifted. Environmental regulations were seen as a burden on businesses and environmentalism was transformed into a liberal agenda item.

To its credit, the modern environmental movement has transformed the world, but the movement has also been criticized for limiting environmentalism to a special interest. In a 2004 essay proclaiming the death of environmentalism, Michael Shellenberger and Ted Nordhaus wrote, "Environmentalism is today more about protecting a supposed 'thing'—'the environment'—than advancing the worldview articulated by Sierra Club founder John Muir, who nearly a

research, one English surgeon, John Lister, began cleaning wounds and using sterilized dressings in his medical practice. He noticed an immediate drop in the number of deaths related to infection among his patients. In the decades that followed, scientists identified the specific microbes that caused diseases such as tuberculosis, malaria, and leprosy, changing the way these diseases were treated.[10]

Not all advances in science are readily accepted. Individuals and communities hold their own beliefs and intuitions about the world. When scientific findings refute our deeply held beliefs, we can have a difficult time accepting new facts.[11] Galileo Galilei for example, was an Italian mathematics professor and astronomer who published major works in the 17th century. By improving the telescope, he was able to make astronomical observations that challenged the conventional scientific and religious beliefs of his day. Galileo's assertions about gravity and the physics of celestial bodies are accepted today, but upset many people during the time he lived and created considerable controversy. At the age of 70, he was imprisoned and put under house arrest for his scientific views.[12]

> *When scientific findings refute our deeply held beliefs, we can have a difficult time accepting new facts.*

century ago observed, 'When we try to pick out anything by itself, we find it hitched to everything else in the Universe.'"[13]

Nevertheless, dedicated activists and scientists continue to drive the movement forward and worldwide support for environmentalism has grown. Milestones of this progress include the signing of the Montreal Protocol in 1987 to address concerns about a massive hole in Earth's ozone layer. The treaty was signed by 191 countries and called for the phase out of man-made ozone-depleting substances such as CFCs. Another milestone occurred with the 1992 Rio Declaration, where United Nations member states established a set of environmental principles, including:

Principle 15

In order to protect the environment, the precautionary approach shall be widely applied by States according to their capabilities.

Where there are threats of serious or irreversible damage, lack of full scientific certainty shall not be used as a reason for postponing cost-effective measures to prevent environmental degradation.

Environmentalism has had a large impact on the world. However, the potential of this social movement may have been limited by several factors. For one, support for environmental causes may depend on current economic circumstances. Communities experiencing an economic boom may have plenty of resources to devote to environmental conservation and stewardship, but when facing an economic recession people in that same community may become more concerned with finding a job, putting food on the table, and keeping a roof over their head. Second, the movement's following has been fractured. Some in the environmental movement have placed the natural environmental above all else, even undertaking criminal ventures to protect nature. Others feel the movement must be sensitive to a wide spectrum of social issues, such as a healthy economy and an educated youth. Third, the environment has been stereotyped as a special interest issue not as pressing as the economy, health care, or social security. Environmental issues can therefore seem like a secondary priority.

Taking Action Today

Youth Today

Every generation is affected by events of their day. For instance, the Silent Generation, born between 1922 and 1943, lived during the Great Depression, racial segregation, the advent of mass production of automobiles, and World War II. Such events helped shape this generation's values and beliefs.[14]

Youth born after 1980 have often been referred to as the *Millennials*. They have been characterized in many different ways. Some see them as confident, self-expressive, liberal, upbeat, and open to change. Others see them as apathetic and concerned mostly about social networking. Within the United States, they are the most ethnically and racially diverse of all generations. Millennials are also known for their constant connection to technology. For example, eight out of ten surveyed sleep with their cell phones and over 60% have a social networking profile online. Statistically, they do not vote as much as past generations, but they do volunteer at the same level as their elders.[15] Millennials have lived through events like the fall of the Berlin Wall, the Iraq War, September 11th, and the technology boom.

There are approximately 1.1 billion youth between the ages of 15 and 24. Youth are over 18% of the world's population.

There are approximately 1.1 billion youth between the ages of 15 and 24. Youth are over 18% of the world's population.[16] The work of economists such as David Bloom suggests that a large working-age population can help drive economic development. For this to happen, it is key that young people have access to good health and education; these tools will support them in finding meaningful employment. When policies don't support such possibilities for young people, the impact is often felt across society. For example, in the Middle East and North Africa the unemployment rate of 15- to 24-year-olds is over 25%. Some believe that the frustration of jobless youth contributed to uprisings in Tahrir Square in Egypt.[17] This movement started on March 23, 2008, when Egyptian activists known as the April 6th Youth Movement called for general support of a strike by textile workers protesting low wages and high food prices.[18]

Youth in Egypt felt the need to take action when their government failed to respond to their needs. What about you? What would make you stand up and take action? Helen Fein, a historical sociologist, has written about the **universe of obligation**. This concept describes the circle of individuals and groups "toward whom obligations are owed, to whom rules apply, and whose injuries call for amends."[19] Your universe of obligation, or responsibility, may be your family, your community, your country, humanity, or the entire natural world. You may feel compelled to help someone or support a cause as a result of religion, culture, or geography.

Sociologists have also studied times when people do not take action. The phenomenon known as the *bystander effect* describes inaction due to the presence of others. People are less likely to take action and help someone in need when a greater number of **bystanders**, or witnesses, are present. When might you intervene in a situation and when might you be less likely to intervene? What if you saw someone getting hurt? What would motivate you to stand up for a person in need of assistance and what might make you not want to get involved?

The Power of Technology

Social media, the ability to use web-based and mobile technologies to support dialogue, can be a powerful tool to take action throughout the world. A study conducted by Philip Howard at the University of Washington showed that social media was key to shaping debates during the series of pro-democracy movements in the Middle East and North Africa known as the

CASE STUDY: Irena Sendler's Universe of Obligation

After Germany was defeated in World War I, the country was required to pay reparations for the damages caused by the war. Attempts to meet this massive debt led to soaring inflation. By 1932, unemployment had doubled and 6 million Germans were out of work. Some people blamed Jews for the hard times Germany experienced and anti-Semitism, or discrimination against Jews, started to rise.

In 1933, the Nazi party and its leader Adolf Hitler came to power in Germany. Hitler was clear about his disdain for Jewish people. His plan, known as the Final Solution, was to rid Germany and other countries in Europe of all Jews as well as other groups deemed undesirable.

Irena Sendler was living in Warsaw, Poland at the time. In 1939, the Nazis invaded Poland and forced 450,000 Jews to leave their homes and move to the Warsaw Ghetto.[20] When she saw what was happening, Irena led a group of 20 people who smuggled Jewish children out of the ghetto from 1940-1943. She knew that if they remained in the ghetto, their lives would be in danger. She was right. By 1943, all those remaining in the Warsaw Ghetto were sent to death camps. Ultimately, Irena Sendler saved 2,500 Jewish children and risked her own life to do so. She wrote the names of all the children she rescued on slips of paper and buried them in jars in her neighbor's yard so that she could help parents find their children after the war ended. Even when the Nazis imprisoned her, she refused to give them the children's names.[21] Irena was Polish and Catholic. Even though many others at the time did not feel a responsibility to help Jews in the Warsaw Ghetto, Irena's universe of obligation prompted her to not be a bystander and to stand up for people who were in danger.

Irena Sendler risked her life to save Jewish children in the Warsaw Ghetto, Poland. This war memorial is dedicated to children from the Czech town of Lidice.

Arab Spring. Because of social media, messages related to freedom and democracy spread quickly throughout the region. In the week before Egyptian president Hosni Mubarak resigned, the total rate of tweets related to political change in Egypt on Twitter increased from 2,300 per day to 230,000 per day.[22]

Social media is used by a whole range of people and in a variety of different ways. It has proven especially useful for social movements because it helps groups of people mobilize quickly around an action. Other technologies have also created new opportunities for political participation. With the rise of the Internet in the early 1990s, millions of people gained Internet access. Two decades later, the number has risen to billions. Cell phones are now widespread in developed and developing countries alike. These technologies have had a big impact on how leaders of social and political movements think and act. In one case, text messaging even helped remove a president from power. On January 17, 2001, during the impeachment trial of Philippine president Joseph Estrada, the country's legislature took an unpopular decision to withhold key

CASE STUDY: Avaaz

With new technology and increased global interdependence, people can now connect to take action in ways they may have not been able to do before. Avaaz is an organization with over 16 million members from 194 countries. Its mission is to "bring people-powered politics to decision-making everywhere."[23] The organization was created in 2007 to close the gap between the world people currently live in and the world they want to create. Avaaz surveys its members each year to determine what the organization's overall priorities should be. In 2012, around 154,000 people from 195 countries took the survey. The top two issues selected by participants were human rights and economic policy for the public good, followed closely by climate change and political corruption.[24]

Avaaz strives to put these principles into action. In recent years, Avaaz has done the following:[25]

- Worked with democracy movements in Syria, Yemen, and Libya to provide high-tech phones and Internet modems so people could connect with global media outlets.

- Helped the Global Commission on Drugs gather public support to end the war on drugs. Avaaz mobilized 600,000 members worldwide to call for an end to this war. As a result of their campaign, 2,000 media articles were written about this issue.

---

evidence against Estrada. Over a million people took to the streets of Manila in protest, many of them mobilized by the receipt of a short text message. The protest was so powerful that the legislature quickly reversed its decision and the trial ultimately removed Estrada from office.[26]

Creating Positive Change

We know eating unhealthy foods and not getting enough sleep or exercise can harm our health. Nevertheless, many of us are guilty of eating junk food, staying up late, and avoiding the gym. What makes these bad habits so hard to break? Sometimes we follow habits due to our surrounding environment. A person who lives in a neighborhood that only has fast food restaurants and grocery stores with limited fruit and vegetable options may not have access to healthy food. Simply telling this person to eat a healthier diet is probably not enough to change his or her behavior; to make a real impact, a change must be made to the surrounding environment.

Meaningful change might be accomplished if enough people in the community petitioned grocery stores to include more healthy food choices. Actions like this often create momentum that can lead to other opportunities for healthy choices in the neighborhood. Imagine what might happen if people did start petitioning. Others might start to become interested in the topic. Then a community center offers a cooking class that showcases healthy and inexpensive meals. Parents and students become more concerned about food in the school cafeteria and lobby for the school district to move toward healthier school gardens. As young people learn about fruits and vegetables at school, they become more invested in learning about where these foods come from and help launch a community garden to grow their own vegetables. Each action can have a profound effect on both individuals and the entire community.

Organizations can help in starting good habits too. Community Health Councils in South Los Angeles helped residents advocate for more healthy food choices in their neighborhood. Through this action, residents supported policies that incentivized restaurants to provide more nutritious food choices, limited the fast food restaurants near schools, and promoted fresher food in grocery stores.[27]

Even when we have the resources, support,

and motivation we need to make a specific change in our lives, change will probably happen slowly. There are often several steps between making a decision to change and achieving your goal. Models like the Transtheoretical Model of Behavior Change created in 1977 by James Prochaska can help us understand all the different parts involved in taking action. Prochaska's model divides the process of changing behavior into five steps: precontemplation, contemplation, preparation, action, and maintenance.[28] Consider the example of healthy eating as it is broken into these five steps, shown to the right.

Change is possible. You don't have to feel overwhelmed by all the issues you see around the world. Choose something you care deeply about, start taking personal actions to address the issue, and create feasible goals you can commit to. Once you start acting on your vision, you'll be amazed at what you can accomplish.

Pathways to Progress: Taking Action

Systems Thinking

Systems are interdependent components that form a whole. Common systems discussed throughout this book have been ecosystems, government systems, food systems, and even education systems. *Systems thinking* is a way to deal with the complexity of these systems. Understanding systems can help us to achieve greater change. When thinking about global issues, we can consider them to also be a part of systems. They require the cooperation of many parts of society: scientists, governments, community groups, businesses, and individuals, just to name a few. The process of creating solutions becomes less daunting when we can identify many places in systems where we can intervene. The late systems thinker Donnella Meadows spoke about ways to intervene in a complex system.[29] She proposed that people could

The Transtheoretical Model of Behavior Change: Healthy Eating

Precontemplation
You don't know anything about nutrition or the importance of eating a well-balanced diet.

Contemplation
You have started to learn about the negative health impacts of eating food that is not nutrious. You see this is an issue in your community. You consider the pros and cons of addressing it.

Preparation
You have started to tell family and friends about the way you will change some of the foods you eat. You inform them of ways they can change their habits too.

Action
You have started to eat healthier foods. You convince your local grocery store to start carrying fresh and more nutritious foods.

Maintenance
You have been practicing this new behavior for almost five months. Now you're starting to consider other ways you can make an impact on your community's health.

intervene through leverage points or optimal places within the system. Consider the example of the global HIV/AIDS pandemic. Read through the following ways you might address this issue and possible ways to intervene that could lead to positive solutions.

There is much to be hopeful about in the world today. Taking a systems approach to global challenges can help change hopes into realities. Countless governments, organizations, and individuals are working to create a sustainable world so that all people today and in the future have the freedom to make choices and enjoy a good quality of life.

Systems Thinking and the Global HIV/AIDS Pandemic

Know how the system behaves.

One of the first steps is to take the time to learn about the spread of HIV/AIDS. Research the history of the disease. Understand its scientific background. It would be a mistake to start addressing the issue without understanding the complexities and nuances of the disease.

Understand what's working well.

Learn about what people are already doing to address HIV/AIDS. For example, there was a 30% decline in new HIV infections in South Africa between 2000 and 2008 due to condom distribution programs and AIDS awareness programs.[30] How were these programs structured in order to be so successful? Similarly, understand what's not working well. People will attempt to create solutions that fail. You can learn from these mistakes; understanding why past efforts failed can help you determine what could work in the future.

Check your assumptions.

We should not assume that there are not already possible solutions to address HIV/AIDS. Check what other people and organizations are doing to address HIV. Be wary of fixating on one possible explanation or hypothesis. Instead, collect as many ideas as possible and think critically about each one. What works in one cultural setting may not be appropriate for another setting. For example, certain AIDS programs designed by the Islamic Medical Association of Uganda worked with imams (mosque leaders) to appoint family AIDS workers to go to Muslim family homes to discuss prevention methods.[31] This form of education was a culturally-specific approach that worked in Uganda.

Present clear and direct information.

When systems go wrong, it is often because of faulty or missing information. It's important to present clear and direct information so people can make informed decisions. If you're working on HIV prevention within a community, share clear information on prevention methods that will support the community's specific needs. You can also help clear up confusion by identifying and addressing false beliefs within the community. In the United States, for example, there was a lot of stigma associated with HIV during the 1980s and many people had misconceptions about how it spread. Educating people about the realities of the disease helped to dispel these myths.

Locate responsibility in the system.

Try to identify the reasons for problems or flaws in HIV prevention efforts. For example, why is there higher incidence of HIV in countries such as Swaziland and Lesotho and lower incidence in Germany and Morocco?

Pay attention to what is important, not just what is quantifiable.

Stigma related to having HIV and AIDS in Swaziland prevented many people living in Swaziland from getting tested. People kept their infection a secret and HIV infection continued to spread. To address the stigma, the government began a new testing campaign called the "love test." The idea was change people's behaviors and encourage couples to go get tested together so that no secrets would be kept between them.[32]

Expand time frames.

The time frame of a solution should extend beyond one generation; it should consider the impact of the current HIV/AIDS situation on future generations. How can a system be designed to take future effects into account? As a result of AIDS, 16 to 18 million children have become orphans.[33] What can be done to account for the livelihood of these children and their futures?[34]

Understand a system's complexity.

All systems are complex. There are often numerous solutions to a system's problems. For example, the following approaches have all been successful with HIV prevention programs: education that prevents transmission, altering norms and behaviors of social groups, social marketing like mass media campaigns, community leadership, political leadership, and community focus on respect for human rights.[35]

Look for the good.

It is important to focus on good things that are happening in the world. Advances in HIV treatments have helped people to live longer and healthier lives. There are so many individuals and organizations committed to HIV prevention around the world. Read articles, books, and the web for stories of success and inspiration.

CAREER PROFILE: Systems Change Consultant

Nalani Linder is an organizational and systems change consultant. She works with organizations and groups who are trying to solve complex problems. Nalani facilitates trainings and coaches clients to help them understand the complex systems they work in so that they can think systemically about how to take action. From early in her life, she was always one to think about interconnections and "the big picture." As she states, "Whenever there's an emergency or accident—an oil spill or a train crash, for instance—I care less about who's to blame, and wonder about some of the seemingly innocent events that led to it, and about the ripple effects that would come from it." Nalani first encountered systems thinking 11 years ago and it changed her life. Systems thinking is a way of seeing the world as a constantly changing web of connections. She was so intrigued by the concept that she went to graduate school to study systems, systems thinking, and leadership. She started to pay attention to how complex problems related to issues at work, in the environment, or in society were commonly described as if they were isolated short-term emergencies rather than the result of a string of interconnected events and relationships. Nalani decided to devote her life to help people see the systems in which we live and work. As she puts it: "Everything impacts everything."

In her work, Nalani has observed people brought together by systems thinking. As people start to look at problems systemically, they naturally turn to others to get multiple perspectives of the issue (because no one person can see the whole system) and to ask for different kinds of help and expertise. She finds this shift to equalizing power an inspiring illustration of sustainability's ideals. Nobody stands alone: students need teachers and teachers need students; leaders need followers and followers need leaders. Nalani offers this advice to youth: "While not every problem in the world requires systems thinking to better understand it, the leaders of today and tomorrow need to take a systems perspective in order to create a just, healthy and sustainable future."

Nalani Linder helps people to see the systems in which we live and work.

The Power of...You!

Each chapter of this book has featured young people taking action to address global issues. You have the capability to make change too, no matter how young or old you are. Consider your universe of obligation. Think about what it means to belong to a family, school, community, city, country, and world. What kinds of responsibilities come with your membership in these different groups? What are ways you can meaningfully participate in each group? You and the millions of youth today will be leaders in years to come. Your civic engagement can have a powerful impact throughout your lifetime. Consider the skills you might develop to help you take action on issues you care about. For example, if you are passionate about governance, you might read about effective leadership or participate in a youth leadership program. Or if you care deeply about public health and want to learn how to document people's health care stories, you might take classes to learn about documentary filmmaking. There are ample opportunities for you to explore your interests and determine where you want to head.

Youth featured throughout this book have committed to making change both locally and globally. They found an issue they cared deeply about and were determined to create positive, lasting change. If you haven't already read their profiles within each chapter, here are several of their stories to get you started.

You can also be a part of creating a sustainable world. What moves you? What choices will you make? What actions will you take? It's never too late!

Youth Making a Difference

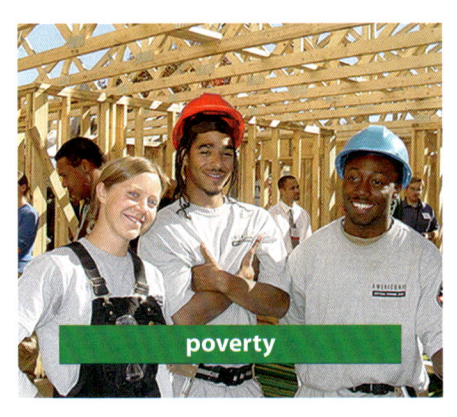

community development	gender	global issues
economics	globalization	human rights
poverty	food	water
biodiversity	oceans	energy

Glossary

A

acidification—A decrease in the pH level of a body of water; an increase in acidity.

AIDS (Acquired Immunodeficiency Syndrome)—A disease caused by the Human Immunodeficiency Virus (HIV) in which the immune system is weakened and therefore less able to fight infections and diseases; AIDS is transmitted through contaminated body fluids, especially via sexual contact or contaminated needles.

air pollution—The concentration of gases, dust, fumes, or odors in amounts that can harm human, animal, and plant health.

aquaculture—The farming of plants and animals that live in water, such as fish, shellfish, and algae.

aquaponics—A method for growing food sustainably in which hydroponics is combined with fish farming; the waste from fish provides nutrients for plants and plants filter water for fish.

aquifer—A permeable underground layer of rock, sand, or soil that stores a significant amount of freshwater.

asylum-seeker—A person who applies for protection and the right of residence in a foreign country.

atmosphere—The blanket of air that surrounds Earth, composed of a combination of gases such as nitrogen, oxygen, and carbon dioxide.

B

base population—The starting population from which a statistic such as birth rate or fertility rate is determined.

bioaccumulation—The process in which chemicals are taken up by an organism directly from their environment or by eating from a food supply that contains the chemicals.

biodiversity—The variety of life in all its forms, levels, and combinations, including ecosystem diversity, species diversity, and genetic diversity.

biodiversity hotspot—A region that has at least 1,500 species of vascular plants that are endemic (the species is limited to a certain geographic area) and has lost 70 percent of its original habitat.

biomimicry—A field of science in which nature is used as model to help create sustainable, human-designed products and systems.

bystander—A person that witnesses but does not participate in an event.

C

carbon footprint—A measure of human impacts on Earth's climate through activities that release carbon dioxide (a greenhouse gas) into the atmosphere; usually reported as weight of carbon dioxide released.

carbon sink—A natural or human-made system that absorbs and stores more carbon dioxide from the atmosphere than it releases.

carbon source—A natural or human-made system that releases more carbon dioxide into the atmosphere than it absorbs and stores.

carrying capacity—The number of people Earth can support without using natural resources faster than the planet can replenish them.

chronic disease—A disease that lasts a long time such as heart disease or diabetes.

civic participation—Individual or community participation in decisions around issues that affect public life.

civil society—The set of voluntary, non-governmental associations formed by people around a common interest, including groups such as labor unions, churches, and charities.

climate change—A significant shift in Earth's overall climate over an extended period of time.

colonization—The act of establishing a population in new territory that maintains allegiance to the parent country.

common resource—Those resources that are collectively owned or shared among many communities; a resource rival in consumption (one person's use of the resource limits use by another) but not excludable (one person's use of the resource does not prevent another's use).

community—A group of people that share some commonality, often based on where they live (the Minneapolis community), what they do (the student community), a shared social characteristic (the Cuban-American community), or shared interests (the small business community).

community development—The process of building ties between community members to create a network that can successfully adapt to challenges or opportunities.

community organizing—A way for people to work together to influence decisions that affect them and their neighbors.

comparative advantage—The ability of a country or business to produce a good at a lower opportunity cost than another country or business.

conflict—A state of opposition between people, ideas, or interests.

consumerism—The cultural orientation that leads people to find meaning, satisfaction, and acceptance through what they consume.

consumption—The process of using natural resources, materials, or finished products to satisfy human wants or needs.

D

dead zone—An area in a body of water that has such a low concentration of oxygen that it is unable to support life.

developed country—A country with a high level of economic development, high life expectancy, and low rate of poverty.

developing country—A country that has a low level of economic development, low life expectancy, and high rate of poverty.

discrimination—The unjust treatment of different groups of people.

E

ecological footprint—The area of the Earth's productive surface that it takes to produce the goods and services necessary to support a particular lifestyle.

ecological overshoot—When a population uses more natural resources each year than Earth can support or supply, measured as the gap between the human demand for natural resources (our collective ecological footprint) and Earth's available supply (biocapacity).

economic development—The process of raising the level of prosperity in a society by increasing per capita income, reducing poverty, and enhancing individual economic opportunities.

economic water scarcity—A type of water scarcity that exists because of a lack of investment in water resources, typically characterized by a lack of infrastructure and an unequal distribution of water.

economy—The system of production, distribution, and consumption of goods and services.

ecosystem services—The benefits, services and goods provided by ecosystems such as food, fuel, and medicines.

electricity—A form of energy generated by the movement of charged particles; generally produced as a secondary form of energy by converting other forms of energy (such as coal or wind) into electricity.

endangered species—Animals or plants that are in danger of extinction.

energy—The capacity to do work or cause change; energy can also refer to sources of energy (such as fossil fuels, water, wind, solar, etc.) that power various aspects of human life (such as transportation, industry, heating, lights and electrical devices, etc.).

energy conservation—Behaviors and actions that save or use less energy, such as turning off the lights when you leave a room.

energy efficiency—Completing a specific task with less energy input than usual, such as using an energy-efficient LED light bulb which uses less energy than other light bulbs to produce the same amount of light.

environmental justice—The equitable treatment of all people, regardless of race, income, culture, or social class, with respect to the development, implementation, and enforcement of environmental laws, regulations, and policies.

evolution—Genetic changes in a population of organisms that are inherited and passed on over many generations.

externality—The positive or negative effect on an uninvolved third party when two individuals or groups of people conduct a transaction.

F

fair trade—A trading partnership that supports greater equity in international trade by improving conditions for those who produce goods in developing countries.

family planning services—Services such as education or medical care that provide families with support to make choices about reproduction.

feminization of poverty—The widening gap between the number of men and the number of women in poverty.

fertility rate—The average number of children born to each woman.

food security—The state in which all people have sufficient physical and economic access to nutritious food to maintain a healthy and active life.

fossil fuel—A non-renewable energy source such as coal, oil, or natural gas created over a long period of time by the decomposition and compression of plants and animals.

free trade—The policy of unrestricted international trade in which goods, capital, and labor can flow freely between countries without the imposition of tariffs, subsidies, or quotas.

G

gender—The range of characteristics such as attitudes, behaviors, roles, and attributes that a society associates with men and women.

gender equity—When men and women are treated fairly in accordance with their differing needs.

genetically modified organisms (GMOs)—Animals, plants, or bacteria whose genetic makeup is altered by combining their genes with genes from other organisms.

genocide—The systematic and deliberate extermination of an entire national, racial, political, or ethnic group.

germ theory of disease—The theory that some diseases are caused by microorganisms (germs) within the body.

global awareness—An understanding of different nations, people, and cultures around the world and an appreciation of the impact of interconnected global issues. A globally aware person can learn from and work collaboratively with individuals from diverse cultures, religions, and lifestyles.

global health—The collaboration among several different countries in research and practice in order to promote the health of all people.

global issue—An issue that is transnational and transboundary, persists over time, affects large numbers of people, has underlying causes, and is connected to other global issues.

globalization—An increased interconnectedness and interdependence of peoples and countries; generally understood to include the opening of borders to increasingly fast flows of goods, services, finance, people and ideas, as well as changes in national and international institutions and policies to facilitate or promote such flows.

governance—The traditions, institutions, and processes that determine how power is exercised, how citizens are given a voice, and how decisions are made on issues of public concern; governance includes not only government, but also the business sector and civil society.

government—The official governing organization or system that has the power to make and enforce laws for a certain territory.

green building—The practice of making structures that are environmentally responsible and resource efficient for the entire life cycle of the building, from choosing a building site to deconstruction of the structure.

green jobs—Typically career-track jobs that improve the environment and pay a livable wage; sometimes also called green-collar jobs.

Green Revolution—Agricultural practices and technologies developed in the 1950s to increase food production through the use of machines, fertilizer, pesticides, irrigation, and the growth of hybrid varieties of rice, wheat, and corn.

greenhouse effect—The process by which gases in Earth's atmosphere retain infrared radiation (heat) from the sun, warming Earth's surface.

greenhouse gas—A gas found in Earth's atmosphere that both absorbs and re-emits infrared radiation.

gross domestic product (GDP)—The total value of goods and services produced by and within a country.

gross national happiness (GNH)—A holistic measure of quality of life in a country that considers factors beyond economic progress.

groundwater—Water beneath the Earth's surface that has seeped down into the soil and porous rock that sits above non-permeable bedrock.

gyres—Large-scale circular systems of ocean currents.

H

human development—The process of creating an environment that enables people to live long, healthy, and creative lives.

human migration—The permanent or semi-permanent relocation of a person or group of people from one location to another.

human rights—The basic rights and freedoms to which all humans are entitled, often held to include the right to life and liberty, freedom of thought and expression, and equality before the law.

human security—The state in which people are free from danger, poverty, or apprehension. The concept of human security extends beyond the absence of conflict to include economic development, social justice, environmental protection, good governance, access to education and health care, and respect for human rights.

human trafficking—The illegal recruitment or trading of human beings through force, fraud, or coercion, in order to compel them to perform labor or services; often called modern-day slavery.

hydroponics—A technique used to grow plants using nutrient-rich water instead of soil.

I

infrastructure—The basic facilities, services, and installations needed for the functioning of a community or society, such as transportation and communications systems, water and power lines, and public institutions such as schools, post offices, and prisons.

interconnectedness—A fundamental principle of sustainability which states that natural and human-constructed systems interact with and impact each other and therefore cannot be separated.

intergenerational responsibility—A fundamental principle of sustainability which states that the current generation has a responsibility to leave ample resources for future generations on Earth.

internally displaced persons—People who are forced to leave their homes because of conflict, food scarcity, or other crisis but who remain within their country.

interstate war—A state of open, armed, and often prolonged combat between the regular military forces of two or more different countries, or between a country or countries and a group of people.

intrastate or **civil war**—A state of sustained armed combat between factions or regions within the same country.

invasive species or **alien species**—An organism not naturally found in a given ecosystem whose introduction to the ecosystem could be harmful to the environment, human health, or the economy.

J K L

keystone species—A species that has a disproportionately larger effect on their ecosystem than its abundance might suggest.

life expectancy—The expected number of years a person will live.

M

macroeconomics—A branch of economics that studies an entire economy and the issues that affect that economy, such as inflation, economic growth, and unemployment.

malnutrition—A state of poor nutrition; it can result from an insufficient, excessive, or unbalanced diet or an inability to absorb foods.

market—A system or structure through which buyers and sellers exchange goods, services, or information.

Maslow's hierarchy of needs—A theory of motivation put forth by Abraham Maslow that is based on the organization of human needs from most basic to more complex.

materials economy—the system of extracting raw materials, turning them into manufactured products, and selling them to consumers who use and dispose of them.

maternal health care—The health care women receive during pregnancy, childbirth, and after childbirth.

media literacy—An ability to access and evaluate media messages of all kinds in order to understand how these messages create meaning and what impact they have on society.

microeconomics—A branch of economics that studies the behavior of individuals and firms with the market, especially how people decide to purchase certain goods and services.

Millennium Development Goals (MGDs)—Eight goals set by the United Nations Development Program in 2000 to be achieved by 2015 in order to improve the quality of life of the world's poorest people. They are: end poverty and hunger, ensure all children complete primary school, eliminate gender inequality in education, improve child and maternal health, combat HIV/AIDS, promote environmental sustainability, and develop global partnerships for economic development.

mortality rate—The number of deaths per unit of population in a given place and time, often measured per 1,000 live births.

multiculturalism—The idea that people from many different cultural and ethnic backgrounds can coexist peacefully and equitably in one country.

multinational corporation—A corporation that has operations or provides goods or services in more than one country.

N O

nation-state—A political unit that exercises control and sovereignty over a defined geographic area and provides a socio-cultural identity for its people.

non-renewable—Refers to a limited resource, such as coal or oil, that cannot be replaced as quickly as it is used.

ozone layer—A layer in the upper atmosphere (approximately 20 miles above the Earth's surface) that contains a concentration of ozone sufficient to block most ultraviolet radiation from the sun.

P

pandemic—An outbreak of disease that reaches across the globe or a large geographic region.

passive solar design—Design techniques and building materials that naturally collect, store, and distribute heat rather than using energy to run mechanical and electrical systems.

pathogen—A disease-causing organism such as a bacterium or virus.

patriarchal society—A society in which the male is the dominant authority figure.

peace—A state in which conflict is absent and differences among people are respected and embraced.

personal solution—A way in which an individual can act to alleviate a problem.

physical water scarcity—A type of water scarcity that exists when the demand for water is greater than local water resources can provide.

phytoplankton—Tiny marine organisms that perform photosynthesis and reside near the surface of the ocean.

population density—The number of people in a given geographic area.

population growth rate—The rate of increase in population over a period of time, often expressed as a percentage.

potable—Safe to drink.

poverty—A state when people lack the means to meet their basic needs. Poverty is defined and measured in a number of different ways based on factors such as income, human development, and relative deprivation.

private sector—The part of the economy consisting of non-governmental businesses and individuals who trade products and services for profit.

public health—The science and art of protecting and improving the health of communities.

Q

quality of life—A holistic measure of the well-being of individuals and societies that takes into account a variety of economic, social, and environmental factors.

R

reciprocity—A relationship characterized by a mutual dependence, action, or influence in which two or more parties benefit by doing things for one another.

refugees—People who have fled their country because they have a well-founded fear of persecution for reasons of race, religion, nationality, membership in a particular social group, or political opinion.

renewable—Refers to a resource, such sunlight, wind, water, or fish, that can be replaced quickly and naturally.

replacement rate—The fertility rate required to maintain a stable population.

reproductive rights—Legal rights and freedoms regarding reproduction and reproductive health.

reserves—Stores of energy resources that can be extracted economically using current technology.

resource curse—The situation describing a country that has an abundance of natural resources but does not experience economic growth or development.

resource scarcity—A condition of limited resources such as a lack of sufficient food, water, or fertile soil.

S

self-determination—The right of all nations to govern themselves without foreign rule or interference.

social capital—The networks, norms, and mutual trust that allow people to coordinate and cooperate for the benefit of a community.

social determinants of health—The social, environmental, and economic conditions of the community in which we live that impact our health.

social movement—A type of group action that focuses on change at a systemic level.

standard of living—The level of comfort and material wealth of an individual or society.

stereotypes—Widely held and oversimplified beliefs about people and things.

stormwater runoff—The snow or rainfall that flows over impervious surfaces, such as roads, as it travels into stormwater drainage systems or directly into bodies of water like lakes, streams, wetlands, or coastal waters.

structural solution—A solution that makes changes within a system in order to alleviate a problem.

subsidy—Direct or indirect payment from a government to businesses, citizens, or institutions in order to encourage people do something the government believes is desirable.

sustainability—The principle of meeting current needs without limiting the ability of future generations to meet their needs.

sustainable actions—Actions that help meet the needs of future generations while meeting the needs of current ones; at their best, they address the three facets of sustainability—environment, society, and economy to create long-lasting change.

sustainable design—Creating products and buildings in a way that maximizes benefits to the environment, economy, and society.

sustainable development—A process of economic, social, and political transformation using practices that meet the needs and desires of the current generation without decreasing the ability of future generations to meet their needs.

systems thinking—A field of study that looks carefully at all important components of a system and how they connect to each other.

T

tariff—A fee (like a tax) that a government imposes on imports or exports.

terrorism—The calculated use of violence or the threat of violence against civilians in order to attain goals that are political, religious, or ideological in nature; this is done through intimidation or instilling fear.

UVW

Universal Declaration of Human Rights—A global declaration of the universal rights that all people are born with, adopted by the General Assembly of the United Nations in response to the conflict that occurred during World War II.

universe of obligation—According to the historical sociologist Helen Fein, the circle of individuals and groups toward whom one feels a sense of responsibility.

urban planning or city planning—A branch of architecture focused on the design and organization of urban space and activities.

virtual water—The amount of water consumed or polluted to produce a product.

water scarcity—A lack of access to enough water to meet human and environmental needs.

water table—The depth that a well must reach in order to find water; the top surface of a groundwater supply.

worldview—A set of assumptions, perspectives, and beliefs held by individuals, cultures, and societies through which we make sense of our lives and the world.

Endnotes

Chapter 1: Global Issues

1. Simon Partner, "The promise of global youth culture," *Chronicle*, February 25, 2011, http://dukechronicle.com/article/promise-global-youth-culture.
2. "Global Shapers Community," World Economic Forum, accessed November 26, 2012, http://www.weforum.org/videos/global-shapers-community.
3. Farhana Hossain, "Snapshot: Global Migration," *New York Times*, June 22, 2007, http://www.nytimes.com/ref/world/20070622_CAPEVERDE_GRAPHIC.html.
4. "Dominican Republic," National Geographic, under Nat Geo Music, accessed November 26, 2012, http://worldmusic.nationalgeographic.com/view/page.basic/country/content.country/dominican_republic_864.
5. "Pop Culture," Globalization 101, project of The Levin Institute, State University of New York, accessed November 26, 2012, http://www.globalization101.org/pop-culture/.
6. Tim Arango, "World Falls for American Media, Even as It Sours on America," *New York Times*, November 30, 2008, http://www.nytimes.com/2008/12/01/business/media/01soft.html.
7. Sheela Bongir, "What India Hands to the World," *NewGeography*, March 7, 2011, http://www.newgeography.com/content/002098-what-india-hands-world.
8. Susan Gigli, *Children, Youth and Media Around the World: An Overview of Trends & Issues*, report presented at the 4th World Summit on Media for Children and Adolescents, Rio de Janeiro, April 2004, available at UNICEF, http://www.unicef.org/videoaudio/intermedia_revised.pdf.
9. "TVs outnumber fridges," *Economist*, April 28, 2011, http://www.economist.com/blogs/americasview/2011/04/mexico%E2%80%99s_census.
10. "Pop Culture."
11. "Technology and Globalization," Globalization 101, accessed November 26, 2012, http://www.globalization101.org/uploads/File/Technology/tech2011.pdf.
12. "Exhibits: Internet History," Computer History Museum, under Exhibits, accessed November 26, 2012, http://www.computerhistory.org/internet_history/.
13. Nielsen//Net Ratings, "Three out of Four Americans Have Access to the Internet according to Nielsen//NetRatings," press release, March 18, 2004, http://www.nielsen-online.com/pr/pr_040318.pdf.
14. "China Tops World in Internet Users," *CNN Tech*, January 14, 2009, http://articles.cnn.com/2009-01-14/tech/china.internet_1_china-tops-world-xinhua-news-service-chinese-government?_s=PM:TECH.
15. Christine Rosen, "Our Cell Phones, Ourselves," *New Atlantis*, Summer 2004, http://www.thenewatlantis.com/publications/our-cell-phones-ourselves.
16. Shanta Devarajan, "More cell phones than toilets," *Africa can… end poverty* (blog), December 4, 2010, http://blogs.worldbank.org/africacan/more-cell-phones-than-toilets.
17. International Campaign to Ban Landmines website, accessed November 26, 2012, http://www.icbl.org/.
18. "Jody Williams—USA, 1997," Nobel Women's Initiative, under Meet the Laureates, accessed November 26, 2012, http://nobelwomensinitiative.org/meet-the-laureates/jody-williams/.
19. Elisabeth Malkin, "Nafta's Promise, Unfulfilled," *New York Times*, March 23, 2009, http://www.nytimes.com/2009/03/24/business/worldbusiness/24peso.html?_r=1&ref=northamericanfreetradeagreement#.
20. James E. Harf and Mark Owen Lombardi, eds., *Taking Sides: Clashing Views on Global Issues* (New York: McGraw Hill, 2010).
21. Frank Laczko and Elizabeth Collett, "Assessing the Tsunami's Effects on Migration," Migration Information Source, project of the Migration Policy Institute, April 2005, http://www.migrationinformation.org/USfocus/display.cfm?id=299.
22. Education Development Center, "Global Youth Survey Explores Perspectives on Social, Cultural Identity," press release, September 19, 2006, http://www.edc.org/newsroom/press_releases/global_youth_survey_explores_perspectives_social_cultural_identity.
23. Women's Commission for Refugee Women and Children, *Education in Darfur: A critical Component of humanitarian response*, (New York: Dec 2006), http://www.crin.org/docs/wom_com_ed_darfur.pdf.
24. How Big is an Iceberg?," Sea Ice Physics and Ecosystem Experiment (SIPEX), under Education: Teacher's Toolbox, accessed November 30, 2012, http://www.acecrc.sipex.aq/access/page/?page=85fd6cc8-bc6f-102a-8ea7-0019b9ea7c60.
25. Edward T. Hall, *Beyond Culture* (New York: Anchor books, a division of Random House, 1976).
26. "Mission," Peace Corps, last updated July 16, 2012, http://www.peacecorps.gov/index.cfm?shell=about.mission.
27. These materials were adapted from *Voices from the Field: Reading and Writing about the World, Ourselves, and Others* (Washington, D.C.: Peace Corps/Coverdell World Wise Schools, September 2006), http://www.peacecorps.gov/wws/stories/stories.cfm?psid=1&rid=afric.
28. Caitlin A. Johnson, "Cutting through Advertising Clutter," *CBS News*, September 17, 2006, http://www.cbsnews.com/stories/2006/09/17/sunday/main2015684.shtml.
29. "China Micro-Blogging Sites Censor 'Egypt'," *Discovery News*, January 29, 2011, http://news.discovery.com/tech/china-censors-egypt-110129.html.
30. "Skills Framework: Global Awareness," Partnership for 21st Century Skills, under Overview: Skills Framework, accessed November 26, 2012, http://www.p21.org/index.php?option=com_content&task=view&id=256&Itemid=120.
31. Ricki Ptakowski, "Back on My Feet," Philadelphia 76ers, under Community News, accessed November 26, 2012, http://www.nba.com/sixers/community/back_on_my_feet.html.
32. "We Won!," Urban Youth Collaborative, under News, June 18, 2010, http://www.urbanyouthcollaborative.org/category/news/.
33. Jamais Cascio, "Leapfrog 101," Worldchanging, December 15, 2004, http://www.worldchanging.com/archives/001743.html.
34. James Hall, "Good to Talk," *New Internationalist 365* (March 2004), http://www.newint.org/columns/currents/2004/03/01/talk/.

Chapter 2: Sustainability

1. Jarid Manos (Founder and CEO of Great Plains Restoration Council), personal communication, July 18, 2009; "Mission," Great Plains Restoration Council, accessed November 28, 2012, http://gprc.org/mission.html.

2. UNICEF, "Children Living in Poverty," *Childhood Under Threat: The State of the World's Children 2005*, accessed June 22, 2012, http://www.unicef.org/sowc05/english/poverty.html.
3. Jared Diamond, *Collapse: How Societies Choose to Fail or Succeed* (New York: Penguin, 2005).
4. UN General Assembly, Meeting no. 102, "Process of preparation of the Environmental Perspective to the Year 2000 and Beyond" (A/RES/38/161), December 19, 1983, http://www.un.org/documents/ga/res/38/a38r161.htm.
5. World Commission on Environment and Development, *Our Common Future* (Oxford: Oxford University Press, March 1987).
6. E.g., Andres Edwards, *The Sustainability Revolution* (Gabriola Island, Canada: New Society Publishers, 2005).
7. "What is Wiser.org? (also known as WiserEarth or WE by our community)," WiserEarth, under About Us, accessed May 9, 2011, http://www.wiserearth.org/article/About.
8. Denise Scribner (ecology teacher, Goddard School District), personal communication, August 16, 2011.
9. "Mission and History," American College & University Presidents' Climate Commitment, accessed June 6, 2011, http://www.presidentsclimatecommitment.org/about/mission-history.
10. "DESD India," UN Decade of Education for Sustainable Development (DESD) 2005-2014, accessed August 17, 2011, http://www.desd.org/Esd_india.htm.
11. Gillian Conahan, "Green Reality: Crunching the numbers on the clean economy," *Discover* (August 2011): 60.
12. Jeanne Hoffman, "Sustainable Madison" (slideshow), City of Madison, under Sustainable Madison Community: Learn what Madison has done in the past about sustainability, accessed May 10, 2011, http://www.cityofmadison.com/sustainability/community/index.cfm.
13. D. W. Fahey et al., "2002 Scientific Assessment Report: Twenty Questions and Answers about the Ozone Layer," UN Environment Programme Ozone Secretariat, accessed May 10, 2011, http://ozone.unep.org/Frequently_Asked_Questions/eeapfaq2002.pdf.
14. Lawrence Troster, "Judaism," in *Berkshire Encyclopedia of Sustainability: The Spirit of Sustainability* (Great Barrington, MA: Berkshire, 2010), available at GreenFaith, http://greenfaith.org/religious-teachings/jewish-statements-on-the-environment/judaism-and-sustainability-rabbi-lawrence-troster-1.
15. Mary Evelyn Tucker and John Grim, "Overview of World Religions and Ecology," Forum on Religion and Ecology at Yale, project of the Yale School of Forestry and Environmental Studies, 2009, http://fore.research.yale.edu/information/index.html.
16. "Alliance of Religions and Conservation—History," Alliance of Religions and Conservation, under About ARC: History, accessed May 18, 2011, http://www.arcworld.org/about.asp?pageID=2.
17. UN Environment Programme (UNEP), "The United Nations Environmental Sabbath Service," from *Only One Earth*, (New York: UNEP DC2-803, June 1990), available at Earth Ministry, May 18, 2011, http://earthministry.org/resources/worship-aids/sample-worship-services/the-united-nations-environmental-sabbath-service.
18. Parliament of the World's Religions, *Declaration Toward a Global Ethic* (Chicago: September 4, 1993), available at http://www.parliamentofreligions.org/_includes/FCKcontent/File/TowardsAGlobalEthic.pdf.
19. "What is a Sustainable Community?," Institute for Sustainable Communities, under What We Do, accessed June 21, 2012, http://www.iscvt.org/what_we_do/sustainable_community/.
20. "Turning Crisis to Opportunity," Institute for Sustainable Communities, under How We've Helped, accessed June 2, 2011, http://www.iscvt.org/how_weve_helped/moss_point/.
21. Snow Leopard Trust website, accessed December 7, 2012, http://www.snowleopard.org/.
22. Global Youth Service Day website, accessed June 26, 2012, http://gysd.org/.

Chapter 3: Food

1. "Food Security," World Health Organization (WHO), accessed December 5, 2012, http://www.who.int/trade/glossary/story028/en/.
2. Rami Zurayk, "Use your loaf: Why food prices were crucial in the Arab spring," *Observer*, July 16, 2011, http://www.globalpolicy.org/component/article/217-hunger/50456-use-your-loaf-why-food-prices-were-crucial-in-the-arab-spring.html.
3. Associated Press, "Egyptians clash with police in bread riot," *MSNBC News*, June 8, 2008, http://www.msnbc.msn.com/id/25048249/ns/world_news-mideast_n_africa/t/egyptians-clash-police-bread-riot/.
4. Annia Ciezadlo, "Let Them Eat Bread: How Food Subsidies Prevent (and Provoke) Revolutions in the Middle East," *Foreign Affairs*, March 23, 2011, http://www.foreignaffairs.com/articles/67672/annia-ciezadlo/let-them-eat-bread?page=show.
5. E.g., Based on corn to cattle numbers (3,000-3,200 pounds of corn to produce a 1,250-1,350 pound cow) from R. Stillman, M. Haley, and K. Matthews, "Grain Prices Impact Entire Livestock Production Cycle," *Amber Waves*, U.S. Department of Agriculture magazine, March 2009, http://webarchives.cdlib.org/sw1vh5dg3r/http://ers.usda.gov/AmberWaves/March09/Features/GrainPrices.htm; an average carcass weight of 60% of the slaughter weight and 50-65% yield of finished meat from carcass after processing, as reported in "Beef Processing," Blue Valley Brand and Pony Express Ranch, accessed June 16, 2011, http://www.bluevalleybrand.com/beef_processing.asp.
6. E.g., Between 1982 and 2007 the rate of farmland conversion to development was 1 acre/minute, amounting to an area the size of Indiana. As reported by the American Farmland Trust, based on statistics from the Farmland Information Center's *2007 National Resources Inventory*, accessed September 29, 2011, http://www.farmland.org/resources/fote/default.asp.
7. M.L. Parry et al., eds., *Climate Change 2007: Impacts, Adaptation and Vulnerability; Contribution of Working Group II to the Fourth Assessment Report of the Intergovernmental Panel on Climate Change* (Cambridge, UK: Cambridge University Press, 2007), available at http://www.ipcc.ch/publications_and_data/publications_ipcc_fourth_assessment_report_wg2_report_impacts_adaptation_and_vulnerability.htm.
8. "FAQs," World Food Programme, under Hunger, accessed January 22, 2013, http://www.wfp.org/hunger/causes.
9. "FAO Insists on Food as a Human Right," *UNFAO Newsroom*, October 16, 2007, http://www.fao.org/newsroom/en/news/2007/1000680/index.html.
10. David Christian, *Maps of Time: An Introduction to Big History* (Berkeley: University of California Press, 2004).
11. Ibid.
12. Ibid.
13. Kevin Krajick, "Ancestors of Science: Green Farming by the Incas?," *Science Magazine*, November 4, 2005, http://sciencecareers.sciencemag.org/career_magazine/previous_issues/articles/2005_11_04/noDOI.12247974335185312452.
14. Mel Landers, "Indigenous Farming Methods: Mitigating the Effects of Climate Change While Boosting Food Production," *Nourishing the Planet* (blog), October 5, 2010, http://blogs.worldwatch.org/nourishingtheplanet/indigenous-farming-methods-mitigating-the-effects-of-climate-change-while-boosting-food-production/.

15 Donald Worster, "Grass to Dust: The Great Plains in the 1930s," *Environmental Review* 1, no. 3 (1976): 2-11.

16 Ibid.

17 "The Dust Bowl," Library of Congress, American Memory Timeline, a student guide to the Library of Congress online collections, under The Great Depression and World War II, 1929-1945, accessed June 26, 2012, http://www.loc.gov/teachers/classroommaterials/presentationsandactivities/presentations/timeline/depwwii/dustbowl/.

18 Mararet Mellon and Jane Rissler, "Environmental Effects of Genetically Modified Food Crops—Recent Experiences," paper presented at the conference Genetically Modified Foods—the American Experience, Denmark, June 12-13, 2003, http://www.ucsusa.org/food_and_agriculture/science_and_impacts/impacts_genetic_engineering/environmental-effects-of.html.

19 Saritha Rai, "India-U.S. Fight on Basmati Rice Is Mostly Settled," *New York Times,* August 25, 2001, http://www.nytimes.com/2001/08/25/business/india-us-fight-on-basmati-rice-is-mostly-settled.html.

20 "Percy Schmeiser," Monsanto, accessed June 30, 2011, http://www.monsanto.com/newsviews/Pages/percy-schmeiser.aspx; "Percy Schmeiser's Battle," *CBC News Online,* May 21, 2004, http://www.cbc.ca/news/background/genetics_modification/percyschmeiser.html.

21 P. P. Chivenge et al., "Long-term impact of reduced tillage and residue management on soil carbon stabilization: Implications for conservation agriculture on contrasting soils," *Soil & Tillage Research* 94 (2007): 328-33, http://ucanr.org/sites/ct/files/44368.pdf.

22 "Toxic Hazards," WHO, under Health and Environment Linkages Initiative, accessed June 30, 2011, http://www.who.int/heli/risks/toxics/chemicals/en/index.html.

23 *Vital Water Graphics: An Overview of the state of the World Fresh and Marine Waters,* 2nd Edition, Executive Summary, (Nairobi, Kenya: UN Environment Programme, 2008), available at http://www.unep.org/dewa/vitalwater/article186.html.

24 "Groundwater Depletion," U.S. Geological Survey, last modified October 31 2012, http://ga.water.usgs.gov/edu/gwdepletion.html.

25 Matthew Cimitile, "Amazon Deforestation: Earth's Heart and Lungs Dismembered," *Live Science,* January 9, 2009, http://www.livescience.com/3201-amazon-deforestation-earth-heart-lungs-dismembered.html.

26 Henning Steinfeld et al., *Livestock's Long Shadow: Environmental Issues and Options,* UNFAO report of the Livestock, Environment and Development (LEAD) Initiative (Rome: 2006), available at http://www.fao.org/docrep/010/a0701e/a0701e00.HTM.

27 Estimates based on world cereal production numbers from UNFAO *Food Outlook,* June 2011 (2007-2009 average was 2.2 billion tonnes), 2011 world population estimate (6.9 billion), and caloric estimate for grain (1 kg grain provides about 3,500 calories) provided by Worldwatch Institute.

28 "Crops," Environmental Literacy Council, last updated April 3, 2008, http://www.enviroliteracy.org/subcategory.php/2.html.

29 "Meat Production Continues to Rise," Worldwatch Institute, accessed July 15, 2011, http://www.worldwatch.org/node/5443#notes.

30 Christopher L. Delgado, "Rising Consumption of Meat and Milk in Developing Countries Has Created a New Food Revolution," *The Journal of Nutrition* 133, no. 11 (November 2003): 3907S-3910S, available at http://jn.nutrition.org/content/133/11/3907S.full.

31 "Malnutrition," WHO, accessed June 20, 2012, http://www.who.int/water_sanitation_health/diseases/malnutrition/en/.

32 Richard H. Weil, "Levels of Overweight on the Rise," Worldwatch Institute, June 14, 2001, http://vitalsigns.worldwatch.org/vs-trend/levels-overweight-rise.

33 Associated Press, "Study: Global Obesity Rates Double Since 1980," *CBS News,* February 4, 2011, http://www.cbsnews.com/stories/2011/02/03/health/main7315733.shtml; "Understanding Adult Obesity," Weight-control Information Network, an information service of the National Institute of Diabetes and Digestive and Kidney Diseases, accessed July 17, 2011, http://win.niddk.nih.gov/publications/understanding.htm.

34 Sue Horton, Harold Alderman, and Juan Rivera, "Copenhagen Consensus 2008 Challenge Paper: Hunger and Malnutrition," WHO, March 6, 2008, http://www.who.int/pmnch/topics/maternal/hunger_malnutrition/en/.

35 "Food Security," WHO, accessed June 25, 2012, http://www.who.int/trade/glossary/story028/en/.

36 Reuters, "Farmland grab of rich countries threatens Africa food security," *World Bulletin,* last modified July 27, 2011, http://www.worldbulletin.net/?aType=haber&ArticleID=76750.

37 "World Bank/IMF Fact Sheet," Global Exchange, accessed September 3, 2011, http://www.globalexchange.org/campaigns/wbimf/facts.html.

38 "Bangladesh: Growing Interest in Tobacco Farming," Integrated Regional Information Network (IRIN), a service of the UN Office for the Coordination of Humanitarian Affairs, January 26, 2011, http://www.irinnews.org/report.aspx?reportid=91718.

39 UNFAO, "Food Insecurity in the Horn of Africa," *The Elimination of Food Insecurity in the Horn of Africa,* summary report of the Inter-Agency Task Force on the UN Response to Long-Term Food Security, Agricultural Development, and Related Aspects in the Horn of Africa, 2000, http://www.fao.org/docrep/003/x8530e/x8530e02.htm.

40 Hans Lofgren and Alan Richards, "Food Security, Poverty, and Economic Policy in the Middle East and North Africa," *Trade and Macroeconomics Division Discussion Paper,* no. 111 (Washington D.C.: International Food Policy Research Institute, February 2003), www.ifpri.org/sites/default/files/pubs/divs/tmd/dp/papers/tmdp111.pdf.

41 Joel K. Bourne Jr., "Haiti Soil," *National Geographic,* September 2008, http://ngm.nationalgeographic.com/2008/09/soil/bourne-text.

42 "U.S. relations with Sudan," U.S. Department of State, April 8, 2011, http://www.state.gov/r/pa/ei/bgn/5424.htm.

43 "Our Work in South Sudan," Farm-Africa, accessed August 26, 2011, http://www.farmafrica.org.uk/where-we-work/southern-sudan.

44 Global Renewable Fuels Alliance, "GRFA Calls on G20 Ag Ministers to Focus on the Impact of Oil Prices on Food Security," press release, June 11, 2011, http://www.globalrfa.com/pr_062111.php.

45 Gregory White, "The Culprit Behind Rising Food Prices Isn't Emerging Markets, It's Energy," *Business Insider,* April 28, 2011, http://www.businessinsider.com/world-bank-food-prices-2011-4.

46 C. Ford Runge and Benjamin Senauer, "How Biofuels Could Starve the Poor," *Foreign Affairs,* May/June 2007, http://www.foreignaffairs.com/articles/62609/c-ford-runge-and-benjamin-senauer/how-biofuels-could-starve-the-poor.

47 R. Diaz-Chavez et al., *Mapping Food and Bioenergy in Africa,* report prepared on behalf of the Forum for Agricultural Research in Africa (London: May 2010).

48 Norman Church, "Why Our Food Is So Dependent on Oil," Powerswitch UK, April 1, 2005, http://www.powerswitch.org.uk/portal/index.php?option=content&task=view&id=563.

49 Pat Thomas, "Behind the Label: Tomato Ketchup," *Ecologist,* November 23, 2010, http://www.theecologist.org/green_green_living/behind_the_label/686422/behind_the_label_tomato_ketchup.html.

50 Michael Pollan, "We Are What We Eat," Center for Ecoliteracy, accessed December 5 2012, http://www.ecoliteracy.org/essays/we-are-what-we-eat.
51 "2008 Farm Bill Side-by-Side Comparison," USDA Economic Research Service, April 15, 2009, http://webarchives.cdlib.org/sw1vh5dg3r/http://ers.usda.gov/FarmBill/2008/.
52 "Junk food advertising ban," Debatepedia, accessed June 20, 2012, http://debatepedia.idebate.org/en/index.php/Debate:_Junk_food_advertising_ban#Should_junk_food_advertising_be_banned.2C_especially_during_children.27s_television_programs.3F.

Chapter 4: Water

1 Gary L. Chamberlain, *Troubled Waters: Religion, Ethics, and the Global Water Crisis* (Lanham: Rowman & Littlefield Publishers, 2008).
2 "Water Resource," UN-Water, under Statistics, accessed December 6, 2012, http://www.unwater.org/statistics_res.html.
3 Ibid.
4 "Map Details Global Water Stress," *BBC News*, last modified August 21, 2006, http://news.bbc.co.uk/2/hi/science/nature/5269296.stm.
5 "Water Use," UN-Water, under Statistics, accessed December 6, 2012, http://www.unwater.org/statistics_use.html.
6 Michael H. Glantz and Igor S. Zonn, The Aral Sea: Water, Climate, and Environmental Change in Central Asia (Geneva, Switzerland: World Meteorological Organization, 2005), http://library.wmo.int/pmb_ged/wmo_982e.pdf.
7 William E. Roper, Kevin J. Weiss, and James F. Wheeler, *Water Quality Assessment and Monitoring in New Orleans Following Hurricane Katrina* (Washington, DC: U.S. Environmental Protection Agency), accessed December 6, 2012, http://www.epa.gov/oem/docs/oil/fss/fss06/roper_3.pdf.
8 Bryson C. Bates et al., eds., *Climate Change and Water*, technical paper of the Intergovernmental Panel on Climate Change (IPCC) (Geneva, Switzerland: IPCC, June 2008), http://www.ipcc.ch/pdf/technical-papers/climate-change-water-en.pdf.
9 "Water," United Nations, under Global Issues, accessed December 6, 2012, http://www.un.org/en/globalissues/water/.
10 "Map Details Global Water Stress."
11 UN-Water, *Coping with Water Scarcity: Challenge for the 21st Century* (Geneva, Switzerland: 2007), available at http://www.fao.org/nr/water/docs/escarcity.pdf.
12 *Progress on Drinking Water and Sanitation: Special Focus on Sanitation* (New York and Geneva: UNICEF and WHO, 2008), available at http://www.who.int/water_sanitation_health/monitoring/jmp_report_7_10_lores.pdf.
13 Ibid.
14 "Drinking Water and Sanitation," UN-Water, under Statistics, accessed December 6, 2012, http://www.unwater.org/statistics_san.html.
15 Emily Wax, "Dying for Water in Somalia's Drought," *Washington Post*, April 14, 2006, http://www.washingtonpost.com/wp-dyn/content/article/2006/04/13/AR2006041302116.html.
16 "Women," Water.org, under The Crisis: Water Facts, accessed December 6, 2012, http://water.org/water-crisis/water-facts/women/.
17 World Savvy Monitor, "Water as Key to Economic Development," *Water* (November 2009), http://worldsavvy.org/monitor/index.php?option=com_content&view=article&id=713&Itemid=1200.
18 UN Development Program (UNDP), *Human Development Report 2006: Beyond Scarcity; Power, Poverty, and the Global Water Crisis* (Geneva, Switzerland: 2008), available at waterwiki.net, http://waterwiki.net/index.php/HDR_2006_-_Beyond_Scarcity:_Power,_Poverty_and_the_Global_Water_Crisis.
19 "Economics," Water.org, under The Crisis: Water Facts, accessed December 6, 2012, http://water.org/water-crisis/water-facts/economics/.
20 Dan Burrows, "Drought Has Food Prices Set to Spike in 2013," *InvestorPlace*, October 16, 2012, http://investorplace.com/2012/10/drought-has-food-prices-set-to-spike-in-2013/.
21 "Industrial Water Use," U.S. Geological Survey (USGS), under Water Use, last modified October 31, 2012, http://ga.water.usgs.gov/edu/wuin.html.
22 Mohamed Fawzi El-Shaieb, "Sumer," Ancient History Encyclopedia, http://www.ancient.eu.com/sumer/.
23 Jan van der Crabben, "Mesopotamia," Ancient History Encyclopedia, last reviewed April 28, 2011, http://www.ancient.eu.com/Mesopotamia/.
24 Tevfik Emin Kor, "Tigris-Euphrates River Dispute," Inventory of Conflict and Environment, American University, accessed December 6, 2012, http://www1.american.edu/TED/ice/tigris.htm.
25 Jane Braxton Little, "The Ogallala Aquifer: Saving a Vital U.S. Water Source," *Scientific American*, March 30, 2009, http://www.scientificamerican.com/article.cfm?id=the-ogallala-aquifer.
26 David E. Kromm and Stephen E. White, eds., *Groundwater Exploitation in the High Plains* (Lawrence: University Press of Kansas, 1992).
27 Little, "The Ogallala Aquifer."
28 "Water Use," UN-Water.
29 "United States of America," Water Footprint Network, under National Water Footprints: Your Country, accessed December 6, 2012, http://www.waterfootprint.org/?page=cal/waterfootprintcalculator_national; "The relation between consumption and water use," Water Footprint Network, under Introduction, accessed December 6, 2012, http://www.waterfootprint.org/?page=files/home.
30 "Water Use," UN-Water.
31 "Overview," U.S. Department of Agriculture (USDA) Economic Research Services, under Irrigation and Water Use, last modified July 19, 2012, http://www.ers.usda.gov/topics/farm-practices-management/irrigation-water-use.aspx.
32 "Maize," Water Footprint Network, under Product Water Footprints: Product Gallery, accessed December 6, 2012, http://www.waterfootprint.org/?page=files/productgallery.
33 "Virtual-water content," Water Footprint Network, under Glossary, accessed December 6, 2012, http://www.waterfootprint.org/?page=files/Glossary.
34 "How Much H2O is Embedded in Everyday Life?" *National Geographic*, under Environment: Freshwater; The Hidden Water We Use, accessed December 6, 2012, http://environment.nationalgeographic.com/environment/freshwater/embedded-water/.
35 "Irrigation Water Use," U.S. Geological Survey (USGS), under Water Use, accessed December 6, 2012, http://ga.water.usgs.gov/edu/wuir.html.
36 "Micro Irrigation Brings Life Changing Alternatives to Hondurans," International Development Enterprises, under Our Results: Success Stories; iDE Honduras Introduces Drip Irrigation, accessed December 6, 2012, http://www.ideorg.org/OurResults/SuccessStories/Honduras.aspx.
37 Peter H. Gleick et al., "Freshwater Withdrawal by Country and Sector," data table in *The World's Water*, Volume 7 (Washington D.C.: Island Press, October 2011), available at http://www.worldwater.org/datav7/data_table_2_freshwater_withdrawal_by_country_and_sector.pdf.

38 "The Connections Between Our Energy and Water," Union of Concerned Scientists, under Clean Energy: Our Energy Choices: Energy and Water Use, last modified November 16, 2011, http://www.ucsusa.org/clean_energy/our-energy-choices/energy-and-water-use/energy-and-water.html.

39 UN Environment Programme (UNEP), "More water evaporates from reservoirs than is consumed by humans," *Vital Water Graphics—An Overview of the State of the World's Fresh and Marine Waters,* 2nd Edition (Nairobi, Kenya: UNEP, 2008), http://www.unep.org/dewa/vitalwater/.

40 "Drinking Water and Sanitation," UN-Water, under Statistics, accessed December 7, 2012, http://www.unwater.org/statistics_san.html.

41 "Dam Solutions—Easing agricultural pressure," WWF Global, under What We Do: Reducing Impacts; Dams, accessed January 21, 2013, http://wwf.panda.org/what_we_do/footprint/water/dams_initiative/dams/agriculture/.

42 UN-Water, "Drinking Water and Sanitation."

43 "Water Supply in the US," WaterSense, an Environmental Protection Agency Partnership Program, accessed December 7, 2012, http://www.epa.gov/WaterSense/pubs/supply.html.

44 Jane Braxton Little, "The Lake and the 'Hood'," *YES! Magazine,* no. 28 (Winter 2004): pp.22-25, www.yesmagazine.org.

45 "WaterSense Labeled High-Efficiency Lavatory (Bathroom Sink) Faucet Specification," WaterSense, an EPA Partnership Program, under Frequently Asked Questions, September 2007, http://www.epa.gov/WaterSense/docs/ws_faq_faucet508.pdf.

46 "Fix A Leak Week," WaterSense, an EPA Partnership Program, accessed December 7, 2012, http://www.epa.gov/WaterSense/pubs/fixleak.html.

47 "Indoor Water Use in the United States," WaterSense, accessed November 15, 2012, http://www.epa.gov/WaterSense/pubs/indoor.html.

48 "The WaterSense Label," WaterSense, under About Use, accessed December 7, 2012, http://www.epa.gov/WaterSense/about_us/watersense_label.html.

49 "What is water governance?" UNDP Water Governance Facility, accessed December 7, 2012, http://www.watergovernance.org/whatiswatergovernance.

50 Gary L. Chamberlain, *Troubled Waters.*

51 World Savvy Monitor, "Privatization of Water," *Water* (November 2009), http://worldsavvy.org/monitor/index.php?option=com_content&view=article&id=715&Itemid=1202.

52 UN-Water, *Status Report on Integrated Water Resources Management and Water Efficiency Plans,* report prepared for the 16th session of the Commission on Sustainable Development (UN-Water, May 2008), http://www.unwater.org/downloads/UNW_Status_Report_IWRM.pdf.

53 "Bottled Water and Energy: A Fact Sheet," Pacific Institute, under Water: Bottled Water; Further Reading, accessed December 7, 2012, http://www.pacinst.org/topics/water_and_sustainability/bottled_water/bottled_water_and_energy.html.

54 "Toilets," WaterSense, under Products, accessed December 7, 2012, http://www.epa.gov/watersense/products/toilets.html.

55 Warren Kagarise, "King County OKs rainwater as sole drinking water source," Issaquah Press, July 22, 2011, http://www.issaquahpress.com/2011/07/22/king-county-oks-rainwater-as-sole-drinking-water-source/.

56 Nicholas Riccardi, "Who owns Colorado's rainwater?" *Los Angeles Times,* March 18, 2009, http://articles.latimes.com/2009/mar/18/nation/na-contested-rainwater18.

57 "About greywater reuse," Greywater Action, under Our Work: Greywater Recycling, accessed December 7, 2012, http://greywateraction.org/content/about-greywater-reuse.

58 "Aynalem Takes Charge to Own its Project," Water.org, under Featured Projects: Ethiopia, accessed December 7, 2012, http://water.org/post/aynalem-takes-charge-own-its-project/.

59 International Commission for the Protection of the Danube River (ICPDR), *Joint Action Programme for the Danube River Basin,* January 2001 to December 2005 (Vienna, Austria: ICPDR, 2001), http://www.icpdr.org/icpdr-pages/pub_programmes.htm.

60 ICPDR, *Danube River Basin Management Plan: Part A—Basin-wide overview,* Final Version (Vienna, Austria: ICPDR, 2009), http://www.icpdr.org/main/publications/danube-river-basin-management-plan.

61 "Events in 2012," Danube Day, accessed November 15, 2012, http://www.danubeday.org/events.

62 "The New Oil," *Newsweek Magazine,* October 8, 2010, http://www.thedailybeast.com/newsweek/2010/10/08/the-race-to-buy-up-the-world-s-water.html

63 World Savvy, "Privatization of Water," accessed January 3, 2012, http://worldsavvy.org/monitor/index.php?option=com_content&view=article&id=715&Itemid=1202

64 Ibid.

65 *Newsweek Magazine,* The New Oil.

Chapter 5: Air

1 "Air Pressure," physics.org, project of the Institute of Physics, under Facts, accessed February 10, 2012, http://www.physics.org/facts/air-really.asp; Ruth Netting, "It's a Breeze: How Air Pressure Affects You," NASA, under Earth: For Kids Only, accessed December 14, 2012, http://kids.earth.nasa.gov/archive/air_pressure/index.html.

2 Tom Benson, ed., "Air Properties Definitions," NASA Glenn Research Center, under The Beginners Guide to Aeronautics, accessed December 14, 2012, http://www.grc.nasa.gov/WWW/k-12/airplane/airprop.html.

3 "The Troposphere," Windows to the Universe, project of the National Earth Science Teachers Association, accessed December 14, 2012, http://www.windows2universe.org/earth/Atmosphere/troposphere.html.

4 "Layers of the Atmosphere," National Weather Service, under JetStream: Online School for Weather, last modified July 11, 2011, http://www.srh.noaa.gov/jetstream/atmos/layers.htm.

5 "The Ozone Layer," National Oceanic and Atmospheric Association (NOAA), accessed December 8, 2011, http://www.oar.noaa.gov/climate/t_ozonelayer.html.

6 U.S. Environmental Protection Agency (EPA), *Ozone—Good Up High, Bad Nearby* (Washington D.C.: EPA-451/K-03-001, June 2003), available at http://www.epa.gov/oaqps001/gooduphigh/ozone.pdf.

7 "Welfare Effect—Stratospheric Ozone Depletion," EPA, under the Air Pollution Control Orientation Course, accessed November 28, 2012, http://www.epa.gov/apti/course422/ap7b3.html.

8 EPA Office of Air Quality Planning and Standards, "Air Pollution," *Our Nation's Air: Status and Trends Through 2011* (Research Triangle Park, NC: EPA-454/R-12-001, February 2012), accessed December 14, 2012, available at http://www.epa.gov/airtrends/2011/report/fullreport.pdf.

9 Jane Beitler, "Tracking Nature's Contribution to Pollution," NASA Earth Observatory, October 17, 2006, http://earthobservatory.nasa.gov/Features/ContributionPollution/.

10 Occupational Safety and Health Administration (OSHA), "Carbon Monoxide Poisoning" fact sheet, 2002, available at http://www.osha.gov/OshDoc/data_General_Facts/carbonmonoxide-factsheet.pdf.

11 Beitler, "Tracking Nature's Contribution to Pollution."
12 "Sources of Pollution in the Ambient Air," EPA, under the Air Pollution Control Orientation Course, accessed December 14, 2012, http://www.epa.gov/apti/course422/ap3.html.
13 S.A. Ewing et al., "Lead isotopes as an indicator of the Asian contribution to particulate air pollution in urban California," Environmental Science and Technology 44, no. 23 (October 29, 2010): 8911-8916, http://dx.doi.org/10.1021/es101450t.
14 E.g. "International Programs, Bilateral and International Agreements," EPA, under International Programs, accessed December 14, 2012, http://www.epa.gov/oia/air/agreements.htm.
15 N. Gregory Mankiw, Principles of Economics, 4th Edition (Mason, Ohio: Thomson South-Western, 2007).
16 Ibid.
17 Cynthia T. Fowler, "Human Health Impacts of Forest Fires in the Southern United States: A Literature Review," Journal of Ecological Anthropology 7 (2003): 39-59, http://www.srs.fs.usda.gov/pubs/ja/ja_fowler001.pdf.
18 Albert Lowe and Gilda Haas, eds., The Shame of the City: Slum Housing and the Critical Threat to the Health of L.A. Children and Families (Los Angeles: Strategic Actions for a Just Economy, April 2007).
19 Partners Healthcare Asthma Center, "Poverty and Asthma," Best of Breath of Fresh Air: 1995-2000, under Featured Articles, accessed December 14, 2012, http://www.asthma.partners.org/NewFiles/BoFAChapter15.html.
20 "Asthma Facts and Figures," Asthma and Allergy Foundation of America, accessed December 14, 2012, http://www.aafa.org/display.cfm?id=8&sub=42#_ftn19.
21 World Bank and State Environmental Protection Administration of the P.R. of China, The Cost of Pollution in China: Economic Estimates of Physical Damages (Washington, D.C. and Beijing: World Bank, 2007), available at http://siteresources.worldbank.org/INTEAPREGTOPENVIRONMENT/Resources/China_Cost_of_Pollution.pdf.
22 Carolynne Wheeler, "Air pollution hazardous to China's economic health," Globe and Mail, January 3, 2012, http://www.theglobeandmail.com/report-on-business/international-news/air-pollution-hazardous-to-chinas-economic-health/article2279684/.
23 Muhammed Mahadi, "The role of plants as indicators for air pollution," Khulna University (2009), http://www.scribd.com/doc/17257460/The-Role-of-Plants-as-Indicator-for-Air-Pollution-Mahadi-.
24 "Air Pollution," BBC Schools GCSE Bitesize, a student resource (2012), http://www.bbc.co.uk/schools/gcsebitesize/science/ocr_gateway_pre_2011/environment/5_population_sustainability3.shtml.
25 S.B. McLaughlin, "Effects of air pollution on forests: A critical review," Journal of the Air Pollution Control Association 35, no. 5 (May 1985), http://www.tandfonline.com/doi/pdf/10.1080/00022470.1985.10465928.
26 Ibid.
27 E. Borsos et al., "Anthropogenic Air Pollution in the Ancient Times," Acta Climatologica Et Chorologica 36, no. 37 (2003): 5-15.
28 Barbara Freese, Coal: A Human History (Cambridge, MA: Perseus Publishing, 2003).
29 Lisa Gardiner, "Peppered Moths: An Example of Natural Selection," Windows to the Universe, last modified May 16, 2005, http://www.windows2universe.org/cool_stuff/tour_evolution_8.html&lang=en.
30 Ann Murray, "Smog Deaths In 1948 Led To Clean Air Laws," NPR, April 22, 2009, http://www.npr.org/templates/story/story.php?storyId=103359330.
31 Christopher Klein, "The Killer Fog That Blanketed London, 60 Years Ago," History Channel, under News, December 6, 2012, http://www.history.com/news/the-killer-fog-that-blanketed-london-60-years-ago.
32 "History of significant air pollution events," online curriculum for Lyndon State College Atmospheric Sciences course MET130 Survey of Meteorology, accessed December 14, 2012, http://apollo.lsc.vsc.edu/classes/met130/notes/chapter18/history.html.
33 Chirag Trivedi, "The Great Smog of London," BBC News, December 5, 2002, http://news.bbc.co.uk/2/hi/uk_news/england/2545759.stm.
34 "Air Quality and Health Question and Answer," World Health Organization (WHO), accessed December 14, 2012, http://www.who.int/phe/air_quality_q&a.pdf.
35 EPA and U.S. Consumer Product Safety Commission, The Inside Story: A Guide to Indoor Air Quality, accessed December 28, 2011, http://www.epa.gov/iaq/pubs/insidestory.html#Intro.
36 WHO, "Indoor air pollution and health," fact sheet no. 292, September 2011, http://www.who.int/mediacentre/factsheets/fs292/en/.
37 Esther Duflo, Michael Greenstone, and Rema Hanna, "Cooking Stoves, Indoor Air Pollution, and Respiratory Health in Rural Orissa," Economic & Political Weekly 43, no. 32 (2008): 71-76, http://web.mit.edu/ceepr/www/publications/reprints/Reprint_205_WC.pdf.
38 Chris Mackay (Co-founder and Executive Director of Crooked Trails), personal communication, February 13, 2012.
39 WHO, "Indoor air pollution and health."
40 B.C. Wolverton, Anne Johnson, and Keith Bounds, Interior Landscape Plants for Indoor Air Pollution Abatement, NASA report, September 15, 1989, available at http://ntrs.nasa.gov/archive/nasa/casi.ntrs.nasa.gov/19930073077_1993073077.pdf.
41 "A Citizen's Guide to Radon: The Guide to Protecting Yourself and Your Family From Radon," EPA, accessed December 30, 2011, http://www.epa.gov/radon/pubs/citguide.html.
42 "Carbon Monoxide," EPA, under An Introduction to Indoor Air Quality, accessed December 30, 2011, http://www.epa.gov/iaq/co.html.
43 "Volatile Organic Compounds," EPA, under An Introduction to Indoor Air Quality, accessed December 30, 2011, http://www.epa.gov/iaq/voc.html.
44 California Integrated Waste Management Board, Building Materials Emissions Study, Executive Summary (Sacramento, CA: November 2003), available at http://www.calrecycle.ca.gov/Greenbuilding/Specs/Section01350/METExecSum.pdf.
45 Minnesota Department of Health, Volatile Organic Compounds in Your Home, fact sheet, April 2010, http://www.health.state.mn.us/divs/eh/indoorair/voc/vocfactsheet.pdf.
46 Gayle C. Wyndham et al., "Autism Spectrum Disorders in Relation to Distribution of Hazardous Air Pollutants in the San Francisco Bay Area," Environmental Health Perspective 114, no. 9 (September 2006): 1438–1444, http://www.ncbi.nlm.nih.gov/pmc/articles/PMC1570060/.
47 Blake Morrison and Brad Heath, "Young students often most vulnerable to toxic air," USA Today, December 22, 2008, http://usatoday30.usatoday.com/news/nation/environment/2008-12-21-youngkids_N.htm.
48 Sharon LaFraniere, "Lead Poisoning in China: The Hidden Scourge," New York Times, June 15, 2011, http://www.nytimes.com/2011/06/15/world/asia/15lead.html?_r=1&pagewanted=1&nl=todaysheadlines&emc=tha2.

49 Enrico Rossi, "Low-level Environmental Lead Exposure: A Continuing Challenge," *Clinical Biochemist Reviews* 29, no. 2 (May 2008): 63–70, available at the National Center for Biotechnology Information, http://www.ncbi.nlm.nih.gov/pmc/articles/PMC2533151/?tool=pmcentrez.

50 WHO, "Dioxins and the their effect on human health," fact sheet no. 225, May 2010, http://www.who.int/mediacentre/factsheets/fs225/en/.

51 Brian P. Leaderer et al., "Low-level ozone and particulate matter pollution is associated with respiratory symptoms in children with asthma," *Journal of the American Medical Association* 290 (2003): 1859-1867, http://www.niehs.nih.gov/research/supported/sep/2003/ozone/index.cfm.

52 "Stratospheric Ozone, the Protector," from an online teaching module created by LEARN: Atmospheric Science Explorers, accessed September 21, 2012, http://www.ucar.edu/learn/1_6_1.htm.

53 Marciela Yip and Pierre Madl, "Air Pollution in Mexico City," International Laboratory for Air Quality and Health (Brisbane, Australia: Queensland University of Technology, 2002), http://biophysics.sbg.ac.at/mexico/air.htm.

54 Priscilla Connolly, "Urban Slum Reports: The Case of Mexico City, Mexico," case study for the UN-Habitat report *The Challenge of Slums: Global Report on Human Settlements 2003* (London and Sterling, VA: Earthscan), available at http://www.ucl.ac.uk/dpu-projects/Global_Report/pdfs/Mexico.pdf.

55 Peter Zeihan, "Shrinking Ozone Threatens Nations Down Under," *ABC News*, October 20, 2008, http://abcnews.go.com/International/story?id=82183#.UMwE9RzWp40.

56 D. W. Fahey et al., "Twenty Questions and Answers about the Ozone Layer: 2006 Update," from the *2002 Scientific Assessment Report* (UN Environment Programme, 2002), http://ozone.unep.org/Assessment_Panels/SAP/Scientific_Assessment_2006/Twenty_Questions.pdf.

57 Patrick Barry and Tony Phillips, "Good news and a puzzle: Earth's Ozone layer appears to be on the road to recovery," *NASA Science News*, May 26, 2006, http://science.nasa.gov/science-news/science-at-nasa/2006/26may_ozone/.

58 "Effects of Acid Rain," EPA, last modified December 4, 2012, http://epa.gov/acidrain/effects/index.html.

59 "CAFE—Fuel Economy," National Highway Traffic Safety Administration, under Laws and Regulations, accessed September 21, 2012, http://www.nhtsa.gov/fuel-economy.

60 John L. Stoddard et al., *Response of Surface Water Chemistry to the Clean Air Act Amendments of 1990* (Research Triangle Park, NC, January: EPA 620/R-03/001, 2003), available at http://www.epa.gov/ord/htm/CAAA-2002-report-2col-rev-4.pdf.

61 "Interior Paints: Our new tests reveal surprises about what paint-makers claim and what you get," *Consumer Reports*, March 2009, http://www.consumerreports.org/cro/magazine-archive/march-2009/home-garden/interior-paints/overview/interior-paints-ov.htm.

62 "Trees Reduce Air Pollution," Maryland Department of Natural Resources Forest Service, accessed December 13, 2012, http://www.dnr.state.md.us/forests/publications/urban2.html.

63 David J. Nowak, "The Effects of Urban Trees on Air Quality," U.S. Department of Agriculture (USDA) Forest Service, accessed January 5, 2012, http://nrs.fs.fed.us/units/urban/local-resources/downloads/Tree_Air_Qual.pdf.

64 Joseph C. Cooke, "How to avoid air pollution while exercising in the city," *Medical News Today*, April 6, 2006, http://www.medicalnewstoday.com/releases/41060.php.

65 "Environmental Justice," EPA, accessed December 19, 2011, http://www.epa.gov/environmentaljustice/.

66 "Carbon Emissions: Cap-and-trade vs. Carbon Tax," Debatepedia.org, accessed January 13, 2012, http://debatepedia.idebate.org/en/index.php/Carbon_Emissions:_Cap-and-trade_versus_Carbon_Tax_%28arguments%29.

Chapter 6: Energy

1 Saumya Vaishampayan, "Anatomy of a Blackout: August 14, 2003," *Boston Globe*, February 3, 2012, http://articles.boston.com/2012-02-05/magazine/31020073_1_blackout-high-voltage-lines-power-plant.

2 David Barstow, "The Blackout of 2003: New York City; In Frustration, Humor and Greed, A Powerless New York Endures," *New York Times*, August 15, 2003, http://www.nytimes.com/2003/08/15/nyregion/blackout-2003-new-york-city-frustration-humor-greed-powerless-new-york-endures.html?pagewanted=all&src=pm.

3 Vaishampayan, "Anatomy of a Blackout."

4 "Fuel Economy: Where Energy Goes," U.S. Department of Energy (DOE), accessed May 25, 2012, http://www.fueleconomy.gov/feg/atv.shtml.

5 The National Energy Education Development (NEED) Project, "Electricity," *Secondary Energy Infobook*, 2012, http://www.need.org/Energy-Infobooks.

6 American Association for the Advancement of Science, "The Designed World," *Science for all Americans* (New York: Oxford University Press, 1990).

7 "How We Use Energy," National Academy of Sciences, under What You Need To Know About Energy, 2009, http://needtoknow.nas.edu/energy/energy-use/.

8 S. Kalyana Ramanathan, "India to Top in Car Volumes by 2050," *Rediff India Abroad*, October 23, 2004, http://www.rediff.com/money/2004/oct/23car.htm.

9 Ban Ki-moon, "Sustainable Energy for All," *Vision Statement by the Secretary-General of the United Nations*, November 2011, http://www.un.org/wcm/webdav/site/sustainableenergyforall/shared/Documents/SG_Sustainable_Energy_for_All_vision_final_clean.pdf.

10 Ibid.

11 International Energy Agency, "Energy Poverty: How to make modern energy access universal?," early excerpt of *World Energy Outlook 2010 for the UN General Assembly on the Millennium Development Goals*, September 2010, http://www.un-energy.org/sites/default/files/share/une/energy_poverty_excerpt_weo2010.pdf.

12 Ibid.

13 Alison Rae, *Oil, Plastics, and Power* (Mankato, MN: Smart Apple Media, 2010).

14 Ibid.

15 National Oceanic and Atmospheric Administration, "Chemical measurements confirm official estimate of Gulf oil spill rate: New NOAA-led analysis shows gases and oil in three chemically different mixtures deep underwater, in the surface slick, in the air," January 9, 2012, http://www.noaanews.noaa.gov/stories2012/20120109_dwhflowrate.html.

16 DOE, *Energy Literacy: Essential Principles and Fundamental Concepts for Energy Education* (Washington, DC: March 2012).

17 Alfred W. Crosby, *Children of the Sun: A History of Humanity's Unappeasable Appetite for Energy* (New York: W.W. Norton & Company, 2006).

18 "Energy Special, Part 4: How Energy Allowed Britannia to Rule the Waves," transcript and MP3 of Radio Live Public Address Science broadcast, October 13, 2007, available at *Southerly* (blog), David Haywood, http://publicaddress.net/southerly/energy-special-part-4-how-energy-allowed/.

19 Crosby, *Children of the Sun*.
20 "Energy Special, Part 4."
21 Crosby, *Children of the Sun*.
22 "Energy Special, Part 6: The Age of Thermodynamics," transcript and MP3 of Radio Live Public Address Science broadcast, November 17, 2007, available at *Southerly* (blog), David Haywood, http://publicaddress.net/southerly/energy-special-part-6-the-age-of-thermodynamics/.
23 DOE, *Energy Literacy*.
24 Ibid.
25 "The History: Vast Reserves, Small-Scale Use," PBS, under *Extreme Oil* (tv series), accessed May 30, 2012, http://www.pbs.org/wnet/extremeoil/history/prehistory.html.
26 "Milestones: 1969-1976," U.S. Department of State Office of the Historian, accessed May 30, 2012, http://history.state.gov/milestones/1969-1976/OPEC.
27 Donald A. Watt, "Arab Oil Embargo of 1973" *American Business*, December 10, 2010, http://american-business.org/2300-arab-oil-embargo-of-1973.html.
28 "Petroleum & Other Liquids: Petroleum Chronology of Events 1970-2000," U.S. Energy Information Administration (EIA), under Publications, May 2002, http://www.eia.gov/pub/oil_gas/petroleum/analysis_publications/chronology/petroleumchronology2000.htm.
29 "The History: Vast Reserves, Small-Scale Use," PBS.
30 DOE, *The History of Nuclear Energy* (Washington DC: DOE/NE-0088), accessed June 11, 2012, http://www.nuclear.energy.gov/pdfFiles/History.pdf.
31 "1945: US drops atomic bomb on Hiroshima," *BBC News*, under On This Day, accessed April 17, 2012, http://news.bbc.co.uk/onthisday/hi/dates/stories/august/6/newsid_3602000/3602189.stm.
32 DOE, *The History of Nuclear Energy*.
33 "2011 in review," British Petroleum (BP) Global, under Reports and Publications: Statistical Review of World Energy 2012, accessed December 5, 2012, http://www.bp.com/sectionbodycopy.do?categoryId=7500&contentId=7068481.
34 Rae, *Oil, Plastics, and Power*.
35 BP, *BP Statistical Review of World Energy June 2012* (London, 2012), http://www.bp.com/liveassets/bp_internet/globalbp/globalbp_uk_english/reports_and_publications/statistical_energy_review_2011/STAGING/local_assets/pdf/statistical_review_of_world_energy_full_report_2012.pdf.
36 "Peak Oil Primer," Post Carbon Institute, under Energy Bulletin, accessed June 8, 2012, http://www.energybulletin.net/primer.php.
37 Dawn Anderson, "Natural Gas," Environmental Literacy Council, accessed June 11, 2012, http://www.enviroliteracy.org/article.php/68.html.
38 The NEED Project, "Natural Gas," *Secondary Energy Infobook*, 2012, http://www.need.org/Energy-Infobooks.
39 "How Natural Gas Works," Union of Concerned Scientists, under Clean Energy, accessed November 29, 2012, http://www.ucsusa.org/clean_energy/technology_and_impacts/energy_technologies/how-natural-gas-works.html.
40 The NEED Project, "Natural Gas."
41 "About U.S. Natural Gas Pipelines—Transporting Natural Gas," EIA, June 2007, http://www.eia.gov/pub/oil_gas/natural_gas/analysis_publications/ngpipeline/index.html.
42 Rae, *Oil, Plastics, and Power*.
43 Ibid.
44 "What is shale gas and why is it important?," EIA, under Energy in Brief, accessed November 29, 2012, http://www.eia.gov/energy_in_brief/about_shale_gas.cfm.
45 World Energy Council, *2010 Survey of Energy Resources*, 2010, http://www.worldenergy.org/documents/ser_2010_report_1.pdf.
46 Ibid.
47 "Coal," EIA, under Energy Kids: Energy Source; Nonrenewable, accessed June 12, 2012, http://www.eia.gov/kids/energy.cfm?page=coal_home.
48 Ibid.
49 "How Coal Works," Union of Concerned Scientists, under Clean Energy, last revised December 15, 2009, http://www.ucsusa.org/clean_energy/technology_and_impacts/energy_technologies/how-coal-works.html.
50 "Coal," EIA.
51 "Nuclear Power in the World Today," World Nuclear Association, accessed May 31, 2012, http://www.world-nuclear.org/info/inf01.html.
52 "Uranium (nuclear)," EIA, under Energy Kids: Energy Sources; Nonrenewable, accessed June 10, 2012, http://www.eia.gov/kids/energy.cfm?page=nuclear_home-basics.
53 "How Nuclear Power Works," Union of Concerned Scientists, under Nuclear Power, last revised February 11, 2003, http://www.ucsusa.org/nuclear_power/nuclear_power_technology/how-nuclear-power-works.html.
54 Dr. Edwin Lyman, *Statement to the Senate Environment and Public Works Committee*, March 16, 2011, http://www.ucsusa.org/assets/documents/nuclear_power/lyman-senate-epw-3-16-11.pdf.
55 "Fukushima Accident 2011," World Nuclear Association, updated November 2012, http://www.world-nuclear.org/info/fukushima_accident_inf129.html.
56 "Uranium (nuclear)," EIA.
57 "Tidal Power," EIA, under Energy Explained: Renewable Sources; Hydropower, last modified October 10, 2012, http://www.eia.gov/energyexplained/index.cfm?page=hydropower_tidal.
58 The NEED Project, "Hydropower," *Secondary Energy Infobook*, 2012, http://www.need.org/Energy-Infobooks.
59 "Tidal Power," EIA.
60 "Hydroelectric power water use," U.S. Geological Survey, under The USGS Water Science School, last modified October 31, 2012, http://ga.water.usgs.gov/edu/wuhy.html; "Three Gorges Dam Hydroelectric Power Plant, China," Power-Technology.com, accessed December 2, 2012, http://www.power-technology.com/projects/gorges/.
61 "Three Gorges Dam Hydroelectric Power Plant, China."
62 The NEED Project, "Hydropower."
63 Peter Ford, "Controversial Three Gorges Dam has problems, admits China," *Christian Science Monitor*, May 19, 2011, http://www.csmonitor.com/World/Asia-Pacific/2011/0519/Controversial-Three-Gorges-dam-has-problems-admits-China.
64 "Elwha River Restoration," National Park Service, under Olympic National Park Washington, accessed December 2, 2012, http://www.nps.gov/olym/naturescience/elwha-ecosystem-restoration.htm; "Decisions to Remove Dams," Elwha Watershed Information Resource, under Elwha River Watershed: Dam Removal, a website developed by the University of Idaho, accessed December 2, 2012, http://www.elwhainfo.org/elwha-river-watershed/dam-removal/decisions-remove-dams.
65 "Biomass Energy Basics," National Renewable Energy Laboratory, under Learning About Renewable Energy, last modified May 30, 2012, http://www.nrel.gov/learning/re_biomass.html.
66 Lindsey Valich, "Passion for the environment fuels students' biodiesel production," Medill Reports – Chicago, Northwestern University, March 4, 2011, http://news.medill.northwestern.edu/chicago/news.aspx?id=182016.

67 The NEED Project, "Wind," *Secondary Energy Infobook*, 2012, http://www.need.org/Energy-Infobooks.
68 "How Wind Energy Works," Union of Concerned Scientists, under Clean Energy: Our Energy Choices; Renewable Energy, last modified December 15, 2009, http://www.ucsusa.org/clean_energy/our-energy-choices/renewable-energy/how-wind-energy-works.html.
69 "The Smart Grid," SmartGrid.gov, a product of the DOE, under What is the smart grid?, accessed December 3, 2012, http://www.smartgrid.gov/the_smart_grid/#smart_grid.
70 J. Matthew Roney, "Offshore Wind Development Picking Up Pace," Earth Policy Institute, August 16, 2012, http://www.earth-policy.org/plan_b_updates/2012/update106.
71 Ibid.
72 "How Geothermal Energy Works," Union of Concerned Scientists, under Clean Energy: Our Energy Choices; Renewable Energy, last modified December 16, 2009, http://www.ucsusa.org/clean_energy/our-energy-choices/renewable-energy/how-geothermal-energy-works.html.
73 Wendell A. Duffield and John H. Sass, *Geothermal Energy— Clean Power From the Earth's Heat* (Reston, U.S. Geological Survey, 2003), http://pubs.usgs.gov/circ/2004/c1249/c1249.pdf.
74 Rae, *Oil, Plastics, and Power*.
75 Ibid; Leah Bissonette, personal communication, June 27, 2012.
76 DOE, *The History of Solar*, accessed June 13, 2012, http://www1.eere.energy.gov/solar/pdfs/solar_timeline.pdf.
77 The NEED Project, "Solar," *Secondary Energy Infobook*, 2012, http://www.need.org/Energy-Infobooks.
78 Ibid.
79 Ibid.
80 "How Solar Energy Works," Union of Concerned Scientists, under Clean Energy, last modified December 16, 2009, http://www.ucsusa.org/clean_energy/technology_and_impacts/energy_technologies/how-solar-energy-works.html.
81 Excerpt written by Kimberly Corrigan (former U.S. Affiliate for the Earth Charter Center for Education for Sustainable Development) based on a November 2010 visit to Barefoot College campus in Tilonia, India, October 2012.; Barefoot College website, accessed December 28 2012, http://www.barefootcollege.org/.
82 Haris Alibasic, "How Energy Efficiency Strategy Pays Off in Grand Rapids," *Triple Pundit*, August 30, 2012, http://www.triplepundit.com/2012/08/energy-efficiency-strategy-pays-grand-rapids/.
83 DOE, *Energy Literacy*.
84 "History of Energy Star," Energy Star, under About Energy Star, accessed December 6, 2012, http://www.energystar.gov/index.cfm?c=about.ab_history.
85 "Light Bulbs," Energy Star, under Products: Find Energy Star Products; Lighting, accessed December 6, 2012, http://www.energystar.gov/index.cfm?fuseaction=find_a_product.showProductGroup&pgw_code=LB.
86 "CAFE—Fuel Economy," National Highway Traffic Safety Administration, under Laws and Regulations, accessed December 6, 2012, http://www.nhtsa.gov/fuel-economy.
87 The NEED Project. "Efficiency and Conservation," *Secondary Energy Infobook*, 2012, http://www.need.org/Energy-Infobooks.
88 The White House, "Obama Administration Finalizes Historic 54.5 MPG Fuel Efficiency Standards," press release, August 28, 2012, http://www.whitehouse.gov/the-press-office/2012/08/28/obama-administration-finalizes-historic-545-mpg-fuel-efficiency-standard.
89 International Energy Agency, *Technology Roadmap: Fuel Economy of Road Vehicles* (Paris: 2012), http://www.iea.org/publications/fueleconomy_2012_final_web.pdf.
90 EIA, Federal Financial Interventions and Subsidies in Energy Markets 1999: *Energy Transformation and End Use* (Washington D.C.: DC: SR/OIAF/2000-02, May 2000) http://www.eia.gov/oiaf/servicerpt/subsidy1/introd.html.
91 DOE, *Energy Literacy*.
92 Environmental and Energy Study Institute, *DoD's Energy Efficiency and Renewable Energy Initiatives*, fact sheet, July 2011, http://files.eesi.org/dod_eere_factsheet_072711.pdf.
93 Andrew Nikiforuk, "Idea #1: The Green Hawks Are Coming," *Tyee*, December 20, 2010, http://thetyee.ca/News/2010/12/20/Greenhawks/.
94 Ibid.
95 Patrick Moore, "Going Nuclear: A Green Makes the Case," *Washington Post*, April 16, 2006, http://www.washingtonpost.com/wp-dyn/content/article/2006/04/14/AR2006041401209_pf.html.
96 Ibid.
97 "Safety of Nuclear Power Plants," World Nuclear Association, last modified October 10, 2012, http://www.world-nuclear.org/info/inf06.html.
98 Ibid
99 "Nuclear's Fatal Flaws: Waste," Public Citizen, accessed December 6, 2012, http://www.citizen.org/cmep/article_redirect.cfm?ID=15210.
100 "Bandwagons and busts," *Economist*, March 10, 2012, http://www.economist.com/node/21549094.
101 Stefan Lovgren, "Chernobyl Disaster's Health Impact Remains Cloudy," *National Geographic News*, April 26, 2004, http://news.nationalgeographic.com/news/2004/04/0426_040426_chernobyl.html.

Chapter 7: Population

1 U.S. Census Bureau, "World Population," accessed September 5, 2012, http://www.census.gov/population/international/data/worldpop/table_population.php; "As world passes 7 billion milestone, UN urges action to meet key challenges," *UN News Centre*, October 31, 2012, http://www.un.org/apps/news/story.asp?NewsID=40257#.UMzlbRzWp40.
2 *Seven Billion*, film produced for National Geographic magazine's year-long series on population (2011), http://ngm.nationalgeographic.com/7-billion.
3 "Qatar Demographic Profile 2012," IndexMundi, accessed December 14, 2012, http://www.indexmundi.com/qatar/demographics_profile.html.
4 "Country Comparison: GDP Per Capita (PPP)," Central Intelligence Agency World Factbook, updated weekly, accessed December 14, 2012, https://www.cia.gov/library/publications/the-world-factbook/rankorder/2004rank.html.
5 "Qatar Demographic Profile 2012," IndexMundi.
6 Population Reference Bureau, *2011 World Population Data Sheet*, (Washington, DC: Population Reference Bureau, 2011), http://www.prb.org/pdf11/2011population-data-sheet_eng.pdf.
7 UN Department of Economic and Social Affairs, Population Division, *The World at Six Billion* (New York: October 12, 1999), http://www.un.org/esa/population/publications/sixbillion/sixbillion.htm.
8 Linda Booth Sweeney, *When a Butterfly Sneezes* (Waltham, MA: Pegasus Communications, Inc., 2001).
9 As found in: Facing the Future, *Global Issues & Sustainable Solutions*, (Seattle, WA: Facing the Future, 2004).
10 Seven Billion.

11 Thomas Malthus, *An Essay on the Principle of Population: As It Affects the Future Improvement of Society, with Remarks on the Speculations of Mr. Godwin, M. Condorcet, and Other Writers* (London: J. Johnson, in St. Paul's Church-yard, 1798), accessed November 13, 2012, http://www.econlib.org/library/Malthus/malPop.html.
12 Robert Kunzig, "Population 7 Billion," *National Geographic*, January 2011, http://ngm.nationalgeographic.com/2011/01/seven-billion/kunzig-text.
13 Jeffrey Gettleman, "U.N. Says Somalia Famine Has Ended, but Warns That Crisis Isn't Over," *New York Times*, February 3, 2012, http://www.nytimes.com/2012/02/04/world/africa/un-says-famine-in-somalia-is-over-but-risks-remain.html.
14 Steve Connor, "Overpopulation is 'main threat to planet,'" *Independent*, January 7, 2006, http://www.independent.co.uk/environment/overpopulation-is-main-threat-to-planet-521925.html.
15 "The Black Death: Bubonic Plague," MiddleAges.net, accessed September 12, 2012, http://www.themiddleages.net/plague.html.
16 Molly Billings, "The Influenza Pandemic of 1918," Stanford University, June 1997, http://www.stanford.edu/group/virus/uda/.
17 Morabia, "Epidemic and population patterns in the Chinese Empire (243 B.C.E. to 1911 C.E.): quantitative analysis of a unique but neglected epidemic catalogue," *Epidemiology & Infection* 137 (2009): 1361-1368, DOI: 10.1017/S0950268809990136, http://www.qc.cuny.edu/Academics/Degrees/DMNS/Faculty%20Documents/Morabia5.pdf.
18 Population Reference Bureau, *2012 World Population Datasheet* (Washington, D.C.: 2012), http://www.prb.org/pdf12/2012-population-data-sheet_eng.pdf.
19 Engr. I. K. Musa, "Saving Lake Chad," paper based on proceedings of Sirte Roundtable, Libya, December 17, 2008, http://afrwg.icidonline.org/save_lakechad.pdf.
20 "Massive African lake could dry up, U.N. agency says," *CNN*, October 15, 2009, http://edition.cnn.com/2009/WORLD/africa/10/15/lake.chad/index.html.
21 E. g. Gail Stewart, *Population: Ripped from the Headlines, the Environment* (South Dakota: Erickson Press, 2008).
22 David Hunter et al., *International Environmental Law and Policy* (Thompson-West, 2007).
23 Population Reference Bureau, *2011 World Population Data Sheet* (Washington, D.C.: 2011), http://www.prb.org/pdf11/2011population-data-sheet_eng.pdf.
24 David Christian, *This Fleeting World* (Great Barrington, MA: Berkshire Publishing Group, 2008).
25 David Christian, *Maps of Time: An Introduction to Big History* (Berkeley, CA: University of California Press, 2004).
26 Christian, *This Fleeting World*.
27 Christian, *Maps of Time*.
28 Ibid.
29 Ibid.
30 UN Department of Economic and Social Affairs, Population Division, *World Urbanization Prospects: The 2009 Revision* (New York: UN, 2010), http://esa.un.org/unpd/wup/Documents/WUP2009_Highlights_Final.pdf.
31 F. Kraas, "Megacities as Global Risk Areas," *Petermanns Geographische Mitteilungern* 147, no. 4 (2003): 6-15.
32 Eric Sanderson, "Eric Sanderson pictures New York—before the City," TED Talks, under TEDGlobal 2009, (audio recording), July 2009, http://video.ted.com/talk/podcast/2009G/None/EricSanderson_2009G.mp4.
33 "History and Politics of New York," accessed September 10, 2012, http://www.ny.com/histfacts/.
34 "Coming to America," PBS Kids, under Big Apple History, accessed September 10, 2012, http://pbskids.org/bigapplehistory/immigration/topic2.html.
35 Sanderson, "Eric Sanderson pictures New York."
36 Population and area numbers derived from New York City Department of City Planning, accessed March 1, 2011, http://home2.nyc.gov/html/dcp/home.html.
37 UN, *World Urbanization Prospects*.
38 Population Reference Bureau, *2012 World Population Data Sheet*.
39 Jeffrey Passel and D'Vera Cohn, "Immigration to Play Lead Role In Future U.S. Growth: U.S. Population Projections; 2005-2050," Pew Research Center, February 11, 2008, http://pewresearch.org/pubs/729/united-states-population-projections.
40 "Go Forth and Multiply a Lot Less," *The Economist*, October 29, 2009, http://www.economist.com/node/14743589.; Population Reference Bureau, *2012 World Population Data Sheet*, (Washington D.C., 2012), accessed online, http://www.prb.org/pdf12/2012-population-data-sheet_eng.pdf.
41 Country Statistics: India and Zimbabwe," UNICEF, under Statistics and Monitoring, accessed January 22, 2013, http://www.unicef.org/statistics/index_countrystats.html.
42 United Nations Department of Economic and Social Affairs, Population Division, *World Population Prospects: The 2008 Revision*, accessed online November 1, 2012, http://www.un.org/esa/population/publications/wpp2008/wpp2008_highlights.pdf.
43 Population Reference Bureau, *2012 World Population Data Sheet*.
44 United Nations Statistics Division, UN Data, accessed September 10, 2012, http://data.un.org/.
45 Economist Intelligence Unit, "Manning the Barricades," accessed April 11, 2011, http://viewswire.eiu.com/site_info.asp?info_name=instability_map&page=noads.
46 Data based on 2009 UN Development Report and 2008 CIA World Factbook.
47 Population Reference Bureau, *2012 World Population Data Sheet*.
48 "Nov 12, 1954: Ellis Island closes," History Channel, under This Day in History, accessed December 14, 2012, http://www.history.com/this-day-in-history/ellis-island-closes.
49 Passel and Cohn, "Immigration to Play Lead Role In Future U.S. Growth."
50 Image generated from the U.S. Census Bureau International Data Base, Population Pyramids, accessed July 18, 2011, http://www.census.gov/ipc/www/idb/informationGateway.php.
51 Lori S. Ashford, "Africa's Youthful Population: Risk or Opportunity," Population Reference Bureau, June 2007, http://www.prb.org/pdf07/africayouth.pdf.
52 Elizabeth Leahy et al., *The Shape of Things to Come: Why Age Structure Matters To A Safer, More Equitable World* (Population Action International, April 11, 2007), http://populationaction.org/wp-content/uploads/2012/01/SOTC.pdf.
53 Tukufu Zuberi and Kevin J.A. Thomas, "Demographic Projections, the Environment and Food Security in Sub-Saharan Africa," working paper for the UNDP Regional Bureau for Africa, February 2012, http://web.undp.org/africa/knowledge/WP-2012-001-zuberi-thomas-demography-environment.pdf.
54 Image generated from the U.S. Census Bureau International Data Base, Population Pyramids, accessed July 18, 2011, http://www.census.gov/ipc/www/idb/informationGateway.php.
55 Farzaneh Roudi-Fahimi, *Iran's Family Planning Program: Responding to a Nation's Need* (Washington, DC: Population Reference Bureau, 2002). http://www.prb.org/pdf/IransFamPlanProg_Eng.pdf.
56 "Iran's Leader Introduces Plan to Encourage Population Growth by Paying Families," *New York Times*, July 27, 2010, http://www.nytimes.com/2010/07/28/world/middleeast/28iran.html; "Iran urges baby boom, slashes birth control problems," *USA Today*, July 29, 2012, http://www.usatoday.com/news/world/story/2012-07-29/iran-baby-boom/56576830/1.

57 Feng Wang, "China's Population Destiny: The Looming Crisis," Brookings Institution, September 2010, http://www.brookings.edu/articles/2010/09_china_population_wang.aspx.
58 E.g. Tracey Bushnik and Rochelle Garner, "The Children of Older First-Time Mothers in Canada: Their Health and Development," Statistics Canada, September 9, 2004, accessed February 24, 2011, http://www.statcan.gc.ca/pub/89-599-m/2008005/5200192-eng.htm.
59 "The dearth of births: Why are so few young Japanese willing to procreate?" *Economist*, November 18, 2010, http://www.economist.com/node/17492838.
60 "China promises more care for the elderly," *People's Daily*, April 14, 2009, http://english.peopledaily.com.cn/90001/90776/90785/6636770.html.
61 Wang, "China's Population Destiny."
62 "Map: Parenthood policies in Europe," *BBC News*, March 24, 2006, http://news.bbc.co.uk/2/hi/europe/4837422.stm#sweden.
63 Population Reference Bureau, *2012 World Population Data Sheet*.
64 Adisa Banjanovic, "Russia's new immigration policy will boost the population," *Euromonitor International*, June 14, 2007, http://blog.euromonitor.com/2007/06/russias-new-immigration-policy-will-boost-the-population.html.
65 UN World Population Day website, http://www.un.org/en/events/populationday/.
66 Ibid.
67 Population Services International website, accessed December 14, 2012, http://www.psi.org/.
68 UNICEF, *The State of the World's Children 2004* (New York: UNICEF, 2003), http://www.unicef.org/sowc04/files/SOWC_O4_eng.pdf.
69 "Cool School Challenge," National Wildlife Federation, accessed March 14, 2011, http://www.coolschoolchallenge.org/whos-cool.aspx.
70 Batonga Foundation website, Batonga Girls, http://www.batongafoundation.org/see/batonga-girls/.
71 Annie Leonard, "Facts from the Story of Stuff," accessed September 9, 2012, http://www.storyofstuff.org/wp-content/uploads/2011/03/annie_leonard_facts.pdf.
72 "Food Waste in America," Society of St. Andrew, accessed September 8, 2012, http://endhunger.org/food_waste.htm.
73 Massoud Hayoun, "Understanding China's One-child Policy," *National Interest*, August 15, 2012, http://nationalinterest.org/commentary/understanding-chinas-one-child-policy-7330.
74 Information Office of the State Council of the People's Republic of China, "Family Planning in China," August 1995, http://www.fmprc.gov.cn/ce/cegv/eng/bjzl/t176938.htm.
75 Andrew Jacobs, "China's one-child policy has exemptions for quake victims' parents," *New York Times*, May 27, 2008, http://www.nytimes.com/2008/05/27/world/asia/27iht-27child.13232512.html?_r=1.
76 Debatepedia, "Is China's 'one child' policy sensible?" accessed January 12, 2013, http://dbp.idebate.org/en/index.php/Debate:_China_%22one_child%22_policy.
77 "China will outlaw selective abortions," *NBC News*, July 7, 2005, http://www.msnbc.msn.com/id/6800405/#.UEzuxhzFaDk.
78 "China faces growing gender imbalance," *BBC News*, January 11, 2010, http://news.bbc.co.uk/2/hi/asia-pacific/8451289.stm.
79 Paul Wiseman, "China thrown off balance as boys outnumber girls," *USA Today*, June 19, 2002, http://usatoday30.usatoday.com/news/world/2002/06/19/china-usat.htm.
80 "The Brutal Truth: A shocking case of forced abortion fuels resentment against China's one-policy," *Economist*, June 23, 2012, http://www.economist.com/node/21557369.

Chapter 8: Consumption

1 Louise Story, "Anywhere the Eye Can See, It's Likely to See an Ad," *New York Times*, January 15, 2007, http://www.nytimes.com/2007/01/15/business/media/15everywhere.html?pagewanted=all.
2 Erik Assadourian, "The Rise and Fall of Consumer Cultures," in *2010 State of the World: Transforming Cultures from Consumerism to Sustainability*, ed. Worldwatch Institute (New York: W. W. Norton & Company, 2010).
3 Juliet B. Schor, *Born to Buy* (New York: Scribner, 2004).
4 Chris Hails, ed., *Living Planet Report 2008* (Gland, Switzerland: World Wildlife Fund, October 2008), http://awsassets.panda.org/downloads/living_planet_report_2008.pdf.
5 Ibid.
6 "United Arab Emirates," Global Footprint Network, under Resources: Case Stories, accessed November 5, 2010, http://www.footprintnetwork.org/en/index.php/GFN/page/uae_case_story.
7 David Christian, *Maps of Time: An Introduction to Big History* (Berkeley, CA: University of California Press, 2004).
8 Annenberg Learner, "Renaissance: Exploration and Trade," accessed December 21, 2010, http://www.learner.org/interactives/renaissance/exploration.html.
9 Christian, *Maps of Time*.
10 "Ford installs first moving assembly line, 1913," PBS, under *A Science Odyssey: People and Places* (tv series), accessed September 13, 2011, http://www.pbs.org/wgbh/aso/databank/entries/dt13as.html.
11 David Christian, *This Fleeting World: A Short History of Humanity* (Great Barrington, MA: Berkshire Publishing Group, 2008).
12 Richard E. Schumann, "Compensation from World War II through the Great Society," originally printed in the Fall 2001 issue of *Compensation and Working Conditions*, available at Bureau of Labor Statistics, http://www.bls.gov/opub/cwc/cm20030124ar04p1.htm.
13 "The Rise of American Consumerism," PBS, under *American Experience* (tv series), accessed November 1, 2012, http://www.pbs.org/wgbh/americanexperience/features/general-article/tupperware-consumer/.
14 Gary Gardner, Erik Assadourian, and Radhika Sarin, "The State of Consumption Today," in *State of the World 2004: Special Focus; The Consumer Society*, ed. WorldWatch Institute (New York: W.W. Norton & Company): 3-21.
15 Jason McLennan, "The Righteous Small House: Challenging House Size and the Irresponsible American Dream," *Yes! Magazine*, January 29, 2010, http://www.yesmagazine.org/planet/the-righteous-small-house-challenging-house-size-and-the-irresponsible-american-dream.
16 Gardner, Assadourian, and Sarin, "The State of Consumption Today."
17 Annie Leonard, *The Story of Stuff* (New York: Free Press, 2010).
18 "Cell Phone Life Cycle," Environmental Literacy Council, accessed December 7, 2009, http://www.enviroliteracy.org/article.php/1119.php.
19 Brook Larmer, "The Real Price of Gold," *National Geographic*, January 2009, http://ngm.nationalgeographic.com/2009/01/gold/larmer-text/1.
20 Mineral Policy Center (now known as EARTHWORKS), *Cyanide Leaching Packet*, August 2000, available at http://www.earthworksaction.org/files/publications/Cyanide_Leach_Packet.pdf.
21 John C. Ryan and Alan Thein Durning, *Stuff: The Secret Lives of Everyday Things* (Seattle, WA: Sightline Institute, 1997).

22. Ibid.
23. Greenhouse Gas Equivalencies Calculator, U.S. Environmental Protection Agency (EPA), accessed September 14, 2010, http://www.epa.gov/cleanenergy/energy-resources/calculator.html.
24. "The story behind Apple's environmental footprint," Apple, under Apple and the Environment, accessed December 5, 2012, http://www.apple.com/environment/#manufacturing.
25. "Secrets, Lies, and Sweatshops," *BloombergBusinessweek Magazine*, November 26, 2006, www.businessweek.com/magazine/content/06_48/b4011001.htm.
26. Adam Matthews, "China's Bloody Factories: A Problem Bigger than Foxconn," Pulitzer Center on Crisis Reporting, March 29, 2012, http://pulitzercenter.org/reporting/china-electronics-factories-injuries-labor-rights-foxconn-wintek-mike-daisey.
27. Garrett Brown, "Global Electronics Factories in Spotlight," *Occupational Health and Safety*, August 4, 2010, http://ohsonline.com/articles/2010/08/04/global-electronics-factories-in-spotlight.aspx.
28. "China 'buried smog death finding,'" *BBC News*, July 3, 2007, http://news.bbc.co.uk/2/hi/asia-pacific/6265098.stm.
29. "History," Silicon Valley Toxic Coalition, accessed November 12, 2012, http://svtc.org/about-us/history/.
30. T.J. Blasing and Sonja Jones, "Atmospheric Carbon Dioxide Concentrations at 10 Locations Spanning Latitudes 82°N to 90°S," with contributions by C.D. Keeling and T.P. Whorf (Oak Ridge, Tennessee: Carbon Dioxide Information Analysis Center, December 2004), DOI: 10.3334/CDIAC/atg.ndp001.2004, http://cdiac.ornl.gov/ftp/ndp001a/ndp001a.pdf.
31. M.L. Parry et al., *Climate Change 2007: Impacts, Adaptation and Vulnerability; Contribution of Working Group II to the Fourth Assessment Report of the Intergovernmental Panel on Climate Change*, ed. M.L. Parry et al. (Cambridge, UK: Cambridge University Press, 2007), available at http://www.ipcc.ch/publications_and_data/publications_ipcc_fourth_assessment_report_wg2_report_impacts_adaptation_and_vulnerability.htm.
32. American Association of State Highway and Transportation Officials, *Transportation: Invest in Our Future; America's Freight Challenge*, report produced for the National Surface Transportation Policy and Revenue Study Commission, (Washington D.C.: May 2007), available at http://www.transportation1.org/tif3report/.
33. James J. Corbett et al., "Mortality from Ship Emissions: A Global Assessment," *Environmental Science & Technology* 41, no. 24 (2007): 8512-8518.
34. Mike Hanlon, "The world's largest container ship launched," *Gizmag*, June 10, 2006, http://www.gizmag.com/go/5853/.
35. Daniel Machalaba and Bruce Stanley, "Massive new container ships carry huge loads," *Pittsburg Post-Gazette*, October 10, 2006, http://www.post-gazette.com/pg/06283/728846-28.stm.
36. Nolly Andriou and Lee Weiss, "Transport Mode and Network Architecture: Carbon Footprint as a New Decision Metric," master's thesis, MIT, June 2008, http://dspace.mit.edu/handle/1721.1/45250.
37. U.S. Energy Information Administration website, accessed October 17, 2010, http://www.eia.doe.gov/cneaf/electricity/epm/epm_sum.html.
38. Based on a minimum wage of U.S.$7.25/hour for 2,080 hours/year, with a federal poverty level of $14,570 for a family of two (one parent, one child).
39. Leonard, *The Story of Stuff*.
40. World Bank, "Global Purchasing Parities and Real Expenditures," 2005 International Comparison Programme Report, (Washington D.C.: 2008).
41. U.S. Department of Labor, Bureau of Labor Statistics, "American Time Use Survey—2008 Results," news release, June 29, 2009, http://www.bls.gov/news.release/archives/atus_06242009.pdf.
42. Mark Whitehouse, "Number of the Week: Americans Buy More Stuff They Don't Need," *Real Time Economics* (blog), April 23, 2011, http://blogs.wsj.com/economics/2011/04/23/number-of-the-week-americans-buy-more-stuff-they-dont-need/.
43. Computer Industry Almanac Inc., "Worldwide PC Market—A market research report with perspectives and a top-down view of the PC industry—past, present and future trends," press release, accessed October 19, 2010, http://www.c-i-a.com/worldwideuseexec.htm.
44. Matt Elliot, "A computer's life expectancy," *CNet*, under Ask the Editors, last modified February 15, 2005, http://reviews.cnet.com/4520-10166_7-5543710-1.html; Shawn M. J. Mann, "What is the Lifespan of a Desktop Computer?" Bright Hub, last modified May 23, 2011, http://www.brighthub.com/computing/hardware/articles/14363.aspx.
45. Nielson Company, "U.S. Ad Spending Fell 2.6% in 2008, Nielson Reports," press release, March 13, 2009, http://blog.nielsen.com/nielsenwire/wp-content/uploads/2009/03/nielsen2008adspend-release.pdf.
46. Schor, *Born to Buy*.
47. Ibid.
48. EPA Office of Solid Waste, *Electronics Waste Management in the United States: Approach 1* (Washington D.C.: EPA, July 2008), http://www.epa.gov/osw/conserve/materials/ecycling/docs/app-1.pdf.
49. Elizabeth Royte, *Garbage Land: On the Secret Trail of Trash* (New York: Little Brown and Co., 2005).
50. "Safety and Health Topics: Toxic Metals," U.S. Department of Labor, under Occupational Safety & Health Administration, accessed May 24, 2010, www.osha.gov/SLTC/metalsheavy/index.html.
51. World Health Organization, "Dioxins and Their Effects on Human Health," fact sheet no. 225, May 2010, www.who.int/mediacentre/factsheets/fs225/en/index.html.
52. Chris Carroll, "High-Tech Trash," *National Geographic*, January 2008.
53. "Following the Trail of Toxic E-Waste," *CBS News*, under 60 Minutes (tv series), August 30, 2009, http://www.cbsnews.com/stories/2008/11/06/60minutes/main4579229.shtml?tag=contentMain;contentBody.
54. Evan Osnos, "Your cheap sweater's real cost," *Chicago Tribune*, December 16, 2006, http://www.chicagotribune.com/chi-china-cashmere-htmlstory,0,7007933.htmlstory.
55. "Footprint Basics—Overview," Global Footprint Network, accessed December 5, 2012, http://www.footprintnetwork.org/en/index.php/GFN/page/footprint_basics_overview/.
56. David Muir and Christine Brozyna, "Family Sells $1.5 Million Home for One That's Half Price," *ABC World News*, February 8, 2010, http://abcnews.go.com/WN/family-sells-15-million-home-half-price-village/story?id=9780698&page=1.
57. Ibid.
58. BALLE website, accessed September 20, 2011, http://www.livingeconomies.org/.
59. Brower Youth Awards website, accessed October 20, 2010, http://broweryouthawards.org/userdata_display.php?modin=50&uid=101.
60. Dara O'Rourke, "Consumers Can Get Results," *New York Times*, July 30, 2012, http://www.nytimes.com/roomfordebate/2012/07/30/responsible-shoppers-but-bad-citizens/the-power-of-environmentally-conscious-shopping.

61 Annie Leonard, "Individual Actions Just Don't Add Up," *New York Times*, July 31, 2012, http://www.nytimes.com/roomfordebate/2012/07/30/responsible-shoppers-but-bad-citizens/individual-actions-just-dont-add-up-to-environmental-change.

Chapter 9: Climate Change

1 Emmanuel Vaughan-Lee and Alan Zulch, "A Thousand Suns: The View from the Ethiopian Highlands," in Our World 2.0, a project of United Nations University, April 5, 2010, http://ourworld.unu.edu/en/a-thousand-suns-the-view-from-ethiopia's-gamo- highlands/; "The Changing Climate in Gamo Highlands," video produced by InsightShare, accessed December 16, 2012, http://insightshare.org/watch/video/changing-climate-gamo-highlands.

2 Milagros Salazar, "Peruvian Andes elders interpret climate changes," *Business Mirror*, June 2, 2012, http://businessmirror.com.ph/home/green/27998-peruvian-andes-elders-interpretclimate-changes; Jere L. Gilles and Corinne Valdivia, "Local Forecast Communication in the Altiplano," *Bulletin of the American Meteorological Society* 90, no. 1 (January 2009): 85-91, available at USAID, http://pdf.usaid.gov/pdf_docs/PNADU404.pdf; Rebecca Clements, Marlo Cossio, and Jonathan Ensor, eds., *Climate Change Adaptation in Peru: The local experiences* (Lima: Soluciones Prácticas, February 2010), http://www.preventionweb.net/files/13927_doc18005contenido.pdf.

3 Nunavut Tunngavik Inc., "Elder's Conference on Climate Change: Final Report," Nunavut Tunngavik Elder's Conference, Cambridge Bay, Nunavut, March 29-31, 2001, http://www.tunngavik.com/documents/publications/2001-03-21-Elders-Report-on-Climate-Change-English.pdf.

4 Collin Namoliki, "Effects on Climate Change on Nukulaelae, Tuvalu," University of the South Pacific, project report, January 2011, http://www.usp.ac.fj/fileadmin/files/faculties/fste/geography/Earthcaching/students/Collin/Collin_Full_Report.pdf.

5 National Center for Atmospheric Research (NCAR), "Earth's Atmosphere," Spark, 2011, http://spark.ucar.edu/shortcontent/earths-atmosphere.

6 H. Le Treut et al., "Historical Overview of Climate Change Science," in Climate Change 2007: *The Physical Science Basis; Contribution of Working Group I to the Fourth Assessment Report of the Intergovernmental Panel on Climate Change*, ed. S. Solomon et al. (Cambridge and New York: Cambridge University Press, 2007): 93-128, http://www.ipcc.ch/pdf/assessment-report/ar4/wg1/ar4-wg1-chapter1.pdf.

7 Laurie David and Cambria Gordon, *The Down-to-Earth Guide to Global Warming* (New York: Scholastic Inc., 2007); "Carbon Cycle," Environmental Literacy Council, last modified August 7, 2008, http://www.enviroliteracy.org/article.php/478.html.

8 "Sources & Sinks," Environmental Literacy Council, last modified, August 19, 2008, http://www.enviroliteracy.org/article.php/439.html.

9 "Carbon Dioxide Emissions," EPA, under Climate Change: Greenhouse Gas Emissions, last modified June 14, 2012, http://www.epa.gov/climatechange/ghgemissions/gases/co2.html.

10 R. A. Houghton, "Terrestrial carbon sinks–uncertain explanations," *Biologist* 49, no. 4 (2002): 155-160, http://www.whrc.org/resources/publications/pdf/HoughtonBiologist.02.pdf.

11 R. A. Houghton and C. L. Goodale, "Effects of Land-Use Change on the Carbon Balance of Terrestrial Ecosystems," *Geophysical Monograph Series* 153 (American Geophysical Union, 2004), available at Wood Hole Research Center, http://www.whrc.org/resources/publications/pdf/HoughtonGoodaleAGUbook.04.pdf.

12 "What is Soil Carbon Sequestration," UN Food and Agriculture Organization (FAO), under Land Resources,: Sustainable Land Management, accessed December 22, 2012, http://www.fao.org/nr/land/sustainable-land-management/soil-carbon-sequestration/en/.

13 "Global Greenhouse Gas Data," U.S. Environmental Protection Agency (EPA), accessed July 10, 2012, http://www.epa.gov/climatechange/ghgemissions/global.html.

14 "Carbon Dioxide Emissions," EPA.

15 "Nitrous Oxide Emissions," EPA, under Climate Change: Greenhouse Gas Emissions, last modified June 14, 2012, http://www.epa.gov/climatechange/ghgemissions/gases/n2o.html.

16 "Methane Emissions," EPA, under Climate Change: Greenhouse Gas Emissions, last modified June 14, 2012, http://www.epa.gov/climatechange/ghgemissions/gases/ch4.html; "RuminantLivestock," EPA, accessed April 6, 2012, http://www.epa.gov/rlep/.

17 "Greenhouse Gases: Frequently Asked Questions," National Oceanic and Atmospheric Administration (NOAA) website, accessed July 10, 2012, http://www.ncdc.noaa.gov/oa/climate/gases.html.

18 NOAA et al., *Scientific Assessment of Ozone Depletion: 2010; Executive Summary* (Geneva, Switzerland: World Meteorological Organization, 2011), http://www.esrl.noaa.gov/csd/assessments/ozone/2010/executivesummary/booklet.pdf.

19 "Global Warming: Abrupt Climate Change," Union of Concerned Scientists, July 9, 2004, http://www.ucsusa.org/global_warming/science_and_impacts/science/abrupt-climate-change.html#cooler.

20 Lucy A. Hawkes et al., "Climate Change and Marine Turtles," *Endangered Species Research* 7 (May 2009): 137-154, http://www.int-res.com/articles/esr2009/7/n007p137.pdf.

21 Ben German, "Insurance giant cites climate in rising North American disaster costs," E2Wire: The Hill's Energy and Environment Blog, October 17, 2012, http://thehill.com/blogs/e2-wire/e2-wire/262627-insurance-giant-cites-climatein-rising-north-american-disaster-costs; World Bank et al., "Fishing and Aquaculture in a Changing Climate," policy brief prepared for UNFCCC COP15, Copenhagen, December 2009, http://siteresources.worldbank.org/EXTARD/Resources/336681-1224775570533/MultiagencyPolicyBriefCOP15.pdf; "Wine Harvest," *National Geographic*, under Nat Geo TV (video), 2011, http://video.nationalgeographic.com/video/news/ng-today/092611-wine-harvest-ngtoday/.

22 Kyle Hopkins, "Encroaching river set clock ticking on Newtok," *Anchorage Daily News*, August 29, 2009, http://www.adn.com/2009/08/29/915958/encroaching-river-set-clock-ticking.html.

23 Kirsten Feifel and Rachel M. Gregg, "Relocating the Village of Newtok, Alaska due to Coastal Erosion," Climate Adaptation Knowledge Exchange, July 3, 2010, http://www.cakex.org/casestudies/1588.

24 Albina Kovalyova and Alissa de Carbonnel, "Arctic ice melt lifts hopes for Russian maritime trade," *Reuters*, January 27, 2012, http://us.mobile.reuters.com/article/economicNews/idUSL5E8CU-2VF20120130.

25 "A bad climate for development," *Economist*, September 17, 2009, http://www.economist.com/node/14447171.

26 Dale Mackenzie Brown, "The Fate of Greenland's Vikings," *Archaeology* online feature, February 28, 2000, http://www.archaeology.org/online/features/greenland/; Jared Diamond, *Collapse: How Societies Choose to Fail or Succeed* (New York: Viking, 2005).

27 Holli Riebeek, "Paleoclimatology: The Ice Core Record," NASA Earth Observatory, December 19, 2005, http://earthobservatory.nasa.gov/Features/Paleoclimatology_IceCores/.

28 J.T. Houghton et al., "2.3.2.1 Palaeoclimate proxy indicators," *Climate Change 2001: The Scientific Basis* (Cambridge and New York: Cambridge University Press, 2011), http://www.grida.no/publications/other/ipcc_tar/?src=/climate/ipcc_tar/wg1/068.htm.

29 "Mauna Loa Observatory," NOAA, under Earth System Research Laboratory: Global Monitoring Division, accessed January 7, 2013, http://www.esrl.noaa.gov/gmd/obop/mlo/.

30 "IPCC, 2007: Summary for Policymakers."

31 Ibid.

32 Ibid.

33 Barbara Freese, *Coal: A Human History* (Cambridge, MA: Perseus Publishing, 2003).

34 Dave Reay, Michael Pidwirny, and C. Michael Hogan, "Carbon dioxide," in *Encyclopedia of Earth*, ed. Cutler J. Cleveland (Washington, D.C.: Environmental Information Coalition, May 17, 2010), http://www.eoearth.org/article/Carbon_dioxide.

35 Adam Vaughan, "Carbon emissions per person, by country," *Guardian*, September 2, 2009, http://www.guardian.co.uk/environment/datablog/2009/sep/02/carbon-emissions-per-personcapital.

36 "Cool School Challenge," National Wildlife Federation, accessed June 22, 2011, http://www.coolschoolchallenge.org/about-us.aspx.

37 Maggie Villiger, "The Artic—Our Global Thermastat," PBS, under *Scientific American Frontiers: Hot Times in Alaska* (tv series), January 15, 2004, http://www.pbs.org/saf/1404/features/thermostat.htm.

38 "Projections of Future Changes in Climate," in *Climate Change 2007: The Physical Science Basis, Contribution of Working Group I to the Fourth Assessment Report of the Intergovernmental Panel on Climate Change*, ed. S. Soloman et al., http://www.ipcc.ch/publications_and_data/ar4/wg1/en/spmsspm-projections-of.html.

39 "Climate Change," World Health Organization, under the Health and Environment Linkages Initiative, accessed December 22, 2012, http://www.who.int/heli/risks/climate/climatechange/en/.

40 U. B. Confalonieri et al., "Human Health," in *Climate Change 2007: Impacts, Adaptation and Vulnerability, Contribution of Working Group II to the Fourth Assessment Report of the Intergovernmental Panel on Climate Change*, ed. M.L. Parry et al. 391–431, http://www.ipcc.ch/publications_and_data/ar4/wg2/en/contents.html.

41 Brian Reed, "Preparing for Sea Level Rise, Islands Leave Home," NPR, February 17, 2011, http://www.npr.org/2011/02/17/133681251/preparing-for-sea-level-rise-islanders-leave-home.

42 Oli Brown, "Climate change and forced migration: Observations, projections and implications," in *Human Development Report 2007/2008: Fighting Climate Change; Human Solidarity in a divided world*, United Nations Development Programme, accessed July 20, 2012, http://hdr.undp.org/en/reports/global/hdr2007-2008/papers/brown_oli.pdf.

43 Mason Inman, "Carbon is forever," *Nature Reports: Climate Change*, November 20, 2008, http://www.nature.com/climate/2008/0812/full/climate.2008.122.html.

44 "Part Two: Action taken by the Conference of the Parties serving as the meeting of the Parties to the Kyoto Protocol at its seventh session," addendum to *Report of the Conference of the Parties serving as the meeting of the Parties to the Kyoto Protocol on its seventh session*, Durban, South Africa, November 28 to December 11, 2011, March 15, 2012, FCCC/KP/CMP/2011/10/Add.1, http://unfccc.int/resource/docs/2011/cmp7/eng/10a01.pdf.

45 Ibid.

46 International Institute for Sustainable Development, "Summary of the Durban Climate Change Conference: 28 November—11 December 2011," *Earth Negotiations Bulletin* 12, no. 534 (December 13, 2011), http://www.iisd.ca/download/pdf/enb12534e.pdf.

47 John Vidal, "Could an artificial volcano cool the planet by dimming the sun?" *Guardian Environment* Blog, February 6, 2012, http://www.guardian.co.uk/environment/blog/2012/feb/06/artificial-volcano-cool-planet-sun; Tim Appenzeller, "The Case of the Missing Carbon," *National Geographic*, http://environment.nationalgeographic.com/environment/global-warming/missingcarbon/#page=9.

48 Michael Grubb, "The Economics of the Kyoto Protocol," *World Economics* 4, no. 3 (July 2003): 143-189, http://ynccf.net/pdf/CDM/The_economic_of_Kyoto_protocol.pdf.

49 Kevin A Baumert, Tim Herzog, and Jonathan Pershing, "Cumulative Emissions," in *Navigating the Numbers: Greenhouse Gas Data and International Climate Policy;* Part I (Washington, D.C.: World Resources Institute, December 2005), http://pdf.wri.org/navigating_numbers_chapter6.pdf.

50 "A bad climate for development."

51 "Climate Analysis Indicator Tools," World Resources Institute, under Our Work: Climate, Energy, and Transport, accessed July 14, 2012, http://www.wri.org/project/cait.

52 Lisa Evans and Simon Rogers, "World carbon dioxide emissions data by country: China speeds ahead of the rest," *Guardian*, January 31, 2011, http://www.guardian.co.uk/news/datablog/2011/jan/31/world-carbon-dioxide-emissions-countrydata-co2#zoomed-picture.

53 International Energy Agency, CO_2 *Emissions From Fuel Combustion: Highlights*, 2012 Edition (Paris, France: IEA, 2012), http://www.iea.org/publications/freepublications/publication/CO2emissionfromfuelcombustionHIGHLIGHTS.pdf.

Chapter 10: Biodiversity

1 Peter H. Meserve, "Bioregions," in The National Geographic Desk Reference (Washington D.C.: National Geographic Society, 1999).

2 "Continental Drift," National Geographic Education online encyclopedia, accessed November 6, 2012, http://education.nationalgeographic.com/education/encyclopedia/continental-drift/?ar_a=1.

3 Michael Pidwirny and Scott Jones, "Introduction to the Biosphere," Fundamentals of Physical Geography, 2nd Edition (eBook), accessed July 28, 2011, http://www.physicalgeography.net/fundamentals/9h.html.

4 Bryan Walsh, "Dozens of New Species Found in Island Crater," Time Magazine, September 9, 2009, http://www.time.com/time/magazine/article/0,9171,1921586,00.html.

5 "Kingdoms of Living Things," Cliff Notes, accessed December 14, 2012, http://www.cliffsnotes.com/study_guide/Kingdoms-of-Living-Things.topicArticleId-8741,articleId-8651.html.

6 Meserve, "Bioregions."

7. Carl R. Woese, Otto Kandler, and Mark L. Wheelis, "Toward a natural systems of organisms: Proposal for the domains Archaea, Bacteria, and Eucarya," Proceeding of the National Academy of Sciences 87 (June 1990): 4576-4579, http://www.pnas.org/content/87/12/4576.full.pdf.
8. "Ecosystems—Overview," San Franscisco Environment, accessed December 10, 2012, http://sfenvironment.org/ecosystems/overview/ecosystems-overview.
9. "Fast Facts about Biodiversity," National Wildlife Federation, accessed December 10, 2012, http://www.nwf.org/Eco-Schools-USA/Become-an-Eco-School/Pathways/Biodiversity/Facts.aspx.
10. Guido R. Rahr, "Why Is Salmon Conservation Important?" Wild Salmon Center, accessed October 31, 2011, http://www.wildsalmoncenter.org/about/whySalmon.php.
11. E.g. Luke M. Brander, Raymond J.G.M. Florax, and Jan E. Vermaat, "The Empirics of Wetland Valuation: A Comprehensive Summary and a Meta-Analysis of the Literature," Environmental & Resource Economics 33 (2006): 223-250, http://www.environmental-expert.com/Files%5C6063%5Carticles%5C9162%5C1.pdf.
12. Lindsey, Rebecca, "Tropical Deforestation," Earth Observatory, project of NASA, March 2007, http://earthobservatory.nasa.gov/Features/Deforestation/.
13. Robert Constanza et al., "The value of the world's ecosystem services and natural capital," Nature 387 (May 1997), http://www.cbd.int/doc/external/academic/constanza-es-1997-en.pdf.
14. A. Garibaldi and N. Turner, "Cultural keystone species: Implications for ecological conservation and restoration," Ecology and Society 9, no.3 (2004), http://www.ecologyandsociety.org/vol9/iss3/art1/.
15. Nicola Beaumont et al., Marine Biodiversity, An economic valuation (Plymoth, UK: Department for Environment, Food and Rural Affairs, July 2006), http://earthmind.net/marine/docs/uk-marine-valuation.pdf.
16. "The Extinction Crisis," Center for Biological Diversity, under Programs: Biodiversity; Elements of Biodiversity, accessed December 12, 2012, http://www.biologicaldiversity.org/programs/biodiversity/elements_of_biodiversity/extinction_crisis/index.html.
17. "Mass Extinction," Discovery Earth, accessed July 28, 2011, http://dsc.discovery.com/earth/wide-angle/mass-extinctions-timeline.html.
18. "Big Five mass extinction events," BBC, under Nature: Prehistoric Life, accessed December 11, 2012, http://www.bbc.co.uk/nature/extinction_events.
19. Juliette Jowitt, "Humans driving extinction faster than species can evolve, say experts," Guardian, March 7, 2010, http://www.guardian.co.uk/environment/2010/mar/07/extinction-species-evolve.
20. "Tamarisk Leaf Beetle," National Parks Service, Glen Caynon Nature Recreation Area, under Nature & Science, last modified December 5, 2012, http://www.nps.gov/glca/naturescience/tamarisk-leaf-beetle.htm; Steven Law, "Beetles killing tamarisk trees," KSL News, October 5, 2011, http://ksl.deseretdigital.com/?sid=17525823&nid=1012; "Tamarisk Frequently Asked Questions," Discover Moab, accessed December 10, 2012, http://www.discovermoab.com/tamarisk.htm.
21. Bob Berwyn, "Environment: Tamarisk biocontrol may work after all," Summit County Citizens Voice, July 18, 2012, http://summitcountyvoice.com/2012/07/18/environment-tamarisk-biocontrol-may-work-after-all/; Ran Meng et al., "Detection of tamarisk defoliation by the northern tamarisk beetle based on multitemporal Landsat 5 thematic mapper imagery," GIScience and Remote Sensing 49, no. 4 (2012): 510-537.
22. Achim Steiner, "Counting the cost of alien invasions," BBC News, April 13, 2010, http://news.bbc.co.uk/2/hi/science/nature/8615398.stm.
23. Ibid.
24. Ecological Society of America, "Ecologists Put Price Tag on Invasive Species," press release, April 20, 2009, http://www.esa.org/pao/newsroom/pressReleases2009/0420-2009.php.
25. "Anaplophora chinensis," species factsheet in the DAISIE Database, accessed November 18, 2011, http://www.europe-aliens.org/speciesFactsheet.do?speciesId=51319#.
26. David Pimentel, Rodolfo Zuniga, and Doug Morrison, "Update on the environmental and economic costs associated with alien-invasive species in the United States," Ecological Economics 52 (2005): 273-288.
27. Rhett Butler, "Controlling the Ranching Boom that Threatens the Amazon," Yale Environment 360, August 10, 2009, http://e360.yale.edu/feature/controlling_the_ranching_boom_that_threatens_the_amazon/2176/.
28. "Endocrine Disruptors," Center for Biological Diversity, accessed December 11, 2012, http://www.biologicaldiversity.org/campaigns/pesticides_reduction/endocrine_disruptors/index.html.
29. Ibid.
30. "Endocrine disrupting compounds in the coastal environment," Marine Biodiversity Wiki, part of the Marine Biodiversity and Ecosystem Functioning EU Network of Excellence, accessed November 1, 2011, http://www.marbef.org/wiki/Endocrine_disrupting_compounds_in_the_coastal_environment.
31. David Hewitt, "Larger predators at greatest risk from environmental changes, study finds," Earth Times, November 25, 2010, http://www.earthtimes.org/conservation/larger-predators-environmental-changes-study/59/.
32. Graham Smith, "Coral species may be extinct within 50 years, warn scientists as they reveal most endangered," Daily Mail, January 11, 2011, http://www.dailymail.co.uk/sciencetech/article-1346088/Coral-species-extinct-50-years-warn-scientists-reveal-endangered.html.
33. "Coral bleaching—will global warming kill the reefs?" Nova: Science in the News, project of the Australian Academy of Science, April 2003, http://www.science.org.au/nova/076/076key.htm.
34. Jonathan H. Adler, "Property Rights and Tragedy of the Commons," Atlantic, May 22, 2012, http://www.theatlantic.com/business/archive/2012/05/property-rights-and-the-tragedy-of-the-commons/257549/.
35. Pervaze A. Sheikh and M. Lynne Corn, "Implementation of CITES: Successes and Problems," Convention on International Trade in Endangered Species of Wild Fauna and Flora (CITES): Background and Issues, CRS Report for Congress (Order Code RL32751), February 1, 2005, http://www.nationalaglawcenter.org/assets/crs/RL32751.pdf.
36. "Hotspots Defined," Conservation International, under Where We Work: Piority Areas; Biodiversity Hotspots, 2007, http://www.conservation.org/where/priority_areas/hotspots/Pages/hotspots_defined.aspx.
37. "Tropical Andes," Conservation International, under Where We Work: Priority Areas; Biodiversity Hotspots, 2007, http://www.conservation.org/where/priority_areas/hotspots/south_america/Tropical-Andes/Pages/default.aspx.
38. "Tropical Andes: Species," Conservation International, under Where We Work: South America; Priorities, accessed January 11, 2012, http://www.conservation.org/where/priority_areas/hotspots/south_america/Tropical-Andes/Pages/biodiversity.aspx.

39 Peter Kareiva and Michelle Marvier, "Conserving Biodiversity Coldspots," *American Scientist* 97, no. 6 (December 2009), http://www.americanscientist.org/issues/id.869,y.2003,no.4,content.true,page.6,css.print/issue.aspx.
40 "What is CITES?," Convention on International Trade in Endangered Species of Wild Fauna and Flora (CITES), accessed July 29, 2011, http://www.cites.org/eng/disc/what.php.
41 "Summary of the Endangered Species Act," U.S. Environmental Protection Agency, accessed November 9, 2011, http://www.epa.gov/lawsregs/laws/esa.html.
42 U.S. Fish and Wildlife Service, "Species Profile: Whooping crane (Grus americana)," Environmental Conservation Online System, accessed November 9, 2011, http://ecos.fws.gov/speciesProfile/profile/speciesProfile.action?spcode=B003.
43 International Whaling Commission website, accessed October 6, 2011, http://www.iwcoffice.org/home.
44 Kenneth R. Weiss and Karen Kaplan, "Gray whale recovery called incorrect," *Los Angeles Times*, September 11, 2007, http://articles.latimes.com/2007/sep/11/science/sci-whales11.
45 S. Elizabeth Alter, Eric Rynes, and Stephen R. Palumbi, "Have Grey Whales Recovered From Whaling?" *Lenfest Ocean Program Research Series*, August 2007, http://www.stanford.edu/group/Palumbi/PNAS/LenfestRS.pdf.
46 International Union for Conservation of Nature Red List of Threatened Species, accessed July 29, 2011, http://www.iucnredlist.org.
47 "Poachers-turned-Protectors in Zambia," Wildlife Conservation Society, accessed July 29, 2011, http://www.wcs.org/conservation-challenges/local-livelihoods/community-based-conservation/poachers-turned-protectors-in-zambia.aspx.
48 "Introducing the Millennium Seed Bank Partnership," *Kew Royal Botanic Gardens*, December 9, 2012, http://www.kew.org/science-conservation/save-seed-prosper/millennium-seed-bank/index.htm.
49 "Svalbard Global Seed Vault," Global Crop Diversity Trust, accessed July 30, 2011, http://www.croptrust.org/content/svalbard-global-seed-vault.
50 Anand Jagatia, "Zoos urged to join forces in conserving biodiversity," Bluesci, *Cambridge University Science Magazine*, March 30, 2011, http://www.bluesci.org/?p=2715.
51 "Recovery Efforts: Reintroduction," Black-Footed Ferret Recovery Program, accessed July 30, 2011, http://www.blackfootedferret.org/reintroduction.
52 "US Highway 93 Wildlife Overpasses 2011," *Arizona Game and Fish Department*, February 14, 2011, http://www.azgfd.gov/w_c/research_maintain_sheep.shtml.
53 Susan Cosier, "Reintroducing Wolves into National Parks Could Restore Ecosystems," *Audubon Magazine*, February 2, 2010, http://magblog.audubon.org/reintroducing-wolves-national-parks-could-restore-ecosystems.
54 Shannon Dininny, "Ranchers, Wolves Are Uneasy Neighbors," Bulletin, September 13, 2011, http://www.bendbulletin.com/article/20110913/NEWS0107/109130371/.

Chapter 11: Oceans

1 Robert Poole, "Earthrise, seen for the first time by human eyes," in *Earthrise: How Man First Saw the Earth* (New Haven, CT: Yale University Press, 2008), http://yalepress.yale.edu/yupbooks/excerpts/poole_earthrise.pdf.
2 Peter Frances and Angeles Gavira Guerrero, eds., *Oceans: The World's Last Wilderness Revealed* (London: American Museum of Natural History, 2006).
3 Ibid.
4 "La Nina's Distant Effects in East Africa: Droughts and Floods Are Remote-Controlled Climate Effects," *Science Daily*, August 4, 2011, http://www.sciencedaily.com/releases/2011/08/110804141754.htm.
5 Elizabeth Kolbert, "The Acid Sea," *National Geographic*, April 2011, http://ngm.nationalgeographic.com/2011/04/ocean-acidification/kolbert-text/1.
6 Environmental Justice Foundation, *Mangroves: Nature's defense against Tsunamis; a report on the impact of mangrove loss and shrimp farm development on coastal development* (London: EJF, 2006).
7 Ibid.
8 Frances and Guerrero.
9 Kennedy Warne, "Forests of the Tide," *National Geographic*, February 2007, http://ngm.nationalgeographic.com/2007/02/mangroves/warne-text/1.
10 "Interdisciplinary research on submarine volcanoes," Interactive Oceans, project of the University of Washington School of Oceanography, accessed September 25, 2012, http://www.interactiveoceans.washington.edu/story/Volcanoes+and+Life%3A+Axial+Seamount.
11 "Tubeworms," To the Depths of Discovery, project of the University of Delaware College of Earth, Ocean, and Environment, accessed October 8, 2012, http://www.ceoe.udel.edu/extreme2003/creatures/tubeworms/index.html.
12 "Chemosynthesis," Extreme 2000: Voyage to the Deep, accessed November 25, 2012, http://www.ceoe.udel.edu/deepsea/level-2/chemistry/chemo.html.
13 Jacqueline S. Mitchell, "Life Above Boiling," PBS, under Beneath the Sea (tv series), accessed November 19, 2012, http://www.pbs.org/saf/1207/features/113.htm.
14 Frances and Guerrero.
15 Enric Sala, "Ocean Ecosystem Services Can Increase—But Only if We Take Less," *National Geographic*, April 2011, http://newswatch.nationalgeographic.com/2011/04/05/ocean-productivity-can-increase-but-only-if-we-take-less/.
16 Andrew Dyck and U. Rashid Sumaila, "Marine Fisheries and the World Economy," Ocean Science Series, research summary (Washington, D.C.: Pew Environment Group, September 2010), http://www.pewenvironment.org/uploadedFiles/PEG/Publications/Report/Pew_OSS_World_Economy.pdf.
17 UN Food and Agriculture Organization, "General situation of world fish stocks," data derived from The State of World Fisheries and Aquaculture (Rome, Italy: UNFAO, 2010), http://www.fao.org/newsroom/common/ecg/1000505/en/stocks.pdf.
18 Nell Greenfieldboyce, "Study: 634 Million People at Risk from Rising Seas," *NPR*, March 28, 2007, http://www.npr.org/templates/story/story.php?storyId=9162438.
19 Edith Widder, "The Mystery of Bioluminescence," TED Talk: Galapagos Islands, April 2010, http://www.ted.com/talks/edith_widder_glowing_life_in_an_underwater_world.html.
20 "The Challenger Expedition," History of Oceanography, accessed November 19, 2012, http://www.divediscover.whoi.edu/history-ocean/challenger.html.
21 Ker Than, "James Cameron Completes Record-Breaking Mariana Trench Dive," National Geographic News, March 25, 2012, http://news.nationalgeographic.com/news/2012/03/120325-james-cameron-mariana-trench-challenger-deepest-returns-science-sub/.
22 Ocean Observatories Initiative website, accessed September 25, 2012, www.oceanobservatories.org.
23 "Marine Problems: Pollution," WWF Global, accessed October 8, 2012, http://wwf.panda.org/about_our_earth/blue_planet/problems/pollution/.

24 Ken Olsen, "Orcas on the Edge," National Wildlife, October 1, 2006, http://www.nwf.org/News-and-Magazines/National-Wildlife/Animals/Archives/2006/Orcas-on-the-Edge.aspx.
25 Jenny Coberly, "Environment: Gulf dead zone could be the largest ever," Summit County Citizens Voice, June 19, 2011, http://summitcountyvoice.com/2011/06/19/environment-gulf-dead-zone-could-be-the-largest-ever/.
26 Lindsey Hoshaw, "Afloat in the Ocean, Expanding Islands of Trash," New York Times, November 9, 2009, http://www.nytimes.com/2009/11/10/science/10patch.html?_r=0.
27 Tamara Keith, "Oyster Businesses Still Plagued by Gulf Oil Spill," NPR, December 6, 2010, http://www.npr.org/2010/12/06/131736305/oyster-businesses-still-plagued-by-gulf-oil-spill; Debbie Elliot and Marisa Peñaloza, "BP Oil Well Capped, But Trauma Still Flowing," NPR, November 30, 2010, http://www.npr.org/2010/11/29/131667797/bp-oil-well-capped-but-trauma-still-flowing?ps=rs.
28 Mark Kinver, "BP oil spill: The environmental impact one year on," BBC News, April 19, 2012, http://www.bbc.co.uk/news/science-environment-13123036.
29 Tom Fowler, "Experts Weigh Spill's Lasting Effects," Wall Street Journal, April 12, 2012, http://online.wsj.com/article/SB10001424052702303624004577339943866694420.html.
30 "BP oil spill seriously harmed deep-sea corals, scientists warn," Guardian, March 26, 2012, http://www.guardian.co.uk/environment/2012/mar/26/bp-oil-spill-deepwater-horizon.
31 "Fish consumption reaches all-time high," UN Food and Agriculture Organization, under Media Center, January 31, 2011, http://www.fao.org/news/story/en/item/50260/icode/.
32 John Sackton, "Hilborn says eliminating global fishing would mean plowing world's rainforests 22 times over," Seafood.com, under News, accessed July 9, 2011, http://www.savingseafood.org/conservation-environment/hilborn-says-eliminating-global-fishing-would-mean-plowing-worlds-rainforests-22-times-3.html.
33 National Oceanic and Atmospheric Administration (NOAA), "Atlantic Bluefin Tuna," in FishWatch—U.S. Sea Food Facts, May 26, 2011, http://www.fishwatch.gov/seafood_profiles/species/tuna/species_pages/atl_bluefin_tuna.htm.
34 Richard T. Wright, Environmental Science, 10th Edition (New Jersey: Pearson Prentice Hall, 2008).
35 "Shellfish Aquaculture Benefits," East Coast Shellfish Growers Association, brochure, accessed October 10, 2012, http://www.ecsga.org/Pages/Sustainability/BenefitsBrochure.pdf.
36 Nichola Meserve, "Risks of Farmed Fish," Aquaculture in America, Biology 217 class project, Duke University, Spring 2005, http://www.biology.duke.edu/bio217/2005/ncm3/risks.htm.
37 "Sea Turtles," Sea World, accessed November 19, 2012, http://www.seaworld.org/animal-info/info-books/sea-turtle/reproduction.htm.
38 "Coastal Development," SEE Turtles, accessed November 19, 2012, http://www.seeturtles.org/1131/coastal-development.html.
39 "Coastal Development," NOAA, accessed November 19, 2012, http://www.yoto98.noaa.gov/facts/cdevel.htm.
40 "Five Effects of Climate Change on the Ocean," Conservation International, 2007, http://www.conservation.org/Documents/Climate%20Change%20on%20the%20Ocean.pdf.
41 E.g. "Implementation of Marine Protection Treaties and International Agreements," Environmental Protection Agency, under International Programs, accessed July 8, 2011, http://www.epa.gov/oia/water/marine/treaties.html.
42 "Frequently Asked Questions," International Maritime Organization, accessed July 9, 2011, http://www.imo.org/About/Pages/FAQs.aspx.
43 NOAA, US Regional Fisheries Management Councils: Opportunities & Challenges (2009), http://www.fisherycouncils.org/USFMCsections/USRFMCintro.pdf.
44 "About Us," Marine Stewardship Council, accessed June 10, 2011, http://www.msc.org/about-us.
45 "Seafood Watch," Monterey Bay Aquarium, accessed July 11, 2011, http://www.montereybayaquarium.org/cr/seafoodwatch.aspx.
46 "MPA Definition," NOAA, under National Marine Protected Areas Center, June 2011, http://www.mpa.gov/aboutmpas/definition/.
47 "MPA Case Studies: Florida Keys National Marine Sanctuary," NOAA, under National Marine Protected Areas Center, accessed August 12, 2011, http://www.mpa.gov/aboutmpas/casestudies/floridakeys/.
48 "Working Together: Making the World Safer For Fish," Marine Conservation Alliance Foundation, newsletter, 2010, http://www.marineconservationalliance.org/sea_alliance/email_template/marine_debris_newsletter.html.
49 Blue Ocean Society for Marine Conservation website, accessed July 11, 2011, http://www.blueoceansociety.org/Research/schedule.html.
50 The Government of St. Vincent and Grenadines, "Bequian Whaling: A Statement of Needs," May 2012, http://www.iwcoffice.org/index.php?cID=2975&cType=document.
51 Stephen R. Braund & Associates, "Quantification of Subsistence and Cultural Need for Bowhead Whales by Alaskan Eskimos," report prepared for the Alaska Eskimo Whaling Commission, Anchorage, AK, May 2012, http://www.iwcoffice.org/cache/downloads/dqmdqrcj93c48ogooko8k0gs8/64-ASW%203.pdf.
52 Ed Andrews, "Sea Shepherd exposes mass whale slaughter: Conservation charity captures images of ritualistic killings," Huck, July 23, 2010, http://www.huckmagazine.com/blog/shepherd-exposes-whale/.
53 "Whale Defenders," Greenpeace, accessed November 19, 2012, http://www.greenpeace.org/usa/en/campaigns/oceans/whale-defenders/?__utma=1.1861249736.1349933246.1349933246.1353396832.2&__utmb=1.2.10.1353396832&__utmc=1&__utmx=-&__utmz=1.1349933246.1.1.utmcsr=(direct)|utmccn=(direct)|utmcmd=(none)&__utmv=-&__utmk=193427373.

Chapter 12: Quality of Life

1 John de Graaf and David K Batker, What's the Economy For, Anyway? Why It's Time to Stop Chasing Growth and Start Pursuing Happiness, (New York: Bloomsbury Press, 2011).
2 Robert Putnam, "Bowling Alone: America's Declining Social Capital," Journal of Democracy 6, no. 1 (January 1995): 65-78, http://xroads.virginia.edu/~HYPER/DETOC/assoc/bowling.html.
3 "Connection and Happiness," PBS, under This Emotional Life (tv series), accessed August 23, 2011, http://www.pbs.org/thisemotionallife/topic/connecting/connection-happiness.
4 "What Makes Teens Happy?," CBS News, February 11, 2009, http://www.cbsnews.com/stories/2007/11/12/earlyshow/living/parenting/main3486964.shtml.
5 Juliet Schor, "Sustainable Work Schedules for All" in 2010 State of the World: Transforming Cultures: From Consumerism to Sustainability, ed. WorldWatch Institute (New York: W.W. Norton & Company, 2010).
6 Rob Kanter, "Trees, Green Space, and Human Well-Being," transcript of Environmental Almanac, a radio show produced by the University of Illinois School of Earth, Society, and Environment, July 7, 2005, http://lhhl.illinois.edu/media/2005.07_kanter.htm.

7. "Respiratory Health and Air Pollution," Centers for Disease Control and Prevention, under Healthy Places: Health Impact Assessment, accessed on July 15, 2012, http://www.cdc.gov/healthyplaces/healthtopics/airpollution.htm.
8. Richard A. Easterlin, "The Worldwide Standard of Living Since 1800," *Journal of Economic Perspectives 14*, no. 1 (Winter 2000): 7-26, http://www.vedegylet.hu/fejkrit/szvggyujt/Easterlin_WorldwidestandarOfLIvingSince1800.pdf.
9. "India," Central Intelligence Agency (CIA) World Factbook, updated weekly, accessed June 25, 2012, https://www.cia.gov/library/publications/the-world-factbook/geos/xx.html.
10. UNESCO Institute for Statistics, "School enrollment, secondary (% net)," World Bank, under Data: Indicators, accessed August 24, 2011, http://data.worldbank.org/indicator/SE.SEC.NENR.
11. John Maynard Keynes, "Economic Possibilities for our Grandchildren," *Essays in Persuasion* (New York: W.W. Norton & Co., 1963), available at http://www.econ.yale.edu/smith/econ116a/keynes1.pdf.
12. Schor, "Sustainable Work Schedules."
13. Ibid.
14. "100 Best Companies to Work For: #3 SAS Institute," *CNN Money*, February 6, 2012, http://money.cnn.com/magazines/fortune/best-companies/2012/snapshots/3.html.
15. "About," OECD Better Life Index, accessed February 16, 2012, http://oecdbetterlifeindex.org/about/better-life-initiative/.
16. UN Development Programme (UNDP), "Regional and National Trends in the *Human Development Index 1970-2010*," *Human Development Report 2011: Sustainability and Equity; A Better Future for All* (New York: Palgrave Macmillan, 2011), under Indices & Data: HDI Trends, http://hdr.undp.org/en/data/trends/.
17. "About Human Development," UNDP Human Development Reports, under Human Development, http://hdr.undp.org/en/humandev/.
18. "Country Profiles," UNDP Human Development Reports, under Indices & Data.
19. CIA World Factbook, https://www.cia.gov/library/publications/the-world-factbook/.
20. Francesca Levy, "Table: The World's Happiest Countries," *Forbes*, July 14, 2010, http://www.forbes.com/2010/07/14/world-happiest-countries-lifestyle-realestate-gallup-table.html.
21. "Average Temperatures—Copenhagen," Holiday Weather.com, accessed August 22, 2011, http://www.holiday-weather.com/copenhagen/averages/#avg_sunshine_hours.
22. "Denmark," CIA World Factbook, updated weekly, accessed August 23, 2011, https://www.cia.gov/library/publications/the-world-factbook/geos/da.html.
23. Bill Weir and Sylvia Johnson, "Denmark: The Happiest Place on Earth," *ABC News 20/20*, January 8, 2007, http://abcnews.go.com/2020/story?id=4006092&page=1#.UDFfyiCXT0U.
24. University of Leicester, "University of Leicester Produces the first ever World Map of Happiness," press release, July 28, 2006, http://www2.le.ac.uk/ebulletin/news/press-releases/2000-2009/2006/07/nparticle.2006-07-28.2448323827.
25. "Health," OECD Better Life Index, under Topics, accessed March 5, 2012, http://oecdbetterlifeindex.org/topics/health/.
26. Alexandra Williams, "Eco latrines improve quality of life in earthquake-affected communities in Rwanda," UNICEF, under Where We Work: Eastern and Southern Africa; Rwanda; News, March 15, 2011, http://www.unicef.org/wash/rwanda_57928.html.
27. "Rethinking the Good Life," Worldwatch Institute, accessed December 2, 2012, http://www.worldwatch.org/node/815.
28. "About," Step Up Savannah, accessed August 25, 2011, http://www.stepupsavannah.org/about-step-savannah.
29. Putnam, "Bowling Alone."
30. David Villano, "Building a Better Citizen," *Pacific Standard*, November 2, 2009, http://www.psmag.com/politics/building-a-better-citizen-3361/.
31. Council on Virginia's Future, "Civic Engagement," Virginia Performs, last modified September 6, 2012, http://vaperforms.virginia.gov/indicators/govtcitizens/civicEngagement.php.
32. Springer Science+Business Media, "Young Teens who Play Sports Feel Healthier and Happier About Life," *Science Daily*, October 14, 2010, http://www.sciencedaily.com/releases/2010/09/100922082330.htm.
33. Putnam, "Bowling Alone."
34. Council on Virginia's Future, "Civic Engagement."
35. "Rethinking the Good Life."
36. Lisa Gale Garrigues, "Why is Costa Rica Smiling?" *Yes! Magazine 25* (Winter 2010), http://www.yesmagazine.org/issues/climate-action/why-is-costa-rica-smiling.
37. Ibid.
38. James Painter, "Why Costa Rica Scores Well on the Happiness Index," *BBC News*, February 2010, http://news.bbc.co.uk/2/hi/americas/8498456.stm.
39. "UN Partners on MDG: Background," UN Millennium Development Goals, accessed August 25, 2011, http://www.un.org/millenniumgoals/bkgd.shtml.
40. Ibid.
41. "NYC Service: Blueprint in Civic Engagement" (powerpoint), NYC Service, under About: NYC Service Reports, 2009, http://www.newyorkersvolunteer.ny.gov/docfiles/ProgDirTraining09/NYC%20Service%20Presentation.pdf.
42. Michael R. Bloomberg and Diahann Billings-Burford, *NYC Service 2011 Annual Report*, accessed December 2, 2012, www.nycservice.org/liberty/download/file/942.
43. Saguaro Seminar on Civic Engagement in America, "Sidebar: Habitat for Humanity," in the report *BetterTogether*, (Cambridge, MA: December 2000, http://bettertogether.org/pdfs/HabitatSidebar.pdf.
44. Excerpt written by John de Graaf, July 12, 2012.
45. Elizabeth W. Dunn, Daniel T. Gilbert, and Timothy D. Wilson, "If money doesn't make you happy, then you probably aren't spending it right," *Journal of Consumer Psychology 21*, no.2 (April 2011), http://www.wjh.harvard.edu/~dtg/DUNN%20GILBERT%20&%20WILSON%20(2011).pdf.
46. Ibid.
47. Michael Norton and Elizabeth Dunn, "How to buy happiness," *CNN Opinion*, July 1, 2012, http://www.cnn.com/2012/07/01/opinion/norton-how-to-buy-happiness/index.html.
48. Leslie Carr, "Why Money Can't Buy Happiness: Feeling Respected Matters More," *Atlantic*, June 27, 2012, http://www.theatlantic.com/health/archive/2012/06/why-money-cant-buy-happiness-feeling-respected-matters-more/259032/.

Chapter 13: Governance

1. Center for Civic Education website, accessed November 16, 2011, http://www.civiced.org/index.php?page=state_campaigns&&p=113&&st=WA.
2. UN Development Programme (UNDP), *Good Governance and Sustainable Human Development*, UNDP policy document, January 1997, http://mirror.undp.org/magnet/policy/chapter1.htm.

3. UN Development Programme (UNDP), Good Governance and Sustainable Human Development, UNDP policy document, January 1997, http://mirror.undp.org/magnet/policy/chapter1.htm.
4. Ibid.
5. Ibid.
6. Shalendra D. Sharma, "Democracy, Good Governance, and Economic Development," *Taiwan Journal of Democracy* 3, no. 1 (July 2007): 29-62, www.tfd.org.tw/docs/dj0301_new/029-062-Shalendra D. Sharma.pdf.
7. Nicholas Shaxson, "Angola's Homegrown Answers to the 'Resource Curse,'" in *Governance of Oil in Africa: Unfinished Business*, ed. Jacques Lesourne and William C. Ramsay (Paris: Institut Francais des Relations Internationales, 2009), http://www.ifri.org/files/Energie/SHAXSON.pdf.
8. Michael R. Ross, "The Political Economy of the Resource Curse," *World Politics* 51 (January 1999): 297-322, http://www.sscnet.ucla.edu/polisci/faculty/ross/paper.pdf.
9. "Good Governance and Human Rights," Office of the UN High Commissioner for Human Rights, under Your Human Rights: Development; Good Governance, accessed November 18, 2012, http://www.ohchr.org/EN/Issues/Development/GoodGovernance/Pages/GoodGovernanceIndex.aspx.
10. Donald P. Moynihan, "The Response to Hurricane Katrina," International Risk Governance Council (IRGC) case study, prepared for the report *Risk Governance Deficits: An analysis and illustration of the most common deficits in risk governance* (Geneva, Switzerland: IRGC, 2009), http://www.irgc.org/IMG/pdf/Hurricane_Katrina_full_case_study_web.pdf.
11. UN Environment Programme, *Environmental governance* (Nairobi, Kenya: 2010), http://www.unep.org/pdf/brochures/EnvironmentalGovernance.pdf.
12. Raymond Colitt, "Cattle drives Amazon deforestation," *Reuters*, April 14, 2009, http://www.reuters.com/article/2009/04/14/us-brazil-amazon-idUSTRE53D65C20090414.
13. Robert D. Bullard et al., *Toxic Wastes and Race at Twenty: 1987-2007; A Report Prepared for the United Church of Christ Justice & Witness Ministries* (Cleveland, OH: The United Church of Christ, March 2007), available at http://www.ucc.org/assets/pdfs/toxic20.pdf.
14. T. Christian Miller, "Ecuador: Texaco Leaves Trail of Destruction", *Los Angeles Times*, November 30, 2003, available at Global Policy Forum, http://www.globalpolicy.org/component/content/article/221/46935.html.
15. Thomas Hartmann, "Government," Scholastic, accessed December 15, 2012, http://www.scholastic.com/teachers/article/government.
16. Jane Burbank and Frederick Cooper, *Empires in World History: Power and the Politics of Difference* (Princeton, NJ: Princeton University Press, 2010).
17. Shashi Tharoor, "The Messy Afterlife of Colonialism," *Global Governance* 8, no. 1 (January-March 2003).
18. Fred Anderson and Andrew Cayton, *The Dominion of War: Empire and Liberty in North America, 1500-2000* (New York: Penguin, 2005).
19. Hakan Alitnay, "Global Governance: A Work in Progress," *Yale Global Online*, a publication of Yale Center for the Study of Globalization, January 26, 2010, http://yaleglobal.yale.edu/about/altinay.jsp.
20. "History of the United Nations," United Nations, under UN at a Glance: History, accessed September 18, 2010, http://www.un.org/aboutun/history.htm.
21. Ibid.
22. "UN at a Glance," United Nations, accessed November 20, 2012, http://www.un.org/en/aboutun/index.shtml.
23. Stefan Halper, *A Miasma of Corruption: The United Nations at 50*, Cato Policy Analysis no. 253 (Washington D.C.: April 30, 1996), http://www.cato.org/pubs/pas/pa-253.html.
24. Vijayendra Rao and Paromita Sanyal, "Dignity through Discourse: Poverty and the Culture of Deliberation in Indian Village Democracies," *The World Bank Policy Research Working Paper*, no. 4924 (May 2009), http://www-wds.worldbank.org/external/default/WDSContentServer/IW3P/IB/2009/05/05/000158349_20090505113505/Rendered/PDF/WPS4924.pdf.
25. "Promoting Community-Based Development," World Bank, under IDA at Work: Afghanistan, last modified August 28, 2009, http://web.worldbank.org/WBSITE/EXTERNAL/EXTABOUTUS/IDA/0,,contentMDK:21296643~menuPK:4754051~pagePK:51236175~piPK:437394~theSitePK:73154,00.html.
26. Yama Torabi, *Assessing the National Solidarity Program: The Role of Accountability in Reconstruction*, (London: Integrity Watch Afghanistan, 2007), available at http://www.iwaweb.org/reports/PDF/AfghanNSP.pdf.
27. Robertson Work, "Overview of Decentralization Worldwide: A Stepping Stone to Improved Governance and Human Development," paper presented at 2nd International Conference on Decentralization, Manila, Philippines, July 25-27, 2002, http://unpan1.un.org/intradoc/groups/public/documents/un/unpan030965.pdf.
28. Ibid.
29. Pierre-Guillaume Meón and Khalid Sekkat, "Does corruption grease or sand the wheels of growth?" *Public Choice* 122, no. 1 (2005): 69-97, http://202.120.43.103/downloads2/b3b3faf7-922a-4168-bd30-3eb2dd4061cf.pdf.
30. Marc Lacey, "Nicaragua: Ex-Leader to Fight for Seized Funds," *New York Times*, December 29, 2006, http://query.nytimes.com/gst/fullpage.html?res=9B00E3D71F31F93AA15751C1A9609C8B63&ref=arnoldoaleman.
31. Magali Rheault, "Stability, Good Governance Boost Confidence in Botswana," *Gallup World*, July 26, 2007, http://www.gallup.com/poll/28228/stability-good-governance-boost-confidence-botswana.aspx.
32. Christian von Soest, "Stagnation of a 'Miracle': Botswana's Governance Record Revisited," *German Institute for Global and Area Studies Working Papers*, no. 99 (April 2009), http://repec.giga-hamburg.de/pdf/giga_09_wp99_von-soest.pdf.
33. ONE website, accessed November 16, 2011, http://www.one.org/us/.
34. "Living Proof Project: AIDS Education through Personal Experience and Music," Bill and Melinda Gates Foundation, accessed November 16, 2011, http://www.gatesfoundation.org/livingproofproject/Pages/aids-education-in-ghana.aspx#image=8.
35. "Fighting Hunger in Guatemala: One Man's Vision to Feed a Nation," The Alliance to End Hunger, under Creating Global Connections, accessed January 15, 2012, http://alliancetoendhunger.org/creating-global-connections/national-partners/guatemala.html.
36. "History of the Little Rock Nine & *Brown* v. *Board of Education*," Arkansas Department of Parks and Tourism, under History, accessed September 12, 2012, http://www.arkansas.com/central-high/history/default.asp.
37. "Debate: Direct democracy," Debatepedia, accessed November 20, 2012, http://debatepedia.idebate.org/en/index.php/Debate:_Direct_democracy.

Chapter 14: Health

1. *Toward a Healthy Future:* Second Report on the Health of Canadians, Executive Summary, prepared by the Federal, Provincial and Territorial Advisory Committee on Population Health for the Meeting of Ministers of Health, Charlottetown, P.E.I., Canada, September 1999, http://nccdh.ca/resources/entry/toward-ahealthy-future.
2. World Health Organization (WHO), *Preamble to the Constitution of the World Health Organization,* as adopted by the International Health Conference, New York, June 19- July 22, 1946, http://www.who.int/suggestions/faq/en/index.html.
3. May Linda Samuel, "The Link between Human Health and Sustainability," Forum on Public Policy 2 (2008), http://www.forumonpublicpolicy.com/summer08papers/archivesummer08/samuel.may.pdf.
4. Health Canada, "Health and the Environment: Critical Pathways," *Health Policy Research Bulletin* 4 (October 2002), http://www.hc-sc.gc.ca/sr-sr/pubs/hpr-rpms/bull/2002-4-environ/indexeng.php.
5. Organization of Economic Co-operation and Development (OECD), "How Does the United States Compare," *OECD Health Data 2012—Country Notes,* June 2012, http://www.oecd.org/unitedstates/BriefingNoteUSA2012.pdf.
6. OECD, "How Does the United Kingdom Compare," *OECD Health Data 2012—Country Notes,* June 2012, http://www.oecd.org/unitedkingdom/BriefingNoteUNITEDKINGDOM2012.pdf.
7. Julio Frenk, "Health and the economy: A vital relationship," OECD *Observer,* May 2004, http://www.oecdobserver.org/news/archivestory.php/aid/1241/Health_and_the_economy:_A_vital_relationship_.html.
8. Desiree A. Teoth, "Medicine in Ancient China: the Impact of Religion and Philosophy on Health Promotion," paper from the 9th Annual Proceedings of Medicine Days (Calgary, Canada: University of Calgary, March 2000), http://www.scribd.com/doc/24019043/Teoth-D-A-Medicine-in-Ancient-China-the-Impactof-Religion-and-Philosophy-on-Health-Promotion.
9. National Institute of Health, "Islamic Culture and Medical Arts: Hospitals," online exhibition in the U.S. National Library of Medicine, last modified December 15, 2011, http://www.nlm.nih.gov/exhibition/islamic_medical/islamic_12.html.
10. "Plague: The Black Death," National Geographic, under Science: Health and the Human Body; Disease, accessed October 5, 2012, http://science.nationalgeographic.com/science/health-andhuman-body/human-diseases/plague-article/.
11. Joseph A. Montagna, "The Industrial Revolution," *An Interdisciplinary Approach to British Studies,* Volume 2 (Yale-New Haven Teachers Institute, 1981), http://www.yale.edu/ynhti/curriculum/units/1981/2/81.02.06.x.html.
12. Bruce Haley, *The Healthy Body and Victorian Culture* (Cambridge, MA: Harvard University Press, 1978).
13. Harvard University Open Collections Program, "Germ Theory," *Contagion: Historical Views of Diseases and Epidemics,* accessed December 22, 2012, http://ocp.hul.harvard.edu/contagion/germtheory.html.
14. Miguel A. Faria, Jr., "Medical History—Hygiene and Sanitation," *Medical Sentinel* 7, no. 4 (2002): 122-123, http://www.haciendapublishing.com/medicalsentinel/medical-history-hygieneand-sanitation.
15. Charles A. Bertrand, "Life Span in the 20th Century," Medicine up to the Minute, 2010, http://www.medicineuptotheminute.com/lifespan.html.
16. "Fertility and Living Standards: Go forth and multiply a lot less," *Economist,* October 29, 2009, http://www.economist.com/node/14743589.
17. "Life Expectancy," Gapminder (powerpoint), accessed December 22, 2012, http://www.gapminder.org/downloads/life-expectancyppt/.
18. "10 facts on malaria," WHO, April 2012, http://www.who.int/features/factfiles/malaria/en/index.html.
19. "Diarrhoeal Disease," WHO fact sheet no. 330, August 2009, http://www.who.int/mediacentre/factsheets/fs330/en/index.html.
20. "About Bed Nets," Nothing but Nets, accessed November 28, 2012, http://www.nothingbutnets.net/nets-save-lives/about-bednets.html.
21. UN Habitat, "Slums: Some Definitions," *State of the World's Cities* 2006/7 (Geneva, Switzerland: 2007), http://www.unhabitat.org/documents/media_centre/sowcr2006/SOWCR%205.pdf.
22. Richard Wilkinson and Michael Marmot, eds., *Social Determinants of Health: The Solid Facts,* 2nd Edition, (Geneva, Switzerland: WHO, 2003).
23. "Overweight or obesity," in *OECD Factbook 2011-2012: Economic, Environmental, and Social Statistics* (OECD Publishing: 2012), available online, http://www.oecd-ilibrary.org/sites/factbook-2011-en/12/02/03/index.html?contentType=&itemId=/content/chapter/factbook-2011-109-en&containerItemId=/content/serial/18147364&accessItemIds=&mimeType=text/html.
24. John Casey, "Body Fat Measurement: Percentage vs. Body Mass" WebMD, 2011, http://www.webmd.com/diet/features/body-fat-measurement.
25. Organization for Economic Co-operation and Development (OECD), "Obesity and the Economics of Prevention: Executive Summary" OECD Policy Brief, 2010, http://www.oecd.org/dataoecd/21/19/46004918.pdf.
26. "How Does Obesity in Adults Affect Spending on Health Care?" Congressional Budget Office, issue brief, September 8, 2010, http://www.cbo.gov/ftpdocs/118xx/doc11810/09-08-Obesity_brief.pdf.
27. Robert H. Eckel, "Obesity and Heart Disease: A Statement for Healthcare Professionals From the Nutrition Committee, American Heart Association," *Circulation* 96 (1997): 3248-3250, http://circ.ahajournals.org/content/96/9/3248.full.
28. Franco Sassi and Jeremy Hurst, *The Prevention of Lifestyle-Related Chronic Diseases: An Economic Framework,* OECD Health working paper no. 32 (Paris, France: OECD, 2008), http://www.oecd.org/dataoecd/57/14/40324263.pdf.
29. U.S. National Center for Health Statistics, "Deaths: Final Data for 2007," *National Vital Statistics Reports* 58, no. 19 (May 2010).
30. "The U.S. and the World," *Unnatural Causes* (tv series), December 22, 2012, http://www.unnaturalcauses.org/amazing_facts.php.
31. Rachel Pomerance, "Most and Least Obese U.S. States," *US News,* August 16, 2012, http://health.usnews.com/health-news/articles/2012/08/16/most-and-least-obese-us-states.
32. Arias, E. United States life tables, 2007. National vital statistics reports; vol 59 no 9. Hyattsville, MD: National Center for Health Statistics. 2011. http://www.cdc.gov/nchs/data/nvsr/nvsr59/nvsr59_09.pdf.
33. Anna Tibaijuka, "Cities without Slums," *Our Planet* 16, no. 1 (2005), http://www.unep.org/ourplanet/imgversn/161/tibaijuka.html.
34. Elisabeth Rosenthal, "Diseases spreading with faster world travel," *New York Times,* August 23, 2007, http://www.nytimes.com/2007/08/23/health/23iht-health.4.7231596.html.
35. "Origin and development of health cooperation," WHO, under Programs and Projects: Global Health Histories, accessed October 42, 2011, http://www.who.int/global_health_histories/background/en/index.html.
36. Alexandra Sifferlin, "H1N1's Death Toll: 15 Times Higher than Previously Thought," *Time Magazine,* June 26, 2012, http://healthland.time.com/2012/06/26/h1n1s-death-toll-15-timeshigher-than-previously-thought/#ixzz28HRgyy2S.

37 WHO, "Report of the Review Committee on the Functioning of the International Health Regulations (2005) and on Pandemic Influenza A (H1N1) 2009," discussion paper for meeting of the Review Committee, March 7, 2011, http://www.who.int/ihr/preview_report_review_committee_mar2011_en.pdf.
38 AVERT website, accessed November 20, 2012, http://www.avert.org.
39 Centers for Disease Control (CDC), "HIV and AIDS—United States, 1981-2000," *Morbidity and Mortality Weekly Report* 50, no. 21 (June 1, 2001): 430-434, http://www.cdc.gov/mmwr/pdf/wk/mm5021.pdf.
40 "HIV in the United States," CDC factsheet, November 2011, http://www.cdc.gov/hiv/resources/factsheets/PDF/us.pdf.
41 "HIV/AIDS," WHO, under Global Health Observatory, accessed October 5, 2012, http://www.who.int/gho/hiv/en/index.html.
42 "About HIV/AIDS," AmfAR, under Statistics: Worldwide, accessed December 22, 2012, http://www.amfar.org/About_HIV_and_AIDS/Facts_and_Stats/Statistics__Worldwide/.
43 UNAIDS, AIDS at 30: *Nations at the Crossroads* (Geneva, Switzerland: UNAIDS, 2011), http://www.unaids.org/unaids_resources/aidsat30/aids-at-30.pdf.
44 UNAIDS, *Report on the Global AIDS epidemic: A UNAIDS 10th Anniversary*, Executive Summary (Geneva, Switzerland: UNAIDS, 2006), http://data.unaids.org/pub/GlobalReport/2006/2006_gr-executivesummary_en.pdf.
45 "HIV/AIDS: Antiretroviral therapy," WHO, under HIV/AIDS Topics, accessed October 5, 2012, http://www.who.int/hiv/topics/treatment/data/en/index2.html.
46 "Questions and Answers about Tuberculosis," CDC, last modified December 21, 2012, http://www.cdc.gov/tb/publications/faqs/qa_introduction.htm#Intro1.
47 Megan Burks, "Community Farm Grows Refugee Businesses," Speak City Heights, June 18, 2011, http://www.speakcityheights.org/2011/06/community-farm-grows-refugee-businesses/.
48 Charles Mpaka, "Village Chief Leads Fight for Maternal Health," *Inter Press Service News Agency*, September 24, 2010, http://ipsnews.net/africa/nota.asp?idnews=52965.
49 Robert Beaglehole and Ruth Bonita, "What is Global Health?" *Global Health Action*, invited editorial, 2010, http://globalhealthcenter.umn.edu/documents/whatisglobalhealth.pdf.
50 Emeline Cokelet and Rachel Wilson, *Advocacy to Improve Public Health: Strategies and Stories from the Field* (Washington, D.C.: PATH, 2009), http://www.path.org/publications/files/ER_advo_wrkbk_stories_field.pdf.
51 "Tuberculosis and MDR-TB," Partners in Health, accessed December 22, 2012, http://www.pih.org/pages/tuberculosis-andmdr-tb/.
52 "PIH Russia," Partners in Health, accessed November 20, 2012, http://www.pih.org/where/pages/russia.
53 Ebonne Ruffins, "Recycling hotel soap to save lives," *CNN*, under CNN Heroes, June 16, 2011, http://www.cnn.com/2011/US/06/16/cnnheroes.kayongo.hotel.soap/index.html?hpt=hp_t2.
54 Adapted from the Debatepedia.org article "Single-payer Universal Health Care," accessed October 10, 2011, http://debatepedia.idebate.org/en/index.php/Debate:_Single-payer_universal_health_care.

Chapter 15: Peace and Conflict

1 "Creation of the State of Israel, 1948," Harry S. Truman Library and Museum, accessed June 15, 2012, http://www.trumanlibrary.org/israel/timeline.htm.
2 "The Arab-Israeli conflict, 1947-present," USA Today online, August 28, 2001, http://www.usatoday.com/news/world/mideast/timeline.htm.
3 World Health Organization (WHO), *World report on violence and health: summary* (Geneva, Switzerland: WHO, 2002) http://www.who.int/violence_injury_prevention/violence/world_report/en/summary_en.pdf.
4 "What health risks do refugees face?," BBC, under Health, accessed June 15, 2012, http://www.bbc.co.uk/health/physical_health/conditions/refugee_health.shtml.
5 Jessica Adley and Andrea Grant, "The Environmental Consequences of War," Sierra Club of Canada, accessed June 29, 2011, http://www.sierraclub.ca/national/postings/war-and-environment.html.
6 Mark Thompson, "The Iraq War Comes Home," *Time*, October 19, 2005, http://www.time.com/time/nation/article/0,8599,1120140,00.html.
7 Adley and Grant.
8 "Rwanda: A Historical Chronology," PBS, under *Frontline* (tv series), accessed August 25, 2011, http://www.pbs.org/wgbh/pages/frontline/shows/rwanda/etc/cron.html.
9 "What is Genocide?," The Holocaust Encyclopedia, an online student resource created by the U.S. Holocaust Memorial Museum, January 2011, http://www.ushmm.org/wlc/en/article.php?ModuleId=10007043.
10 "About the Victims," US Holocaust Memorial Museum, under Research: Frequently Asked Questions, accessed August 25, 2011, http://www.ushmm.org/research/library/faq/details.php?lang=en&topic=03#02.
11 Department of Defense Dictionary of Military Terms website, accessed December 15, 2012, http://www.dtic.mil/doctrine/dod_dictionary/?zoom_query=terrorism&zoom_sort=0&zoom_per_page=10&zoom_and=1.
12 Kathryn Gregory, "Shining Path, Tupac Amaru (Peru, leftists)," Council on Foreign Relations backgrounder, August 27, 2009, http://www.cfr.org/terrorism/shining-path-tupac-amaru-peru-leftists/p9276.
13 "Profile: Peru's Shining Path," *BBC News*, November 5, 2004, http://news.bbc.co.uk/2/hi/americas/3985659.stm.
14 "Foreign Terrorist Organizations," US Department of State, accessed January 27, 2012, http://www.state.gov/j/ct/rls/other/des/123085.htm.
15 Al McKay, "The Study of Modern Intrastate War," e-International Relations, February 3, 2011, http://www.e-ir.info/?p=6758.
16 Halvard Buhaug et al., "Global trends in armed conflict," Centre for the study of civil war, International Peace Research Institute, Oslo, Norway, 2006, available at http://www.regjeringen.no/nb/dep/ud/kampanjer/refleks/innspill/engasjement/prio.html?id=492941.
17 Virginia Page Fortna, "Where Have All the Victories Gone? Peacekeeping and War Outcomes," Columbia University, August 2009, http://www.columbia.edu/~vpf4/victories%20Sept%202009.pdf.
18 Patrick Reagan, "Conditions of Successful Third-Party Intervention in Intrastate Conflicts," Journal of Conflict Resolution 40, no. 2 (June 1996): 336-359.
19 *Environmental Degradation as a Cause of Conflict in Darfur*, conference proceedings, UN University for Peace, Kartoum, Darfur, December 2004 (Geneva, Switzerland: UN University for Peace, 2006), http://www.upeace.org/library/documents/darfur_cp.pdf.
20 Ibid.
21 Tobias Debiel and Ulf Terlinden, *Promoting Good Governance in Post-Conflict Societies*, a discussion paper commissioned by the German Ministry for Economic Cooperation and Development (Eschborn, Germany: German Agency for Technical Cooperation, 2005), accessed August 25, 2011, http://www2.gtz.de/dokumente/bib/05-0032.pdf.

22 J. Habyarimana et al., "Is Ethnic Conflict Inevitable?: Parting Ways Over Nationalism and Separatism," *Foreign Affairs* (July/August 2008), http://www.foreignaffairs.com/articles/64457/james-habyarimana-macartan-humphreys-daniel-posner-jeremy-weinst/is-ethnic-conflict-inevitable?page=2.
23 "'Just 20 Minutes More': Writing a New Constitution," Facing History and Ourselves, accessed June 10, 2012, http://www.facinghistory.org/reading/just-20-minutes-more.
24 David Pottebaum, *Conflict, Poverty, Inequality, and Economic Growth*, a publication prepared for the U.S. Agency for International Development (Development Alternatives, Inc., January 2005), http://pdf.usaid.gov/pdf_docs/PNADK690.pdf.
25 "London Riots 2011: Could Such Disturbances Happen in the U.S.?," *International Business Times*, August 13, 2011, http://m.ibtimes.com/uk-riots-london-us-197342.html.
26 "About the Court," International Criminal Court, accessed August 23, 2011, http://www.icc-cpi.int/Menus/ICC/About+the+Court/.
27 "Profile: DR Congo militia leader Thomas Lubanga," *BBC News*, January 23, 2009, http://news.bbc.co.uk/2/hi/6131516.stm.
28 "Afghanistan's Environmental Recovery: A post-conflict plan for people and their natural resources," UN Environment Programme, August 2006, http://postconflict.unep.ch/publications/UNEP_afghanistan_lr.pdf.
29 Basic Education Coalition website, accessed June 5, 2012, http://www.basiced.org/.
30 "Anderson Sa," SourceWatch, project of the Center for Media and Democracy, accessed June 15, 2012, http://www.sourcewatch.org/index.php?title=Anderson_Sa.
31 Ibid.
32 "About Seeds of Peace," Seeds of Peace, accessed July 15, 2012, http://www.seedsofpeace.org/about.
33 *Youth Helping America: The Role of Social Institutions in Teen Volunteering*, Corporation for National Community Service issue brief (Washington DC: November 2005), accessed August 26, 2011, http://www.polk-fl.net/community/volunteers/documents/servicelearning/FactSheet_ROSITV.pdf.
34 Christian P. Scherrer, "Preventing Genocide: The Role of the International Community," Prevent Genocide International, accessed July 24, 2012, http://preventgenocide.org/prevent/scherrer.htm; "The Global Regime for Armed Conflict," Council on Foreign Relations issue brief, last updated July 25, 2012, http://www.cfr.org/global-governance/global-regime-armed-conflict/p24180.

Chapter 16: Human Rights

1 "History," Free the Children, accessed July 30, 2012, http://www.freethechildren.com/aboutus/history/.
2 "Your Human Rights," Office of the UN High Commissioner for Human Rights (OHCHR), accessed July 30, 2012, http://www.ohchr.org/en/issues/Pages/WhatareHumanRights.aspx.
3 Michelle Dowst, "Working with Civil Society in Fragile States," briefing paper for the International NGO Training and Research Centre, May 2009, http://www.intrac.org/data/files/resources/621/Briefing-Paper-23-Working-with-Civil-Society-in-Fragile-States.pdf.
4 David Kinley and Devin T. Stewart, "Civilizing Globalization: Human Rights and the Global Economy," Policy Innovations, October 6, 2009, http://www.policyinnovations.org/ideas/briefings/data/000145.
5 "Human Rights and the Environment," UN Environment Programme, under Division of Environmental Law and Conventions (DELC), accessed June 30, 2012, http://www.unep.org/delc/HumanRightsandTheEnvironment/tabid/54409/Default.aspx.
6 "A Brief History of Human Rights," United for Human Rights, accessed July 19, 2011, http://www.humanrights.com/what-are-human-rights/brief-history/cyrus-cylinder.html.
7 Andrew Clapham, *Human Rights: A Very Short Introduction* (New York: Oxford University Press, 2007).
8 Micheline R. Ishay, *The History of Human Rights: From Ancient Times to the Globalization Era* (Berkeley, CA: University of California Press, 2008).
9 Ibid.
10 UN General Assembly, "Universal Declaration of Human Rights" (A/RES/217(III)A), December 10, 1948, http://www.un.org/en/documents/udhr/index.shtml.
11 Clapham, Human Rights.
12 Clapham, Human Rights.
13 Ibid.
14 Micheline R. Ishay, *The History of Human Rights* (London: University of California Press, 2008).
15 "Dandi: A 'War' on Salt Tax," *Times of India*, March 2005, http://timesofindia.indiatimes.com/india/Dandi-A-war-on-salt-tax/articleshow/1050405.cms.
16 "Timeline: India and Pakistan Split," PBS, under Newshour: *India and Pakistan; 60 Years of Independence* (tv series), August 14, 2007, http://www.pbs.org/newshour/indepth_coverage/asia/partition/timeline/index.html.
17 James Risen and Eric Lichtblau, "Bush Lets U.S. Spy on Callers Without Courts," *New York Times*, December 16, 2005, http://www.nytimes.com/2005/12/16/politics/16program.html?pagewanted=all&_r=0.
18 Ibid.
19 "The Berlin Wall," Newseum, accessed January 5, 2011, http://www.newseum.org/berlinwall/.
20 Jon Henley, "The Berlin Wall: A Short History," *Guardian*, October 26, 2009, http://www.guardian.co.uk/world/2009/oct/27/berlin-wall-short-history.
21 "Timeline: Berlin Wall," *BBC News*, August 12, 2001, http://news.bbc.co.uk/2/hi/europe/1484769.stm.
22 "The Human Rights of Women," UN Population Fund, accessed August 29, 2012, http://www.unfpa.org/rights/women.htm.
23 Faye Bowers, "Saudi Women, Long Silent, Gain a Quiet Voice," *Christian Science Monitor*, January 13, 2004, http://www.csmonitor.com/2004/0113/p07s01-wome.html.
24 "Property Rights for Women," Habitat for Humanity, accessed February 7, 2011, http://www.habitat.org/wb/international/advocacy.aspx.
25 David E. Bloom and Mark Weston, "Girls' Education in Developing Countries: Mind the Gap," PBS, under *Wide Angle* (tv series), August 25, 2003, http://www.pbs.org/wnet/wideangle/uncategorized/time-for-school-essay-girls-education-in-developing-countries-mind-the-gap/1612/.
26 Jina Moore, "Congo War leaves legacy of sexual violence against women," *Christian Science Monitor*, June 30, 2010, http://www.csmonitor.com/World/Africa/2010/0630/Congo-war-leaves-legacy-of-sexual-violence-against-women.
27 Andrew Morrison, Dhushyanth Raju, and Nistha Sinha, "Gender Equality *Is* Good for the Poor," *Poverty in Focus* 13 (January 2008), http://www.ipc-undp.org/pub/IPCPovertyInFocus13.pdf.
28 Zineb Touimi-Benjelloun, "A New Family Law in Morocco: 'Patience is Bitter, But its Fruit is Sweet,'" UN Women, under Stories from the Field, December 19, 2003, http://www.unifem.org/gender_issues/voices_from_the_field/story.php?StoryID=264 "Stop Child and Forced Labor," International Labor Rights Forum, under Cocoa Campaign, accessed January 10, 2011, http://www.laborrights.org/stop-child-labor/cocoa-campaign.

29. International Labor Organization, *Facts and Figures on Child Labour* (Geneva, Switzerland: 1999), available at the World Bank, accessed March 4, 2011, http://info.worldbank.org/etools/docs/library/237384/toolkitfr/pdf/facts.pdf.
30. "Cote D'Ivoire," Central Intelligence Agency (CIA) World Factbook, updated weekly, accessed August 29, 2012, https://www.cia.gov/library/publications/the-world-factbook/geos/iv.html.
31. Paola Roggero et al., "The Health Impact of Child Labor in Developing Countries: Evidence from Cross-Country Data," *American Journal of Public Health* 97, no. 2 (February 2007): 271-275, DOI 10.2105/AJPH.2005.066829, http://www.ncbi.nlm.nih.gov/pmc/articles/PMC1781398/.
32. "Factsheet: Child Soldiers," UNICEF, accessed March 4, 2011, http://www.unicef.org/emerg/files/childsoldiers.pdf.
33. International Labor Organization, *Facts and Figures on Child Labour* (Geneva, Switzerland: 1999), available at the World Bank, accessed March 4, 2011, http://info.worldbank.org/etools/docs/library/237384/toolkitfr/pdf/facts.pdf.
34. "Child Marriage: What We Know," PBS, under *Child Brides: Stolen Lives* (tv series), accessed March 4, 2011, http://www.pbs.org/now/shows/341/facts.html.
35. "20 Years: The Conventions on the Rights of the Child," UNICEF, accessed February 9, 2011, http://www.unicef.org/rightsite/.
36. Daniel Kaufman, "Human Rights, Governance, and Development: an empirical perspective," *Development Outreach* (World Bank Institute, October 2006): 15-20, http://siteresources.worldbank.org/EXTSITETOOLS/Resources/KaufmannDevtOutreach.pdf.
37. "Apartheid Timeline," UN Cyber Schoolbus, accessed January 10, 2011, http://cyberschoolbus.un.org/discrim/race_b_at_print.asp.
38. "Apartheid Timeline," UN Cyber Schoolbus, accessed January 10, 2011, http://cyberschoolbus.un.org/discrim/race_b_at_print.asp.
39. "France," CIA World Factbook, updated weekly, accessed February 9, 2011, https://www.cia.gov/library/publications/the-world-factbook/geos/fr.html.
40. Eric Brahm, "Religion and Conflict," Beyond Intractability, project of the University of Colorado Conflict Information Consortium, November 2005, http://www.beyondintractability.org/bi-essay/religion-and-conflict.
41. Emile Lester and Patrick S. Roberts, *Learning About World Religions in Public Schools: The Impact on Student Attitudes and Community Acceptance in Modesto, Calif.* (Nashville, TN: First Amendment Center, 2006), available at http://iis-db.stanford.edu/pubs/21196/FirstForum_ModestoWorldReligions.pdf.
42. "Health and Human Rights," World Health Organization, accessed January 13, 2011, http://www.who.int/hhr/en/.
43. Dara Carr, "Improving the Health of the World's Poorest People," *Health Bulletin* 1 (February 2004) available at the Population Reference Bureau, accessed March 3, 2011, http://www.prb.org/pdf/ImprovingtheHealthWorld_Eng.pdf.
44. Ibid.
45. "What We Do," Partners in Health, under The PIH Model, accessed January 15, 2011, http://www.pih.org/pages/what-we-do/.
46. "Rights on the Line: Human Rights Watch Work on Abuses against Migrants in 2010," Human Rights Watch, December 12, 2010, http://www.hrw.org/sites/default/files/reports/wrd1210webwcover.pdf.
47. Andrew Cockburn, "21st Century Slaves," *National Geographic*, September 2003, http://ngm.nationalgeographic.com/ngm/0309/feature1/.
48. Corydon Ireland, "Slavery in 2010," *Harvard Gazette*, February 19, 2010, http://news.harvard.edu/gazette/story/2010/02/slavery-in-2010/.
49. "Forced Labor Statistics," Cornell University ILR School, January 2006, http://digitalcommons.ilr.cornell.edu/cgi/viewcontent.cgi?article=1019&context=forcedlabor.
50. Manuel Velasquez, "UNOCAL in Burma," Santa Clara University Markkula Center for Applied Ethics, November 3, 2005, http://www.scu.edu/ethics/practicing/focusareas/business/Unocal-in-Burma.html.
51. Clapham, Human Rights.
52. "Who We Are," Amnesty International, accessed January 18, 2011, http://www.amnesty.org/en/who-we-are/about-amnesty-international.
53. "What is Transitional Justice?" International Center for Transitional Justice, accessed February 11, 2011, http://ictj.org/about/transitional-justice.
54. "Life in Japanese Internment Camps," Oracle ThinkQuest Library, accessed February 24, 2011, http://library.thinkquest.org/TQ0312008/bhjic.html.
55. "WWII Internment Timeline," PBS, under *Children of the Camps* (documentary), accessed April 1, 2011, http://www.pbs.org/childofcamp/history/timeline.html.
56. OHCHR, *Good Governance Practices for the Protection of Human Rights*, (New York and Geneva, Switzerland: UN, 2007), http://www.ohchr.org/Documents/Publications/GoodGovernance.pdf.
57. Ibid.
58. *We Are A Global Community*, Free the Children Annual Report 2011, accessed July 30, 2012, http://www.freethechildren.com/wp-content/uploads/2012/09/Free_The_Children-Annual_Report-20112.pdf.
59. "Debate: Security vs. Liberty," Debatepedia, accessed July 12, 2012, http://debatepedia.idebate.org/en/index.php/Debate:_Security_vs._liberty.

Chapter 17: Gender

1. Micheline Maynard, "The Kicking Queen," *New York Times*, October 3, 2011, http://www.nytimes.com/2011/10/04/sports/homecoming-queen-and-winning-field-goal-on-same-night.html.
2. Monica Brasted, "Care Bears vs. Transformers: Gender Stereotypes in Advertisements," *Socjournal*, February 17, 2010, http://www.sociology.org/media-studies/care-bears-vs-transformers-gender-stereotypes-in-advertisements.
3. "National Statistics," Youth Violence Project, research project of the University of Virginia Curry School of Education, accessed July 31, 2011, http://curry.virginia.edu/research/projects/violence-in-schools/national-statistics.
4. "Mental Health," World Health Organization (WHO), accessed July 30, 2011, http://www.who.int/mental_health/prevention/suicide/suicide_rates_chart/en/index.html.
5. Mary Beth Marklein, "College gender gap widens: 57% are women," *USA Today*, October 19, 2005, http://www.usatoday.com/news/education/2005-10-19-male-college-cover_x.htm.
6. Central Intelligence Agency (CIA) World Factbook, updated weekly, accessed June 25, 2012, https://www.cia.gov/library/publications/the-world-factbook/geos/xx.html.
7. "Women in National Parliaments: World Average," The Inter-Parliamentary Union, October 31, 2012, accessed December 5, 2012, http://www.ipu.org/wmn-e/world.htm.
8. "Facts & Figures on Women, Poverty & Economics," UN Women, under Gender Issues, accessed July 30, 2011, http://www.unifem.org/gender_issues/women_poverty_economics/facts_figures.php#2.
9. Ibid.

10 Fedwa Malti-Douglas, *Encyclopedia of Sex and Gender* (Detroit, MI: Macmillan, 2007).

11 UN Population Fund (UNFPA), "Partnering with Boys and Men," *World Population 2005: The Promise of Equality; Gender Equity, Reproductive Health, and the Millennium Development Goals* (New York: 2005): 57-63, http://www.unfpa.org/webdav/site/global/shared/documents/publications/2005/swp05_eng.pdf.

12 Karen Messing and Piroska Östlin, *Gender Equality, Work and Health: A Review of the Evidence* (Geneva, Switzerland: WHO Press, 2006), http://www.who.int/gender/documents/Genderworkhealth.pdf.

13 "Agriculture & Food Security," International Center for Research and Women, accessed December 10, 2011, http://www.icrw.org/what-we-do/agriculture-food-security.

14 Takyiwaa Manuh, "Women in Africa's Development: Overcoming obstacles, pushing for progress," Africa Recovery Briefing Paper #11 (New York: UN, April 1998).

15 "The Gobal View," *Wall Street Journal*, April 10, 2011, http://online.wsj.com/article/SB10001424052748704013604576246292633371136.html.

16 Viviana Zelizer, "The Gender of Money," *Ideas Market* (blog), January 27, 2011, http://blogs.wsj.com/ideas-market/2011/01/27/the-gender-of-money/.

17 Ibid.

18 Robert J. Barro, "Determinants of Democracy," *Journal of Political Economy* 107, no. S6 (1999): 158-183, http://nrs.harvard.edu/urn-3:HUL.InstRepos:3451297.

19 The Green Belt Movement website, accessed December 20, 2011, http://www.greenbeltmovement.org.

20 "The plough and the now: Deep seated attitudes to women have roots in ancient agriculture," *Economist*, July 21, 2011, http://www.economist.com/node/18986073.

21 Jeanne Boydston, "Cult of True Womanhood," PBS, under *Not for Ourselves Alone: The Story of Elizabeth Cady Stanton and Susan B. Anthony* (documentary), accessed December 9, 2011, http://www.pbs.org/stantonanthony/resources/index.html?body=culthood.html.

22 Grolier, "Women's Suffrage," Scholastic, under Student Activities, accessed August 1, 2011, http://teacher.scholastic.com/activities/suffrage/history.htm.

23 Jeffrey Fleishman, "Saudi Arabia to allow women to vote," *Los Angeles Times*, September 25, 2011, http://articles.latimes.com/2011/sep/25/world/la-fg-saudi-women-vote-20110926.

24 "Women's Rights Timeline," Leonore Annenberg Institute for Civics, Annenberg Classroom, accessed December 10, 2011, http://www.annenbergclassroom.org/Files/Documents/Timelines/WomensRightstimeline.pdf.

25 Nadia Steinzor, "Women's Property and Inheritance Rights: Improving Lives and Changing Times; Final Synthesis and Conference Proceedings Paper" (Washington D.C.: Women in Development Technical Assistance Project, March 2003), available at the US Agency for International Development, http://pdf.usaid.gov/pdf_docs/PNADA958.pdf.

26 "Supporting the Constellation of Reproductive Rights," UNFPA, under Human Rights, accessed December 10, 2011, http://www.unfpa.org/rights/rights.htm.

27 UN Development and Human Rights Section, *Women: The Right to Reproductive and Sexual Health* (New York: UN Department of Public Information, February 1997), accessed December 10, 2011, http://www.un.org/ecosocdev/geninfo/women/womrepro.htm.

28 National Center for Education Statistics, "Total fall enrollment in degree-granting institutions, by sex, age, and attendance status: Selected years, 1970 through 2016," accessed January 11, 2013, http://nces.ed.gov/programs/digest/d07/tables/dt07_181.asp.

29 Lorraine Ethington, interview by Allison Liddell, Casa Grande, Arizona, 1989.

30 Hanna Rosin, "The End of Men," *Atlantic Magazine* (July/August, 2010), http://www.theatlantic.com/magazine/archive/2010/07/the-end-of-men/8135/2/.

31 "Catalyst Quick Take: Statistical Overview of Women in the Workplace," Catalyst, October 17, 2012, http://www.catalyst.org/publication/219/statistical-overview-of-women-in-the-workplace.

32 Terry Kirby, "It's a Woman's World," *Independent*, March 8, 2006, http://www.independent.co.uk/news/world/politics/its-a-womans-world-469102.html.

33 Elizabeth Powley, "Rwanda: Women Hold Up Half the Parliament," in *Women in Parliament: Beyond Numbers*, ed. Julie Ballington and Azza Karam (Stockholm, Sweden: International Institute for Democracy and Electoral Assistance, 2005): 154-163, http://www.idea.int/publications/wip2/upload/Rwanda.pdf.

34 Ruth Levine et al., "Girls Count: A Global Investment & Action Agenda" (Washington, D.C.: The Center for Global Development, 2009), http://www.cgdev.org/files/15154_file_GirlsCount.pdf.

35 "Slavery Today," Free The Slaves, under About Slavery: Modern Slavery, accessed December 20, 2011, https://www.freetheslaves.net/SSLPage.aspx?pid=301.

36 "Estimating the Numbers," PBS, under Frontline: Sex Slaves (tv series), February 7, 2006, http://www.pbs.org/wgbh/pages/frontline/slaves/etc/stats.html.

37 "Invisible: Slavery Today," National Underground Railroad Freedom Center, accessed October 3, 2011, http://www.freedomcenter.org/slavery-today/.

38 "Cambodia," HumanTrafficking.org, project of the Academy for Education Development (now known as FHI 360), 2006, accessed August 5, 2011, http://www.humantrafficking.org/countries/cambodia.

39 "Prosecution," HumanTrafficking.org, accessed December 21, 2011, http://www.humantrafficking.org/combat_trafficking/prosecution.

40 Maddy Berry and Will Putnam (students, Overlake School), personal communication, May 25th, 2011.

41 Claudia García-Moreno et al., *WHO Multi-country Study on Women's Health and Domestic Violence against Women* (Geneva, Switzerland: WHO, 2005), http://www.who.int/gender/violence/who_multicountry_study/en/.

42 WHO, *Violence against women*, fact sheet no. 239, 2009, http://www.who.int/mediacentre/factsheets/fs239/en/.

43 Mark Doyle, "DR Congo death toll more than 5m," *BBC News*, January 22, 2008, http://news.bbc.co.uk/2/hi/africa/7202384.stm.

44 "2012 UNHCR country operations profile: Democratic Republic of the Congo," Office of the UN High Commissioner for Refugees, accessed January 9, 2012, http://www.unhcr.org/pages/49e45c366.html.

45 Karen Allen, "Bleak future for Congo's child soldiers," *BBC News*, July 25, 2006, http://news.bbc.co.uk/2/hi/africa/5213996.stm.

46 "Democratic Republic of the Congo," Central Intelligence Agency (CIA) World Factbook, updated weekly, accessed December 7, 2012, https://www.cia.gov/library/publications/the-world-factbook/geos/cg.html.

47 "Gender and Justice," HEAL Africa, under Women, accessed December 12, 2011, http://www.healafrica.org/empowering-women/gender-and-justice/.

48 "Maternal and newborn health," UNICEF, under What We Do: Health; UNICEF in action, last modified June 21, 2012, http://www.unicef.org/health/index_maternalhealth.html.

49 WHO, "Maternal deaths worldwide drop by third," news release, September 15, 2010, http://www.who.int/mediacentre/news/releases/2010/maternal_mortality_20100915/en/index.html.
50 "Child Marriage: What We Know," PBS, under NOW: *Child Brides* (tv series), accessed August 5, 2011, http://www.pbs.org/now/shows/341/facts.html.
51 Ibid.
52 Charlotte Feldman-Jacobs, *Do Empowered Mothers Foster Gender Equity and Better Reproductive Health in the Next Generation? A qualitative analysis from rural Bangladesh*, policy brief for the Interagency Gender Working Group (Washington D.C.: Population Reference Bureau, 2005), http://www.prb.org/pdf05/DoEmpoweredMothers.pdf.
53 "Child Marriage: What We Know."
54 John Cloud, "If Women Were More Like Men: Why Females Earn Less," *Time Magazine*, October 3, 2008, http://www.time.com/time/nation/article/0,8599,1847194,00.html.
55 UN Division for the Advancement of Women and UN Department of Public Information, "The Feminization of Poverty," fact sheet no. 1. (DPI/2035A—May 2010), press kit for the UN General Assembly Special Session "Women 2000: Gender Equality, Development and Peace for the Twenty-first Century," New York, June 5-9, 2000, accessed December 7, 2012, http://www.un.org/womenwatch/daw/followup/session/presskit/fc1.htm.
56 "Asia: The role of women's workload in passing on poverty (to) the next generation," adapted from the draft paper *Rural Poverty Assessment: Asia and the Pacific Region* (Rome: International Fund for Agricultural Development, September 1999), available at http://www.ifad.org/gender/learning/role/workload/in_generation.htm.
57 "Boys in School," PBS Parents, under Issues & Advice: Understanding and Raising Boys, accessed December 12, 2011, http://www.pbs.org/parents/raisingboys/school.html.
58 Bruce Western and Becky Pettit, "Incarceration & social inequality," *Daedalus* 139, no. 3 (Summer 2010): 8-19, http://www.mitpressjournals.org/doi/abs/10.1162/DAED_a_00019.
59 "Introduction," Self Employed Women's Association, under About Us, accessed August 18, 2011, http://www.sewa.org/About_Us.asp.
60 Nancy Gibbs, "To Fight Poverty, Invest in Girls," *Time Magazine*, February 14, 2011, http://www.time.com/time/printout/0,8816,2046045,00.html#.
61 Ibid.
62 "Girls' Education," World Bank, under Topics in Development: Education for All, accessed December 10, 2011, http://web.worldbank.org/WBSITE/EXTERNAL/TOPICS/EXTEDUCATION/0,,contentMDK:20298916~menuPK:617572~pagePK:148956~piPK:216618~theSitePK:282386,00.html#why.
63 Girl Up website, accessed December 12, 2011, http://www.girlup.org.
64 "Promoting Reproductive Health," UN Foundation, under What We Do: Issues; Global Health, accessed August 18, 2011, http://www.unfoundation.org/what-we-do/issues/women-and-population/sexual-repro-health.html.
65 WHO, *Violence Prevention: The Evidence; Promoting gender equality to prevent violence against women*, series of briefings (Geneva, Switzerland: 2009), available at http://www.who.int/violence_injury_prevention/violence/gender.pdf.
66 Reel Grrls website, accessed December 14, 2011, http://www.reelgrrls.org/.
67 Liza Jansen, "Rights: Women's Treaty a Powerful Force for Equality," *Inter Press Service News Agency*, December 4, 2009, http://www.ipsnews.net/2009/12/rights-womens-treaty-a-powerful-force-for-equality/.
68 UNFPA, "Partnering with Boys and Men."
69 "Single-Sex Schools: Separate but Equal?," *New York Times*, under Room for Debate (web feature), October 17, 2011, http://www.nytimes.com/roomfordebate/2011/10/17/single-sex-schools-separate-but-equal.
70 Vincent A. Anfara, Jr. and Steven B. Mertens, "What Research Says: Do Single-Sex Classes and Schools Make a Difference?," *Middle School Journal* (November 2008), http://curriculumstudies.pbworks.com/f/Single+Sex+Classrooms+-+Anfara,+V,+Mertens,+S.pdf.
71 "Single-Sex vs. Coed: The Evidence," National Association for Single Sex Public Education, accessed July 15, 2012, http://www.singlesexschools.org/research-singlesexvscoed.htm.
72 Amy Novotney, "Coed versus single-sex ed," *American Psychological Association* 42, no. 2 (February 2011), http://www.apa.org/monitor/2011/02/coed.aspx.
73 "Single-Sex Education: Fertile Ground for Discrimination," National Coalition for Women and Girls in Education, accessed July 15, 2012, http://www.ncwge.org/TitleIX40/Single-Sex.pdf.

Chapter 18: Human Migration

1 Khalid Koser, *International Migration: A Very Short Introduction* (Oxford: Oxford University Press, 2007).
2 Farhana Hossain, "Snapshot: Global Migration," *New York Times*, June 22, 2007, http://www.nytimes.com/ref/world/20070622_CAPEVERDE_GRAPHIC.html.
3 Ernesto Friedrich Amaral and Wilson Fusco, "Shaping Brazil: The Role of International Migration," Migration Information Source, project of the Migration Policy Institute, under Country Profiles, June 2005, http://www.migrationinformation.org/Profiles/display.cfm?ID=311.
4 Everett S. Lee, "A Theory of Migration," *Demography 3*, no. 1 (1966): 47-57, http://www.students.uni-mainz.de/jkissel/Skripte/Lee.pdf.
5 Global Commission on International Migration, *Migration in an Interconnected World: New Directions for Action* (Switzerland: SRO-Kundig, October 2005), accessed online at Office of the UN High Commissioner for Refugees (UNHCR), http://www.unhcr.org/refworld/docid/435f81814.html.
6 Russell King, *People on the Move: An Atlas of Migration* (Berkeley and Los Angeles: University of California Press, 2010).
7 Matt Mabe, "The World's Most Global Cities," *Bloomberg Businessweek*, October 29, 2008, http://www.businessweek.com/globalbiz/content/oct2008/gb20081029_679467.htm.
8 King, *People on the Move*.
9 Jonathan Crush and Sujata Ramachandran, *Xenophobia, International Migration and Human Development*, UN Development Programme Human Development Research Paper no. 47 (September 2009), http://hdr.undp.org/en/reports/global/hdr2009/papers/HDRP_2009_47.pdf.
10 Satsuki Ina, "Internment History," PBS, under *Children of the Camps* (documentary), 1999, http://www.pbs.org/childofcamp/history/index.html.
11 Will Kymlicka, "Multiculturalism: Success, Failure, and The Future," *Migration Policy Institute* (Washington D.C.: February 2012), http://www.migrationpolicy.org/pubs/Multiculturalism.pdf.
12 "Viewpoints and the headscarf," *BBC News*, February 2004, http://news.bbc.co.uk/2/hi/europe/3459963.stm#Rachida.
13 Angelique Chrisafis, "Nicolas Sarkozy says Islamic veils are not welcome in France," *Guardian*, June 22, 2009, http://www.guardian.co.uk/world/2009/jun/22/islamic-veils-sarkozy-speech-france.

14 Damien Cave, "After Quake, Haitians with Dreams Look for an Exit," *New York Times,* July 8, 2010, http://www.nytimes.com/2010/07/09/world/americas/09haiti.html?pagewanted=all.
15 Karen Fragala Smith, "Haiti: A Historical Perspective," *Newsweek,* January 2010, http://www.newsweek.com/2010/01/15/haiti-a-historical-perspective.html.
16 Patrick Gavingan, "Migration Emergencies and Human Rights in Haiti," paper prepared for the Conference on Regional Responses to Forced Migration in Central America and the Caribbean, Department of International Legal Affairs, Washington D.C., September 30 to October 1, 1997, available at the Organization for American States, http://www.oas.org/juridico/english/gavigane.html.
17 Henriette Lunde, "Youth and Education in Haiti: Disincentives, vulnerabilities and constraints," Fafo paper no. 26 (Oslo, Norway: Fafo, 2008), http://www.fafo.no/pub/rapp/10070/10070.pdf.
18 "Haiti," Central Intelligence Agency (CIA) World Factbook, updated weekly, accessed December 10, 2010, https://www.cia.gov/library/publications/the-world-factbook/geos/ha.html.
19 James Cox, "Economy in Haiti on life support," *USA Today,* February 26, 2004, http://www.usatoday.com/money/world/2004-02-26-haitiecon_x.htm.
20 Margarita Puerto Gomez and Asger Christensen, "The Impacts of Refugees on Neighboring Countries: A Development Challenge," July 29, 2010, a background note for *The World Development Report 2011: Conflict, Security, and Development* (Washington D.C.: World Bank, May 26, 2011), http://siteresources.worldbank.org/EXTWDR2011/Resources/6406082-1283882418764/WDR_Background_Paper_Refugees.pdf.
21 Guy Gugliotta, "The Great Human Migration," *Smithsonian Magazine* (July 2008) http://www.smithsonianmag.com/history-archaeology/human-migration.html?c=y&page=1.
22 King, *People on the Move.*
23 Ibid.
24 Wayne Curtis, "The Magic that is Trinidad," *New York Times,* November 21, 2004, http://travel.nytimes.com/2004/11/21/travel/sophisticated/21STTRINIDAD.html?pagewanted=1&_r=2.
25 "Trinidad and Tobago," CIA World Factbook, updated weekly, accessed https://www.cia.gov/library/publications/the-world-factbook/geos/td.html.
26 King, *People on the Move.*
27 Julia Preston, "Many Visas Are Sought for Skilled Immigrants," *New York Times,* April 11, 2008, http://www.nytimes.com/2008/04/11/us/11immig.html.
28 "United Arab Emirates (UAE) Events of 2009," Human Rights Watch, accessed July 20, 2012, http://www.hrw.org/world-report-2010/united-arab-emirates-uae.
29 King, *People on the Move.*
30 Koser, *International Migration.*
31 "Global Statistics," Internal Displacement Monitoring Centre, under Countries, accessed April 11, 2011, http://www.internal-displacement.org/8025708F004CE90B/%28httpPages%29/22FB1D4E2B196DAA802570BB005E787C.
32 "2012 UNHCR country operations profile—Sudan," UNHCR, under Where We Work, accessed July 20, 2012, http://www.unhcr.org/cgi-bin/texis/vtx/page?page=49e483b76.
33 "2012 UNHCR country operations profile—Columbia," UNHCR, under Where We Work, accessed July 20, 2012, http://www.unhcr.org/cgi-bin/texis/vtx/page?page=49e492ad6.
34 Koser, *International Migration.*
35 Ibid.
36 "Anatomy of a refugee camp," *CBC News,* June 2007, http://www.cbc.ca/news/background/refugeecamp/.
37 Ibid.
38 Rosemarie North, "Darfur's refugees in Chad," *Magazine of the International Red Cross and Red Crescent Movement* 2 (2005), http://www.redcross.int/EN/mag/magazine2005_2/22-23.html.
39 "Sudan-Chad: Sudanese refugees and Chadian hosts share scarce water," Integrated Regional Information Network (IRIN), a service of the UN Office for the Coordination of Humanitarian Affairs, September 2006, http://www.irinnews.org/InDepthMain.aspx?InDepthId=13&ReportId=61032.
40 King, *People on the Move.*
41 Ibid.
42 Jason DeParle, "Global Migration: A World Ever More on the Move," *New York Times,* June 26, 2010, http://www.nytimes.com/2010/06/27/weekinreview/27deparle.html?ref=weekinreview.
43 "Human Trafficking and Migrant Smuggling," UN Office on Drugs and Crime, accessed December 8, 2010, http://www.unodc.org/unodc/en/human-trafficking/index.html.
44 "Human Trafficking: the Facts," UN Global Initiative to Fight Human Trafficking, accessed December 8, 2010, http://www.unglobalcompact.org/docs/Issues_doc/labour/Forced_labour/HUMAN_TRAFFICKING_-_THE_FACTS_-_final.pdf.
45 "About SMF," Somaly Mam Foundation, accessed July 15, 2011, http://www.somaly.org/somaly-mam.
46 "Our Story," Sierra Leone's Refugee All Stars, accessed December 13, 2010, http://www.sierraleonesrefugeeallstars.com/fr_home.cfm.
47 "Environment—Looking After the Land," UNHCR, under What We Do, accessed December 13, 2011, http://www.unhcr.org/pages/49c3646c10a.html.
48 Grace Wong, "Fighting Africa's Brain Drain," *CNN,* June 22, 2009, http://edition.cnn.com/2009/HEALTH/06/22/africa.brain.drain/index.html.
49 "Basic Information about the DREAM Act Legislation," DREAM Act Portal, July 16, 2010, http://dreamact.info/students.
50 "North Carolina scholars implore Hagan & Burr: Support the Dream Act," Blue NC, December 15, 2010, http://www.bluenc.com/north-carolina-scholars-implore-hagan-burr-support-dream-act.
51 Ian Lovett, "California Court Backs Illegal Immigrant Students," *New York Times,* November 15, 2010, http://www.nytimes.com/2010/11/16/us/16immig.html.
52 W.W., "The message the DREAM Act sends," *Economist,* November 21, 2010, http://www.economist.com/blogs/democracyinamerica/2010/11/amnesty_and_decency.
53 Steven A. Camarota, *Estimating the Impact of the DREAM Act,* Center for Immigration Studies memorandum (Washington D.C.: November 2010), http://cis.org/dream-act-costs.
54 David Frum, "A DREAM bill that's more like a nightmare," *Week,* November 25, 2010, http://theweek.com/bullpen/column/209766/a-dream-bill-thats-more-like-a-nightmare.

Chapter 19: Economics

1 Lindsay M. Howden and Julie A. Meyer, *Age and Sex Composition: 2010; 2010 Census Briefs* (Washington D.C.: U.S. Census Bureau, May 2011), http://www.census.gov/prod/cen2010/briefs/c2010br-03.pdf.
2 "How U.S. Teens Spend Their Time and Money," Institute For Global Labour and Human Rights, March 10, 2007, www.globallabourrights.org/reports?id=0626.

3 International Labour Organization, *Facts and Figures on Child Labour* (Geneva, Switzerland: 1999), available at the World Bank, accessed July 20, 2012, http://info.worldbank.org/etools/docs/library/164047/howknow/..%5Cpdf%5Cfacts.pdf.
4 E.g. Robert Costanza, Joshua Farley, and Ida Kubuszewski, "Adapting Institutions for Life in a Full World," in *2010 State of the World: Transforming Cultures from Consumerism to Sustainability*, ed. Worldwatch Institute (New York: W.W. Norton & Company, 2010).
5 "Pew Campaign for Responsible Mining," Pew Environment Group, accessed March 28, 2011, http://www.pewenvironment.org/campaigns/pew-campaign-for-responsible-mining/id/328473/.
6 "How Countries Spend Their Money," Visual Economics, accessed March 14, 2012, http://visualeconomics.creditloan.com/how-countries-spend-their-money/.
7 Associated Press, "India urged to double health spending to aid its impoverished sick," *National*, June 9, 2011, http://www.thenational.ae/news/world/south-asia/india-urged-to-double-health-spending-to-aid-its-impoverished-sick#page1.
8 David Lewit, "Porto Alegre's Budget—Of, By, and For the People," *YES!* Magazine 24 (Winter 2003): 21-22.
9 Robert E. Lucas, Jr., *Lectures on Economic Growth* (Cambridge: Harvard University Press, 2002).
10 Dr. Davut Ates, "Industrial Revolution: Impetus Behind the Globalization Process," Management and Economics 15, no. 2 (2008), http://www2.bayar.edu.tr/yonetimekonomi/dergi/pdf/C15S22008/31_48.pdf.
11 "Glass-Steagall Act (1933)," *New York Times*, accessed March 14, 2010, http://topics.nytimes.com/topics/reference/timestopics/subjects/g/glass_steagall_act_1933/index.html.
12 Roya Wolverson, "GDP and Economic Policy," *Renewing America* (blog), September 10, 2010, http://www.cfr.org/economics/gdp-economic-policy/p22922.
13 Wolverson, "GDP and Economic Policy."
14 Michael Watts, "What is a Market Economy," InfoUSA, project of the Bureau of International Information Programs, U.S. Department of State, accessed August 30, 2012, http://usinfo.org/enus/economy/overview/mktec1.html.
15 "Command Economy, Planned Economy," Economy Watch, October 14, 2010, http://www.economywatch.com/economy-articles/command-economy.html.
16 Wolverson, "GDP and Economic Policy."
17 Richard A. Easterlin, "Does Economic Growth Improve the Human Lot? Some Empirical Evidence," *Nations and Households in Economic Growth: Essays in Honor of Moses Abramowitz*, eds. Paul A. David and Melvin W. Reder (New York: Academic Press, 1974): 89-125, available at http://graphics8.nytimes.com/images/2008/04/16/business/Easterlin1974.pdf.
18 Edward S. Herman, "The Threat of Globalization," *New Politics* 26 (Winter 1999), http://nova.wpunj.edu/newpolitics/issue26/herman26.htm.
19 Jeremy Brecher and Tim Costello, *Global Village or Global Pillage: Economic Reconstruction from the Bottom Up* (Cambridge, MA: South End Press, 1994).
20 David D. Driscoll, "The IMF and the World Bank: How Do They Differ?" International Monetary Fund, accessed April 5, 2012, http://www.imf.org/external/pubs/ft/exrp/differ/differ.htm.
21 "Drop the Debt," Make Poverty History, accessed July 5, 2012, http://www.makepovertyhistory.org/whatwewant/debt.shtml.
22 Clifford Cobb, Gary Sue Goodman, and Mathis Wackernagel, *Why Bigger Isn't Better: The Genuine Progress Indicator—1999 Update*, (San Francisco, CA: Redefining Progress, November 1999), available at http://www.nber.org/~rosenbla/econ302/lecture/GPI-GDP/gpi1999.pdf.
23 UN Development Programme, "Regional and National Trends in the Human Development Index 1970-2010," *Human Development Report 2011: Sustainability and Equity; A Better Future for All* (New York: Palgrave Macmillan, 2011), under Indices & Data: HDI Trends, http://hdr.undp.org/en/data/trends/.
24 "The Index of Social Health," Institute for Innovation in Social Policy, accessed March 29, 2011, http://iisp.vassar.edu/ish.html.
25 Ibid.
26 "Our History," The Body Shop, accessed December 2, 2012, http://www.thebodyshop.com/content/services/aboutus_history.aspx.
27 Nicolás Estupinán et al., "Affordability and Subsidies in Public Urban Transport: What Do We Mean, What Can Be Done?" World Bank policy researching working paper no. 4440, December 2007, http://elibrary.worldbank.org/docserver/download/4440.pdf?expires=1356750605&id=id&accname=guest&checksum=47A9FF655D2281B68154A3A65A89F9DF.
28 "Financial Literacy Facts," Money U, accessed December 2, 2012, http://moneyu.com/index.php/financial-literacy-facts.
29 "10 Generation Next entrepreneurs to watch: Nikhil Arora and Alejandro Velez," *CNN Money*, July 7, 2011, http://money.cnn.com/galleries/2011/smallbusiness/1107/gallery.generation_next_entrepreneurs/3.html.
30 Judith D. Schwartz, "Is GDP an obsolete measure of progress?" *Time*, January 30, 2010, http://www.time.com/time/business/article/0,8599,1957746,00.html.

Chapter 20: Poverty

1 Washington CASH, communication, August 26, 2009; Washington CASH website, accessed December 13, 2012, http://www.washingtoncash.org.
2 Harold R. Kerbo, World Poverty: *Global Inequality and the Modern World System* (New York: McGraw Hill, 2006).
3 "Regional aggregation using 2005 PPP and $1.25/day poverty line," The World Bank, accessed September 7, 2011, http://iresearch.worldbank.org/PovcalNet/povDuplic.html.
4 Jeffrey Sachs, "Who and Where are the Poor?" in *The End of Poverty: How We Can Make it Happen in Our Lifetime* (London: Penguin, 2005).
5 "2012 HHS Poverty Guidelines," U.S. Department of Health and Human Services, accessed July 12, 2012, http://aspe.hhs.gov/poverty/12poverty.shtml/.
6 Gordon Green and John Coder, *Household Income Trends: January 2012* (Sentier Research, January 2012), http://www.sentierresearch.com/reports/Sentier_Research_Household_Income_Trends_Report_January_2012_12_03_01.pdf.
7 Robert Rector and Rachel Sheffield, "Air Conditioning, Cable TV, and an Xbox: What is Poverty in the United States Today?," Heritage Foundation, July 19, 2011, http://www.caledonia.org.uk/papers/Who-and-Where-are-the-Poor.pdf.
8 UN Development Programme (UNDP), *Human Development Report 2003* (New York: Oxford University Press, 2003), http://hdr.undp.org/en/media/hdr03_complete.pdf.
9 "Economics focus: A Wealth of Data, A Useful New Way to Capture the Many Aspects of Poverty," *Economist*, July 29, 2010, http://www.economist.com/node/16693283/.
10 UNDP, *Human Development Report 1990* (New York: Oxford University Press, 1990), http://hdr.undp.org/en/media/hdr_1990_en_front.pdf.
11 "Economics focus."

12 "Millennium Development Goals," UNICEF, accessed September 8, 2011, http://www.unicef.org/mdg/poverty.html.
13 Servaas van der Berg, *Poverty and education*, International Institute for Educational Planning poverty and education booklet series no. 10 (e-book), 2008, accessed September 13, 2011, http://www.iiep.unesco.org/fileadmin/user_upload/Info_Services_Publications/pdf/2009/EdPol10.pdf.
14 UN Department of Economic and Social Affairs, *Rethinking Poverty: Report on The World Social Situation 2010* (New York: UN, 2009), http://www.un.org/esa/socdev/rwss/docs/2010/fullreport.pdf.
15 Ibid.
16 "Life Expectancy in most U.S. counties fall behind world's healthiest nations," Institute for Health Metrics and Evaluation, June 15, 2011, http://www.healthmetricsandevaluation.org/news-events/news-release/life-expectancy-in-us-counties-2011.
17 Tom Paulson, "Life Span Shorter in Parts of the U.S.," *Seattle Post-Intelligencer,* April 21, 2008, http://www.seattlepi.com/national/article/Life-span-shorter-in-parts-of-U-S-1270994.php.
18 Duncan Green, "Are Women Really 70% of the World's Poor? How do we know?" *From Poverty to Power* (blog), February 3, 2010, http://www.oxfamblogs.org/fp2p/?p=1797.
19 "Facts & Figures on Women, Poverty & Economics," UN Women, accessed September 8, 2011, http://www.unifem.org/gender_issues/women_poverty_economics/facts_figures.php.
20 "Review of International Operations: Tarkwa Gold Mine," Gold Fields, December 31, 2011, http://www.goldfields.co.za/ops_int_tarkwa.php.
21 "Wassa District," No Dirty Gold, accessed August 9, 2011, http://www.nodirtygold.org/wassa_district_ghana.cfm.
22 Krishna Ramanujan, "Gro Harlem Brundtland discusses sustainable development at Iscol lecture," *Cornell University News Service,* May 4, 2005, http://www.news.cornell.edu/stories/May05/Iscol.Brundtland.kr.html.
23 Sriram Ramgopal, "Introduction: Slums in India," *Sangam* India, accessed August 11, 2011, http://www.sangamIndia.org/index.php?page=introduction-slums-in-india.
24 "Urbanization: A Majority in Cities," UN Population Fund, accessed September 12, 2011, http://www.unfpa.org/pds/urbanization.htm.
25 "How We Work," Agros International, accessed June 27, 2011, http://www.agros.org/ag/how-we-work/frequently-asked-questions/.
26 *Human Development Report,* 2003.
27 Anup Shah, "Poverty Facts and Stats," *Global Issues* (blog), September 20, 2010, http://www.globalissues.org/article/26/poverty-facts-and-stats.
28 Jeffrey D. Sachs, "The End of Poverty," *Time Magazine,* March 6, 2005, http://www.time.com/time/magazine/article/0,9171,1034738,00.html
29 Steven M. Beaudoin, *Poverty in World History* (New York: Taylor & Francis, 2007).
30 Ibid.
31 "Exploration," Oswego City School District's Regents Exam Prep Center, accessed June 27, 2011, http://regentsprep.org/Regents/global/themes/change/exp.cfm.
32 "The Story of... Steel," PBS, under *Guns, Germs, and Steel* (tv series), accessed June 27, 2011, http://www.pbs.org/gunsgermssteel/variables/steel.htm.
33 "European Colonization of the Americas," New World Encyclopedia, accessed June 16, 2011, http://www.newworldencyclopedia.org/entry/European_Colonization_of_the_Americas.
34 Kerbo, *World Poverty.*

35 "A Brief History of the Berlin Conference," Pine Crest International Relations Club, accessed June 8, 2011, http://teacherweb.ftl.pinecrest.edu/snyderd/MWH/Projects/mun-bc/History.htm.
36 Republic of South Africa National Planning Commission, *Diagnostic Overview* (2011), accessed June 9 2011, http://www.npconline.co.za/MediaLib/Downloads/Home/Tabs/Diagnostic/Diagnostic%20Overview.pdf.
37 World Savvy Monitor, "Global Poverty: Why?" *Global Poverty and International Development* 5 (October 2008) accessed June 9, 2011, http://worldsavvy.org/monitor/index.php?option=com_content&view=article&id=350&Itemid=539.
38 "South Africa: Inequality not so black and white," Integrated Regional Information Network (IRIN), a service of the UN Office for the Coordination of Humanitarian Affairs, February 8, 2010, http://irinnews.org/Report.aspx?ReportId=88038.
39 Regina Birner, *Improving Governance to Eradicate Poverty and Hunger,* International Food Policy Research Institute 2020 Focus brief on the world's poor and hungry people no. 35 (December 2007), http://www.ifpri.org/sites/default/files/publications/beijingbrief_birner.pdf.
40 Punam Chuhan-Pole and Manka Angwafo, eds., *Yes Africa Can: Success Stories From a Dynamic Continent* (Washington D.C.: World Bank, 2011).
41 Mona Serageldin, Elda Solloso, and Luis Valenzuela, "Local Government Actions to Reduce Poverty and Achieve the Millennium Development Goals," *Global Urban Development* 2 (March 2006), http://www.globalurban.org/GUDMag06Vol2Iss1/Serageldin,%20Solloso,%20&%20Valenzuela.htm.
42 Ibid.
43 "Global Poverty Info Bank," Global Poverty Project, accessed June 14, 2011, http://www.globalpovertyproject.com/infobank/conflict.
44 Centre for International Cooperation and Security, *The Impact of Armed Violence on poverty and development: Full report of the Armed Violence and Poverty Initiative* (Bradford, UK: University of Bradford, March 2005), http://www.brad.ac.uk/acad/cics/publications/AVPI/pove3rty/AVPI_Synthesis_Report.pdf.
45 David Pottebaum, "Conflict, Poverty, Inequality, and Economic Growth," in *Pro-Poor Economic Growth Issues Papers,* Volume 2 (Washington, D.C.: U.S. Agency for International Development, January 2005), available at http://pdf.usaid.gov/pdf_docs/PNACY515.pdf.
46 "Food for Life: Zero Hunger," *Against the Odds: Making a Difference in Global Health,* online exhibition in the National Library of Medicine, accessed September 8, 2011, http://apps.nlm.nih.gov/againsttheodds/exhibit/food_for_life/zero_hunger.cfm; Claire Hastings, ed., *Water Rights and Wrongs: A Young People's Summary of the United Nations Human Development Report 2006; Beyond Scarcity: Power, Poverty, and the Global Water Crisis* (Buntingford: UNDP and Peace Child International, 2007), accessed June 15, 2011, http://hdr.undp.org/en/media/water_rights_and_wrongs_english.pdf.
47 Joanna M. Foster, "Food Prize Goes to Ex-Leaders of Ghana and Brazil," *New York Times,* June 21, 2011, http://green.blogs.nytimes.com/2011/06/21/food-prize-goes-to-ex-leaders-of-ghana-and-brazil/.
48 UNDP, *Human Development Report 2006: Beyond Scarcity; Power, Poverty, and the Global Water Crisis* (New York: UNDP, 2006), http://hdr.undp.org/en/media/HDR06-complete.pdf.
49 Ibid.
50 World Savvy Monitor, "Global Poverty."
51 "Structural Adjustment Programmes (SAPs)," World Health Organization, under Programmes and projects: Trade, foreign policy, diplomacy and health, accessed July 12, 2012, http://www.who.int/trade/glossary/story084/en/index.html.

52 YouthBuild USA website, accessed September 5, 2011, https://youthbuild.org/
53 "Biography of Dr. Muhammad Yunus," Grameen Bank, accessed September 7, 2011, http://www.grameen-info.org/index.php?option=com_content&task=view&id=329&Itemid=363.
54 "At a Glance," Grameen Bank, accessed September 5, 2011, http://www.grameen-info.org/index.php?option=com_content&task=view&id=26&Itemid=175.
55 Wang Sangui, Li Zhou, and Ren Yanshun, "The 8-7 National Poverty Reduction Program in China—The National Strategy and Its Impact," case study from *Reducing Poverty, Sustaining Growth: What Works, What Doesn't, and Why A Global Exchange for Scaling Up Success*, conference submission, Scaling Up Poverty Reduction: A Global Learning Process and Conference, Shanghai, May 2004 (World Bank, 2004), http://info.worldbank.org/etools/docs/reducingpoverty/case/33/fullcase/China%208-7%20Full%20Study.pdf.
56 "About Us," Kiva, accessed June 23, 2011, http://www.kiva.org/about.
57 Jessica Jackley, "Poverty, Money, and Love," TED Talks (video), accessed June 23, 2011, http://www.ted.com/talks/lang/eng/jessica_jackley_poverty_money_and_love.html.
58 Sangui, "The 8-7 National Poverty Reduction Program in China"
59 "The Millennium Development Goals Work!: Brief examples of country progress," briefing paper for Plenary Meeting of the UN General Assembly, UN Summit, New York, September 20-22, 2010, http://www.un.org/en/mdg/summit2010/successstories.shtml.
60 *Millennium Development Goals: At a Glance* (UN Department of Public Information, April 2010), http://www.un.org/millenniumgoals/pdf/mdgs_glance_factsheet.pdf.
61 Peter M. Haas, John A. Hird, and Beth McBratney, eds., *Controversies in Globalization* (Washington, DC: CQ Press, 2009).
62 Initiative for Global Development, *Building a Better World: A New Global Development Strategy to End Extreme Poverty*, policy brief (Seattle, WA: January 2004), http://www.igdleaders.org/documents/IGD_PolicyBrief_05.pdf.
63 "Cancellation of developing world debt," Debatepedia, an online forum of the International Debate Education Association, accessed May 14, 2012, http://debatepedia.idebate.org/en/index.php/Debate:_Cancellation_of_developing_world_debt.
64 Ibid.

Chapter 21: Globalization

1 "Glossary of globalization, trade and health terms," World Health Organization, accessed July 20, 2011, http://www.who.int/trade/glossary/en/.
2 "The Footprint Chronicles," Patagonia, accessed April 14, 2011, http://www.patagonia.com/us/footprint/.
3 "Environment," Globalization 101, project of the Levin Institute, State University of New York, accessed April 14, 2011, http://www.globalization101.org/category/issues-in-depth/environment/.
4 Ibid.
5 Gary Clyde Hufbauer, "Globalization Facts and Consequences," notes from a debate at Williams College, Williamstown, MA, October 12, 2000, available at Peterson Institute for International Economics, accessed April 19, 2011, http://www.iie.com/publications/papers/paper.cfm?ResearchID=388.

6 Nicolas Meisel, *Governance Culture and Development: A Different Perspective on Corporate Governance* (OECD Development Center Studies, 2004), available at http://www.proparco.fr/jahia/webdav/site/afd/shared/PORTAILS/RECHERCHE/Meisel/Meisel-Etude2004%20E-Governance%20CultureVA.pdf.
7 "Britain's e-waste illegally leaking into West Africa," *BBC News*, May 16, 2011, http://news.bbc.co.uk/panorama/hi/front_page/newsid_9483000/9483148.stm.
8 "Following the Trail of Toxic E-Waste," 60 minutes, *CBS News*, accessed April 20, 2011, http://www.cbsnews.com/stories/2008/11/06/60minutes/main4579229.shtml?tag=contentMain;contentBody.
9 Chris Carroll, "High Tech Trash," *National Geographic* (January 2008): 64-81.
10 "Hazardous E-Waste Surging in Developing Countries," *Science Daily*, February 23, 2010, http://www.sciencedaily.com/releases/2010/02/100222081911.htm.
11 Dan Koeppel, "Yes We Will Have No Bananas," *New York Times*, June 18, 2008, http://www.nytimes.com/2008/06/18/opinion/18koeppel.html?ref=bananas.
12 Laurel Singleton and Caroline Starbird, eds., *Get It! Global Education to Improve Tomorrow: Curriculum Guide* (Little Rock, AR: Heifer International, 2004).
13 "Vikings: sea-raiders and traders," British Museum, accessed April 25, 2011, http://www.britishmuseum.org/explore/highlights/article_index/v/vikings_sea-raiders_and_trade.aspx.
14 "Primer 1: The Economics of International Trade," Globalization 101, accessed October 6, 2011, http://www.globalization101.org/primer-1-the-economics-of-international-trade/.
15 Andrew Bergmann, "World's Largest Economies," *CNN Money*, accessed April 25, 2011, http://money.cnn.com/news/economy/world_economies_gdp/.
16 "World could face severe economic downturn, new UN report suggests," *UN News Centre*, May 15, 2008, http://www.un.org/apps/news/story.asp?NewsID=26686&Cr=desa&Cr1.
17 Kelly Leong, ed., "GATT/WTO," Duke University School of Law, under J. Michael Goodson Law Library Research Guides, revised October 2011, http://law.duke.edu/lib/researchguides/gatt.
18 "EU cuts import tariffs in a bid to end 'banana wars,'" *BBC News*, December 15, 2009, http://news.bbc.co.uk/2/hi/business/8391752.stm.
19 World Trade Organization (WTO), *10 benefits of the WTO Trading System* (Geneva, Switzerland: WTO, 2008), accessed May 8, 2012, www.wto.org/english/res_e/doload_e/10b_e.pdf.
20 "How the EU Works," European Union, accessed August 1, 2012, http://europa.eu/about-eu/eu-history/index_en.htm.
21 Uri Dadush and Bennett Stancil, "The G20 in 2050," *International Economic Bulletin*, a publication of the Carnegie Endowment for International Peace, November 19, 2009, http://carnegieendowment.org/2009/11/19/g20%2Din%2D2050/lp4.
22 Abul Kalam Azad, "Rock 'n Roll in Bangladesh: Protecting Intellectual Property Rights in Music," in *Managing the Challenges of WTO Participation*, WTO case study no. 3, accessed September 21, 2011, http://www.wto.org/english/res_e/booksp_e/casestudies_e/case3_e.htm.
23 Josiane Georges, "Trade and the Disappearance of Domestic Rice," TED case study no. 725 (June 2004), http://www1.american.edu/TED/haitirice.htm.
24 "Internet 2010 in numbers" *Royal Pingdom* (blog), accessed April 26, 2011, http://royal.pingdom.com/2011/01/12/internet-2010-in-numbers/.

25. Bianca Consunji, "Hashtags Help Coordinate Relief Efforts in Philippine Floods," *Mashable US and World*, August 7, 2012, http://mashable.com/2012/08/07/philippine-floods/.
26. Lauren F. Landsburg, "Comparative Advantage," Library of Economics and Liberty, accessed April 28, 2011, http://www.econlib.org/library/Topics/Details/comparativeadvantage.html.
27. Daniel Griswold, "The Blessings and Challenges of Globalization," Cato Institute, September 1, 2000, http://www.cato.org/pub_display.php?pub_id=10891.
28. Nicholas D. Kristof, "Where Sweatshops Are a Dream," *New York Times*, January 14, 2009, http://www.nytimes.com/2009/01/15/opinion/15kristof.html.
29. WITNESS website, accessed July 15, 2012, www.witness.org/.
30. World Savvy Monitor, "NAFTA: Does the North American Trade Agreement really promote free trade?" *Mexico* 10 (August 2009), http://worldsavvy.org/monitor/index.php?option=com_content&view=article&id=682&Itemid=1147.
31. Ibid.
32. World Savvy Monitor, "Maquiladoras," *Mexico* 10 (August 2009), http://worldsavvy.org/monitor/index.php?option=com_content&view=article&id=684&Itemid=1147.
33. Elyse Bolsterstein, "Environmental Justice Case Study: Maquiladora Workers and Border Issues," student case study for *Environmental Justice: Domestic and International*, a course at the University of Michigan's School of Natural Resources and Environment, accessed October 7, 2011, http://www.umich.edu/~snre492/Jones/maquiladora.htm.
34. Moisés Naím, "Five Wars of Globalization," *Foreign Policy*, January 1, 2003, http://www.foreignpolicy.com/articles/2003/01/01/five_wars_of_globalization.
35. Adil Najam, David Runnalls, and Mark Halle, "Environment and Globalization: Five Propositions," International Institute for Sustainable Development, accessed August 25, 2012, http://www.iisd.org/pdf/2007/trade_environment_globalization.pdf.
36. "From English to Chinglish: The Globalization of Languages," Globalization 101, July 23, 2008, http://www.globalization101.org/from-english-to-chinglish-the-globalization-of-languages/.
37. Brennan Edwardes and Frank Frizelle, "Globalisation and its impact on the South Pacific," *New Zealand Medical Journal* 122, no. 1291 (March 2009), http://www.nzma.org.nz/journal/122-1291/3518/.
38. Jack Robertiello, "The Lemon Ice King of Corona," *New York Magazine*, accessed May 15, 2011, http://nymag.com/listings/restaurant/ben_faremo_the_lemon_ice_king_of_corona/.
39. "Products, Banana Farmers," Equal Exchange, accessed October 6, 2011, http://www.beyondthepeel.com/bananas.html#guabo.
40. Laurence Chandy and Geoffrey Gertz, "With Little Notice, Globalization Reduced Poverty," *Yale Global Online*, July 5, 2011, http://yaleglobal.yale.edu/content/little-notice-globalization-reduced-poverty.
41. WTO, "Free trade helps reduce poverty, says new WTO secretariat study," press release, June 13, 2000, http://www.wto.org/english/news_e/pres00_e/pr181_e.htm.
42. Nicole Hassoun, "Free Trade, Poverty, and the Environment," *Public Affairs Quarterly* 22, no. 4 (October 2008): 353-380, http://www.hss.cmu.edu/philosophy/hassoun/papers/Paper_FreeTradePovertyEnvironment.pdf.
43. Jagadeesh Gokhale, *Globalization: Curse or Cure? Policies to Harness Global Economic Integration Solve Our Economic Challenge*, Cato Policy Analysis no. 659 (Washington D.C.: February 1, 2010), http://www.cato.org/pubs/pas/html/pa659/pa659index.html.

Chapter 22: Community Development

1. "Core Programs," Peace Players International, under Middle East, accessed November 11, 2011, http://www.peaceplayersintl.org/locations/middle-east.
2. "Testimonials," Peace Players International, accessed June 12, 2012, http://www.peaceplayersintl.org/about/testimonials.
3. "Our Chapters," Boston Youth Organizing Project, under Who We Are, accessed December 18, 2011, http://byop.org/who/chapters.php.
4. Will Allen, "Community Resilience and Adaptation," learningforsustainability.net, under Sustainable Development, accessed January 4, 2012, http://learningforsustainability.net/susdev/resilience.php; "Resilient Communities," Ontario Healthy Communities Coalition, under Position Papers and Factsheets, accessed December 5, 2012, http://www.ohcc-ccso.ca/en/resilient-communities.
5. "Managing a Networked Job Search," Harvard College Office of Career Services, accessed June 26, 2012, http://www.ocs.fas.harvard.edu/students/jobs_networking.htm.
6. Robert Putnam, "Bowling Alone: America's Declining Social Capital," *Journal of Democracy* 6, no. 1 (January 1995): 65-78, http://xroads.virginia.edu/~HYPER/DETOC/assoc/bowling.html.
7. Anirudh Krishna, "How Does Social Capital Grow? A Seven-Year Study of Villages in India," *Journal of Politics* 69, no. 4 (November 2007): 941-956, http://sitemason.vanderbilt.edu/files/bQQjQY/Social%20Capital%20KRISHNA.pdf.
8. B. Walisser, B. Mueller, and C. McLean, "The Resilient City," Vancouver Working Group Discussion Paper prepared for the World Urban Economic Forum 2006 in *The World Urban Forum 2006: Vancouver Working Group Discussion Paper* (Ministry of Community Aboriginal and Women's Services, Government of British Columbia, 2005), accessed December 3, 2012, http://www.cscd.gov.bc.ca/lgd/intergov_relations/library/wuf_the_resilient_city.pdf.
9. John Wisely and Todd Spangler, "Motor City Population Declines 25%," *USA Today*, March 24, 2011, http://www.usatoday.com/news/nation/census/2011-03-22-michigan-census_N.htm.
10. Dudley Street Neighborhood Initiative, *Annual Report: July 1, 2010-June 30, 2011*, accessed November 7, 2011, http://www.dsni.org/sites/default/files/dnsi_files/2010%20Annual%20Report.pdf.
11. "History Timeline," Blackfeet Nation, accessed January 4, 2012, http://www.blackfeetnation.com/index.php?option=com_content&view=article&id=28:history-timeline&catid=1:about-the-blackfeet-nation&Itemid=4.
12. "History of the Settlement Movement," Columbus Federation of Settlements, 2009, accessed January 4, 2012, http://www.cfsettlements.org/The_Settlement_Movement.html.
13. "History," Back of the Yards Neighborhood Council, accessed January 4, 2012, http://bync.org/?page_id=20.
14. Putnam, "Bowling Alone."
15. Stephen Valocchi, "A Way of Thinking about the History of Community Organizing," Trinity College, accessed January 4, 2012, http://www.trincoll.edu/depts/tcn/valocchi.htm.
16. Ibid.
17. Ibid.
18. "Youth Volunteering on the Rise," *Philanthropy Journal*, September 23, 2009, http://www.philanthropyjournal.org/news/youth-volunteering-rise.
19. Robert Putnam, "E Plurbis Unum: Diversity and Community in the 21st Century," *Journal of Scandinavian Political Studies* 30, no. 2 (2007): 137-174.

20 Jennifer Cheeseman Day, "National Population Projections," in *Integrated Public Use Microdata Series* (machine-readable database) (Minneapolis: University of Minnesota, 2011), accessed January 4, 2012, http://cps.ipums.org/cps/resources/cpr/2_ps.pdf.
21 "Effects of Poverty, Hunger, and Homelessness on Children and Youth," American Psychological Association, accessed November 11, 2011, http://www.apa.org/pi/families/poverty.aspx.
22 "Our Work in Schools," Communities in Schools, accessed December 5, 2012, http://www.communitiesinschools.org/our-work/in-schools.
23 The steps of community development laid out here are adapted from Greg Wise, *Definitions: Community development, community-based education, and the environment,* discussion paper developed for EPA/USDA Partnership to Support Community-Based Education, 1998, http://www.uwex.edu/erc/pdf/AppA_CommunityEdDefinitions.pdf.
24 "Programs Offered," Communities in Schools Seattle, accessed December 5, 2012, http://www.seattle.ciswa.org/about-us/programsoffered.
25 "Our Work in Schools," Communities in Schools.
26 "Programs Offered," Communities in Schools Seattle.
27 Ibid.
28 Ibid.
29 "History," Dudley Street Neighborhood Initiative, accessed November 12, 2011, http://www.dsni.org/history.
30 Putnam, "E Plurbis Unum."
31 Sherry R. Arnstein, "A Ladder of Citizen Participation," *Journal of the American Planning Association* 35, no. 4 (1969): 216-224, http://www.planning.org/pas/memo/2007/mar/pdf/JAPA35No4.pdf.
32 "History," Harlem Children's Zone, under About Us, accessed November 13, 2011, http://www.hcz.org/about-us/history.
33 "What is a Promise Neighborhood?," Promise Neighborhood Institute, accessed November 13, 2011, http://www.promiseneighborhoodsinstitute.org/What-is-a-Promise-Neighborhood.
34 Unless otherwise cited, these examples are from Robert D. Putnam and Lewis M. Feldstein, *Better Together: Restoring the American Community* (New York: Simon and Schuster, 2003).
35 "Los Angeles Urban Rural Roundtable," Roots of Change, under Activities, accessed November 28, 2011, http://rootsofchange.org/content/los-angeles-urban-rural-roundtable.
36 "Social Capital: Definitions," bettertogether.org, project of the Saguaro Seminar on Civic Engagement in America, Harvard University's Kennedy School of Government, accessed November 13, 2011, http://bettertogether.org/socialcapital.htm.
37 Gerald R. Pitzel et al., "Rural Revitalization in New Mexico: A Grass Roots Initiative Involving School and Community," *Rural Educator* 9 (2007), http://www.ruraleducator.net/archive/28-3/28-3_Pitzel.pdf.
38 "Area state legislators announce $200,000 Rural Areas Revitalization Program Grant to CHRIC," *Dunkirk Observer*, May 31, 2009, http://www.observertoday.com/page/content.detail/id/524436.html.
39 Susan Arterian Chang, "Best Job in the Neighborhood— and They Own It," *YES! Magazine*, Fall 2011, http://www.yesmagazine.org/issues/new-livelihoods/best-job-in-the-neighborhood-and-they-own-it.
40 Tina Rosenberg, "Where All Work is Created Equal," *Opinionator* (blog), September 15, 2011, http://opinionator.blogs.nytimes.com/2011/09/15/where-all-work-is-created-equal/.
41 Anabel Quan-Haase and Barry Wellman, "How does the Internet affect social capital?" in *Social Capital and Information Technology*, ed. Marleen Huysman and Volker Wulf (Cambridge, MA: MIT University Press, 2004): 113-132.
42 R. E. Kraut et al., "Social impact of the Internet: What Does It Mean?," *Communications of the ACM* 41, no. 12 (December 1998), DOI: 10.1145/290133.290140.

Chapter 23: Sustainable Design

1 "EPA Green Buildings," U.S. Environmental Protection Agency (EPA), under Greening EPA, accessed December 10, 2012, http://www.epa.gov/oaintrnt/projects/index.htm.
2 "Basic Information," EPA, under Green Building, accessed December 10, 2012, http://www.epa.gov/greenbuilding/pubs/about.htm.
3 Ibid.
4 "Biomimicry," Designboom, accessed December 10, 2012, http://www.designboom.com/contemporary/biomimicry.html; Jill Fehrenbacher, "Biomimetic Architecture: Green Building in Zimbabwe Modeled After Termite Mounds," Inhabitat, November 29, 2012, http://inhabitat.com/building-modelled-on-termites-eastgate-centre-in-zimbabwe/.
5 Ibid.
6 "Indoor Air Quality," GreenBuilding.com, under Knowledge Base, accessed December 10, 2012, http://www.greenbuilding.com/knowledge-base/indoor-air-quality.
7 Ibid.
8 World Health Organization (WHO), *Health in the green economy: Co-benefits of climate change mitigation; Housing sector*, executive summary (Geneva, Switzerland: 2011), http://www.who.int/hia/brochure_housing.pdf.
9 Ibid.
10 "Green schools enhance learning," Center for Green Schools, under Why: Better for learning, accessed December 10, 2012, http://www.centerforgreenschools.org/better-for-learning.aspx.
11 Ibid.
12 Norbert Schoenauer, *6,000 Years of Housing*, Revised and Expanded Edition (New York: W.W. Norton and Company, 2000).
13 Ibid.
14 "Cliff Dwellings," Mesa Verde Colorado, under Discover: Points of Interest, accessed December 10, 2012, http://www.visitmesaverde.com/vacation-attractions/cliff-dwellings.aspx; "Keeping Cool Through the Ages: Slideshow," History.com, under News, July 22, 2011, http://www.history.com/news/2011/07/22/keeping-cool-through-the-ages-slideshow/.
15 "Basic Information," EPA.
16 Sustainable Energy Authority Victoria, "Sustainable Energy Info Fact Sheet: Thermal Mass," accessed December 10, 2012, http://www.sustainability.vic.gov.au/resources/documents/Thermal_mass.pdf.
17 Schoenauer, *6,000 Years of Housing*.
18 Robert Cassidy, ed., *White Paper on Sustainability: A Report on the Green Building Movement* (Oak Brook, IL: Building Design & Construction, November 2003), available at http://www.usgbc.org/Docs/Resources/BDCWhitePaperR2.pdf.
19 "Home and Building Technologies," U.S. Department of Energy (DOE): Energy Efficiency & Renewable Energy, under Energy Basics: Homes & Buildings, last modified December 3, 2012, http://www.eere.energy.gov/basics/buildings/passive_solar_design.html.
20 Cassidy, *White Paper on Sustainability*.
21 Ibid.
22 "LEED," U.S. Green Building Council (USGBC), accessed December 10, 2012, https://new.usgbc.org/leed.
23 Ibid.
24 Cassidy, White Paper on Sustainability.

25 "LEED Green Building Rating Systems," USGBC, under LEED: Rating systems; Overview, accessed December 10, 2012, https://new.usgbc.org/leed/rating-systems.
26 Ibid.
27 "LEED International Roundtable," USGBC, under LEED: Learn About LEED, accessed December 10, 2012, https://new.usgbc.org/about/committees/international.
28 Cassidy, *White Paper on Sustainability*.
29 International Living Future Institute, *Living Building Challenge 2.1: A Visionary Path to a Restorative Future* (Seattle, WA: May 2012), https://ilbi.org/lbc/LBC%20Documents/lbc-2.1.
30 "EPEA GmbH," Environmental Protection and Encouragement Agency (EPEA), accessed December 10, 2012, http://epea-hamburg.org/index.php?id=47&L=0.
31 "Principles," EPEA, under Cradle to Cradle: Principles and Implementation, accessed December 10, 2012, http://epea-hamburg.org/index.php?id=155&L=0#c1550.
32 "Van Houtum," EPEA, under Cradle to Cradle: Case Studies, accessed December 10, 2012, http://epea-hamburg.org/index.php?id=206&L=0.
33 Vance Freymann, John Tessicini, and Martine Dion, *Planning for Construction Waste Reduction*, USGBC white paper, accessed December 10, 2012, http://www.modular.org/marketing/documents/USGBC_WhitePaper_PlanningConstructionWasteReduction.pdf.
34 Ibid.
35 "Field Services—Overview," RE Store, accessed December 10, 2012, http://www.re-store.org/index.php?option=com_content&view=article&id=54:salvage-services&catid=40&Itemid=59.
36 USGBC, *LEED 2009 for New Construction and Major Renovations Rating System* (Washington D.C.: 2009), http://www.usgbc.org/ShowFile.aspx?DocumentID=8868.
37 "How We Use Energy," U.S. Energy Information Administration, under Energy Kids: Energy Use Basics, accessed December 10, 2012, http://www.eia.gov/kids/energy.cfm?page=us_energy_use_basics.
38 Laney White, "Your Green Corner: DIY Winter Weatherization," *Global Green USA: Build It Back Green* (blog), December 9, 2011, http://globalgreen.org/blogs/global/?p=2751.
39 Karyn Maier, "Energy-Efficient Fluorescent Light Bulbs," *National Geographic*, under Environment: The Green Guide; Green Living, http://greenliving.nationalgeographic.com/energyefficient-fluorescent-light-bulbs-2458.html.
40 "About the Campaign," and "Save Water Today, Make a Difference Tomorrow," Save Water Today, accessed December 10, 2012, http://www.savewatertoday.org/.
41 Larry Cummings, "Facts about Aluminum Recycling," Earth911.com, April 2, 2007, http://earth911.com/news/2007/04/02/facts-about-aluminum-recycling/.
42 "Composting Terminology," Composting 101, under Terminology, accessed December 10, 2012, http://www.composting101.com/words-to-know.html.
43 "Food Waste Basics," EPA, under Resource Conservation: Reducing Food Waste, last modified November 26, 2012, http://epa.gov/waste/conserve/foodwaste/.
44 Tristan Baurick, "Students Take Lead in Successful Composting Initiative at Bainbridge High," *Kitsap Sun*, June 13, 2010, http://www.kitsapsun.com/news/2010/jun/13/students-take-lead-in-successful-composting-at/.
45 "Passive Solar Home Design," DOE, under Energy Savers, an energy efficiency and renewable energy resource, accessed July 23, 2012, http://www.energysavers.gov/your_home/designing_remodeling/index.cfm/mytopic=10250.

46 Keya Lea Horiuchi, "Orientation/South Facing Windows," Green Passive Solar Magazine, under Passive Solar Overview: Building Characteristics, accessed December 10, 2012, http://greenpassivesolar.com/passive-solar/building-characteristics/orientation-south-facing-windows/.
47 "Walkable Neighborhoods," Walk Score, under Why It Matters, accessed December 11, 2012, http://www.walkscore.com/walkable-neighborhoods.shtml.
48 "Students Shout Out for the Living Building Challenge and the Bertschi School's New Science Wing," *Building Capacity* (blog), February 16, 2011, http://buildingcapacity.typepad.com/blog/2011/02/students-shout-out-for-the-living-building-challenge-and-the-bertschi-schools-new-science-wing.html.
49 GGLO, *Sustainable Design Case Study: Bertschi School Science Wing* (Seattle, WA: GGLO), accessed August 10, 2012, http://www.gglo.com/files/Downloads/PDF/Bertschi%20Living%20Building%20Science%20Wing.pdf.
50 Ibid.
51 "Bertschi School Living Science Building," Whole Building Design Guide, under Documents & References: Case Studies, accessed December 12, 2012, http://www.wbdg.org/references/cs_bslsb.php.
52 Bertschi School website, accessed August 10, 2012, http://www.bertschi.org/campus/science.html.
53 "Walkable Neighborhoods," Walk Score.
54 "Jane Jacobs," Project for Public Spaces, under Resources: Placemaker Profiles, accessed December 11, 2012, http://www.pps.org/reference/jjacobs-2/.
55 Jane Jacobs, *The Death and Life of Great American Cities* (New York: Vintage Books, 1992).
56 Ibid.
57 "What is District Energy?," International District Energy Association, under District Energy, accessed December 11, 2012, http://www.districtenergy.org/what-is-district-energy.
58 Ibid.
59 "What is CHP?" International District Energy Association, under About District Energy, accessed December 11, 2012, http://www.districtenergy.org/what-is-chp.
60 UN Department of Economic and Social Affairs/Population Division, *World Urbanization Prospects: The 2011 Revision*, Highlights (New York: UN, March 2012), http://www.slideshare.net/undesa/wup2011-highlights.
61 WHO, *Health Indicators of sustainable cities in the Context of the Rio+20 UN Conference on Sustainable Development*, initial findings from WHO expert consultation (WHO/HSE/PHE/7.6.2012f, May2012), http://www.who.int/hia/green_economy/indicators_cities.pdf.
62 M. Kinyanjui, P. Mukungu, and G. Mboup, "Development Context and the Millennium Agenda," in *The Challenge of Slums: Global Report on Human Settlements 2003*, revised and updated version (New York: UN Habitat, April 2010), http://www.unhabitat.org/downloads/docs/GRHS_2003_Chapter_01_Revised_2010.pdf.
63 "Heat Island Effect," EPA, under State and Local Climate and Energy Program, last modified November 20, 2012, http://www.epa.gov/hiri/.
64 Ibid.
65 American Society of Landscape Architects, "Chicago City Hall Green Roof: Chicago, Illinois," press release, October 19, 2002, http://www.asla.org/meetings/awards/awds02/chicagocityhall.html.
66 "Heat Island Effect," EPA.
67 "Fact Sheet: Climate Change," Smart Growth America, under Programs: National Complete Streets Coalition; Fundamentals, accessed December 11, 2012, http://www.smartgrowthamerica.org/complete-streets/complete-streets-fundamentals/factsheets.

68 "Fundamentals," Smart Growth America, under Programs: National Complete Streets Coalition, accessed December 11, 2012, http://www.completestreets.org/complete-streets-fundamentals/complete-streets-faq/.
69 Mary Logan Barmeyer, "Transportation/New York, New York," *National Resources Defense Council: Smarter Cities* (blog), February 23, 2011, http://smartercities.nrdc.org/topic/transportation/new-york-new-york-0.
70 New York Metropolitan Transportation Authority, *2012 Sustainability Report* (April 2012), http://www.mta.info/sustainability/pdf/2012Report.pdf.
71 New York City Department of Transportation, "About DOT," press release no, 10-043, September 22, 2010, http://www.nyc.gov/html/dot/html/pr2010/pr10_043.shtml.
72 City of Vancouver, *Greenest City 2020: Action Plan,* accessed December 11, 2012, https://vancouver.ca/files/cov/Greenest-city-action-plan.pdf.
73 Ibid.
74 Ibid.
75 Ibid.
76 Jennifer Langston, "Mandatory recycling program working well," *Seattle Post-Intelligencer,* March 14, 2006, http://www.seattlepi.com/local/article/Mandatory-recycling-program-working-well-1198413.php.
77 "Composting Benefits," Seattle Public Utilities, under My Services: Food & Yard, Apartment/Condo Residents, accessed December 11, 2012, http://www.seattle.gov/util/MyServices/FoodYard/FoodYardWaste-ApartmentResidents/CompostingBenefits/index.htm.
78 Lucien Steil, Nikos A. Salingaros, and Michael W. Mehaffy, "Growing Sustainable Suburbs: An Incremental Strategy for Reconstructing Sprawl," for publication in *New Urbanism and Beyond: Contemporary and Future Trends in Urban Design,* preliminary version, ed. Tigran Haas, accessed December 11, 2012, http://zeta.math.utsa.edu/~yxk833/suburbia.pdf.
79 Andres Duany, Elizabeth Plater-Zyberk, and Jeff Speck, *Suburban Nation: The Rise of Sprawl and the Decline of the American Dream* (New York: North Point Press, 2000).
80 Ibid.
81 Steil, Salingaros, and Mehaffy, "Growing Sustainable Suburbs."
82 Ibid.
83 "What is Rural?" U.S. Department of Agriculture (USDA) Economic Research Service, under Topics: Rural Economy & Population; Rural Classifications, last modified May 30, 2012, http://www.ers.usda.gov/topics/rural-economy-population/rural-classifications/what-is-rural.aspx.
84 Partnership for Sustainable Communities and USDA, *Supporting Sustainable Rural Communities* (Fall 2011), http://www.epa.gov/dced/pdf/2011_11_supporting-sustainable-rural-communities.pdf.
85 Ibid.
86 Ibid; Stephen J. Horsman (Rural Development Specialist, USDA), personal communication, Summer 2012.
87 "Saving Lives with Solar-Powered Lights," *CNN,* February 12, 2010, http://www.cnn.com/2010/LIVING/02/11/cnnheroes.wadongo/.
88 "Architects—What They Do," StudentScholarships.org, under Career & Salary Information, accessed December 11, 2012, http://www.studentscholarships.org/salary/556/architects.php.
89 The Institution of Structural Engineers, *Careers in Structural Engineering: an opportunity to transform our world* (London: Institute of Structural Engineers), accessed December 11, 2012, http://www.istructe.org/webtest/files/61/61104179-8334-4652-891a-8641fd772d64.pdf.
90 *CNN,* "Saving Lives with Solar-Powered Lights."; "Benefits," Just 1 Lamp, accessed December 11, 2012, http://www.justonelamp.com/benefits/.
91 American Institute of Architecture, *Architects and Climate Change,* fact sheet, accessed December 11, 2012, http://www.aia.org/aiaucmp/groups/aia/documents/pdf/aias078740.pdf.
92 Ibid.
93 Alejandra Roman, "Curitiba, Brazil," Encyclopedia of Earth, last modified January 30, 2011, http://www.eoearth.org/article/Curitiba,_Brazil.
94 "Solutions: citizenship," PBS, under *Frontline/World: Brazil–Curitiba's Urban Experiment* (tv series), December 2003, http://www.pbs.org/frontlineworld/fellows/brazil1203/citizenship.html.
95 Alejandra Roman, "Curitiba, Brazil."
96 Mithun, *South Lincoln Redevelopment Master Plan* (Seattle, WA: Mithun, January 2010), http://www.denverhousing.org/development/SouthLincoln/Documents/B.%20Exec%20Summ%20-%20SoLi-FinalReport%20JAN%202010.pdf.
97 Kaid Benfield, "How the Feds Are Building More Sustainable Cities," *Atlantic,* June 28, 2012, http://www.theatlanticcities.com/politics/2012/06/how-feds-are-building-more-sustainable-cities/2404/.
98 Alex Aylett, "Changing a City: Inside Portland's 80 Percent by 2050 Target," Worldchanging, November 3, 2009, http://www.worldchanging.com/archives/010712.html.
99 The City of Portland and Multnomah County, *Climate Action Plan 2009,* accessed December 11, 2012, http://www.portlandoregon.gov/bps/article/268612.
100 Ibid.
101 "The Environmental Value of Building Reuse," National Trust for Historic Preservation, accessed September 23, 2012, http://www.preservationnation.org/information-center/sustainable-communities/sustainability/green-lab/valuing-building-reuse.html.
102 "Old School Buildings: Prehistoric or Worth Preserving?" Education World, accessed September 23, 2012, http://www.educationworld.com/a_issues/issues172.shtml.
103 Randall Mason, "Economics and Historic Preservation: A Guide and Review of the Literature," discussion paper prepared for the Brookings Institution Metropolitan Policy Program (Washington D.C.: The Brookings Institution, September 2005), http://www.brookings.edu/~/media/research/files/reports/2005/9/metropolitanpolicy%20mason%2020050926_preservation.
104 David W. Look, Terry Wong, and Sylvia Rose Augustus, "The Seismic Retrofit of Historic Buildings Keeping Preservation in the Forefront," U.S. National Park Service Technical Preservation Series, preservation brief no. 41, accessed September 24, 2012, http://www.nps.gov/hps/tps/briefs/brief41.htm.

Chapter 24: Taking Action

1 "Jane Goodall Biography," *Encyclopedia of World Biography,* accessed October 24, 2012, http://www.notablebiographies.com/Gi-He/Goodall-Jane.html#b.
2 A. H. Maslow, "A Theory of Motivation," *Psychological Review* 50 (1943): 370-396, available at Classics in the History of Psychology, accessed December 7, 2012, http://psychclassics.yorku.ca/Maslow/motivation.htm.
3 Thomas S. Kuhn, *The Structure of Scientific Revolutions,* 3rd Edition (Chicago: The University of Chicago Press, 1996).
4 John Farndon, *The Great Scientists: From Euclid to Stephen Hawking* (New York: Metro Books & Arcturus Publishing Limited, 2005).

5. Ibid.
6. "Our Mission," NAACP, accessed November 5, 2012, http://www.naacp.org/pages/our-mission.
7. John Farndon, *The Great Scientists: From Euclid to Stephen Hawking* (New York: Metro Books & Arcturus Publishing Limited, 2005).
8. "Timeline: The Modern Environmental Movement," PBS, under *American Experience Online* (tv series), accessed October 3, 2012, http://www.pbs.org/wgbh/americanexperience/features/timeline/earthdays/1/.
9. Ibid.
10. Farndon, *The Great Scientists: From Euclid to Stephen Hawking*.
11. Jonah Lehrer, "Why don't we believe in Science?" New Yorker, June 7, 2012, http://www.newyorker.com/online/blogs/frontalcortex/2012/06/brain-experiments-why-we-dont-believe-science.html.
12. Robert Charles Stewart, "The Rise of Modern Science: The Metaphysics of Evolution," Shattering the Sacred Myths (The Academy of Evolutionary Metaphysics, 2005), http://www.evolutionary-metaphysics.net/rise_of_modern_science.html.
13. Ted Nordhaus and Michael Schellenberger, "The Death of Environmentalism: Global warming politics in the post-environmental world," paper presented at a meeting of the Environmental Grantmakers Association, October 2004, available at The Breakthrough, http://www.thebreakthrough.org/images/Death_of_Environmentalism.pdf.
14. Gail Lukasik, "Step aside Boomers, Silent Generation has much to offer," *USA Today*, accessed December 20, 2012, http://usatoday30.usatoday.com/news/opinion/letters/2010-11-23-letters23_ST_N.htm.
15. Pew Research Center, *Millennials: A Portrait of Generation Next* (February 2010), http://pewsocialtrends.org/files/2010/10/millennials-confident-connected-open-to-change.pdf.
16. "Youth and the State of the World," Advocates for Youth, accessed October 10, 2012. http://www.advocatesforyouth.org/publications/455?task=view.
17. Charles Kenny, "Sweet Bird of Youth! The Case for Optimism," *Time Magazine*, March 17, 2011, http://www.time.com/time/specials/packages/printout/0,29239,2059521_2059564_2059561,00.html#.
18. "April 6 Youth Movement," PBS, under Frontline: Revolution in Cairo (tv series), accessed October 8, 2012, http://www.pbs.org/wgbh/pages/frontline/revolution-in-cairo/inside-april6-movement/.
19. "Universal Declaration of Human Rights 2: Universe of Obligation," lesson idea, Facing History and Ourselves, accessed October 29, 2012, http://www.facinghistory.org/resources/lesson_ideas/udhr-2-universe-obligation.
20. Dennis Hevesi, "Irena Sendler, Lifeline to Young Jews, Is Dead at 98," *New York Times*, May 13, 2008, http://www.nytimes.com/2008/05/13/world/europe/13sendler.html?_r=0.
21. "Poland honors woman who saved 2,500 Jews," NBC News, March 14, 2007, http://www.msnbc.msn.com/id/17607715/ns/world_news-europe/t/poland-honors-woman-who-saved-jews/#.UJlYqMXA_8E.
22. Catherine O'Donnell, "New study quantifies use of social media in Arab Spring," University of Washington, news release, September 12, 2011, http://www.washington.edu/news/2011/09/12/new-study-quantifies-use-of-social-media-in-arab-spring/.
23. Avaaz website, accessed December 7, 2012, http://www.avaaz.org.
24. Ibid.
25. "Highlights," Avaaz, accessed December 7, 2012, http://www.avaaz.org/en/highlights.php.
26. Clay Shirky, "The Political Power of Social Media: Technology, the Public Sphere, and Political Change," Foreign Affairs 90, no. 1 (January/February 2011), accessed October 4, 2012, http://www.foreignaffairs.com/articles/67038/clay-shirky/the-political-power-of-social-media.
27. "I Want More Healthy Food Choices in South L.A.!," online petition, Community Health Councils, accessed October 12, 2012, http://org2.democracyinaction.org/o/5382/p/dia/action/public/index.sjs?action_KEY=11249.
28. Gretchen L. Zimmerman, Cynthia G. Olsen, and Michael F. Bosworth, "A 'Stages of Change' Approach to Helping Patients Change Behavior," *American Family Physician* 61 (March 2000) 1409-1416, http://www.aafp.org/afp/2000/0301/p1409.html.
29. Donella Meadows, "Dancing with Systems," Donella Meadows Institute, http://www.donellameadows.org/archives/dancing-with-systems/.
30. Jason Beaubien, "Prevention Programs Curb New HIV Infections in South Africa," NPR, July 25, 2012, http://www.npr.org/blogs/health/2012/07/25/157297530/prevention-programs-curb-new-hiv-infections-in-south-africa.
31. Sue Alford, Nicole Cheetham, and Debra Hauser, *Science and Success in Developing Countries: Holistic Programs that Work to Prevent Teen Pregnancy, HIV & Sexually-Transmitted Infections, Executive Summary* (Washington, D.C.: Advocates for Youth, 2005), accessed October 9, 2012, http://www.advocatesforyouth.org/publications/610?task=view.
32. "HIV and AIDS in Swaziland," AVERT, accessed October 9, 2012, http://www.avert.org/aids-swaziland.htm#contentTable0.
33. "Children orphaned by HIV and AIDS," AVERT, accessed October 9, 2012, http://www.avert.org/aids-orphans.htm.
34. "AIDS Orphans," AVERT, accessed October 9, 2012, http://www.avert.org/aids-orphans.htm.
35. Global HIV Prevention Working Group, *Behavior Change and HIV Prevention: [Re]Considerations for the 21st Century* (August 2008), http://www.globalhivprevention.org/pdfs/PWG_behavior%20report_FINAL.pdf.

Thank you to all the inspiring individuals who contributed their stories for our youth and career profiles.